A HISTORY OF ENGLISH GEORGIC WRITING

The interconnected themes of land and labour were a common recourse for English literary writers between the sixteenth and twentieth centuries, and in the twenty-first they have become pressing again in the work of nature writers, environmentalists, poets, novelists and dramatists. Written by a team of sixteen subject specialists, this volume surveys the literature of rural working lives and landscapes written in English between 1500 and the present day, offering a range of scholarly perspectives on the georgic tradition, with insights from literary criticism, historical scholarship, classics, post-colonial studies, rural studies and ecocriticism. Providing an overview of the current scholarship in georgic literature and criticism, this collection argues that the work of people and animals in farming communities, and the land as it is understood through that work, has provided writers in English with one of their most complex and enduring themes.

PADDY BULLARD is Associate Professor of English Literature and Book History at the University of Reading. He is the author of *Edmund Burke and the Art of Rhetoric* (Cambridge University Press, 2011), and editor of *The Oxford Handbook of Eighteenth-Century Satire* (2019). With James McLaverty, he co-edited *Jonathan Swift and the Eighteenth-Century Book* (Cambridge University Press, 2013), and with Alexis Tadié, *Ancients and Moderns in Europe* (2016). With Timothy Michael, he is co-editor of volume 15 (*Later Prose*) of The Oxford Edition of the Works of Alexander Pope.

A HISTORY OF ENGLISH GEORGIC WRITING

EDITED BY
PADDY BULLARD
University of Reading

Shaftesbury Road, Cambridge CB2 8EA, United Kingdom

One Liberty Plaza, 20th Floor, New York, NY 10006, USA

477 Williamstown Road, Port Melbourne, VIC 3207, Australia

314–321, 3rd Floor, Plot 3, Splendor Forum, Jasola District Centre, New Delhi – 110025, India

103 Penang Road, #05–06/07, Visioncrest Commercial, Singapore 238467

Cambridge University Press is part of Cambridge University Press & Assessment, a department of the University of Cambridge.

We share the University's mission to contribute to society through the pursuit of education, learning and research at the highest international levels of excellence.

www.cambridge.org
Information on this title: www.cambridge.org/9781009011297

DOI: 10.1017/9781009019507

© Cambridge University Press & Assessment 2023

This publication is in copyright. Subject to statutory exception and to the provisions of relevant collective licensing agreements, no reproduction of any part may take place without the written permission of Cambridge University Press & Assessment.

First published 2023
First paperback edition 2025

A catalogue record for this publication is available from the British Library

ISBN 978-1-316-51987-5 Hardback
ISBN 978-1-009-01129-7 Paperback

Cambridge University Press & Assessment has no responsibility for the persistence or accuracy of URLs for external or third-party internet websites referred to in this publication and does not guarantee that any content on such websites is, or will remain, accurate or appropriate.

Contents

List of Contributors	*page* vii
A Note on National Designations	xii
List of Abbreviations	xiii

Introduction: A Survey of English Georgic
Writing, 1521–2021   1
Paddy Bullard

PART I   TURNINGS

1 Hesiod, Virgil and the Ambitions of Georgic   39
 Philip Thibodeau

2 Turning, Flying: The Rural Year   57
 Alexandra Harris

3 Farm Diaries, 1770–1990   79
 Jeremy Burchardt

4 Twentieth-Century Georgic and Agricultural Technology   99
 Paul Brassley

PART II   TIMES

5 Jacobean Georgic   121
 Andrew McRae

6 'Varieties too Regular for Chance': John Evelyn, John Dryden
 and Their Contemporaries   140
 Melissa Schoenberger

7   Enlightenment, Improvement and Experimentation:
    Jethro Tull and His Contemporaries   155
    Frans De Bruyn

8   Georgic, Romanticism and Complaint: John Clare
    and His Contemporaries   177
    Tess Somervell

9   Rural Labour in an Age of Industry: William Cobbett
    and Some Contemporaries   197
    James Grande

10 Labour Isn't Working: The (F)ailing Georgics of Hardy's
    Wessex Novels   215
    Andrew Radford

11 Twentieth-Century Georgic: V. Sackville-West   235
    Juan Christian Pellicer

12 Rags and Tatters: Hughes, Oswald and
    Their Contemporaries   255
    Jack Thacker

PART III   TERRITORIES

13 Low Lands: Fen Georgic   275
    Paddy Bullard

14 Between the Georgic and the Pastoral: The British Weald   296
    Suzanne Joinson

15 American Georgic   316
    Sarah Wagner-McCoy

16 Environment and Empire: Georgic through Time   344
    Charlie Kerrigan

Bibliography   362
Index   382

Contributors

PAUL BRASSLEY is Honorary University Fellow in the Centre for Rural Policy Research at the University of Exeter. Since 2009 he has been working there on a project to investigate the process of technical change in English agriculture, the results of which were published as *The Real Agricultural Revolution: The Transformation of English Farming 1939–1985*, by Paul Brassley, David Harvey, Matt Lobley and Michael Winter (Boydell, 2021). His other recent books are *Agriculture: A Very Short Introduction* (with Richard Soffe, Oxford University Press, 2016) and, as contributor and editor, *Transforming the Countryside: The Electrification of Rural Britain* (with Jeremy Burchardt and Karen Sayer, Routledge, 2017).

FRANS DE BRUYN is Professor Emeritus of English at the University of Ottawa. He has published extensively on georgic writing in the eighteenth century, as well as articles on a range of other subjects, from the South Sea Bubble to the reception of Shakespeare and Cervantes. He is the author of *The Political Genres of Edmund Burke* (Clarendon Press, 1996). His most recent publications are *Comedy and Crisis: Pieter Langendijk, the Dutch, and the Speculative Bubbles of 1720* (with Joyce Goggin, Liverpool University Press, 2020) and *The Cambridge Companion to Eighteenth-Century Thought* (Cambridge University Press, 2021).

PADDY BULLARD is Associate Professor of English Literature and Book History at the University of Reading. He is the author of *Edmund Burke and the Art of Rhetoric* (Cambridge University Press, 2011) and editor of *The Oxford Handbook of Eighteenth-Century Satire* (Oxford University Press, 2019). He co-edited *Jonathan Swift and the Eighteenth-Century Book* (with James McLaverty, Cambridge University Press, 2013) and *Ancients and Moderns in Europe* (with Alexis Tadié, Voltaire Foundation, 2016). He is co-editor of volume 15 (Later Prose) of *The*

Oxford Edition of the Works of Alexander Pope (with Timothy Michael, Oxford University Press, forthcoming).

JEREMY BURCHARDT is Associate Professor in Rural History at the University of Reading. His research focuses on the historical experience of landscape and the social and cultural history of the nineteenth- and twentieth-century English countryside. He is the author of *Lifescapes: The Experience of Landscape in Britain, 1870–1960* (Cambridge University Press, 2022), *The Allotment Movement in England, 1793–1873* (Boydell & Brewer, 2002), *Paradise Lost: Rural Idyll and Social Change* (I. B. Tauris, 2002) and various articles and edited books, among them *Transforming the Countryside: The Electrification of Rural Britain* (with Paul Brassley and Karen Sayer, Routledge, 2016) and 'The Rural Idyll: A Critique', in Verity Elson and Rosemary Shirley, eds., *Creating the Countryside: The Rural Idyll Past and Present* (Paul Holberton Publishing, 2017).

JAMES GRANDE is Senior Lecturer in Eighteenth-Century Literature and Culture at King's College London. He is the author of *William Cobbett, the Press and Rural England: Radicalism and the Fourth Estate, 1792–1835* (Palgrave Macmillan, 2014) and co-editor of *The Opinions of William Cobbett* (Ashgate, 2013) and *William Cobbett, Romanticism and the Enlightenment: Contexts and Legacy* (Pickering & Chatto, 2015). His next monograph, *Articulate Sounds: Music, Dissent, and Literary Culture, 1789–1840*, is forthcoming from the British Academy and Oxford University Press. He is a trustee of the Keats-Shelley Memorial Association and editor of the *Keats-Shelley Review*.

ALEXANDRA HARRIS is Professorial Fellow at the University of Birmingham, where she co-convenes the Arts of Place network, and a Fellow of the Royal Society of Literature. She is the author of *Romantic Moderns* (Thames and Hudson, 2015) and *Weatherland: Writers and Artists under English Skies* (Thames and Hudson, 2016) and many essays on British art, literature and landscape. Her *Time and Place: The Art of Calendars* (Little Toller, 2019) is part of a Common Ground project to encourage the making of contemporary calendars. Her next book, forthcoming with Faber & Faber, tells stories from a few square miles of Sussex, asking how people have inhabited one area over centuries.

SUZANNE JOINSON is a prize-winning novelist, creative non-fiction writer and Reader in Creative Writing at the University of Chichester. Her novels include *A Lady Cyclist's Guide to Kashgar* (Bloomsbury, 2012) and *The Photographer's Wife* (Bloomsbury, 2016). She regularly reviews for the *New York Times* and writes for many publications, including *The Guardian*, *Aeon*, BBC Radio 4, *LitHub* and others. She teaches fiction and non-fiction, with a strong interest in landscape. She held a Fellowship at the Museum of English Rural Life, University of Reading, in 2018–19, and works closely with a range of museums in the south of England exploring links between cultural memory and creative narratives. She is the National Life Stories Goodison Fellow at the British Library 2020–22.

CHARLIE KERRIGAN is a research fellow in the Department of Classics at Trinity College, Dublin, where he teaches Latin language and literature. His monograph, *Virgil's Map: Geography, Empire, and the Georgics*, was published by Bloomsbury in 2020.

ANDREW MCRAE is Professor of Renaissance Studies in the Department of English, University of Exeter. He is author of books including *God Speed the Plough: The Representation of Agrarian England, 1500–1660* (Cambridge University Press, 1996), *Literature, Satire and the Early Stuart State* (Cambridge University Press, 2004) and *Literature and Domestic Travel in Early Modern England* (Cambridge University Press, 2008). He is co-editor of *Early Stuart Libels* (Arts & Humanities Research Council, 2005) and *The Writing of Rural England, 1500–1800* (Palgrave Macmillan, 2003). He is currently completing, with Philip Schwyzer, a new scholarly edition of Michael Drayton's *Poly-Olbion*, and in 2019 he was co-director of the *Places of Poetry* project. His interest in early modern georgic writing dates back to his doctoral research and has been a recurrent strand in his work over three decades since then.

JUAN CHRISTIAN PELLICER is Professor of English at the University of Oslo. He is the author of *Preposterous Virgil: Reading through Stoppard, Auden, Wordsworth, Heaney* (Bloomsbury, 2022), as well as numerous articles on eighteenth-century poetry and classical reception.

ANDREW RADFORD is Senior Lecturer in Critical Studies at the University of Glasgow. He is a co-editor of *The Occult Imagination 1890–1947* (Routledge, 2018) and *Modernist Women Writers and Spirituality: A Piercing Darkness* (Palgrave Macmillan, 2017). He has also published *Mary Butts and British Neo-Romanticism: The Enchantment of Place* (Bloomsbury, 2014) as well as essays and books reviews on Katherine Mansfield, Mina Loy, Dion Fortune, James Joyce, Joseph Conrad and Rudyard Kipling. He is currently researching the literary career of independent publisher and anti-censorship campaigner John Calder. His new essay collection *British Experimental Women's Fiction 1945–1975: 'Slipping Through the Labels'* was published by Palgrave in 2021.

MELISSA SCHOENBERGER is Associate Professor of English at the College of the Holy Cross in Worcester, MA, where she specializes in Restoration and eighteenth-century poetry. She is the author of *Cultivating Peace: The Virgilian Georgic in English, 1650–1750* (Bucknell University Press, 2019). She has published articles in *Restoration*, *Translation and Literature* and *Philological Quarterly*. Her current monograph-in-progress considers long poems by Alexander Pope, Christopher Smart and William Cowper.

TESS SOMERVELL is a lecturer in English at Worcester College, University of Oxford. Previously she held a British Academy Postdoctoral Fellowship at the University of Leeds, working on a project titled 'Georgic Climates: Writing the Weather in Eighteenth-Century Poetry'. She completed her PhD, on the poetry of Milton, Thomson and Wordsworth, at the University of Cambridge. Her research interests include poetry from 1660 to 1830, science and literature, genre, reception and allusion, and ecocriticism.

JACK THACKER is a poet and researcher based in Sheffield and has previously published articles on Ted Hughes and Alice Oswald. In 2016, he was the winner of the Charles Causley International Poetry Competition. He has since been writer in residence at the Museum of English Rural Life, University of Reading, and at the Lighthouse Arts Centre. His debut pamphlet-length collection is *Handling* (Two Rivers Press, 2018).

PHILIP THIBODEAU is Associate Professor of Classics at Brooklyn College, CUNY. His areas of expertise include early Greek cosmology, ancient agricultural science, and Virgil, Horace and Augustan poetry. His is the author of *Playing the Farmer: Representations of Rural Life in Vergil's Georgics* (University of California Press, 2011) and he co-edited *Being There Together: Essays in Honor of Michael C. J. Putnam on the Occasion of His Seventieth Birthday* (with H. Haskell, Afton Press, 2003).

SARAH WAGNER-MCCOY is Assistant Professor of English and Humanities at Reed College. She received her PhD from Harvard University, MA from University College Dublin and BA from Columbia College. She is currently editing the complete short stories of Charles W. Chesnutt for Oxford University Press with generous support from the National Endowment for the Humanities. In 2013 she published the first in-depth study of Chesnutt's use of classical literature in English Literary History, drawing on her doctoral work on transatlantic pastoral fiction, for which she received the Helen Choate Bell Dissertation Prize. She has received support for her research from the 2016 Graves Award in the Humanities, administered by Pomona College under the auspices of the American Council of Learned Societies, to recognize excellence in teaching, and from the Bridging Cultures initiative at the NEH in 2014.

A Note on National Designations

The historical timeframe of *A History of English Georgic Writing* is broad: it focuses on the last five centuries, but has an ancient hinterland. As a consequence, the different national designations used in its chapters vary, and should be understood in the context of particular periods. There are important points of discontinuity and realignment. These include: the formation of the Kingdom of Great Britain in 1707; the declaration of independence of American Continental Congress in 1776; the formation of the Kingdom of Great Britain and Ireland in 1801; and the creation of the Irish Free State in 1922. In this volume, 'English georgic' refers to literary writing about work on the land written in modern vernacular English. The chapters focus on texts by English, Scottish, Irish, Welsh and American writers who operated within a generic frame that recalled ancient Greece and Rome. For an account of how land law was used across this period by British and Anglo-American powers in the spatial politics and geographical formation of developing countries, see Patrick McAuslan, 'Property and Empire: From Colonialism to Globalization and Back', *Social and Legal Studies*, 24 (2015), 339–57.

Abbreviations

Works cited with a pre-1900 publication date are published in London, unless otherwise stated.

AHEW	*The Agrarian History of England and Wales*, gen. ed. J. Thirsk, 8 vols. in 11 (Cambridge University Press, 1967–2000)
Georgics	Latin text of the *Georgics* as given in the Loeb Classical Library edition, as referenced under the abbreviation '*Georgics* (Fairclough)' in the following text, unless another edition is specified
Georgics (Dryden)	*The Works of John Dryden. Vol. 5: Poems: The Works of Virgil in English, 1697*, ed. W. Frost and V.A. Dearing (Berkeley: University of California Press, 1987)
Georgics (Fairclough)	Virgil, *Eclogues, Georgics, Aeneid I–VI*, tr. H.R. Fairclough, rev. G.P. Gould (1935; Cambridge, MA: Harvard University Press, 1999)
Georgics (Fallon)	Virgil, *Georgics*, tr. P. Fallon (Oxford University Press, 2009)
Georgics (Ferry)	*The Georgics of Virgil*, tr. D. Ferry (New York: Farrar, Straus and Giroux, 2005)
Georgics (Johnson)	*The Georgics: A Poem of the Land*, tr. K. Johnson (London: Penguin, 2010)
ODNB	*The Oxford Dictionary of National Biography*
OED	*The Oxford English Dictionary*

Introduction
A Survey of English Georgic Writing, 1521–2021
Paddy Bullard

This book is a history of English literary writing about the work of people and animals in farming communities, and about the land as it is understood through that work. Since the sixteenth century, English authors with rural interests have looked to a four-part didactic poem called the *Georgics* (29 BCE) by the Roman poet Virgil as a model for this kind of text. The classical and late medieval inheritance of agricultural writing is itself diverse and very ancient, as Philip Thibodeau shows in the first chapter of this collection. Yet it is Virgil's poem that has lent its title most often as a general label for farming literature, and it does again for this history.[1]

There are two broad categories of English georgic writing. The first is a category of genre, made up by imitations and adaptations of Virgil's *Georgics*. These tend to be long, mixed poems about rural work in which a didactic authorial voice allows itself to be sidetracked at regular intervals into passages of historical narration, of philosophical discussion, of local description or of rhapsody. They were especially prestigious and widely read in Europe and America between the middle of the seventeenth and the beginning of the nineteenth centuries.[2] Some poems of this kind make their lineage obvious, such as James Thomson's *The Seasons* (1726–46), which features sections of direct imitation of the *Georgics*, and shares its four-part structure and rural outlook. In others, the agricultural content has fallen away from recognizable formal georgic structures, as is the case with John Milton's *Paradise Regained* (1671), for example, or with John Gay's entirely urban *Trivia: or, The Art of Walking the Streets of London* (1716). The second category of georgic is one of theme and mode, and it covers all sorts of literary texts, in poetry, prose and drama, that deal with life on the land in a practical way. Usually they share with Virgil's *Georgics* a distinctive circle of concerns: unremitting labour as human fate; the clash between progressive civilization and natural rhythms that are cyclical and recursive; the bonds between humans and companion species; the persistence of local attachments in national or imperial political contexts.

These themes are prominent, for example, in certain novels by Thomas Hardy, as discussed by Andrew Radford in Chapter 10 of this volume – although there is no formal georgic among Hardy's surviving poems. The essays collected in this volume trace a literary history shared by these two categories of georgic writing. Together they show how georgic has been an ever-present and vital green force in English literary history from the sixteenth into the twenty-first century.

A growing body of literary criticism has recognized the variety and significance of English georgic writing.[3] Other kinds of literature rise and evolve, or stay tied to some ancient precedent or well-defined form. Georgic is a different sort of tradition: fragmented and discontinuous, each iteration starting in a new direction, it is always too absorbed in external things – in natural processes and in human practices – to worry about formal conventions. Georgic is thought of sometimes as an interrupted genre, an abandoned literary form.[4] This book argues on the contrary that it has been a constant presence in English and American culture over the last five hundred years. Yet you must know how to read and recognize it. *A History of English Georgic Writing* shows how, and gives a map of the territory.

Virgil's *Georgics* is arranged in four parts, and foursquareness is a characteristic feature of georgic poetics. This *History of English Georgic Writing* has a correspondingly quadrilateral design, its sixteen chapters arranged in groups of four and eight. The first quarter ('Turnings') is made up of four chapters on different scales of change in rural writing: from ancient to modern, from season to season, from day to day, from tradition to technology. The second and third quarters ('Times') give a historical overview of English georgic writing in eight chapters. These feature readings of the principal georgic texts for each period, and specialist scholars find in each a scheme of wider contexts for period-specific knowledge. The final quarter ('Territories') looks at English georgic writing from the special perspectives of landscape and environment over four chapters: from home, the perspectives of rich lowland fen and open highland weald; from abroad, the perspectives of America, and of Britain's history as a former colonial power.

This introductory chapter is a headland to the larger field. It is set aside for a general survey of English georgic writing, as viewed through the contexts of agrarian history in the British Isles, and of non-literary agricultural writing published over the last five centuries. The aim is to draw out some historical patterns, and to fill in some of the literary gaps between chapters. What none of the contributors to this volume proposes, however, is a continuous narrative of development in English georgic writing. This frees us from having to begin the survey at the very beginning. We can start instead with a triptych of modern georgic snapshots, featuring three contemporary British writers. They will give us a sense of what formal resources the georgic tradition can afford to writers today.

Three Modern Georgic Snapshots

The first snapshot features the poet Simon Armitage. In May 2016, Armitage wrote a series of poems to accompany an exhibition at the Norfolk and Norwich Festival, featuring early aerial photography from the First World War. Most of the photographs are landscape 'obliques', unpopulated panoramic images taken during reconnaissance of the Somme battlefields. Armitage's texts are translations from the *Georgics*, focused on Virgil's darker passages, but still resolutely agricultural. The poems were printed onto transparent fascia fixed an inch in front of the enlarged military photographs, 'to suggest an aerial detachment and perspective', as Armitage explains it, 'to bring about a form of "oblique" refraction'.[5] This displacement makes sense of the photographs' odd perspectives, and it matches the *Georgics* as well: Virgil designed his poem 'to suggest a Truth indirectly', wrote Joseph Addison in 1697, 'and without giving us a full and open view of it: To let us see just so much as will naturally lead the Imagination into all the parts that lie conceal'd'.[6] Like the wartime 'obliques', Armitage's translations are down-to-earth and straight-talking. Yet they hold back from reading the missing soldiers and their bloody actions onto the battlefields. These they insist on seeing as agricultural landscapes, ready for seedtime, plough and harvest. The solemn didactic poetry leads our imaginations into war, but Armitage does not want us to approach too closely. Like Euridice ascending from death behind Orpheus in the fourth *Georgic*, the past only follows us until we turn to look straight at it.

A second georgic snapshot, more fleeting this time, features the novelist Ali Smith. In summer 2021 the Royal Academy of Arts exhibited a new series of works by David Hockney, 'The Arrival of Spring', painted by the artist at his home in Normandy the previous year using an iPad and stylus. Smith had published her novel *Spring* the year before. Like the other volumes in her 'Seasonal Quartet', the cover of *Spring* features a striking half-jacket image of a particular lane in Yorkshire painted by Hockney. So Smith was the obvious person to introduce the artist's new work with an article for the *RA Magazine*. She illustrates her commentary on Hockney with vernal poetry by Thomas Carew, T. S. Eliot, Emily Dickinson and e.e. cummings, but her main exhibit is a passage from Virgil's second *Georgic* (lines 336–42) in Kimberly Johnson's translation:

> Such days, I fancy, dawned upon the birth
> of the infant earth, and such a course they kept:
> spring it was, spring the wide world observed –
> the eastwinds spared their wintry blasts,
> when first the cattle drank in light, and the earthen line
> of men reared up its head from the stiff fields
> and beasts were released to forests and stars released to sky.⁷

The lines capture not only the beginning of all life on earth, but also the moment of respite between frost and heat when human consciousness at last looks up at it all – 'the first noticing moment', as Smith puts it. She sees it in Hockney's pictures as well, when he captures the season's 'merry falling-over-itself, the swing of a branch loaded with not-snow, spring like the hinge on the seasonal door'. Georgics are poems about the pleasures and revelations of the everyday, according to Smith. They form a mediating genre, hemmed in between the heedless amorousness of pastoral and the pride of epic violence. They are still full of myth, but stripped of illusions. Armitage turns to georgic for a poetic mode at once ironic and deadly serious in its realism; Smith finds in it a trace of the generative pause in which true poetic attentiveness began.

In a third snapshot of contemporary georgic, the Virgilian inheritance lines up with modern British agricultural and environmental thinking. James Rebanks lives and works on an upland mixed rotational farm in Matterdale, near Ullswater in the English Lake District. There is nothing in the title of his second book, *English Pastoral* (2020), to surprise readers of his bestselling memoir *The Shepherd's Life* (2015), which described the author's annual cycle of work with a flock of tough Herdwick sheep (Suzanne Joinson discusses *The Shepherd's Life* in Chapter 14 of this collection). However, it turns out that *English Pastoral*'s title is a little misleading: its contents are less pastoral – particularly 'beseeming shepherds', as Samuel Johnson defined it – than deeply georgic.⁸ Rebanks is drawn to the hardscrabble belligerence of life on a mixed farm as described by Virgil in the first *Georgic*: 'His [Virgil's] farming philosophy was that we had to take things from nature by using our wisdom and our tools, because the alternative was defeat and starvation.'⁹ He notices, as do many of the earlier writers discussed in this collection, that Virgil describes the plough and hoe as weapons (*arma*) in a war, and that by the same analogy the technology of modern agribusiness would be 'something more comparable to tanks, jet fighters, and chemical and nuclear weapon systems'.¹⁰ Unremitting labour, learning through practice and commitment to a plot of ground are central georgic themes. Rebanks brings them together in the figure of his grandfather, who was 'rooted in work, connected to the soil and the crops and the animals upon it'.[11] He represents an inheritance of traditional knowledge embedded in farming landscapes, bloodstock lines and working communities.

English Pastoral wants to pass on some of that knowledge, but Virgilian didactic is hardly an option for mass-market non-fiction. So rather than offering direct instruction, Rebanks tells the story of his own schooling in the land. The policy-level argument here is that small marginal holdings like his are crucial components in the jigsaw of diversified British agriculture. They are repositories for the older understandings of land management and food production, knowledge that conventional farming needs to ensure its own sustainability at a time of recalibration for the agricultural sector.[12] At the end of the era of Common Agricultural Policy subsidies, as government looks to reward farmers for environmental stewardship as much as productivity, the argument is especially timely.

These snapshots show three high-profile contemporary writers drawing on the georgic tradition in different contexts. All three deploy Virgil's poem as a catalyst to bring alive stubborn cultural materials. Armitage's ghostly images from the military archive, Smith's poems and paintings of a fugitive season, Rebanks's passed-over agricultural ecologies: each is looking for a vivifying connection to the realm of everyday human practice in the natural world. In all three snapshots the perspective offered is oblique, reflecting georgic's characteristic poetics of openness and indirection. Georgic cannot think of a thing, a place or a process without thinking of its analogue or opposite at the same time. Battlefield and farm, painting and poem, rooted labour and abstracted technology, each is displayed as part of a larger scheme of natural patterns. Each involve historical artefacts – reconnaissance photographs, seventeenth-century lyrics, a shed of old farm tools – that require a serious attentiveness, an engagement stripped clean of nostalgia. Each represents a particular natural environment, and lets it stand in for somewhere else as well, for any landscape the reader has worked in and belonged to. It is a cluster of poetic functions that georgic is uniquely well equipped to perform. This collection of essays shows that English writers have been using the georgic mode to these ends for over five hundred years, and that in the second decade of the twenty-first century that georgic inheritance is as valuable and fruitful as it has ever been.

The Sixteenth Century

If Armitage, Smith and Rebanks give us a glimpse of where English georgic finds itself today, where does the story begin? Looking back in 1659 on the history of vernacular agricultural writing, the educational reformer and horticulturalist Samuel Hartlib found nothing to challenge the primacy of his own *Discourse of the Whole Art of Husbandry* – at least, he argued, there was no earlier '*Systema* or compleat book' of agriculture in English. 'Till the latter end of Queen *Elizabeths* days', he wrote,

> I suppose that there was scarce a book wrote of this subject; I never saw or heard of any. About that time: *Tusser* made his verses, and *Scot* wrote about a Hop-garden, *Gouge* translated some things.[13]

Hartlib's dismissive remark at least gives us some leads on the origins of English georgic. He was right: signs of the first growth of agricultural writing in the Tudor period are hard to spot. The *Georgics* themselves were familiar to scholarly readers at the start of the sixteenth century, and supplied hortulan themes to English humanist writers from the 1520s onwards. In fact, a Scots poet got there before anyone writing in English: the 'Prologues' of Gavin Douglas's *Eneados* (completed 1513) have a georgic frame of reference and characteristically georgic themes – labour, didactics of practice, landscape and seasonality.[14] There are georgic glimmerings in Sir Thomas More's *Utopia* (1516). The laws of the Utopians permit the invasion of neighbouring peoples who leave their fields idle and waste, a colonial extrapolation from Virgil's 'neu segnes iaceant terrae'.[15] The Utopians are also self-sufficient horticulturalists, and More seems to have shared his contemporary Sir Thomas Elyot's appreciation of the variety of cultivation discussed in the *Georgics*, 'the divers graynes, herbes, and flowres, that be there described', as Elyot put it in *The Governour* (1531), 'that redig therin hit semeth to a man to be in a delectable gardeine or paradise'.[16]

The musician and farmer Thomas Tusser first 'made his verses' in 1557, though Hartlib's true dawn for English georgic is the Elizabethan 1570s, when Tusser expanded *A Hundreth* into *Fiue Hundreth Points of Good Husbandry* (1573). They are discussed by Alexandra Harris in Chapter 2 and by Andrew McRae in Chapter 5. Hartlib also mentions Reynolde Scot's *Perfite Platforme of a Hoppe Garden*, which appeared a year later, and Barnabe Googe's *Foure bookes of husbandry, collected by M. Conradus Heresbachius*, which followed in 1557. In 1570, Roger Ascham had invoked 'that perfite worke of the *Georgickes*' as his model for poetic 'epitome'. Virgil 'used daily, whan he had written *40* or *50* verses, not to cease cutting, paring, and polishing of them, till he had brought them to the number of *x* or *xii*' – the quartering proportions of the *Georgics* were always significant to the humanists.[17] By the end of the decade, Edmund Spenser was incorporating georgic features into the pastoral of the *Shepheardes Calender*

(1579): his shepherds are 'mortal men, that swincke and sweate', while Virgil is remembered as one who left his sheepwalks 'and laboured lands to yield the timely eare'.[18] So Hartlib's first shoots of English agricultural writing appeared among the established greenery of humanist literary georgic.

The Seventeenth Century

Hartlib goes on to mention 'divers small Treatises' on agriculture written later by 'divers, as Sir *Hugh Platts, Gab. Platts, Markham, Blith*, and *Butler*, who do well in divers things'.[19] Two of these 'divers' (i.e., partial and unsystematic) books belong to the first decade of the seventeenth century, and are happy still to cite Virgil's *Georgics* as a technical authority. Sir Hugh Platts's *New and Admirable Arte of Setting of Corne* (1600) refers to Virgil's strictures on the selection and preservation of seed stock, while Charles Butler's enduringly popular *The Feminine Monarchie, or a Treatise Concerning Bees* (1609) quotes extensively from the fourth *Georgic*.[20] Edward Maxey's *Nevv Instuction [sic] of Plowing and Setting of Corne* (1601) is another late Elizabethan book advocating rectilinear regularity in farming practice, while *A Surveyor's Dialogue* (1607) by John Norden, a topographer and mapmaker with much experience of crown estates, stands out, according to Joan Thirsk, as an early Jacobean work remarkable for the precision and range of its local information on soil types and social patterns.[21]

Is it a coincidence that this flourishing of agricultural books during the first decades of the seventeenth century happened at the same time as Francis Bacon turned, in *The Aduancement of Learning* (1605), to the *Georgics* as his model for a new kind of progressive inquiry that no longer 'dispised to be conuersant in ordinary and common matters'? After all, wrote Bacon, Virgil got as much literary fame from his observations on husbandry as he did from his epic poetry:

> *Nec sum animi dubius verbis ea vincere magnum,*
> *Quam sit & angustis his addere rebus honorem.*

> And surely if the purpose be in good earnest not to write at leasure that which men may read at leasure, but really to instruct and suborne Action and actiue life, these Georgickes of the mind concerning the husbandry & tillage therof, are no lesse worthy then the heroical descriptions of *vertue, duty,* & *felicity.*[22]

Where the *Aeneid* depends for its moral power on a precarious process of exemplarity, according to Bacon, the *Georgics* has a method (and perhaps even a psychology) of education built into it.[23] Earlier in the *Aduancement*

Bacon had quoted Virgil's famous distinction in the second *Georgic* between the contentment of the rustic and the happiness of the Epicurean philosopher ('Felix, qui potuit rerum cognoscere causas' – 'Blessed is he who has succeeded in learning the laws of nature's working').[24] In her influential reading of these passages, Annabel Patterson argues that Bacon was advancing a new blend of inward-looking pastoralism (Stoic in origin, rooted in the 'cultura animi' tradition) with a distinctly georgic emphasis on human labour and inventiveness – 'a principled synthesis of two conceptual structures'.[25] The prominence of these quotations in Bacon's text suggest that the psychological and therapeutic components of his programme, as well as the practical ones, could be supplied out of the *Georgics*, without bothering too much about Virgil's own strictly pastoral writings.[26]

Of the remaining three agricultural writers mentioned ('*Gab. Platts, Markham, Blith*'), Gervase Markham belongs more to the Jacobean flush of English georgic writing than to Hartlib's own mid-century moment. In the first of his agricultural books, *The English Husbandman* (1613; followed by a *Second Book*, 1614; and a *Farwell to Hvsbandry*, 1620), Markham claimed that it was an English paraphrase of the *Georgics* – presumably Abraham Fleming's translation (or 'mere crib') of 1589 – that provoked him to write. He objected to Virgil's methods on account not of their ancientness, but of their 'onely belonging to the Italian climbe, & nothing agreeable to ours'.[27] Thomas Fuller later reported that the poet Samuel Daniel took up farming at around the same time, but with doubtful success, blamed once again on the inappropriate continental influence of Virgil:

> For though he [Daniel] was well vers'd in *Virgil*, his fellow *Husbandman-Poet*, yet there is more required to make a rich Farmer, than only to say his *Georgicks* by heart, and I question whether his *Italian* will fit our *English* Husbandry.[28]

Over the same decade in which Daniel turned farmer and Markham published the *English Husbandman* volumes, Michael Drayton produced the first great English chorographical georgic, *Poly-Olbion* (1612, 1622). Drayton goes even further than Markham in scolding 'this lunatique Age' for entertaining 'fantasies of forraine inventions'.[29] British specificity is a necessary first step towards Drayton's real theme in *Poly-Olbion*, which is the particularity of regions within a diverse national prospect. In Drayton's poetics, each landscape and feature has a name and a voice with which to reveal itself. The general perspectives of earlier antiquaries are folded into particular descriptions, 'making the various places themselves recite England's chronicle history', as Richard Helgerson puts it.[30] In

Chapter 5 of this volume, Andrew McRae's assessment is that for Drayton and his contemporaries the *Georgics* changed from a stable, universal classical authority into a dynamic catalyst for understanding a time of precarious national politics: 'Georgic did not so much present a model for understanding their world', he concludes, 'as provide resources that helped them to think for themselves'. In the first two decades of the seventeenth century, georgic came into its early modernity.

The next historical hotspot for English georgic was the 1650s and 1660s, the age of Hartlib himself and of our two remaining authors ('*Gab. Platts*' and '*Blith*'). Gabriel Plattes is best known today as the author of an early Baconian utopia with much to say about agricultural improvement, *A Description of Macaria* (1641), and for the role he played in Hartlib's correspondence network.[31] Plattes first published on agriculture in the late 1630s, but his main contribution to the subject was his 1656 treatise *Practical Husbandry Improved*, very much a work of the 1650s, with its restless emphasis on technical innovation and experiment.[32] Another member of the network was Leicestershire farmer and 'lover of ingenuity' Walter Blith. In his 1649 treatise *The English Improover*, Blith recommended six basic methods of fertilization, drainage and ploughing, none of them especially original. Yet by the time he revised his book as *The English Improver Improved* (1652) three years later, he had found half a dozen new techniques to promote, including the cultivation of special crops for fodder, textiles, seed oil and dyeing.[33] Hartlib was also responsible for the publication of Sir Richard Weston's *Discours of Husbandrie used in Brabant and Flanders* (1650), the earliest English work to promote the use of turnips and clover in crop rotations on marginal land. The *Discours* is another instance of Hartlib's inclusive, expansive cultural energies: Weston wrote his treatise as a Royalist exile in the Low Countries, but in Hartlib's hands it was converted to the Commonwealthsman's cause by the addition of material from one of his lieutenants, Cressy Dimock, the circle's most enthusiastic advocate of land reform, mechanical innovation and agricultural education. Turning to the classically georgic topic of apiculture, Hartlib published another book that converted Charles Butler's 'feminine monarchie' of the hive into a republicanized 'Common-wealth of Bees', fit to produce industrial quantities of honey and wax.[34]

The restoration of the Stuart monarchy in 1660 and Hartlib's death two years later threatened to dissipate the georgic energies of the previous decade, but in the event they were converted and extended once again. Two years after its foundation in 1662 the Royal Society convened a 'Georgical Committee', with old Hartlib correspondents John Evelyn and

Ralph Austen among its thirty-two members.³⁵ A year after that Austen carefully updated his *Treatise of Fruit-Trees* (1653), apparently trimming it for the new Caroline regime. In its first edition, published under the Protectorate, Austen had advocated the cultivation of apple orchards for the sake of economic development and the employment of the poor. In a new preface to the 1665 edition, now dedicated to Robert Boyle and the work of the Royal Society, Austen changed his emphasis to the promotion of well-regulated and profitable cider production for the benefit of proprietors.³⁶ A few years later the innovations that Walter Blith had proposed in 1653 were swallowed whole and then extended by John Worlidge in his *Systema agriculturae* (1669), the most compendious farming publication of the age.³⁷ Another work revised across a series of editions that spanned the restoration was Izaak Walton's *Compleat Angler* (1653; final authorial edition 1676), a sporting miscellany containing prose dialogue, natural history and tavern balladry, concerned more with riverside recreation rather than agricultural labour – but its mode is unmistakably didactic and georgic.³⁸

Once again, there are circumstantial connections between these Hartlibian continuities and the further development of georgic modalities in post-Restoration literary culture. In *Paradise Lost* (1667), Hartlib's friend John Milton places georgic labour at the heart of the prelapsarian everyday, and develops the theme further as a marker of what changes after the fall.³⁹ A case can be made for the georgic formalism of Milton's four-book *Paradise Regained* (1671), which is at very least, as Alastair Fowler puts it, a 'brief epic with georgic modulation'.⁴⁰ In the plans for the funeral of Oliver Cromwell in 1658, Hartlib and Milton are seen walking with another poet, Andrew Marvell.⁴¹ The beneficent floods that feature in Marvell's poems 'Upon Appleton House' (written 1651) and 'The First Anniversary' (1655) have long been connected with georgic techniques for levelling and fertilizing water meadows by floating them with silty water, as set out by Sir Richard Weston and Walter Blith.⁴² As Melissa Schoenberger shows in Chapter 6 of this volume, the georgic tradition emerged in its full agrarian form at several seventeenth-century moments, while at others its presence constituted 'merely part of a looser georgic mode that winds and weaves its way through various genres and forms'.

So in the mid-seventeenth century we see moments of convergence between literary georgic and practical agricultural instruction. The georgic poetry of this period is characterized by its efforts 'to extend the exegesis of Virgil's text into the practice of agriculture', as Douglas Chambers has drily put it.⁴³ Yet poetry and instruction are set far apart at the turn of the eighteenth century by John Dryden's era-defining translation of the *Georgics*. It appears in Dryden's *Works of Virgil* (1697), a grand folio volume published by Jacob Tonson, where it is supported by an essay on georgic by a rising protégé of Dryden's, Joseph Addison, still a student at Oxford when he wrote the piece in 1693. Addison asserts the dignity of Virgil's poem, although he cannot do so without a finicking shudder of irony: the Mantuan 'breaks the Clods and tosses the Dung about with an air of gracefulness'.[44] Dryden had prepared the ground for all this activity by commissioning a sequence of appetizer translations from the *Georgics* by some of his most fashionable and aristocratic collaborators. They appear across the six volumes of the *Dryden-Tonson Miscellanies* (1684–1709), their authors including the Earl of Mulgrave, Knightley Chetwood, two successive Earls of Lauderdale, Addison's college friend Henry Sacheverell, and Addison himself.[45]

These grand literary performances contrast strikingly with the most innovative agricultural publication of the same period, which is a humble one, despite its elite institutional associations. *A Collection of Letters for the Improvement of Husbandry and Trade* was one of the very first encyclopaedic periodicals, appearing monthly between September 1681 and 1683, and again, as a modest folio sheet, between March 1692 and September 1703.[46] Its editor was John Houghton, a rare Fellow of the Royal Society who did not claim the rank of gentleman (he was an apothecary by trade) and a member of the revived Georgical Committee. Houghton solicited letters on agricultural innovation from a wide network, ranging from his fellow FRSs to farmers, countrywomen and agricultural merchants, and contributors were rewarded with free subscriptions to the periodical. The *Collection of Letters* is full of reforming optimism, but it is also a document of the depressed and therefore hard-working agricultural economy of the period 1664 to 1691, witness to the 'great improvement made of lands since our inhuman civil wars, when our gentry, who before hardly knew what it was to think, then fell to such an industry, and caused such an improvement as England never knew before'.[47] Houghton always struggled to find a paying readership for his uncostly periodical, resorting in the end to advertisements and news-mongering.[48] By contrast, Dryden's *Virgil* was, like his *Miscellanies*, a bold commercial experiment in leveraging elite cultural and social capital against a lucrative subscription system.[49]

The Eighteenth Century

A more modest classicism and a mercantile spirit had converged once more, however, by the first decade of the eighteenth century, in the first formal English imitation of the *Georgics*: John Philips's two-part poem *Cyder* (1708). Looking forward to the 'sweet prospect of a mutual gain' represented by the 1707 Anglo-Scottish Act of Union, Philips anticipates a century of 'uncontrol'd' naval dominance and colonial plenty, crowned by some unlikely British exports: 'to the utmost Bounds of this | Wide Universe, *Silurian* Cyder borne | Shall please all Tasts, and triumph o'er the Vine'.[50] Joseph Addison himself used a passage from the first *Georgic* (lines 54–61, on the special productivities of different lands) as the epigram for *Spectator* 69 (19 May 1711), his famous essay on the cosmopolitan Royal Exchange.[51] These texts are examples of a distinctively georgic trajectory of focus. The poet's attention starts off at home, or at least among domestic landscapes – which can now be urban too, as in *Spectator* 69, or in Jonathan Swift's prognosticating 'Description of a City Shower' (1710), or in the urban digressions on georgic mythography of John Gay's *Trivia* (1716).[52] Then it shifts outwards to a dispersed scene of consumption and use that hides its evidently imperial logic by stressing reconciliation, mutual adaptation and copious supply: 'trade, without enlarging the British Territories', Addison concludes, 'has given us a kind of additional Empire'.[53] This georgic sequencing of attention finds its most characteristic expression in Alexander Pope's *Windsor Forest* (1713). From the 'rich Industry' of Pope's native Loddon valley, where '*Ceres*' Gifts in waving Prospect stand, | And nodding tempt the joyful Reaper's Hand', to 'Earth's distant Ends', and the further prospect of a time when 'Conquest cease, and Slav'ry be no more', *Windsor Forest* hopes to reshape the overweening energies of a recent European war into a peaceful, wealthy and multifarious georgic order.[54]

A century after Plattes's *Setting Corne* was published, and fifty years after the period of Hartlib's information-sharing activity, English farmers of the early eighteenth century were enjoying increases in agricultural productivity unparalleled in Europe. As the economist Robert C. Allen sums it up, the output-to-worker ratios for British farming in 1600 were at the low end of the continental norm, but by 1750 they had risen sharply to the leading position.[55] An average English cornfield that had yielded ten bushels per acre in 1600 was yielding twenty bushels or more by the early eighteenth century, and national productivity continued to rise over the following fifty years as more waste land (particularly in the East Anglian fens) was brought into cultivation and fallow reduced.[56] Georgic poets and agricultural writers were on hand to bear witness to these improvements, and to make their contribution to the diffusion of progressive practice that helped propel them. It is also significant that these extraordinary rises in farming productivity had levelled by about 1750 – that is, before the fabled period of British agricultural improvement, parliamentary enclosure and industrial revolution, throughout which farm outputs remained stable, spread through an expanding rural population. It makes more sense to see the golden age of English georgic writing – if that is not too grand a label for the period c.1697–c.1767 – as a literary reflection of these gathering energies, than as anticipations of a slightly later agrarian revolution.

There is another contextual factor that muddies the eighteenth-century picture: steadily increasing productivity did not always mean economic prosperity. A succession of big harvests through the second quarter of the eighteenth century led to tumbling farm prices and emptying rent rolls, and the consequence was a sustained agricultural depression in 1725–50.[57] These challenging years help to account for the grit one finds mixed in with even the most optimistic eighteenth-century georgic writing. The jarring disjunction between georgic abundance and grinding economic adversity marks the labouring-class complaint literature of the 1730s, most famously in *The Thresher's Labour* (1730) by Stephen Duck, and Mary Collier's answer to it, *The Woman's Labour* (1739) – the latter opening a new domestic prospect for georgic drudgery half-hidden, as Alexandra Harris argues in Chapter 2 of this collection, by Virgil.[58] It casts a shadow over passages of satire against agricultural innovation in Jonathan Swift's *Gulliver's Travels* (1726), itself another deeply worked literary experiment in georgic form.[59] The bitterness of the ad hominem exchanges between Jethro Tull and Stephen Switzer, horse-hoeing modernizer and champion of ancient agronomy, respectively, suggest the heightened tensions of straitened times. Frans De Bruyn tells their story in Chapter 7.[60]

The most popular and hopeful of all eighteenth-century English georgics was James Thomson's four-part poem *The Seasons* (1726–30). A few months after its publication in 1730, Queen Caroline struck a coin commemorating the life of Sir Isaac Newton which bore the inscription 'felix cognoscere causas' – the georgic motto adopted by Bacon, here reflecting the scientific optimism that Thomson's poem was doing much to popularize.[61] Yet it is striking how many of *The Seasons*' frequent Virgilian allusions are to darker and more threatening passages from the *Georgics*. Admittedly, several of *The Seasons*' set pieces – the awakening of ploughed land in 'Spring', the scenes of 'happy Labour, Love, and social Glee' and the extended patriotic hymn in 'Summer', the prophesy of British commercial greatness at the start of 'Autumn' – seem if anything to soften their sources in the first *Georgic*.[62] Yet representations of nature at its most threatening, toilsome and tragic, often with allusions to Virgil, are frequent: the

Nightingale's robbed nest and the lover's agonies in 'Spring'; the stinging insects, fires and serpents of 'Summer'; the sublime storms of 'Winter'.[63] Thomson's moral ideals of social love and charity could prevail easily over vice, if only humanity could pay proper attention to

> the thousand nameless Ills,
> That one incessant Struggle render Life,
> One Scene of Toil, of Suffering, and of Fate.[64]

When Thomson imitates the joyful 'O fortunatos nimium' section from the second *Georgic* in 'Autumn', it is significant that he largely replaces the modest and unknowingly lucky farmer focused on by Virgil with the figure of a rhapsodizing rural philosopher-poet.[65] Expanding prospects and productive abundance explain the hopefulness of Thomson's patriot ideology. Yet the lived experience of rural workers during the second quarter of the eighteenth century could only bare so much hopeful scrutiny.

As farm prices rose again after 1750 there was a flush of substantial new georgic poems, lineal descendants from Philips, Pope and Thomson. First to appear was a pair of Virgilian imitations that stuck to an agricultural brief: Christopher Smart's 'The Hop Garden: A Georgic' (1752), and Robert Dodsley's 'Agriculture', the latter published as the first instalment of a larger, never-to-be-finished work, *Public Virtue*, in 1753. The painter and farmer John Dyer, an old friend of Thomson, published *The Fleece* in 1757, the physician James Grainger issued his Caribbean georgic *The Sugar-Cane* in 1764, and finally came the Warwickshire clergyman Richard Jago's topographic georgic *Edge-Hill* in 1767. These georgic poems have attracted more critical attention than their profile on publication would seem to warrant, perhaps because they are such a coherent set poetically and ideologically, and because they fit so promisingly into larger historical narratives about agricultural and industrial revolution. No other group of writers took on so willingly the work of securing moral and aesthetic connections between farming, industry and empire.[66] They were more optimistic than earlier georgic writers about the capacity of human labour to overcome nature's tendency to entropy.[67] Indeed, their appearance 'marks the point at which the morality attached to frugality and self-limitation is exchanged for the morality of improvement', writes Clare Bucknell, 'and the georgic poet rejects the genre's traditional investment in modest ambition and difficult circumstances'.[68] They also present a kind of literary mystery. If the mid-century fashion for full-scale georgic poems answered so directly to the cultural and economic questions of the age, and if those questions only became more urgent through to the nineteenth century, why did the literary fashion for georgic end so abruptly with Jago's *Edge-Hill*?

Many different explanations have been proposed for the sudden eclipse of patriot-spirited georgic poetry after 1767. John Barrell and Juan Christian Pellicer have pointed to the development of sentimental novels and political economy as modes of writing that handled the moral and industrial components in georgic separately and more effectively, not having to negotiate their poetic entanglement in an ancient literary genre.[69] Kurt Heinzelman and Frans De Bruyn both attribute it to a slipping of didactic confidence in the unity of scientific knowledge, as an age of encyclopaedism gave way to one of romantic fragmentation.[70] Karen O'Brien and Barrell agree that growing national shame over the dependence of British imperial economics on slave labour – a problem woven deeply into Virgil's text – drove mid-century georgic to rapid obsolescence.[71] Each of these explanations is significant, and together they do much to explain the genre's decline. Yet none of them considers the one sufficient cause for the fading of mid-eighteenth-century georgic. These sorts of poems stopped appearing because the only London bookseller who was willing to underwrite the publication of long-format georgics died in 1764. That bookseller was Robert Dodsley, who we have met already as the author of 'Agriculture'.[72] Dodsley was behind the financing or publication of every mid-century example of the genre.[73] These were prestigious but expensive quarto-format poems that did not sell well.[74] Dodsley was willing to risk financing them, or to use them as loss leaders, out of a real cultural commitment to didactic poetry on rural themes. He was also committed to a patriotic, manufacture-focused, physiocratic agenda in economics that his georgic authors tended to share.[75] The true context for mid-century georgic is the wider publishing catalogue of Dodsley's bookshop at the sign of Tully's Head. It features three separate translations or editions of Virgil's *Georgics* (and the distribution of a third) between 1750 and 1767.[76] It also connects literary georgic with some important agricultural publications of the day. Dodsley published Edward Lisle's *Observations in Husbandry*, edited posthumously by his son in 1757, and distributed Walter Harte's *Essays on Husbandry* (1763). It would be hard to write a coherent history of English georgic writing if Robert Dodsley had not drawn together so many of its strands in the middle of the eighteenth century.

The Romantic and Victorian Periods

As we have seen, it is a paradox of economic history that levels of agricultural productivity (as measured by output-per-worker) in England plateaued during the later part of the eighteenth century, the great age of agricultural improvement and enclosure, having risen steeply and steadily between 1600 and 1750. It is often assumed that parliamentary enclosures drove country people off the land during the second half of the eighteenth century, but again the historical record suggests the opposite: between 1751 and 1789 a population increase averaging at 22 per cent was recorded in sixteen English counties in which there was no major industrial development.[77] In 1784, the young Marquis de la Rochefoucauld toured Norfolk with the age's most prolific advocate of improvement, Arthur Young, author of a series of *Tours* of agricultural England and the bestselling *Farmer's Kalendar* (1771), which went through ten editions to 1820. Rochefoucauld was especially impressed by the region's large-scale tenant farmers, who speak 'with more intelligence than one would expect from peasants' – one is reminded of the alert and well-informed young farmer Robert Martin, and of the patronizing social judgements that he faces, in Jane Austen's novel *Emma* (1815).[78] Population in rural counties grew even faster at 27 per cent between 1789 and 1815 – the early Romantic period in literary history – and farm prices rose strongly as well, pushed by the Napoleonic wars.[79] The agricultural economy remained precarious, however: 1794–5, 1799–1800 and 1810–11 were years of scarcity, inflation and ultimately famine, with government slow in its efforts to buy compensatory stock from abroad.[80] Still, this era saw the height of the improving spirit: government took an increasing interest in farming with the foundation of the Board of Agriculture in 1793, and advanced farming practices were disseminated more quickly than ever by journals such as the wide-reaching *Farmer's Magazine* (founded 1800).[81] Then after Waterloo the fortunes of British farming changed suddenly and gravely for the worse: further population increases and falling farm prices led to significant civil conflict and rural unrest during the period 1815–37, especially the Swing Riots (1830–1).

English georgic writing during the Romantic period maps unevenly onto this historical terrain. The voices of writers and rural workers come closest together during the dark years for British farming after 1815. The correspondence is evident in the development of John Clare's writing between *The Village Minstrel* (1821), *The Shepherd's Calendar* (1827) and his unpublished *The Parish*, where local elegy is apt to turn swiftly into social protest, and protest to harden again into satire. It is articulated especially clearly, and with a distinctly georgic emphasis, in William Cobbett's *Cottage Economy* (1821–2) and *Rural Rides* (1822–6). Cobbett feels that country people are far better off in marginal and afforested landscapes, where they can keep a pig in the woods, or continue to enjoy ancient common rights to turbary (peat-cutting), estover (fire-wood) or fiscary (fishing), than they are in the prosperous and enclosed landscapes such as Clare's Northamptonshire. In Chapter 9, James Grande ascribes Cobbett's sympathetic attention to the difficulties and obstacles overcome by rural workers to a georgic spirit: 'History is not buried in *Rural Rides*', he writes, 'but continually uncovered', as it is uncovered at the close of the first *Georgic*.

Yet social protest had been the dominant note in English georgic writing during earlier improving decades as well: 'In the Romantic period', Tess Somervell argues in Chapter 8 of this collection, 'to the role of the georgic poet – observing and describing the natural environment of the countryside and the traditional ways of working it, and instructing the reader in those ways – was added the task of rural complaint.' This is especially evident in the line of displaced country voices that dominate the moral landscape of early Romantic literature: the economic emigrants of Oliver Goldsmith's *Deserted Village* (1770); the sojourners in blighted, infertile east Suffolk of George Crabbe's *The Village* (1783); impoverished Margaret and her absent husband in Wordsworth's 'The Ruined Cottage' (written 1797); and the now-disillusioned 'early worshipper at Nature's shrine' of Charlotte Smith's *Beachy Head* (1807).[82] These works correspond in different ways to historical evidence that the growth of rural economy in the Romantic period was purchased at the cost of widening social divisions: between big farmers and struggling small operations, between landlords and tenants, and between the national farming interest and the rural labourer.[83]

The second half of the nineteenth century was an era of boom and bust in British farming, and a period in which the line of georgic literature grows more faint.[84] After the repeal of the protectionist Corn Laws in 1846 there began a golden age for agriculture, the period of 'High Farming', during which improvement was underpinned by (among other things) a thoroughly scientific foundation, the introduction of mechanized reaping and mowing machines, and a significant increase in capital inputs.[85] At the beginning of his period, R. S. Surtees wrote his third novel featuring the Cockney grocer Mr Jorrocks, *Hillingdon Hall* (serialized 1843–4), to satirize the laissez-faire economics of the Whig agricultural interest. Surtees does not want to discourage progress in farming, but rather to 'repress the wild schemes of theoretical men'. Jorrocks offers the improving Duke of Donkeyton the sensible concession that 'drainin's a grand diskivery, your Greece, it's the foundation of all agricultural improvement'.[86] Representing the progressive party in these years is Alfred Tennyson's character Sir Walter Vivian, the 'great broad-shouldered genial Englishman' who we see opening his similarly broad lawns for a kind of local science fair in 'The Princess' (1847):

> A lord of fat prize-oxen and of sheep,
> A raiser of huge melons and of pine,
> A patron of some thirty charities,
> A pamphleteer on guano and on grain.[87]

A touch of satire is felt still, but the progressives were clearly set up on the winning side of the argument for the third quarter of the century. Yet from the 1870s into the early twentieth century British farming suffered one of its most sustained economic depressions.[88] Few were left untouched. The power of landowner-aristocrats such as Sir Walter was eventually broken, and many farmers and workers followed the sad advice given by Thomas Hardy in his study of the Depression's impact, 'The Dorsetshire Labourer' (1883): 'to adopt the remedy of locomotion for the evils of oppression and poverty – charms which compensate in some measure for the lost sense of home'.[89] As Andrew Radford shows in Chapter 10 of this collection, Hardy and the essayist Richard Jefferies are examples of writers who resisted the tendency to pastoralize the representation of rural work during the decades of depression, providing instead an 'excavation of those partially concealed patterns of civic strife, exploitation and bare subsistence that comprise the farmer's lot'.

The Twentieth Century

The early decades of the twentieth century were another historical hotspot for English georgic writing. Once again this reflects a period of continuing difficulties for British farming. When the adventure writer and Norfolk landowner Henry Rider Haggard completed his tour of twenty-seven English agricultural counties in 1906, his general impression was one of depopulation and rural dereliction, a picture that he swathed with biblical gloom:

> Everywhere the young men and women are leaving the villages where they were born and flocking into the towns ... This is certain—for I have noted it several times—some parts of England are becoming almost as lonesome as the veld of Africa. There 'the highways lie waste, the wayfaring man ceaseth'. The farm labourer is looked down upon, especially by young women of his own class, and consequently looks down upon himself. He is at the very bottom of the social scale.[90]

There was a countervailing trend as well: city-dwellers flowed from towns into new suburban villas – built often on plots that had been received as enclosure allotments and then sold on by former cottagers – and the countryside was rediscovered by a new class of residents with no immediate interest in the land. The account that George Sturt gave of these changes to his semi-rural corner of Surrey in 1912 was an influential one:

'The population of some five hundred twenty years ago has increased to over two thousand; the final shabby patches of the old heath are disappearing; on all hands glimpses of new building and raw new roads defy you to persuade yourself that you are in a country place'.[91] Sturt was one of a generation of memoirists scrabbling to record what remained of a traditional way of life connected to the land. Writers had been complaining about the retreat of these rural cultures for centuries, but the losses of the early twentieth century really were of an extreme order. Sturt's concern was with the vanishing rural crafts-knowledge of wheelwrights and blacksmiths; others dedicated themselves to national societies for the preservation of folk-lore (founded 1878), folk-song (founded 1898) and folk-dance (founded 1911). These projects often have a sense of belatedness hanging over them, and a suspicion that their middle-class organizers are making what remains of a deep-rooted rural culture even more hollowed-out by virtue of their participation. It is harder to hear the voices of working country people in early twentieth-century rural literature than it had been in the age of Bloomfield and Clare a century earlier. Rider Haggard, for example, was conspicuously reluctant to extend his rural surveys to labouring-class countrymen or their representatives, as readers noticed at the time.[92] Even Sturt was not excepted from Raymond Williams's cutting verdict, that since the beginning of the century 'we have had country writing that moves, at times grossly, at times imperceptibly, from record to convention and back again, until these seem inextricable'.[93] The problematic conventions were those of myth, nostalgia, 'half-history', and the literary canon: even an allusion to Virgil's *Georgics* was enough turn off Williams in dismay.[94]

In economic terms, the 1920s were especially hard years for agriculture, following the 'Great Betrayal' of the Conservative coalition government, which dropped guaranteed farm prices in 1921. From a September 1920 peak of over three times the levels seen at the beginning of the Great War in 1911, prices fell swiftly by almost 50 per cent to the end of 1922, and continued to contract nearly to pre-war levels by 1933.[95] Writing in 1939, A. G. Street observed that 'even today the burden of that piece of political treachery presses hardly on some farmers' and, remarkably, the events of 1921 are still being invoked as a warning in the farming press today.[96] It was during the 1920s that Vita Sackville-West wrote *The Land* (1926), a late, prize-winning and bestselling coda to the line of full-scale English georgic poems that runs back to Thomson's *Seasons*, as Juan Christian Pellicer shows in Chapter 11 of this volume. Her georgic poetry 'from first to last ... develops Virgil's fundamental idea that agriculture is an alternative form of warfare', writes Pellicer, 'waged not against human adversaries but against a recalcitrant natural world bent on speeding everything towards the worse ("in peius ruere", *Georgics* I, 200)'. A direct commentary on the experience of farming in the 1920s is given in Street's memoir *Farmer's Glory* (1932). Street belonged to a generation made briefly rich by high war-time prices ('farmers swanked', he recalls), but for whom, by the mid-1920s, 'ruin gibbered in the background not so very far away'.[97] Only a wholesale switch from arable to dairy and the lucky adoption of a new mobile milking rig saved him from bankruptcy. The trilogy of farming memoirs written in the same years by Adrian Bell (*Corduroy*, 1930; *The Silver Ley*, 1931; *The Cherry Tree*, 1932) are more recognizably georgic in the sharp lyricism of their descriptions of land and crop. Yet there is also the sense in these books of the author as a well-resourced incomer reluctant to look squarely at the adversity that his neighbours and employees were obliged to face. In Chapter 4 of this collection Paul Brassley concludes from his survey of these books that they leave the ambivalent and characteristically georgic impression 'that a life in farming might mean fulfilling daily involvement with satisfying and technically advanced work for some of its practitioners, but that for others, possibly the majority, it was about struggle and worry'.

By the mid-1920s writing with a georgic accent was making a relatively small contribution, despite Sackville-West, to the general chorus of rural literature and commentary. The loudest voice of all was heard in a much-reported speech of 6 May 1924 by the prime minister, Stanley Baldwin, to the Royal Society of St George. The same noises of lost rural labour that George Sturt had recalled the year before in *The Wheelwright's Shop* (1923) still chink and clank through Baldwin's patriotic declamation:

> The sounds and sights of England—the tinkle of the hammer on the anvil in a country smithy, the corncrake in the dewy morning, the sound of the scythe against the whetstone, and the sight of a plough team coming over the brow of the hill; the wild anemones in the woods in April, the last load of hay being drawn down the lane in twilight, and, most moving, the smell of the wood smoke going up in the autumn evening. Those things struck down to the very depths of our feelings. Those were the things that made England, and they ought to be the inheritance of every child born into this country.[98]

Baldwin had been in coalition government at the time of the great betrayal of 1921, so it was daring of him to imagine a British (or at least English) agricultural sector pitched backwards into the pre-mechanized past. Four years later Baldwin spoke at another annual dinner, this time for the Royal Literary Fund, and mentioned as an example of neglected rural writing the novels of Mary Webb: 'her characters really are the creation of the country' – and that is why, Baldwin imagined, 'the appeal fails' for a generation no longer in touch with country smithies and plough teams.[99] Baldwin's recommendation caused such a demand for novels by Webb, who had died the year before, that a new collected edition was swiftly published, with the prime minister providing a ghost-written preface to *Precious Bane* (1924), Webb's story about ambition and passion in a remote Shropshire village.[100] However, the posthumous success of Webb's novels, and of similarly turbulent rural romances written by Sheila Kaye-Smith, author of *Sussex Gorse* (1916) and *Susan Spray* (1931), precipitated another reaction. In 1932, Stella Gibbons published *Cold Comfort Farm*, a determinedly urbane satire on Webb, Kaye-Smith and a line of wild-eyed, heathery rural novelists going back through the Powys brothers, D. H. Lawrence and Hardy to Emily Brontë.[101] Susanne Joinson places *Cold Comfort Farm* precisely in its upland setting in Chapter 14 of this collection. Gibbons was not the only one exasperated by the excesses of rural writing. Mr Salter, foreign editor of *the Daily Beast* in Evelyn Waugh's satire *Scoop* (1938), finds the logical counterpoint to Baldwin's nostalgic, cacophonous patriotism: 'there was something un-English and not quite right about "the country"', according to Salter, 'with its solitude and self-sufficiency, its bloody recreations, its darkness and silence and sudden, inexplicable noises'.[102] Early twentieth-century georgic receded into the widening gap between conservative sentiment, agricultural science and modernistic satire.

In the second half of the twentieth century any connections that remained between changes in the UK agricultural sector and literary writing that reflected them became increasingly complicated and irregular. As Paul Brassley notes in this volume, rural fiction written for adult readers 'has been much less prominent since the Second World War than it was in the interwar years', when a little over two hundred rural novels (by Glen Cavaliero's estimate) were published.[103] Raymond Williams noticed during his lifetime an inverse proportion 'between the relative importance of the working rural economy and the cultural importance of rural ideas'.[104] When he wrote this in 1973, the balance was perhaps finer than he thought. The farming sector enjoyed the importance of success. It had made extraordinary gains after the war, with outputs per worker rising 46 per cent over just ten years after 1949, and British wheat yields going up by as much as 67 per cent between 1945 and 1960, powered by the development of artificial fertilizers, herbicides and pest controls.[105] Wheat fields that yielded 2 tonnes of grain per acre during the Second World War were producing over 7 tonnes per acre by the 1990s.[106] However, they did so in a diminishing human context, and at great ecological cost. In 1945–50 there were 865,000 agricultural workers on British farms; by 1981–5 there were 314,000, shrinking to 200,000 by the 1990s.[107]

Even the small pockets of precious landscape subject to environmental protection as SSIs (Sites of Special Scientific Interest) were often damaged or destroyed by high-input intensive farming.[108] Throughout this period the rural ideas to which Williams ascribed significance in 1973 – the enduring iconicity of country houses, the poetics of natural description, the resonance of rural memoir – were fairly prominent, especially the third category, which included widely distributed works such as Flora Thompson's *Lark Rise to Candleford* (1945) and Ronald Blythe's Suffolk composite *Akenfield* (1969). Yet their cultural impact was small in comparison with their equivalents today, as we will see in the next section.

What did remain strong across the middle of the century was a connection between high modernism in literature and advanced agricultural thinking. In Chapter 2 Alexandra Harris makes the case for reading Ford Madox Ford through a georgic lens. Lines of positive influence have been found between the writings of modernist poets such as T. S. Eliot and Ezra Pound and the organic movement as it emerged during the 1940s and 1950s.[109] At the time Edmund Wilson assumed that Virgil's didactics were antithetical to the poetics of 'pure vision' that Eliot set out in his early critical essays. Yet Eliot himself saw the *Georgics* as vitally relevant to his age, arguing that 'the attitude towards the soil, and the labour of the soil' that they expressed 'is something that we ought to find particularly intelligible now, when urban agglomeration, the flight from the land, the pillage of the earth, and the squandering of natural resources are beginning to attract attention'.[110] In Chapter 12 of this collection Jack Thacker shows how the *Georgics* continued to operate as an influence on the generation of poets that succeeded Eliot, lingering 'at the margins of the literary mainstream, albeit in a diminished form and largely unrecognised'. They are a shadowy presence in Ted Hughes's *Moortown Diary* (1979) and, Thacker argues, in Alice Oswald's river-haunting topographical poem *Dart* (2002). Their significance has been acknowledged more directly in recent Irish poetry, where the Virgil scholar Richard F. Thomas has found a pointed 'georgics of resistance' in work by Patrick Kavanagh, Seamus Heaney and Peter Fallon, tougher and darker than the English strain of modernist georgic.[111]

The Twenty-First Century

The inverted proportions between the economic power of British farming and the cultural power of ruralism detected by Raymond Williams in 1973 has become even more pronounced in recent decades. Membership numbers at the National Trust, a common index for the interest in country houses that Williams identified especially with British rural ideas, has risen from 226,200 in 1970 to a high-point of 5.95 million in 2019–20.[112] On 7 February 2016, a peak of 9.6 million viewers were tuned in to the BBC1 rural affairs magazine *Countryfile*, far outnumbering the 5.7 million viewers who watched a big-budget adaptation of *War and Peace* on the same day.[113] Each year a growing number of popular rural and 'New Nature Writing' titles appear in bookshops, supported by their own national award (the Wainwright Prize was founded in 2014) and by specialist publishers.[114] While country-facing culture has boomed, the relative economic significance of the agricultural sector has been shrinking, to the point that rural cultural services now contribute more to the nation's coffers than big agribusiness. In 1973, agriculture accounted for 2.6 per cent of the UK economy; by 2020 that contribution had shrunk to under 0.5 per cent.[115] Total income from UK farming was valued at £4.1 billion, less than a tenth of the £48 billion impact that English domestic tourism has on the UK economy, and slightly less than the £5.5 billion contributed to it from England's National Parks alone in 2017.[116] Agricultural holdings take up almost three-quarters of the UK's total land area, but their position in the economy looks increasingly marginal.

There is no way to estimate what proportion of the UK's rural culture can be described meaningfully as georgic – that is, concerned with productive work connected with the land – but it cannot be a large part. As far as literary culture is concerned, books on farming are outnumbered vastly by popular titles that focus on rural recreation, on nature cures of various kinds, or on evocations of the wilder parts of the countryside. Conventional farming makes only rare appearances on the New Nature Writing stage, cast typically as the villain of the piece.[117] However, there are signs that this may be changing. Bella Bathurst's *Field Work* (2021) is a deeply attentive portrait of modern British farming, unflinching before the daily horrors faced by stock-keepers, vets and knackermen, undeterred by the defensiveness and secrecy of the sector. Elizabeth-Jane Burnett's experimental memoir *The Grassling* (2019) digs its fingers deeply into the redland clay of Ide, the Devon village where she grew up and her forebears farmed, working to articulate 'a sense of self so deeply tangled in the soil that it is impossible to say who owns who'.[118] Melissa Harrison's novels dwell often on the joys of paying close attention to otherwise unnoticed British farming landscapes. In her second, *At Hawthorn Time* (2015), Culverkeys Farm is a recently lost component in the village life of Lodeshill, glimpsed at a closure sale; in her third, *All Among the Barley*

(2018), set in the 1930s, Wych Farm moves centre stage, as Harrison explores the different sorts of love – fierce, proprietorial, ideological – that her characters have for a small plot of East Anglian clay.[119] Other recent novels with georgic colourings include Tom Bullough's *Addlands* (2016), in which the pugilistic Radnorshire farmer Oliver Hamer becomes the unwitting subject of georgic (or 'Post-Pastoral') poetry by his lover Naomi Chance, and Ross Raisin's *God's Own Country* (2008), in which the teenage son of a hill farmer, Sam Marsdyke, descends into psychosis among the North Yorkshire moors. As the relative contribution of British agriculture to the national economy diminishes, these books show that farming communities remain the key component in contemporary representations of the land.

The idea of georgic is likely to be more useful for readers today as a frame for interpretation than as an essential category of literary genre. As we have seen, georgic writing has a well-defined set of themes: the demands of unremitting labour that recursive nature makes on productive communities; the relationship that human settlements have with unsettling histories of violence or usurpation; the reciprocal moral demands that humans and companion species make upon one another. Sometimes the reoccurrence of these themes in modern georgic literature is a matter of direct influence or of tacit cultural convention, in which case it makes sense to think of it in terms of genre or mode. However, they refer also to logics of human practice that are interconnected in ways that georgic writing has itself evolved to reflect: the anthropology of European land settlement connects with western legal codes relating to labour and property rights; the law of conflict resolution connects with the politics of nation and empire; the genetics of seed crops and domesticated animals connect with the economics of food production. It is inevitable that writers should follow the interconnections between these topics independently of literary convention.

This means that books with an apparently anti-georgic character – including rural memoirs critical of modern farming practices – can have a georgic structure of ideas. An example is George Monbiot's *Feral* (2013), which advocates for rewilding in the UK. The book is angry at how modern British agriculture excludes people from access to the countryside and reduces natural environments to monocultures. Yet the author's ethic of strenuous engagement with the natural world has its own georgic character. His dangerous and exhausting kayak expeditions to fish for mackerel in Cardigan Bay, for example, show all the spirit of Virgil's famous simile for the tenure of humans in the natural world:

>   like one whose oar can scarcely thrust his skiff upstream;
>   if perchance he slack his arms, sternward
>   the coursing water drags him down the rapids.[120]

In a later chapter, Monbiot gives a sympathetic hearing to Dafydd Morris-Jones, a Cambrian hill farmer who makes an eloquent case against rewilding, and for the undocumented culture of his disappearing community.[121] Placing a book like *Feral* in a georgic frame sets off the pragmatic human scale of its proposals, as distinct from the more radical exclusions of deep ecologists – whatever farmers might think about Monbiot's proposals for (re-)introducing megafauna such as wisent and elephants to the British countryside. The descriptive didactics of the English georgic tradition have been succeeded by the auto-didactics of the new nature writers.

In the third decade of the twenty-first century, our idea of the history of English georgic writing has two especially powerful forces reshaping the frame it gives us on working rural environments in the British Isles. The first is the changing understanding readers have of how the strenuous, anti-atrophic energy registered in domestic georgic writing should be identified with the expansive and expropriating energy of imperialism. This understanding is likely to continue to shape our sense of the English georgic canon. James Grainger's plantation didactic *The Sugar-Cane* (1764) has been the subject over recent years of more monographic academic articles than any other English georgic, taking a central position in post-imperial readings of the genre.[122] It is not clear, however, whether Grainger's blithe and self-exonerating representations of the Caribbean slave economy will find a place in tomorrow's de-colonized research programmes.[123] In the concluding chapter of this collection, Charlie Kerrigan looks again at how georgic 'has been implicated in imperial politics, imagining the world and its peoples from imperial centres in ways which appear to normalize and promote the subjection of imperial subjects'.

A second force that is shaping the course of contemporary English georgic writing is the influence of American agrarianism. In Chapter 15 of this collection, Sarah Wagner-McCoy traces a tradition of American georgic writing that displays more ethical intensity and more moral jeopardy than its British equivalents. From the ideally virtuous husbandman of Thomas Jefferson to the sainted bean-hoeing intellectual of Henry David Thoreau, agrarian writers have taken up the task of imagining an American model for citizenship and selfhood in the figure of the small farmer. Yet the Civil War-era georgics of Frederick Law Olmsted, Charles Carter Lee and Charles Chesnutt discussed by Wagner-McCoy reveal intractable complications behind the ideology of agricultural independence: 'Like Virgil's

Georgics, which holds out the promise of progress in a fallen world but shows the human and environmental costs of the hard work it seems to promote', she writes, 'complex US adaptations of the georgic mode illuminate the destructive forces of agricultural labour, and the moral ambiguities of imperial expansion and racialized labour.' Chesnutt in particular uses Virgilian models 'to represent the experience of black labourers whose knowledge and skills shaped and were shaped by the land'. The discourse of American agrarianism is more urgent and direct than its British equivalent, because the topics of American agrarianism are more deeply contested, and play out for higher moral stakes.

It may be a consequence of these heightened circumstances that writers of international standing have emerged from American farming communities during the second half of the twentieth century. Their influence is felt increasingly in contemporary English georgic writing. The Kentucky farmer-poet Wendell Berry is the most celebrated of these American voices. His agrarian essays set out a complementary vision of ecological stewardship and faithfulness to place. Berry's writings on agriculture, along with those of his contemporaries Gary Snyder and Wes Jackson, advocate passionate dwelling in local environments, with a commitment to the land so intense that some atonement might even begin for the historical abuse of enslaved workers and indigenes.[124] Their agendas are full of georgic themes, particularly in their shared concern for the ethics of agricultural work. Other American environmentalist thinkers have developed the positions taken by Berry and Snyder, criticizing how some ecologists have idealized wilderness states in the natural world. Wherever nature is represented negatively in terms of human exclusion, writes William Cronon, 'we leave ourselves little hope of discovering what an ethical, sustainable, *honourable* human place in nature might actually look like'.[125] Personal labour is central once again to these theorizations of an 'everyday nature': 'we cannot come to terms with nature', suggests Richard White, 'without coming to terms with our own work, our own bodies, our own bodily labour'.[126] This is a characteristically georgic line of thinking, and it corresponds with arguments made by two very different contemporary British writers for whom Wendell Berry has been an important influence. One is Paul Kingsnorth, in his recent accounts of retreating from environmental activism into a laborious new life on a smallholding in the west of Ireland: 'I am learning what to make of it', he reports, 'slowly and clumsily and often impatiently, and it is work that I will never get enough of, and I will never master.'[127] The other, to complete the long circuit of this introductory survey, is James Rebanks, who acknowledges Berry's influence on his own writing in *English Pastoral*. One characteristic distinction between recent agricultural writing from the British Isles and its American forebears is the former's responsiveness to the much older landscapes in which it is set. 'Our land is like a poem', writes Rebanks, 'in a patchwork landscape of other poems, written by hundreds of people, both those here now and the many hundreds that came before us, with each generation adding new layers of meaning and experience'.[128] This book tells the five-hundred-year story of how writers have read the signs of husbandry, labour and cultivation – sometimes much older than their own working traditions – as a poem left upon a particular plot of land.

Notes

1 An important predecessor for Virgil was Hesiod's *Works and Days*, the oldest Western didactic poem, discussed by Philip Thibodeau in Chapter 1 of this volume. As Andrew McRae notes in Chapter 5, when George Chapman published the first English translation of Hesiod in 1618, it appeared with the title *Hesiod's Georgicks*.
2 On the seventeenth- and eighteenth-century 'poem of mixed genre, variously mingling satire, the epistle, and the didactic poem whether philosophical or georgic', see J. Barrell and H. Guest, 'On the Uses of Contradiction: Economics and Morality in the Eighteenth-Century Long Poem', in *The New 18th Century: Theory, Politics, English Literature*, ed. F. Nussbaum and L. Brown (New York: Methuen, 1987), pp. 121–42.
3 This volume's select bibliography lists around two hundred books and articles that discuss modern georgic literature. One indication of the rising profile of georgic studies is that Terry Gifford has inserted a new chapter on it into the second edition of his widely distributed *Pastoral* (Abingdon: Routledge, 2020), pp. 149–66. Three twentieth-century surveys have been especially influential: D. L. Durling, *Georgic Tradition in English Poetry* (New York: Columbia University Press, 1935); J. Chalker, *The English Georgic: A Study in the Development of a Form* (London: Routledge and Kegan Paul, 1969); and A. Low, *The Georgic Revolution* (Princeton University Press, 1985). L. P. Wilkinson, *The Georgics of Virgil: A Critical Survey* (Cambridge University Press, 1969), pp. 270–312, offers a synoptic account of 'The "Georgics" in Aftertimes'. For a contemporary perspective see P. Marland, D. McCracken and T. Somervell, '"Down on the Farm" – Introduction to the Special Issue on Agriculture and Environment', *Green Letters*, 24 (2020), 335–43.
4 See, for example, R. Robertson, *Mock-Epic Poetry from Pope to Heine* (Oxford University Press, 2009), p. 12: 'Genres certainly do cease to exist: who now writes georgic poetry or pastoral drama?'; for the idea that English georgic disappeared after c.1770 see the later section subtitled 'The Eighteenth Century'.
5 S. Armitage, *Still: A Poetic Response to Photographs of the Somme Battlefield* (London: Enitharmon Press, 2016), p. 5.

6 J. Addison, 'An Essay on the Georgics', in Virgil, *Georgics* (Dryden), pp. 145–53, at p. 147.
7 A. Smith, 'The Poetry of Budding Life', *The Royal Academy Magazine: RA*, 150 (Spring 2021), 49; *Georgics* (Johnson), p. 59.
8 S. Johnson, *A Dictionary of the English Language*, 2 vols. (1755), vol. II, 'PA'STORAL, *adj.*'
9 J. Rebanks, *English Pastoral: An Inheritance* (London: Allen Lane, 2020), pp. 33–4.
10 Rebanks, *English Pastoral*, p. 158.
11 Rebanks, *English Pastoral*, p. 17.
12 Rebanks, *English Pastoral*, pp. 176–9, 203, 240; for a vision of future sustainability for farms like Rebanks's, see D. Helm, *Green and Prosperous Land: A Blueprint for Rescuing the British Countryside* (London: William Collins, 2020), pp. 105–26.
13 S. Hartlib, *The Compleat Husband-Man: or, A Discourse of the Whole Art of Husbandry* (1659), p. 75.
14 A. Fowler, 'The Beginnings of English Georgic', in *Renaissance Genres*, ed. B. K. Lewalski (Cambridge, MA: Harvard University Press, 1986), pp. 105–25, at p. 114.
15 *The Yale Edition of the Complete Works of St Thomas More, Volume 4: Utopia*, ed. E. Surtz, S.J. and J. H. Hexter (New Haven: Yale University Press, 1965), pp. 136–7; cf. Virgil, *Georgics* (Fairclough), p. 139 (*Georgics*, II. 37): 'and let not your soil lie idle'.
16 T. Elyot, *The Book Named the Governor, 1531* (Menston: Scholars Press, 1970), fol. 32^v.
17 R. Ascham, *The Scholemaster* (1570), p. 45; on the rational fourfold structure of the *Georgics*, see *The Logike of the Moste Excellent Philosopher P. Ramus*, tr. R. MacIlmaine (1574), pp. 55, 97.
18 E. Spenser, *The Poetical Works of Edmund Spenser*, ed. E. De Selincourt, 3 vols. (Oxford University Press, 1910), vol. I, p. 110 ('November', line 154), p. 98 ('October', line 58); for Spenser and georgic, see Low, *Georgic Revolution*, pp. 35–70, and K. Hiltner, *What Else Is Pastoral?: Renaissance Literature and the Environment* (Ithaca: Cornell University Press, 2011), pp. 156–73.
19 Hartlib, *Compleat Husband-Man*, p. 75; 'diverse' is, apart from Hartlib's sarcastically repeated usage here, a word much used by Francis Bacon, e.g., 'diuers particular sciences', *The Oxford Francis Bacon IV: The Advancement of Learning*, ed. M. Kiernan (Oxford: Clarendon Press, 2000), p. 62.
20 C. Butler, *The Feminine Monarchie or a Treatise Concerning Bees, and the Due Ordering of Them* (Oxford, 1609), A2^r, quoting *Georgics*, IV. 210–28; A4^r, quoting *Georgics*, IV. 219–21; G2^{r-v}, quoting *Georgics*, IV. 170–8.
21 J. Thirsk, 'Agricultural Innovations and Their Diffusion', *AHEW*, vol. V.ii, pp. 534, 540.
22 Bacon, *Advancement of Learning*, pp. 134–5, quoting *Georgics*, III. 289–90, 'And well I know how hard it is to win with words a triumph herein, and thus to crown with glory a lowly theme'; for the broader structure of georgic metaphor here, see B. Vickers, *Francis Bacon and Renaissance Prose* (Cambridge

University Press, 1968), pp. 187–98, and S. E. Fish, *Self-Consuming Artefacts: The Experience of Seventeenth-Century Literature* (Berkeley: University of California Press, 1972), pp. 78–155.

23 See A. Wallace, 'Virgil and Bacon in the Schoolroom', *ELH*, 73 (2006), 161–185, at 172.

24 Bacon, *Advancement of Learning*, p. 50: 'And therefore *Virgill* did excellently, and profoundlye couple the knowledge of causes, and the Conquest of all fears, together, as *Concomitantia*'.

25 A. Patterson, 'Pastoral versus Georgic: The Politics of Virgilian Quotation', in *Renaissance Genres*, ed. Lewalski, pp. 241–67, at p. 245; for the *cultura animi* tradition, see M. Sharpe, 'Georgics of the Mind and the Architecture of Fortune: Francis Bacon's Therapeutic Ethics', *Philosophical Papers*, 43 (2014), 89–121.

26 On Virgil's Epicureanism, see M. Gale, *Virgil on the Nature of Things: The Georgics, Lucretius and the Didactic Tradition* (Cambridge University Press, 2006), pp. 38–43, who notes that Virgil refuses to guarantee a Lucretian promise that knowledge of the causes of things can free us from 'metus' (fear) or 'labor'.

27 G. Markham, *The English Husbandman* (1613), sig. A1r; on Fleming's translation, see Wilkinson, *Georgics of Virgil*, p. 296.

28 T. Fuller, *The History of the Worthies of England* (1662), 'Somersetshire', pp. 28–9.

29 M. Drayton, *The Works of Michael Drayton*, ed. J. W. Hebel, 5 vols. (Oxford: Blackwell, 1931–41), vol. IV, p. v* (*Poly-Olbion*, 'To the Generall *Reader*').

30 R. Helgerson, 'The Land Speaks: Cartography, Chorography, and Subversion in Renaissance England', *Representations*, 16 (1986), 50–85, at 76.

31 C. Webster, 'The Authorship and Significance of *Macaria*', *Past & Present*, 56 (1972), 34–48.

32 *ODNB*, 'Plattes, Gabriel (c. 1600–1644)' mentions a 1638 title, *A Treatise of Husbandry*, but there is no record of it on ESTC; it seems to be one of three untraced titles by Plattes discussed by G. E. Fussell, *The Old English Farming Books*, 5 vols. (London: Crosby Lockwood, [1947?] 1991), vol. I, pp. 36–7; Plattes's 1639 agricultural title *A Discovery of Infinite Treasvre, Hidden since the Worlds Beginning* does survive.

33 J. Thirsk, 'Plough and Pen: Agricultural Writers in the Seventeenth Century', in *Social Relations and Ideas: Essays in Honour of R. H. Hilton*, ed. T. H. Aston et al. (Cambridge University Press, 1983), pp. 295–317, at pp. 307–12.

34 S. Hartlib, *The Reformed Common-Wealth of Bees* (1655), pp. 45–6.

35 T. Birch, *The History of the Royal Society*, 4 vols. (1756–7), vol. I, pp. 212–19.

36 See Thirsk, 'Agricultural Innovations', p. 560.

37 Thirsk, 'Plough and Pen', pp. 314–17.

38 J. R. Cooper, *The Art of 'The Compleat Angler'* (Durham: Duke University Press, 1968), pp. 42, 47, 75–6.

39 See K. Goodman, '"Wasted Labor"? Milton's Eve, the Poet's Work, and the Challenge of Sympathy', *ELH*, 64 (1997), 415–46; J. C. Pellicer, 'Virgil's Georgics II in *Paradise Lost*', *Translation and Literature*, 14 (2005), 129–47; and S. Lobis, 'Milton's Tended Garden and the Georgic Fall', *Milton Studies*, 55 (2014), 89–111.

40 L. L. Martz, '*Paradise Regained:* Georgic Form, Georgic Style', *Milton Studies*, 32 (2002), 7–25; Fowler 'Beginnings of English Georgic', p. 123.
41 British Library, Lansdowne MS 95, no. 2, ff.1–15, cited by B. K. Lewalski, *The Life of John Milton: A Critical Biography* (Oxford: Blackwell, 2000), p. 655.
42 Low, *Georgic Revolution*, pp. 280–5, 289–90.
43 D. Chambers, '"Wild Pastorall Encounter": John Evelyn, John Beale and the Renegotiation of Pastoral in the Mid-Seventeenth Century', in *Culture and Cultivation in Early Modern England*, ed. M. Leslie and T. Raylor (Leicester University Press, 1992), pp. 173–94, at p. 185.
44 J. Dryden, *Annus mirabilis, The Year of Wonders* (1667), *A*8^v; Addison, 'Essay on the Georgics', p. 151.
45 John Dennis and Joseph Trapp also contributed translations from the *Georgics*: see attributions in J. Dryden, *The Dryden-Tonson Miscellanies, 1684–1709*, ed. S. Gillespie and D. Hopkins, 6 vols. (London: Routledge, 2008), vol. I, p. cviii; vol. II, p. viii; vol. VI, p. ix.
46 M. Hunter, *The Royal Society and Its Fellows 1660–1700: The Morphology of an Early Scientific Institution*, 2nd ed. ([Stanford in the Vale]: British Society for the History of Science, 1994), p. 63 [F361].
47 J. Houghton, *Husbandry and Trade Improv'd*, 4 vols. (1728), vol. IV, p. 56.
48 A. Johns, *The Nature of the Book: Print and Knowledge in the Making* (Chicago University Press, 1998), pp. 108, 537–8.
49 J. Barnard, 'Dryden, Tonson, and Subscriptions for the 1697 *Virgil*', *Papers of the Bibliographical Society of America*, 57 (1963), 129–51; P. Hammond, 'The Printing of the Dryden–Tonson *Miscellany Poems* (1684) and *Sylvae* (1685)', *Papers of the Bibliographical Society of America*, 84 (1990), 405–12.
50 J. Philips, *Cyder: A Poem: In Two Books* (1708), pp. 87, 89; see K. O'Brien, 'Imperial Georgic, 1660–1789', in *The Country and the City Revisited: England and the Politics of Culture, 1550–1850*, ed. G. MacLean, D. Landry and J. P. Ward (Cambridge University Press, 1999), pp. 160–79; J. C. Pellicer, 'Celebrating Queen Anne and the Union of 1707 in Great Britain's First Georgic', *Journal for Eighteenth-Century Studies*, 37 (2014), 217–27.
51 *The Spectator*, ed. D. F. Bond, 5 vols. (Oxford: Clarendon Press), vol. I, p. 292; the *Georgics* provided epigrams for nineteen further numbers, including the manifesto essay of *Spectator* no. 10 (vol. I, p. 44); it is discussed in three of the 'Pleasures of the Imagination' essays (vol. III, pp. 549, 560, 565).
52 B. O Hehir, 'The Meaning of Swift's "Description of a City Shower"', *ELH*, 27 (1960), 194–207; H. Power, 'Virgil, Horace, and Gay's Art of Walking the Streets', *Cambridge Quarterly*, 38 (2009), 338–67.
53 *The Spectator*, vol. I, p. 296.
54 A. Pope, *Windsor Forest*, in *The Twickenham Edition of the Poems of Alexander Pope*, ed. J. Butt et al., 11 vols. (London: Methuen, 1939–69), vol. I, pp. 152, 191–2 (lines 39–40, 401, 408); see P. Rogers, 'John Philips, Pope, and Political Georgic', *Modern Language Quarterly*, 66, 4 (2005), 411–42.
55 R. C. Allen, 'Economic Structure and Agricultural Productivity in Europe, 1300–1800', *European Review of Economic History*, 4 (2000), 1–25, at 21.

56 R. C. Allen, 'Agriculture during the Industrial Revolution, 1700–1850', in *The Cambridge Economic History of Modern Britain*, ed. R. Floud and P. Johnson (Cambridge University Press, 2004), pp. 96–116, at p. 108.

57 P. J. Bowden, 'Agricultural Prices, Wages, Farm Profits, and Rents', *AHEW*, vol. V.ii, p. 9; G. E. Mingay, 'The Agricultural Depression, 1730–1750', *Economic History Review*, n.s., 8 (1956), 323–38.

58 See B. Keegan, 'Georgic Transformations and Stephen Duck's "The Thresher's Labour"', *SEL: Studies in English Literature 1500–1900*, 41 (2001), 545–62; C. E. Andrews, '"Work" Poems: Assessing the Georgic Mode of Eighteenth-Century Working-Class Poetry', in *Experiments in Genre in Eighteenth-Century Poetry*, ed. Sandro Jung (Lebanon, NH: Academia Press, 2011), pp. 105–33.

59 J. Swift, *The Cambridge Edition of the Works of Jonathan Swift. 16: Gulliver's Travels*, ed. D. Womersley (Cambridge University Press, 2012), pp. 194, 253 (Lord Munodi's tour of his estates, doomed to be ruined by agricultural innovation); M. A. Doody, 'Insects, Vermin, and Horses: *Gulliver's Travels* and Virgil's *Georgics*', in *Augustan Studies: Essays in Honour of Irvin Ehrenpreis*, ed. D. L. Patey and T. Keegan (Newark: University of Delaware Press, 1985), pp. 147–74; see also D. L. Patey, 'Swift's Satire on "Science" and the Structure of Gulliver's Travels', *ELH*, 58 (1991), 809–39, at 828.

60 See also F. De Bruyn, 'Reading Virgil's *Georgics* as a Scientific Text: The Eighteenth-Century Debate between Jethro Tull and Stephen Switzer', *ELH*, 71 (2004), 661–89.

61 Referring to Virgil, *Georgics*, II. 490, 'felix qui potuit rerum cognoscere causas', the poem's most Lucretian and scientistic passage; cf. J. Thomson, *The Seasons*, ed. J. Sambrook (Oxford: Clarendon Press, 1981), p. 192, 'Autumn' lines 1133–7; for Caroline's coin, see P. Fara and D. Money, 'Isaac Newton and Augustan Anglo-Latin Poetry', *Studies in the History and Philosophy of Science*, 35 (2004), 549–71, at 567; for Thomson's association with Queen Caroline, see Philip Connell, *Secular Chains: Poetry and the Politics of Religion from Milton to Pope* (Oxford University Press, 2016), pp. 199–207.

62 Thomson, *Seasons*, pp. 4–6, 'Spring' lines 32–77 (imitating *Georgics*, I. 44–6, 63–5); pp. 78–82, 'Summer' lines 352–431, and pp. 125–33, lines 1442–619 (*Georgics*, II. 138–76); pp. 146–50, 'Autumn' lines 43–150 (*Georgics*, I. 125–46).

63 Thomson, *Seasons*, p. 36, 'Spring' lines 714–28 (imitating *Georgics*, IV. 511–15) and p. 52, lines 1067–73 (*Georgics*, III. 258–63); p. 84, 'Summer' lines 498–505 (*Georgics*, III. 146–51), p. 90, lines 628–42 (*Georgics*, II. 303–11) and p. 102, lines 898–907 (*Georgics*, II., 153–4); 'Winter', p. 206, lines 72–80 (*Georgic*, I. 322–31, 351–456).

64 Thomson, *Seasons*, p. 219, 'Winter' lines 349–51; see also p. 44, 'Spring' lines 878–93, for the diffusion of God's 'creative bounty' through social love.

65 This point is made by Sambrook in his notes to *Seasons*, 'Autumn' lines 1235–1373 and 1352–1373, which imitate *Georgics*, II. 458–542 and II. 457–86, respectively.

66 O'Brien, 'Imperial Georgic', p. 161.

67 D. Fairer makes this point regarding Dyer in '"Where Fuming Trees Refresh the Thirsty Air": The World of Eco-Georgic', *Studies in Eighteenth-Century Culture*, 40 (2011), 201–18, at 204; see D. Griffin, *Patriotism and Poetry in Eighteenth-Century Britain* (Cambridge University Press, 2002), p. 196, for a similar assessment.
68 C. Bucknell, 'The Mid-Eighteenth-Century Georgic and Agricultural Improvement', *Journal for Eighteenth-Century Studies* 36 (2013), 335–52, at 340.
69 J. Barrell, 'Afterword: Moving Stories, Still Lives', in *The Country and the City Revisited*, ed. MacLean et al., pp. 231–48, at p. 245; Juan Christian Pellicer, 'The Georgic at Mid-Eighteenth Century and the Case of Dodsley's "Agriculture"', *RES*, 54, 213 (2003), 67–93, at 91–2.
70 F. De Bruyn, 'From Virgilian Georgic to Agricultural Science: An Instance in the Transvaluation of Literature in Eighteenth-Century Britain', in *Augustan Subjects: Essays in Honor of Martin C. Battestin*, ed. A. J. Rivero (Newark, NJ: University of Delaware Press, 1997), pp. 47–67, at p. 63; K. Heinzelman, 'Roman Georgic in the Georgian Age: A Theory of Romantic Genre', *Texas Studies in Literature and Language*, 33 (1991), 182–214, at 190; see also R. Beck, 'From Industrial Georgic to Industrial Sublime: English Poetry and the Early Stages of the Industrial Revolution', *British Journal for Eighteenth-Century Studies*, 27 (2004), 17–36.
71 O'Brien, 'Imperial Georgic', p. 174; Barrell, 'Afterword', p. 245.
72 Dodsley's more cautious brother James published Jago's *Edge-Hill* three years later in 1767, part-financing it by subscription, but the poem had a long and difficult gestation in which Robert was involved; see William Shenstone to Jago, 18 December 1762, *Correspondence of Thomas Percy and William Shenstone*, ed. C. Brooks (New Haven: Yale University Press, 1977), p. 232.
73 Dodsley's name does not appear on the title page of Smart's *Poems on Several Occasions* (1752), where 'The Hop-Garden' first appeared, but recently discovered correspondence confirms that he managed its publication by subscription: see C. Donaldson, 'Another Smart Letter', *Notes and Queries*, 59 (2012), 338–40. The other georgics all have Dodsley's Tully's Head imprint.
74 None of them reached a second monographic edition; Grainger's *Sugar-Cane* is an apparent exception, but the 12mo edition of 1766 was a Dublin piracy by William Sleater with a false London imprint.
75 Evidence for this commitment can be found in every aspect of Dodsley's professional, cultural and associational life, as I show in a forthcoming book, *Enlightenment Mock-Arts*.
76 Virgil, *The Georgics of Virgil. Attempted in English Verse* (1750), an anonymous translation of the first georgic; Virgil, *The Works of Virgil*, ed. J. Warton, 4 vols. (1753); and *The Georgics of Virgil*, tr. T. Neville (Cambridge, 1767), which Dodsley helped distribute. John Baskerville's typographically innovative Latin Virgil appeared in 1757, with Dodsley as London agent and distributor; see *Correspondence of Robert Dodsley, 1733–1764*, ed. J. E. Tierney (Cambridge University Press, 1988), pp. 264–5, 273.

77 W. A. Armstrong, 'The Countryside', in *The Cambridge Social History of Britain, 1750–1950*, ed. F. M. L. Thompson (Cambridge University Press, 1990), pp. 87–154, at p. 96.
78 *A Frenchman in England, 1784: Being the 'Mélanges sur l'Angleterre' of François de la Rochefoucauld* (Cambridge University Press, 1933), pp. 233–4.
79 *AHEW*, vol. VI.ii, p. 642.
80 R. Wells, *Wretched Faces: Famine in Wartime England, 1793–1801* (New York: St Martin's Press, 1988).
81 N. Goddard, 'Agricultural Literature and Societies', *AHEW*, vol. VI.i, pp. 367, 379–83.
82 C. Smith, *Beachy Head: with Other Poems* (1807), p. 24.
83 G. E. Mingay, 'Conclusion: The Progress of Agriculture, 1750–1850', *AHEW*, vol. VI.ii, p. 971.
84 An exception is K. Hadley's article '"Tulips on Dunghills": Regendering the Georgic in Barrett Browning's *Aurora Leigh*', *Victorian Poetry*, 52 (2014), 465–82.
85 E. L. Jones, 'The Changing Basis of English Agricultural Prosperity, 1853–1873', *Agricultural History Review*, 10 (1962), 102–19; P. J. Perry, 'High Farming in Victorian Britain: The Financial Foundations', *Agricultural History*, 52 (1978), 364–79.
86 R. S. Surtees, *Hillingdon Hall: Or, The Cockney Squire*, 3 vols. (London, 1845), vol. I, p. 216; see C. R. Vanden Bossche, *Reform Acts: Chartism, Social Agency, and the Victorian Novel, 1832–1867* (Baltimore: Johns Hopkins University Press, 2014), pp. 75–127, especially pp. 102–13 on Surtees.
87 *Tennyson: A Selected Edition*, ed. C. Ricks, rev. ed. (Abingdon: Routledge, 2007), pp. 329–30 ('The Princess', 'Conclusion', lines 85–9).
88 R. Perren, *Agriculture in Depression, 1870–1940* (Cambridge University Press, 1995), pp. 7–11; T. W. Fletcher's analysis indicates that the Great Depression was also a readjustment that did have winners (livestock, liquid milk producers), see 'The Great Depression of English Agriculture, 1873–1896', *Economic History Review*, 13 (1961), 417–32.
89 T. Hardy, 'The Dorsetshire Labourer', *Longman's Magazine*, Vol. II (May–October 1883), p. 264.
90 H. Rider Haggard, *Rural England: Being an Account of Agricultural and Social Researches Carried Out in the Years 1901 and 1902*, 2 vols. (1906; Cambridge University Press, 2011) vol. II, pp. 539, 540.
91 G. Sturt, *Change in the Village* (1912; Cambridge University Press, 2010), pp. 6–7; for Sturt's influence among F. R. Leavis and his students, see P. Bullard, 'Restoring the Wheelwright's Shop', *Journal of Modern Craft*, 13 (2020), 161–78, at 162.
92 See M. Freeman, 'Rider Haggard and "Rural England": Methods of Social Enquiry in the English Countryside', *Social History*, 26 (2001), 209–16.
93 R. Williams, *The Country and the City* (1973; London: Vintage, 2016), p. 375.
94 Williams, *Country and City*, pp. 19, 375, the incriminating cliché being 'a way of life that has come down to us from the days of Virgil', which he attributes to George Ewart Evans's *The Pattern under the Plough* (1966).

95 *AHEW*, vol. VIII, pp. 142, 230; E. H. Whetham, 'The Agriculture Act, 1920 and Its Repeal – the "Great Betrayal"', *Agricultural History Review*, 22 (1974), 36–49.
96 *Farmer's Weekly*, 13 October 1939, p. 16; W. Evans, 'Opinion: Let's not Repeat the "Great Betrayal" of 1921', *Farmer's Weekly*, 18 January 2020, www.fwi.co.uk/news/opinion-lets-not-repeat-the-great-betrayal-of-1921 (accessed 22 September 2012).
97 A. G. Street, *Farmer's Glory* (1932; Oxford University Press, 1983), pp. 206, 215.
98 'English Traits', *The Times*, 7 May 1924, p. 16.
99 'Royal Literary Fund', *The Times*, 26 April 1928, p. 18.
100 *Baldwin Papers: A Conservative Statesman, 1908–1947*, ed. P. Williamson and E. Baldwin (Cambridge University Press, 2004), p. 193.
101 F. Hammill, 'Cold Comfort Farm, D. H. Lawrence, and English Literary Culture Between the Wars', *Modern Fiction Studies*, 47 (2001), 831–54.
102 E. Waugh, *Scoop* (1938; London: Eyre Methuen, 1978), p. 36.
103 G. Cavaliero, *The Rural Tradition in the English Novel 1900–1939* (London: Macmillan, 1977), pp. 227–31.
104 Williams, *Country and City*, p. 356.
105 Mingay, 'Conclusion', *AHEW*, vol. VI.ii, p. 951; P. Brassley, 'Output and Technical Change in Twentieth-Century British Agriculture', *Agricultural History Review*, 48 (2000), 60–84, at 71.
106 J. Martin, *The Development of Modern Agriculture: British Farming since 1931* (Basingstoke: Palgrave Macmillan, 2000), p. 98.
107 H. F. Marks, *A Hundred Years of British Food and Farming: A Statistical Survey* (London: Taylor & Francis, 1989), p. 138, quoted by A. Howkins, *The Death of Rural England: A Social History of the English Countryside since 1900* (London: Routledge, 2003), p. 164.
108 G. Harvey, *The Killing of the Countryside* (London: Cape, 1997), pp. 50–65, at p. 52.
109 J. Diaper, 'Ill Fares the Land: The Literary Influences and Agricultural Poetics of the Organic Husbandry Movement in the 1930s–50s', *Literature and History*, 27 (2018), 167–88; J. Diaper, *T. S. Eliot and Organicism* (Clemson University Press, 2018); J. Diaper, 'Farming and Agriculture in Literary Modernism', *Modernist Cultures*, 16 (2021), 86–113.
110 E. Wilson, *Axel's Castle: A Study in the Imaginative literature of 1870–1930* (New York: Scribner, 1931), p. 120; T. S. Eliot, 'Virgil and the Christian World' (1951), quoted by G. Reeves, *T. S. Eliot: A Virgilian Poet* (Basingstoke: Macmillan, 1989), p. 89; on the georgic character of Eliot's poem 'East Coker', see T. Ziolkowski, *Virgil and the Moderns* (Princeton University Press, 1993), p. 128.
111 R. F. Thomas, in 'The "Georgics" of Resistance: From Virgil to Heaney', *Vergilius*, 47 (2001), 117–47.
112 *National Trust Annual Report 2019–20*, https://nt.global.ssl.fastly.net/documents/annual-report-201920.pdf (accessed 23 September 2020).

113 'Countryfile Beats War and Peace', 8 February 2016, *Radio Times*, www.radiotimes.com/tv/entertainment/countryfile-beats-war-and-peace-finale-and-call-the-midwife-with-record-tv-audience/ (accessed 23 September 2021).

114 On the impact and cultural politics of this movement, see J. Smith, *The New Nature Writing: Rethinking the Literature of Place* (London: Bloomsbury, 2017), pp. 22–32; see also P. Marland, 'Rewilding, Wilding, and the New Georgic in Contemporary Nature Writing', *Green Letters*, 24 (2020), 421–36.

115 'Changes in the Economy since 1970', www.ons.gov.uk/economy/economicoutputandproductivity/output/articles/changesintheeconomysincethe1970s/2019-09-02 (accessed 23 September 2021).

116 'Agriculture in the UK 2020', www.gov.uk/government/statistics/agriculture-in-the-united-kingdom-2020 (accessed 23 September 2021), 9; 'England Tourism Factsheet 2019', www.visitbritain.org/sites/default/files/vb-corporate/Documents-Library/documents/England-documents/england_tourism_factsheet_2019_website.docx (accessed 23 September 2021); 'Gross Value Added of England's National Parks', www.nationalparksengland.org.uk/__data/assets/pdf_file/0015/29040/Gross-Value-Added-for-England-National-Parks-2017-Update.pdf (accessed 23 September 2021).

117 For example J. Lewis-Stempel's portrait of his agribusiness neighbours 'the Chemical Brothers' in *The Running Hare: The Secret Life of Farmland* (London: Doubleday, 2016), pp. 35–41; similarly damning in its assessment of modern farmers is M. McCarthy, *The Moth Snowstorm: Nature and Joy* (London: John Murray, 2015), Ch. 3, 'The Bond and the Losses'.

118 E.-J. Burnett, *The Grassling: A Geological Memoir* (2019; London: Penguin, 2020), p. 11; cf. pp. 67–9, 74–8.

119 For a discussion on Harrison's work, see Dominic Head, 'The Farming Community Revisited: Complex Nostalgia in Sarah Hall and Melissa Harrison', *Green Letters*, 24 (2020), 354–66.

120 *Georgics* (Johnson), p. 17 (*Georgics*, I. 201–3); cf. G. Monbiot, *Feral: Rewilding the Land, the Sea, and Human Life* (2013; London: Penguin, 2014), pp. 23–34. Since this volume went into production, George Monbiot has published a more direct and comprehensive critique of modern farming in *Regenesis: Feeding the World without Devouring the Planet* (Allen Lane, 2022); the editor regrets missing the opportunity to discuss this major intervention here.

121 Monbiot, *Feral*, pp. 167–85; Morris-Jones is one of the farmers interviewed by Patrick Barkham in 'The Reality of Modern Farming: Three Farmers in Conversation', *Green Letters*, 24 (2020), 344–53.

122 Examples include M. Ellis, 'Incessant labour: Georgic Poetry and the Problem of Slavery', in *Discourses of Slavery and Abolition: Britain and its Colonies, 1760–1838*, ed. B. Carey, M. Ellis and S Salih (Basingstoke: Palgrave Macmillan, 2004), pp. 45–62; D. Fairer, 'A Caribbean Georgic: James Grainger's The Sugar-Cane', *Kunapipi: Journal of Post-Colonial Writing*, 25 (2003), 21–8; A. M. Foy, 'Grainger and the "Sordid Master": Plantocratic

Alliance in *The Sugar-Cane* and Its Manuscript', *RES*, ns, 68 (2017), 708–33; S. Irlam, '"Wish You Were Here": Exporting England in James Grainger's *Sugar-Cane*', *ELH*, 68 (2001), 377–96; S. Kaul, 'On Intersections between Empire, Colony, Nation, and Province in Eighteenth-Century British Poetry', *Eighteenth-Century Novel*, 6–7 (2009), 138–44; C. Plasa, *Slaves to Sweetness: British and Caribbean Literatures of Sugar* (Liverpool University Press, 2009), especially '"Muse Suppress the Tale": James Grainger's *The Sugar-Cane* and the Poetry of Refinement', pp. 8–32; B. P. Randhawa, 'The Inhospitable Muse: Locating Creole Identity in James Grainger's *The Sugar-Cane*', *ECTI*, 49 (2008), 67–85; K. Sandiford, *The Cultural Politics of Sugar: Caribbean Slavery and Narratives of Colonialism* (Cambridge University Press, 2000), especially 'Grainger: Creolizing the Muse', pp. 67–87; C. Silva, 'Georgic Fantasies: James Grainger and the Poetry of Colonial Dislocation', *ELH*, 83 (2016), 127–56.

123 A positive model is the *Digital Grainger* project, an online edition of *The Sugar-Cane* that includes an auto-critical section designed 'to enable counter-plantation readings of the poem that work against the grain of Grainger's pro-slavery narrative', https://digital-grainger.github.io/grainger/about.html (accessed 23 September 2021).

124 G. Snyder, 'Reinhabitation', *A Place in Space: Ethics, Aesthetics, and Watersheds* (Washington, DC: Counterpoint, 1995), pp. 183–92; W. Berry, *The Art of the Commonplace: The Agrarian Essays of Wendell Berry*, ed. N. Wirzba (Berkeley: Counterpoint, 2002), especially 'People, Land, and Community', pp. 182–94, and 'The Whole Horse', pp. 236–48; see the essays collected in W. Vitek and W. Jackson, ed., *Rooted in the Land: Essays on Community and Place* (New Haven: Yale University Press, 1996), especially Jackson's 'Matfield Green', pp. 95–103.

125 W. Cronon, 'The Trouble with Wilderness; or, Getting Back to the Wrong Nature', in *Uncommon Ground: Rethinking the Human Place in Nature*, ed. W. Cronon (New York: Norton, 1996), pp. 69–91, at p. 81; cf. W. Jackson, 'Wilderness as Saint', *Aperture*, 120 (1990), 50: 'without civilization, wilderness is doomed'.

126 R. White, 'Are You an Environmentalist or Do You Work for a Living? Work and Nature', in *Uncommon Ground*, ed. Cronon, pp. 171–85, at p. 173; S. Hess, 'Imagining an Everyday Nature', *ISLE*, 17 (2010), 85–112, with discussions of the georgic tradition at p. 102.

127 P. Kingsnorth, 'Learning What to Make of It', in *Confessions of a Recovering Environmentalist* (London: Faber, 2017), pp. 90–106, at p. 105, an essay framed by Kingsnorth's reading of Berry's correspondence with Snyder; see also 'Dark Ecology', pp. 119–49.

128 Rebanks, *English Pastoral*, p. 197.

PART I

Turnings

CHAPTER I

Hesiod, Virgil and the Ambitions of Georgic
Philip Thibodeau

Living outside of cities in landscapes overwhelmingly shaped by natural forces has been the norm for the vast majority of the human population until recently. It is an experience that embraces a colourful range of lifestyles, from the pirate and the robber to the shepherd and the hunter, the hermit and the holy man – and also the farmer, plantation owner and gardener, whose concerns lie at the heart of georgic literature. As a genre, georgic writing is a contingent thing, waxing and waning in popularity for reasons that are not easy to discern. Within the European–Mediterranean world it flourished first in Carthage, Greece and Rome, then, later, in Byzantium and the Islamic kingdoms, and from the Renaissance onward among the nations of Europe. This chapter tells the story of its early efflorescence, with the hope that this will allow the reader to judge, through comparison, which aspects of modern, Anglophone georgic are genuinely old or new.

If the question is raised regarding when and where georgic first arose, the answers will depend to a certain extent on the criteria one uses to define the genre. Its very existence presupposes mastery of the written word and some degree of systematization of agronomical lore. One good candidate for the genre's earliest surviving instance is a short text discovered in 1908 at the ancient site of Gezer, just west of Jerusalem, written in Semitic letters on a limestone slab. It is a calendar that begins in early autumn and divides the agricultural year into eight short seasons, four of two months and four of one. The text of the inscription reads, in its entirety:

> Two months for the harvest,
> two months for the planting of grain,
> two months for late-planting,
> one month for the flax harvest,
> one month for the barley harvest,
> one month for harvest and feasting,
> two months for tending to vines,
> and one month for summer fruit.

Consensus is lacking regarding the language of the document (Phoenician? Hebrew?) as well as its date, although it is conventionally assigned to the tenth century BCE. Even the motive for its inscription is unclear. Yet it is a written record of farm lore, with its monthly scheme betraying an incipient impulse to systemization.[1]

Yet if we press harder on the term 'literature' and take it to refer to texts committed to perishable media that are subsequently copied, circulated and handed down, then, with all due respect to its anonymous author, the Gezer calendar no longer qualifies. By this stricter definition, there appears not to have been a Hebrew georgic tradition. It is certainly true that the Jewish holy books contain passages, such as the story of Eden in Genesis or the rural delights of the Song of Songs, that left a profound mark on later georgic, yet no book from ancient Israel deals specifically with farmwork. The Egyptian corpus of sacred texts and wisdom literature likewise does not include anything that attends consistently to farming. That we know as much about Egyptian agriculture as we do is a tribute to its visual artists, whose many colourful representations of gardening and other rural tasks form a kind of pictorial georgic tradition.[2]

At one point in antiquity, the city of Carthage housed a large collection of georgic literature that was written in Punic and ascribed to a man named Mago. When the Romans sacked Carthage in 146 BCE, they seized its libraries and distributed their contents to the heads of local African kingdoms – except for Mago's twenty-eight books on farming, which were shipped back to Rome. There the Senate appointed a certain Decimus Junius Silanus to head a committee charged with translating these writings into Latin. (What became of their efforts is, unfortunately, a mystery.) Another translation of Mago's books was made a century later, this time into Greek, and it is from this effort that some sixteen quotations and paraphrases of Mago's collection have come down to us, including the opening sentence of its first book: 'A man who has purchased a farm should sell his townhouse, lest he prefer his urban home to his rural one; a man who is fond of his city residence has no need of a country estate.'[3] The name Mago evokes a king of the same name who founded the Magonid dynasty at Carthage in the sixth century BCE; many of the fragments seem too sophisticated for the time period, however, which would imply that the collection was mostly the work of a later author or authors, now anonymous. The subjects that are treated point to writers with a broad range of expertise, including grain milling, viticulture, oleoculture, animal husbandry, the gathering of wild plants and beekeeping. One can only lament our lack of access to this detailed portrait of farming and farm life in the ancient Maghreb. Dan-el Padilla Peralta

Greek Georgic Writing

has recently cited the loss of Mago's collection as a prime illustration of the workings of 'epistemocide' – the extinction of bodies of local knowledge that often follows in the wake of imperialism.[4]

The fact that ancient Mediterranean georgic only survives in Greek and Latin is thus a by-product of Roman imperialism. Fortunately the Greek and Roman traditions evince their own remarkable richness and variety. As we turn to consider their character, it will make sense to start with the Greek tradition, not just because it is the older of the two, but also because the word 'georgic' is itself of Greek origin. A compound of *gē* ('earth, land') and *ergon* ('work'), it originally denoted the various activities assorted with grain cultivation – ploughing, sowing, harvesting – its field of reference only gradually expanding to include the many subjects we now think of as 'georgic'. The earliest treatise to bear the title *Georgika* or *Georgiē* was written around the time of the Peloponnesian War by the Presocratic philosopher Democritus of Abdera; surviving fragments discuss the economics of stone walls and fencing, and the relationship between water sources and landscape.[5] Other treatises on agronomy soon followed, written by authors who maintained that the farmer should have a firm theoretical understanding of the elements of the natural world. We know about them because their approach was criticized by Xenophon of Athens, a contemporary of Plato whose essay on rural estate management, the *Oeconomicus*, takes a less stringent approach to expertise. Xenophon maintained, *pace* his predecessors, that cultivation is not at all difficult to master because one can learn what needs to be done simply by observing the behaviour of crops and considering how they respond to different environments; a walk through the countryside at planting or harvest time is all one needs to learn the basics of technique. Xenophon composed the first of what would soon become many encomia to the life of the farmer, praising it as a means of acquiring wealth approved of by both men and gods. He specifically described running a country estate as the best way to become a 'gentleman' (*kalos k'agathos*), thus initiating the discourse of the 'gentleman farmer'. Xenophon seems to have practised what he preached, spending most of his later life on a large estate in the Peloponnese, which he had acquired after being forced into exile from his native Athens.[6]

In the three centuries after Xenophon's death, Greek culture spread across the eastern Mediterranean thanks to the conquests of Alexander the Great. Meanwhile, in the Greek homeland, there was an efflorescence of georgic writing in both prose and poetry. The names of more than forty authorities from this period are preserved, although the ravages of time have left only the most exiguous of fragments from their works. One author about whom we are somewhat better informed was the poet Nicander of Colophon, c.200 BCE. Nicander is perhaps best known today for his two short epic poems on snakes and cures for animal bites, which are remarkable for their exquisite handling of morbid themes. He also composed a *Georgica*, the extant fragments of which point to extended discussions of flower and vegetable gardening:

> In its roots the dwarf iris resembles the hyacinth,
> that lamented blossom; when they rise, its swallowlike flowers
> run the same course as swallows. From their hearts
> they pour forth swordlike leaves, and newborn buds
> like drooping mouths ...
> You should cut gourds in half, string them on cords,
> dry them in the air, and hang them over smoke
> so your servants in winter can fill a spacious pot
> and chow down at leisure after the mill-woman
> has measured a mixture of beans for the soup.

While ostensibly concerned with practical advice, the poem is filled with finely observed portraits of animals, plants and rural life. One gets the impression of a move into description for its own sake, anticipating what today we tend to call 'nature writing'.[7]

Aestheticism was far from the rule, however; authors of Hellenistic georgic were often very serious about their pursuit. Pliny the Elder tells us of one writer, a beekeeper named Aristomachus of Soli, who did nothing but raise bees for fifty-eight years of his life, and alludes to a certain Philiscus of Thasos 'who kept bees on abandoned lands and so earned for himself the nickname "Wild Man"'.[8] Some followed Xenophon in reflecting on the significance of the rural way of life, defending its priority over its urban alternative:

> Menander of Heraclea has claimed that farmers are the sole surviving remnant of the race of Saturn, while Epigenes of Rhodes has shown through various proofs that country life is much more ancient than city life. Diophanes of Nicaea tells us that agriculture was the origin of nobility, because men who were thought superior to others in that pursuit wanted to be herdsmen, so that they could, in a way, exercise rule over other living beings.[9]

Despite their brevity, one can detect in these paraphrases of georgic writers the influence of contemporary Greek mythography (Menander), history (Epigenes) and anthropology (Diophanes). Around the middle of the first century CE, the Stoic philosopher Musonius Rufus wrote an essay making the case that the best way for a philosopher to support himself was as a farmer or a shepherd: 'Is it not "living more in accord with nature" to draw one's sustenance directly from the earth, which is the nurse and mother of us all, rather than from some other source? Is it not more like the life of a man to live in the country than to sit idly in the city, like the sophists?'[10] In a rather grim twist, Nero had Musonius arrested and sent to Corinth to join the digging crew tasked with constructing a canal across the isthmus.

One development that was of critical importance for the genre, and in some respects presaged its decline, was the creation of the georgic anthology. The first such work was made at the start of the first century BCE by Dionysius of Utica, the Greek writer who was also responsible for translating Mago. He dedicated it to his patron, a governor of Africa named Sextilius – it is probably no coincidence that it was a Roman who commissioned a treatise that would extract the practical nuggets from a vast and confusing literature. Further anthologies and epitomes of anthologies followed, each of these works, while of real value and reflecting individual judgement, serving somewhat to depersonalize the genre. Over time the tradition of Greek georgic writing became a tradition of Greek georgic anthologies, which were recomposed and updated every few hundred years or so, as the need arose. Under the emperor Marcus Aurelius, the twin brothers Quintilii, two former consuls whose ruined villa still looms over the fifth mile mark on the Via Appia outside of Rome, composed a *Georgica* designed to replace Dionysius' work. Its successor was composed by Vindonius Anatolius of Beirut late in the fourth century CE; Vindonius' work was in turn revised by one Cassianus Bassus in the seventh century; and Bassus' *Geoponica*, as it was called, formed the basis for the larger encyclopaedia of agriculture, also called *Geoponica*, that survives today, a labour of love by unknown scholars who enjoyed the patronage of the tenth-century Byzantine emperor Constantine VII.[11] This last *Geoponica* represents both the culmination and the end of the ancient Greek tradition, a dazzling array of recipes and short essays neatly organized by topic, starting with weather forecasts and ending with pisciculture. The authorities for each are dutifully cited, giving the whole an impressive air of erudition and authority; but the personal voice is wholly absent.[12]

The *Works and Days* of Hesiod

We have now surveyed, in broad strokes, the entire Greek georgic tradition – except for one short, idiosyncratic work, first composed a millennium and a half before the *Geoponica*, that towered above everything that came after it: Hesiod's *Works and Days*. First set down on paper around the time that texts of Homer's *Iliad* and *Odyssey* began to circulate, it quickly became part of the canon. In Aristophanes' *Frogs*, the character Aeschylus describes the practical value of the old poets in the following terms: Orpheus introduced initiation rituals, Musaeus gave men charms and oracles, Homer teaches about war, while 'Hesiod showed us how to work the earth, plus the seasons of grain and plowing.' Hesiod's poem was subsequently quoted and commented on with such frequency as to suggest that among literate Greeks at least, acquaintance with it was nearly universal.[13]

The popularity of *Works and Days* is hard to account for if one focuses strictly on its farming advice. True, it describes many of the tasks involving in grain raising, comments on the varieties of wood best suited to ploughs and wagons, offers advice on managing members of one's household, including slaves, and spells out when during the year and month crucial tasks should be done. Yet it has almost nothing to say on such vital topics (particularly from a Greek point of view) as viticulture and olive cultivation. Other than noting the day of the month when bulls should be castrated, it is nearly silent on matters of animal care. Xenophon, Democritus and their successors offered advice on the best location for a farm, irrigation, soil fertility and other such matters, but Hesiod did not. What then accounts for his extraordinary popularity?

A proximate explanation lies in the fact that *Works and Days* had become part of the school curriculum. Said curriculum was not imposed by the state: throughout classical antiquity, schooling in literature was handled by private teachers. Yet from the fifth century onward, Greek 'grammatici' and 'musici', teachers of letters and music, included *Works* and its companion poem, *Theogony*, on a short list of authors taught alongside Homer, Euripides, Plato, Demosthenes and so on.[14] Once ensconced in the canon, it benefitted from the conservative disposition of the 'grammatici' to find a captive audience everywhere Greek literacy was inculcated.

Yet this consideration begs the question why *Works and Days* was chosen as a teaching text in the first place – and why it retained that status despite competition from treatises far superior to it in coverage and relevance. Here we must come to grips with its special language and form. Like the Homeric epics, the Hesiodic poems were the product of an ancient tradition of oral poetry; *Works* is virtually identical in dialect, style and idiom to the *Iliad* and *Odyssey*, despite pursuing such different narrative ends. Hesiod employs the same weighty epithets and formulae as Homer, whereby Zeus becomes 'the son of Cronus' and wheat 'the sacred corn of

Demeter' (18, 597). He embraces hymnic elements, imitating the language of prayer in the opening address to Zeus and the Muses (1–10). The poem features a wide panoply of soundplay and rhetorical figures, such as the anaphora in this commentary on the farmer's morning tasks (578–81):

> Dawn portions out a third part of the workday,
> dawn moves your travels, moves your work along,
> dawn shines and sets the feet of many a man
> upon the road, and lays a yoke on many oxen.

In short, *Works* was an example not just of georgic, but also of 'epos', epic, the supreme literary genre.

Besides its language, Hesiod's poem also draws on the mythology articulated by its precursor poem, *Theogony*, and the Homeric epics. The story of Pandora, Prometheus' theft of fire, the Greek expedition against Troy, the birth of Apollo – all serve as points of reference for the narrator, and thus, by extension, for his farmer-reader. Surely one source of the appeal of *Works* was that it formed a kind of diptych with *Theogony*, the two poems serving to define the cosmos of the early Greeks at its extremes of remoteness and familiarity. *Theogony* strives constantly for the sublime as it describes how the gods came into being out of primordial chaos and brought order, often through indescribable violence, to a monster-filled world. *Works* by contrast talks about life in the hardscrabble Boeotian village of Ascra, a place where farmers worry about their plough-beams breaking and scan the weeds for the first snail of spring, and which was, in Hesiod's memorable description, 'hot in summer, cold in winter, and never any good' (640). The quotidian is not only ennobled by its juxtaposition with the elevated world of myth, but also thrown in high relief by the contrast.

Another feature of *Works and Days* that endeared it to ancient 'grammatici' and philosophers alike was its gnomic character. One would in fact be quite justified in regarding the poem, not as the exemplar of georgic, but as a specimen of wisdom literature, which is how Martin West, the editor of the best modern commentary on the poem, presents it in his introduction.[15] Most of the advice on farming proper falls in the calendar of the seasons, which starts in the middle of the poem and stretches for 232 lines, in a work that is more than three times as long. Whether this section on husbandry constitutes the climax of Hesiod's advice or is a sort of extended digression is an academic question – the poet was simply juxtaposing related-seeming materials. Yet there is no denying that the recitation of useful maxims and the lecturing of Hesiod's brother Perses that frames it take up more space than the advice on working the soil. The modern reader who comes to *Works* looking for discussion of nature must first wade through Hesiod's thoughts on idleness, stinginess, neighbours and bribery, in addition to much rancid stereotyping of women. The reception of the poem shows just how popular this material was. Hesiod's ethical maxims are constantly quoted, while his instructions on, say, plough construction draw little comment.[16] It may almost seem paradoxical that *Works and Days* could be the *ne plus ultra* of georgic, yet have less to say about agriculture proper than any other member of the genre. To defuse the paradox, one must bear in mind that georgic literature takes as its subject the *life* of the farmer, which involves much more than farming in the strict sense of the word.

A final factor recommending the poem to its audiences was the nobility and beauty of its verses, which were thought to bring out what was noble and beautiful in its subject. This is a treacherous topic for modern scholars, since what Hesiod has to say about women, for example, is often so ugly. Fortunately we possess an ancient witness who made the case for its aesthetic merits in terms we can still accept. The sophist Alcidamas, an older contemporary of Plato, composed a short fictional exercise called *The Contest of Hesiod and Homer*, which has come down to us more or less in its original form.[17] The contest it imagines pits the two poets against each other in a battle of wits and verses, showing them answering each other's riddles and capping each other's lines. At the end of their competition, the two are invited to recite the verses they consider most *kalos*, that is, most beautiful or noble. Homer rises to the challenge by giving a description of Greek warriors poised to fight, while Hesiod recites the following from *Works and Days* (383–92):

> As the Pleiades, Atlas' family, are rising,
> start your harvest; start plowing when they set.
> Remember, for forty nights and days they lie
> in hiding, appearing yet again once the year
> comes round, the first time that you whet your blade.
> This rule obtains for plains, and those who dwell
> close to the sea, and those who occupy
> folded glens, rich soil far from the salt waves.
> Strip down to sow, strip down to plow, strip down
> to reap, whenever each task is in season.

These are the first lines of Hesiod's farmer's calendar and include one of the most remarkable verses in the entire poem, a line (383) of just three words: 'Plēiadōn Atlāgeneōn epitellomenaōn'. At this point the common people in the audience vote by acclamation to have Homer crowned the superior poet. However, the event's sponsor, King Panedes, overrules them, giving the honour to Hesiod on the grounds that it is right for a man who extols the arts of farming and peace to win, not the proponent of war. What Alcidamas shows us here is not just that these lines were considered aesthetically brilliant, but that their brilliance valorizes their subject matter in ways that can have significant ethical and political ramifications.

The Roman Georgic Tradition

Now to Rome. What we think of as Latin literature was the fruit of a belated cultural effort to translate, inherit and rival the major genres of Greek literature.[18] Accordingly, the comedies of Terence were revisions of Greek New Comedy, Cicero endeavoured at various times to become Rome's Demosthenes or Rome's Plato, while Virgil with his *Aeneid* undertook a complex revision of Homer's *Iliad* and *Odyssey*. The same is true of the oldest surviving work of Latin prose, the *de Agricultura* of Cato the Elder, a treatise meant to function as a no-nonsense Italic substitute for Xenophon's essay. Like Xenophon, Cato underscores the virtuousness of the farmer's lifestyle and means of pursuing wealth. Yet he does so in distinctively Roman terms by invoking the ways of the ancestors and values enshrined in Roman law. His treatise – and Roman prose literature in general – opens with the following words:

> There are times when the best way to acquire wealth is through trade – if only it were not so risky – or through money-lending – if only it was respectable. Our ancestors held this view and enshrined it in law, fining a thief twice the sum in question, and a money-lender, four times as much; from this one can infer how much worse than a thief they thought a money-lending citizen was. And when they wanted to praise a good man, they did so in these terms, calling him a 'good farmer and cultivator'; anyone praised in these terms was considered to have received very high praise. Now in my view a trader is stubborn and eager to acquire things, but, as I just said, he is exposed to risk and disaster. The bravest men and the most stubborn soldiers come from the class of farmers, and their gains are especially honest and steady, the least prone to cause envy, and men who engage in that pursuit are the least prone to evil thoughts.[19]

Cato's case for farming, like Xenophon's, speaks to his reader's presumed desire for financial gain as well as their longing for respectability. What is new is the appeal to tradition, and the idea that being a farmer is a good thing now precisely because it used to be a good thing once upon a time.

Subsequent Roman writings on farming and farm life seek to inherit the Greek tradition and improve on Cato, each in their own way. Of the dozens of treatises composed by the great polymath Varro of Reate, the sole one to come down to us complete is his three-book opus *On Country Things* (*de Rebus Rusticis*). Like Xenophon he frames his work as a dialogue, or, more precisely, three dialogues that depict notable Roman landowners and agronomists at their leisure and talking about farming. Along the way, Varro provides us with a brief history of Hellenistic georgic and occasionally quotes from authorities such as Mago. His first book is devoted to crops, his second to livestock and his third to raising small animals for the specialty market such as birds, snails, dormice and honeybees. The author's forced march through all the essential information on breeding, feeding and cultivation is spelled by frequent anecdotes and ethnographic observations, such as the story of a giant Lusitanian sow that yielded cuts of pork one foot thick, or a recital of the appearances of oxen in Greek myth.[20]

The *de Re Rustica* of the Spanish writer Lucius Junius Moderatus Columella is perhaps the most comprehensive and informative of all the Latin treatises; it is elegantly written but mostly avoids literary pretensions, save for the occasional quotation from Virgil and a book on gardening written in verse, *à la* Nicander. The eighteenth book of Pliny's *Natural History* is essentially a long essay on farming and is a valuable source of information on such matters as ancient grain varieties. The last of the surviving Latin treatises on agriculture was the *Opus Agriculturae* of Palladius Rutilius Taurus Aemilianus. Drawing on materials from Columella and the lost writer Gargilius Martialis, as well as the author's own experience farming in southern Italy and Sardinia, it is helpfully organized as a farmer's calendar, with one book per month describing what work needs to be done.[21]

All the Latin georgic writers came from the upper class: Cato and Varro were senators, Columella, Pliny and Virgil, knights; and Palladius was said to be a *vir illustris*, which probably indicates senatorial rank. Since class was a function of wealth at Rome, we may infer that all our writers came from the top 0.1 per cent of households in the Empire. In practice most of this wealth would have been invested in land. Thus it comes as no surprise that the authors envision holdings on a much larger scale than those typically assumed by the Greeks – no hardscrabble peasants here. Cato details the equipment and staff needed for an olive farm of 260 'iugera' and a vineyard of 100 'iugera' (65 and 25 ha., respectively), and assumes that one will have a portfolio of such properties.[22] Among the interlocutors of Varro's second book we encounter Titus Pomponius Atticus, who was not just Cicero's best friend but also one of the wealthiest men of his generation, the owner of several enormous cattle and horse ranches in Epirus. Pliny remarked indignantly that in his day, 'six landlords own half of Africa'. Yet it did not matter if you were an absentee owner who had never touched a mattock: being a landowner made you an *agricola*, a farmer, and brought with it all the prestige that Cato tells us was associated with the term. This was rustic life at an almost comically large and abstract scale.[23]

The *Georgics* of Virgil

One very Greek feature of the Roman tradition was that it had as its centrepiece a poem which, while not terribly edifying about the particulars of practice, outshone the rest in terms of its literary and cultural influence. I am of course referring here to Virgil's *Georgics*. Because of his fame, we know more about Virgil's life than any other georgic author from antiquity with the possible exception of Xenophon, who left us a partial autobiography in his *Anabasis*. Virgil's biography is worth reviewing because issues involving land loom large in it. Born in 70 BCE in the north Italian town of Mantua, he was a young man when Rome was torn apart by a civil conflict that pitted the armies of Julius Caesar against soldiers loyal to Pompey the Great and the Roman Senate. One of the crises that led Rome to this pass was the long-running failure of the Senate to provide demobilized soldiers with land where they could redirect their prodigious energies towards more peaceful ends. Caesar's soldiers, motivated in part by dreams of farming, defeated Pompey's, only to see their leader assassinated on the Ides of March. Caesar's nephew Octavian inherited his obligations as well as his uncle's estate, and set about finding land for his soldiers on the rich soil of the Po valley. Much of the property assigned to the veterans was already owned, and among those who lost property in the confiscation was Virgil's family. The poet made an appeal to Octavian that proved successful; in gratitude he paid tribute to Caesar's heir in his *Bucolics*, the pastoral poems that first put Virgil's genius on display and lay the ground for his achievements in the genres of georgic and epic.[24]

The civil wars continued to churn, however, as Octavian and Marc Antony fought each other for the right to rule the empire. For traditionalist senators it was a gloomy time, as there was no longer any prospect of the Senate assuming the prerogatives it had enjoyed since the foundation of the Republic. Senators lost their honour and prestige – yet continued to be Italy's main rural landlords. It was in effect Virgil's job – suggested to him by Maecenas, Octavian's cultured advisor – to present farming as such an honourable profession that it could adequately make up for the lost pride and success that the once-free Republic used to provide.[25]

Such were the circumstances under which Virgil's *Georgics* was composed. The poet wanted it to be an 'Ascraean song', a Roman version of Hesiod's *Works and Days*, just as his *Bucolics* had been a version of Theocritus' *Idylls*. Yet it is Hesiodic in spirit rather than letter; direct imitations of his predecessor constitute only a small fraction of the poem. Virgil took full advantage of the vogue for Hellenistic georgic, immersing himself in this literature as well as the writings of his Roman predecessors Cato and Varro. By selectively alluding to a large number of farm practices and specialist opinions, the narrator manages to create an impression of immense learning. Hesiod touched on the basics of grain farming, while Xenophon spoke largely about wheat and vine cultivation; Virgil devotes attention to such matters as crop rotation, grafting techniques, the diseases of sheep and the siting of beehives. Yet for all his sophistication, he handles these topics so efficiently and with such a light touch that the poem is only about twice as long as Hesiod's.[26]

The *Georgics* is in fact far more than a versified how-to manual. When Dryden called the *Georgics* 'the best poem by the best poet', he was thinking of the great artistry of the poem, which manifests itself in the symphonic arrangement of its sections, the intricate charm of its word music and the variety of its contents.[27] At various points Virgil's narrator digresses to contemplate the physics of air pressure, the wonders of Scythian anthropology, a great pestilence affecting the animals in Noricum and the bounties of nature on display in Italy. His panegyric for Octavian is appended to a lament for civil war. Like a more decorous version of Eliot's *The Waste Land*, it shifts constantly through voices and registers, now indulging a bit of Nicandrian portrait painting (*Georgics*, I. 291–6):

> A certain man stays up all night by the fire
> of his winter's lamp, carving wheat-shaped torches with a sharp knife.
> As he does so, his wife soothes her work with song,
> running her whistling shuttle through the threaded loom,
> or boils sweet must down to sap on the fire,
> skimming the froth from the bubbling pot with leaves.

Now easing into pastoral, now dabbling in mock epic, as in this description of a divided bee swarm that is meant to recall 'The Troubles' of Virgil's own day (*Georgics*, IV. 67–76):

> Often, when there are two kings, Discord enters
> the scene attended by a great uproar
> and soon their spirits and every heart
> is beating for war, as you might know in advance.
> For a war song comes from the bright loud bronze

> to scold the malingerers, and sounds imitating
> the syncopated tooting of a trumpet
> are heard. The bees in expectation join
> together, wings flashing, sharpening their stings,
> flexing their muscles, and around the king,
> his royal tent, they mingle in a throng,
> calling on their enemy with a great shout.

The last half of the fourth book abandons the didactic mode entirely in favour of a mythical narrative – part Homeric epic, part Latin love elegy – that relates how the hero Aristaeus lost his bees after attempting to rape Orpheus' wife Eurydice. The old man of the sea, Proteus, serves as Aristaeus' oracle, identifying his fault and relating how Orpheus had attempted, unsuccessfully, to bring his wife back from the dead, and how he met his tragic end, torn apart by Maenads, his limbs thrown into the Thracian river Hebrus (*Georgics*, IV. 532–7):

> Even then his head, torn from its marble neck,
> was carried by the Hebrus amidst its seething waves,
> rolling; his voice itself and cold tongue cried,
> as his spirit fled, 'Eurydice, ah poor Eurydice!' –
> 'Eurydice', the banks echoed all along the river.

Why Virgil chose to end his poem on farming with this myth is a puzzle that need not detain us here. Yet it is worth noting that a direct line of inheritance can be traced from this narrative to Gluck's opera *Orfeo ed Euridice* – an artistic legacy no other work of ancient georgic can come close to matching.[28]

What Virgil seems to have learned from Hesiod, in short, was that the best way to make the life of the country dweller appealing was not to enumerate all the many tasks and rules that such persons must keep constantly in mind. Instead, it was to provide just enough detail and insight to validate the author's credentials as an expert, while dwelling more on the larger political, ethical and mythical themes that inform and enrich rural life.

If one had to venture a criticism of Virgil's poem, it would be that it was too successful *qua* work of art. For while it was quickly ushered into the canon by the Roman *grammatici* – and Octavian's endorsement certainly did not hurt – it was greeted with silence and occasional contempt by experts in cultivation. Columella was a fan, certainly, but Pliny is quite critical, and authorities such as the philosopher Seneca and the polymath Celsus also dissented from his advice.[29] The situation in the late fourth century CE is especially revealing. This was Virgil's heyday, a time when

Servius was composing his indispensible commentary on the poems and Macrobius was exploring the depths of Virgil's erudition in his *Saturnalia*, affording the *Georgics* as much attention as the *Aeneid* and the *Bucolics*.[30] Poets such as Proba and Ausonius had internalized his verses so thoroughly that they could compose centos – poems made of nothing but Virgilian lines and phrases – on topics such as the life of Christ, full of *Georgic* echoes. When the pagan Roman senator Symmachus crafted his famous plea for religious tolerance, his *Relation on the Altar of Victory*, he ornamented his speech with phrase after phrase drawn from the *Georgics*. Yet the agronomist Palladius, who was a contemporary of those just named, makes only a single reference to Virgil in his treatise, alluding to the bard's view that pears can be grafted on ash trees.[31] The poem had risen so high in literary prestige that it was in a sense no longer regarded as an essay on rural life or farming at all, but a work of secular scripture.

Then the *Georgics* vanishes from sight, for nearly a millennium. While the *Aeneid* retained its authority and fame in the Middle Ages, its precursor, as Lancelot Wilkinson has demonstrated, was squeezed out of the canon of preferred pagan texts.[32] The *Georgics* was still quoted and its manuscripts copied, but with far less frequency than before; and it was never imitated. Monks labouring in the fields were advised to look to Palladius, not Virgil, for advice on farming. Rural life continued to find itself reflected in the mirror of medieval literature, but without the mediation of the *Georgics*; and the georgic genre itself was in abeyance. Appreciation of the poem's virtues did not return until the Renaissance, when the curiosity of figures such as Petrarch caused the pagan canon to expand once again. The first georgic poem soon followed: Poliziano's *Rusticus*, composed in 1483 as a kind of advertisement for his lectures on Hesiod and Virgil.[33]

The fortunes of Hesiod's *Works and Days* followed a similar trajectory in the Byzantine empire. Knowledge of Greek sufficient to parse Hesiod's text vanished from the western Mediterranean sometime after the death of Boethius, and so it was up to the scholars of the east to transmit the poem to posterity. While it was assiduously copied and occasionally commented on, it endured a shadowy afterlife, the text of a suspect pagan mythographer. Its gnomic sections proved most popular, perhaps because they echoed the wisdom books of the Old Testament. In Byzantine literary circles, georgic did not completely die out, but took the form of monuments such as the *Geoponica*, encyclopaedic and impersonal. It is interesting to see Hesiod quoted just once in this tome, for the opinion that the wine in the middle of a jar is better than that which touches the lid and the dregs (7.6.7). Like Virgil, Hesiod seems to have been reclassified as a 'wise man', rather than an authority on rural living. There was a great vogue for gardens in the courts and palaces of Byzantium, but inspired by the garden of Eden, a rural setting as unlike Ascra as one could possibly imagine.[34]

Hesiod's poems were being read in Italy again c.1400, though the circle of scholars qualified to do so was at first very small, all students of the Byzantine ambassador Manuel Chrysoloras, who was based in Florence. For several decades Hesiod was read mainly in Latin translation, but by the end of the century most humanists had acquired some mastery of Greek. In February 1496, Aldus Manutius published the definitive edition of Hesiod's works in Venice. This marked the first time in nearly a millennium that the two most famous ancient georgic poems were part of the same common culture. The seeds for a renewal of the genre had been planted, and quickly sprouted, in Italy, France and, soon enough, England as well.

Notes

1 See W. F. Albright, 'The Gezer Calendar', *Bulletin of the American Schools of Oriental Research*, 92 (1943), 16–26; D. Sivan, 'The Gezer Calendar and Northwest Semitic Linguistics', *Israel Exploration Journal*, 48 (1998), 101–5.
2 W. Wetterstrom and M. A. Murray, 'Agriculture', in *The Oxford Encyclopedia of Ancient Egypt*, ed. D. B. Redford, 3 vols. (Oxford University Press, 2001), vol. I, pp. 36–44.
3 On Silanus, see Pliny the Elder, *Natural History, Volume V: Books 17–19*, tr. H. Rackham (Cambridge, MA: Harvard University Press, 1950), pp. 202–5 (Pliny, *Natural History*, XVIII. 22–3); Columella, *On Agriculture, Volume I*, tr. Harrison Boyd Ash (Cambridge, MA: Harvard University Press, 1941), pp. 36–7 (I. 'Preface', 18) gives the quotation of Mago's first line; the fragments are collected in F. Speranza, *Scriptorum Romanorum de re rustica reliquiae* (Messina: Università degli studi, 1974–).
4 D. Padilla Peralta, 'Epistemicide: The Roman Case', *Classica*, 33 (2020), 151–86.
5 Columella, *On Agriculture, Volume III: Books 10–12*, tr. E. S. Forster and E. H. Heffner (Cambridge, MA: Harvard University Press, 1955), pp. 130–1 (11.3.2); *Geoponika: Farm Work*, tr. A. Dalby (Totnes: Prospect, 2011) (1.6). Given their pragmatic character, it seems to me unlikely that either of these fragments derive from the magical precepts ascribed to Democritus by Bolus of Mendes, *pace* M. Wellmann, *Die Georgika des Demokritos* (Berlin: Verlag der Akademie der Wissenschaften, 1921); cf. J. P. Hershbell, 'Democritus and the Beginnings of Greek Alchemy', *Ambix*, 34 (1987), 5–20.
6 Xenophon, *Oeconomicus: A Social and Historical Commentary, with a New English Translation*, tr. S. B. Pomeroy (Oxford: Clarendon Press, 1994), 'encomium for farming', 5; 'gentleman farmer', 6.8; 'scientific knowledge unneeded', 16.1.
7 Nicander, *The Poems and Poetical Fragments*, tr. A. S. F. Gow and A. F. Scholfield (1953; London: Bristol Classical Press, 1997), fragments 72 and 74.

8 Pliny, *Natural History, Volume III: Books 8–11*, tr. H. Rackham (Cambridge, MA: Harvard University Press, 1940), pp. 444–5 (11.9).
9 Pseudo-Plutarch, *On Nobility*, 20, quoted by P. Thibodeau, *Playing the Farmer. Representations of Rural Life in Vergil's Georgics* (Berkeley: University of California Press, 2011), 90.
10 C. Musonius Rufus, *That One Should Disdain Hardships: The Teachings of a Roman Stoic*, tr. C. E. Lutz (New Haven: Yale University Press, 2020), p. 54 (lecture 11).
11 On the *Geoponica*'s predecessors and its social context, see R. Rodgers, '*Kepopoiia*: Garden Making and Garden Culture in the *Geoponika*', in *Byzantine Garden Culture*, ed. A. Littlewood, H. Maguire and J. Wolschke-Bulman (Washington, DC: Dumbarton Oaks Research Library and Collection, 2002), pp. 159–75.
12 For a fuller account of these developments, see P. Thibodeau, 'Ancient Agronomy as a Literature of Best Practices', in *The Oxford Handbook of Science and Medicine in the Classical World*, ed. P. T. Keyser and J. Scarborough (Oxford University Press, 2018), pp. 463–80.
13 *Aristophanes: Frogs; Assemblywomen; Wealth*, tr. J. Henderson (Cambridge, MA: Harvard University Press, 2002), pp. 164–5 (*Frogs*, 1032–4). The literature on the *Works and Days* is extensive: see, Hesiod, *Works and Days*, ed. M.L. West (Oxford: Clarendon Press, 1978) for edition and commentary; J. S. Clay, *Hesiod's Cosmos* (Cambridge University Press, 2009) for authorial design and relation to the *Theogony*; S. Nelson, *God and the Land: The Metaphysics of Farming in Hesiod and Vergil* (Oxford University Press, 1998) for its georgic facets; A.T. Edwards, *Hesiod's Ascra* (Berkeley: University of California Press, 2004) for its use as a historical document of peasant life; R. Hunter, *Hesiodic Voices: Studies in the Ancient Reception of Hesiod's Works and Days* (Cambridge University Press, 2014) for its reception; and A. Loney and S. Scully, eds., *The Oxford Handbook of Hesiod* (Oxford University Press, 2018).
14 For a provocative history of canon formation in ancient Greece, see now R. Netz, *Scale, Space and Canon in Ancient Literary Culture* (Cambridge University Press, 2020).
15 West, *Hesiod: Works and Days*, pp. 1–25.
16 See the revealing charts in H. H. Koning, *Hesiod, the Other Poet: Ancient Reception of a Cultural Icon* (Leiden: Brill, 2010), p. 20.
17 Hesiod, *The Homeric Hymns, and Homerica*, tr. H. G. Evelyn-White (1914; Cambridge, MA: Harvard University Press, 1982), pp. 565ff.
18 As described most fully by D. Feeney, *Beyond Greek. The Beginnings of Latin Literature* (Cambridge, MA: Harvard University Press, 2016).
19 For a treatment of the work in the context of Cato's life, see A. E. Astin, *Cato the Censor* (Oxford: Clarendon Press, 1978); B. Reay, 'Agriculture, Writing, and Cato's Aristocratic Self-Fashioning', *Classical Antiquity*, 24 (2005), 331–61 is also very insightful.

20 *Cato and Varro: On Agriculture*, tr. W. D. Hooper and H. B. Ash (Cambridge, MA: Harvard University Press, 1934) pp. 356–9, 368–9 (Varro, 2.4.11; 2.5.5). On Varro, see J. E. Skydsgaard, *Varro the Scholar: Studies in the First Book of Varro's De re rustica* (Copenhagen: Hafniae Munksgaard, 1968).

21 K. D. White, *Roman Farming* (Ithaca: Cornell University Press, 1970) offers an invaluable survey of Roman farming and these treatises. For Columella, see J. Henderson, 'Columella's Living Hedge: The Roman Gardening Book', *Journal of Roman Studies*, 92 (2002), 110–33.

22 *Cato and Varro: On Agriculture*, pp. 22–5 (Cato, 10–11).

23 Pliny, *Natural History, Volume V*, pp. 212–13 (18.35). For statistics on wealth, see R. MacMullen, *Roman Social Relations, 50 B. C. to A. D. 284* (New Haven: Yale University Press, 1974) and I. Shatzman, *Senatorial Wealth and Roman Politics* (Bruxelles: Latomus, 1975); Thibodeau, *Playing the Farmer*, pp. 17–37, discusses the social significance of the term *agricola*.

24 See L. Keppie, *Colonisation and Veteran Settlement in Italy, 47–14 B.C.* (London: British School at Rome, 1983) on veteran settlement; see J. Osgood, *Caesar's Legacy. Civil War and the Emergence of the Roman Empire* (Cambridge University Press, 2006) and R. Syme, *The Roman Revolution* (Oxford: Clarendon Press, 1939) for a narrative of the times. The most detailed recent study of the evidence for Virgil's life is N. Horsfall, *A Companion to the Study of Virgil* (1995; Leiden: Brill, 2000), pp. 1–27, whose scepticism about the reliability of our sources is excessive.

25 So Thibodeau, *Playing the Farmer*, pp. 74–115.

26 There are many perceptive literary-critical studies of the *Georgics*. Especially good on particular sources and allusions are: D. O. Ross, *Virgil's Elements: Physics and Poetry in the Georgics* (Princeton University Press, 1987); R. F. Thomas, 'Virgil's *Georgics* and the Art of Reference', *Harvard Studies in Classical Philology*, 90 (1986), 171–98; R. F. Thomas, *Virgil. Georgics*, 2 vols. (Cambridge University Press, 1988); R. A. B. Mynors, *Virgil. Georgics* (Oxford: Clarendon Press, 1990); and J. Farrell, *Vergil's Georgics and the Traditions of Ancient Epic* (Oxford University Press, 1991). M. C. J. Putnam, *Virgil's Poem of the Earth: Studies in the Georgics* (Princeton University Press, 1979), G. B. Miles, *Virgil's Georgics: A New Interpretation* (Berkeley: University of California Press, 1980), C. G. Perkell, *The Poet's Truth: A Study of the Poet in Virgil's Georgics* (Berkeley: University of California Press, 1989), and C. Nappa, *Reading After Actium: Vergil's Georgics, Octavian, and Rome* (Ann Arbor: University of Michigan Press, 2005) offer more discursive mixes of close reading and reflection.

27 'Dedication' in Virgil, *Georgics* (Dryden), p. 137; L. P. Wilkinson, *Golden Latin Artistry* (1963; Norman: University of Oklahoma Press, 1985) and Thomas, *Georgics*, offer some of the best analysis of Virgil's patterning and verbal art.

28 Of the many scholarly efforts to tackle this question, see especially J. Griffin, 'The Fourth Georgic, Virgil, and Rome', *Greece & Rome*, 26 (1979), 61–80, and G. B. Conte, 'Aristaeus, Orpheus, and the *Georgics*: Once Again', in *The*

Poetry of Pathos. Studies in Virgilian Epic, ed. G. B. Conte (Oxford University Press, 2007), pp. 123–49; M. O. Lee, *Virgil as Orpheus: A Study of the Georgics* (Albany: SUNY Press, 1996) helpfully expounds on the connections between the *Georgics* and opera.

29 E. Christmann, 'Zur Antiken Georgica-Rezeption', *Würzburger Jahrbücher für die Altertumswissenschaft*, 8 (1982), 57–67, and A. Doody, 'Virgil the Farmer? Critiques of the *Georgics* in Columella and Pliny', *Classical Philology*, 102 (2007), 180–97, review ancient criticisms of Virgil.

30 See the essays in R. Rees, ed., *Romane Memento: Vergil in the Fourth Century* (London: Duckworth Press, 2004) for a fine introduction to the many ways Virgil pervaded Roman culture at this time.

31 Palladius, *Palladii Rutilii Tauri Aemiliani viri inlustris opus agriculturae*, ed. Robert H. Rodgers (Leipzig: Teubener, 1975), p. 97 ('Februarius', 3.25.7).

32 L. P. Wilkinson, *The Georgics of Virgil: A Critical Survey* (1969; Bristol Classical Press, 1997), pp. 273–90.

33 For a good introduction to Poliziano's poem, see T. A. Wimperis, 'Genre and Rhetoric in the Reception of Virgil's Georgics: Poliziano's Rusticus as Didaxis and Epideixis', dissertation, University of North Carolina at Chapel Hill (2013).

34 For Hesiod's image in Byzantium, see N. Zorzi, 'Hesiod in the Byzantine and Early Renaissance Periods', in *Oxford Handbook of Hesiod*, pp. 413–30. R. Rodgers, '*Kepopoiia*', pp. 159–75, gives a fine introduction to Byzantine garden culture. Hesiod's return to western Europe is the subject of J. Wolfe, 'Hesiod and Christian Humanism, 1471–1667', in *Oxford Handbook of Hesiod*, pp. 431–44.

CHAPTER 2

Turning, Flying
The Rural Year

Alexandra Harris

Virgil promises a calendar of times and tasks. He will sing the pattern of the year's labour: 'beneath what star to turn | the soil, Maecenas, when to wed vines | to the elms'.¹ The *Georgics* is often referred to as a kind of almanac. 'It resembles a farmer's calendar of work', says Simon Schama; Raymond Williams calls it 'a prolonged and detailed description and celebration of the farmer's year'.² The poem emphasizes the proper alignment of agricultural process with the turning of the heavens and the weather; it acknowledges the skill and labour involved in timely husbandry; it heralds the bounty that comes when the journey through the year is wisely made. Virgil places his faith in the tools and techniques that allow the good farmer to counter aberrant forces (weeds, diseases, untimely weathers) and thus keep on a steady path.

Yet as Williams also observes, it has a 'complicated movement'. A reader trying to consult it for a list of tasks would be driven to giddiness by its leaps, its sudden doublings back, its folding and expanding of time. In this it establishes richly productive dynamics that will keep moving and changing through later writing about the rural year – between handbook-style usefulness and imaginative shaping, between the fixed elements of the natural cycle and all their variations, between the power of repetition and the appeal of unpredictability, originality, eccentric creativity. There is, too, another conversation deep in the make-up of Virgil's poem: between the collective identity of Roman farmers, who may all benefit from the same knowledge, whose feeling for cultivation comes largely from a shared culture, and on the other hand an idea of individual, subjective experience. This will become one of the most powerful elements of rural time as it is described and reshaped by English writers from William Cowper in his garden to Ford Madox Ford planting by the moon and Katherine Swift, stalled by high summer, hanging 'like a water beetle in the meniscus of time'.³

The stability–instability of the calendar in the *Georgics* is there in its defining verb 'vertere', which famously introduces the doubling of ploughman and poet: the ploughman turning at the headland, the poet turning at the end of each line. The analogy suggests regularity in the poem – the kind of regularity you get when a plough is led by oxen moving heavily through clay and not likely to make quick detours. 'Turn! Turn! Turn!' sang the Byrds in the 1960s, Pete Seeger's song marrying with superb concision Virgil's poem of the land with the 'time for every purpose' passage of Ecclesiastes, partner texts through a great deal of georgic writing. Steer steadily, the time will come, they say, as the world turns and the seasons turn, and children turn to adults. Yet in the *Georgics* things can 'turn' unexpectedly into other things. Most astonishingly the solid innards of an ox can liquify and then send swarms of bees flying into the sky. The trudging beast of the plough has metamorphosed into something airborne. Releasing himself from calendar instruction into mythic story-telling, and from soil into air, Virgil asserts a degree of creative freedom that English georgic writers would not often claim for themselves. Yet much of the power of their work, like his, will lie in its fusion of rhythmically predictable and newly imagined turns in the wheel of the year.

It is not solely Virgil's influence that has established calendars of agricultural work as a strong tradition in English culture and a powerful means of expressing ideas about time, change, effort and social order. A defined iconography of annual tasks was well established through Western Europe by the thirteenth century. The 'labours of the months' appeared consistently in the calendar pages of illuminated psalters and carved on church facades or fonts for all to see. The imagery proved remarkably enduring, so that when Edmund Spenser conceived his *Shepheardes Calender* in the 1570s he was well aware of drawing together distinct but intriguingly contiguous traditions: one Virgilian (the Virgil of both *Eclogues* and *Georgics*) and the other to be found among the anonymous pictures and personifications in popular almanacs, old prayerbooks and stained-glass windows. Two hundred and fifty years later, with both kinds of material thriving more than ever, John Clare published a *Shepherd's Calendar* that was deeply responsive to the Virgilian georgic mode in eighteenth-century English poetry and was also, as Hugh Haughton and Adam Phillips put it, 'a latter-day English book of hours and robust illuminated diary of the agricultural year'.[4]

The 'labours of the months' have not previously been discussed in relation to English georgic writing, but I want to begin by suggesting that they provide a fruitful context for thinking about the depiction of rural work in literature. I shall bear them in mind as helpful comparatives, if not direct influences, as I go on to explore some of the central dynamics in writing about the agricultural year. Focusing on texts with at least some element of calendrical form, I want to feel for the shapes writers find in the annual cycle, their approach to variation and unpredictability, their rendering of despair, drudgery and satisfaction, and their sense of netting time in a reliable schedule – and watching it escape their grasp.

Labours

Open a psalter, or an illuminated book of hours, and you will find that a month-to-view calendar is proffered as essential equipment in organizing one's life of prayer. Holy feasts will be marked against the appropriate days, but the accompanying pictures will probably not show St Thomas or St Swithin. Instead they will show one of the established activities for this month and the sign of the zodiac. The effect will be a gathering together of prayer, the history of the church, the community of saints, the annual springing and withering of nature, the turning of the heavens, and – deeply woven into this pattern – the yearly narrative of work on the land.[5]

The pictures may appear in small medallions, as they do, say, in the mid-thirteenth-century Oscott Psalter made for use somewhere in the Midlands.[6] The page for each month features an image of the appropriate zodiac symbol and a single figure performing a 'labour' or (for some months) not labouring at all but feasting or admiring the flowers. Two-faced January drinks from a horn; February stirs a cauldron and warms his feet; March takes a pruning knife to curling vines; April holds flowers and leaves; May is hunting with a hawk; June is weeding (and warm enough to take off a layer); July is mowing with a scythe; August harvests corn; September is stripped to drawers for the physical strain of threshing; October starts the autumn sowing; November kills a fattened pig; December makes wine (a woman's role: brewing and malting would remain women's labours for as long as they were done at home). The resulting drink will fill the horn-cup of future Januaries, so that the circle begins again.

March, June, July, August, September, October, November, December: details from 'The Oscott Psalter', English, 1265–70. Copyright The British Library Board, BL Add Ms 50000.

Each series is idiosyncratic and expressive, but the point is that the pictures should be immediately recognizable, and should conjure a stable idea of the months. As a sequence of symbols, reprised by artists across Europe, they are almost as fixed as the zodiac signs, though with adjustments to accommodate the timing of tasks according to the climate in different regions. Ram, Crab, Centaur; pruning, hay-making, pannaging or slaughtering pigs. Though the pictures could be emblematically concise, there were also highly elaborate versions of them, as in the volume known as Queen Mary's Psalter. These scenes evolved into an artistic genre, reaching its height in northern Europe in the fifteenth and sixteenth centuries where the figures moved out from stylized gilded backgrounds into the open air and closely observed orchards, wattle-fenced gardens and woods browning with the autumn. Depictions of Flemish villages and fields were exported across the continent. These were expensive books, owned by people who would not themselves be lifting a sickle or even directing operations on an estate. Occasionally the images are adapted to occupations of courtly or gentry life, but the core of the sequence remains farming. Rural work is a subject on which high- and low-born alike are asked to meditate. The 'labours' tradition is a kind of visual georgic, more ethical than practical in its teaching, instructing that human beings must strive on the earth in the well-ordered way that is their fate and duty in a fallen world. Like the classical georgics, this tradition is keenly concerned with relationships between art, practical work, and philosophical or spiritual reflection.

The 'labours' are among the great sequences of Christian imagery, like the Fall from Eden and the Passion, or indeed the Doom and the Sufferings of Hell: the pruners and threshers share parchment pages and church walls with these. Among theologically alert audiences, the figures seem to have been understood as allegories for the work of the liturgical year – the work of worship through the hours, the making of timely spiritual progress.[7] This linking of spiritual and physical discipline was deeply embedded in monastic, and especially Cistercian, practices of manual work and worship. The 'labours' appeared regularly in calendars setting out the liturgical year for religious houses, and in the psalters intended to help lay readers emulate a version of regulated monastic life.

In this sense the calendar pictures were not secular at all, and yet to look up at a chancel arch and see a weeder appearing in recognizable clothes, bending in a way that is familiar to anyone who has weeded, is to see a representative of ordinary people moving among the sacred stories. No miracle is occurring; no-one is blessed or damned. They are all just getting on with their jobs for May or September. It is clear that artists, clerical patrons and congregations took pleasure in the portrayal of this work, and in seeing earthly tasks in the sacred scheme. This conception of the 'labours' is no less spiritually powerful, and it is closely connected with scripture. 'To every thing there is a season', teaches Ecclesiastes: 'a time to plant, and a time to pluck up that which is planted' (or in the Latin bibles of pre-Reformation England, 'tempus plantandi et tempus evellendi quod plantatum est').[8] The 'labours' make art of that timeliness, and that sense of each task contributing to the cycle of the whole. The first curse on Adam and Eve condemned them to a long struggle with vegetable life. 'Cursed is the ground for thy sake': 'Thorns also and thistles shall it bring forth to thee, and thou shalt eat the herb of the field.'[9] The figure of the 'weeder', tugging at thistles in the corn, appears in this context as a direct descendent of Adam, and an appropriate representative of all those of us whose task is not weeding but some other struggle or act of vigilance by which we might work our way to our hoped-for harvest.

This connection with the curses of the Old Testament, however, brings out something distinctive about the 'labours'. They are not pictures of suffering. As the historian Bridget Henisch observes, 'this is one of the few places in medieval art where serenity, not suffering, is the order of the day'.[10] Serenity for the viewer and – so far as we can tell – in the attitude of the figures to their occupations. What we have here is not only an established sequence of activities and conventional places to represent them, but also an attitude to the idea of work itself, a leaning towards its rightness and satisfaction. In early modern and later accounts of seasonal work, this inherited iconography converges with interest in the classical georgics of Hesiod, Varro and particularly Virgil.

There is no evidence of 'labours' imagery being adapted in relation to Virgil, or vice versa, before the fifteenth century. From then on, with the rise of illustrated editions of The *Georgics*, it is hard to tell who is influencing whom. There has been very little acknowledgement of these overlaps. In an unpublished but very valuable thesis, Kristi Eastin identifies at least thirty illustrated versions from the fifteenth century, most with scenes showing the defining Virgilian 'labours' of ploughing and beekeeping, often several activities shown at once (not usual in the medieval sequences). She argues that the artists of the *Très Riches Heures* calendar pictures 'were inspired at least in part by this pictorial georgic tradition'.[11] Michael Liversidge has shown how ideas moved in the other direction too, with the new fame of the *Georgics* helping to shape the development of Dutch and Flemish rural landscape painting as it grew out from the medieval 'labours' into another genre of its own. Bruegel's sequence *The Months* (1565) emerges from these converging patterns of thought, and stands as inexhuastible testament to what might happen at the crossroads.[12] 'Serenity', for one thing, tips into dramatized stories of struggle and effort in vividly realized landscapes and in palpable conditions of sultry midday heat or the dim light of early spring. The workers who prune trees and harvest the corn are individualized people, thinking or joking or concentrating on which branch to cut. Nature and men set traps for each other. There are cruel fates, but there is an overriding sense of ordered enterprise. The scenes have a scale and grandeur that suggests we are witnessing the work of the world. As we look, we feel at once the busyness and contemplative spaciousness of the pictures. In each, time is both held and moving, each season emblematically separate and yet turning, turning, with the wheel of the year.

Hundreds of Points

The 'labours' tradition depends on simplicity; the emblematic succession of figures insists on a knowable sequence. Yet each task is singled out from all the other tasks to be undertaken at roughly the same time. Many hundreds of distinct 'occupations' will be necessary each month on even a modest smallholding, and once one includes the work of different kinds of farmers (to Virgil's wine-growers and stockmen we might add hop growers, orchardmen and silkworm breeders, all of whom received special attention from early georgic writers in English), great panoplies of possible subjects come into view along with calendrical correlations between them.[13] In terms of both visual iconography and literary form, there is a challenge here: so much must be done at once. How is a writer to select points of focus and make them tell on each other?

Thomas Tusser, author of the most popular sixteenth-century farming poetry in English, emphasized the multitude of tasks to be incorporated in each month's husbandry. His 1573 *Five Hundred Points of Good Husbandrie* may not have offered a full four hundred new instructions to readers of his original *One Hundred Points* (1556), but his titles advertised amplitude and his rhymed tutorials proliferated because there was so much to advise upon. Readers compared Tusser with Virgil and Varro, and Tusser himself was conscious of the georgic tradition, but he also presented himself as defiantly removed from high literariness and courtly poetry.[14] As a practising farmer (albeit with a dubious record of success), his interest was not in choosing a few symbolically expressive seasonal tasks to represent the year, but in the need to coordinate numerous activities going on at once. He enumerates and details. He delights in lists – of tools, herbs for salad, herbs for strewing. Yet his concern is always, also, with concision and coherence. The 'good husbandrie' he promotes is tightly organized and thrifty, and his poetry aspires that way too. The prodigious to-do lists are given in tersely epigrammatic couplets, and the summings-up of each month's labour play a virtuosic game of compression. He envisages the book as an orchard tree, well-pruned and offering plentiful fruit.[15]

March in the 'labours' is usually digging or pruning. March for Tusser, and for the independent smallholders he wanted to reach, is potentially giddying but you must keep your head. 'White peason sowe, | scare hungry crow.' Barley needs to be sown in the dry, then the field rolled, mown and raked. This is also a crucial time for hops: 'March drie or wet | hop ground go set.'[16] It is time for grafting fruit trees (except in East wind), and time to sow summer plants and vegetables in well-prepared tilth. None of these jobs can be forgotten once done, since the vulnerable new grafts and seedlings must be painstakingly guarded: 'Things graffed or planted, the greatest and least, | defend against tempest, the bird, and the beast'.[17] All this raising and protecting fits with the traditional calendar correspondences between the seasons and human ages, and Tusser affirms the connection: 'The yeere I compare, as I find for a truth, | the Spring unto childhood, the Sommer to youth'.[18] Yet his many 'points' make clear that in spring the farmer needs to do the complicated parenting rather than going off to play.

Part of the appeal to rural readers was that they recognized their multifarious work in Tusser's book. Even the most small-scale gardener knows that, far from the single iconic tasks represented in psalters and emblem books, the year's cultivation might be imagined more like an orrery, with multiple sequences of events on separate but related orbits. Working on a simple vegetable patch, you must hold in mind the relation between the different trajectories of the carrots and the beetroot, knowing which will crowd or shade the other, which will attract what pests when. Consider the operation of a mixed farm and you must be alert to more simultaneous timescales than many a modernist novel, remembering and anticipating the arcs of intersecting plots. Virgil treats distinct kinds of farming in turn, arable then viniculture then livestock; cattle and goat-herding are separated out, their special timetables honoured. Yet part of the pleasure in reading the poem is the work of overlaying these sections until one can feel all the calendars going on at once. Tusser favours the integration of tasks in almanac sequence, or at least the attempt, and his many revised editions brought systems of cross-reference advising the reader to calibrate the advice for woodland and 'champion' country as required.

Tusser's most distinctive step towards an integrated calendar was his inclusion of women's work. His *Hundreth Points of Good Huswiferie* appeared separately at first, but soon he was 'marrying' the two, printing the texts for men and women back-to-back as well as including (marked with pilcrows) seasonal kinds of housewifery in the main sequence of each month's husbandry. There is plenty of blaming the dairymaid ('If cheeses in dairie have Argusses eies | tell Cisley the fault in hir huswiferie lies') and many points addressed to the reading husband who will be keeping the wife in check.[19] Still, it is rare for such attention to be paid to women's work, and worth noticing how Tusser's 'calendar of rural and domestic economy' presents the rhythm of the housewife's year.

He acknowledges that it is relentless:

> Though husbandrie seemeth to bring in the gaines,
> Yet huswiferie labours seeme equall in paines.
> Some respit to husbands the weather may send,
> But huswives affaires have never an end.[20]

Whereas 'husbandrie' is arranged month by month, most 'huswiferie labours' cannot so easily and pleasingly be distributed that way because they go on and on. Instead we have headings such as Baking, Scouring, Brewing, Washing, Malting. There are entries for each day's regular work: Morning, Afternoon, Evening, Supper and then (in case you were thinking of bed) 'After Supper Matters'. All these domestic tasks should be carried out with a thrifty eye on future needs and repurposed leftovers. Resourceful management depends on consciousness of each task as part of the complex whole. You might be cooking, but think how you can help the cowherd and carter: 'Save droppings and skimmings, how ever ye doo, | for medcine for cattel, for cart and for shoo'.[21]

The idea of the year's work being punctuated by holiday feasts, the idea that periods of intense effort culminate in relief and relaxation thanks to a beautifully patterned calendrical cycle, simply does not hold up when the work in question is domestic. Tusser is unusual in observing this, though he is not too concerned. 'Forget not the feastes that belong to the plough', he instructs the housewife: Plough Monday, Sheep-Shearing and Harvest Home – 'For all this good feasting, yet art thou not loose, | till ploughman thou givest his harvest home goose'.[22] Not only on high days but also twice every week the labouring man should feel free to demand his due: 'Good ploughmen looke weekly, of custome and right, | for roast meat on Sundaies and Thursdaies at night.' The great feasts of the year are not, of course, arranged to celebrate and reward domestic work, which just carries on. Come November, Cisley is still in the dairy and trying to get the cheese right: 'From April beginning, til Andrew be past, | so long with good huswife, hir dairy doth last'.[23]

Nearly two hundred years later, when Mary Collier ('Now a washerwoman, at Petersfield in Hampshire') responded to Stephen Duck's belittling of women's harvest work in his 1730 poem *The Thresher's Labour*, she stressed both the major contribution of women to seasonal agricultural tasks and their parallel lives of year-round domestic chores. She was saying, from experience and with exasperated fury in her voice, what Tusser had said: 'huswives' affairs have never an end'. She was calling the attention of georgic poets and readers to the other kinds of work that go on around the central narrative of sowing, scything, threshing, those biblically sanctioned, mythically satisfactory labours that had such a powerful hold on artists, writers and clerics. Women are there in the central narrative ('throwing, turning, making hay', reaping and gleaning in the cornfield with children in tow), but there is work when they get home after sunset, and work stretches out long after the harvest is brought in.[24] Collier describes the long winter days of domestic service – washing linens, scouring saucepans, brewing beer. Working in darkness before sunrise and piercing 'summer's day with candle-light', she describes lives cut off from the natural rhythms that variegate the year's husbandry, and work without shape, lacking culmination or pause.[25]

Virgil offered no model for treating this different kind of rural year. In the very beautiful winter evening scene of his *Georgics* (and it is a 'scene', held still in the current of the book's ongoing instructions and turning stars), the labouring man is at last indoors after the year's action in the open air. For a moment the curtain is lifted on indoor work. The woman is there, and she has been there all along:

> One man before the late flame of a winter lamp
> lingers wakeful, and with his axe's edge tapers torchpoles
> while, consoling her long toil with song,
> his wife with shrill shuttle zips across the warp
> or at the hearth reduces grape's sweet juices,
> skimming off the pot's rolling current with a frond.[26]

Weaving and skimming, she serves here as the background tune to the farmer's winter tasks. For the man to come indoors is to work alongside women. It is as if Virgil, like the farmer, is suddenly aware of her, so that she becomes the foreground and for a moment we seem to watch and listen to her with brief wonder at the patient song of her 'longum laborem'.

Pauses, Pivots, Culminations

Both men and women labour on. Voluntarily, or without much choice in the matter, they keep at it, answering Hesiod's summative instruction to 'work': 'work upon work'.[27] Georgic writers, feeling for the shapes and rhythms of these working years, are deeply interested in the kind of narrative that the annual 'rotation' makes. Their material is cyclical, while literary works are necessarily linear in the sense of one phrase following the next. The resulting relationship between circle and line is at the heart of the art form. The georgic writer must decide where the story begins and ends. Is the cycle really a tragic arc, soaring to a zenith, tipping over and irremediably declining? A. E. Housman, among the most melancholy of georgic poets, understands the year as 'beautiful and death-struck', bearing a mortal wound as it treads at a walking pace through the seasons.[28] For others the year is a comedy of renewal, an ascent to a culminating moment, or a series of chapters with equal worth and weight.

Joseph Addison expressed his impatience with Hesiod's chronological treatment of tasks in *Works and Days*: 'too grave and simple', he thinks; 'it takes off from the surprize and variety of the Poem, and makes the whole look but like a modern Almanack in Verse'.[29] Virgil's departure from the timetable impressed him much more. Virgil makes us feel the beat of turning time while emphasizing contiguities that are conceptual and emotional, rather than calendrical. When his poem intensifies into passages of pulsing concentration it is not generally in relation to harvest-home or grape-pressing but things not marked on an almanac, things suddenly perceived: a vision of civil war, or a perception of the animal kingdom's united sexual power. British georgic writers have learned from both models. The seasonal sequence exerts a powerful hold; its gravity and simplicity are part of its meaning. Writers have also insisted on the year's infinite 'surprise and variety'.

'There's no beginning to the farmer's year', Vita Sackville-West observes in her 1926 poem *The Land*, cutting off the corner as she turns from her winter section to spring, not wanting to impose divisions that have no place in nature or in work.[30] Yet human beings make sense of time by inventing beginnings, or starting over, or turning the page. Hesiod's first emphatic instruction about timing is to reap when the Pleiades rise before the sun and to begin ploughing when they set; an arc through autumn and winter, from reaping to first ploughing forms in the mind in parallel with the arc of the stars in the sky.[31] He then sets out in earnest with the ploughing, though first you must have made your plough and have your oxen ready. After ploughing: woodcutting, pruning, reaping, threshing, summer sailing.

Virgil looks to the melting of Alpine snow for his cue to begin. 'In new spring, when from snowy peaks the run-off flows': this is the time to hitch the oxen and break open the earth.[32] It is a vividly localized gesture of timekeeping. We look up from field to distant mountains as if looking across a whole landscape view, and we imagine people throughout the region looking likewise. For Virgil's English admirers, 'vere novo' must therefore be the start, and James Thomson in *The Seasons* makes a mobile, delicate drama of the give-and-take between winter and spring over marshes and hills. 'As yet the trembling year is unconfirmed', he writes; it is late April before warm airs 'unbind' the frosty earth and the 'impatient husbandman' can plough.[33]

Thomas Tusser begins in August, after the wheat harvest, in the first version of his *Points of Husbandrie*; in later editions he revised that to September. Because land was customarily leased annually from Michaelmas, farmers arrived on new plots (or renewed their commitment to the same place) in the autumn.[34] The harvest was packed or stored like the furniture, and the ground awaited. Tusser's first lines in 'Septembers Abstract' are perhaps the best of the book: 'Now enter John, | old fermer is gone.' Here's the new man, starting out, looking around. It all begins here, according to contract. As we all know from the rhythm of school years, which still reflect that ancient legal pattern determined by harvests, the chill in the air becomes associated with first days, sharp pencils, assessing the situation.

Yet it is Januarius who has the doorkey to unlock the new year, and he who has the threshold gift of retrospect and foresight. Centuries of classical and Christian culture have accustomed us to the trajectory of a year that begins in deep winter – sometimes at the solstice, sometimes at Christmas, most often with the end of Christmastide and return to work (which was near the end of January in the Middle Ages and later moved up to the beginning of the month and Plough Monday). Discussing the 'Menologium', an eleventh-century calendar poem, Carolyne Larrington observes that 'the church's year virtually suppresses the seasonal cycle, beginning with the birth of Christ in December'.[35] The sense of birth in that dead-seeming winter still-point has irresistible potency. Yet there is not even a snowdrop and it is far too early to plough or prune.

So there emerges a pattern of seasonal georgics starting ahead of time, preparing, waiting, protecting. John Clare opens *The Shepeherd's Calendar* by hurrying us indoors: 'Withering and keen the winter comes | While comfort flyes to close shut rooms.'[36] Wonderfully, in two lines, we feel both the weather and the shelter, though not everyone is at the tavern like the 'labours of the months' January figures. The thresher goes out in darkness. The foddering boy goes 'shuffling thro' the sinking snows | blowing his fingers as he goes'. He is at once a winter figure from a calendar picture and a particular living boy on the path between rimy hedges, towards a known field.[37]

Vita Sackville-West was always moved by winter imagery and makes the most of starting in stillness. Her farmer is imagined with emblematic clarity, sitting at the kitchen table under lamplight, planning. This is Virgil's 'breather', though like Clare she includes the 'desultory' outdoor tasks quietly and firmly undertaken.[38] She visualizes (and hears and smells) the dung-cart's 'reasty load', the horses standing by with 'nostrils smoking on the air', the 'wedge-shaped hale of roots' to be portioned out into the feeding troughs.[39] There can be no turning of one's back. Katherine Swift in *The Morville Hours* (2008), an intricately plotted account of her Shropshire garden calibrated to the labours of the months and the monastic hours, starts with customary precision. It is a moment before the striking of midnight on New Year's Eve. 'Listen.' The chapter is called 'Vigils' – the hour of waiting and watching.[40] As if adjusting our eyes to darkness, we learn to look at the place when it has least on show. Before digging begins, there is time for thought, preparation, historical reading.

In the classical and medieval system of correspondences between the ages of man and the times of the year, June and July are associated with man being at the height of his powers and summer is at the top of the wheel of time.[41] In the calendar illustrations, people are mowing the hay and tending the corn; the world is green and burgeoning, and perhaps there is time to sit under a hedge enjoying the sun. For the most part, this tallies with modern ideas about summer. Yet the high point has long brought mixed feelings. 'All country dwellers know the small despair | Of the year's summit', writes Sackville-West. There can be no sinking into melancholy: 'the yeoman now | Has little time for vain regrets'.[42] A little past the summit come the dog days, classically dreaded for their heat, now more dreaded in England for the likelihood of rain when holiday weather is most yearned for. For gardeners, the July gap can be lowering. Skill can plug the vacancies, but the season's underlying character is tiredness and uncertainty. Katherine Swift writes of losing her nerve and losing her way in high summer. The roses brown, galega capsizes, ox-eye daisies collapse: 'We teeter daily on the brink of disaster, the garden and I – horticulturally, aesthetically, financially, physically, emotionally.'[43] Her lostness, and sense of loss, lead her to recollections of John Clare losing his bearings in an altered countryside, and the modern tearing up of hedges, the forgetting of the land's stories.

So where does the culmination of the year's story come? Sackville-West's winter beginning allows her to turn full circle and end in late autumn with the gathering of Kent's most prized crops: apples and hops. John Philips in his 1708 georgic *Cyder* had dramatized a similarly fruitful climax of the productive year in Herefordshire (which he elects as representative of Britain, Cyder-Land). He elevates orchards and their resulting cider to match the status accorded by Virgil to Italian vineyards and their wine. 'Thrice happy time, | Best portion of the various year', the autumn orchard is an Eden of ambrosial fruits. Yet 'Inclement winter dwells | Contiguous', like a threatening neighbour who may at any moment appear. 'Now, now's the time' – to pick, to prepare the presses.[44] This laden moment holds within it knowledge of all the work and uncertainty that has made it: the pruning, grafting, thinning, the fight against droughts and diseases, the anxious watching for nature's delicate coordination of blossom with the warmth that will bring bees flying to the pollen.

William Cowper in *The Task* revised the pattern of the georgic year to reflect his own life as a small-scale gardener, indoor writer, walking thinker. Since the 'task' to which Cowper responds is a call to 'sing the sofa', and since the whole poem is an apologia for rural retirement, *The Task* is in some respects an anti-georgic, in others a mock-georgic.[45] Yet most of all it is genuinely georgic, steadfast and unsatirical in its feeling for repetition, for long attachment to a well-studied patch, and for an understanding of life in which work is the bulwark that humans keep building against chaos. Cowper is profoundly sympathetic to Virgil's emphasis on hard-won order. He sings 'th'employs of rural life | Reiterated as the wheel of time | Runs round, still ending and beginning still'.[46]

His central labour is that of writing, and his time of intensity and fruitfulness is winter – so much so that three books of *The Task*, the latter half of the poem, are devoted to it, following a single winter day so that time seems to slow and each moment is distinct. Cowper welcomes the grand old man Winter, 'ruler of th' inverted year'. His delighted injunction to 'wheel the sofa round' picks up the image of the running wheel of time. Yet his imaginative work is sustained by the physical tasks of the gardening year. Virgil left gardening to a dashing *occupatio*, imagining what he would include, briefly mooting the cucumber as a plumply temping subject. Cowper takes him up on the suggestion: 'To raise the prickly and green-coated gourd ... is an art | That toiling ages have but just matured, | And at this moment unassay'd in song'.[47] The cucumber gets an inset georgic of its own, a miniature *Task*, in keeping with the giant effort the fruit demands.

The cucumber imposes a calendar. In November 'the task begins' with the manure pile and placing of the hot frame. As when building a house, one must consider siting and materials. Then be patient: 'Thrice must the voluble and restless earth | Spin round upon her axle 'ere the warmth | Slow gathering in the midst, through the square mass | Diffused, attain the surface.'[48] It is like Virgil's enigmatic instruction to let the ploughed earth feel sun and frost twice before sowing; Cowper is as solicitous of his hot frame as Virgil of Roman fields. Both ask us to visualize the movement of the cosmos, and our own small field or frame within it. 'Slow gathering' has in it an echo of the mist 'fast gathering at the heels' of the homebound worker proleptically envisaged at the close of *Paradise Lost*. Now here, in the fallen world, a fog is rising at man's will, controlled by modern skill, filling the hot frame which becomes a microcosm under human care. Once the seed is placed, there ensues 'the ticklish balance of suspense' in steering safely to the fruiting of the plant.

Cowper does not need to grow this cucumber; nothing and nobody depends upon it. Yet nor are these occupations entirely trivial. They require Cowper to follow timetables other than his own. With these efforts of steady attentiveness, he fights off or wrestles down the disorder he perceived in the world and the madness from which he suffered – no less so than Virgil advocating the use of sickle instead of sword against the wars of his time.

Lucky Days

Hesiod devotes the final section of his *Works and Days* to a list of dates on which tasks should and should not be done. He teaches that days matter; works and days must be choreographed for agricultural success. For instance, 'avoid the 13th of the standing moon for beginning sowing; but it is the best day for bedding in vines'.[49] The schedule is extensive, and liable to stop the farmer from doing a task at just the moment when season, weather and preparation are all aligned. Hesiod attributes the character of days to Zeus, who has ordained their usefulness. It is often suggested that Virgil includes guidance on propitious dates according to the Roman calendar as a kind of tribute to his forebear, and is not himself so convinced of their influence.[50] Still, he keeps the faith, if faith it is: 'Distinct days with distinct phases the Moon herself | has consecrated auspicious for work.'[51] 'Felicis operam': auspicious, or happy, or lucky for work. The calendar of luck was determined not only by the moon's phases, but also by anniversaries of divine triumphs and disasters: 'Avoid | the fifth: then Earth spawned forth pale Orcus | and the Furies'.[52] Virgil understands it as part of the farmer's proud art to negotiate between the preordained framework of dates and the ever-changing weather. If the fifth is unlucky, but you have a field ready to harvest and signs of coming rain, you must be wise enough to choose.

The Christian calendars used in medieval England still marked two unlucky days each month (known as 'Egyptian days' or *dies mali*), though the church never quite condoned these pagan relics. As for luck, best choose your saint. Religious anniversaries accrued around them much varied thinking about their felicity, or otherwise. Belief in the luck of particular days for certain tasks was suppressed after the Reformation, but superstitions, more or less attached to logical factors of season and sequence, continued to thrive in rural communities.

All of which gives a complex charge to notions of auspicious timing in English georgic. John Aubrey did a characteristically clear-headed bit of disentangling, and pointed out that the same dates kept being used in relation to calendars working on different principles, the numbers having floated free from any former connection with moon or zodiac: 'Thus may divers be mistaken who superstitiously observe certain times'.[53] He and other members of the Royal Society 'Georgical Committee' would honour Virgil by recording modern agricultural knowledge, not by enshrining antiquarian folklore. There is no talk of dates in the enlightened georgics of Philips or Thomson or Cowper.

However, 'I have always had luck when gardening' reports Ford Madox Ford in his part-fictionalized memoir *It Was the Nightingale* (signed and dedicated 'on the feast of St Eulogius, 1933'): 'I imagine it is because I observe the rules of the game of gardening life.' Ford affirms his adherence to rituals of timing: 'I always seed while the moon is waxing; I never begin a planting on a Friday or a 13th, but always on a 9th, an 18th, or a 27th. I attach superstitious reverence to certain favourite plants or beds. If there is a wishing-well in the neighbourhood I fetch a bottleful of it to start my first watering of the spring.'[54]

Ford is the most georgically inclined of the great modernists, preoccupied with the moral good of frugality and manual work, nurturing all his life an ideal image of himself as smallholder and author. He is, partly, the Gringoire of *No Enemy* (1929) who proposes 'to save the world by intensive kitchen gardening and exquisite but economical cookery' and is ever on the verge of writing a manual on the keeping of goats.[55] He is, partly,

Marie-Léonie in *Last Post* (1928), running her cottage estate in England as only the French know how. Ford's accounts of his husbandry come in tones of pride, amused self-satire and woundedness at being overlooked as an agriculturalist, the inventor no less of a new method for sowing corn. Ezra Pound was sceptical about his friend's rural life, but glad of expert guidance on matters of vine nomenclature and oxen in *The Cantos*. 'Dear Hesiod', he wrote from Paris in March 1922 when Ford sent georgically oriented notes on his manuscript, 'Thanks orfully'.[56]

Ford's mind echoed with freighted dates. He would rig things to fit them, misremembering moments of literary inspiration to line them up with the Feast of St Catherine.[57] He would let them haunt him year on year, as 4 August tolls fatefully through *The Good Soldier*. Like masons' marks, or the lesser-known rules in Debrett's, the days for husbandry are the code of a profession and community. Ford displays his badge of honour as a countryman. Sowing on the 18th, he is expressing his kinship with those who have planted and watered over the centuries, watching the moon for a spring blessing on a new crop.

There are local variations in the calendar code, but many aspects continue to be observed in rural communities across Europe. When the Sussex sheep farmer Chris Stewart moved to southern Spain and bought a farm stretching over terraced hillsides and down into a remote valley of the Alpujarra, long-time residents of the area noted his loose adherence to the proper times:

> 'What's that you're sowing?'
> 'Broad beans.'
> 'They'll be no good.'
> 'Why not, for heavens' sake?'
> 'Wrong phase of the moon.'[58]

Driving over Lemons, Stewart's account of starting the farm and learning the particularities of the region – social, topographical, agricultural – was a bestseller in Britain. Part of what has appealed so much to readers (apart from the dandling of plump lemons in northern minds, and the oil flowing after the olive harvest) is Stewart's voice as both expert and novice. This is a kind of georgic writing in which didacticism, studentship and anthropological watching take equal parts. In the matter of preordained timings, he sets out the Alpujarran custom and his failure to comply:

> All rural occupations in the Alpujarras have their allotted day, with the odd adjustment to accommodate the waxing and waning of the moon or the falling of a Friday. Thus the year always starts with the sowing of

garlic on the 1st of January; then you prune your vines on the 24th or 25th depending on where you live. Most tasks are governed by the saint's day, as are many meteorological and cosmic phenomena such as the disappearance on St John's Day of the clouds of horseflies that plague the village of Fregenite.[59]

Stewart agrees that 'the system is perfectly logical' – in the sense that the filigree of association between the day, the saint and the task helps everyone remember what to do next and brings a deal of certainty to a complicated timetable. This is the kind of logic that characterized almanacs in England for centuries and survives, much diminished, in a few axioms. Yet for the Alpujarran farmers the 'system' is about much more than handy aide-memoires and it is deployed in a way that has nothing to do with logic. Josefina from the village raises an eyebrow at the incomer:

> 'You should prune vines on the 25th'.
> 'I know but I'm only four days late. That's not too bad is it?'
> 'We always prune ours on the 25th, rain or shine; that way we don't get any pests or diseases.'
> 'You mean you don't have to use any sprays or chemicals?'
> 'Are you mad? We blast them with every fungicide we can lay our hands on.'[60]

For Josefina, and for Ford in Sussex, the art and the rightness of farming lies in precise compliance with immemorial laws. Vita Sackville-West is a firm representative of the opposite persuasion: for her the art lies in independent judgement and responsiveness to the moment. 'Therefore let no man say "Peas shall be sown | This month or that; now shall the harrow go".' She will not pin tasks to a month, let alone a day: ''Tis farmer, not the date, that calls the time. | Better dry August hay than wet in June'. Hers is the determinedly rational view that has been dominant in British georgic writing. Saints' days offer no special aura for the sower: 'Such arbitrary dates and rules are vain; | Not thus the year's arithmetic is planned'.[61] Part of the farmer's central skill is to be 'sharp on the minute when the minute's come', weighing each year's unfolding circumstances day by day. Accordingly, Sackville-West's poem takes its energy from the interplay of set structures and continual variation that makes no two farming years alike.

Spring to Spring

When Sackville-West reaches Michaelmas, Tusser's starting point, she reflects on this autumnal threshold. Strikingly, she perceives it as a twin to January:

> Now retrospect and prospect have their equal share,
> For autumn like the Janus of the year
> Holds spring to spring in double-handed keeping.[62]

The farmer looks back at the successes and shortcomings of the recent harvest and plans for winter crops. It is not a still-point: 'no respite comes'. One must immediately begin again, 'and bring new life to earth'. Imagining the arms that hold two springs together, and the similarities that connect Michaelmas with New Year, Sackville-West makes firm spokes crossing time's wheel.

The expression of kinship between times, the binding of opposite seasons, the articulation of future harvests that wait curled tight within buds: these are special arts of georgic writing. These are the means by which the year is shown to turn, not merely pass, and these are tools that help us get our bearings. Hesiod's repeated technique is to coil the future inside his instructions. Plough and sow in the right way, and 'the ears may nod towards the earth with thickness … and you may banish the cobwebs from the storage jars'.[63] It is a method of motivation – envisaging the future reward from the very moment of starting out. Virgil is less concerned to play the goading coach, and more interested in the poetry of juxtaposition. The bees, for instance, swarm in spring more densely than hail, or acorns raining down 'from the shaken oak'.[64] Spring swarm, winter hail, autumn acorns (the knocking down of acorns to feed pigs brought to the woods for pannage would become one of the key 'labours' for November in medieval cycles). Virgil has packed the seasons tight together like the bees, so that for a moment the year seems to hang before us in a humming ball of energy.

Cowper does not need motivation but steady hope, the balancing of opposites and affirmation of the goodness in his chosen domestic way of life. In the 'Winter Evening' section of *The Task*, like the winter evening passage of Virgil's *Georgics*, a woman is at work: 'here the needle plies its busy task'.[65] A flower is unfolding in the embroidery. Cowper binds this task to summer, as if stretching a thread from the winter solstice across the circle to midsummer. The winter flower blooms indoors, in memory and anticipation of the summer garden.

Cowper attends in late winter to fruit trees espaliered on the garden wall. Applying his own moral creed to pruning, he cuts away large showy branches in favour of 'neighb'ring twigs | Less ostentatious, and yet studded thick | With hopeful gems'.[66] The year's growth and fruit is all contained there in those shiny tight-furled buds. The interrelatedness of each task and season appeals to Cowper deeply, and his marking of this coherence is weighed against the urban activities which seem to him fragmentary, leading nowhere. The espaliers, by contrast, hold the promise of next autumn in their bare winter twigs. The subject of staking attracts him too. The practice of supporting plants with stakes unites new growth to old poles, the beginnings and ends of vegetable life and of the year:

> Few self-supported flow'rs endure the wind
> Uninjur'd, but expect th' upholding aid
> Of the smooth-shaven prop, and, neatly tied,
> Are wedded thus, like beauty to old age,
> For int'rest sake, the living to the dead.[67]

Symbolically it has a beautiful concision. He borrows the theme from Virgil, who advertises it in the first lines of his poem ('when to wed vines to elms'). Cowper weds his new work to the strong support of Virgil's precedent.

'Meanwhile it flies, time flies, irretrievably'.[68] The year is thickly wrought with tasks, associations, instructions, memories and hopes; it is gem-studded, staked, embroidered, held in place. Yet time slips away and is airborne, flying flying.

Notes

I am extremely grateful to the Leverhulme Trust for funding that allowed me time to work on this chapter. For discussions and comments that helped to shape the arguments here, I would like to thank Paddy Bullard, Jessica Fay and Ali Smith.

1 *Georgics* (Johnson), p. 5 (*Georgics*, I. 1–3).
2 R. Williams, *The Country and the City* (1973; London: Vintage, 2016), p. 25; S. Schama, *Landscape and Memory* (London: Fontana, 1996), p. 528.
3 K. Swift, *The Morville Hours* (London: Bloomsbury, 2009), p. 207.
4 H. Haughton and A. Phillips, 'Introduction', *John Clare in Context* (Cambridge University Press, 1994), pp. 1–28, at p. 5.
5 See B. A. Henisch, *The Medieval Calendar Year* (Pennsylvania: Penn State University Press, 1999). A comprehensive record of labours sequences is to be found in Colum Hourihane, ed., *Time in the Medieval World: Occupations of the Months and Signs of the Zodiac in the Index of Christian Art* (Princeton University Press, 2007).
6 Oscott Psalter, *c.*1265–70, British Library Add. Ms 5000.
7 Writing about the painted labours at Salisbury Cathedral, M. M. Reeve gives theological contexts for this allegorical significance in *Thirteenth-Century Wall Painting of Salisbury Cathedral* (Woodbridge: Boydell, 2008), pp. 99–100. Thanks to Jessica Fay for seeing the connection with monastic work, and the significance of it.
8 Ecclesiastes 3: 1–2.
9 Genesis 3: 17–18.

10 Henisch, *Medieval Calendar*, p. 10.
11 K. A. Eastin, 'Virgil and the Visual Imagination: Illustrative Programs from Antiquity to John Ogilby', unpublished PhD thesis, Brown University (2009), p. 65.
12 M. Liversidge, 'Virgil in Art', *The Cambridge Companion to Virgil*, ed. C. Martindale (Cambridge University Press, 1997), pp. 91–103, at p. 100.
13 For different kinds of farming in English georgics, see e.g., T. Moffet's *The Silkewormes* (1599), J. Philips' celebration of fruit-growing in *Cyder* (1708), and C. Smart's 'The Hop-Garden' (1752). Silkworms reappeared in English literature with *The Silkworm: A Poem* (1750), S. Pullein's translation of *De bombycum cura et usu* by M. H. Vida (1527).
14 See S. Oldenburg, 'Thomas Tusser and the Poetics of the Plow', *English Literary Renaissance*, 49 (2019), 273–303.
15 Dedicatory poem 'To the Right Honorable Lord Thomas Paget', in T. Tusser, *Five Hundred Points of Good Husbandry*, ed. G. Grigson (Oxford University Press, 1984), p. 6.
16 Tusser, *Husbandry*, 'Marches Abstract', pp. 86–7.
17 Tusser, *Husbandry*, 'Marches Husbandrie', p. 95.
18 Tusser, *Husbandry*, 'A Description of Time and the Yeare', p. 59.
19 Tusser, *Husbandry*, 'A Lesson for Dairie Maid Cisley', p. 101.
20 Tusser, *Husbandry*, 'The Preface to the boke of Huswiferie', p. 157.
21 Tusser, *Husbandry*, 'After Noone Workes', p. 172.
22 Tusser, *Husbandry*, 'The Ploughman's Feasting Daies', pp. 177, 178.
23 Tusser, *Husbandry*, 'Aprils Husbandrie', p. 99.
24 M. Collier, *The Woman's Labour: An Epistle to Mr Stephen Duck* (1739), p. 8.
25 Collier, *Labour*, p. 14.
26 *Georgics* (Johnson), pp. 21, 23 (*Georgics*, I. 291–6).
27 Hesiod, *Works and Days*, trans. M. L. West (Oxford University Press, 1988), p. 48.
28 A. E. Housman, 'In My Own Shire, If I Was Sad', in *Works*, ed. M. Irwin (London: Wordsworth, 2005), p. 56.
29 J. Addison, 'An Essay on the Georgics', in Virgil, *Georgics* (Dryden), p. 150.
30 V. Sackville-West, *The Land* (London: Heinemann, 1926), p. 25.
31 Hesiod, *Works and Days*, p. 48: 'When the Pleiades born of Atlas rise before the sun, begin the reaping; the ploughing, when they set'.
32 *Georgics* (Johnson), p. 60 (*Georgics*, I. 43).
33 J. Thomson, *The Seasons*, ed. James Sambrook (Oxford: Clarendon Press, 1972), p. 4 ('Spring', lines 18, 33).
34 A. McRae notes the significance of Tusser's altered starting point and its relation to tenant farming and 'improvement': *God Speed the Plough* (Cambridge University Press, 1996), p. 147. I have discussed Michaelmas moving in 'Moving House', *Lives of Houses*, ed. K. Kennedy and H. Lee (Princeton University Press, 2020).
35 C. Larrington, *A Store of Common Sense: Gnomic Theme and Style in Old Icelandic and Old English Wisdom Poetry* (Oxford: Clarendon Press, 1993), p. 167.

36 J. Clare, *The Shepherd's Calendar*, ed. Eric Robinson (Oxford University Press, 1993), p. 1 ('January', lines 1–2).
37 Clare, *Calendar*, p. 2 ('January', lines 39–40).
38 *Georgics* (Johnson), p. 23 (*Georgics*, I. 299). Virgil has 'hiems ignava colono'.
39 Sackville-West, *Land*, p. 18.
40 Swift, *Morville*, p. 17.
41 On the extent and implication of this tradition, see M. Dove, *The Perfect Age of Man's Life* (Cambridge University Press, 1986), pp. 67–100.
42 Sackville-West, *Land*, p. 55.
43 Swift, *Morville*, pp. 207–8.
44 J. Philips, *Cyder: A Poem: In Two Books* (1708), p. 53.
45 W. Cowper, *The Task* (Book 1, line 1), in *The Poems of William Cowper*, ed. J. D. Baird and C. Ryskamp, 2 vols. (Oxford University Press, 1995), vol. II, p. 117. All subsequent quotations from this edition.
46 Cowper, *Task*, p. 178 (Book 3, lines 625–7), echoing *Georgics*, II. 401–2: 'redit agricolis labor actus in orbem, atque in se sua per vestigial voluitur annus'.
47 *Georgics*, IV. 122; Cowper, *Task*, p. 174 (Book 3, lines 446, 451).
48 Cowper, *Task*, p. 175 (Book 3, lines 490–3). Smart's allusion to the same lines in *The Hop-Garden* sounds (like most of the poem) unproductively affected: 'When twice bright Phoebus' vivifying ray', 'The Hop-Garden: A Georgic', in C. Smart, *Poems on Several Occasions* (1752), p. 115. Cowper, while obviously enjoying the literary game, also catches the real physicality of the microcosm he describes.
49 Hesiod, *Works and Days*, p. 60.
50 On Virgil's lip-service to an outdated calendar, see e.g., L. P. Wilkinson, *The Georgics of Virgil* (Cambridge University Press, 1969), pp. 57–8: 'It is clear that [Virgil] attached no importance to [the calendar of auspicious days] except as a reminder of Hesiod'.
51 *Georgics* I. 275–6.
52 *Georgics* I. 284.
53 J. Aubrey, *Remaines of Gentilisme and Judaisme*, quoted in B. Blackburn and L. Holford-Strevens, *The Oxford Companion to the Year* (Oxford University Press, 1999), p. 595.
54 F. M. Ford, *It Was the Nightingale* (London: Heinemann, 1934), p. 111.
55 F. M. Ford, *No Enemy: A Tale of Reconstruction* (1929), ed. P. Skinner (Manchester: Carcanet, 2002), p. 8.
56 E. Pound to F. M. Ford, 21 March 1922, *Pound/Ford: The Story of a Literary Friendship*, ed. B. Lindberg-Seyersted (London: Faber, 1982), p. 65. Thanks to Max Saunders for this reference.
57 Ford, *Nightingale*, p. 174.
58 C. Stewart, *Driving over Lemons* (New York: Pantheon, 1999), p. 75.
59 Stewart, *Lemons*, p. 75.
60 Stewart, *Lemons*, p. 76.
61 Sackville-West, *Land*, p. 56.
62 Sackville-West, *Land*, p. 77.

63 Hesiod, *Works and Days*, p. 49.
64 *Georgics* (Johnson), p. 123 (*Georgics*, IV. 77).
65 Cowper, *Task*, p. 190 (Book 4, line 150).
66 Cowper, *Task*, p. 173 (Book 3, lines 419–21).
67 Cowper, *Task*, p. 179 (Book 3, lines 656–61, alluding to *Georgics* II. 358).
68 *Georgics* (Johnson), p. 95 (*Georgics*, III. 284).

CHAPTER 3

Farm Diaries, 1770–1990

Jeremy Burchardt

The gap between rural labour and its representation is less in farm diaries than in any other kind of georgic. Typologically, then, the farm diary could be regarded as the most basic, even foundational, form of georgic writing. Yet considered in relation to the evolution of georgic as a genre, farm diaries are peripheral, sometimes even detached: the cultural traffic between them and other forms of georgic was sparse in both directions. Farm diaries therefore offer a unique vantage point for assessing other georgic writing and for engaging with related questions of the representation of rural labour and landscape.

This chapter falls into two parts. The first is a broad overview that seeks to define the farm diary and draw attention to some recurrent characteristics. The second explores how rural work and landscape, and the relationship between them, are represented in eight contrasting farm diaries. In concluding, I will consider how a survey of farm diaries affects our understanding of georgic and pastoral, and the adequacy or otherwise of these lenses for looking at the representation and experience of rural work and landscape.

Surveys such as this can easily become platitudinous exercises based on a wide but superficial overview. I have sought to avoid that by drawing principally on eight farm diaries which I have read, considered and, insofar as space allows, analysed in depth. Standing behind these, and shaping my interpretation of them, is the largely invisible presence of the many other diaries, farm and non-farm, that I have encountered over the last twenty years while researching the experience of landscape in nineteenth- and twentieth-century England. The eight diaries are those of: Mary Hardy, who farmed and brewed with her husband William at Coltishall, Norfolk, 1773–1809; William Hodkin, a farmer from Beeley on the Chatsworth Estate, 1864–66; Cornelius Stovin, Methodist lay preacher and tenant of Binbrook Hall Farm, Lincolnshire 1871–5; William Carter Swan, farm apprentice at Dial Post Farm, Sussex, 1909–10; Maria Gyte, of the Devonshire Arms Inn and Farm at Sheldon, Derbyshire, 1913–20; Anne McEntegart, farm and milk-round worker at New Park Farm, Brockenhurst, Hampshire, 1943–5; Doreen Strange, a land girl on the Burnham Grove Estate, 1948; and Ivan Turner, a farmworker at Netherwood, Herefordshire, 1971–87. There is a good gender and occupational balance here (four women, four men; four farmworkers, four farmers), and a broad if hardly even geographical and chronological range. Nevertheless it should be acknowledged that a study based on a different selection of farm diaries would undoubtedly reach different conclusions in some respects.

With regard to ethnicity, unfortunately all the farm diaries I have been able to identify were written by white British men or women. This is not surprising because throughout the period under study there was little ethnic diversity in the stable, year-round English agricultural workforce, who were best placed to write diaries and whose diaries are most likely to have been preserved. However, Romani, Irish and, mainly in the twenty-first century, eastern European workers have played a notable role, often under conditions of extreme exploitation, as a casual labour force, especially during harvest. More fully recovering the experiences of such workers would be a project of prime historical value, although one that would almost certainly have to draw on sources such as oral history, rather than diaries.

What Is a Farm Diary?

As with all diary genres, the boundaries of the farm diary are indistinct, merging into other kinds of diary such as the nature diary, 'sporting' (i.e., hunting and shooting) diaries and the looser category of the country diary.[1] Farm diaries also blur into other kinds of life writing, record keeping and communication: memoirs, log books and accounts, letters and instructional texts. Stovin copied letters he had written to his wife into his diary, while Swan's diary was written partly as an aide-memoire to help him remember what he was learning as a farm apprentice.[2]

As a genre, the farm diary therefore has a wide, fuzzy border. Pursuing precision in this area is neither necessary nor fruitful. Fortunately, however, the core of the genre can be reasonably easily defined. I would suggest that a farm diary is a record consisting of dated – not necessarily daily – entries; that it must be written by a farmer, farmworker or other person engaged at the time of writing in agricultural work; and that it must be concerned at least in part with farming (excluding, therefore, pure nature or sporting diaries, even if written by agriculturalists).[3]

Despite the fluidity and variability of the diary as a literary form, almost all the farm diaries I have looked at share three characteristics. First, the weather is mentioned in every entry. This is true for most non-farm diaries too. The daily weather record is an anchoring device, providing an element of structure akin to the bar lines in musical notation, and an external context for the fickle subjectivity of the diarist's words. In farm diaries, however, the weather record serves other significant purposes too. In particular, it often explains and is always relevant to their second characteristic feature – the daily record of tasks. This is much less frequent in non-farm diaries, where work typically manifests as merely one dimension among others, having no special priority, and is often pushed to the margins in favour of a focus on leisure activities. The extraordinary diaries of William Hallam, for example, run to eighty-two volumes across sixty-seven years, from 1886 to 1952, but refer to the GWR's Swindon Works, where he was employed for almost all that time, only in passing.[4]

This second core characteristic of farm diaries is in turn involved in their third defining feature: the daily record of tasks is almost always locationally specific. Where the work was done is virtually inseparable from what was done:

> Wm. Downs John and Richard went shearing in the morning I went to little brook and took the stirks to the Lydget brought the gees from the Lydget and the Hoggs out of the Morton Greave and took them in the wood close and hiring gate, then helped the others to finish shearing caught 3 rabbits and one leverit. Father covering the stack that was made on Thursday, a fine harvest day.[5]

More consistently, then, than most other kinds of life writing, farm diaries are grounded in the fundamental verities of time, place, weather and task. These recurring elements constitute the warp from which farm diaries are woven. The weft is formed by non-daily incidents and events shot through this framework. These are highly variable but even here some patterns can be discerned. Perhaps the most obvious is the reports of accidents and mishaps that feature intermittently in most farm diaries, testifying to the dangerous, unpredictable and never entirely standardized nature of farmwork. Other recurring elements depend on the position of the writer in relation to the production process. Records of sales and purchases and of payments made and received are a prominent element of diaries written by farmers, bailiffs and farm managers:

> A Wett Morng, fine Afternoon. New Labourer at Ingworth. R[obert] M[anning] at Lessingham, sent Cash £10 10s 0d. J Davison here, paid cash £7 10s 0d. Ann Gay here, paid Cash £3 0s 0d … Bought 2 young Geese 2/-.[6]

The allocation of labour on the farm features frequently in such diaries too:

> A nice day today. Anthony, Tony and Wilf Goodwin spreading lime on moor this morning. Tom carting stone and gravel from Magpie for meres. Wm. Gould carting clay. Tony and Wilf Goodwin picking potatoes this afternoon (to sell) some going bad.[7]

Journeys to market and elsewhere, visits to and from other farmers and traders, and occasional social events also figure recurrently in farmers' diaries:

> John ploughing I was making bills out in the morning, went to Edensor and Pilsley with flour &c and recvd. Mr Halls and Mr Spencers and Mrs Turners and Mr Buckleys bills, then went to Bakewell with a cow to be ready for the show tied her in Mr Ormes cowhouse at night.[8]

These elements are much less pronounced in diaries written by farmworkers. Conversely, a wary preoccupation with the character, mood and decisions of 'the boss' throws into sharp relief the power imbalance inherent in all employment relations but often especially stark in agriculture:

> The gaffer cheerfully going up to the woods with saw in hand, came back a little later looking black and disgruntled. Afterwards we found out why. He had some time previously picked out a Christmas tree for himself and on going up to cut it down, found it had gone. Not knowing he had his eye on it, one of us had beaten him to it ... Not a sensible thing for us to have done as this sort of thing can lead to bad gaffer-worker relationships.[9]

Or more painfully in William Carter Swan's anxious entries:

> The governor is in a very good temper this evening. (7th June 1909)
> The governor is rather cross today. (14th June 1909)
> I have my first experience of loading [hay] and the governor is very pleased with same. (19th June 1909)
> Mrs Venn [the 'governor's' wife] rather ill-tempered today. (17th September 1909)
> I ask the gov. for a little extra for Sunday work, but tis no go, it seems rather hard. (1st January 1910)[10]

Other minor tribulations Swan endured included an evening 'lecture on the ways of men employed on the farm, very edifying of course (Oh yes)' and being evicted from his room to make way for Mr Venn's brother, who then went off with his bicycle without deigning to ask.[11] The tone fluctuates between indignation, sarcasm and injury.

Practical difficulties in completing assigned tasks are another leitmotif of farmworkers' diaries:

> I took the red tractor & trailer & carted a load of straw to Britwell yard (nearly got stuck – it was an awful mess, like a bog), & then went up to

the sheep dip with a load. This yard was ½ cleared out, but the other half (not very noticeable) was very wet & thick with dung, & I got really stuck there. Tom Rose came along, just as I was starting to unhitch the tractor, & he wanted me to try & get out with the trailer, which of course I couldn't, & kept telling me what to do, & finally we unhitched & still I couldn't get out. He put hurdles behind the wheels, sloping upwards & smooth & I just open. Then off he tootled to get Micky & his tractor to draw me out & when he'd gone I took the dung from under the hurdles to slope them downhill a bit, & covered them with thick straw & came out OK & was just about to draw the trailer out backwards with the big chain when he & Micky arrived! They were astonished to see I'd got out on my own! I don't think I've ever had to be drawn out of a mess by another tractor yet.[12]

Perhaps the most interesting difference between farmers' and farmworkers' diaries, however, is the contrast in geographical scales. Although locational specificity is a critical element in virtually all farm diaries, in those written by farmers this is typically at the level of the parish or neighbourhood, extending to adjacent villages, the local market town and often beyond. The scale registered in farmworkers' diaries is often microscopic by comparison, almost always looking inward within the farm, at the level of the individual field rather than the farm or parish:

> We went out to a field opposite the Grove & cut three boxes of broccoli, & eight boxes of curly kale until dinner time. It was lovely out there – sheltered from the wild wind, & bright & sunny, with a nice cosy view of the golf course & the green slopes around.[13]

Often what is seen and recorded is at even higher resolution, at the scale of a particular tree or field corner:

> Sitting in the crawler having tea under the solitary oak tree in the middle of the field, where the big orchard used to be, a little owl came down out of the tree and preceded to investigate the crawler, walking along the tracks, peering about as he went ... It had the most inquiring eyes I've ever seen in man or beast.[14]

This respectful, ground-level observation recalls the writing of a better-known farmworker, although one who lived and wrote more than a century earlier: John Clare. Almost all writing about animals in the English tradition falls into one of three categories: the instrumental, the appropriating or anthropomorphizing and the distancing or objectifying. What is so unusual and distinctive in the way Clare and the crawler driver Ivan Turner write about animals is that they avoid all three modes. They do so through their positioning, placing themselves physically and normatively on the same level as, and extending a friendly egalitarian recognition to, the animals they encounter, but one that avoids appropriation because it neither expects nor requires a response. When Clare writes about 'all lifes little crowd | That haunt the waters fields & woods', he includes himself within it; in his view 'the pismires round the hill' are 'full as blest as I'.[15] Similarly, Turner assimilates 'man' and 'beast' to a single non-hierarchical frame of reference as he searches for a way to register the little owl's alert curiosity. He looks at the owl and the owl looks at the tractor in which he is sitting; each remains themselves.

Strongly reminiscent though Turner's writing can be of Clare, however, direct influence is highly unlikely. Turner left school at fifteen, and seems to have read little thereafter: when he wanted to identify a flint he had found, the best reference source available to him was a children's encyclopaedia.[16] If he and Clare saw similar things in a similar way, the explanation is less likely to be cultural transmission than their positioning in the social and material landscape, which was sufficiently close that there was much overlap between their respective fields of view.

In the farm diaries I have looked at, these similarities and contrasts in relation to the production process are more pronounced than those due to gender, education or even time, although a more extended study would undoubtedly bring out further patterning in these and other dimensions.

Farm Diaries, Work and Landscape

Beyond the defining features identified earlier, farm diaries, like other diaries, often consist of little more than a bare outline of events. Some, however, are much richer and in the remaining part of this chapter I want to look at two themes of particular significance in connection with georgic: work and landscape.

Work

As might be expected, plenty of evidence of discomfort and danger in relation to the labour process can be gleaned from farm diaries. Anne McEntegart describes how she was viciously kicked by a cow:

> I was just stooping down to wipe her off [prior to milking] when she landed me a terrific crippling blow on the knee and followed with six more, quick as lightning from the middle of my calf to the top of my thigh and I was in such pain I just stood rooted to the spot, unable to move. It was agony.[17]

More serious accidents occurred too:

> Poor old Sybil, who worked on the farm there [Elmstone, Kent], who I often saw on a trailer behind a Ferguson tractor, chucking out cow food, was killed falling off it somehow – she died in 1½ hours.[18]

Farming was, and remains, a dangerous occupation but even in farming, fatal accidents were exceptional. Tiredness and exhaustion, by contrast, were an almost daily occurrence. Swan found this especially difficult to endure: he was only sixteen when he began his apprenticeship and perhaps lacked the strength and stamina for some of the tasks assigned to him. One of the worst, he found, was loading hay:

> I have another hard day's loading … My feet again pain me very much.[19]

Nearly as bad was 'pitching' (setting out) sheep folds, which made his arms ache, while dusty barn work left him with an itchy head in the evening.[20]

For all this, most farm diaries, including those written by farmworkers, place more emphasis on the pleasures than the pains of agricultural labour. Perhaps the physical demands of the job became less onerous once workers were accustomed to them, or simply so familiar that they were rarely thought worthy of comment. Discomfort did not always preclude enjoyment, as McEntegart found when weeding kale:

> On and on I went … It was most rewarding and satisfying, and the only difficulty was that I got an ache in the small of my back with bending hour after hour.[21]

Strange too took pleasure in her work:

> I went with Tom wood carting … & enjoyed myself driving the David Brown along to the woods where timber haulers were working, & helping load up the smaller pieces they'd left in the pile, & taking it to Britwell where the men were sawing it up on the circular saw … It was lovely in the woods, with the sun shining through the mist in beams between the trees. I love working in woods in the winter.[22]

It is perhaps less surprising that a large farmer such as Stovin relished agricultural work, since in the main his role was to direct rather than participate in manual labour. Nevertheless, his delight in witnessing it was the purest georgic:

> This has been a fine harvest day. My oat crop is cutting up magnificently. It waves all golden in the breeze and falls prostrate before the march of the reaper. The ring and rattle and bustle of the reaper is a joy to the husbandman.[23]

As this suggests, he embraced mechanization eagerly:

> The reaper, the steam engine, and thrashing apparatus, the double plough, are Divine gifts to the agriculture of the nineteenth century.[24]

These 'Divine gifts' naturally brought their pious purchaser tangible earthly rewards:

> This is somewhat of an eventful year in my farming career. The year 1871 marks the era of the double plough on the farm. In availing myself of it, I have been able to dispense with the third waggoner, also with two draught horses ... The keep of two horses will make a considerable difference to my oatsack.[25]

Stovin's celebration of the nineteenth-century 'march of the mind' was unusually effusive but many farm diaries record the purchase, or occasionally construction, of new equipment and machinery with a degree of emphasis, suggesting that it was regarded as a noteworthy. Mary Hardy and her husband William, for example, paid for the construction of a wherry (a large sailing barge) to take their malt down the River Bure from Coltishall to the port of Great Yarmouth. They named it the *William and Mary* and Mary's diary follows its building and launch closely.[26] Maria Gyte's diary mentions a new swath-turner which 'acted pretty well', a new mowing-machine/reaper, a new self-binder and a new oil engine.[27] Ivan Turner describes the difficulties he had operating a newly arrived Massey-Ferguson combine harvester for the first time.[28]

For all the excitement their purchase generated, however, none of the innovations mentioned in the previous paragraph can compare with the significance accorded to tractors in farm diaries written from the mid-twentieth century onward. Almost every entry in Turner's diary features the crawler tractor he drove or is written from his vantage point as he sat on it. For McEntegart, learning to plough with a tractor was an exhilarating experience:

> Presently, he [the 'Boss'] went away and I realised my dream had last come true. Here I was alone with my tractor, ploughing up a piece of Mac's England. I looked and saw the green strips getting thinner as I added furrow after furrow to the brown rectangle. I stood up very straight and the tractor purred on tirelessly ... There was now left only a narrow strip of green two or three feet wide along the hedge – the rest I had turned into a billowing sea of brown and shiny waves. Have I ever felt so proud? But I felt exhausted also, with excitement and fatigue. It is a heavy job and my shoulders and arms ached.[29]

Agricultural historians have, with good reason, dwelt on the transformative impact of tractors on the productivity of English agriculture during and after the Second World War.³⁰ Yet their equally transformative impact on work experience seems largely to have escaped notice. Notwithstanding stereotypical assumptions about the nexus between men and tractors, this is registered most vividly in women's farm diaries, and never more compellingly than by Strange. She had worked with tractors on arable farms, mainly in Sussex, during the Second World War but her diary covers only her last year in the Women's Land Army, from January 1948 to March 1949, when she was employed on an arable and market gardening farm in Buckinghamshire. Unfortunately the farm manager wanted her to drive a 'midget' Ransome's tractor in the market garden, rather than the Fordson (which she christened 'Smoky Joe') on the arable:

> It was a lovely day … I thought of the chain harrowing that was needed, while I was doing these footling jobs not that I actually minded digging leaks or lifting up frames, but Smoky Joe was calling me. But about 11:30 Mr Rose [the foreman] … came along & seeing us standing in the sun with nothing to do … said I could go & get my Smoky Joe ready, & after dinner go chain harrowing. Did I go from there in a hurry? I got to my Smoky Joe in less than hardly anytime … I spent a happy afternoon doing a job I could see on a tractor I could get hold of. Quite a simple job perhaps, with not much skill to it … but after a couple of days in the market garden it's heaven to me.³¹

In early March she made a rather half-hearted effort to reconcile herself to market gardening:

> I was cultivating etc all day on the midget. I felt a bit happier about it today – it's quite interesting sort of work if you've never known the joy of proper farming & haven't got such a passion for arable fields as I have.³²

Yet the sight of arable fields from a train window on a visit home a few days later brought her true feelings surging back:

> The rich ploughed fields laying straight & even, & some already cultivated, made me ache with longing. It's no good – heaven to me will always consist of just that – the good earth & the work cultivating & ploughing it, days spent on the wide fields under the night sky, on my beloved tractor. (That I haven't got now).³³

By dint of leaping at every opportunity, Strange managed to spend more time than had initially seemed likely on the big tractors at Burnham Grove. Yet a new difficulty now arose. She was keen to move on to the next stage of her life, which in her eyes meant marriage and children, but neither she nor her fiancée Charles believed this was compatible with farmwork. Her diary registers the conflict with painful intensity:

> When I finished Tom let me do two turns of ploughing & drive back with the baby one on the trailer, which I put away in the shed. It was good to have even such a tiny bit with the tractor, though in a way it makes it harder. To think that I have to snatch such crumbs when not so long ago it was my daily work. I never realised how much a part of me it had become & how much I love it. I don't know how I'm going to give it up to get married, I really don't (though of course, I'd rather that than give up Charles, which is impossible!) But all the same, I dread the day when I'm no longer a tractor driver & hate it that I can't spend these last few months doing the job I love ... I wish I was a man – I'd get married & <u>never never</u> stop driving a tractor on the farm, & I'd get a job on a farm near download with wide fields & plenty of work, & plough & harrow & roll & cut corn & hay as the seasons came & want nothing more.[34]

As the end approached, Strange cherished every minute she got on the big tractors:

> I had a treat after dinner – Micky had half a day off just right & I took over his tractor & fetched in the grass from the orchard all afternoon – every time I get an odd hour or so tractoring these days I wonder if it's the last time (as it might well be), & that makes the pleasure all the keener, but all the more sad, so to speak. I wish I could go on everyday like I used to. When I get on a tractor again, all that's come between me & the days when it was my everyday job, just fall away, & it doesn't seem as if I'd ever stopped – behind it is the knowledge that it's gone really – the dear familiar ways of the farm & the work with the tractor, – so many years of it that I can hardly believe it's as good as over for me, unless anything very unforeseen happens. I wish I didn't love it so much, not being a man, & able to carry on after being married. I know lots of girls go on working, but that's neither Charles's nor my idea of being married, & I shall just have to forget all that & try & concentrate on being a wife. It couldn't have always been my job, anyway, but that doesn't make it any easier somehow. It just comes over me like an ache sometimes.[35]

Although she gave her tractor a nickname, the joy Strange found in driving it came not through emotional projection or identification, but from the work itself and the connection with the landscape around her. McEntegart also named her tractor but in her case this was indicative of a much closer emotional entanglement, one that she experienced as a form of union and for which romantic metaphors were appropriate:

> That thrilling, exciting period of courtship is over. Elizabeth and I have been together for one whole week and our romance has resolved itself into something infinitely deep and wonderful. I have come to know her and sense her every mood. Every sound and movement betrays her inner emotions and with the intuition of true love, I find myself dealing with her

instinctively. How wonderful life can be when we are together and alone, in the wide open spaces.[36]

The pattern of work at New Park Farm consisted of alternating periods on the arable and the milk round. Strikingly, McEntegart experienced feelings of unison with Peter, the pony who pulled her milk float, that were closely comparable to those she had known with 'Elizabeth'. Following one such occasion, she described how she had felt 'a deep feeling of peace ever since'.[37] The following autumn, Peter ran away with some of the ponies that roamed freely over the New Forest and was lost for several days. When he was found again, McEntegart rode him back to the farm:

> We knew each other so perfectly and were in complete unison and being on his back was so much better than being in the float. We raced along and each time I spoke to him his ears pricked and he gave little snorts of pleasure. All along the chalky soil, on the high ridge of moorland we cantered. Flat out, like a streak in wonderful harmony. I sensed his joy at being no longer lost and lonely and that 8 miles home was rapturous.[38]

Farm diaries, then, register not only the hardships and dangers of agricultural work but also the deep rewards and satisfactions it could sometimes bring.

Landscape

Although Sidney Smith infamously claimed that ploughmen had 'nothing more nearly approaching to [sentiment], than the ideas of broiled bacon and mashed potatoes', a study of farm diaries quickly refutes such facile stereotypes.[39] Nowhere is this more apparent than in the responsiveness many farmworkers, and farmers, showed towards landscape. Here is Turner, reaching for a characteristically idiosyncratic metaphor to express his pleasure in autumn colour:

> The hedges had not yet been trimmed and the leaves were still on, in vivid contrasting colours. Often one farmer on one side of the road will cut his hedge, the other not, so the balance is gone; but just this once the colours worked together, and I felt as if I was driving between a pair of twisting multi-coloured caterpillars as the morning sun shone on the dewy hedgerows.[40]

A few days later in the year, but just over a century earlier, Stovin offered an equally analytical assessment of a more understated autumnal scene:

> The Autumnal glory has not yet faded from the landscape. Some trees still tenaciously hold remnants of their summer robes, but their change of dye indicates their approaching fall, the revolutions in colouring produced by

the dyeing processes of Autumn, the infinitely various light and shade, the gentle and unabrupt mingling of all possible shades of rainbow hues. The sunshine is not so glaring but flows through the valleys and clothes the hills with a mild and gentle radiance. There are no sharp contrasts of dark green and brown. It is the multitudinous character of the tints that create such a charm to the eye and imagination.[41]

The colours and light effects of autumn seem to have wrought even more powerfully on Strange. Her rendering of the impressions that infused her mind while working in the fields on 5 November 1948 breathes quiet exhilaration:

> It was bright and clear all day, and just perfect about 4 o/c – a clear pale blue sky going into green and purple round the edges, with great pinky cream cauliflower clouds with violet shadows, and grey wisps of smaller clouds about the sky and the sunshine putting a golden coat over everything – the drills of wheat shining, every one clear cut against the earth, and all the oaks and elms with their autumn browns and yellows and russets intensified in the clear gold light, and a touch of blue distance between – a magic day, when all the spirit of the autumn seems to be gathered in a few hours – the autumn that's almost winter, but has just that richness that lingers from the summer warmth. Sometimes a day in November can be more beautiful than one in June.[42]

For all the special appeal of autumn, there is no lack of responsiveness to the distinctive qualities of other seasons in farm diaries. Space permits only one further quotation, in which McEntegart exults in the beauty of the New Forest on a midsummer morning:

> I wakened at quarter to four, to see a red dawn lighting the sky and three hours later, when I was cycling along the narrow bumpy track to my work across the Moor, the sun was already bright and warm and the air like ice – a glorious morning. And what a wonderful ride across the dew-laden moor then into the dark, still forest and along the wide cart track to the farm.[43]

Clearly, farmers and farmworkers were every bit as capable of perceiving beauty in the landscape as any other group of people. Certainly they appreciated fine crops and livestock too but the evidence of farm diaries indicates that this complemented rather than precluded or displaced a non-instrumental relationship to landscape. Stovin articulates this quite explicitly:

> Both grass and clover fields are a mass of blossom. It is a summer to kindle the poet's vision as well as cheer and gladden the farmer's heart. As we have never enjoyed one so rich in landscape beauty neither have we known one so profitable in sheep.[44]

Indeed, far from there being an antithesis between the appreciation of landscape and rural labour, farm diaries demonstrate that the first often arose in the context of, or was even elicited by, the second. Sometimes this was expressed in terms that could be construed as pastoral:

> I took the cows to Queen's Meadow, this time through a hazy forest dripping with rain, and leaves shining with water. It was very beautiful. I love this evening excursion and feast my eyes on the scene and love the noise of the cows and the shouting of the boys.[45]

The diaphanous light, verdure, placid cattle and youthful cowherds, evidently relishing their leisurely labour, could come from one of Claude's paintings or the long tradition of literary pastoral that inspired them. At other times, the mood is paradigmatically georgic in its evocation of the aesthetic and existential rewards of strenuous agricultural work, represented as virtuous, public-spirited and patriotic:

> The Park looked most glorious – 300 acres of yellow corn, glowing in the golden evening sunshine, surrounded by great oaks and the reaper and binder carving its way through the tall oats with red and green wings moving in circles. How thrilled I felt to feel that here I was helping to secure Britain's food! I worked like a Trojan.[46]

At its height, doubtless overrepresented in farm diaries, the joy of work brought the landscape to life, as for Strange when she managed to get back on her tractor one bright morning:

> It was a glorious day, and Good Friday. And it was a Good Friday for me too – I went and got my Smoky Joe ready and found the plough, and sallied forth in the golden dawn along the lanes bursting into new leaves, until I got to the field by Elm Tree Cottage, where it was already set out, across the old ploughing. It was like new life to me to be back on the old tractor and I felt like a million dollars, except for the little sad undercurrent, because I knew it was only for a day, when it used to be my everyday work, and I love it so, there's nothing on earth that is so good to me – at least, as far as work is concerned.[47]

Conversely, for some the beauty of the landscape, absorbed perhaps often below the threshold of conscious attention through long hours working in the fields, was a vital element in the satisfaction they derived from agricultural labour. McEntegart put it best:

> [I] rejoice in … the transforming effect it [ploughing] has on the landscape – rich bands of deep brown soil appearing over large areas of pale stubble and widening each day until the whole is one uniform colour. The beauty of the scenery around me is a great part of the joy that I get out of my work. I am

> forever conscious of it and I absorb it, so that I am now able to recall visually any work I have done over nearly two years. My mind is a kaleidoscope of scenes in spring, summer, autumn and winter as the crops and the colours have changed.[48]

As this suggests, for those working on the land (and many who did not), the beauty perceived in the landscape was indivisible from the changing imprint of the seasons. In Turner's words:

> The autumn song of the robin is so full of meaning for me as if nature itself had been captured in its notes, a reminder that the seasons are constantly changing and that summer does not last through 12 months of the year.[49]

Seen in a casual glance, through a camera's lens or framed in a gallery, a landscape may appear to be a single moment frozen in time, but in diaries written by those who worked on it, and indeed helped to create it, landscape is represented as inherently temporal – a flow of experience rather than static 'scenery':

> What used to be about 17 fields of different shapes and sizes, is now only four. While travelling backwards and forwards, it seemed I was ploughing 15 acres of memories a day, visualising in my mind's eye, all the different spots where things had happened 40 years ago … There are clear pictures in my mind when I travelled over where these small fields used to be.[50]

Landscape both inscribes memory and testifies to loss, sometimes directly, as here, and sometimes, as Strange found at Burnham, through its perceived resemblance to other landscapes:

> I worked all day as happy as a sandboy in the open air, and in spite of the rain – I'd rather put up with rain sometimes than the lid all the time – it was a treat to drive, and made me think of the old days at Warnham (I suppose the meadow, which was in front of the big house, was like the park and fields at Warnham).[51]

For someone like Turner, intimately familiar with every undulation of fields that he had worked in since he was fifteen, the landscape bore witness to the unfolding of time over much longer timescales too. He found his first flint in 1971 and thereafter built up an impressive collection of flints, pottery shards, floor tiles, coins and clay pipes, all gathered from the land as he worked it:

> What pleased me most was the variation and time range of the different archaeological finds, which made me feel very humble. I thought of the different people from years past who had lived in the valley, looked on similar sunsets, sun rises and moons … These thoughts make one person's life span seem very small indeed.[52]

Just as Turner's deep embeddedness in the landscape gave him a sense of his place within a vast panoply of time, in the same way it enabled him to understand himself and humanity as only one element, and not necessarily the most significant, in the totality of life:

> We humans think we're the be-all-and-end-all of everything, but perhaps birds and animals have an affinity with things and places and a past that has in one form or another handed down to them. One evening at dusk I was walking down the side of Rabbitbury Copse under the tall overhanging ash trees, and I had the feeling that the trees with their roots deep in the soil belonged more to the earth and the world than ever we humans. We seem such temporary, fragile things, scampering over the world like a lot of ants.[53]

The salient feature of the history of twentieth-century English farmwork is the decline in the number of farmworkers and the ensuing shift from collective to solitary work. Eminent scholars such as Newby and Howkins have lamented this, attributing to it the decline of agricultural trade unionism, the inability of farmworkers to improve their relative socio-economic position and the loss of a distinctive work-based rural culture.[54] Farm diaries, however, suggest there may also have been gains, albeit hardly perhaps commensurate with the undoubted losses. Among these gains may have been a quality of attentiveness to the non-human world that can arise from long periods of solitary immersion in it. As Turner explains:

> While ploughing long periods by oneself, one develops an affection for the birds and animals that one sees and hears.[55]

Or again:

> Sitting quietly under a hedge, one realises with how many creatures and things one shares the world.[56]

Turner's deeply reciprocal understanding of his relationship with the other inhabitants of the Netherwood landscape informed his interpretation of their behaviour:

> Mouse on top of my bait bag hung on the fence, top Calves Hill; a gift from the kestrel that was catching mice that I was discing up in the stubble? This was not a one-off coincidence, for the same thing happened when working in the Parks field. My bait bag was again hanging on the fence with a dead mouse carefully placed on top. I suppose the kestrel had seen me many times get this bag off the fence, sit down and proceed to eat out of it. Maybe it was its way of saying 'thank you' for making many mice available over the years of ploughing and such![57]

Whether the kestrel genuinely reciprocated Turner's egalitarian goodwill is open to question but there is no doubt another of the small and comparatively powerless inhabitants of his landscape did:

> When working behind Netherwood Cottages, a cup of tea would be brought out by one or other from the cottages. One girl, Christiana, instead of going to sleep this once, would each time I came up the field, put a different doll in the window behind her bedroom curtains for me to see in the headlights. Next morning a sleepy head peeped out and gave me a wave before going off to school.[58]

Reciprocity implies care, for the landscape and everything in it, and this is abundantly evident in Turner's diary. He went to great lengths to locate and move peewits' nests before ploughing the ground where they had been and was distraught when he was the inadvertent agent of destruction:

> Harrowed over and killed two baby hares, causing me to weep in frustration at having done this.[59]

In Turner's experience, farmers, especially those who came and went, rarely shared his deep affective investment in the landscape. He describes finding the bodies of some crows he had been fond of under a tree, 'blasted with a 12-bore shotgun', the cutting down of a gnarled elm that had reminded him of trees in children's picture books, and the mutilation of an ash tree to extract a swarm of bees:

> It hurt me for years afterwards to see this disfigured tree, empty and sad, on the skyline ... I was getting to the stage of making a point of not liking anything in case it disappeared. The selling of the historic part of Netherwood Manor hurt me, as did the closing of the footpaths on Netherwood. I don't suppose that the then farmer even thought that anyone would be attached to any of these things.[60]

What this remarkable diary demonstrates above all is the complete identification with and depth of care for a landscape that can arise through working in it over many decades, qualities epitomized by Turner's diary entry for 7 January 1981:

> I felt a welling up of loving feelings for Netherwood inside me when going up Netherwood drive ... It was totally unexpected. I wasn't feeling any different; just looking up towards Netherwood house in the woods behind. The feeling was like being in love with a girl and you see her coming towards you and want to put your arms around her, and hold her tight. This was the feeling I had for this place; only for a second or two, but enough for me to imagine I had great long arms and was able to hold the whole of Netherwood close for a while.[61]

Conclusion

Social historians have emphasized the misery and degradation of agricultural labour. Yet farm diaries show that, although usually arduous, it could also be deeply rewarding. This underlines the sheer waste of the centuries of exploitation and oppression, and the poverty and degradation they caused: had it not been for this, the materials of a good life were there. It also perhaps provides some retrospective consolation. Although history's wrongs are irreparable, some of those who, in an English context, suffered most may have derived more satisfaction from their work than might have been imagined.

Similarly, the demise of horse-drawn agriculture, and the loss of skill, tradition, occupational diversity and independence this entailed, has been much lamented. There is ample evidence to support these contentions but the further claim that the disappearance of the working horse from English agriculture drastically impoverished the affective experience of farmwork is more questionable.[62] Farm diaries show that for women as well as men, tractors could substitute affectively for horses much more fully and satisfactorily than might have been expected. It seems possible that the introduction of tractor cabs in fact had more drastic consequences for the quality of the work experience. The tractor cab (and its precursor the roll bar) saved many lives but cut the direct connection between farmworkers and their environment. '[T]hat thing oppresses and cramps me', Strange declaimed, 'I'd rather get frozen with wind and damp with rain.'[63] Looking back on the same change decades later, John Lewis-Stempel's verdict was even more damning:

> They killed farming ... by putting cabs on tractors. No longer was the farmer alive to the elements, or even close to the earth. All he did now was sit in a little mobile office, complete with heater and radio, pulling levers.[64]

Furthermore, aesthetic enjoyment of rural landscapes is often cast as a superficial attribute of 'urban outsiders'; by contrast, farmers and farmworkers were supposedly too busy and hard pressed to allow sentiment to distort their down-to-earth and practical attitude to the land. To an extent this maps onto the distinction between pastoral and georgic, with pastoral implicated in a celebration of idyllic rural landscapes detached from agricultural realities, and georgic founded on a recognition of the centrality of labour to rural life. However, such assumptions and distinctions do not correspond to how farmers and farmworkers represented landscape in their diaries. On the contrary, many farm diaries contain lush, even ecstatic, descriptions of landscape that, if they had been penned by a townsperson, would be dismissed as shallow pastoral expressions of the 'rural idyll'. Yet often the perceptions represented in these passages arise in the context of work, sometimes even because of it. Furthermore, these landscape sensibilities are continuous, not in tension, with other passages that fuse the experience of work and the apprehension of landscape. The distinction between pastoral and georgic constantly collapses as we read farm diaries, as does the related assumption that there is a stable, useful or even tenable distinction to be made between 'urban' and 'rural' attitudes to landscape. Few if any widespread 'urban attitudes' were not also available to, and commonly held by, the inhabitants of the modern English countryside. This is not surprising, since farmers and farmworkers were not hermetically sealed from the rest of the population in terms of demography, education or culture.

However, although rural and urban dwellers largely shared a common culture in nineteenth- and twentieth-century England, they did not share common experiences. What comes through most strongly in studying farm diaries is the depth of engagement of those who wrote them with land and landscape. Yet there is little sense of a conscious tradition. Now and again, a farm diary may be informed by rural fiction, agricultural writing or landscape painting, but few were in dialogue with each other, or even with the wider diary canon, beyond the most basic conventions of the genre. It seems likely that the recurrent features of farm diaries mainly derive from the shared situations, affordances, challenges and rewards inherent in farmwork itself. How far these recurrent experiences find their way, independently of inherited convention, into other kinds of georgic writing and contribute to its defining tropes is a question that perhaps deserves consideration.

Notes

1 On nature diaries, see M. E. Bellanca, *Daybooks of Discovery: Nature Diaries in Britain, 1770–1870* (Charlottesville: University of Virginia Press, 2007).
2 J. Stovin, ed., *Journals of a* Methodist Farmer *1871–1875* (London: Croom Helm, 1982), pp. 108–18; W. C. Swan, *The Diary of a Farm Apprentice. William Carter Swan 1909–1910*, E. E. Swan (Gloucester: Alan Sutton, 1984).
3 On the dated entry, see M. Hewitt, 'Diary, Autobiography and the Practice of Life History', in D. Amigoni, ed., *Life Writing and Victorian Culture* (Aldershot: Ashgate, 2006), p. 31.
4 The Hallam Diaries, Berkshire Record Office, D/EX 1415.
5 W. Hodkin, *A Victorian Farmer's Diary. William Hodkin's Diary 1864–66. Life in and around Beeley on the Chatsworth Estate*, ed. T. A. Burden (n.p.: Derbyshire County Council Cultural & Community Services Department, 2003), p. 47, 27 August 1864. Stirks are heifers or bullocks.

6 M. Hardy, *The Diary of Mary Hardy 1773–1809. Diary I, 1773–1781. Public House and Waterway*, ed. M. Bird (Kingston upon Thames: Burnham Press, 2013), p. 36, 7 May 1774.
7 M. Gyta, *The Diaries of Maria Gyte of Sheldon, Derbyshire, 1913–1920*, ed. G. Phizackerley (Cromford: Scarthin Books, 1999), p. 6, 27 November 1913. 'Magpie' was a local lead mine. A mere, in this context, is pond for watering cattle and sheep.
8 Hodkin, *A Victorian Farmer's Diary*, p. 52, 5 October 1864.
9 I. Turner, *Riding on a Plough* (Upton upon Severn: Square One Publications, 1994), pp. 217–18, 16 December 1986.
10 Swan, *Farm Apprentice*, pp. 36–8, 56, 77.
11 Swan, *Farm Apprentice*, pp. 39, 72, 61.
12 Burnham Historians, *A Land Girl's Diary: Burnham 1948* (Taplow: Burnham Historians, 1999), pp. 119–20, 18 October 1948.
13 Burnham Historians, *Land Girl's Diary*, p. 51, 1 April 1948.
14 Turner, *Riding on a Plough*, p. 179, 26 October 1981.
15 John Clare, 'Emmonsales Heath', in *The Major Poems*, ed. Eric Robinson and David Powell (Oxford University Press, 1984), pp. 181–3, lines 73–4 and 83–4. Pismires are ants.
16 Turner, *Riding on a Plough*, p. 115, 23 October 1971.
17 Anne McEntegart, *The Milk Lady at New Park Farm. The Wartime Diary of Anne McEntegart, June 1943–February 1945* (Sheffield: RMC Books, 2011), p. 128, Christmas 1944.
18 Burnham Historians, *Land Girl's Diary*, p. 98, 22 August 1948.
19 Swan, *Farm Apprentice*, p. 42, 3 July 1909.
20 Swan, *Farm Apprentice*, pp. 30, 62.
21 McEntegart, *The Milk Lady at New Park Farm*, p. 42, 2 August 1943.
22 Burnham Historians, *Land Girl's Diary*, p. 25, 28 January 1948.
23 Stovin, *Methodist Farmer*, p. 26, 22 August 1871.
24 Stovin, *Methodist Farmer*, p. 47, 6 January 1872.
25 Stovin, *Methodist Farmer*, p. 23, 18 August 1871.
26 Hardy, *Diary of Mary Hardy*, pp. 168, 172–3, 175–6, 186, 191.
27 Gyte, *Diaries of Maria Gyte*, pp. 59, 79, 243.
28 Turner, *Riding on a Plough*, p. 112, 16 August 1971.
29 [McEntegart], *The Milk Lady at New Park Farm*, p. 84, 5 April 1944. 'Mac' was Anne's husband Bernard, who was serving with the RAF in the Middle East.
30 See Paul Brassley, 'Twentieth Century Georgic and Agricultural Technology', Chapter 4 in this book.
31 Burnham Historians, *Land Girl's Diary*, p. 32, 12 February 1948.
32 Burnham Historians, *Land Girl's Diary*, p. 40, 2 March 1948.
33 Burnham Historians, *Land Girl's Diary*, p. 41, 6 March 1948.
34 Burnham Historians, *Land Girl's Diary*, p. 42, 9 March 1948.
35 Burnham Historians, *Land Girl's Diary*, p. 71, 2 June 1948.
36 McEntegart, *Milk Lady*, p. 84, 16 April 1944.
37 McEntegart, *Milk Lady*, p. 55, 16 September 1943.
38 McEntegart, *Milk Lady*, p. 121, September 1944.

39 [Sydney Smith], 'Poor Laws', *Edinburgh Review*, 66 (1820), p. 106. See the excoriating critiques of the 'Hodge' stereotype of farmworkers perpetuated by Smith and other writers in K. D. M. Snell, *Annals of the Labouring Poor: Social Change and Agrarian England, 1660–1900* (Cambridge University Press, 1985), pp. 1–14 and M. Freeman, 'The Agricultural Labourer and the "Hodge" Stereotype', *Agricultural History Review*, 49 (2001), 172–86.
40 Turner, *Riding on a Plough*, p. 145, 20 October 1975.
41 Stovin, *Methodist Farmer*, p. 38, 3 November 1871.
42 Burnham Historians, *Land Girl's Diary*, p. 126, 5 November 1948.
43 McEntegart, *Milk Lady*, p. 14, 29 June 1943.
44 Stovin, *Methodist Farmer*, p. 71, 10 July 1872. See also p. 79, 2 August 1872.
45 McEntegart, *Milk Lady*, p. 32, 21 July 1943.
46 McEntegart, *Milk Lady*, p. 39, 30 July 1943.
47 Burnham Historians, *Land Girl's Diary*, p. 49, 26 March 1948.
48 McEntegart, *Milk Lady*, pp. 123–4, November 1944. 'Also' in addition to the doing of the work itself.
49 Turner, *Riding on a Plough*, p. 162, 1 September 1979. See also McEntegart, *The Milk Lady*, pp. 103–4: 'It has been a good year, a year of great gain because in it I have learned to know the seasons.'
50 Turner, *Riding on a Plough*, p. 216, 1 October 1986.
51 Burnham Historians, *Land Girl's Diary*, p. 29, 5 February 1948. The 'lid' was the removable tractor cab, which Strange loathed.
52 Turner, *Riding on a Plough*, p. 118, 23 October 1971.
53 Turner, *Riding on a Plough*, p. 201, October 1984.
54 Howard Newby, *The Deferential Worker: A Study of Farm Workers in East Anglia* (London: Allen Lane, 1977); A. Howkins, *The Death of Rural England: A Social History of the Countryside since 1900* (London: Routledge, 2003).
55 Turner, *Riding on a Plough*, p. 174, 12 January 1981.
56 Turner, *Riding on a Plough*, p. 166, 3 June 1980.
57 Turner, *Riding on a Plough*, p. 192, 10 September 1983.
58 Turner, *Riding on a Plough*, p. 153, 14 October 1977.
59 Turner, *Riding on a Plough*, p. 143, 3 May 1975.
60 Turner, *Riding on a Plough*, pp. 140–1, 21 December 1974.
61 Turner, *Riding on a Plough*, p. 173, 7 January 1981.
62 G. E. Evans, *The Horse in the Furrow* (London: Faber, 1960). See also Tim Pears's West Country Trilogy: *The Horseman* (2017), *The Wanderer* (2018) and *The Redeemed* (2019).
63 Burnham Historians, *Land Girl's Diary*, pp. 25, 124.
64 J. Lewis-Stempel, *Meadowland* (London: Black Swan, 2015), p. 170.

CHAPTER 4

Twentieth-Century Georgic and Agricultural Technology

Paul Brassley

> Only a man harrowing clods
> In a slow silent walk ...
> Yet this will go onward the same

So wrote Thomas Hardy in 1915, whereas in 1952 the ascetic Welsh parish priest and poet R. S. Thomas invited us to

> see Cynddylan on a tractor.
> Gone the old look that yoked him to the soil;
> He's a new man now, part of the machine

and he goes on to explore the tractor's impact on the driver and the landscape in which he drives.[1] Which is closer to reality: Thomas Hardy or the hardy R. S. Thomas? Continuity, or change? This chapter contends that they both reflect their times, and that the concerns of georgic writing changed around the years of the Second World War. Pre-war georgic, as exemplified by Adrian Bell and A. G. Street, was part of a rich seam of rural writing that emphasized the power of tradition and its resultant problems. Post-war writers in general were less concerned with the countryside. Technical change in agriculture was of greater interest to its practitioners than to the general reader.

In 1939 agriculture, in Britain as in other European countries, was still heavily dependent upon the muscles of men, women and horses for much of its power. Many of the farmers attending the centenary Royal Show in 1939, Edith Whetham suggested, were using the same type of implements as those at the jubilee show in 1889, and that was inevitable as long as the horse remained the principal power source on most farms.[2] The steam engines that had transformed urban industry were ill-suited to the more dispersed power requirements of farms, except for their use with threshing machines. The drills, mowers, rakes and self-binding reapers that had increased the productivity of farm labour from the nineteenth century onwards were still pulled, in the main, by horses.[3] Cows were still milked by hand on most farms. Only one farm in five had a mains electricity supply, often used only to provide electric light in the farmhouse.[4]

'Probably one of the hardest things for farmers to realize to-day is that they are considered unimportant people by the majority of the community', wrote A. G. Street in 1931 in the epilogue to *Farmer's Glory*. 'As a result of this the farmer has no pride in his occupation. The zest has gone out of farming'. In 1950 Street wrote another epilogue for the Penguin edition of his book, and found that his 1931 epilogue 'makes queer reading to-day ... Instead of farmers and their employees hoeing their lowly rows, unwept, unhonoured, and unsung, they are now so publicized that they are in danger of suffering from swelled head.' A new kind of high-input/high-output farming was taking over, based on 'the work of the scientist, the engineer and the plant breeder'. What brought about the change? 'There is little doubt', wrote Street, 'that the present prosperity of British farming is mainly due to one man, who is now dead. His name was Adolf Hitler'.[5]

Over the fifty years from the beginning of the Second World War farming changed dramatically. The use of fertilizers and purchased feeding-stuffs, with which farmers were already familiar, increased. New technologies were introduced: higher-yielding crop varieties, protected from weeds, insects and fungi by new pesticides, new crops, such as oilseed rape, and a change in the principal power source from the muscles of horses to the internal combustion engines of tractors. In 1940 there were ten times as many horses as tractors on British farms; twenty years later the numbers were reversed. New breeds of dairy cow were milked in new milking parlours, and new breeds of pigs and poultry living in controlled environments and fed by automatic feeders produced more meat and eggs. The number of farmworkers more than halved, and the volume of agricultural output more than doubled. Whereas in earlier centuries the annual growth rate in output was less than 1 per cent, between 1946 and 1965 it rose to 2.8 per cent.[6]

Analysing twentieth-century writing about agriculture, whether or not it is 'put into a pleasing dress' (as Addison suggested that georgic should be) or idealizes the satisfactions of rural work, should concentrate on the impact of technical change, if only because it is the dominant feature of twentieth-century agriculture.[7] Its hesitant adoption before the Second World War, and greater significance during the war and afterwards, provides the framework for the remainder of this chapter, initially in discussing agricultural textbooks and surveys, and subsequently in examining memoirs and fiction.

Textbooks and Surveys

The stream of writing on agriculture, from classical times to the eighteenth century, had dwindled by the mid-nineteenth century.[8] When Henry Stephens published *The Book of the Farm* in 1844, specifically aimed at the needs of farm pupils, one reviewer could claim that there was less demand for works on agriculture than for any other kind of book.[9] Nevertheless, as the nineteenth century drew to a close and agricultural education began to expand, the Royal Agricultural Society of England (RASE) felt that there was a need for a comprehensive and affordable agricultural textbook. William Fream, a lecturer at the College of Agriculture at Downton and the editor of the Society's journal, was commissioned to write it.[10]

Fream's *Elements of Agriculture*, first published in 1892, was an immediate success, with seven editions and a total print run of 46,000 in the author's lifetime.[11] The earlier editions of Fream's *Elements* contained nothing on the management of farms, and it was perhaps this absence which prompted Watson and More, academics in the Department of Agriculture at Edinburgh University, to produce the first edition of their textbook *Agriculture: The Science and Practice of Farming* in 1924, for apart from its final section on farm organization and management its structure was remarkably similar to Fream's, beginning with the soil and its management and continuing through crops and livestock. It went through eleven editions by the time Watson died in 1966. Although its authors had been at the forefront of agricultural research from the 1930s to the 1950s, read today that final 1962 edition appears in many ways to be a summary of an agricultural tradition that went back to the nineteenth century, with only a few pages on pesticides and the retention of detailed discussions of the threshing machines and farm horses that had virtually disappeared by the time of its publication.[12]

It was replaced by later editions of Primrose McConnell's *Agricultural Notebook*. McConnell was a farmer, lecturer and writer, who, as a student, 'oftentimes felt the great want of a book containing all the data connected with the subject he was studying'. It was only after his death in 1931 that subsequent editors and publishers gradually expanded what had begun as a slim pocket-sized notebook into a fatter and more discursive work, while still retaining its original character as a small-format rapid reference book. After they realized, in the early 1980s, that the absence of recent editions of Fream's *Elements* and Watson and More's *Agriculture* had left a gap in the market, the 17th edition of the *Notebook* emerged as a comprehensive multi-authored textbook and continued as such through subsequent editions.[13] It is not the only available introductory textbook but it remains prominent.[14]

The *Notebook*'s continued publication indicates that publishers still find a big enough market among students, farmers and those in associated industries to make the production of a general textbook worthwhile, but throughout the twentieth century such general works were accompanied by more specialist books. Russell's *Soil Conditions and Plant Growth*, Percival, and later Gill and Vear on *Agricultural Botany*, Culpin on *Farm Machinery*, Halnan and Garner on *Feeding Farm Animals*, followed later by McDonald, Edwards and Greenhalgh on *Animal Nutrition* were just some of the better-known examples that went through several editions.[15] These were the books used in university and college courses and read by students and advisory specialists. Their function was to summarize and promulgate the results of the agricultural research that was expanding from the end of the nineteenth century onwards, a process begun at the start of the twentieth century by Sir Daniel Hall's summary of the results of the work that had been undertaken at the Rothamsted research station since its establishment in the 1840s.[16] They were therefore almost entirely written by academics and research scientists and only a few spread beyond the textbook market into higher sales volumes. One that did was Dexter and Barber's *Farming For Profits*, which essentially explained the methods being used in the 1960s and 1970s by farm management advisers. The first edition sold about 25,000 copies, many of them to farmers.[17]

The same split between the economically depressed and technically conservative years before 1939 and the subsequent more expansive period can also be seen in various surveys of UK agriculture. Henry Rider Haggard, who undertook a tour of twenty-seven mainly arable counties in the years 1901 and 1902, formed the overall impression of 'failure to cope with these difficult times' leading to 'grave problems' for agriculture, although in three tours undertaken between 1910 and 1912 Daniel Hall found much to praise in traditional farming.[18] Further surveys followed in the late 1930s, some judicious and considered, some more polemical.[19] 'Does [agriculture] really matter to a town people?' asked A. G. Street. 'Is it a great industry ... using the latest discoveries of science and mechanical invention ... or just an old-fashioned ... relic of our history?'[20] That became, as Astor and Rowntree perceived, an essentially political question: 'what sort of role is it that agriculture should properly play in our national life?'[21] What emerged from these interwar surveys was the clear impression that a life in farming might mean fulfilling daily involvement with satisfying and technically advanced work for some of its practitioners, but that for others, possibly the majority, it was about struggle and worry. Hugh Barrett remembered seeing, at the sale of a farm that had gone bankrupt in 1933, the farmer standing by a carthorse 'with tears streaming down his face, stroking the animal's neck ... a man utterly crushed by economic forces he had no understanding of or control over'.[22] While machinery and fertilizers and new farming systems were being developed by some farmers, there were many who were too close to the daily routine, or operating on too small a scale, or too short of capital, to make significant changes.

Another thirty years, however, and a different picture emerged. Jack and Frances Donaldson's work, written at the end of the 1960s, resembled an updating of Astor and Rowntree's 1930s work, and contrasted the farming of 'England today with its trim hedges, arable and ley farming, highly capitalized and intensively used buildings' with the 'broken-backed appearance of yesterday'. It was a revolution, they argued, produced by scientists in Europe and the USA, engineers, plant and animal breeders, promulgated by advisers, and 'animated by the farmers themselves [which] owed its beginning, its speed and its completion to the vast sums of money poured into the industry in the form of subsidies and capital grants'.[23] A few years later Tristram Beresford made the same case, that the post-war change had been revolutionary, that farming had recovered 'its spirit, its zest, its vocation ... It has dug up its buried talent and put it to work.'[24] The war, the resultant changes in government policies that produced the grants and subsidies, and some confidence that these policies would continue, meant that what Street had called 'the rotten state of things in the agricultural world' remained only as memories.[25] Yet while in being, that rotten state had been a powerful influence on georgic literature.

Memoirs and Novels Written before the Second World War

Something of the same division around the Second World War years evident in the surveys of agriculture can be found in farming memoirs and novels, although it is clearly an over-simplification to see anything written before 1939, or about the pre-war period, as disparaging, and everything post-1939 as celebratory. Primrose McConnell, introducing his *Diary of a Working Farmer* in 1906, captured some of the excitement and satisfaction he found in farming. Despite its alternations of 'hopes and fears, of sunshine and rain', it was 'a life which carries with it much of the joy of living, which gives great comfort to the one who lives it in many ways, though it never yields big dividends in cash'. Part of his excitement arose from the belief that farming had a 'great future' of technical progress, and some of his satisfaction from the pleasure he took in physical work on the farm. His diary entry for 31 March noted that he was 'full of spring work' so that he could not 'sit still to write any more'.[26]

The existence of a readership for McConnell's magazine *Farm Life* is evidence of the rising interest in rural literature in the late nineteenth and early twentieth centuries. Following industrialization, the factory, not the farm, became the 'defining metaphor for human toil', so as workers left agriculture a romanticized view of the rural appeared 'in the gap of expanding naiveté'.[27] It led to a great outpouring of rural writing between the wars – Cavaliero listed 217 novels, only a few of them published before 1918. Most of it was hardly georgic, and still less concerned with twentieth-century changes in agricultural technology.[28] Farms and farming, when they appeared, did so as settings for interpersonal or family conflicts, or struggles between rich and poor, weak and strong, the stuff of fiction in general. Sheila Kaye-Smith's *Joanna Godden* (1921), for example, set on Walland Marsh near Rye in Sussex, is essentially concerned with the romantic life of a farmer's daughter who sets out to run the farm after her father's death, despite family and neighbours insisting that it is no job for a woman. Where the farm enters the novel it is there as a metaphor for honesty and virtue; unchanging farming tradition is therefore what matters.[29] Similarly H. E. Bates's *The Fallow Land* (1932) is essentially an exploration of human strengths, embodied in the central character Deborah, and weaknesses, as demonstrated by her husband and son in the years before and after the First World War. The farm, and the technical details of farming, are used as signals of the human relationships. A failing farm represents a failing marriage. Unrealistic expectations foretell doom, as when Deborah's son promises to buy a tractor and 'plough the big field twice over before you milk one cow'. Inevitably the tractor requires spares, the last breeding sow is sold to pay for them, and within four pages the farm is bankrupt and the son's wife has left him.[30] Given the style and subject matter of many of the authors discussed by Cavaliero, especially Mary Webb, Constance Holme and T. F. Powys, it is not difficult to see why their detractors lumped them together as the 'loam and lovechild' school, or to identify the inspiration for the mocking comedy of *Cold Comfort Farm*.[31]

Leaving aside Vita Sackville-West's long poem *The Land* (discussed in Chapter 11), the two major figures of interwar georgic writing were Adrian Bell and A. G. Street. They both dealt with the impact of declining postwar cereal prices, which they portrayed as creating fundamental shifts in the rural economy and society. Adrian Bell, brought up in London, went as a farm pupil in 1920 to work on Farley Hall, a large Suffolk arable farm run by 'Mr Colville', the epitome of traditional arable farming expertise.[32] The first of what Ronald Blythe called his 'quietly novelized' memoir trilogy (*Corduroy*, *Silver Ley* and *The Cherry Tree*) is an account of Bell's apprenticeship under Mr Colville, and an engaging account of East Anglian arable farming as it had been practised since the late nineteenth century, with many features reminiscent of the farming methods later recorded from the memories of farm labourers by the pioneering oral historian George Ewart Evans.[33] At the end of his pupillage, Mr Colville helped Bell to buy a small farm near Farley Hall, and the remaining two books of the trilogy cover his experiences in farming it. He made the sensible decision, as cereal prices fell, to decrease the arable area, grow potatoes and sugar beet on what remained, and increase his livestock. Having been trained in Mr Colville's style of farming, he regretted the change: 'It had died away – the old bluff, hospitable life of the countryside – like a summer's day.'[34] Yet like his mentor Mr Colville, he stuck with established muscle-powered technology, arguing that 'nature imposes her limits … The tractor wheels skid helplessly upon the softened earth … Variability only can cope with variability. Agriculture needs legs and arms.'[35] It was a conflict he later returned to in a novel, *By-Road*, in which the leading character buys an unpromising heavy-land farm and produces milk and fruit using the most modern technology, motorized wherever possible. His revolutionary 'chromium and asbestos enterprise' is contrasted throughout the story with the 'progressive' mixed high farming exemplified by Mr Colville's style of agriculture.[36] The ability of large-scale horse-based Suffolk arable farming to survive the stresses imposed on it by low cereal prices was also demonstrated, from the labourer's perspective, in Hugh Barrett's account of his first year on a farm in 1933.[37]

A. G. Street was a Wiltshire farmer's son. He wrote his first book, *Farmer's Glory* (1932), at the age of forty, and its structure reflected the pattern of his life up to that point.[38] The first part is an affectionate portrait of the rural life and farming of his youth, with its annual cycle of ploughing, sowing, harvesting and threshing, lambing and calving, sheep sales and harvest suppers. The farmworkers of those pre-First World War years are his heroes, and he celebrates an era in which one did one's duty by the land, farmed according to local customs and took one's proper place in rural society. It was a time made even more attractive by its contrast with what came next: first a few years of immensely hard work in Canada, and then the struggle to avoid bankruptcy in the hard economic climate of the interwar years. In contrast to Bell, he embraced one of the more successful innovations of the time: the milking bail. This was a mobile milking parlour developed by the Hosier brothers. They too responded to low interwar cereal prices by converting cheaply available arable land to dairying. As well as farming, they actually made the bails, and sold them to other farmers, along with their other products such as hay sweeps. By 1939 they farmed about 5,000 acres, with twelve dairy herds and a large acreage of cereals, and after the war they wrote a book explaining how their ideas, practices and inventions had developed between 1910 and 1950.[39]

Keeping a dairy herd on his formerly arable land and selling milk door to door gradually brought Street's business back into profit, although he admitted that this third section of the book, entitled 'The Waning of the Glory', 'lacks charm as compared with the earlier pages. I am afraid that this is only too true ... I think that it was the placid unchanging well-being of years ago, which made rural life so charming.'[40] Becoming a successful and prolific author also increased his income. Much of his journalism was polemical, and he also wrote novels to argue a case. The *Gentleman of the Party* (1936) was written in praise of the loyal farmworker, and *Strawberry Roan* (1932) condemns the short-sighted post-First World War hedonism of which he was himself guilty. *Sweetacres* (1956) was largely a post-Second World War attack on the 'Russian methods' of the County Agricultural Executive Committees (earlier John Moore made the same case, with more wit and charm, in *The Blue Field*, 1948), although he also used it to argue the advantages of mechanization and pesticides.[41]

While Bell Street, and the Hosiers were coping with low cereal prices in the arable districts of the south and east, farmers were under less pressure in the livestock areas of the north and west, as Street found when touring England in autumn 1936. Devon and Somerset farmers had 'been able to withstand the recent depression in agriculture better than most parts of England'; those in north Lancashire were 'less afraid than most to meet their bank managers'; a Cheshire dairy farm could 'stand a depression better than most'; and Lake District sheep farms were 'thriving'.[42] The same more positive picture emerged from accounts of farming in the most difficult conditions. Thomas Firbanks's *I Bought a Mountain* (1940) tells the story of a couple in their twenties learning to run a hill farm in Snowdonia in the 1930s with the help of their workers and neighbours, who are portrayed with affection and respect. Although the environment ensured that they had to stick to the tradition of sheep and cattle rearing – pig and poultry enterprises failed – they were keen to adopt new technology when they could. They introduced the Burdizzo castrator, liver-fluke drenches, a second-hand Fordson tractor to pull the mower, hydroelectricity and breeding for hardiness in their ewe flock, and took great pride in the way they had improved their holding by building repairs, fencing, ditching and better grassland management.[43] Similarly, Frank Fraser Darling and his wife improved an island croft off the west coast of Scotland between 1938 and 1942 by the use of lime-rich coral sand and basic slag, controlling the rushes and mechanising with a two-wheel tractor.[44]

From the late 1930s onwards, the expectation of war, and especially its outbreak, raised both farm prices and the status of farmers. The tenant farmer Robert Homewood, who began farming in 1929, wrote about the difficulties he faced on his first two farms, but then in the mid-1930s moved to a Sussex dairy farm where life was made easier by the establishment of the Milk Marketing Board, the availability of fertilizer subsidies and his adoption of machine milking. To his great satisfaction, the coming of war required him to increase production, and in consequence he found farming 'a fine way of life; since our new growth in stature, completely satisfying'.[45]

Wartime and Post-War Georgic

The sense that agriculture, technically conservative or even backward, might *only* be important as a repository of worthwhile values and traditions, began to dissipate among writers of the 1940s. It was still there when C. Henry Warren opposed the 'sibilant scythe' with its 'silvery whisper' to the 'rackety-clack of the binder'.[46] Other writers perhaps felt that their readers might be interested in how the country could produce more food to cope with wartime scarcities. John Stewart Collis's *While Following the Plough* shows farming technology changing in the 1940s.[47] It is especially valuable because it was written by a man who, when he began, knew nothing about farming. Experts often forget, or find it difficult to believe, that the reader may be ignorant of what they consider to be basic information. Collis could write clearly, for that was his trade.[48] In 1940, and at the age of 40, rather than taking up a home administrative post in the Army, he decided to go to work on a farm. He had never previously worked in agriculture, and arrived on a farm at Stonegate in Sussex in April 1940 feeling 'like a new boy at school'. He admits that his approach to writing about farming 'is one of genuine ignorance, and I have described many operations and implements as if the reader was as fresh to them as I was'. In these descriptions, especially of operations no longer carried out or implements no longer used, lies some of the value of his book. He explains how much skill was required to successfully accomplish apparently simple jobs such as broadcasting seed or fertilizer, or ploughing a straight furrow with a horse plough ('I immediately felt in need of four hands'), or how much back strain resulted from hand-planting potatoes, so that 'I would cast a favourable eye on any man who appeared with a potato planter'.[49]

In March 1942 Collis moved to a large dairy and arable farm at Tarrant Hinton in Dorset, where a potato planter was indeed used, and he explains how much easier and more rapid it made the job. On this farm, under the pressures of wartime labour shortages, and with the advantage of higher prices, new technology was replacing the old. Cereals were sown by a combined (seed and fertilizer) tractor-drawn drill, cows were machine-milked, hay was collected by hay-sweeps attached to cars, and on one occasion a field of barley was harvested by a hired combine-harvester instead of the more usual binder.[50] On this, and also in relation to milking, he meditates upon mechanization, and wonders what is done with the time saved, concluding that it is more to the advantage of the employer than the worker. Not that he is at all sentimental about rural labour. He notes the 'tendency of writers on country themes to assume that the countryman alone is splendid, the townsman a poor specimen. This view can be overdone ... It is superficial to suppose that the man who has dealings with animals, with sheep or cows or horses, is thereby more human or humanized than the man dealing solely with machines.'[51]

The humanization or otherwise of such men was an important issue for members of the Kinship in Husbandry, a group of prominent writers, landowners and farmers led by the ecological campaigner and forester Rolf Gardiner and the writer H. J. Massingham. Some of them felt that the tractor was 'alien to the land' while others saw it as a solution to agriculture's 'antiquated and inefficient methods'.[52] Henry Williamson, then farming in north Norfolk, was one of the latter, praising 'Mr Ferguson's magnificent tractor', a Model A Ferguson, to judge from his description: 'half the weight of an ordinary tractor, built of aluminium and of immensely strong steel, and it carried its twin-furrow plow under its tail, on three steel arms'. Its performance immediately impressed his initially sceptical farmworkers, and he writes enthusiastically about the pleasures of ploughing and drilling corn with it, and explains how he had horse-drawn implements converted to a tractor hitch by the local blacksmith.[53] Thanks to their association with both pioneer advocates of organic farming and far-right political organizations, the Kinship in Husbandry has perhaps received more attention from historians than its contemporary significance merited.[54] They were ignored in the numerous editions of *The Farming Ladder*, George Henderson's account of the success that he and his brother had in making a living from 85 acres of poor land on the edge of the Cotswolds, near Enstone in Oxfordshire. The Hendersons might have appeared to be adherents of the organic movement, as they were 'great believers in natural manure and humus' and preferred cultivations to herbicides for controlling weeds. Yet they could 'not condemn artificial manures', which did 'no harm if used in conjunction with farmyard manure and ploughed-in green crops', and they were enthusiasts for all sorts of new technologies that were only beginning to enter farming during their first twenty years. They bought their first tractor, second-hand, for £30, in 1925, 'which put us right on top of our work', and enthused over electric fences, silage, tripods for haymaking, new grass and fodder beet varieties, and lucerne.[55] In his second book, a kind of textbook for his farm pupils, Henderson asserted that 'the greatest contribution in recent years has been the full mechanization and installation of electricity. On this small farm of 85 acres ... there are no less than thirty-four electric motors, every one doing some essential job, saving time and manual labour'.[56]

Ruth Janette Ruck was one of Henderson's farm pupils. Like him she came from an urban background. At the end of the war she and her parents bought a small hill farm in North Wales, and her books give a vivid and moving account of the way in which hill farming responded to the postwar combination of agricultural optimism and supportive agricultural policy. Hers 'was only one farm of many which benefitted from the Hill Farming Act', which supported building and road improvements, fencing, liming of acid pastures and bracken cutting, and in her case allowed additional enterprises in the form of poultry and seed potato production.[57]

Unlike her, but as with the Hendersons, many of the other writers who published after 1945 began their farming careers in the interwar years. Like Henderson, they captured the excitement and optimism of farming in a period in which agricultural policy was encouraging increased output. The zest which was missing between the wars, according to A. G. Street, began to return during the war and continued afterwards. Much of John Laity's *Profitable Ley Farming* (1948) was about the management of his Cornish farm from 1920, when he took over from his father, but the emphasis was not on survival in difficult times but on the way he managed his land to build fertility and maximize production. That was what other farmers would need to do in future, he argued.[58] John Cherrington, too, echoed Street's opinion: 'The war did not of itself mend the fortunes of British farming', he wrote, 'but it did restore its confidence.' He was farming 2,000 acres by the mid-1950s and admitted that one of the problems of operating on such a large scale was 'finding something for the boss to do', because his management style simply involved finding the right employees and leaving them to get on with the job. He solved his own employment problem by taking up journalism and broadcasting, which gave him an extensive overview of farming in Britain and Europe, but apart from pointing out that cereal yields at least doubled between the 1930s and the 1970s, his engaging memoirs have more to say about technical changes before the war (he was one of those who adopted Hosier's milking bail on downland), when he was more personally involved day to day.[59]

Farmers who operated on the scale of John Cherrington were often prominent, and featured in the farming press, but they did not represent the majority. As the number of permanently employed workers fell much more rapidly than the number of farmers, family farming businesses, run by a man and wife, their children, and sometimes one or two employees, were much more common than Hosier-sized enterprises in the fifty years after the war. As Michael Winter has observed, this was the period in which family farming emerged simultaneously as 'a cultural ideal, a political project, and a socio-economic reality'.[60] This is not to imply that family farmers were necessarily less technically progressive. Advisory officers and the farming press ensured that they were aware of technical developments, and agricultural policy up to 1985 promoted output increases. Tony Harman, who began farming in Buckinghamshire between the wars on about 150 acres, had expanded to about 800 acres by 1980, but still only employed three men. He attributed the 'huge surge' in agricultural output between the 1940s and the 1980s to the 1947 Agriculture Act. Whereas some farmers, conditioned by years of low prices and lack of investment between the wars, had to be coerced into adopting new methods in the 1940s and early 1950s, 'by the early sixties we had quite a different attitude … Instead of nurturing strictly limited ambitions about what we could achieve, almost anything seemed possible.' Whereas the first two-thirds of his book chart the various ways in which he survived in farming before the war, the last part celebrates the impact of new technologies: drainage, mechanization, ley farming, pesticides, fertilizers, new breeds of livestock – he was instrumental in the importation of Charolais beef sires – and specialization in 'the things that we perhaps do best: beef cattle, wheat and barley'. He celebrated the result: 'When my father bought Grove Farm in 1919, 18 cwt to the acre was a good yield of wheat in this area. Just before the Second World War we got it up to 35 cwt, nearly double. Now we're disappointed if we don't get 70 cwt to the acre. So yield has quadrupled in my lifetime.'[61]

Similarly Arthur Court, a dairy farmer on the Somerset-Wiltshire border, devoted a chapter of his memoirs to recording the 'tremendous advances' that had transformed farming in his seventy-year career: mechanization, pesticides, silage, mechanized materials handling, effective veterinary medicines, and new breeds of beef and dairy cattle.[62] A different impression emerges from Ronald Blythe's *Akenfield* (1969). Based on his knowledge of the people living in the area north of Ipswich in Suffolk, Akenfield was a composite of several villages, and Blythe's purpose was to present a portrait of rural life in his time as a whole. His real interest was in the working of a rural society, although of course farming was a part of that. His farmers and farmworkers emphasized the struggle involved in farming more than the satisfaction, and although they recognized the extent of post-war technical change, they were not excited by it in the same way that Tony Harman or Arthur Court were.[63]

In fiction, the georgic theme has been much less prominent since the Second World War than it was in the interwar years. In recent years novelists have been more interested in the helplessness of farmers in the face of impersonal (but personalized) social and economic forces. Jane Beeson's *Scarhill* (1995) and Sam North's *The Lie of the Land* (1998), both set on Dartmoor farms, are more about property, planning permission, and tensions between incomers and existing residents than about farming.[64] Christopher Hart's *The Harvest* is an anti-pastoral, exploring the problems of a rural underclass, with virtually no farming involved at all, and another anti-pastoral, Magnus Mills's black comedy *The Restraint of Beasts* (1998) uses fencing contractors as symbols of the disappearance of the supportive rural community.[65] Several of Penelope Lively's novels are set in rural communities, and in the course of exploring the lives of her characters makes some perceptive points about late twentieth-century rural life, but changes in farming technology are hardly central concerns.[66] Tim Pears's more recent West Country trilogy and Melissa Harrison's *All Among the Barley* (2018) are all set in earlier periods, either before the Second or the First World Wars.[67] The Welsh border novels of Bruce Chatwin and Tom Bullough certainly use farmwork as a source of incident and technical change as a marker of time, but their main focus always is on the influence of places, especially remote places, on people.[68]

By the beginning of the present century, advanced-technology commercial agriculture was on the defensive. In part this can perhaps be traced to the gradual disappearance of small family farms in the face of hard commercial reality, a process covered in Richard Benson's memoir, *The Farm* (2005).[69] It must also have something to do with critiques of the impact of farming on animal welfare and the environment. In 1963, Rachel Carson published *Silent Spring*, condemning the effect of pesticides in US agriculture, and in 1964 Ruth Harrison wrote *Animal Machines*.[70] It is often remembered as an attack on the animal welfare implications of intensive livestock, but it is worth remembering that she was also concerned with its landscape impact, contrasting the 'visual pleasure' produced by the traditional farm with the way in which new farm buildings 'jar on the eye and rob the countryside of much of its charm'. Against this background, it is hardly surprising that James Rebanks, one of the most popular farmer-writers of recent years, celebrated the traditional aspects of Lake District sheep farming more than its adoption of new technologies.[71] Indeed, it is tempting to see much modern rural writing as anti-georgic, either arguing for a return to older technologies or for the cessation of farming in favour of rewilding.[72] At the same time, there remains a flourishing niche market in periodicals catering for people interested in maintaining or restoring vintage farm machinery, and Old Pond Publishing produces books aimed at 'enthusiasts for the land-based industries' with titles such as *Seventy Years of Farm Tractors, 1930–2000*, or *Oily Hands and the Smell of Diesel*.[73]

Conclusions

This chapter cannot claim to be a comprehensive survey and analysis of all the twentieth-century literature that might possibly be classified as georgic. Such an enterprise would require much more space than is available here, and in any case the emphasis here has been on the response to technical change rather than on any of the other possible concerns of georgic literature, such as the relationship of farmers and their families with employees, or the impact of government agricultural policy on farming. Some writers, especially from the Second World War and immediate post-war period, have been neglected entirely.[74]

These caveats notwithstanding, it does seem safe to conclude that there was a difference between pre- and post-Second World War georgic writing. From the beginning of the century rural writing in its widest sense was flourishing, even if it might be dismissed by some historians as 'a kind of escapist cult'.[75] Within the wider category georgic was a significant strand in the pre-war period. It is undeniable that some of its more prominent figures fed the escapist market through the attractiveness of their portraits of traditional farming methods and people, even if, for some of them, the purpose was to argue a case for greater respect for farming and farmers. Respect from the wider population, and increased self-respect within agriculture emerged from the wartime and immediate post-war expansion of farm output, as Clare Griffiths has argued, and was reflected in the content of georgic writing and the extent to which both memoirs and textbooks were published.[76] What this represented, however, was, as Cavaliero argued, 'a general movement away from imaginative abstraction towards documentation, as can be seen from the virtual demise of any significant rural fiction after the end of the Second World War'.[77] Serious fiction had to wait until the twenty-first century and by then, stimulated by increasing environmental awareness, was more anti-georgic, as was much non-fiction writing. Yet if there were no serious novelists, and not many memoirists, to commemorate the dramatic technical changes that transformed agriculture in the second half of the twentieth century, the flourishing niche market for vintage machinery magazines, books and videos suggests that those involved at the time are proud to remember their achievements.

Notes

1 T. Hardy, 'In Time of "The Breaking of Nations"', in *The New Oxford Book of English Verse*, ed. H. Gardner (Oxford University Press, 1972), p. 771; R. S. Thomas, *An Acre of Land* (Newtown: Montgomeryshire Printing Co., 1952).
2 *AHEW*, vol. VIII, p. 331.
3 The significance of different power sources is explored in J. Auderset and P. Moser, 'Mechanisation and Motorisation: Natural Resources, Knowledge, Politics and Technology in 19th- and 20th-century Agriculture', in *Agriculture in Capitalist Europe, 1945–1960: From Food Shortages to Food Surpluse*, ed. C. Martiin, J. Pan-Montojo and P. Brassley (London: Routledge, 2016), pp. 145–64.
4 P. Brassley, 'Electrifying Farms in England', in *Transforming the Countryside: The Electrification of Rural Britain*, ed. P. Brassley, J. Burchardt and K. Sayer (London: Routledge, 2017), pp. 83–114, at p. 92.
5 A. G. Street, *Farmer's Glory* (London: Penguin, 1951), pp. 210, 222, 224.
6 P. Brassley, 'Output and Technical Change in Twentieth-Century British Agriculture', *Agricultural History Review*, 48 (2000) 60–84; P. Brassley, 'Britain, 1750–2000', in *Rural Economy and Society in North-Western Europe, 500–2000. Struggling with the Environment: Land Use and Productivity*, ed. E. Thoen and T. Soens (Turnhout: Brepols, 2015), pp. 109–46.
7 Addison is quoted in W. J. Keith, *The Rural Tradition: William Cobbett, Gilbert White and Other Non-Fiction Prose Writers of the English Countryside* (Hassocks: Harvester, 1975), p. 5; See also John Barrell and John Bull, eds., *The Penguin Book of English Pastoral Verse* (Harmondsworth: Penguin, 1982), p. 10.
8 G. E. Fussell, *The Classical Tradition in West European Farming* (Newton Abbot: David and Charles, 1972); G. E. Fussell, *The Old English Farming Books* (London: Crosby Lockwood, 1947) pp. 129–38; G. E. Fussell, *More Old English Farming Books* (London: Crosby Lockwood, 1950) pp. 171–82. Fussell went on to publish three more volumes on the subject with the Pindar Press (*The Old English Farming Books*, 5 vols., 1991) taking his account up to 1900.

9. N. Goddard, 'Agricultural Institutions: Societies, Associations and the Press', in *AHEW*, vol. VII.i, p. 683.
10. G. E. Jones, 'William Fream (1854–1906): A Biographical Essay', in *Fream's Agriculture*, ed. C. Spedding (16th ed., London: John Murray, 1983) pp. xvii–xix.
11. Goddard, 'Agricultural Institutions', p. 683.
12. J. A. S. Watson and J. A. More, *Agriculture: The Science and Practice of Farming* (1924; Edinburgh: Oliver and Boyd, 1962).
13. P. Brassley, 'Primrose McConnell: A brief biographical sketch', in *The Agricultural Notebook*, ed. R. J. Soffe, 20th ed. (Oxford: Blackwell Science, 2003) pp. xi–xii. The 21st edition was published in 2021.
14. Other texts range from the very small, such as P. Brassley and R. Soffe, *Agriculture: A Very Short Introduction* (Oxford University Press, 2016) to the more internationally focused C. Martiin, *The World of Agricultural Economics: An Introduction* (London: Routledge, 2013).
15. E. J. Russell, *Soil Conditions and Plant Growth* (London: Longmans, Green, 1912; 11th ed., Harlow: Longman, 1988); J. Percival, *Agricultural Botany* (London: Duckworth, 1900; 8th ed., 1936); N. T. Gill and K. C. Vear, *Agricultural Botany* (Duckworth, 1958; 3rd ed., 1980); C. Culpin, *Farm Machinery* (London: Lockwood, 1938; 12th ed., Oxford: Blackwell, 1992); E. T. Halnan and F. H. Garner, *The Principles and Practice of Feeding Farm Animals* (London: Longmans Green, 1940; 5th ed., London: Estates Gazette, 1966); P. Mcdonald, R. A. Edwards and J. F. D. Greenhalgh, *Animal Nutrition* (Edinburgh: Oliver and Boyd, 1966; 7th ed., Harlow: Pearson, 2011).
16. A. D. Hall, *The Book of the Rothamsted Experiments* (London: John Murray, 1905).
17. K. Dexter and D. Barber, *Farming for Profits* (Harmondsworth: Penguin, 1961; 2nd ed., London: Iliffe, 1967).
18. H. Rider Haggard, *Rural England: Being an Account of Agricultural and Social Researches Carried Out in the Years 1901 and 1902*, 2 vols. (London: Longman, 1906), vol. I, pp. xxxiv, xxxvi, 58; A. D. Hall, *A Pilgrimage of British Farming* (London: John Murray, 1913), pp. vii, 431, 439.
19. M. Hessell Tiltman, *English Earth* (London: Harrap, 1935); *Agriculture in the Twentieth Century: Essays on Research, Practice, and Organization to be presented to Sir Daniel Hall* (Oxford: Clarendon Press, 1939); J. P. Maxton, ed., *Regional Types of British Agriculture* (London: Allen and Unwin, 1936).
20. A. G. Street, *Farming England* (London: Batsford, 1937), p. 10.
21. W. A Astor and B. S. Rowntree, *British Agriculture: the Principles of Future Policy* (Harmondsworth: Penguin, 1939), p. 39. This was preceded by two similar enquiries: W. A. Astor and K. A. H. Murray, *The Planning of Agriculture* (Oxford University Press, 1933), and W. Astor and B. S. Rowntree, *The Agricultural Dilemma: A Report of an Enquiry* (London: King, 1935).
22. H. Barrett, *Early to Rise: A Suffolk Morning* (London: Faber & Faber, 1967), p. 103.

23 J. G. S. and Frances Donaldson, in association with Derek Barber, *Farming in Britain Today* (Harmondsworth: Penguin, 1969), pp. xiii–xv. Frances Donaldson had farmed during and after the war, and produced three previous accounts of her experiences. See M. Winter, 'Farming Tales: Narratives of Farming and Food Security in Mid-Twentieth-Century Britain', in *A Cultural History of Famine: Food Security and the Environment in India and Britain*, ed. A. Mukherjee (London: Routledge, 2019), pp. 151–66, at pp. 163–4.
24 T. Beresford, *We Plough the Fields: British Farming Today* (Harmondsworth: Penguin, 1975), p. 7.
25 A. G. Street, *Farmer's Glory* (London: Faber, 1932), pp. 225–6.
26 P. McConnell, *The Diary of a Working Farmer: Being the True History of a Year's Farming in Essex* (London: Cable, 1906), pp. xv–xvi, 144. The *Diary* was formed of the collected weekly entries published in the magazine *Farm Life*, which McConnell edited and published from 1905. See P. Brassley, '"A Pioneer in Everything": Primrose McConnell, 1856–1931', *Journal of the Royal Agricultural Society of England*, 156 (1995), 172–8. I am most grateful to Richard Soffe for the loan of his copy of the *Diary*.
27 A. Carey, 'This Land', in *Creating the Countryside: The Rural Idyll Past and Present*, ed. V. Elson and R. Shirley (London: Paul Holberton, 2017), pp. 79–87, at p. 79.
28 G. Cavaliero, *The Rural Tradition in the English Novel 1900–1939* (London: Macmillan, 1977), pp. 227–31. See also D. Head, *Modernity and the English Rural Novel* (Cambridge University Press, 2017).
29 S. Kaye-Smith, *Joanna Godden* (London: Cassell, 1921).
30 H. E. Bates, *The Fallow Land* (London: Cape, 1932), pp. 206, 223, 227.
31 S. Gibbons, *Cold Comfort Farm* (London: Longman, 1932).
32 A. Bell, *Corduroy* (1930), *Silver Ley* (1931) and *The Cherry Tree* (1932) were all initially published by Cobden-Sanderson. R. Blythe, 'Introduction', in A. Bell, *Men and the Fields* (Wimborne Minster: Little Toller Books, 2009), p. 8.
33 G. E. Evans, *Ask the Fellows Who Cut the Hay* (London: Faber, 1956); G. E. Evans, *The Horse in the Furrow* (London: Faber, 1960).
34 Bell, *Cherry Tree*, p. 27.
35 Bell, *Corduroy*, p. 120.
36 A. Bell, *By-Road* (London: Bodley Head, 1937), pp. 105, 266.
37 Barrett, *Early to Rise*.
38 Street, *Farmer's Glory*.
39 A. J. Hosier and F. H. Hosier, *Hosier's Farming System* (London: Crosby Lockwood, 1951), p. 43.
40 Street, *Farmer's Glory*, p. 218.
41 A. G. Street, *Strawberry Roan* (London: Faber, 1932); A. G. Street, *The Gentleman of the Party* (London: Faber, 1936); A. G. Street, *Sweetacres* (London: Michael Joseph, 1956), pp. 111, 216. Some of Street's journalism was collected in *Hedge Trimmings* (London: Faber, 1933); J. Moore, *The Blue Field* (London: Collins, 1948).
42 Street, *Farming England*, pp. 26, 71, 95, 99.

43 T. Firbank, *I Bought a Mountain* (London: Harrap, 1940), pp. 78–9, 146–9, 240, 249–50.
44 F. F. Darling, *Island Farm* (London: Bell, 1943). Fraser Darling was later commissioned to write a series of advisory articles, based on his own experience, which were published as *Crofting Agriculture: Its Practice in the West Highlands and Islands* (London: Oliver and Boyd, 1945).
45 R. A. Homewood, *Three Farms* (London: Latimer House, 1947), pp. 127, 139, 146, 186–8.
46 C. H. Warren, *England is a Village* (London: Eyre and Spottiswoode, 1940), p. 126.
47 J. S. Collis, *While Following the Plough* (London: Cape, 1946). Collis later wrote *Down to Earth* (London: Cape, 1947) and the two books were combined and published as *The Worm Forgives the Plough* (London: Charles Knight, 1973, reprinted by Penguin, 1975). Subsequent references are to the Penguin edition.
48 M. Drabble, 'Collis, John Stewart', in *The Oxford Companion to English Literature*, ed. M. Drabble (Oxford University Press, 1985), p. 215.
49 Collis, *Worm*, pp. 11, 15, 17, 19.
50 Collis, *Worm*, pp. 67, 79, 86, 99, 128, 192.
51 Collis, *Worm*, pp. 69, 193–6.
52 J. E. Hosking, 'Mechanization and the Land' in *The Natural Order: Essays in the Return to Husbandry*, ed. H. J. Massingham (London: Dent, 1945), pp. 100–10; J. Wentworth Day, *The New Yeomen of England* (London: Harrap, 1952), pp. 22–3, 185.
53 H. Williamson, *The Story of a Norfolk Farm* (London: Faber, 1941), pp. 198, 213, 256, 401, discussed at greater length in Head, *Modernity and the English Rural Novel*, pp. 86–90. The ease of driving a Ferguson is emphasised in R. A. E. Linney, *Peter and Pauline at Hollyhock Farm* (Coventry: Harry Ferguson Ltd, 1951), reprinted by Old Pond Publishing, 2008.
54 Among the large literature on these topics, see R. J. Moore-Colyer, 'Back to Basics: Rolf Gardiner, H. J. Massingham and "A Kinship in Husbandry"', *Rural History*, 12 (2001), 85–108; R. Moore-Colyer and Philip Conford, 'A "Secret Society"? The Internal and External Relations of the Kinship in Husbandry, 1941–52', *Rural History*, 15 (2004), 189–206.
55 G. Henderson, *The Farming Ladder* (1944; London: Faber, 1956), pp. 9, 15, 48, 115, 124, 187, 235–6.
56 G. Henderson, *Farmer's Progress* (London: Faber, 1950), p. 95.
57 R. J. Ruck, *Place of Stones* (London: Faber, 1961), p. 80. Her other books were *Hill Farm Story* (London: Faber, 1966) and *Along Came a Llama* (London: Faber, 1978).
58 J. Laity, *Profitable Ley Farming* (London: Crosby Lockwood, 1948), p. 21.
59 J. Cherrington, *On the Smell of an Oily Rag* (1933; London: Northwood Publications, 1979), pp. 88–9, 142.
60 Winter, 'Farming Tales', p. 155.
61 T. Harman, *Seventy Summers: The Story of a Farm* (London: BBC, 1986), pp. 8, 207–12, 16, 226–32.

62 A. Court, *Seedtime to Harvest: A Farmer's Life* (Bradford on Avon: Ex Libris Press, 1987), pp. 108–13.
63 R. Blythe, *Akenfield: Portrait of an English Village* (Harmondsworth: Penguin, 1969).
64 J. Beeson, *Scarhill* (London: Mandarin, 1995); S. North, *The Lie of the Land* (London: Secker and Warburg, 1998).
65 C. Hart, *The Harvest* (London: Faber, 1999); M. Mills, *The Restraint of Beasts* (London: Flamingo, 1998).
66 P. Lively, *Next to Nature, Art* (London: Heinemann, 1982); P. Lively, *Passing On* (London: Andre Deutsch, 1989); P. Lively, *Heat Wave* (London: Viking, 1996); P. Lively, *Spiderweb* (London: Viking, 1998). I once suggested to her, at a literary festival, that these novels might be seen as a 'condition of rural England' series. She disagreed.
67 T. Pears, *The Horseman* (2017), *The Wanderers* (2018) and *The Redeemed* (2019), all published in London by Bloomsbury. M. Harrison, *All Among the Barley* (London: Bloomsbury, 2018).
68 B. Chatwin, *On the Black Hill* (London: Cape, 1982); T. Bullough, *The Claude Glass* (London: Sort of Books, 2007); T. Bullough, *Addlands* (London: Granta, 2016).
69 R. Benson, *The Farm: The Story of One Family and the English Countryside* (London: Hamish Hamilton, 2005).
70 R. Carson, *Silent Spring* (London: Hamish Hamilton, 1963); R. Harrison, *Animal Machines: The New Factory Farming Industry* (London: Vincent Stuart, 1964), figures 2 and 3.
71 J. Rebanks, *The Shepherd's Life: A Tale of the Lake District* (London: Allen Lane, 2015); J. Rebanks, *English Pastoral: An Inheritance* (London: Allen Lane, 2020).
72 J. Lewis-Stempel, *The Running Hare: The Secret Life of Farmland* (London: Doubleday, 2016); I. Tree, *Wilding: The Return of Nature to a British Farm* (London: Picador, 2018).
73 B. Bell, *Seventy Years of Farm Tractors, 1930–2000* (Chichester: Old Pond Publishing, 2020); D. Harris, *Oily Hands and the Smell of Diesel* (Chichester: Old Pond Publishing, 2017). Examples of periodicals are found at www.kelsey.co.uk/brand/commercial-vehicles/tractor-world/ and www.classictractormagazine.co.uk/this-month/ (both accessed 10 January 2021). (In the interests of full disclosure the author confesses to owning a half share of a 1953 Ferguson TE20 tractor.)
74 See Winter, 'Farming Tales', p. 152.
75 G. E. Mingay, quoted by M. Shaw, 'Cold Comfort Times: Women Rural Writers in the Interwar Period', in *The English Countryside Between the Wars: Regeneration or Decline?*, ed. P. Brassley, J. Burchardt and L. Thomson (Woodbridge: Boydell Press, 2006), pp. 73–86, at p. 74.
76 C. Griffiths, 'Heroes of the Reconstruction? Images of British Farmers in War and Peace', in, *War, Agriculture, and Food: Rural Europe from the 1930s to the 1950s*, ed. P. Brassley, Y. Segers and L. Van Molle (London: Routledge, 2012), pp. 209–28.
77 Cavaliero, *The Rural Tradition*, p. x.

PART II
Times

CHAPTER 5

Jacobean Georgic

Andrew McRae

In 1618, George Chapman published the first English translation from the Greek of Hesiod's *Works and Days*. Signalling the much greater contemporary awareness of Virgil's Latin work, Chapman titled the book *The Georgicks of Hesiod*, containing 'Doctrine of Husbandrie, Moralitie, and Pietie'. As well as establishing a minor landmark in the assimilation of Greek literature into English culture, Chapman's volume also framed a loose but noteworthy intellectual community. He dedicated the book to Francis Bacon, citing the dedicatee's own writings and asserting that there are few men 'that live now' who so combine '*Honour* and *Learning*'. It was prefaced with commendatory poems by two of the most prominent poets of the Jacobean era: Ben Jonson and Michael Drayton. While Bacon's works would revolutionize scientific understandings of the natural world, Jonson and Drayton are key figures within any literary history of rural England. Jonson returned repeatedly to the land, confronting issues of social and economic change in a number of poems, plays and masques. Drayton was working across the first two decades of the seventeenth century on one of the most audacious exercises of national description ever attempted: the epic poem *Poly-Olbion*, published in two parts, in 1612 and 1622.

All four of the authors who contributed to this book – Hesiod, Chapman, Jonson, Drayton – focus attention on labour. Jonson admires the 'free labours' and 'travell' (i.e., travail) undertaken by Chapman (sig. A4r). Drayton celebrates the 'returnes' of the translator's endeavours, such that 'now of all men, it is called thy Trade' (sig. A4v). In the poem itself, Hesiod confronts more forthrightly the labours of agriculture, and the desire of a farmer for financial gain. In a pivotal passage late in the first book, the poem upbraids 'The slothfull man', while affirming that 'With Labour Men become | Herd-full and rich'. Indeed through labour, '*Glorie* and *vertue* into consort fall | With *wealth*'. Significantly, Chapman pauses on this passage in a marginal note, commenting that Hesiod has adopted this line of argument 'to perswade his unwise brother to follow his busines', although Hesiod himself 'prefers labor alone, joind with love of vertue and Justice, and the good expense of a mans time; before wealth, and honour with *Covetousnes* and *Contention*' (p. 15). The note of unease about the legitimate ends of labour is telling, for this was a period in which the values of work in rural England were matters of intense contestation. Did one work on account of a commitment to virtue and community, or fuelled by competition and self-interest? Should one aim to uphold customary practices in the fields, or seek ways to innovate and as a result transform the agrarian landscape?

This chapter considers the status and shape of georgic in this period and in the context of these questions. While Alastair Fowler has argued that the publication of Chapman's Hesiod was a 'turning point' for English georgic, I would suggest that at the time it was more important for the way in which it clarified the issues at stake.[1] The debates about the values of rural labour that Chapman acknowledges generated a vocabulary that echoed throughout writing about the land. By the time that formal georgic enjoyed its greatest moment of prominence, from the late seventeenth century into the eighteenth century, these debates had largely been settled in the interests of agrarian capitalism. Some of the greatest changes to rural land use in the nation's history were by then underway, in parallel with a reconceptualization of the bonds between landowners, agricultural workers and the land itself. Yet at the time that Hesiod, Chapman, Bacon, Drayton and Jonson were yoked together within a volume titled *Georgicks*, these outcomes were by no means certain. The period that I want to consider here – roughly, the reign in England of James I (1603–25) – was shaped by fundamental debates about the values of the land, and the lives of those who owned and worked it. Poets had to consider quite how the resources of georgic related to these upheavals.

The chapter begins with a review of existing criticism on georgic in this period, in order to demonstrate the breadth of existing views. The subsequent section considers contemporary debates concerning economic and environmental change, the values of rural labour, and the status of the English nation. The final section considers Jacobean works by Jonson and Drayton. These poets appreciated the arguments in favour of rural change, but achieved in their respective works rather different, distinctive accommodations with georgic.

Making Sense of Renaissance Georgic

According to narratives of literary history that held sway until the latter decades of the twentieth century, georgic largely bypassed the English Renaissance.[2] Granted, people were familiar with Virgil's *Georgics*, a text that was consistently printed, translated and read; one Elizabethan gentleman in fact declared himself so impressed that 'I could find it in my hart to drive the plough.'[3] Yet while Virgil's *Eclogues* provided the inspiration for countless works of Renaissance pastoral, poets made few overt efforts to import classical models of georgic into a native context. While the study of georgic in this period remains as a result a decidedly minority interest, it has benefited considerably from efforts to reconceive the literary canon, and think more creatively about genre. Scholars have posed the question: in an era in which nobody self-declared as a georgic poet, and there were no agreed definitions of what constitutes georgic, what cultural work might georgic nonetheless have been doing? Their approaches have prompted readers to look beyond poems that overtly proclaim their alignment with georgic, as would become the fashion during several decades subsequent to the 1697 publication of Dryden's translation of Virgil. That period reshaped conceptions of English georgic, yet was in truth a relatively brief moment in English literary history. Georgic has always had other ways of making its presence felt.

Two critics, in particular, established the foundations for fresh understandings of georgic in this period. Fowler proposed that 'we think in terms of Renaissance generic conceptions', attending to the ways in which writers of the time addressed topics of rural work rather than anachronistically imposing models from a later era.[4] Meanwhile, Anthony Low approached georgic less as a formal genre and more as a mode: 'It is an informing spirit, an attitude towards life, and a set of themes and images rather than anything so definite, say, as a four-book, didactic poem of two thousand lines on the subject of agriculture.'[5] Georgic influences might thus be evident in the ethical stance of a text: as Low puts it, in a characteristic stress on 'the value of intensive and persistent labour against hardships and difficulties'.[6] They might equally be apparent in a text's purpose, assumed audience, or social politics. These various approaches to georgic on the one hand have facilitated a reassessment of canonical texts. Low's monograph is book-ended by Edmund Spenser and John Milton; others, demonstrating the inexorable centripetal logic of Renaissance studies, have gravitated towards Shakespeare.[7] On the other hand, critical attention has been drawn beyond the usual canonical suspects, to a wide range of descriptive and didactic poems (and prose) 'containing precepts, instruction in an art, or meditation on the good life'.[8]

Since the work of Low and Fowler, scholars have looked afresh at writing on husbandry from the Elizabethan and Jacobean periods. In his essay published with Dryden's translation of Virgil, Joseph Addison set the tone for centuries of criticism by acknowledging the tension within georgic between its didactic and aesthetic imperatives, but settling on the primacy of the latter. He declared: '*A Georgic therefore is some part of the Science of Husbandry put into a pleasing Dress, and set off with the Beauties and Embellishments of Poetry.*'[9] Yet for readers who have refocused their gaze onto content – writing about the 'Science of Husbandry' – the century that precedes Addison has presented itself as especially rich. Even Low, in a book that is otherwise predominantly canonical in its interests, considers the 'new science' writings, specifically the works of Bacon and his followers, to be georgic in character. Similarly, the prose husbandry manuals that proliferated in this era were often positioned as literary works, and reward attention in this frame; for example, Conrad Heresbach's *Foure Bookes of Husbandry*, translated for an Elizabethan audience by Barnabe Googe, included a prefatory list of authorities that had informed the text, including classical authors such as Virgil, Xenophon and Ovid.[10] Wendy Wall has demonstrated how Gervase Markham, one of the most energetic authors of the early seventeenth century, gave shape in a series of overlapping prose publications on aspects of agriculture and rural life in England to a 'low' form of georgic.[11]

Other writers were pursuing similar ends in poetry, and have as a result posed challenges to histories of georgic built on Addisonian foundations. Thomas Tusser, author of the book that was initially published as *A Hundreth Good Pointes of Husbandrie*, but expanded over the course of its twenty-three editions between 1557 and 1638 to become *Five Hundred Points of Good Husbandry*, presents a test-case for the study of georgic.[12] For Low, Tusser's work should be left at the margins of literary history; it is a mere 'mixture of didacticism, forehead-knuckling, and greed'.[13] Yet when Francis Meres surveyed his nation's literary scene in 1598, he formed a more generous opinion: 'As *Hesiod* writ learnedly of husbandry in Greeke: so hath *Tusser* very wittily and experimentally written of it in English.'[14] Interestingly, Meres looks to Hesiod rather than Virgil for a point of comparison, then stresses two qualities: Tusser's 'wit', in accord with the literary values of the time; and his writing from direct experience (the meaning at this time of 'experimentally').[15] Indeed, later editions of the book contain a long autobiographical poem, recounting Tusser's struggles as a farmer in East Anglia. The core of the work is a calendar of farming life, to which was added in later editions a section on the housewife (organized around the cycle of a day), and a range of miscellaneous reflections on husbandry. Although there has never been any consensus on the question of who was buying Tusser's book, nor the extent to which they were reading it either as entertainment or didacticism, it became (by the assessment of one historian) one of the fifteen biggest selling books of the reign of Elizabeth I.[16]

By acknowledging the claims of writers such as Tusser and Markham to a place within a tradition of georgic writing, scholars have been able to ask fresh questions about the cultural functions of the mode. Crucially, if georgic is characterized by its endorsement of labour, what is the purpose of that labour? Tusser's overt self-interest may appear out of line with the dogged labour of a ploughman within the constraints of his estate, as celebrated by moral and religious writers from the Middle Ages through to the Tudor period.[17] It also stands askew from the heroic labour of Spenser's Red Cross Knight in *The Faerie Queene*: a character who bears the name 'Georgos' on account of his upbringing, as a foundling, by a ploughman.[18] Yet, as I have argued elsewhere, Tusser's version of georgic provided a model for writers in subsequent decades, in both its populist appeal and its embrace of competition and expansion. This strain of georgic economics was extended most powerfully in the early seventeenth century by John Taylor, whose own experience of labour was as a waterman on the Thames, but who wrote more widely about work and the economy.[19] For instance, *Taylors Pastoral* is really a georgic about the cloth industry. *The Praise of Hemp-Seed*, meanwhile, is an expansive and miscellaneous work, inspired by a fascination with the economic activity generated by a seed.[20] As a number of recent studies have demonstrated, Taylor's writing celebrates the energy of commoners and the economic functions of competition and mobility; it is perhaps no wonder that it was written out of Addisonian histories of the mode.[21]

Others have attended to the role of georgic within debates over the contours of English nationhood. To the extent that Virgil's poem is about rural work – the focus for the majority of critics of georgic in this period – the poet's commitment to an expansive Roman empire is often positioned as an afterthought. Yet work is always to some end, and farmers operate within nations. Shakespeare grasped this point as well as anyone in his period, and it is notable that some of the most thoughtful consideration of the national functions of georgic has been made by readers of the history plays.[22] Hence Katherine Bootle Attié has identified a thematic contest in the second tetralogy, culminating in *Henry V*, between pastoral idleness and georgic labour, with the latter ultimately underpinning national renewal.[23] Dermot Cavanagh identifies a more authoritarian logic, noting that Virgil's poem is framed by 'panegyric to Octavian as a divine sovereign whose "care for our lands" will restore their fertility', and arguing that

Shakespeare follows the Roman author in linking the necessity of ordering and disciplining the fields with an endorsement of authoritarian domination over people, within and beyond the nation.[24] While the equation of England with Augustan Rome was not common at this time – too audacious, perhaps, for even the most sycophantic of court poets – the idea that it might become a colonizing force was a matter of live debate. Early proponents, such as the Elizabethan Richard Hakluyt and the Jacobean Samuel Purchas, associated classical learning in a country with a propensity to colonial success.[25] The former's *Discourse of Western Planting*, like Francis Bacon's essay 'On Plantations', fused colonial settlement with the georgic acts of ploughing and planting.[26]

Finally, the emergence of ecocriticism in Renaissance studies has lent further depth to understandings of georgic in this period. Ecocriticism alters the perspective; if previous approaches to georgic had focused on the activity of human agents, ecocritics invite reflection on the environment within which they were working. They attend to the effects of rural labour, whether it involves the continuation of traditional agricultural cycles, or the transformation of practices and landscapes in the interests of increased returns. Ecocritics have demonstrated that Renaissance writers, though they may speak about the natural world in ways that may sound unfamiliar to ears attuned to the Romantics and their heirs, might nonetheless be offering powerful reflections on human engagement with the land. We may just need to learn to listen to them.[27] While there may not yet have been a definitive ecocritical study of Renaissance georgic, this movement has clarified what was at stake when the mode was translated into English fields. It thus creates a context within which to ask some of the questions raised in the subsequent sections of this chapter: questions about the ends of labour and the ethics of agriculture. For there is a continuum of sorts between a celebration of the honest labour of the ploughman, an exhortation to a husbandman to consider the best use of his lands, and the promises of radically increased returns made by a fen-drainer. Georgic may be useful to any of them.

If there is a single lesson to take forward from these successive generations of scholarship on Renaissance georgic, it is the mode's malleability. If the achievement of Dryden and Addison was to define a dominant, authorized model of georgic as a literary genre, the task for those who came before them was to make sense of what georgic might mean in their context. The results are various and uncertain; georgic was not so much a fixed set of poetic practices and ethical values, as an assortment of cultural resources, open to writers of different kinds, with disparate interests. The risk in such circumstances is that the literary historian selects scraps of evidence to support an argument, and neglects all else. The challenge is to appreciate the complexity, and indeed the importance, of the debates into which georgic was enlisted.

The Georgic Debates of Jacobean England

With the benefit of several hundred years' hindsight, processes of social and economic change can appear linear, even inevitable. Feudalism gives way to capitalism, husbandry is transformed from a matter of observing custom into a challenge to maximize returns, and so forth. Yet none of this was obvious to those living in Jacobean England. As will be explored in this section, the debates of this period centred on certain transformative acts, such as the enclosure of common land, the clearing of woods and the draining of fens. They were negotiated through struggles over the value of certain words, such as 'thrift', 'profit' and, above all, 'improvement'.

In the House of Commons in 1601, these issues appeared straightforward. Speaking in support of measures to restrict enclosure, Robert Cecil, Elizabeth's secretary of state, proclaimed: 'I do not dwell in the Country, I am not acquainted with the Plough: But I think that whosoever doth not maintain the Plough, destroys this Kingdom.'[28] The statement's authority was derived from centuries of tradition. The plough represents a structure of arable husbandry geared largely towards self-sufficiency rather than a market economy. It suggests an organization of the countryside into a patchwork of manorial estates, each constituting a stable social hierarchy: 'a little commonwealth', in the words of one contemporary commentator.[29] The fear, articulated brilliantly a century earlier in Thomas More's *Utopia* and rehearsed in the Commons in 1597 by Francis Bacon, was that fields would be enclosed for pastoral farming, and people would be replaced in the landscape by sheep: 'soe in England instead of a whole Towne full of people [there would be] nought but Greenefeildes a Shepheard and his Dogg'.[30] These were stark, powerful images, affirming what was still a dominant political position, but they would soon become dated and unhelpful. Pastoral farming was of course critical to the nation's economy, and had been for centuries. Moreover, enclosure was more complex and variable in its effects than the images of depopulation and deserted villages would suggest; technically, it involved the abolition of common rights over land, and could happen through agreement among landholders rather than merely as a result of a landlord's decree.[31] The countryside was changing in myriad other ways, which were less controversial but equally significant in the longer term. Population increases drove a push to bring new land – such as forests, moors and fens – under cultivation.³² The inexorable development of a market economy for rural produce was also changing minds and practices, driving in particular a rise in specialist crops, such as flax, rape and woad.³³

Cecil's statement is also noteworthy for its casual assumption of authority. The speaker does not live in the country, is not acquainted with the plough, but presumes to impose his received understanding of rural values upon those who do. It reminds us of a nexus of questions concerning authorship and authority that face readers of georgic in any era. Specifically, what is the relationship between the expertise of the author, the power of those who own rural property and the labour of those actually working the fields? From the late seventeenth century, it may be easy to agree that georgic aligned with pastoral in this regard, as a project of the cultural centre, largely separated from the everyday exploitation of natural and human resources.³⁴ Arguably that model aligns with the perspective of Cecil, and with the position of Virgil in relation to agriculture in the Roman world. Yet discourse on husbandry in Jacobean England was notable for its social diversity, in terms of both authorship and intended readership. Knowledge was not necessarily assumed as the preserve of the landed. While 'husbandman' was a term that was socially coded, generally indicating a smallholder of lower than yeoman status, 'husbandry' was an activity common to people involved in agriculture across the social scale.³⁵

Hence, Jacobean writing about husbandry was always complicated in its negotiation between social and technical authority. The conservative position was to represent landlords as intellectual labourers, committed to the successful management of their estates. According to a proverb rehearsed by multiple husbandry manuals, 'the best doung for the feelde is the maisters foote'.³⁶ This is the logic of Robert Herrick's estate poem 'The Hock-Cart', with its dual frames of address: the author's patron, Mildmay Fane, earl of Westmorland, and the workers on his estate. The poem begins:

> Come Sons of Summer, by whose toile,
> We are the Lords of Wine and Oile:
> By whose tough labours, and rough hands,
> We rip up first, then reap our lands.³⁷

As Raymond Williams famously observed, this 'jollying kind of man-management' is notably 'crude in feeling', yet arguably more honest in its acknowledgement of 'the fact of labour' than other contemporary poems.³⁸ Yet labour could also be figured as socially transformational: a point that would not have been lost on Drayton and Jonson, both sons of artisans who were industriously carving out careers as professional writers. Markham packaged knowledge for different audiences: big books on farming and rural sports for the elite; smaller and cheaper manuals aimed at working farmers seeking to improve their conditions. Tusser, meanwhile, unashamedly valorized the labour and aspirations of tenant-farmers. For him there are no easy assumptions of property rights over the land that a husbandman works; his calendar of activities begins not in spring but September, when 'new farmer comes in' to assume a tenancy.[39]

Freely acknowledging that he had not himself enjoyed the success he desired, Tusser's poetry embraces the uncertainty and contestation of husbandry. An introductory poem, 'The Ladder to Thrift', begins:

> To take thy calling thankfully,
> And shun the path to beggery.
> To grudge in youth no drudgery,
> To come by knowledge perfectly.
> To count no travell [labour] slaverie,
> That brings in penie saverlie.
> To folow profit earnestlie
> But meddle not with pilferie.
> To get by honest practisie,
> And keep thy gettings covertlie.[40]

This is tenant-farmer georgic. Embedded in a socially conservative religious discourse of vocations ('To take thy calling thankfully'), it valorizes in turn knowledge, labour and profit. The word 'thrift' develops during the sixteenth century from an identification with 'thriving or prospering; prosperity, success, good-luck' towards meanings which take more account of the individual's efforts, such as 'industry, labour; profitable occupation', and 'economical management, economy'.[41] Tusser's *Five Hundred Points* also contains an early argument – and almost certainly the first statement in verse – in favour of enclosure. His position aligns with the values of individualism that resonate throughout the book; a husbandman has less control over common lands, which are figured as disorderly and unprofitable, preferred on the one hand by poor commoners who 'theevishlie loiter and louke' upon them, and on the other hand by idle landlords. The industrious husbandman will instead prefer enclosed lands: 'Againe what a joie is it knowne, | when men may be bold of their owne!'[42]

Tusser crystallizes the period's debates over the purpose of labour. While Cecil and other opponents of social and economic change in the countryside insisted on labour as a means for sustaining order, Tusser represents the case for its transformational potential. In his view, after enclosure the land could be managed better, the labour of husbandman and housewife could be more effective, and they could quite legitimately hope to be rewarded materially. The key word, for him and so many of his contemporaries, was 'improvement'. Often used to refer specifically to enclosure, the cry of improvement could be used to justify anything from an expanded use of manure to large-scale commercial development.[43] In the reign of James, these arguments were advanced on several fronts. The estate surveyor and agricultural reformer John Norden, for instance, described an imaginary tour of an estate, in which the surveyor explains to a landlord how different kinds of land could be managed more profitably. The assumptions of custom must thus give way to new learning and industry. Meanwhile rural 'projects' were changing ideas of the rural economy, with projectors proposing – and in some instances achieving – previously unthinkable rewards on the back of innovative crops and practices.[44] The fact that some projects became mired in scandals over monopolies, and were as a result the butt of satire – witness the gull in Jonson's play *The Devil is an Ass*, who is conned by the fantasy of becoming 'the duke of drowned land' in a fantastical fen-drainage scheme – merely underscores what was perceived to be at stake.

King James himself appeared confused about the values of the land. The Midlands Revolt of 1607 left him with an abiding fear of 'levellers', but with little apparent concern about enclosure, which had been the main focus of the rioters.[45] He was also supportive of rural projectors for most of his reign, particularly those interested in fen drainage. Yet he was also insistent that members of the traditional landowning degrees, the gentry and nobility, should be managing the land. He fretted about landowners devoting too much of their time to lives of luxury and consumption in the city rather than overseeing their estates. Such 'Gentlemen', he claimed, 'lose their owne thrift for lacke of their owne presence, in seeing to their owne busines at home.'[46] He reiterated this position in a Horatian elegy, addressed to ladies who 'love' London:

> The cuntrey is your Orbe and proper Spheare
> Thence your Revenues rise bestowe them there
> Convert your coach horse to the thrifty plough
> Take knowledge of your sheepe, your corne your cowe
> And thinke it noe disparagement or taxe
> To acquaint your fingers with the wooll & flaxe.[47]

The vision of aristocratic ladies actually getting their fingers calloused in the cloth industry is ludicrous, but stands in the poem as a signifier of the labours of housewifery. Like Markham, who described at length the housewife's ideal role alongside that of the lord, the manorial system depends on 'knowledge', on landowners as managers of labour.

While James's overt lesson may be a conventional model of social order, the language is georgic. The plough is 'thrifty' to the extent that it produces income as well as crops; in a variant version, the subsequent line, 'Take knowledge of your sheepe', is translated into 'make mony of your sheepe'. His poem is an effort to contain the energy of georgic, subsuming the economic impetus of Tusser beneath a model of rigid social hierarchy; however, it recognizes in the process the multiple threats to this order. The land was no longer the locus of stable and accepted values, even to the extent that that ever had been the case. This contestation over the meaning and values of rural life created a distinctive context for Jacobean writers' encounters with georgic. Heavy with classical authority but with no established English tradition, georgic could be deployed by writers with divergent interests, to different ends.

Jacobean Georgics: Ben Jonson and Michael Drayton

Perhaps more than any other poets of this period, the two men who wrote commendatory poems for Chapman's Hesiod in 1618 were engaging with this context, seeking to make sense of it within their writing. Jonson and Drayton were different men politically, the former remaining more loyal than the latter to James and his courtiers, but they were united on several counts. They shared a keen sense of the value of their own labour, they were committed to translating classical literary traditions into contemporary culture, and they were concerned at particular moments with the values and practices of the English countryside. They were entirely in accord with their time in not overtly identifying any of their works as georgic, but each was nonetheless negotiating a position for his work within a tradition that stretches back to Hesiod and Virgil. In order to understand georgic in this period, it is thus worth turning briefly to Jonson's estate poems (or 'country house poems') and Drayton's epic of nationhood, *Poly-Olbion*.

The key word in Jonson's 'To Penshurst' and 'To Sir Robert Wroth', printed second and third in his 1616 collection *The Forest*, is the verb 'to dwell'.[48] The former, which addresses the Penshurst estate itself by way of praising its owner, Sir Robert Sidney, ends with the lines:

> Now, Penshurst, they that will proportion thee
>   With other edifices, when they see
> Those proud, ambitious heaps, and nothing else,
>   May say, their lords have built, but thy lord dwells. (lines 99–102)

In the latter, Jonson offers his addressee the aphorism: 'when man's state is well, | 'Tis better, if he there can dwell' (lines 93–4). These lessons are in part consolatory; Wroth, in particular, was deep in debt, and thus ill-equipped to pursue a career at court or a life of consumption in the city. They are also aligned with James's social policy, and its definitive concern with order in the countryside. Yet 'dwell' is an equivocal verb, gesturing amiably towards the responsibilities of a landowner yet suggesting simultaneously that the order of the estate is loosened from the vicissitudes of rural life. It leans at once towards process and stasis; the ideological trick of the poems is to suggest that this is just the way things are. People and seasons come and go, but the house and its lord maintain a genteel continuity, imprinting order upon the estate not necessarily through his knowledge of agriculture or his management of tenants and labourers, but through the mystery of his presence.[49]

Jonson aligns himself with classical georgic more explicitly in 'To Sir Robert Wroth', in which a central passage is modelled on Virgil's 'O fortunatus nimium' section of his second *Georgic*. This extract was in fact favoured by a succession of poets over subsequent decades, providing a vehicle through which they learned to engage with their native landscape.[50] It was often coupled with Horace's Epode 2, a poem that Jonson himself translated as 'The Praises of a Country Life'.[51] With their emphasis on the pleasures of the land, an approach arguably more akin to the *otium* of the pastoral mode, these classical precedents were the gateway drugs for the English georgic tradition. Crucially, they invite the English poet to define rural life in terms of consumption rather than production. Wroth's estate is 'with unbought provision blest', a statement that underscores the fantasy of a rural place isolated from the business and contestation of economic exchange (line 14). At Penshurst, food has a way of presenting itself to the lord: from the 'painted partridge' that 'for thy mess is willing to be killed', through 'Fat, agèd carps, that run into thy net', to eels that 'leap on land, | Before the fisher, or into his hand' (lines 29–30, 33, 37–8). Jonson depicts the community of the estate ('all come in, the farmer and the clown') approaching the house:

> Some bring a capon, some a rural cake,
>   Some nuts, some apples; some that think they make
> The better cheeses, bring 'em; or else send
>   By their ripe daughters, whom they would commend
> This way to husbands; and whose baskets bear
>   An emblem of themselves, in plum or pear. (lines 48, 51–6)

As Williams observed with passion, this is an act of 'magical recreation', translating an order based on property and the curse of labour into 'a natural bounty' balanced by 'a willing charity: both serving to ratify and bless the country landowner'.[52] It is georgic with the labour taken out. These poems thus co-opt georgic to support a politicized vision of rural England as a locus of unchanging order. Their enduring fascination derives in part from the sense of struggle involved to do so, as though the poet is constraining not only the social and economic realities of his time, but also the potential of a literary mode.

Drayton's 14,000-line description of the history and geography of England and Wales, published with idiosyncratic county maps and (for the first eighteen of thirty songs) historical annotations by John Selden, aligns with the prose genre of chorography.[53] For Fowler, though, *Poly-Olbion* stands as 'a massive georgic poem'. He claims that much of the poem 'could be regarded as an enormous *macrologia* of Virgil's "laus Italiae" passage, describing landscape and towns and local products, in its expansive Elizabethan way'.[54] There is a risk here; most readers of *Poly-Olbion*, myself included, have been guilty of focusing on the passages we find most congenial, and disregarding the rest. Moreover, while georgic tends to look through the processes of the present towards the imagined advances of the future, *Poly-Olbion* is fundamentally more sceptical, even elegiac in its vision. Yet while Fowler's claim is overstated, it is by no means wholly wrong. Indeed, a subsequent generation of critics, particularly those approaching the poem from an ecocritical perspective, have further demonstrated the ways in which it adapts georgic expectations.[55]

While there is anxiety about the present at the heart of Drayton's vision of his native land, its nature differs from that of Jonson or King James. In a departure from chorography, Drayton famously displays little concern for the society of rural England, and reserves even less attention for landowners. His concerns instead are environmental. Notably, Drayton was the first poet to criticize the destruction of ancient woodland in England. His recurrent complaints on this topic combine an economic concern for the sustainability of a natural resource with a profound emotional engagement with the land:

> But mans devouring hand, with all the earth not fed,
> Hath hew'd her timber downe. Which wounded, when it fell,
> By the great noise it made, the workmen seem'd to tell
> The losse that to the Land would shortlie come thereby,
> Where no man ever plants to our posteritie.[56]

In response to Jacobean debates about the exploitation – or 'improvement' – of the land, Drayton thus offers a distinctive and passionate response. He is sceptical about the capacity of human labour to improve anything, and fascinated by the generative powers of the land itself. Set against such images of men destroying woodlands is the figure of a hermit in Warwickshire's Forest of Arden, who describes the natural properties of herbs (13.162–230). For Drayton, knowledge of the land need not necessarily entail destruction of environments.[57]

The point is underscored in passages on England's fenlands. While Drayton does not explicitly engage with debates over fen-drainage, he repeatedly celebrates the fens' fertility and plenitude under traditional methods of management. In the description of Lincolnshire, the fenland region of Holland proclaims the distinct qualities of her 'vast and queachy soyle', beginning her oration with a catalogue of the wildfowl her land sustains, and ending with a catalogue of fish (25.15, 25.53–138, 25.157–91). By conventional measures, the fens frustrate conventional georgic tropes; as the Isle of Ely had stressed in an earlier song, 'My full and batning earth, needs *not* the Plowmans paines' (21.239; italics added). Yet Holland's lesson is that the inhabitants of the numerous settlements that 'upon my Bosome sticke' thrive specifically because they adapt their lives to this distinctive environment:

> The toyling *Fisher* here is tewing of his Net:
> The *Fowler* is imployd his lymed twigs to set.
> One underneath his Horse, to get a shoot doth stalke;
> Another over Dykes upon his Stilts doth walke:
> There other with their Spades, the Peats are squaring out,
> And others from their Carres, are busily about,
> To draw out Sedge and Reed, for Thatch and Stover fit,
> That whosoever would a Landskip rightly hit,
> Beholding but my Fennes, shall with more shapes be stor'd,
> Then *Germany*, or *France*, or *Thuscan* can afford.[58]

Drayton appears uncertain about the register or purpose of this passage, labelling it in a marginal note 'The pleasures of the *Fennes*', and later invoking the newly fashionable art of framing a landscape ('landskip'). Yet it is also a working, productive environment for those accustomed to living within it. The fisher is 'toyling' and the fowler 'employed', while the land affords peat, sedge and reeds to support human and animal life ('stover' is winter food for cattle). While landscape art and poetry may typically have been framed from the perspective of the propertied, Drayton reclaims the dignity of those whose ways of life were threatened by the very improvement schemes that so many of his contemporaries were so keen to promote.[59]

Drayton extends this perspective onto a national scale in Song 23, the centrepiece of which is a survey of the 'sundry soyles' of England presented through the voice of Helidon Hill. Though much of the information is not new, given the wealth of local detail offered throughout the poem, the perspective is significant. Helidon's voice is common, figured as a demotic intrusion into the otherwise polite space of *Poly-Olbion*. His focus is on how different regions will accommodate specific forms of agriculture and life: the 'naturally ... wooddy' southern counties, the 'rich In-land parts' around Wiltshire and the Cotswolds, the sandy soils of Middlesex, the 'Mosses, Fleets, and Fells' of Lancashire, and so forth (23.74, 97, 125, 191). The rest of the song provides a frame for Helidon's speech, realizing the point about human adaptation to an environment through its depiction of Northamptonshire, and ultimately one place within this county. Significantly, there is nothing magically sustaining about this landscape; the 'earth' of Northamptonshire, the opening lines of the song assert, is 'As fruitfull every way, as those by Nature, which | The Husbandman by Art, with Compost doth inrich' (23.2–4). The appreciation of the 'art' – and labour – required of the inhabitants is extended in a speculation on Whittlewood Forest, which has perhaps escaped the 'generall fall' of woodland elsewhere in England on account of the fact that it 'dost naturally produce | More Under wood, and Brake, then Oke for greater use' (23.11, 14–16). In other words, it is a wood managed for the needs of its local community, not exploited for the 'greater' demands of other interests, such as industry or shipping. The song ends with a description of hare-coursing at Kelmarsh. As opposed to hunting, which was restricted to the social elite, the coursing scene is communal; similarly to his representation of the fens, in Song 23 Drayton resists georgic's predominant focus on the aspirations of landowners, creating instead a vision of adaptation, integration and common endeavour.[60]

Admittedly, these are snippets from what is arguably English literature's most miscellaneous epic. If Fowler's ascription of *Poly-Olbion* as georgic has any value, this is due as much to its heterogeneity and manic collection of local details as to any unified vision of the land and its inhabitants. Yet Drayton's sketches of people living and working within distinctive rural places, set alongside his expressions of disgust at the degradation of other environments, nonetheless demonstrate a distinctive perception of the role of rural labour within the nation. Like Jonson, Drayton lived with the pressures of his era's debates about the land. Yet while Jonson leaned towards James's conservative social policy, and perceived the countryside through the interests of his patrons, Drayton admitted different voices and perspectives into his poem. As this chapter has sought to demonstrate, Jacobean georgic defies coherence; it might best be understood as a common store of cultural resources, deployed from various angles in a number of overlapping debates. Within a long narrative of literary history it might indeed be seen as transitional (a word that Fowler reserves specifically for *Poly-Olbion*).[61] Yet Drayton and Jonson did not know they were merely marking generic time; in the view of their contemporary Chapman, they were manifestly great writers of the era, whose place in his translation of Hesiod could valuably raise its profile. Hence the purpose of this chapter has been to consider the reign of James not merely as a point of transition, but as a complicated, contentious period, when georgic performed quite different kinds of cultural work.

In 1606, Drayton wrote a poem to celebrate the English expedition to establish a settlement in Virginia. The ode 'To the Virginia Voyage' is not only somewhat shorter than *Poly-Olbion*, but also less assured as it looks across the ocean towards unknown spaces.[62] Is America a land of pastoral or georgic? The bulk of this unremarkable poem opts for the former, imagining a paradise where the land will produce an abundance of natural produce 'Without your toil' (line 28). Yet the opening of the poem is more candid in confronting the labour that will be required if the New World is to be moulded to English desires:

> You brave Heroique Minds,
> Worthy your Countries Name,
>   That Honour still pursue,
>   Goe, and subdue,
> Whilst loyt'ring Hinds
> Lurke here at home, with shame. (lines 1–6)

There is a note here of a nationally expansive strain of georgic, derived in part from Virgil: the conviction that 'labor omnia vicit improbus' ('toil triumphed over every obstacle'), and that it might underset not only individual success at home but also a form of national regeneration typified by the imposition of authority upon other lands.[63] In the preceding generation, this had been adapted most notably by Spenser, who considered the colonization of Ireland in abstract terms in *The Faerie Queene*, more literally in *A View of the Present State of Ireland*, and in practice as a landowner and colonial administrator.[64] In time this energetic, exploitative, acquisitive approach to colonial spaces would become accepted as an essential component of georgic poetry. Yet for Drayton the hesitancy is critical. In so many ways, he and his contemporaries were constantly assessing the value of georgic for their changing world and its uncertain values. Georgic did not so much present a model for understanding their world as provide resources that helped them to think for themselves.

Notes

1. A. Fowler, 'The Beginnings of English Georgic', in *Renaissance Genres*, ed. B. K. Lewalski (Cambridge, MA: Harvard University Press 1986), pp. 105–25, at p. 117.
2. See esp. D. L. Durling, *Georgic Tradition in English Poetry* (New York: Columbia University Press, 1935); J. Chalker, *The English Georgic: A Study in the Development of a Form* (London: Routledge and Kegan Paul, 1969).
3. Quoted in Fowler, 'Beginnings of English Georgic', p. 107.
4. Fowler, 'Beginnings of English Georgic', p. 106.
5. A. Low, *The Georgic Revolution* (Princeton University Press, 1985), p. 7.
6. Low, *Georgic Revolution*, p. 12.
7. See esp. C. Scott, *Shakespeare's Nature: From Cultivation to Culture* (Oxford University Press, 2014); J. C. Bulman, 'Shakespeare's Georgic Histories', *Shakespeare Survey*, 38 (1985), 37–49.
8. Fowler, 'Beginnings of English Georgic', p. 111; cf. A. McRae, *God Speed the Plough: The Representation of Agrarian England, 1500–1660* (Cambridge University Press, 1996), pp. 198–228.
9. J. Addison, 'Essay on Georgics', in Virgil, *Georgics* (Dryden), p. 146.
10. C. Heresbach, *Foure Bookes of Husbandry*, trans. B. Googe (London, 1577), sig. π4v. See esp. McRae, *God Speed the Plough*, pp. 135–68.
11. W. Wall, 'Renaissance National Husbandry: Gervase Markham and the Publication of England', *Sixteenth Century Journal*, 27 (1996), 767–85, at 768.
12. References are to *Five Hundred Points of Good Husbandry*, ed. G. Grigson (Oxford University Press, 1984).
13. Low, *Georgic Revolution*, p. 33.
14. *Palladis Tamia* (1598), fol. 285v.
15. *OED* 1.
16. L. C. Stevenson, *Praise and Paradox: Merchants and Craftsmen in Elizabethan Popular Literature* (Cambridge University Press, 1984), p. 141; cf. McRae, *God Speed the Plough*, pp. 146–51, 206–8.
17. A. McRae, 'Fashioning a Cultural Icon: The Ploughman in Renaissance Texts', *Parergon*, 14 (1996), 187–204.
18. E. Spenser, *The Faerie Queene*, ed. A. C. Hamilton, 2nd ed. (Harlow: Longman, 2007), 1.10.66.
19. B. Capp, *The World of John Taylor the Water Poet, 1578–1653* (Oxford University Press, 1994).
20. J. Taylor, *Taylors Pastorall, Being Both Historicall and Satyricall. or, The Noble Antiquitie of Shepheards, with the Profitable Use of Sheepe* (1624); *The Praise of Hemp-seed* (1620); McRae, *God Speed the Plough*, pp. 224–6.
21. See esp. L. Ellinghausen, 'The Individualist Project of John Taylor "The Water Poet"', *The Ben Jonson Journal*, 9 (2002), 147–69; C. J. Finlayson, 'John Taylor, the Self-Made Poet, on Merit and Social Mobility in Mercantile

London', *English Studies*, 98, 1–2 (2017), 120–36; A. McRae, *Literature and Domestic Travel in Early Modern England* (Cambridge University Press, 2009), pp. 210–34.
22 Cf. studies of Spenser, most notably W. A. Sessions, 'Spenser's Georgics', *English Literary Renaissance*, 10 (1980), 202–38.
23 K. B. Attié, '"The mettle of your pasture": Georgic Sensibility and English Identity in *Henry V*', *Studies in Philology*, 117 (2020), 769–800.
24 D. Cavanagh, 'Georgic Sovereignty in *Henry V*', in *Shakespeare Survey*, vol. 63, *Shakespeare's English Histories and their Afterlives*, ed. P. Holland (Cambridge University Press, 2010), pp. 114–26.
25 D. Armitage, *The Ideological Origins of the British Empire* (Cambridge University Press, 2000), p. 68.
26 E. R. Hakluyt, *Discourse of Western Planting, 1584*, ed. David Quinn (London: Hakluyt Society, 1999); F. Bacon, *The Essays*, ed. J. Pitcher (London: Penguin, 1985), pp. 162–4.
27 See esp. T. A. Borlik, *Ecocriticism and Early Modern English Literature: Green Pastures* (London: Routledge, 2011); K. Hiltner, *What Else Is Pastoral? Renaissance Literature and the Environment* (Ithaca: Cornell University Press, 2011).
28 Sir S. D'Ewes, *The Journals of All the Parliaments during the Reign of Queen Elizabeth* (1682), p. 674; cf. McRae, *God Speed the Plough*, pp. 7–12.
29 J. Norden, *Surveiors Dialogue* (1610), p. 27.
30 'Hayward Townshend's Journals', ed. A. F. Pollard and M. Blatcher, *Bulletin of the Institute of Historical Research*, 12 (1934–5), 10; cf. T. More, *Utopia: The Complete Works of St. Thomas More, Volume Four*, ed. E. Surtz, S. J., and J. H. Hexter (New Haven and London: Yale University Press, 1965), pp. 65–7.
31 J. Thirsk, 'Enclosing and Engrossing', in *AWEH*, vol. IV, p. 200.
32 J. Thirsk, 'The Farming Regions of England', in *AWEH*, vol. IV, p. 2.
33 J. Thirsk, *Economic Policy and Projects: The Development of a Consumer Society in Early Modern England* (Oxford: Clarendon Press, 1978), p. 7.
34 R. Williams, *The Country and the City* (London: Chatto and Windus, 1973), pp. 46–54; K. O'Brien, 'Imperial Georgic', in *The Country and the City Revisited: England and the Politics of Culture, 1550–1850*, ed. G. Maclean, D. Landry and J. P. Ward (Cambridge University Press, 1999), pp. 160–79, at p. 160.
35 K. Wrightson, *English Society, 1580–1680* (London: Hutchinson, 1982), pp. 17–38.
36 Heresbach, *Foure Bookes of Husbandry*, fol. 3r; Joan Thirsk traces the classical origins of this saying in 'Plough and Pen: Agricultural Writers in the Seventeenth Century', in *Social Relations and Ideas: Essays in Honour of R. H. Hilton*, ed. T. H. Aston et al. (Cambridge University Press, 1983), pp. 295–317, p. 298.
37 R. Herrick, *The Complete Poetry of Robert Herrick*, ed. T. Cain and R. Connolly, 2 vols. (Oxford University Press, 2013), vol. I, p. 96.
38 Williams, *Country and the City*, p. 33; cf. the discussion of Jonson's estate poems below.

39 Tusser, *Five Hundred Points of Good Husbandry*, p.30.
40 Tusser, *Five Hundred Points*, p. 13.
41 *OED* 1a, 1b, 3a; McRae, *God Speed the Plough*, pp. 144–5.
42 Tusser, *Five Hundred Points*, pp. 137–8.
43 Cf. McRae, *God Speed the Plough*, pp. 136–7.
44 Thirsk, *Economic Policy and Projects*; McRae, *God Speed the Plough*, pp. 151–6.
45 'A Speech in the Starre-Chamber' [1616], in *King James VI and I: Political Writings*, ed. J. P. Sommerville (Cambridge University Press, 1995), p. 227.
46 'A Speech in the Starre-Chamber', p. 227.
47 *The Poems of James VI of Scotland*, ed. J. Craigie, 2 vols. (Edinburgh: Scottish Text Society, 1955–8), vol. II, p. 180.
48 B. Jonson, *The Cambridge Edition of the Works of Ben Jonson*, ed. D. Bevington et al., 7 vols. (Cambridge University Press, 2012), vol. V, pp. 209–20.
49 See esp. D. E. Wayne, *Penshurst: The Semiotics of Place and the Poetics of History* (Madison: University of Wisconsin Press, 1984), pp. 45–128.
50 M-S Røstvig, '*The Happy Man*': *Studies in the Metamorphoses of a Classical Ideal. Vol. 1, 1600–1700*, 2nd ed. (Oslo: Norwegian Universities Press, 1962).
51 Jonson, *Cambridge Edition of the Works of Ben Jonson*, vol. 7, pp. 279–85.
52 Williams, *Country and the City*, p. 32.
53 M. Drayton, *The Works of Michael Drayton*, ed. J. W. Hebel, 5 vols. (Oxford: Blackwell, 1931–41), vol. IV.
54 Fowler, 'Beginnings of English Georgic', p. 118; cf. *Georgics*, II. 136–76.
55 See, e.g., T. A. Borlik, 'Bioregional Visions in *Poly-Olbion*', in '*Poly-Olbion*': *New Perspectives*, eds. A. McRae and P. Schwyzer (Cambridge: D. S. Brewer, 2020), pp. 89–111.
56 Drayton, *Works of Michael Drayton*, vol. IV, p. 31 (*Poly-Olbion*, II. 64–8).
57 On woodlands in *Poly-Olbion*, see S. Dasgupta, 'Drayton's "Silent Spring": *Poly-Olbion* and the Politics of Landscape', *Cambridge Quarterly*, 39 (2010), 152–71; A. McRae, 'Tree-Felling in Early Modern England: Michael Drayton's Environmentalism', *RES*, 63 (2012), 410–30; S. Trevisan, 'The Murmuring Woods Euen Shuddred as with Feare': Deforestation in Michael Drayton's *Poly-Olbion*', *The Seventeenth Century*, 26 (2011), 240–63.
58 Drayton, *Works of Drayton*, vol. IV, pp. 518, 514–15 (*Poly-Olbion*, 25.298, 25.139–48).
59 J. Turner, *The Politics of Landscape: Rural Scenery and Society in English Poetry 1630–1660* (Oxford University Press, 1979), pp. 8–35.
60 Cf. McRae, 'Of Albion's "Sundry Varying Soyles": The Land and its Human Occupants in *Poly-Olbion*', in '*Poly-Olbion*': *New Perspectives*, pp. 69–88, at pp. 82–7.
61 Fowler, 'Beginnings of English Georgic', p. 120.
62 Drayton, *Works of Michael Drayton*, vol. II, pp. 363–4.
63 Virgil, *Georgics* (Fairclough), pp. 108–9 (*Georgics*, I. 145).
64 Cf. Sessions, 'Spenser's Georgics'; Hiltner, *What Else Is Pastoral?*, pp. 156–73.

CHAPTER 6

'Varieties too Regular for Chance'
John Evelyn, John Dryden and Their Contemporaries
Melissa Schoenberger

In the introduction to his translation of the *Georgics*, David Ferry reflects on Virgil's vision of life permanently separated from the idyllic ways of the golden age: 'Culture, in the fallen world of Jupiter, is always near the fragile beginnings of its making and always near its potential end. Existence itself is fragile in this world, and the more loved because it is so, having to be so carefully and anxiously constructed and maintained by toil and ingenuity and arts.'[1] Here, Ferry captures perhaps the central reason why this poem endures: its profound sense of human creation hovering between equally delicate states of realization and destruction appeals as much in the early decades of the twenty-first century as it must have in the 30s BCE. Such a notion would certainly have resonated with people living, working and writing in the decades following the English Civil Wars, a period known for diverse forms of cultural creation and exploration: in the sciences, in literature, in music and in evolving conversations about social, political and religious life. The georgic ideal of the 'felix, qui potuit rerum cognoscere causas' – the happy one who knows the causes of things – informed the spirit of experimentation, observation and learning so valued by members of the Royal Society, including those of the 'Georgicall Committee', along with many of their contemporaries.[2] More fundamentally, a georgic sense of perpetual revision and adjustment informed thought and writing in general; consider the decades-long work that John Evelyn – one of the Society's founding members – devoted to his horticultural text *Elysium Britannicum*, which seemed to demand from him the same constant upkeep and attention as a working farm or highly cultivated garden. Even the very language with which seventeenth-century writers argued for incorporating Greco-Roman agricultural writing took georgic turns. In *The Georgic Revolution*, Anthony Low notes in particular Thomas Sprat's acknowledgement of how much 'more fertile' modern agricultural writing could be when nourished by the ancients.[3]

Yet of course, this was a period that faced new shifts and uncertainties of other kinds as well, and in this way is particularly notable for its affinities with the political contexts from which an agricultural text such as Virgil's *Georgics* emerged. As was the case for the Roman poet, writers of georgic literature living in the middle and later decades of the seventeenth century contemplated civil war and its often challenging aftermaths, such as the demise and resurrection of monarchy, the emergence of a deeply factionalized politics and the accelerating development of imperial structures. That a culture already so steeped in ancient texts would appreciate a Latin poem concerned with the precarity of all post-war paths forward should come as no surprise. Moreover, agricultural writing of all kinds typically bore a political charge. As Frances Dolan has observed, seventeenth-century writers often thought about agriculture as a kind of connective tissue for the political state. She draws our attention, for instance, to Walter Blith, whose *English Improver* (1649) and *English Improver Improved* (1652) straddled the difficult period that saw the fall of Charles I and the rise of Oliver Cromwell: 'Commonwealths may replace monarchies, the body politic might change its shape, but husbandry remains the life force and the principle of connection.'[4] The *Georgics* lends itself especially well to such politicized interpretation, imitation and translation, since here the terms of rural cultivation and maintenance frequently transform into the terms of civil conflict and then, as swiftly as the change has come, it recedes again, returning us to the peaceful, though arduous, work of agriculture. As I have discussed elsewhere, for Virgil, farm tools are *arma* – weapons – for labourers bringing unruly vines under control.[5] By the end of the poem's first book, we witness a peasant conscripted into war as rapidly and chaotically as a charioteer who has lost control of his horse's reins; later, the rows of a vineyard appear like soldiers at the ready, with Mars weaving through their ranks, but blink and they become harmless plants again. Such changeability indicates the challenges of maintaining crops and livestock – work itself can be a kind of battle – but I also believe that Virgil means to show us with his agricultural poetry that the objects, spaces and energies of peace and war share more at their roots than we may want to acknowledge.

As the larger history recounted in this volume demonstrates, the *Georgics* and other ancient agricultural texts have not moved through literary-historical time in linear or even clearly discernible ways. They emerge in some places in full form – as large-scale translations or overt imitations – but elsewhere their presence constitutes merely part of a looser georgic mode that winds and weaves its way through various genres and forms. The story of English georgic writing from 1650 to 1700 is no more or less complicated than in other periods, but this half century is indeed notable for sustaining long-held forms of georgic writing at the same time that it began to foster the development of new ones, the roots of which would take firmer hold in the next century.[6] Although Virgil was undoubtedly the most important ancient model for writers working before the eighteenth century, not all texts that we might now read under the heading of 'georgic' in this period engaged seriously or extensively with the *Georgics*. Nevertheless, the Latin poem remains an important touchstone in these decades, and in the following sections, we will encounter it in various guises: as an agricultural authority; a source of political metaphors and ideas; and a poem that fosters thinking about the place and significance of poetry itself. Of course, early modern agricultural, political and poetic writing tend to fold inextricably into one another, so I shall allow various writers' engagements with georgic, and with the *Georgics*, to emerge organically rather than systematically.

Marvell's Militarized Georgics

During the politically ambiguous period after the execution of Charles I, Andrew Marvell appears to have been aware of exactly the kind of cultural fragility Ferry detects in his reading of Virgil.[7] His long poem *Upon Appleton House, To My Lord Fairfax* (1651) is marked by a pervasive sense that the places where people work the earth and those where they battle one another cannot easily be separated. Written while the poet was tutor to Mary Fairfax, whose father Thomas had not long before ceded his post as commander of the New Model Army to Oliver Cromwell, *Upon Appleton House* draws from a variety of genres and sources, but it is clearly shot through with a Virgilian awareness of how agricultural writing can offer access to larger questions. It moves associatively and briskly, beginning by contemplating the property and its praiseworthy owner, moving into familial legend and finally broadening out onto the grounds of the estate. From here, scenes of rural labour give way to private contemplations in a quiet wood. As one might expect, the capaciousness and variety of *Upon Appleton House* has elicited an equally heterogenous critical response. Readers have long been interested in questions of genre, history, politics, gender, military strategy, environmentalism and landscape design as they relate to this poem.[8]

As often occurs in the *Georgics*, here images of rural peaceability sometimes give way suddenly to thoughts of war. For instance, approaching the midpoint of the poem, Marvell laments our separation from an idyllic age of peace and plenty:

> Unhappy! shall we never more
> That sweet *Militia* restore,
> When Gardens only had their Towrs,
> And all the Garrisons were Flowrs,
> When Roses only Arms might bear,
> And Men did rosie Garlands wear?
> Tulips, in several Colours barr'd,
> Were then the *Switzers* of our *Guard*.
>   The *Gardiner* had the *Souldiers* place,
> And his more gentle Forts did trace.
> The Nursery of all things green
> Was then the only *Magazeen*.
> The *Winter Quarters* were the Stoves,
> Where he the tender Plants removes.
> But War all this doth overgrow:
> We Ord'nance Plant and Powder sow.[9]

Marvell fuses these two worlds, one ideal, one fallen: we can receive the golden age only in terms of the warlike visions that now stalk even the most peaceable places. Before the fall, there was a 'sweet Militia', but a militia nonetheless. No image arrives unmarked by the implements of battle, which in the final lines overwhelm the scene, as 'We' seed the ground with weapons and gunpowder. At the same time that this passage insists on a distinction between a lost rural paradise and a militarized present, it refuses any hope that the imaginative work of poetry might offer untroubled respite.

From here we move to a vision of Fairfax as an upright gardener whose cultivation of post-war England would have differed from that of his military successor Cromwell. He arrives as someone who 'with his utmost Skill' could '*Ambition* weed, but *Conscience* till. | *Conscience*, that Heaven-nursed Plant, | Which most our Earthly Gardens want' (lines 353–6); these lines draw on broader classical tropes of the farmer-statesman at the same time that they heighten the poem's associations between English land and the continued reverberations of civil conflict. Moreover, the uncomfortable rhyme between 'Plant' and 'want' suggests a gap between present lack and georgic potential. Ultimately, these images give way to more explicit scenes of rural work, rife with their own threats and risks and characterized by both a sustained commitment to describing labour itself and a sense that every movement indicates something larger.

Also often considered under the aegis of georgic are Marvell's four 'Mower poems', published in the posthumous *Miscellaneous Poems* (1681), but possibly begun in the same period as *Upon Appleton House*.[10] Although generally associated with pastoral – not least because of their speakers' frequent amorous pining – they also acknowledge the arduous and ever-shifting qualities of rural labour. Nigel Smith observes the transitory nature of this work, noting that 'mowers were needed in only two summer months; it was not possible to live as a mower for the whole of the year'. This transitoriness often also overlapped with military work: '[d]uring the civil disruption of the mid-century, travelling labourers who found work as mowers included decommissioned soldiers and uprooted sectaries'.[11] Indeed, these poems, like the mowing scenes of *Upon Appleton House*, indicate a clear sense of the ease with which the work of mowing might lend itself to militarized expression. Sometimes the echoes are faint, as in 'The Mower against Gardens', where the eponymous horticultural critic complains that '"Tis all enforc'd' (line 31), meaning that the garden is highly artificial in contrast to unmanipulated nature. Yet the notion of nature having been 'forc'd' – as well as suffering an ongoing enforcement – strikes an ominous tone. Things get more violent in 'Damon the Mower', which culminates in a gory accident:

> While thus he threw his Elbow round,
> Depopulating all the Ground,
> And, with his whistling Sythe, does cut
> Each stroke between the Earth and Root,
> The edged Stele by careless chance
> Did into his own Ankle glance;
> And there among the Grass fell down,
> By his own Sythe, the Mower mown. (lines 73–80)

The violence begins with the figurative depiction of mowing as 'depopulating' a field, as though each blade of grass were someone standing upright; the language here also indicates that Damon pays little attention to the destructive potential of his tool, otherwise he might not 'thr[o]w' his arms so 'careless[ly]'. Of course, the inherently violent energies of the scythe do eventually bear down on his limbs, but we should hardly be surprised by this turn of events, given the portentous lines Marvell offers us early in the stanza. In these poems, the terms of rural work and those of military violence move into and out of one another as freely as in Virgil's *Georgics*. Yet at the same time, this movement was also characteristic of the period more broadly; for instance, Smith notes that mowing metaphors not infrequently made their way into mid-century accounts of battle.[12] Where questions of land meet civil conflict, the georgic mode tends to emerge.

Evelyn, Cowley and Early Restoration Georgic

The life of John Evelyn represents a similarly Virgilian blending of military and agricultural terms: his extensive work as a garden designer, cultivator and horticultural–agricultural writer was undergirded by a family fortune derived from the gunpowder trade.[13] Like Virgil, the fact of civil war casts its shadows over much of his writing. His *Sylva, or A Discourse of Foresttrees, and the Propagation of Timber in His Majesties Dominions* (1664), which recruits the *Georgics* among other ancient agricultural works as a central reference text, also betrays a deeper sense of why one ought to consider plants and politics together. Framed in terms of preservation and repair, it opens with overt acknowledgements of the recent war, but also takes care to link the circumstances of this work's publication to the conditions under which Virgil wrote. In the 'Preface to the Reader', Evelyn allows his own syntax to slide easily into two lines from the *Georgics*: 'It was the simple *Culture* onely, with so much difficulty retriv'd from the late confusion of an intestine and bloody *War*, like *Ours*, and now put in *Reputation* again, which made the noble *Poet* write –How hard it was | Low Subjects with illustrious words to grace'.[14] Translated from Rome to England, this repairing of arboriculture becomes for Evelyn a way of turning violent energies outward, away from civil strife and towards the strengthening of English naval ships, all in the name of the restored King Charles II. Casting himself even more overtly as an English Virgil, Evelyn frames the main text of *Sylva* with an epigraph reproducing a passage from the second book of the *Georgics* in which the poet invokes his patron, but here Maecenas has been replaced by the Latinized 'CAROLIDE'.

Evelyn also frames his treatise by lamenting that those interested in tree cultivation sometimes come to the practice too late in life, given the long, slow pace of arboreal time. In the second edition (1670), he entreats the landowning 'Reader' addressed in the preface to understand that

> my earnest and humble *Advice* should be, That at their very first coming to their *Estates*, and as soon as they get *Children*, they would seriously think of this work of *Propagation* also: For, I observe there is no part of *Husbandry*, which men commonly more *Fail* in, *neglect*, and have cause to *repent* of, than that they did not begin *Planting betimes*, without which, they can expect neither *Fruit*, *Ornament*, or *Delight* from their *Labours*: Men seldom Plant *Trees* till they begin to be *Wise*, that is, till they grow *Old*, and find by *Experience* the *Prudence* and *Necessity* of it.[15]

This problem of time is a practical one, of course, but it also points to the smallness of human efforts when compared with the massive scale of natural cycles. Evelyn offers an important georgic lesson in this passage: all successful cultivation must happen at the right time (and, as he and his ancient predecessors point out elsewhere, in the right place). In much georgic writing, the right time means the correct part of the year, but here Evelyn gestures towards the larger intersections between a human lifetime and the duration required to bring a tree up from a sapling into fruit. Without instruction from a work like *Sylva*, an otherwise capable propagator might wait until he becomes '*Wise*', and therefore will arrive too late to his task.

This way in which Evelyn couches his instructions – decide early to tend trees, and enjoy their fruits; but wait for inspiration late in life, and leave that pleasure to later generations – aligns with his larger advocacy for deliberate cultivation, rather than natural growth. In various moments, he recalls Virgil's passage on the differences between trees that spring up spontaneously in nature – 'sponte sua' (*Georgics*, II. 47) – and those planted and sown by the farmer. The natural trees harbor a special kind of strength and vitality – 'laeta et fortia surgunt' (*Georgics*, II. 48) – but they bear no fruit. In his Introduction, Evelyn advocates against simply tending to the 'spontaneous supply' of extant forests, urging instead an informed programme of '*Sowing*, or *Planting*'. He goes on to make the point even more explicitly:

> I do affirm upon *Experience*, that an *Acorn* sown by hand in a *Nursery*, or ground where it may be free from these encumbrances, shall in two or three Years out-strip a *Plant* of twice that age, which has either been self-sown in the *Woods*, or removed; unless it fortune, by some favourable accident, to have been scatter'd into a more natural, penetrable, and better qualified place.[16]

The 'encumbrances' Evelyn mentions here result from the randomness of natural growth; some seeds might sprout too close to one another, and others, dropped in less healthy soil, might not thrive. He leaves open the possibility that some, 'scatter'd' into 'better qualified place[s]' may well compete with their cultivated cousins, but insists upon the vitality of trees placed and tended purposefully. Such purpose, however, derives from learning, and the resulting '*Experience*', that a georgic openness to studying 'rerum causas' (*Georgics*, II. 490) – the causes of things – can yield. This notion that the happiest person is one who has achieved such learning, perhaps the *Georgics*' most important lesson, appears in the poem's second book, which is largely devoted to teaching the propagation of trees and vines.

The poet Abraham Cowley shared with his friend Evelyn concerns about the past, present and future of English cultivation, both for its own sake and for its significance for civic life more broadly. Early in his essay 'Of Agriculture', he advocates country life not least because it appears to foster peaceable temperaments. Drawing on conventions of rural peace and contentment, Cowley posits an idealistic vision of those who work the land; they are

> without dispute of all men the most quiet and least apt to be inflamed to the disturbance of the Common-wealth: their manner of Life inclines them, and Interest binds them to love Peace: In our late mad and miserable Civil

> Wars, all other Trades, even to the meanest, set forth whole Troopes … But I do not remember the Name of any one Husbandman who had so considerable a share in the twenty years ruine of his country, as to deserve the Curses of his Country-men.[17]

He also urges increased attention to the task of sharing agricultural knowledge with younger generations, lamenting that landed youth have too many dancing masters and too few teachers of farming:

> I could wish (but cannot in these times much hope to see it) that one Colledge in each University were erected, and appropriated to this study, as well as there are to Medecin, and the Civil Law … The business of these Professors should not be, as is commonly practised in other Arts, onely to read Pompous and Superficial Lectures out of *Virgils Georgickes*, *Pliny*, *Varro*, or *Columella*, but to instruct their Pupils in the whole Method and course of this study.[18]

As his translations and imitations indicate, Cowley fostered a deep appreciation for ancient writers, but here he appears concerned with the difference between more distanced, gentlemanly reading habits – which may or may not result in actual labour – and the application of practical agricultural knowledge in work on the land. This distinction, and Cowley's defence of what we might now call experiential learning, was gaining traction in other fields, too; in the next century, doctors whose training included clinical work at such universities as Edinburgh and Leiden began to rival their colleagues trained at Oxford and Cambridge, where curricula focused more on textual study.[19]

After contemplating politics and education, Cowley turns more explicitly to poetry, suggesting that not only does rural life foster peace, it also nourishes poetry. Taking up the georgic notion of planting in the right soil, he insists that cities 'will bear nothing but the Nettles and Thornes of *Satyre*', and for this reason, 'almost all Poets' choose to write far from the 'Vices and Vanities of the Grand World', taking up instead 'the innocent happiness of a retired Life'. A genealogy of agricultural poetry follows, moving through the Greeks and Romans, culminating in long praise for Horace, and setting the stage for various poems and translations. The first of these is a rendition of the 'o fortunatos nimium' passage from the second book of the *Georgics*, followed by a translation of Horace's 'beatus ille' epode; together, of course, these two poems lie at the heart of much English georgic writing in the later seventeenth century.[20] Cowley adds at least one new line to Virgil's passage; after rendering the poet's wish to know what drives all the wonders of nature – celestial movement, earthquakes, tides – he constructs a conclusion to this section with no basis in the Latin, describing these phenomena together as '*Varieties too regular for chance*'.[21] That Cowley would feel free to add or expand to the original text is not surprising; changes of this kind are typical of seventeenth-century translation. Yet I find this particular alteration remarkable because it appears meant to help us better understand the passage in which it appears; in other words, it constitutes a small additional act of teaching within an already didactic poem. In this way, the line points to the larger aims of the *Georgics* while also commenting on one relatively brief passage.[22] Cowley draws our attention to both the changeability and the orderliness of these natural occurrences. By noting that they can hardly happen by 'chance', he emphasizes the possibility of learning how and why they work. Ideas such as this one grant a sense of hopefulness to both the *Georgics* and georgic writing in general, even though such texts also point to the devastations of failure and mishap. In the Latin text, Virgil moves from this prayer for understanding to an admission that he may never gain it, and will have to accept appreciation for nature instead. Yet Cowley strengthens the poem's belief that we truly can come to know more deeply. This essay and the poems included with it are perhaps most valuable because they make clear the fact that to write 'Of Agriculture' in the seventeenth century is not simply to compose a husbandry manual. It means contemplating politics, history, morality, education and poetry, and it also invites the kind of conversation with the past that only translation can elicit.[23]

Is Paradise Georgic?

'Of Agriculture' is followed by 'The Garden', dedicated to Evelyn. Here Cowley writes that a garden to be tended was 'the first Gift' to man, 'first, ev'n before a Wife' (116.11). Evelyn begins his own *Kalendarium Hortense* with an acknowledgement of the perpetual work inherent even in tending to Paradise: 'As *Paradise* (though of *Gods* own *Planting*) had not been *Paradise* longer then the *Man* was put into it, to *Dress it and to keep it*; so, nor will our *Gardens* (as neer as we can contrive them to the resemblance of that blessed Abode) remain long in their *perfection*, unless they are also continually *cultivated*.'[24] Although often associated with pastoral, paradisical gardens and gardening elements of the georgic mode in this period as well. This was certainly the case for John Milton's conception of Eden in *Paradise Lost*. In his seminal account of a seventeenth-century 'georgic revolution', Low offers an exhaustive catalogue of specific allusions to the *Georgics* and instances of the term 'labour' in Milton's body of work, with sustained attention to the epic.[25] Notably, in Eden Adam and

Eve do not toil for their survival. That, tragically, comes later. Yet they are charged with maintaining the garden, and maintenance, any good reader of georgic writing will know, is a crucial aspect of rural work.

Our modern obsessions with productivity, innovation and disruption tend to elide the significance of custodial efforts, with sometimes disastrous effects. Yet Milton appears to have been keenly aware that maintenance is something to be respected and done with care. After all, Eve's interest in enhancing the productivity of her labour leads to the fateful argument and separation between her and Adam. Low suggests that she 'misinterprets the nature of the work she and Adam have to do, and Adam allows her to have her way; so both share the fault'.[26] Her desire to do more, rather than simply to keep up, suggests that the fall, in Milton's conception of it, is at least partly a georgic failure.[27] Saskia Cornes has advocated for an even stronger and more literally agricultural reading of the poem, urging us to interpret Adam and Eve's 'manuring' of Eden not in sanitized pastoral terms but rather as the very kind of earthy, arduous labour it would have indicated in the seventeenth century. For Cornes, reading in this way allows us to understand Eden 'as a place of eternity without stasis, a place upon which Adam and Eve might have left their godly mark'.[28]

Yet what about the labour that follows the fall? Although not set in a garden, *Paradise Regained* has attracted scholars with interests in georgic, not least because of its four-book structure and relatively frequent allusions to Virgilian poetry. For Low, *Paradise Regained* 'depicts the moment when, for the first time in history, georgic takes on a new and more hopeful significance, as the georgic spirit is given the power to bring Eden back within human reach'.[29] Writing both before and after Low's account, Louis L. Martz proposed georgic approaches to this poem, which has also frequently been characterized in epic terms. His essay of 2002, which makes a sustained case for reading *Paradise Regained* in conversation with the *Georgics*, remains especially valuable for scholars interested in questions of form and genre, particularly because it suggests ways in which epic and georgic need not be taken as mutually exclusive, and because makes a case early on for the notion that not all georgic writing needs to be expressly agricultural.[30]

Fundamentally, the relationship between Paradise and georgic is necessarily a vexed one, though the two concepts find themselves near one another again and again in this period. *Upon Appleton House* concludes with a meditation on Nun Appleton as a kind of Paradise as well. Although the idyllic aspects we associate with such spaces would seem at odds with the harsh realities of rural labour, perhaps paradises appear so often in proximity to georgic elements because of their inherent limitations. In its oldest etymological sense, a paradise is a walled garden, a place inherently circumscribed, and not an endless expanse. This boundedness is perhaps its most georgic aspect: Hesiod and Virgil understood well the limits of control over the land, and by extension, of control over any aspect of life. Hesiod frames the *Works and Days* as a corrective remedy for a failure that has already occurred, teaching his wayward brother how to work more successfully. By the end of Virgil's first georgic, things have spun out of control – devolving into war – but the poet returns them to order by starting over again at the beginning of the second book. The prospect of failure, memories of its various manifestations, and attempts to begin again run through most forms of georgic writing; perhaps these elements remind readers such as Marvell and Milton of paradises lost and regained. Ferry senses these links too, writing that despite the vast gulf of time separating Virgil and Milton:

> The presence of the *Georgics* in one's reading of *Paradise Lost*, and of *Paradise Lost* in one's reading of the *Georgics*, is powerfully felt throughout because these poems are our two great original responses to our common human knowledge, already expressed in the prior mythologies of Genesis and the stories of the Greeks – that we and the nature we inhabit are fallen, and that we must somehow bravely deal with this.[31]

At its best, translation reminds us of the generative power that texts bear within them. The best translators, such as Ferry, sense this capability in the works they render, as well as in those connected to them. The deliberate anachronism of his chiasmic formulation of these two great poems allows us to see the reasons why we remain fascinated by them, and why writers of all kinds perpetually rewrite, reimagine, and recast them as they confront the problems and questions of their own time.

Translating the *Georgics* at the Turn of the Century

In the 'Essay on the *Georgics*', placed before Dryden's translation of the poem in his *Works of Virgil* (1697), Joseph Addison complains in terms that will not be unfamiliar to modern students of georgic, noting that 'the *Georgics* are a Subject which none of the *Criticks* have sufficiently taken into their Consideration; most of 'em passing it over in silence, or casting it under the same head with *Pastoral*'.[32] Of course, from the later decades of the twentieth century onwards, scholarly study of the georgic has gained an ever-increasing momentum and, given the continued problem of climate change, seems poised to keep moving into a more central position. Outside the academy, however, the term 'georgic' means much less even to highly educated general readers than does 'epic' or 'pastoral'. Yet some encouraging signs of change have emerged: the short story collection *Georgic* (2010) by Mariko Nagai connects human beings, history, trauma and the land in rural Japan; it also includes a note expressly distinguishing 'georgic' from 'pastoral'. Nevertheless, 'georgic' remains a specialized term, and some of the work that lies ahead for scholars working in this area will involve making more outward turns, rather than talking only to one another.

In the 1690s, however, writers such as Addison and Dryden enjoyed – and sometimes suffered from – a very different set of assumptions about poetry and public life. To write was nearly always to address public concerns, and most public texts could be read in relation to ongoing political questions. Dryden's *Georgics* appeared at the end of a violent, fractious century and arrived charged with the political tensions of recent years. Having converted to Catholicism in the 1680s, Dryden was also among those who remained loyal to the exiled James II, rather than the new King William III, in the wake of the Glorious Revolution. According to Dryden's biographer James A. Winn, he and his publisher Jacob Tonson 'evidently believed that national pride in having a fine English Virgil would weigh more heavily with readers of all classes than the faith and politics of the translator'.[33] Both judged correctly: before its publication, the *Virgil* was highly anticipated by readers across the political and religious spectrums, and John Barnard has shown in painstaking detail the wide scope of first – or five-guinea – and second – two-guinea – subscribers to the volume. The full list includes Tories and Whigs, as well as a relatively high number of women; in addition to the aristocratic subscribers on the first list, the second included merchants, lawyers, actors, soldiers, tradesmen and others.[34]

This notion of a 'national' English-language Virgil marks a turning point in the history of georgic writing. Although the Latin *Georgics* celebrate Roman land and Rome's nascent imperial power, it is also very much a poem of civil war and social precarity. During the seventeenth century, georgic was put to various political uses, but cannot reliably be tracked as a 'national' mode or genre. Yet in the eighteenth century, this form would prove highly amenable to both a domestic poetics written in celebration of English agricultural production and a related, more outward-facing imperial poetics. Addison's 'Essay' enumerates many of the aspects that would come to define these newer georgics, yet it is appended to a text that is highly attuned to the political uncertainties woven through the Latin poem, and one written by a writer who could hardly be described as a supporter of the relentlessly militaristic ambitions of William III that marked the final years of the seventeenth century. As a result, the *Virgil* bears within it both a theory of georgic that would propel the mode forward into the next century and a translation that at every opportunity prefers to look back upon the challenges of recent English history, recruiting and expanding the original poem's darker strains along the way.

For instance, Addison frequently praises georgic poetry for its descriptive qualities.[35] Yet the didactic *Georgics* tend not to offer sustained observations of things as they are; instead, the posture of teaching leads Virgil, and his translator, to write in consistently subjunctive and imperative terms, suggesting what might be realized, not that which already exists. Whereas the descriptive mode inherently suggests a degree of confidence – it believes that things are stable enough to warrant description – the didactic mode bears within its minute grammatical details the possibility that even the most assiduous learning cannot by itself generate a secure outcome.[36] In this way, we might consider Dryden's translation to stand as a hinge between an older, looser georgic mode – which in England often tended to conjure up memories of or concerns about civil unrest – and a new, increasingly recognizable and definable genre that could be recruited to articulate a more coherent, and therefore imperially potent, national poetics. Although Dryden was well aware of his poetry's place in the larger political landscape, he concludes his translation with a clear sense that the work of a poet lies far away from that of the statesman. Following his typical practice of expanding the Latin, he renders Virgil's 'ignobilis oti' – inglorious or unknown leisure – as work marked by both 'peaceful Days' and 'less noisy Praise' (*Georgics*, IV. 816–17). At the close of the seventeenth century, three years before his death, Dryden lays the georgic down gently, letting it recede into the quiet of the countryside, separating it from the commotions of conquest.

Notes

1. Virgil, *Georgics* (Ferry), p. xv.
2. *Georgics* II. 490.
3. A. Low, *The Georgic Revolution* (Princeton University Press, 1985), p. 118.
4. F. E. Dolan, *Digging the Past: How and Why to Imagine Seventeenth-Century Agriculture* (University of Pennsylvania Press, 2020), p. 4.
5. Schoenberger, *Cultivating Peace: The Virgilian Georgic in English, 1650–1750* (Lewisburg: Bucknell University Press, 2019). I have discussed some aspects of the present essay in this monograph as well.
6. See C. W. Smith, *Empiricist Devotions: Science, Religion, and Poetry in Early Eighteenth-Century England* (University of Virginia Press, 2016), especially chapter 5, 'Georgic Realism, an Empirical-Devotional Poetics'.

7 For broader consideration of Marvell, ancient writers and his more immediate predecessors, see P. Davis, 'Marvell and the Literary Past', in *The Cambridge Companion to Andrew Marvell*, ed. D. Hirst and S. N. Zwicker (Cambridge University Press, 2010), pp. 26–45.
8 For a more expressly ecocritical reading of *Upon Appleton House* and the 'Mower' poems, see A. McRae, 'The Green Marvell', in *The Cambridge Companion to Andrew Marvell*, ed. Hirst and Zwicker, pp. 122–39.
9 *Miscellaneous Poems of Andrew Marvell* (1681), *Early English Books Online*, lines 329–44.
10 Headnote to *The Mower Poems* in A. Marvell, *The Poems of Andrew Marvell*, ed. N. Smith (Abingdon: Routledge, 2007), p. 128.
11 Marvell, *Poems of Marvell*, p. 129.
12 Marvell, *Poems of Marvell*, p. 130.
13 D. D. C. Chambers, 'Evelyn, John (1620–1706)', *ODNB*. See also Levine, 'Between Ancients and Moderns', in *John Evelyn's 'Elysium Britannicum' and European Gardening*, ed. T. O'Malley and J. Wolschke-Bulman (Washington, DC: Dumbarton Oaks, 1997); and G. Parry, 'John Evelyn', in *The Seventeenth Century: The Intellectual and Cultural Context of English Literature, 1603–1700* (Abingdon: Routledge, 1989).
14 John Evelyn, *Sylva, or A Discourse of Forest-trees, and the Propagation of Timber in His Majesties Dominions* (1670), sig. b2^r. The English translation, printed beside the Latin, appears in this edition; in 1644, only the Latin appears.
15 Evelyn, *Sylva*, sig. b^v–b2^r.
16 Evelyn, *Sylva*, p. 3.
17 A. Cowley, 'Of Agriculture', in *The Works of Mr. Abraham Cowley* (1668), pp. 99–100.
18 Cowley, 'Of Agriculture', pp. 101–2.
19 See M. H. Kaufman, *Medical Teaching in Edinburgh during the 18th and 19th Centuries* (Royal College of Surgeons of Edinburgh, 2003); and the prefatory materials in A. Budd, ed., *John Armstrong's 'The Art of Preserving Health': Eighteenth-Century Sensibility in Practice* (Farnham: Ashgate, 2011).
20 Further discussion of these translations, as well as the other poems included with 'Of Agriculture', appear in P. Davis, *Translation and the Poet's Life* (Oxford University Press, 2008), pp. 98–102, and D. Hopkins, *Conversing with Antiquity* (Oxford University Press, 2010), chapter 2.
21 Cowley, 'Of Agriculture', p. 40.
22 Davis reads this line much differently, describing it as a 'smugly rationalist axiom entirely contrary to the tone of the Virgilian passage and italicized for the benefit of readers looking to restock their commonplace books' (*Translation*, p. 101).
23 I draw this term from Hopkins, *Conversing with Antiquity*, see especially 'Introduction: Reception as Conversation'.
24 Evelyn, *Sylva*, p. 55.
25 See Low, *Georgic Revolution*, chapter 7. See also J. C. Pellicer, 'Virgil's *Georgics* II in *Paradise Lost*', *Translation and Literature*, 14 (2005), 129–47.

26 Low, *Georgic Revolution*, 320.
27 See K. Goodman, '"Wasted Labor"? Milton's Eve, the Poet's Work, and the Challenge of Sympathy', *ELH*, 64 (1997), 415–46, and S. Lobis, 'Milton's Tended Garden and the Georgic Fall', *Milton Studies*, 55 (2014), 89–111.
28 S. Cornes, 'Milton's Manuring: Paradise Lost, Husbandry, and the Possibilities of Waste', *Milton Studies*, 61, 1 (2019), p. 66. For an extensive reading of Milton's paradise and its connections to labour of various forms, see J. Picciotto, *Labors of Innocence in Early Modern England* (Cambridge, MA: Harvard University Press, 2010), especially chapter 6, 'Milton and the Paradizable Reader'.
29 Low, *Georgic Revolution*, 322.
30 L. L. Martz, '"*Paradise Regained*": Georgic Form, Georgic Style', *Milton Studies*, 42 (2002), pp. 7–25.
31 Virgil, *Georgics* (Ferry), xvii.
32 J. Addison, 'An Essay on the Georgics', in Virgil, *Georgics* (Dryden), p. 145.
33 J. A. Winn, *John Dryden and His World* (New Haven: Yale University Press, 1987), p. 475.
34 J. Barnard, 'Dryden, Tonson, and the Patrons of *The Works of Virgil* (1697)', in *John Dryden: Tercentenary Essays*, ed. P. Hammond and D. Hopkins (Oxford University Press, 2000), pp. 174–239. See also Winn, *Dryden*, p. 475.
35 For an account of specific distinctions between seventeenth-century georgic writing and eighteenth-century descriptive georgic, see Smith, *Empiricist Devotions*, pp. 174–80.
36 For thorough introductions to classical didactic poetry, see M. Gale, *Virgil on the Nature of Things: The Georgics, Lucretius, and the Didactic Tradition* (Cambridge University Press, 2000), and A. Dalzell, *The Criticism of Didactic Poetry: Essays on Lucretius, Virgil, and Ovid* (University of Toronto Press, 1996).

CHAPTER 7

Enlightenment, Improvement and Experimentation
Jethro Tull and His Contemporaries

Frans De Bruyn

In 1733 Jethro Tull published *The Horse-Hoing Husbandry, or, An Essay on the Principles of Tillage and Vegetation*, a pioneering work of agronomy that outlined an innovative system of mechanical tillage and crop production involving drill husbandry (planting seeds in rows), intensive cultivation of the soil and a minimal use of manure. To implement his system, Tull developed a mechanical seed drill; a horse-hoe or cultivator, to work the soil between the drills or rows of plants; and a four-coultered plough, to prepare the soil for planting. He also developed a theory of plant nutrition to explain the superior efficacy (as he believed) of his 'new husbandry'. Earth, he maintained, was the sole food of plants, and the more finely the soil was divided or pulverized by his horse-hoe, the better plants would absorb nutrients and flourish.

The appearance of *The Horse-Hoing Husbandry* marks an important chapter in the history of agricultural science, but Tull's treatise was destined also to figure in the history of georgic writing owing to his inclusion of a scathing analysis of Virgil's advice on tillage in the first *Georgic* (lines 43–101), which Tull with polemical flair entitled, 'Remarks on the Bad Husbandry, that is so finely Express'd in Virgil's First Georgic'. After subjecting Virgil's precepts on soil cultivation to withering scrutiny, Tull concluded that no scheme of husbandry could be worse, and with a parting shot, he named his new system at the poet's expense: 'Mine Differing from [Virgil's field husbandry] in all respects, warrants me in calling it *anti-Virgilian*.'[1]

A response to Tull's heretical rejection of Virgil was not long in coming. Landscape designer and seedsman Stephen Switzer, styling himself the spokesperson for a 'Society of Husbandmen and Planters', used the final two numbers of a short-lived publication, *The Practical Husbandman and Planter* (1733–4), as a platform for a furious counter-attack on Tull. '[W]ith what Face', demanded Switzer, 'can any Modern Author take upon him to say, that there is not a good Line in all *Virgil's* Works, which relate to Husbandry? Or have the Arrogance to affirm that after a serious Perusal … *they are fit for nothing, but to be laid on a Hand-barrow, and thrown on the Fire?*[2] Switzer's vindication of Virgil's agricultural expertise elicited, in turn, a minute, point-by-point rebuttal from Tull, published in 1736 as *A Supplement to the Essay on Horse-Hoing Husbandry*.

The controversy over Virgil's credentials as an agriculturalist reverberated down the century, with numerous interventions on both sides. In his 1742 translation of the *Georgics*, for example, James Hamilton reaffirmed that notwithstanding Tull's efforts 'to lessen the Esteem of ancient Writers … the World owes the Principles of Agriculture more to *Virgil*, than any who have wrote thereupon for many Ages bypast'. Some two decades later, Walter Harte, while acknowledging the value of Tull's innovations in drill husbandry, sought nonetheless to counter anew the latter's aspersions of Virgil: 'Let the praise therefore of truly correct and spirited writings, in matters of husbandry, remain intirely in the possession of *Virgil* without a rival … For his *Georgics* to this very day are the groundwork of all *Italian* agriculture, and his rules and precepts are followed (traditionally at least) by those who never read him, or heard of him.'[3] As late as the year 1801, a dissenting voice testified to the continuing currency of the debate over Virgil's qualifications: 'I cannot forbear smiling at the idea, that the study of Virgil's *Bucolics* and *Georgics* should be seriously recommended … as likely to improve the modern modes of breeding cattle, or growing corn and turneps.'[4]

Though the full story of this controversy cannot be rehearsed here, it illustrates vividly the scope and ambition of georgic writing in the eighteenth century and the cultural and intellectual weight it enjoyed.[5] No literary period before or since exhibits a like range of experimentation with the georgic form: from translations and formal imitations of the Virgilian original, along with more free-wheeling poetic variations, such as loco-descriptive poems, poems of rural retirement, and didactic treatments of other disciplines and pursuits; to prose essays, pamphlets, treatises, periodicals and technical manuals. Though various in form and purpose, these texts declare their georgic affiliation by the tropes and themes they employ and by the structure of feeling they evoke. This protean richness of the georgic in the eighteenth century is, accordingly, the subject of this chapter: not only the genre's connection with a culture of agricultural and technical innovation, but also its co-optation by writers with a wide range of thematic preoccupations, including (among others) labour, sport, human health, mining, manufacturing, empire, nationhood, political economy and slavery. The georgic, in David Fairer's words, 'offered the eighteenth century not only a poetic model but also a way of thinking about culture, economics, and modernity'.[6]

This diversity of thematic and formal uses in the period reflects the georgic's flexibility as a literary mode, but that very variety complicates a consideration of what counts as georgic writing in the eighteenth century. One indication is what authors themselves signalled about their generic choices, whether through their titles, paratextual statements, or allusions and other textual gestures. Alexander Hunter, for example, a founding member of the York Agricultural Society, titled his collection of agricultural articles *Georgical Essays*, and in his introductory essay on the origins of agriculture, he placed Virgil prominently in the company of ancient agricultural writers. Alluding to Virgil's oft-cited praise of country life in the second *Georgic* (lines 458–512), Hunter advises the 'busy courtier to retire into the country, where he will find peace and plenty. Instead of hunting a shadow through the mazes of a court, bid him leave his ribbon where he found it, and join Hesiod and Mago, Virgil and Cato, from whom one honest look is worth all the smiles of the drawing-room.'[7] In another instance, Alexander Blackwell ascribed to Columella and Virgil whatever 'Merit' his 1741 book on the improvement of wet, clayey, and barren soils might possess: 'In treating this Part of Husbandry, I have followed *Columella* and *Virgil* … believing that in what they say on this Head they are much more judicious and better to be relied on than most of the Moderns.'[8] Blackwell's text confirms his declaration. Of the book's fourteen chapters, seven begin with epigraphs taken from the *Georgics*, and specific passages and precepts in Virgil's poem are cited along the way (and in one instance subjected to detailed analysis) to support the author's recommended techniques for improving barren terrain.[9]

These explicit invocations of the *Georgics* in prose texts have their poetic counterpart in the formal georgics of John Philips (*Cyder*, 1708), John Armstrong (*The Art of Preserving Health*, 1744), Christopher Smart (*The Hop-Garden*, 1752), Robert Dodsley (*Agriculture*, 1753), John Dyer (*The Fleece*, 1757), James Grainger (*The Sugar-Cane*, 1764) and others. These poets declare their generic allegiance by rehearsing and adapting passages in the *Georgics* that were widely acknowledged to be standard set-pieces of the form; for example, the account of agriculture's origins (*Georgics*, I. 118–46), the farmer's calendar or rota of the seasons (*Georgics*, I. 204–350), the praise of the poet's native land (*Georgics*, II. 136–76), the 'happy husbandmen' passage extolling the virtues of country life ('O fortunatos nimium', *Georgics*, II. 459–540), and the interpolated narrative or episode (e.g., the story of Aristaeus, *Georgics*, IV. 315–558).

Beyond such direct invocations of Virgil's poem, a deeper sense of the period's engagement with georgic can be gained by identifying some of the key features that defined the genre for writers and critics at the time – and locating these in contexts not perhaps immediately recognizable to us as georgic. When eighteenth-century writers engaged with the georgic, they did so in ways that reflected their personal, professional and intellectual commitments. Ralph Cohen describes how they adapted and redefined existing formal features to serve new literary ends:

> With regard to the georgic poem, for example, new perceptual techniques are introduced and new subjects are pursued. The georgic poem not only reveals new functions for poetic features so that these become, in time, new conventions, but the form as a whole urges on its readers a new way of responding. Not only is rationalistic and commercial imagery introduced, not only is perception of nature made primary, but these innovations socialize a form that had up to that time been emblematic.[10]

An example of the process Cohen outlines here is Virgil's panegyric on his native land in *Georgics*, II. 136–76, an emblematized survey of Italy's landscape that emphasizes the blessings of its topography, climate, resources and fertility. In poems such as Alexander Pope's *Windsor-Forest* (1713), James Thomson's *The Seasons* (1726–46) and Richard Jago's *Edge-Hill* (1767, 1784), Virgil's rhetorical set-piece, structurally a digression in his poem, reappears in the form of a prospect survey: a description of an actual landscape seen from an identifiable vantage point. As a generic feature, the prospect survey in these topographical poems has been elevated in importance to become structurally central. In the process, a native poetic tradition, originating with John Denham's *Coopers Hill* (1642, 1668), is fused with the georgic to produce one of the eighteenth century's most characteristic poetic forms: a hybrid, descriptive amalgam of georgic and landscape poetry.

In their authorial practice and their critical claims, eighteenth-century georgic writers focus repeatedly on an interrelated cluster of concerns. The first of these is a notable self-consciousness about stylistic means and ends in georgically inspired writing. Closely related to this is the georgic's rhetorical miscellaneity, variously described in terms of its variety and structural digressiveness. These two writerly preoccupations find a correlative in the theme of labour, a recurrent subject that addresses both physical and intellectual activity, and resonates with moral, political and economic implications. The Virgilian georgic's cyclical rhythms, moreover, manifested in the seasonality of the agricultural year and the time-honoured wisdom, lore and arts of the farmer, are challenged by a gathering pace of change in the Enlightenment. Tradition and experience come face to face with a drive to experiment, and cyclical time, with its immemorial repetition, is challenged by an ideology of progress and improvement. In each of these instances, as will appear in the following sections, can be discerned a dynamic process of generic adaptation and transformation in Enlightenment georgic writing.

'Answerable Style'

Joseph Addison's 'Essay on the *Georgics*' (1697), as Juan Christian Pellicer pertinently observes, 'placed the issue of poetic decorum at the head of the georgic agenda for the entire eighteenth century'.[11] '[T]he Precepts of Husbandry', declares Addison, 'are not to be deliver'd with the simplicity of a Plow-Man, but with the Address of a Poet'.[12] The georgic poet must 'be careful of not letting his Subject debase his Stile, and betray him into a meanness of Expression, but every where to keep up his Verse in all the Pomp of Numbers, and Dignity of Words'. Virgil is so successful in this that 'He delivers the meanest of his Precepts with a kind of Grandeur, he breaks the Clods and tosses the Dung about with an air of gracefulness'.[13]

In his essay, Addison elaborates on the verbal means Virgil uses to preserve his lines 'from sinking into a plebian style': these include 'metaphors, Grecisms, and circumlocutions, to give his verse the greater pomp'.[14] If one substitutes 'Latinisms' for 'Grecisms' (or more specifically, a Latinate style mediated by Milton), Addison's inventory accurately anticipates the stylistic repertoire of the eighteenth-century formal georgic. A striking illustration of this is the poetic treatment of that lowest of subjects: manure. On several occasions, poets in the period rose to the challenge implicit in Addison's praise of Virgil's stylistic virtuosity in writing of dung.[15] William Cowper is a case in point; in the third book of *The Task* ('The Garden'), he describes the winter-time cultivation of cucumbers, beginning with an account of the growing medium to be used: 'a stercoraceous heap | Impregnated with quick fermenting salts'.[16] Cowper gives detailed instructions for building a glass-covered hot-bed in which the manure is laid, where it is left to ferment for three days:

> When, behold!
> A pestilent and most corrosive steam,
> Like a gross fog Boeotian, rising fast,
> And fast condensed upon the dewy sash,
> Asks egress; which obtained, the overcharged
> And drench'd conservatory breathes abroad,

> In volumes wheeling slow, the vapor dank,
> And purified, rejoices to have lost
> Its foul inhabitant.[17]

The Latinate language Cowper employs is simultaneously Miltonic and proto-scientific: the 'foul inhabitant' ejected from the fermenting manure bed is both a hellish serpent, evoked by the wheeling 'volumes' or coils of the vapour, and a product of a chemical reaction. Either way, the diction is heavily periphrastic, exposing an opposition between the demands of poetic decorum and the ostensible didactic purposes of georgic poetry. Verbal elaborateness such as this is not a medium for plain communication and instruction.

Cowper's highly wrought verses hark back to the earliest of the blank verse georgics, John Philips's *Cyder* (1708), which pioneered Miltonic imitation as the characteristic voice of English georgic, an idiom mediating heroic and didactic verbal registers. As regards subject matter, the georgic poets of mid-century were in general more frank than Cowper in their embrace of 'low' concerns, practices and processes, but a certain embarrassment about modes of address remained, as evidenced in James Grainger's approach to the subject of composts:

> Of composts shall the Muse descend to sing,
> Nor soil her heavenly plumes? The sacred Muse
> Nought sordid deems, but what is base; nought fair
> Unless true Virtue stamp it with her seal.[18]

Grainger does not shy away from naming forthrightly the ingredients of an efficacious compost – 'ashes … weeds, mould, dung, and stale' – but he does so only after signalling his awareness that he is stooping here to low, unpoetic diction.[19] Joseph Warton summed up the problem in the dedication to his 1753 translation of the *Georgics*: 'the coarse and common words I was necessitated to use … viz. *plough and sow, wheat, dung, ashes, horse and cow*, &c. will, I fear, unconquerably disgust many a delicate reader'.[20]

Stylistic self-reflexiveness is, thus, a key generic marker of georgic writing. In Virgil's first *Georgic*, this authorial self-reflexiveness is figured by an analogy the poet draws between the husbandman's duty to work his fields until the 'plow blade shines as the furrow rubs against it', and the poet's responsibility (in a pun on the Latin word *versus*, which designates both 'furrow' and 'verse') to produce burnished verses that gleam in their expression.[21] An early commentary on the *Georgics* glossed this passage (I. 43–6) with a citation from Cato's advice to his son: 'You can still tell a good farmer by the shine on his tools.'[22]

The same stylistic self-awareness, as writers consider the task of writing in the process of performing it, characterizes the period's prose scientific treatises and technical manuals on husbandry. A case in point is Tull's Preface to *The New Horse-Houghing Husbandry* (1731), in which he excuses the inelegance of his prose in words that knowingly dismantle Virgil's poetic analogy between ploughing and poetry: 'I hope the Farmer will not regard the Roughness of the Stile; because he knows a Plough will go never the better for being polish'd.' Skilful husbandry and fine writing are, in fact, mutually exclusive activities: 'Writing and Ploughing are two different Talents; and he that writes well, must have spent in his Study that time, which is necessary to be spent in the Fields, by him who will be Master of the Art of Cultivating them.'[23] In his translation of the *Georgics*, Hamilton similarly invokes (and inverts) Virgil's conceit, as he excuses the inelegance of his appended remarks: 'I have not made the Choice of Words and Connexion so much my Study, as to render what I have wrote useful, not designing so much to shew elaborate Pages, as desiring to see well laboured Ridges.'[24]

Such meta-reflection on standards of linguistic decorum persisted. In 1775, James Anderson introduced his *Essays Relating to Agriculture and Rural Affairs* with a lengthy reflection on the linguistic register appropriate to his subject: 'Purity of language will not be looked for in a treatise of this nature … It is the matter rather than the form that ought to constitute the principal merit of every didactic performance.' Instead of striving for 'a classical elegance of language', he aims at unornamented clarity.[25] Classical purity implies diction uncontaminated by dialectal peculiarities or the technical jargon of a profession or trade, but Anderson defends the necessity of using 'provincial words' and terms of art for the sake of precision. He is just as sensitive to stylistic ways and means as any georgic poet, but in his *Essays*, as in the agrarian texts of numerous contemporaries, the polarities of literary value laid down by Addison have been reversed, and a key feature of the Virgilian georgic is realigned with new intellectual and professional priorities. Anderson's rejection of rhetorical polish echoes the preference given by the new science to 'res' over 'verba', as in Thomas Sprat's call in *History of the Royal Society* (1667) for a return to a 'primitive purity, and shortness' of style, 'when men deliver'd so many *things*, almost in an equal number of *words*'.[26]

Yet, the agricultural writers did not entirely succeed in liberating themselves from Latinisms and circumlocutions. If Cowper has recourse to the Latinate 'stercoraceous' to describe dung poetically, it is on account of the medical and agricultural writers who introduced this term into English in the mid-eighteenth century. Despite his protestations against unduly learned diction, Tull struggled to explain his theoretical concepts without it. His explanation of how plant roots absorb minute particles of soil is almost comical in its Latinate prolixity: 'The Mouths, or Lacteals, being situate, and opening in the convex Superfices of Roots, they take their Pabulum, being fine particles of Earth, from the Superficies of the Pores, or Cavities, wherein the Roots are included.'[27] Such language met with Arthur Young's disapproval in the 1760s, as he set out on his career as advocate for agricultural improvement. Young felt compelled, in one instance, to censure an otherwise admirable essay on soil improvement for its 'cramp, barbarous terms', many of them borrowed directly from Tull, and he reminds georgical writers that 'one simple rational experiment is worth ten elegantly-flowing periods'.[28]

'Labor Omnia Vicit': Georgic Labour

Another feature of the Virgilian georgic that underwent a significant alteration in the eighteenth century is Virgil's emphasis on the toilsomeness of georgic labour. The arts themselves, we are told, are the products of unending toil, ordained by Jove, the father of the gods, to stimulate human ingenuity: 'Then followed other arts; and everything | Was toil, relentless toil, urged on by need'.[29] Here, too, an analogy is drawn between the farmer and the poet: the art of poetry, we are told, is just as arduous as the art of agriculture. Thus, at a point of transition in the third *Georgic*, when Virgil turns to the culture of sheep and goats, he emphasizes the heroic difficulty of what he is about to undertake:

> Now it is time
> To turn away from the herds and undertake
> My other task, the care of my woolly flock
> And shaggy goats. The task is hard, and so,
> You sturdy shepherds, the fame would be hard won
> And well deserved. Nor am I ignorant
> Of the magnitude of the work of conquering
> A theme like this with words, and winning glory
> When the subject is so lowly.[30]

The Virgilian parallel between the poet's and the countryman's labours may strike the present-day reader as facile, given the picture Virgil himself draws of the farmer's unremitting struggle against entropic forces of nature. Eighteenth-century imitators of Virgil were not unaware of the ironies implicit in the comparison. In *The Thresher's Labour*, Stephen Duck presents the unending, cyclical toil of agricultural work from the perspective of the day-labourer, for whom the annual feast marking the end of the harvest is a chimeric culmination: 'the next Morning soon reveals the Cheat, | When the same Toils we must again repeat'. The cycle of the seasons that orders the farmer's life is for the labourer a recurring nightmare:

> Thus, as the Year's revolving Course goes round,
> No respite from our Labour can be found:
> Like *Sisyphus*, our Work is never done,
> Continually rolls back the restless Stone.[31]

The change in voice and point of view is decisive. The Virgilian farmer in the *Georgics* is a mute figure, to say nothing of Roman labourers or slaves, who remain altogether out of view. Though sympathetic to the husbandman, Virgil views him from above, and he aligns himself with Caesar, whom the poetic speaker invites to join him in pitying the untutored farmer groping to find his way (*Georgics*, I. 41). Whereas Virgil plays with the fiction that he is the expert, set to enlighten readers and ignorant husbandmen, Duck gives voice to the inarticulate, those who actually live the labours of cultivation and experience with their bodies the 'care' ('cura') that Virgil repeatedly urges the farmer to embrace.

In *Cyder*, book 1, Philips gives a facetious account of his laborious research into the improved breeding and propagation of fruit trees, signalling his awareness that equating didactic and physical labour exposes the georgic poet to mock-heroic diminishment. The conceit he invokes, of burning the midnight oil as an emblem of toil, echoes Dryden's translation of Virgil's transition in the third *Georgic* – 'Nor can I doubt what Oyl I must bestow, | To raise my Subject from a Ground so low' – but the glory to be won comes across now, in Philips's lines, as mock-heroic:

> lo! thoughtful of Thy Gain,
> Not of my Own, I all the live-long Day
> Consume in Meditation deep, recluse
> From human Converse, nor, at shut of Eve,
> Enjoy Repose; but oft at Midnight Lamp
> Ply my brain-racking Studies, if by chance
> Thee I may counsel right; and oft this Care
> Disturbs me slumbring. Wilt thou then repine
> To labour for thy Self? and rather chuse
> To lye supinely, hoping, Heav'n will bless
> Thy slighted Fruits, and give thee Bread unearn'd?[32]

The word 'care' in this passage carries the full weight of Virgil's 'cura', meaning serious, heedful attention (taking pains, assuming responsibility, undertaking toil, experiencing mental burdens) but the disturbance of the writer's sleep occasioned by his care appears inconsequentially comical, and his questioning reproof of the reader's indolence is merely playful.

The diversity of subjects addressed in eighteenth-century georgics meant that labour came to be reimagined in unexpected ways. When John Armstrong announces 'exercise' as the subject of the third book of *The Art of Preserving Health*, his transition once again invokes the trope of poetic labour, in echo of Virgil and Philips, but he then strikes off in a new direction. Pausing at the beginning of book 3, Armstrong reviews the 'various toils th' adventurous muse' has accomplished, and he notes that 'half the toil, and more than half, remains'. To advise those in delicate health, the poet compromises his own: 'for you | I tame my youth to philosophic cares, | And grow still paler by the midnight lamps'. By contrast, 'the labourer of the glebe', who 'knows no laws by Esculapius given' and 'studies none', enjoys rude health, immune to the 'midnight fogs' that 'infest' the poet: 'By health the peasant's toil | Is well repaid'.[33]

'Toil, and be strong' is Armstrong's watchword, but toil in *Preserving Health* is reconceived as exercise. 'Go, climb the mountain', he advises his readers, recommending vigorous walks and rural sports, such as hunting, shooting, and angling, or proposing gardening as a domesticated version of farming (*Georgics*, III. 39, 57). Armstrong's meditation on exercise falls in with a lively corpus of eighteenth-century poetry that adapted the georgic to the celebration of rural sports. In the poetry of sport, georgic labour or difficulty is reconceived as the artificial constraints imposed on an activity to make it sporting (such as using artificial flies in angling instead of the nets employed by subsistence fishers). The georgic lineage of these poems is acknowledged in the opening lines of Thomas Scott's *The Anglers* (1758):

> But books or bus'ness, with unpausing care,
> What force of body or of mind can bear?
> The steed, unharness'd from the plow awhile,
> Returns with spirit to his rural toil.
> Sports (like parentheses) may part the Line
> Of labour, without breaking the design.[34]

Sport is here placed within the archetypal georgic scene of agricultural labour, which defines it by antithesis and circumscribes it, for 'sport cannot properly be enjoyed without its opposite, work'.[35]

The most consequential transformation of georgic toil in the eighteenth century, however, occurred at a deeper conceptual level. In the world of the georgic, work is embedded in a cyclical, tradition-bound experience of time and nature. Ceaseless work is the only remedy for a natural world that continuously deteriorates: 'All things by nature are ready to get worse, | Lapse backward, fall away from what they were'.³⁶ In such a world, as both Hesiod and the biblical writer of *Ecclesiastes* advise, every task has its appointed, propitious time or season. This, David Fairer explains, 'is not a matter of personal observation or empirical experience, but rather of "experience" as an inherited body of knowledge based on patterns of repetition, cause and effect, trial and error'.³⁷ Unremitting work is necessary when nature withholds her gifts, but it is also virtuous and even redemptive.

Early eighteenth-century English georgics echo, for the most part, this georgic ethic of 'frugality and self-limitation', as Claire Bucknell terms it, but by mid-century a growing literature of agricultural improvement challenged these constraints, and a new, more forward-looking outlook among agricultural improvers found itself reflected back into the poetic georgics of the 1750s and 1760s. Thus, in *The Fleece*, Dyer affirms that 'much may be perform'd, to check the force | Of Nature's rigour ... | Moors, bogs, and weeping fens, may learn to smile'. The improvers insisted that toil, in alliance with art, could break the cycle of repetition that typified the world of the georgic farmer:

>   'Tis art and toil
>   Gives nature value, multiplies her stores
>   Varies, improves, creates ...
>   What changes cannot toil,
>   With patient art, effect?³⁸

Work, for Dyer (and for Dodsley), as Bucknell notes in citing this passage, is no longer 'a simple matter of cooperating with circumstance and making the best of a bad job, in the way of Hesiod and Virgil's sense of necessary dissatisfaction; instead, it succeeds because it transforms pre-existing conditions and makes its own opportunities'.³⁹

In the latter part of the century, georgic activity, including labour, was increasingly conceptualized in economic rather than ethical terms. The gradual merging of the discourse of georgic into that of economics is illustrated by Adam Smith's *The Wealth of Nations*, a classic of economic theory that, Kurt Heinzelman argues, can also be read as 'the last georgic'.⁴⁰ In his treatise, Smith singles out agriculture as economically foundational: the 'cultivation and improvement of the country', on which society depends for its subsistence, 'must, necessarily, be prior to the increase of the town'.⁴¹ Investment in land is more secure and satisfying than investment in manufactures or trade, and Smith extends this 'predilection' to the work of the farmer, which harnesses not only the productivity of 'labouring servants' and 'labouring cattle', but also that of nature herself, who 'labours along with man' (II.v.12).

Tellingly, Smith celebrates this economic primacy in affective terms drawn directly from Virgil:

> The beauty of the country besides, the pleasure of a country life, the tranquillity of mind which it promises, and wherever the injustice of human laws does not disturb it, the independency which it really affords, have charms that more or less attract everybody; and as to cultivate the ground was the original destination of man, so, in every stage of his existence he seems to retain a predilection for this primitive employment.[42]

This idealization of georgic labour recalls the poet's well-known praise of country life in the second *Georgic*, as well as his story of the Corycian swain (*Georgics*, IV. 125–46), whose cultivation of an unpromising patch of ground makes him as content and independent as any king. Glaringly absent from these pictures is any hint of the slave labour upon which Roman agriculture relied in Virgil's time. 'The astonishing thing about the *Georgics*', notes L. P. Wilkinson, 'is that in the whole poem there is no reference to slavery'.[43] This circumstance puts into perspective James Grainger's decision, in writing *The Sugar-Cane*, to address at length the employment of African slaves in Caribbean sugar cultivation (in book, IV). Grainger's poem disturbs us with its problematic treatment of enslaved labour, but its departure in this respect from its Virgilian model, which elides the subject altogether, is in the eighteenth-century context an act of boldness.[44]

Miscellaneity and Georgic Variety

Addison identifies variety, artful digressiveness and indirection as key features of the Virgilian georgic. These poetic qualities work on the reader psychologically: by merely hinting at a precept or lesson, Virgil engages the understanding, 'which is always delighted with its own Discoveries ... and seems to work out the rest by the strength of her own faculties'. This engagement of the reader in a process of discovery, relieved from time to time (for mental respite) by 'a pleasant and pertinent digression', is the georgic's chief source of aesthetic pleasure. Addison contrasts how prose and poetry operate on the mind. Unlike the georgic poet, the prose writer 'tells us plainly what ought to be done': the rationale of prose is to 'range and dispose [a] body of precepts into a clear and easy method'.[45] The term 'method' here means systematic arrangement, both a logical ordering of ideas for the exposition of a subject and, in logic's rhetorical counterpart, an orderly disposition of topics and ideas in writing.

Yet such 'methods' in scientific writing are illusory; they convey a false sense of certainty and completeness about what we know. In the *Novum Organum*, Francis Bacon had warned against the presentation of scientific subjects 'as if they were in all parts complete and finished'. Methods or systematic arrangements create subject divisions that look impressive but upon closer inspection are nothing more than 'empty cases', since little or nothing may be known about them. In the place of totalizing presentations of knowledge, Bacon champions aphorisms, 'short and scattered sentences, not linked to each other by a rhetorical method of presentation', for, as he explains in *The Advancement of Learning*, 'aphorisms, representing a knowledge broken, do invite men to enquire further; whereas Methods carrying the shew of a total, do secure men, as if they were at furthest'.[46]

What connects Bacon's advocacy of the aphorism (as well as his later adoption of the miscellaneous form of the silva) with Virgilian variety and digressiveness is an underlying conception of miscellaneity as a principle of literary form. This miscellaneity functions quite differently in prose treatises on agriculture than it does in formal georgic poetry. In Alexander Pope's *Windsor-Forest*, for instance, the variety of the Thames Valley landscape reflects a conception of natural and cosmic order characterized by diversity, multiplicity, and plenitude:

> Here Hills and Vales, the Woodland and the Plain,
> Here Earth and Water seem to strive again,
> Not *Chaos*-like together crush'd and bruis'd,
> But as the World, harmoniously confus'd:
> Where Order in Variety we see,
> And where, tho' all things differ, all agree.[47]

The poet guides the reader's eye spatially and encourages reflection, enacting the empirical premises of an eighteenth-century epistemology that understood sensation, perception and mental reflection as the sources of human understanding. *Windsor-Forest* illustrates Addison's conception of georgic miscellaneity, which is aesthetic and reader-centred.

In agricultural writing and other scientific forms of expression, by contrast, miscellaneity is embraced as a rhetorical strategy for avoiding premature synthesis and as a model for productive scientific thinking, which is incremental, experimental and subject to revision. Reconceiving miscellaneity in this way signals a commitment to a new understanding of knowledge and its acquisition: it represents, in effect, an epistemological transformation. John Mills articulates this commitment in the preface to his *Essays Moral, Philosophical, and Political* (1772), in which he decries 'the spirit of system as one of the greatest obstacles to the progress of our knowledge'. The precipitate urge to synthesize 'makes men adopt arbitrary *data*, which will be exploded by posterity'. Sciences founded on experience and observation can advance only by a process of ongoing 'continued analysis'; accordingly, Mills recommends that writers who seek after truth should '[treat] their subjects in small detached essays', a genre avowedly modest and miscellaneous in its ambition, whose very name (from the French *essai*) means 'attempt'. In this spirit, he casts the discussion of agriculture in his treatise in the form of an essay, for, as he writes, 'we cannot see into nature, but by little and little, and by parts'.[48]

James Anderson likewise adopts the tentative form of the essay in his treatise on agriculture, and he meditates at some length on his rationale for so doing. Vanity and excess of imagination have too often led agricultural writers to make unfounded claims to certainty and comprehensiveness, vices that Anderson vows to curb in himself by reporting only such observations as are 'the result of his own experience'. Successful georgic writing is an exercise in self-knowledge, inculcating a modest awareness of the limits of one's abilities and the scope of one's experience. In this spirit, he claims to have 'followed no other plan but to mark down with candour such facts relating to the subjects that he has treated of, as he knew could be relied upon, or such observations as naturally flowed from these; without ever once proposing to give a complete treatise on any one subject'.[49]

For Mills and Anderson, the concept of miscellaneity has come to mean something quite different from the structures of variety and digressiveness characteristic of eighteenth-century georgic and loco-descriptive poetry. Yet generic memory has a way of reasserting itself, as is evidenced in the agricultural surveys or tours of Arthur Young, which revert in interesting ways to eighteenth-century poetic precedent. In the preface to *A Six Months Tour through the North of England* (1771), Young apologizes 'for introducing so many descriptions of houses, paintings, ornamented parks, lakes, &c.'. With an eye, perhaps, to broadening the audience for his publications, Young invokes a rationale for textual variety grounded in georgic pleasure and didacticism: 'Every reader does not seek for the same entertainment, some hastily pass over every page that is not dedicated to ploughing and sowing, – others quickly turn over every leaf that concerns husbandry, and dwell alone on the description of houses and gardens, – and not a few, perhaps, who seek the latter, are accidentally led to more useful passages, and become undesignedly acquainted with agriculture.'[50]

Young offers another reason for his inclusion of passages that would seem to appeal more to the tourist than the agriculturalist: 'I am sensible they have little to do with agriculture, but there is, nevertheless, an utility in their being known. They are a proof, and a very important one, of the riches and the happiness of this kingdom.'[51] Young's language here – 'utility', 'riches', 'happiness' – is that of the economist; indeed, his agricultural 'Tours' signal a generic transition at the end of the century from georgic to a nascent social science of statistics. One way to infer that the agricultural practices of a district are scientific and productive is to look for visible signs of the wealth derived from those practices. The physical appearance of Young's printed pages, in which his descriptive accounts appear as substantial footnotes to his collections of facts, lists and statistical data, illustrates a movement 'from observed particulars, at the top of the page, to a broader discursive context, at the bottom'.[52]

The Muse of Sage Experience: From Experience to Experiment

William Marshall, a contemporary of Young and a rival writer on agriculture, was insistent that agriculture, as a branch of 'natural philosophy', had to be first and foremost an experimental science. He laments, in *Minutes of Agriculture* (1783), that it has instead become '*the hobby-horse of Projectors*, and *the catch-penny of Booksellers*' – a mere '*playmate of Taste*' or 'chit-chat Companion to the FINE ARTS and BELLES LETTRES'. A footnote makes clear that the 'playmate of Taste' Marshall has in mind is Young himself: 'Whoever will look into the celebrated TOURS, may see Corn-Sheaves, Sculpture, and Carrots; Bullocks, Belles Lettres, and Burnet; Paintings, Pigs, and Picturesque Views.'[53] Marshall's dismissal of Young's agricultural publications is as much a literary judgement as a methodological one, illustrating the point that the agricultural revolution was in some respects a problem of reading and writing, a struggle 'to transfer a universe of traditional practice into a coherent body of written authority'.[54]

Marshall shows considerably more admiration for Virgil than for Young, but he finds even Virgil to be deficient in his methods of gathering and augmenting agricultural knowledge: 'EVEN VIRGIL ... who was not only a *practical* agriculturist, but may be supposed to have studied the *written* Agriculture extant in his time, neither appears to have made himself, nor recommends to others, A COURSE OF SCIENTIFIC EXPERIMENTS.'[55] As a consequence, the *Georgics* is more a compendium of traditional lore than a collection of duly tested and evaluated precepts. The problem for the georgic writer is how to negotiate the movement from tradition and experience to experimental progress and improvement.

As Marshall himself observes, countless generations of illiterate farmers held 'the management of their Ancestors sacred as their Faith'.[56] To move forward from this condition of stasis required a codification and evaluation of that tradition. In the eighteenth-century poetic georgic, this process is summed up in the phrase 'sage experience', a trope (or personification) that appears repeatedly and carries a double valence. In *Cyder*, for instance, Philips advises that the orchardist should allow 'sage Experience' to teach the arts of grafting and propagation: 'She will best the Hours | Of Harvest, and Seed-time declare'.[57] Here experience is received, time-tested wisdom, but in a later passage Philips recommends the use of the microscope as a tool to learn more about seeds and the process of reproduction: 'Thus All things by Experience are display'd, | And Most improv'd' (book 1, lines 359–60). This is experience shaped by observation.

To sift tradition and move beyond it requires evaluation, as Dodsley notes in 'Agriculture':

> Yet listen not
> To doubtful precepts, with implicit faith:
> Experience to experience oft oppos'd,
> Leaves truth uncertain.[58]

This passage appears at the conclusion of an exposition of Tull's theories of plant nutrition and his rejection of manure as a fertilizer, precepts that the poet assures us are 'drawn from sage experience'.[59] Sage experience, in Dodsley's characterization, is based on experimentation. It discovers new techniques through a process of trials (Tull's intensive soil cultivation), and it enables a verification of precepts old and new, especially when one conflicts with another ('Experience to experience … oppos'd'). In the case of Tull's new system versus the time-honoured use of manures, Dodsley counsels a combination of techniques, adapted by trial and error to local conditions: 'Join then with Culture the prolific strength | Of such manure as best inclines to aid | Thy failing glebe'.[60]

The only major eighteenth-century formal georgic in which the term 'experiment' appears is *The Sugar-Cane*. 'The skill'd in chemia … | Know from experiment, the fire of truth'.[61] That fire of truth, as Grainger affirms in the poem's preface, is the parent of his agricultural precepts: 'They are the children of Truth, not of Genius; the result of Experience, not the productions of Fancy' (p. 89). Grainger turns his back on 'Genius' and 'Fancy', the wellsprings of poetry, and instead embraces 'Experience' as his muse. As a result, he admits, his poem 'may not be able to please', but it will stand a greater chance of 'instructing the Reader; which … is the nobler end of all poetry' (p. 89). The georgic tension between pleasing readers and enlightening them is especially apparent in *The Sugar-Cane*, which adopts the learned device of the footnote to supplement and complete the selectiveness and indirection with which georgic poetry treats its subject (in effect, mapping Addison's 'By-way' that imparts a 'hint from the Poet').

In a digression halfway through Book 1 (lines 278–306), Grainger defends his rejection of the muse of Fancy in favour of Experience. The 'vast importance' of his subject 'to my native land' emboldens him 'to pluck from Fancy's soaring wing, | A plume to deck Experience' hoary brow'.[62] In Virgilian tradition, Grainger describes his task as laborious, but the labour of the poet now consists in evaluating conflicting precepts in order to advise his readers rightly, scientifically: 'The task how difficult, to cull the best | From thwarting sentiments: and best adorn | What Wisdom chuses, in poetic garb!'[63] Knowledge, for Grainger, is perfectible; 'improvement is the child of time':

> Unprejudic'd, then learn
> Of ancient modes to doubt, and new to try:
> And if Philosophy, with Wisdom, deign
> Thee to enlighten with her useful lore;
> Fair Fame and riches will reward thy toil.[64]

The poet ends his digression by exhorting his readers to 'Attend' to what he now has to say, asserting that the advice which follows is 'The Son of Truth and Time'.[65]

Philips, Dodsley and Grainger play on two, or even three, senses of 'experience', which in the eighteenth century could mean *experiment* or controlled, tested knowledge (as the word *expérience* still does in modern French); knowledge gained through observation; or customary, practical knowledge. These different kinds of experience underlie the period's distinction between science, a body of knowledge based on general principles, and art, a craft or skill gained through practice. Marshall develops this distinction at some length. 'Unintentional Observation', he writes, 'may ... give Art: but Intentional Observation can alone produce Science.' The philosopher 'becomes wise, through Design; the *Mechanic* expert, thro' habit'. The scientist records knowledge and transmits experience to future generations, whereas the artist relies on memory and oral transmission. Thus, 'The scientific Farmer ... not only *observes* and *records* the useful information which occurs to him in the course of his practice, by INCIDENT; but *discovers* by EXPERIMENT, those valuable facts, which never did ... come, *incidentally*, within his knowledge'.[66] On this basis,

Marshall theorizes an entirely new mode of writing agricultural science, one that leaves little room for the preceptive claims of georgic (or indeed for Young's discursive tours, which Marshall dismisses as little more than random collections of incidental experiences).

Feeling Georgic: The Pleasures of Agriculture

Perhaps the most elusive feature of the georgic to trace is the range of emotions it arouses. Virgil is capable of evoking the minutest of feelings, a happiness in small details – 'ecstatic and tender celebrations of the very life in things', in the words of David Ferry, poet and translator of the *Georgics*.[67] Pride in human ingenuity and self-sufficiency surface alongside a powerful sense of precarity, mutability, corruption and death. Dignity of labour and the value of toil come face to face with their unending and often futile trajectories. Love of place, the life of retirement, nostalgia, piety, patriotism – the gamut of feelings Virgil summons up in the course of the *Georgics* is extensive, from the most personal and private to the most public and heroic.

The eighteenth-century georgic poems that most closely match this affective range are not the formal imitations of the *Georgics*, but rather Thomson's *The Seasons* or Cowper's *The Task*. The formal georgics of Dodsley, Dyer and Grainger, with their commitment to energy, progress and improvement, describe a narrower circle of feeling. Nonetheless, it is significant that the prose writers of agricultural improvement regularly introduce their texts with disquisitions on the nobility and patriotism of agricultural pursuits, and the pleasures and satisfactions they afford. Virgilian themes of independence, self-sufficiency, dignity, health and happiness are central in these prefaces. In *The Gentleman Farmer* (1776), Lord Kames proceeds through a familiar and obligatory list of topics:

> In every well-governed state, agriculture has been duly honoured ... Agriculture corresponds to that degree of exercise, which is the best preservative of health ... Agriculture is equally salutary to the mind ... Our gentlemen who live in the country, have become active and industrious. They embellish their fields, improve their lands, and give bread to thousands. Every new day promotes health and spirits; and every new day brings variety of enjoyment. They are happy at home; and they wish happiness to all.[68]

Arthur Young treads the same thematic ground in his essay 'On the Pleasures of Agriculture'. After a review of the many illustrious writers and rulers, ancient and modern, who championed agricultural pursuits, Young concludes, 'If agriculture was a pleasing and highly interesting pursuit in the eyes of these heroes, poets and philosophers, how much more should it be in this age, when a variety of new discoveries have connected it intimately with every branch of experimental philosophy'.[69] In Young's tribute, which proceeds to expatiate on the seasonal pleasures of husbandry, concluding with winter, when the 'elaboratory opens its recesses, and gives to wintry darkness the illumination of science', the classical georgic tradition is seamlessly joined with the enlightenment project of agricultural improvement.[70]

Notes

1 J. Tull, *The Horse-Hoing Husbandry* (1733), p. 44.
2 S. Switzer, Dedication to *The Practical Husbandman and Planter*, 2 vols. (1733), vol. II, sig. c2ᵛ. Switzer quotes J. Tull, *The New Horse-Houghing Husbandry: or, an Essay on the Principles of Tillage and Vegetation* (1731), iv.
3 J. Hamilton, *Virgil's Pastorals Translated into English Prose; as also His Georgicks, with Such Notes and Reflexions as Make Him Appear to Have Wrote like an Excellent Farmer* (Edinburgh, 1742), p. x; W. Harte, *Essays on Husbandry* (Bath, 1764), Essay 1, pp. 206–8.
4 Letter to the editor in *The European Magazine, and London Review* 39 (March 1801), 177–8.
5 For accounts of Tull and the controversies, both agricultural and literary, he provoked, see F. De Bruyn, 'Reading Virgil's *Georgics* as a Scientific Text: The Eighteenth-Century Debate between Jethro Tull and Stephen Switzer', *ELH*, 71 (2004), 661–89; L. Sayre, 'Cultivating Virgil: Jethro Tull and the New Husbandry', in 'Farming by the Book: British Georgic in Prose and Practice, 1697–1820', PhD diss., Princeton University (2002), pp. 109–68; and Sayre, 'The Pre-History of Soil Science: Jethro Tull, the Invention of the Seed Drill, and the Foundations of Modern Agriculture', *Physics and Chemistry of the Earth*, 35 (2010), 851–9.
6 D. Fairer, 'Georgic', in *The Oxford Handbook of British Poetry, 1660–1800*, ed. J. Lynch (Oxford University Press, 2016), pp. 457–72, at p. 457.
7 A. Hunter, *Georgical Essays* (1769), p. 11.
8 A. Blackwell, *A New Method of Improving Cold, Wet, and Barren Lands: Particularly Clayey-Grounds* (1741), iv.
9 See chapter 7 of Blackwell's *New Method*, esp. pp. 49–55, in which Virgil's advice about burning 'barren fields' (*Georgics*, I. 86–93) is examined and endorsed.
10 R. Cohen, 'Innovation and Variation: Literary Change and Georgic Poetry', in *Literature and History: Papers Read at a Clark Library Seminar, March 3, 1973* (Los Angeles: William Andrews Clark Memorial Library, 1974); rpt. in *Genre Theory and Historical Change: Theoretical Essays of Ralph Cohen* (Charlottesville: University of Virginia Press, 2017), pp. 190–1.
11 J. C. Pellicer, 'The Georgic at Mid-Eighteenth Century and the Case of Dodsley's "Agriculture"', *RES*, n.s. 54 (2003), 67–93, at 71.

12 J. Addison, 'An Essay on the *Georgics*', in Virgil, *Georgics* (Dryden), p. 145.
13 Addison, 'Essay on the *Georgics*', pp. 149, 151.
14 Addison, 'Essay on the *Georgics*', p. 149.
15 For a case study of how georgic convention intersected with technical discussions of dung, see A. M. Foy, 'The Convention of Georgic Circumlocution and the Proper Use of Human Dung in Samuel Martin's *Essay upon Plantership*', *Eighteenth-Century Studies*, 49 (2016), 475–506.
16 W. Cowper, 'The Garden', in *The Task*, in *The Poems of William Cowper, Vol. 2: 1782–1785*, ed. J. D. Baird and C. Ryskamp (Oxford University Press, 1995), p. 174 (book 3, lines 463–5).
17 Cowper, *Task*, p. 175 (book 3, lines 493–501).
18 J. Grainger, *The Sugar-Cane*, in John Gilmore, *The Poetics of Empire: A Study of James Grainer's The Sugar Cane (1764)* (London: Athlone Press, 2000), p. 97 (book 1, lines 218–21).
19 Grainger, *Sugar-Cane*, in Gilmore, p. 97 (book 1, lines 225–6).
20 J. Warton, 'Dedication to the Honourable Sir George Lyttelton', in *The Works of Virgil, in Latin and English*, 4 vols. (1753), vol. I, p. vii.
21 Virgil, *Georgics* (Ferry), p. 5 (*Georgics*, I. 46).
22 Quoted in R. A. B. Mynors, 'Commentary', in Virgil, *Georgics*, ed. Mynors (Oxford: Clarendon Press, 1990), p. 11. The text by Cato, *ad filium*, cited in *Servius Danielis*, has not survived; the citation reads, 'Vir bonus est, Marce fili, colendi peritus, cuius ferramenta splendent'.
23 J. Tull, *The New Horse-Houghing Husbandry: or, an Essay on the Principles of Tillage and Vegetation* (1731), pp. xxviii, iii.
24 *Virgil's Pastorals Translated into English Prose; as also his Georgicks*, tr. J. Hamilton (Edinburgh, 1742), p. v.
25 J. Anderson, Preface to *Essays Relating to Agriculture and Rural Affairs* (Edinburgh, 1775), pp. xiv–xv.
26 T. Sprat, *The History of the Royal Society*, ed. Jackson I. Cope and Harold Whitmore Jones (London: Routledge and Kegan Paul, 1959), p. 113.
27 Tull, *Horse-Hoing*, p. 15.
28 A. Young, 'Number LXIII, Of the Improvement of Wet Pastures,' in *Museum Rusticum et Commerciiale*, 6 vols. (1764–6), vol. III, p. 293.
29 Virgil, *Georgics* (Ferry), p. 13 (*Georgics*, I. 145–6).
30 Virgil, *Georgics* (Ferry), p. 115 (*Georgics*, III. 286–90).
31 S. Duck, 'The Thresher's Labour', in *Poems on Several Occasions* (1730), p. 25.
32 Virgil, *Georgics* (Dryden), p. 224; J. Philips, *Cyder. A Poem. In Two Books* (1708), p. 23 (book 1, lines 364–74).
33 J. Armstrong, *John Armstrong's The Art of Preserving Health*, ed. Adam Budd (Farnham: Ashgate, 2011), pp. 85–6 (book 3, lines 1–34).
34 T. Scott, *The Anglers: Eight Dialogues in Verse* (1758), pp. 1–2.
35 F. De Bruyn, 'What Is Sport? Arts of Rural Sport and the Art of Poetry, 1650–1800', in *Sporting Cultures, 1650–1850*, ed. Daniel O'Quinn and Alexis Tadié (University of Toronto Press, 2018), p. 44.
36 Virgil, *Georgics* (Ferry), p. 17 (Blackwell, *New Method*, pp. 199–200).

37 D. Fairer, '"The Year Runs Round": The Poetry of Work in Eighteenth-Century England', in *Ritual, Routine, and Regime: Repetition in Early Modern British and European Cultures*, ed. L. Clymer (University of Toronto Press, 2006), pp. 153–71, at pp. 164–5.
38 J. Dyer, *The Fleece: A Poem in Four Books*, ed. J. Goodridge and J. C. Pellicer (Cheltenham: Cyder Press, 2007), pp. 40–1 (book 2, lines 159–62, 183–91).
39 C. Bucknell, 'The Mid-Eighteenth-Century Georgic and Agricultural Improvement', *Journal for Eighteenth-Century Studies* 36 (2013), 340–2.
40 K. Heinzelman, 'The Last Georgic: *Wealth of Nations* and the Scene of Writing', in *Adam Smith's Wealth of Nations: New Interdisciplinary Essays*, ed. S. Copley and K. Sutherland (Manchester University Press, 1995), pp. 171–94.
41 A. Smith, *An Inquiry into the Nature and Causes of the Wealth of Nations*, ed. R. H. Campbell, A. S. Skinner and W. B. Todd, 2 vols. (Oxford: Clarendon Press, 1976), vol. I, p. 377 (III.i.2).
42 Smith, *Wealth of Nations*, vol. I, p. 378 (III.i.3).
43 L. P. Wilkinson, *The Georgics of Virgil: A Critical Survey* (Cambridge University Press 1969), p. 53.
44 See J. Gilmore's discussion of this issue in the introduction to *The Poetics of Empire: A Study of James Grainger's* The Sugar Cane (London: Athlone Press, 2000), pp. 54–65 ('"Canes and Swains": Slavery, Poetry, and the Modern Reader').
45 Addison, 'Essay on the *Georgics*', pp. 146–8.
46 F. Bacon, *Novum Organum with Other Parts of the Great Instauration*, trans. P. Urbach and J. Gibson (Chicago: Open Court, 1994), p. 96 (book 1, aphorism 86); *Advancement of Learning*, Book 2, in *Francis Bacon*, ed. B. Vickers (Oxford University Press, 1996), p. 235.
47 A. Pope, *Windsor-Forest*, in *The Poems of Alexander Pope*, ed. John Butt, 1 vol., Twickenham ed. (Yale University Press, 1963), p. 195 (lines 11–16).
48 J. Mills, *Essays Moral, Philosophical, and Political* (1772), pp. iii–v, 290.
49 Anderson, Preface to *Essays*, x.
50 A. Young, *A Six Months Tour through the North of England*, 4 vols. (1770), vol. I, pp. x–xi.
51 Young, *A Six Months Tour*, xi.
52 F. De Bruyn, 'From Georgic Poetry to Statistics and Graphs: Eighteenth-Century Representations and the "State" of British Society', *The Yale Journal of Criticism*, 17 (2004), 107–39, at 119.
53 W. Marshall, 'A General View of Farmers and Farming', in *Minutes of Agriculture; with Experiments and Observations* (1783), p. 5. The *Minutes* is in several parts, each with its own pagination. The 'General View' forms the second part or 'Digest of the Minutes'.
54 Sayre, Abstract to 'Farming by the Book', p. iii.
55 Marshall, 'Introduction to the Experiments', in *Minutes*, n.p. (sig. b).
56 Marshall, 'General View', in *Minutes*, p. 5.
57 Philips, *Cyder*, p. 21 (book 1, lines 226, 229–30).
58 R. Dodsley, 'Agriculture', *Public Virtue: A Poem. In Three Books. I. Agriculture. II. Commerce III. Arts* (1753), p. 36 (I.ii.129–32).

59 Dodsley, 'Agriculture', p. 32 (I.i.50).
60 Dodsley, 'Agriculture', p. 37 (I.i.147–9).
61 Grainger, *Sugar-Cane*, in Gilmore, p. 136 (book III, lines 342–3).
62 Grainger, *Sugar-Cane*, in Gilmore, p. 99 (book I, lines 302–6).
63 Grainger, *Sugar-Cane*, in Gilmore, p. 99 (book I, lines 297–9).
64 Grainger, *Sugar-Cane*, in Gilmore, p. 99 (book I, lines 281–5).
65 Grainger, *Sugar-Cane*, in Gilmore, p. 99 (book I, line 307).
66 Marshall, 'General Observations Concerning Scientific Agriculture', in *Minutes*, p. 2 (separately paginated).
67 Virgil, *Georgics* (Ferry), p. xii.
68 H. Home, Lord Kames, *The Gentleman Farmer* (1776), pp. xiv–xviii.
69 A. Young, 'On the Pleasures of Agriculture', in *Annals of Agriculture and Other Useful Arts*, 2 (1784), p. 473.
70 Young, 'Pleasures', 476–8.

CHAPTER 8

Georgic, Romanticism and Complaint
John Clare and His Contemporaries

Tess Somervell

John Clare's *The Village Minstrel* introduces its protagonist, Lubin, in a conventional pastoral pose, reclining in the shade: 'An humble rustic hums his lowly dreams, | Far in the shade where poverty retires'.[1] Lubin spends more time wandering than working, and is more interested in describing rural sports than rural labours, leading Theresa Adams to describe the poem as 'a carnivalesque revision of georgic form ... in which leisure, not labor, is the focus'.[2] However, we are told that Lubin 'a thresher with his sire has been ... he a ploughboy in the fields did maul, | And drudg'd with toil through almost every scene'. Furthermore, Lubin's minstrelsy is presented as a georgic vocation: to record the customs of rural life and to 'trace | Through nature's secrets with unwearied eye'. Here Lubin is presented as Virgil's 'happy man' from *Georgics* II: 'Happy the Man, who, studying Nature's Laws, | Thro' known Effects can trace the secret Cause.'[3] The 'happy man' passage was one of the most persistent tropes of eighteenth-century georgic, adapted from Virgil and from Horace's second epode, both of which extol the pleasures of a farming life (although in Virgil as in *The Village Minstrel*, the precise relationship between the happy man who traces nature's causes and the happy swain who actually works the land is ambiguous).[4] As Clare's allusion suggests, Lubin is more truly a georgic than a pastoral poet, for all his seeming leisure. Yet Lubin's role, as well as to observe and celebrate the countryside, is to 'complain':

> O Poverty! thy frowns were early dealt
> O'er him who mourn'd thee ...
> And as his tears and sighs did erst complain,
> His numbers took it up, and wept it o'er again.

The change that Lubin laments most is enclosure, which has turned open commons into private farmland and increased rural poverty and suffering in the process:

> O samely naked leas, so bleak, so strange!
> How would he wander o'er ye to complain,
> And sigh, and wish he ne'er had known the change,
> To see the ploughshare bury all the plain.

The poem itself, although it only occasionally quotes Lubin directly, increasingly ventriloquizes the complaint that we are told was his, until the distance between Lubin and the speaker almost completely closes: 'Ye fields, ye scenes so dear to Lubin's eye … Ye banish'd trees, ye make me deeply sigh, – | Inclosure came, and all your glories fell'. In the Romantic period, to the role of the georgic poet – observing and describing the natural environment of the countryside and the traditional ways of working it, and instructing the reader in those ways – was added the task of rural complaint. By the 1800s, alongside his or her lines on ploughing, animal husbandry, weather lore and rural sports, the British georgic poet had to include a complaint for the social and economic ills that afflicted the contemporary English (*not* necessarily British) countryside. As georgic poets, both Lubin and Clare fulfil this new georgic task in *The Village Minstrel*.

This chapter traces the emergence of the rural complaint as a new feature of georgic, and ultimately as a georgic form in its own right, in the Romantic period, and explores how recognition of this trend can adjust our understanding of what happens to georgic at the end of the eighteenth century. The most familiar story of georgic in the Romantic period is a story of decline. It is often said that the formal georgic (commonly defined as 'the long didactic and descriptive poem about labour, especially agricultural labour, in imitation of Virgil's *Georgics*') enjoyed its heyday in English in the early and mid-eighteenth century, but 'disappeared … quite suddenly vanished' after 1770.[5] Yet the apparent wane of the formal georgic is simultaneous with increased public and literary interest in the conditions of rural labour and the reality of life in the countryside, essentially georgic themes that are sublimated into lyrical and narrative forms. As a result, critical accounts of Romantic georgic either stress georgic's intractability, its inability to adapt to new economic and social conditions (which explains the defunction of georgic form), or its adaptability, its capacity to infiltrate other genres as a mode (which explains the persistence of georgic subject-matter).

Accounts of the decline of formal georgic often refer to industrialization's disenchantment of labour. By the nineteenth century, as David Fairer puts it, '[d]rudgery was no longer divine'.[6] As Rudolf Beck has shown, even poets who wrote in favour of industrialization did not find the georgic form suitable to their purposes by the turn of the century.[7]

Georgic, although it acknowledges the challenge and pain of labour, is also about the potential rewards of hard work, the benefits of being adaptive and flexible, and the value of the labourer's learned skills: positive aspects of work that appeared lacking in new urban industrial forms of labour and in an increasingly industrialized rural economy. Raymond Williams famously argued that this notion of a recently lost ideal rural life has been a feature of English literature since the early modern period; every generation has indulged in nostalgia for the country life enjoyed by their parents and grandparents.[8] However, others have argued that in late eighteenth-century England the life of the average rural labourer really was demonstrably worse than it had been in recent memory.[9] Social, economic and ecological changes in the late eighteenth century, including growing inequality, enclosure, urban migration, aggressive conscription and food shortages, meant that the georgic conception of rural life seemed increasingly like fantasy. As Rachel Crawford puts it, 'the georgic celebration of a traditionalist scheme that equates happy labor with the soil could not ameliorate the hunger of the poor'.[10] How 'happy' labour is in both classical and neoclassical georgic is debateable, but georgic does depend on the principle that the 'Crop rewards the greedy Peasant's Pains': hard, skilled work produces fruits (material, social, and psychic) for the worker.[11]

Alongside this narrative of the formal georgic's decay, a critical interest in georgic has risen in the twenty-first century, and scholars have been eager to uncover the persistence of georgic themes, moods and energies in Romantic literature. These narratives emphasize georgic's capacity to adapt, particularly 'to autobiographical and lyric forms'.[12] In this version of the narrative, georgic appears almost as a kind of organism, evolving to shed its unwieldy didactic form and its status as a genre to become a mode that makes its habitat within other host genres. Its tendency for adaptation, Tim Burke argues, allowed the georgic 'mode' or 'mood' 'to survive the fading fashion for long formal poems in the Virgilian style as the eighteenth century drew to a close'.[13] Taking cue from Kurt Heinzelmann, Burke identifies georgic's evolution towards autobiography: what he calls 'the new georgicism' is an adaptation of the georgic theme of labour to explore not the cultivation of the land but the cultivation of the poet's self.[14] Romantic poems that have been identified as 'georgics of the mind' include William Cowper's *The Task*, William Wordsworth's *The Prelude* and *The Excursion*, and James Woodhouse's *The Life and Lucubrations of Crispinus Scriblerus*.[15] While the theme of labour persists in these Romantic autobiographical-epic forms, the theme of agriculture persists in Romantic lyric. This is why poems such as Wordsworth's 'Michael' and Keats's 'To

Autumn' are sometimes, but usually only hesitantly, labelled georgic – they take a clear interest in georgic themes of husbandry and harvest, but show little sign of georgic's usual didactic form, or its usual length, and arguably tend more towards pastoral idealism than georgic realism.

However, the persistence and relevance in the Romantic period of georgic form, not just georgic subject-matter, should not be underestimated. There are a handful of Romantic poems that do resemble formal georgics, and examination of these poems is essential to understanding what happens to georgic at the turn of the nineteenth century. What these poems tell us is that our definition of georgic form needs to be expanded in order to understand the Romantic development of the genre and the multiple forms that georgic could take, and could take into itself, in this period. It is true that the georgic form of explicitly didactic poetry recedes in the late eighteenth and early nineteenth century. Yet many poets utilized other formal elements from classical and neoclassical georgic, such as the seasonal or calendrical structure, the 'happy man' formula, and detailed natural description (a form that has become so pervasive that it is easy to forget its roots in eighteenth-century English georgic).

This chapter argues that we see the emergence in the Romantic period of a new georgic form: the rural complaint. It was able to address contemporary changes in rural life that didactic and descriptive georgic forms struggled to acknowledge, and could accommodate both lyrical and autobiographical poetics that were in ascendancy. The first section of this chapter describes how georgic subject-matter, but also elements of georgic form, 'adapted to' or infiltrated the complaint, which had previously been associated with pastoral. Early experiments in rural complaint, most notably Oliver Goldsmith's *The Deserted Village* (1770), were so successful that georgic was able to appropriate the complaint form almost entirely. The rural complaint became a poetic form that was not only used to address georgic themes, but also associated with the long tradition of classical and neoclassical georgic poems. The main evidence for this appropriation, as the second section of this chapter outlines, is that the rural complaint became a formal element of those Romantic poems that most overtly advertised themselves as georgics, as clearly as the 'happy man' interlude or the catalogue of weather signs. Like those tropes, it could be extracted from the longer formal georgic but retain its georgic status. The third and final section of this chapter reads Charlotte Smith's *Beachy Head* in the light of this Romantic meeting of georgic and complaint.

It may seem pedantic to dispute over whether particular Romantic poems, or episodes within poems, are pastoral or georgic: Romantic poets and even Romantic critics were not at pains to distinguish between these genres. Yet it is important to recognize the rural complaint as a specifically georgic form of poetry in this period. First, because the labels of 'pastoral' and 'georgic' are useful tools to us as readers, providing a vocabulary by which we can unpick a poem's inter-weavings of labour and leisure, idealism and realism, and nostalgia and progress. Second, we gain insight into the traditions that poets understood themselves to be working in when writing about the countryside. In the case of Romantic rural complaint poetry, the negotiation between pastoral and georgic becomes a way for poets to navigate between the two poles of (pastoral) pessimistic nostalgia and (georgic) optimistic progress.

The Roots of Rural Complaint

In a complaint, a speaker laments their grievance(s) and expresses their grief, whether in prose or lyrical verse. Often (but not always) the complaint involves a narrative of loss, and takes its impetus from the contrast between past happiness and present misery. Clearly the complaint is closely related to elegy, but the speaker's grievance is not necessarily the death of a loved one. Complaint poems appear as modal interludes in medieval and early modern dramas, romances, epics, ballads and sermons, as well as other forms, and they can be amatory, devotional or political. The lyrical complaint poem as a stand-alone form enjoyed its greatest popularity in the 1590s, and then flourished again, in its political guise, during the English Civil War.[16] The complaint remains an important form into the eighteenth century, however. While early modern complaint is usually understood as Ovidian and biblical in its roots, the complaint is also one of the original pastoral forms in Virgil's *Eclogues* and Theocritus's *Idylls*, and it is this pastoral complaint tradition that comes to the fore in the eighteenth century.

In poems such Nicholas Rowe's 'Colin's Complaint' (1712) and the pastoral complaints of Robert Fergusson, we can see one important effect of this blend of pastoral themes with the complaint form: a redoubled sense of stasis. Both pastoral and complaint are prone to hopelessness, but in themselves *can* offer possibilities either of 'pastures new' in the case of pastoral, or redress in the case of complaint.[17] In combination, however, the form of complaint and genre of pastoral make forward progression extremely difficult. The complaint is pastoral's most backward-looking form, and in turn pastoral idleness stymies the complaint's potential rousing effect. Rowe's Colin finds no prospect of improvement at the end of his complaint:

> Tho' thro' the wide World I should range,
> 'Tis in vain from our Fortune to fly ...
> 'Tis Mine to be constant and die.[18]

Similarly, in Fergusson's (conveniently titled) 'The Complaint. A Pastoral' (1773), the shepherd Damon laments the loss of his contentment since he fell in unrequited love with Stella, and the only solution is his death at the end of the poem: 'He hath sigh'd all his sorrows away'.[19]

In the Romantic period, the complaint undergoes two gradual and related shifts in emphasis away from its predominant eighteenth-century type, which was the pastoral love-complaint. The first is a shift from amatory subject-matter to political (the complaint becomes a popular form for abolitionist poetry, for example). The second, related shift is from pastoral to georgic and the emergence of the 'rural complaint' as a popular version of the complaint form. The past, happier life is no longer one of pastoral ease, lost due to rejection by a mistress, but one of labour that was rewarding and enriching, lost due to social, economic and political change. Arcadia, occupied by shepherds, is replaced by Auburn, occupied (in the past) by 'the labouring swain'. This is the setting established in Oliver Goldsmith's *The Deserted Village* (1770), the best-known and most influential example of the rural complaint: 'Sweet Auburn, lovliest village of the plain, | Where health and plenty cheared the labouring swain'.[20] Although Goldsmith, like Clare, is more interested in describing rural leisure than rural work, and we see in the poem how 'toil remitting lent its turn to play' (line 16), his ideal of village life was defined by the toil as much as by the play. 'Contented Toil' (line 403) and 'smiling toil' (line 222) both enabled and gave value to leisure time, and leisure time in turn 'taught even toil to please' (line 32). The narrator complains that enclosure, rural depopulation and growing inequality have relegated this healthy, balanced way of life to recent history.

The Deserted Village is notoriously difficult to define generically. It appears to be at once pastoral (in its idealizing nostalgia), anti-pastoral (in its depiction of contemporary rural life as painful), georgic (in its emphasis on a fulfilling working life) and anti-georgic (in its relegation of this life to the past). The two most obvious precedents for Goldsmith's rural complaint are Stephen Duck's *The Thresher's Labour* (1730) and Thomas Gray's 'Elegy Written in a Country Churchyard' (1751). Both lament social inequalities in the countryside, but the key difference between their poems and Goldsmith's is the latter's claim for the previous existence of an idyllic rural way of life. Goldsmith constructs what Gary Harrison calls an 'agrarian idyll', 'a composite image of rural England as a place of social harmony, fulfilling labor and blissful simplicity' and, crucially, he locates this idyll in the recent past.[21] Goldsmith's nostalgia for the past takes him closer to pastoral, but Goldsmith's rural complaint exerted greater influence upon the development of the Romantic georgic, and on the emergence of the rural complaint as a georgic form.

Fairer calls *The Deserted Village* the 'obverse' of georgic because it 'sees progress in terms of loss', and 'register[s] change as a sudden, disruptive break with the past'.[22] Despite these anti-georgic qualities of the poem, Goldsmith signals in *The Deserted Village* that he understands himself to be writing a kind of georgic. He includes, for example, the 'happy man' trope: 'How happy he who crowns in shades like these, | A youth of labour with an age of ease' (lines 99–100). This couplet manages to bring georgic and pastoral together in both of its lines – the happy man (who would have reminded contemporary readers of Virgil's second georgic as much as Horace's second epode) with the shades of pastoral in the first, followed by the labour of georgic and the ease of pastoral in the second. *The Deserted Village* signals a turning-point in the development of Romantic pastoral *and* georgic, and their relation to one another. After *c.*1770, the ideal rural life, the traditional sphere of pastoral, is less often one of idle leisure, and more often incorporates the georgic values of rewarding hard work; at the same time, it becomes harder to write georgic poetry that is set in the present-day, as the life of rewarding, fulfilling hard work in the countryside comes to seem like something that was enjoyed by previous generations.

The Deserted Village ends on a wish that poetry's voice may prevail even in and beyond 'these degenerate times' (line 409). The poetry that Goldsmith wishes for is didactic poetry:

> Still let thy voice prevailing over time,
> Redress the rigours of the inclement clime;
> Aid slighted truth, with thy persuasive strain[23]
> Teach erring man to spurn the rage of gain;
> Teach him that states of native strength possest,
> Tho' very poor, may still be very blest[.] (lines 421–6)

Goldsmith is describing his own poem and the effects that he hopes it may have in the future, and simultaneously inviting other poets to write such poetry: poetry that will 'teach' and that will 'redress'. Formal georgic poetry, these lines seem to say, has the capacity to offer the kind of redress that was lacking in the fatalistic pastoral complaint. In these lines, Goldsmith hopes that a quasi-georgic rural complaint such as *The Deserted Village* might not only inform its readers about the changes afflicting the countryside, but also even slow down, halt, or reverse these changes.

In *The Village* (1783), George Crabbe rejects Goldsmith's fantasy of 'contented toils', criticizing the notion of an agrarian idyll, whether that idyll is located in the present or past. Yet the pervasiveness of this narrative in the late eighteenth century is evidenced by the fact that even *The Village* contains glimpses of a better life in the past, characterized by georgic labour that was rewarded by periods of rest and communal leisure: 'Where are the swains, who, daily labour done, | With rural games play'd down the setting sun[?]'.[24] After 1770, the default complaint poem no longer laments a shepherd's lost love, but a farm labourer's decline into poverty. We find short complaint poems such as John Freeth's 'The Cottager's Complaint, on the Intended Bill for Enclosing Sutton-Coldfield' (1778), in which the cottager exclaims 'How happy were the days!' when he grazed his small stock of sheep on the common without fear; but now the 'avaricious plan' of enclosure threatens to force him from home.[25] We find longer rural complaints too, such as William Holloway's *The Peasant's Fate* (1802), which celebrates the place 'where my forefathers spent | Their honest days in labour and content' but complains that 'times grew hard, – too hard indeed to bear! – | And half depopulated was the vale'.[26] In his preface, Holloway cites Thomson, Goldsmith and Cowper as models for a 'rural poetry' that 'speak[s] the language of nature' instead of pursuing 'far-fetched subjects, of the Arcadian cast'.[27] Later, Ebenezer Elliott, the 'corn-law rhymer', would mimic *The Deserted Village* in *The Splendid Village* (1833). This extended complaint similarly recalls a poor and hard-working but happy rural community that has been desecrated by enclosure ('cottages | That, happy once … gaz'd | On poor men's fields, which poor men's cattle graz'd!').[28] Like Goldsmith, Elliott introduces georgic tropes such as the 'happy man': 'Oh, happy, if they knew their bliss, are they | Who, poor themselves, unbounded wealth survey.'[29] Here is evidence that, certainly by 1800, the rural complaint was understood not as a pastoral form with georgic thematic colouring, but, first and foremost, as a way of writing georgic, as a form that automatically invoked the georgic tradition. The clearest evidence for the georgic status of the rural complaint is that it becomes a feature of the long formal georgic, a set-piece within those Romantic poems which overtly advertise themselves as georgic in form as well as content.

Complaint in the Romantic Formal Georgic

If we take the strict definition of 'formal georgic' as the long didactic and descriptive poem about agriculture, there is one clear example in the Romantic period: *British Georgics* (1809) by James Grahame, which is a close imitation of Virgil's *Georgics* in the tradition of eighteenth-century formal georgics such as *Cyder* (1708) and *The Fleece* (1757). There are other poems in the period, by poets from a range of backgrounds, that might not qualify as formal georgics by the narrowest definition, but which were understood as georgic by their writers and readers, and which experiment with formal features of georgic as well as with georgic themes.[30] Richard Payne Knight's *The Landscape: A Didactic Poem* (1794), for example, is georgic in its didactic form but addresses landscape designers rather than farmers. Poems such as *The Farmer's Boy* (1800) by Robert Bloomfield and *The Progress of Agriculture* (1804) by Thomas Batchelor are harder to identify as formal georgics because they are more descriptive than didactic, and less directly imitative of Virgil than Grahame's poem. If we expand our definition of the formal georgic, however, to accommodate the more descriptive forms that were clearly and explicitly identified as georgic, then we gain a clearer view of what happened to georgic in the Romantic period. We find that the first decade of the 1800s, particularly, is a significant blip in the narrative of the decline of georgic, and we find that by the turn of the century the rural complaint was an essential georgic trope.

In his appendix to the third edition of *The Farmer's Boy*, Capel Lofft, Bloomfield's patron and editor, labelled the poem 'our ENGLISH GEORGIC'. In the same appendix, however, he quoted the critic Nathan Drake's argument that, although it did not assume 'the form of an Eclogue', *The Farmer's Boy* was 'peculiarly and exclusively, throughout, a pastoral Composition', presumably due to its idealized conception of rural life.[31] Clearly Lofft accepted that a poem could be both georgic and pastoral at once. This generic blend leads William Christmas to identify the poem as a 'new kind of rural realism', 'devoid of the "harshness" of, say, Duck or Crabbe, but not quite pastoral either, in its attention to accurate, detailed description'.[32] Although the idealizing lack of 'harshness' might seem to disqualify *The Farmer's Boy* from being georgic, the poem clearly invites us to read it in this generic tradition. Bloomfield (a farm-labourer-turned-cobbler) signals the georgic identity of his poem through his deployment of many of the popular set-pieces that the eighteenth-century georgics had adapted from Virgil: the passage on weather forecasting, the sudden summer storm, the 'happy man' section (humorously adapted to describe the happiness of a pig being groomed by birds), the reflection on hunting. These passages are not just forays into a georgic mode; *The Farmer's Boy* is georgic in its overall form and therefore, in that sense, a formal georgic. It adopts the seasonal structure that Thomson had used in his quasi-georgic *The Seasons* (1730), but incorporates more descriptions of agricultural labour and even more Virgilian tropes than had featured in Thomson's poem.

The Farmer's Boy is not explicitly didactic, but its detailed accounts of rural labour indirectly impart advice on best practice.

Another formal feature of georgic that the poem utilizes is its temporal perspective. This may not be immediately obvious: first we are introduced to Giles in the past tense, and then quickly the poem moves into the present indefinite tense, which it sustains for its majority. This has led Bridget Keegan to observe that *The Farmer's Boy* 'exists not in a lost pastoral past, nor in the deferred future of the more prescriptive georgic mode'.[33] It is true that georgic frequently operates in a hypothetical future tense, imagining possible activities that are contingent on various environmental factors. However, georgic also frequently adopts the present indefinite tense, describing eternal or habitual action, particularly when it assumes its descriptive rather than didactic attitude. That present is then framed by past experience and future possibility:

> THE FARMER'S life displays in every part
> A moral lesson to the sensual heart.
> Though in the lap of Plenty, thoughtful still,
> He looks beyond the present good or ill;
> Nor estimates alone one blessing's worth,
> From changeful seasons, or capricious earth;
> But views the future with the present hours,
> And looks for failures as he looks for show'er[s.] (book II, lines 1–8)

The georgic husbandman remembers lessons from the past, and looks forward to the results of his labour even as he carries it out. Looking 'beyond the present good or ill' distinguishes the georgic from the pastoral perspective. As Kevin Binfield observes of *The Farmer's Boy*, 'the present is full of labor, but that present is always vanishing into actual and imagined futures, thereby becoming the past in continuity'.[34] Bloomfield repeatedly stresses the way the farmer imagines the future outcome of his work: 'In fancy sees his trembling oats uprun ... And all his harvest gather'd round his door' (book I, lines 99–102).

The poem's dominant georgic temporal perspective is partly what makes the end of 'Summer' so surprising. Here Bloomfield describes the harvest feast, where 'Distinction low'rs its crest, | The master, servant, and the merry guest, | Are equal all' (book II, lines 323–5). The harvest feast emblematizes the georgic principle of labour rewarded; even Duck celebrates its pleasures in *The Thresher's Labour*, although he laments its brevity. After this present-tense description, however, Bloomfield reveals the influence of Goldsmith, and the speaker reminds us that what he is describing is not the present state of the countryside, but the better past:

> Such were the days, ... of days long past I sing,
> When Pride gave place to mirth without a sting;
> Ere tyrant customs strength sufficient bore
> To violate the feelings of the poor[.] (book II, lines 333–6)

This, several hundred lines into the poem, is the first use of 'I' to refer to the poem's speaker, and signals the poem's turn into the lyrical mode of complaint. The phrase 'of days long past I sing' may only refer to the preceding lines on the feast, when master and labourer could socialize together; or, more worryingly, it may encompass the poem's entire depiction of rural life, and remind us that Giles was introduced in the past tense at the poem's beginning. The complaint interlude does not separate off the political argument into a neat bounded space; it reveals the possibility that all georgic is nostalgic fantasy, and that the whole georgic poem must be read as an elegiac complaint, a record of lost rural life. It is as if here, at the end of 'Summer', Bloomfield remembers a requirement to acknowledge that the happy georgic life no longer exists.

The end of 'Summer' offers us not one complaint, but two: first this brief complaint by the poem's main speaker, and then a reiteration of the same complaint, in even harsher and more politicized terms, in the quoted voice of a 'mourner':

> Methinks I hear the mourner thus impart
> The stifled murmurs of his wounded heart:
> 'Whence comes this change, ungracious, irksome, cold?
> 'Whence the new grandeur that mine eyes behold?
> 'The wid'ning distance which I daily see,
> 'Has Wealth done this? ...
> 'The hope of humble industry is o'er.' (book II, lines 345–54)

This new trope, in which the narrative voice either shifts into lyrical mode in order to deliver his own complaint or introduces another speaker to act as complainant, is also found in other Romantic poems that are recognizable as formal georgics. Thomas Batchelor's *The Progress of Agriculture* is largely forgettable, but it does tell us a good deal about what Batchelor (the son of a tenant farmer and later a writer and researcher for the Board of Agriculture) understood the georgic to be: early on he invokes the goddess 'Ceres, patron of the Georgic train'.[35] His poem is more descriptive than didactic, and is reminiscent of many eighteenth-century georgics in its optimism that commercial forces and technological improvements will make Britain's land more productive. Even this most Whiggish of Romantic georgics, however, contains what Batchelor names in his preface 'The Peasant's Complaint', 'inserted' into the poem to do the job of relaying 'the evils complained of by the peasantry':[36]

> For, hark!—methinks far other notes I hear,
> Which, sad and solemn, strike my wounded ear;
> Beneath yon willow sits a minstrel swain …
> his plaintive notes arise,
> The drops of anguish glisten in his eyes …
> 'Life's smiling prospects must be mine no more!
> 'Ye blissful hours! which once this breast has known,
> When half the village sow'd and reap'd their own'[37]

The peasant complains that smaller farms are being enclosed and replaced by huge pastures for sheep. His posture under the willow indicates a venture into pastoral complaint; but he turns out to be a georgic complainant, allowed into this formal georgic poem because his nostalgic longing is not for a life of ease and reciprocated love, but for an agrarian idyll.

We find another example of the rural complaint interlude in *British Georgics* by James Grahame (a lawyer-turned-curate from Glasgow), the most conventional formal georgic of the Romantic period. As well as identifying itself as georgic in its title, *British Georgics* uses blank verse like many of the eighteenth-century georgics and, unlike Bloomfield's or Batchelor's georgics, is explicitly and overtly didactic. Grahame's georgic is also distinctive in the Romantic period because it clearly describes the contemporary countryside. Grahame is able to resist the Goldsmithian imperative to relocate the georgic life to the recent past, because he argues that even though this life no longer exists in England, it does persist in his native Scotland. Yet even Grahame does not resist the new georgic trope of the rural complaint. Into 'May' he introduces a lament, for both what has happened in England and what he fears will happen in Scotland:

> O simple times
> Of peaceful innocence, fast giving way
> To Trade's encroaching power! Yes, Trade ere long
> Will drive each older custom from the land,
> Will drive each generous passion from the breast.[38]

These examples of rural complaint interludes in Bloomfield, Batchelor and Grahame's georgic poems are not modal incursions by pastoral, but uses of a now standard feature of the georgic genre. These poems demonstrate georgic's capacity to evolve in form as well as content, as Romantic georgics assume or accommodate descriptive and even lyrical forms without losing their georgic identities.

Grahame's use, in his explicitly georgic poem, of the calendar form, an adaptation of the seasonal structure used by Thomson and Bloomfield, encourages us to read Clare's *The Shepherd's Calendar* (1827) as georgic too. Although *The Shepherd's Calendar* is not overtly didactic, it fulfils those same georgic tasks that both Lubin and Clare himself fulfilled in *The Village Minstrel*: recording the rituals of rural life and 'trac[ing] nature's secrets with unwearied eye'. The calendar form also recreates georgic's distinctive temporal perspective of an ongoing present, shaped by the past and shaping the future, which is both reassuringly repetitive and pleasingly variable. Yet because he writes a Romantic georgic, Clare must punctuate this sense of ongoing cyclical time with a complaint interlude, which raises the unsettling possibility that everything the poem describes belongs not to the present but to a lost past. Clare follows Bloomfield in using the topic of the communal feast to introduce a narrative of loss:[39]

> And ale and songs and healths and merry ways
> Keeps up a shadow of old farmers days
> But the old beachen bowl that once supplyd
> Its feast of frumity is thrown aside
> And the old freedom that was living then
> When masters made them merry wi their men
> ...
> All this is past – and soon may pass away
> The time torn remnant of the holiday.[40]

These lines are an argument for a particular kind of freedom: the *old* freedom, in which there are still masters, but the distance between them and their 'men' was less pronounced. The rural complaint is a way for the poet to introduce a political argument into the georgic, but its politics are complicated; the harvest feast, after all, is a motif of feudalism. For all its apparently progressive concern with improving conditions for the working poor, the rural complaint's nostalgic premise is inherently conservative. Christmas observes that, although Bloomfield's mourner's complaint 'earned Bloomfield his only political censure from the anti-Jacobin *British Critic*', his 'conservative tendencies are felt when we recall that this passage is framed within a Goldsmithian lament for a lost golden age'.[41] This conservatism is already latent in the Romantic georgic's tendency to idealize rural labour. As Harrison argues, the agrarian idyll uses a 'strategy of normalization rooted in middle-class conventions of capitalism and industry [that] involves the writing of values, like thrift, patience and industriousness, onto the working-class body'.[42] Similarly, John Murdoch has shown that Virgil's *Georgics* was used in the 1790s to defend a status quo in which

'Labor is inevitable'.[43] For Crawford, an 'anti-progressive impulse' is inherent in georgic itself, not just Romantic georgic: 'the [georgic] poet teeters between his celebration of the new world of commerce founded on progressive farming methods and his yearning for a traditional paternalistic structure'.[44] While social conservatism and the naturalization of working-class labour is prominent in many of the eighteenth-century georgics, the Romantic georgic re-emphasizes these elements through its construction of an agrarian idyll, and then further literalizes that conservatism through its use of the rural complaint form, which relocates the idealization of hard work into a longed-for past.

Yet the potential progressive energy of the rural complaint cannot be dismissed. Harrison goes on to acknowledge that the agrarian idyll did become an effective counter-ideology to industrial and capitalist expansion: 'One can speak ... at least after 1790, of a critical nostalgia ... a new writing of pastoral and georgic that redeploys their conventional epithets and ideologemes – "cheerful toil," "rustic simplicity," the "Noble Savage" – as a vision of not just social harmony, but social equality and political justice.'[45] At the end of *The Deserted Village*, Goldsmith hoped for a poetic that could teach the value of 'native strength' over 'gain', and offer some form of 'redress' that was unavailable within the stasis of the pastoral complaint. In the Romantic georgics, we see that the new trope of the rural complaint enables poets to introduce political arguments into their georgics; we also discover that in turn, the georgic form – the long descriptive or didactic poem that looks forward as well as back – enables them to introduce the possibility of progress into the conservative agrarian idyll.

In these Romantic georgics, after the complaint interlude's nostalgic retrospection, which idealizes the past and laments the present, the georgic temporality is resumed. In *The Shepherd's Calendar* the complaint comes at the end of 'June', unsettling the eternality created by the present indefinite tense used in the rest of the poem. Yet the calendar form means that after June, July comes, and the merry georgic life reasserts itself: 'July resumes her yearly place ... A lovly rest to daily toils'.[46] Whereas a pastoral complaint ends in hopeless stasis or death, a georgic complaint can 'look beyond the present good or ill' to potential forms of redress. 'Lo!' cries Batchelor after his peasant's complaint, 'Hope extends her magic tube, to see | What charms lie hid in dim futurity', and imagines a future 'blissful scene' in which hard work is rewarded by peace and plenty.[47] Grahame ends 'May' with an optimistic georgic image: even where you see weeds, 'rely that there | Grain, pulse, or root, whate'er the crop, will yield | An early and exuberant increase'.[48]

Bloomfield, meanwhile, allows his mourner to close his complaint, and 'Summer', with the injunction, 'Let labour have its due … then peace is mine, | And never, never shall my heart repine.' For Sean Nolan, the mourner's complaint is 'a key moment of change' in *The Farmer's Boy*, after which 'the scenes of farm life become increasingly tied with broader moral reflections pertaining mainly to the collateral damage resulting from landscape refinement'.[49] This overstates the extent of critique in 'Autumn' and 'Winter', but there is still a political dimension to their portrait of a farm where, for both humans and animals, 'each day's labour brings its sure reward' (book IV, line 152). The mourner's (albeit very vague) proposal for a solution means that the rest of the poem *might* describe not the lost past, but a better future. 'Autumn' ends with the declaration that the 'child of poverty' shall not 'despair', but be 'Assur'd … that *Spring* will come' (book III, lines 357–60). The poem ends, at the close of 'Winter', with Giles's georgic prayer, a version of the happy man's wish for knowledge of nature's ways:

> '*Another* SPRING!' his heart exulting cries;
> '*Another* YEAR! with promis'd blessings rise! …
> 'ETERNAL POWER! from whom those blessings flow,
> 'Teach me still more to wonder, more to know.' (book IV, lines 385–88)

On one hand, georgic's ability to move on may neutralize the potentially radical argument of the complaint, by returning to a status quo defined by work. Georgic enables 'evolution' rather than 'revolution', as Fairer puts it.[50] Yet it also enables, in Binfield's formulation, 'sustainability rather than stasis'.[51] It offers a vision of a present and future countryside in which rural customs may be recuperated and labour may have its 'due'.

Understanding the rural complaint as a feature of formal georgic in the Romantic period helps us to understand the strange nostalgic political interludes in overtly georgic poems. It also encourages us to read other rural complaint poems as georgic: when poets lamented the loss of an idealized lifestyle characterized by rewarding rural labour, they were experimenting not just with georgic subject-matter, but also with georgic form.

Beachy Head and Georgic Complaint

By recognizing the complaint as a georgic form, we discover a new generic logic to some of the strangest moments in Romantic poetry. One example, serving here as a kind of case study in how the georgic rural complaint tradition can illuminate poems that are not obviously formal georgics, is

Charlotte Smith's *Beachy Head* (1807). As georgic's critical currency has grown in recent years, so the georgic elements of this generically multifarious poem have attracted greater attention, by critics including Kevis Goodman, Theresa M. Kelley, Tobias Menely and Juan Christian Pellicer.[52] Smith deploys several of the most popular georgic set-pieces in her poem, including the image of labourers turning up ancient bones with their tools, and the 'happy man' trope. Identifying the georgic tradition behind these lines can open up a transformative reading not only of a passage but also of the entire poem, as Pellicer has demonstrated in his reading of these and other georgic tropes in Smith's poem. Similarly, recognizing Smith's use of the rural complaint as an experiment with a *georgic* form opens up *Beachy Head* in interesting ways. It allows us to understand at least one aspect of Smith's logic when a georgic passage on the happy hind, and his difficult but rewarding way of life, turns into a (seemingly pastoral) complaint about the speaker's own personal development:

> I *once* was happy, when while yet a child,
> I learn'd to love these upland solitudes.[53]

Kelley identifies *Beachy Head*'s 'pattern in which early joy gives way to embittered, trapped adulthood' as a function of 'the poem's flawed georgic' ('flawed' in that it questions the eighteenth-century 'confident georgic' emblematized by *The Seasons*).[54] Yet this autobiographical pattern is easily accommodated within Romantic georgic because by the time Smith writes *Beachy Head*, the georgic is a genre in which happiness must be relocated to the past and lamented. Here Smith's complaint is not explicitly longing for a past in which rural labour was better recompensed, but her complaint reminds her to remind us that everything she describes in the poem, including that happy hind and other 'simple scenes of peace and industry', are in fact 'Scenes of fond day dreams'. That is, as in *The Farmer's Boy* and *The Shepherd's Calendar*, this complaint interlude threatens to relocate the rest of the poem's georgic content, and its celebration of a georgic life and landscape, to the past. Whereas Pellicer has argued that Smith's key model is Gray's 'Elegy', and that the poem is unlike *The Deserted Village* because its interest is in individual melancholy rather than 'social disruptions', we can see Goldsmith's influence in Smith's complaint for an idealized agrarian past.[55]

As well as the lament which follows the 'happy hind' sequence, Smith includes another explicit complaint near the end of the poem. Again, the complaint follows another self-consciously georgic image, in which the landscape of past war, in this case a Norman castle, has been turned into farmland:

> But now a tiller of the soil dwells there,
> And of the turret's loop'd and rafter'd halls
> Has made an humbler homestead—Where he sees,
> Instead of armed foemen, herds that graze
> Along his yellow meadows.

This georgic scene is immediately followed by the story of a poet who composes complaints:

> In such a castellated mansion once
> A stranger chose his home; …
> They heard him, as complaining of his fate.

Beachy Head then includes his complaint, a pastoral song in which he imagines himself as a shepherd:

> 'Were I a Shepherd on the hill
> And ever as the mists withdrew'

This is not the rural complaint for a lost agrarian idyll, but the conventional pastoral complaint for lost love. Nevertheless, Smith's formal turn here, from description of the activities of a husbandman to lyrical complaint, whether delivered in the main narrative voice or the quoted voice of a 'mourner', 'minstrel swain' or 'stranger', is enabled by the naturalization of just such a formal turn in contemporary Romantic georgic. The stranger's song ends like an eighteenth-century pastoral complaint, with the imagined death of the speaker. Yet Smith's poem, with its longer form derived from the georgic and topographical traditions, is able to continue with a note of tempered optimism. Despite the stranger's own pastoral forlornness, 'Some future blessings he may yet enjoy … For what is life, when Hope has ceas'd to strew | Her fragile flowers along its thorny way?' *Beachy Head* is sceptical about the possibility of redress for any of its complaining speakers, including the narrator, and the poem ends with another mournful tale. Yet *Beachy Head*'s 'scenes of fond day dreams' are not only memories of a lost past, but also, simultaneously, visions of a wished-for future ('I would recline'). The future the poet wishes for is one in which she may contemplate Nature's works, and record the ways of local working people – in other words, in which she may be a georgic poet.

Georgic should not be relegated from genre to mode in the Romantic period, because the formal georgic did not disappear. It absorbed the rural complaint and in turn transformed the rural complaint into a new georgic form. The rural complaint features as a naturalized set-piece in the Romantic poems that are most clearly attempts at formal georgic, and it can also stand alone as a georgic form, with full invocation of this generic tradition. Recognizing this, we see that the autobiographical narratives of *Beachy Head*, *The Task* and *The Prelude*, as well as the lyrical forms and elegiac tones of poems such as 'Michael', 'The Ruined Cottage', 'To Autumn' and again *Beachy Head*, are not at odds with these poems' georgic elements. They are closely bound up with georgic's Romantic development into a genre that aimed to 'redress the rigours of the inclement clime'.

Notes

1 J. Clare, *The Village Minstrel and Other Poems*, 2 vols. (1821), vol. I, p. 3. Subsequent references to *The Village Minstrel* are to this edition.
2 T. Adams, 'Representing Rural Leisure: John Clare and the Politics of Popular Culture', *Studies in Romanticism*, 47 (2008), 371–92, at 380.
3 Virgil, *Georgics* (Dryden), p. 203 (II, lines 698–9) (*Georgics*, II. 494–5).
4 On the development of this trope, see M.-S. Røstvig, *The Happy Man: Studies in the Metamorphoses of a Classical Ideal*, 2 vols. (Oslo: Akademisk Forlag, and Oxford: Blackwell, 1954–8).
5 K. Heinzelman, 'Roman Georgic in the Georgian Age: A Theory of Romantic Genre', *Texas Studies in Literature and Language*, 33 (1991), 182–214, at 182.
6 D. Fairer, '"The Year Runs Round": The Poetry of Work in Eighteenth-Century England' in *Ritual, Routine, and Regime: Repetition in Early Modern British and European Cultures*, ed. L. Clyne (University of Toronto Press, 2006), pp. 153–71, at p. 154.
7 R. Beck, 'From Industrial Georgic to Industrial Sublime: English Poetry and the Early Stages of the Industrial Revolution', *British Journal for Eighteenth-Century Studies*, 27 (2004), 17–36.
8 R. Williams, *The Country and the City* (New York: Oxford University Press, 1973), pp. 9–45.
9 See, for example, G. L. Harrison, *Wordsworth's Vagrant Muse: Poetry, Poverty and Power* (Detroit: Wayne State University Press, 1994), pp. 27–8.
10 R. Crawford, 'English Georgic and British Nationhood', *ELH*, 65 (1998), 123–58, at 135.
11 Virgil, *Georgics* (Dryden), p. 157 (I, line 72) (*Georgics*, I. 47–8).
12 J. C. Pellicer, 'Virgil's Eclogues and Georgics in Charlotte Smith's Beachy Head', in *Romans and Romantics*, ed. T. Saunders et al. (Oxford University Press, 2012), pp. 161–82, at p. 163.
13 T. Burke, 'The Romantic Georgic and the Work of Writing', in *A Companion to Romantic Poetry*, ed. C. Mahoney (Chichester: Wiley-Blackwell, 2011), pp. 140–58, at p. 143.
14 Burke, 'Romantic Georgic', p. 144. See Heinzelman, 'Roman Georgic'.
15 I am grateful to Adam Bridgen for drawing my attention to Woodhouse.
16 R. Smith, M. O'Callaghan and S. C. E. Ross, 'Complaint' in *A Companion to Renaissance Poetry*, ed. C. Bates (Hoboken: Wiley, 2018), pp. 339–52.

17 F. Stafford, 'The Shepherd's Calendar', *Victoriographies*, 2 (2012), 103–27, at 124, and R. Smith, 'Cultures of Complaint: Protest and Redress in the Age of #Metoo', *Australian Humanities Review*, 63 (2018), 172–84.
18 N. Rowe, *Poems on Several Occasions*, 3rd ed. (1714), p. 30.
19 R. Fergusson, *The Works of Robert Fergusson* (Edinburgh, 1805), p. 14.
20 O. Goldsmith, *The Collected Works of Oliver Goldsmith*, ed. A. Friedman, 5 vols. (Oxford: Clarendon Press, 1966), vol. IV, p. 287, lines 1–2. All subsequent references to *The Deserted Village* are to this edition.
21 Harrison, *Wordsworth's Vagrant Muse*, p. 48.
22 D. Fairer, 'Georgic' in *The Oxford Handbook of British Poetry, 1660–1800*, ed. Jack Lynch (Oxford University Press, 2016), pp. 457–72, at p. 466.
23 Several editions have 'And' for 'Aid', which suggests that 'slighted truth', rather than poetry, is asked to teach. However, most editions including the first have 'Aid' so I have used 'Aid' here.
24 G. Crabbe, *The Complete Poetical Works*, ed. N. Dalrymple-Champneys and A. Pollard, 3 vols. (Oxford: Clarendon Press, 1988), vol. I, p. 159 (book I, lines 93–4).
25 R. Palmer, *A Ballad History of England from 1588 to the Present Day* (London: B. T. Batsford, 1979), p. 68.
26 W. Holloway, *The Peasant's Fate: A Rural Poem* (Boston: Hosea Sprague, 1802), pp. 4, 28.
27 Holloway, *The Peasant's Fate*, 'Preface', unpaginated.
28 E. Elliott, *The Splendid Village: Corn Law Rhymes; and Other Poems* (1833), p. 24.
29 Elliott, *Splendid Village*, p. 37.
30 For the importance of georgic as a framework for labouring-class writers particularly, see D. Landry, 'Georgic Ecology' in *Robert Bloomfield: Lyric, Class, and the Romantic Canon*, ed. S. White, J. Goodridge, and B. Keegan (Lewisburg: Bucknell University Press), pp. 253–68.
31 R. Bloomfield, *The Farmer's Boy: A Rural Poem*, 3rd ed. (London: Vernor and Hood, 1800), pp. 121, 114. Subsequent references to *The Farmer's Boy* are to this edition.
32 W. J. Christmas, '*The Farmer's Boy* and Contemporary Politics', in *Robert Bloomfield*, ed. White et al., pp. 27–48, at p. 32.
33 B. Keegan, *British Labouring-Class Nature Poetry, 1730–1837* (Basingstoke: Palgrave Macmillan, 2008), p. 29.
34 K. Binfield, 'Labor and an Ethic of Variety in *The Farmer's Boy*', in *Robert Bloomfield*, ed. White et al., pp. 70–88, at p. 76.
35 T. Batchelor, *Village Scenes, The Progress of Agriculture, and Other Poems* (1804), p. 69.
36 Batchelor, *Village Scenes*, 'Preface' (unpaginated).
37 Batchelor, *Village Scenes*, p. 88.
38 J. Grahame, *British Georgics* (Edinburgh, 1809), pp. 90–1. For a study of Grahame's reworking of georgic, see D. M. Zimmerman, 'The Last Georgic, or James Grahame's Revision of Eighteenth-Century Rural Labour', *Scottish Studies*, 45 (2010), 244–52.

39 Later, Elliott would also use the village feast as the emblem of the lost happy georgic life in *The Splendid Village*.
40 J. Clare, *The Shepherd's Calendar*, ed. E. Robinson and G. Summerfield (Oxford University Press, 1964), pp. 68–9.
41 Christmas, '*The Farmer's Boy* and Contemporary Politics', p. 43.
42 Harrison, *Wordsworth's Vagrant Muse*, p. 29.
43 J. Murdoch, 'The Landscape of Labor: Transformations of the Georgic', in *Romantic Revolutions: Criticism and Theory*, ed. K. R. Johnston et al. (Bloomington: Indiana University Press, 1990), pp. 176–93, at p. 180.
44 Crawford, *English Georgic*, p. 135.
45 Harrison, *Wordsworth's Vagrant Muse*, p. 50.
46 Clare, *Shepherd's Calendar*, p. 70.
47 Batchelor, *Village Scenes*, pp. 98–9.
48 Grahame, *British Georgics*, p. 100.
49 S. Nolan, '"The Task that Leads the Wilder'd Mind": Robert Bloomfield, Humble Industry, and Studious Leisure', *European Romantic Review*, 31 (2020), 573–85, at 577.
50 Fairer, 'Georgic', p. 466.
51 Binfield, 'Labor and an Ethic of Variety', p. 70.
52 K. Goodman, *Georgic Modernity and British Romanticism* (Cambridge University Press, 2004), p. 1; T. M. Kelley, 'Romantic Histories: Charlotte Smith and *Beachy Head*', *Nineteenth-Century Literature*, 59 (2004), 281–314, at 290, 295, 301, 311; T. Menely, 'Late Holocene Poetics: Genre and Geohistory in *Beachy Head*', *European Romantic Review*, 28 (2017), 307–14, at 308, 310; and Pellicer, 'Virgil's Eclogues and Georgics'.
53 C. Smith, *Beachy Head: with Other Poems* (1807), p. 20. Subsequent references to *Beachy Head* are to this edition.
54 Kelley, 'Romantic Histories', p. 301.
55 Pellicer, 'Virgil's Eclogues and Georgics', p. 177.

CHAPTER 9

Rural Labour in an Age of Industry
William Cobbett and Some Contemporaries

James Grande

In 'Three around Farnham', a famous chapter in his classic study *The Country and the City* (1973), Raymond Williams takes the reader on an imagined journey 'round a thirty-mile triangle of roads, in the turning years of the late eighteenth and early nineteenth centuries ... on the borders of Hampshire and Surrey: six miles from Selborne to Chawton; ten miles from Chawton to Farnham; fourteen miles from Farnham back to Selborne'. This narrow triangle encompasses three rural writers, 'overlapping within a generation ... who could hardly be more different': Gilbert White, Jane Austen and William Cobbett. For Williams, these writers offer 'a complex of different ways of seeing even the same local life', from White's detailed, proto-scientific observations of the natural world to Austen's novels of gentry life and the thick social description of Cobbett's itinerant journalism.[1] These differences are partly determined, in Williams's account, by their contrasting perspectives: Austen was 'writing from a very different point of view, from inside the houses that Cobbett was passing on the road'. The paradoxical achievement of Austen's fiction was to maintain a 'remarkable unity of tone' while describing a historical period of often bewildering change, as an agrarian economy became enmeshed within the wider networks of a commercial society.[2]

This chapter re-visits Williams's imagined journey to explore the meanings of georgic in a period of rapid urbanization and industrialization. Representations of rural labour in this historical moment might seem to occupy the category that Williams defines elsewhere as the 'residual', running counter to narratives of progressive change.[3] Such a reading fails, however, to account for the complexity of such representations and the cultural work they perform. To take one example from Austen's oeuvre, a survey of George Knightley's estate of Donwell Abbey during the strawberry-picking scene of *Emma* (1815) leads to an unexpectedly charged moment of national identification:

> It was hot; and after walking some time over the gardens in a scattered, dispersed way, scarcely any three together, they insensibly followed one another to the delicious shade of a broad short avenue of limes, which stretching beyond the garden at an equal distance from the river, seemed the finish of the pleasure grounds. ... The considerable slope, at nearly the foot of which the Abbey stood, gradually acquired a steeper form beyond its grounds; and at half a mile distant was a bank of considerable abruptness and grandeur, well clothed with wood;—and at the bottom of this bank, favourably placed and sheltered, rose the Abbey-Mill Farm, with meadows in front, and the river making a close and handsome curve around it.
>
> It was a sweet view—sweet to the eye and the mind. English verdure, English culture, English comfort, seen under a sun bright, without being oppressive.[4]

Emma represents (among other things) Austen's response to the new genre of the 'national tale' developed by Walter Scott and Maria Edgeworth in the early years of the nineteenth century. In her anglicizing of this genre, 'English verdure, English culture, English comfort' conveys a form of national identification that is rooted in a particular landscape. If the village of Highbury often appears as an oppressively claustrophobic environment through the narrative lens of Emma Woodhouse, whose attitude to the wider world verges on the agoraphobic, here the view opens to a wider prospect. In narrative terms, the sweetness of this view signals the appropriateness of the marriage between Emma's friend Harriet Smith and Robert Martin, Mr Knightley's tenant farmer at Abbey-Mill Farm. Emma had previously tried to obstruct this match, dismissing 'A young farmer, whether on horseback or on foot' as beyond her pale of interest: 'The yeomanry are precisely the order of people with whom I feel I can have nothing to do.'[5] The ultimate approbation of their union is at one with the socially conservative vision of *Emma*, governed by a form of moderation that is distinctly English even in climatological terms: 'seen under a sun bright, without being oppressive'.

Austen's celebration of the sweetness of 'English verdure' seems to affirm a sense of national belonging rooted in the cultivated landscape of the southern counties. It is a rare but telling flash of patriotic feeling, and one that might be taken to reflect a confident, optimistic national mood at the end of the long years of the Napoleonic Wars. By contrast, the writing of Austen's Hampshire neighbour William Cobbett gives us a much bleaker account of the post-war landscape and the state of rural labour and the rural economy. In what follows, I want to suggest that Cobbett might be productively read as a writer engaged with the georgic mode. Cobbett has long occupied an awkward place in literary history, as a popular, even demagogic, journalist and political writer, who started out as a loyalist, anti-Jacobin pamphleteer and scourge of revolutionaries on both sides of the Atlantic, before becoming a committed radical, vociferous campaigner for parliamentary reform, and virtual embodiment of rural England. To Thomas Carlyle, Cobbett was 'the pattern John Bull of his century', while Karl Marx described him as 'the purest incarnation of Old England and the most audacious initiator of Young England'.[6] Cobbett might not seem like an obvious writer to think about in connection with the categories of classical poetics, given his remoteness from elite literary culture and frequent disparagement of classical learning. Cobbett ridiculed 'those dens of dunces called Colleges and Universities', insisting *what they call the* LEARNED LANGUAGES *are improperly so called; and that, as a part of general education, they are worse than useless*' – a claim that started a long-running controversy in the pages of his *Political Register*.[7] Nonetheless, his writing on rural England contains recognizably pastoral and georgic themes, tropes and rhetorical strategies.

The rural ideal was one that Cobbett did not merely write about but also attempted to inhabit. He claimed, with characteristic hyperbole, to have been 'bred at the plough-tail, and in the Hop-Gardens of Farnham in Surrey, my native place, and which spot, as it so happened, is the neatest in England, and, I believe, in the whole world. All there is a garden'.[8] After leaving Farnham and enlisting in the army, he spent two decades away from rural England at Chatham, New Brunswick, northern France and Philadelphia, where he launched his literary career as a political pamphleteer. In 1805, however, having returned to England, and on the cusp of the transition between his early anti-Jacobinism and mature radicalism, he purchased a farm at Botley, outside Southampton. From this point on, his new identity as a Hampshire farmer was a sign of his independence from the nexus of political and financial corruption he associated with the city and contemptuously described as 'the THING'.[9] Alongside the angry fusillades of his weekly journalism, there was now another side to Cobbett's self-identity, existing in apparent pastoral seclusion.

One of the most vivid descriptions of Cobbett in this phase of his career is from the author and dramatist Mary Russell Mitford, looking back from mid-century in *Recollections of a Literary Life, or Books, Places and People* (1852). She remembers how Cobbett,

> had at that time a large house at Botley, with a lawn and gardens sweeping down to the Bursledon River ... large, high, massive, red, and square, and perched on a considerable eminence—[it] always struck me as not being unlike its proprietor ... He was a tall, stout man, fair, and sunburnt, with a

bright smile, and an air compounded of the soldier and the farmer, to which his habit of wearing an eternal red waistcoat contributed not a little. He was, I think, the most athletic and vigorous person that I have ever known.

Mitford was visiting Botley with her father, who had met Cobbett hare coursing and invited him to a meeting near their home in the village of Three Mile Cross, Berkshire. They were now repaying the visit and found Cobbett's house 'filled ... almost to overflowing', with guests including the naval hero and radical politician Lord Cochrane, 'in the very height of his warlike fame' but 'as unlike the common notion of a warrior as could be. A gentle, quiet, mild young man, was this burner of French fleets and cutter-out of Spanish vessels ... He lay about under the trees reading Selden on the Dominion of the Seas', appearing almost as a version of Austen's Captain Wentworth in *Persuasion* (1818).

For Mitford, the defining quality of Cobbett's English ruralism is his unaffected hospitality, which transcends the divisions of social class and embraces both the naval captain and the local farmer:

> there was a large fluctuating series of guests for the hour or guests for the day, of almost all ranks and descriptions, from the Earl and his Countess to the farmer and his dame ... I never saw hospitality more genuine, more simple, or more thoroughly successful in the great end of hospitality, the putting every body completely at ease. There was not the slightest attempt at finery, or display, or gentility. They called it a farmhouse, and everything was in accordance with the largest idea of a great English yeoman of the old time.

Mitford compares William and Nancy Cobbett to Dandie and Ailie Dinmont, the hearty Borders farmer and his wife in Walter Scott's *Guy Mannering* (1815). This hospitality is set within a bucolic scene and Mitford gives a rich description of Cobbett's horticultural skill:

> The fields lay along the Bursledon River, and might have been shown to a foreigner as a specimen of the richest and loveliest English scenery. In the cultivation of his garden, too, he displayed the same taste. Few persons excelled him in the management of vegetables, fruit, and flowers. His green Indian corn—his Carolina beans—his water-melons, could hardly have been exceeded at New York. His wall-fruit was equally splendid, and ... I never saw a more glowing or a more fragrant autumn garden than that at Botley, with its pyramids of hollyhocks, and its masses of china-asters, of cloves, of mignionette, and of variegated geranium.[10]

Mitford's portrait of Cobbett at Botley is insistently apolitical, even ahistorical, recalling the rural idylls of Mitford's influential collection of stories, *Our Village: Sketches of Rural Character and Scenery*, which were first serialized in the *Lady's Magazine* and published in successive volumes between 1824 and 1832.¹¹ It is an unusually static view of Cobbett, who, as his most perceptive readers have noticed, spent much of his life in a state of continual motion: John Barrell has described him as 'an habitually *itinerant* man', for David Simpson, he 'has a commitment to the local but the habits of a cosmopolitan', while Linda Colley has drawn attention to 'how substantially un-English his life experience was, and the impact this had on his ideas'.¹² These readings run counter to Mitford's portrait – or, indeed, to Raymond Williams's account of Cobbett as the supreme localist. It is this pastoral and static scene that would be disrupted over the next decade by the government's relentless persecution of Cobbett's radical journalism.

In 1810, Cobbett was sentenced to two years in Newgate prison and issued with heavy fines and sureties after being convicted of seditious libel for an article in the *Political Register* attacking the practice of flogging in the army. Cobbett's children took turns to stay with him in Newgate and assist him with the continued production of the *Political Register* and his daughter Anne gave a vivid description of her father exercising on the roof of the prison each morning, above the yard where executions took place, by acting out agricultural labour: going through 'the motions of digging, raking, mowing etc with a dumb bell in each hand'.¹³ This image simultaneously suggests an imaginative escape from Newgate and an ascetic daily regime, rooted in rural life and labour. Reduced to going through the motions of agricultural labour on the roof of the prison, Cobbett nonetheless tried to retain complete control over work at Botley and his letters from Newgate are filled with sketches, plans and instructions, covering every detail of work on the farm. Cobbett's rural economy would be disrupted again in 1817 by the government's suspension of habeas corpus. Convinced that he would be imprisoned again, he fled to America and established himself on Long Island, declaring 'my intention to be a downright farmer', in marked contrast to his American sojourn in the 1790s when he had launched himself into the fiercely partisan world of Philadelphia politics and print culture as the anti-Jacobin pamphleteer 'Peter Porcupine'.¹⁴ Once again, Cobbett continued the *Political Register* during his American exile, contending with the six-week lag-time between sending his articles from Long Island and publication in Britain. His Long Island farmyard became at once a place of pastoral exile and an extension of Cobbett's England, with his new identity as an American farmer standing for his continued commitment to his rural audience at home.

Cobbett returned to England at the end of 1819, accompanied by the mortal remains of Thomas Paine, which he had dug up and brought back to serve as a rallying point for reform. This project came to nothing (notoriously, Cobbett ultimately lost track of Paine's bones) and within a few months of his return Cobbett was declared bankrupt and forced to sell the Botley farm. His new base was a four-acre smallholding and nursery-garden at Kensington, on what is now the High Street Kensington station of the London Underground. This was then at the edge of what Cobbett described as the 'Great Wen' of London: Samuel Johnson's *Dictionary* defines a 'wen' as 'a dangerous fleshy excrescence' and Cobbett viewed the city as a morbid swelling on the body politic. His large-scale farming ambitions were now effectively over, but this was still the site of impressive feats of productivity, as he boasted to a friend:

> I think I have *a million of trees*; and, in the paths between the beds, I have enough vegetables for two or three families, and enough for *cow* and pigs, and green stuff enough for horses (they like fine cabbages) besides ... We have raised, 12 ducks, 10 chickens, and *18 Turkeys*, the two former came against our will. My sow had 11 pigs last Monday three weeks. I killed 5 yesterday, that weighed 8 ¾ lb each. I shall kill three more of them, and keep 3 to kill for bacon in March. I have now 3 of her *January* farrow, for bacon in the winter and spring. So much for my farming.[15]

His main project at Kensington was 'to form a Nursery for American Forest-Trees, and Apple trees', with Cobbett 'very anxious to keep my foot on the American soil' in case he had to flee England again.[16] Having left his son James on Long Island to coordinate the American side of the venture, Kensington soon became the headquarters of a transatlantic seed business.

This project provided Cobbett with an alternative source of income at a time when the government were determined to suppress radical publications through taxes and prosecutions. Cobbett seems to have viewed it as a necessary venture, as the government increased the tax on cheap publications and limited his circulation and profits. Within a few years, his publications carried advertisements for American apple trees ('I hope to be able to shew such apples as have never been seen in England before'), hickory, black walnut, persimmon, occidental plane, tulip trees, white oak, sweet chestnut, paper birch, catalpa and althea frutex shrubs, and locust trees.[17] As he explained to James, in distinctly pastoral idiom, 'it is prudent and pleasant to be independent of courts and courtiers.—And, besides, I take great delight in trees and gardens, and it gives me great pleasure to introduce and spread things of this sort.'[18] In the *Political Register*, he reflected that the 'melancholy, mean fellow, DOCTOR JOHNSON, observes, that when a man *plants a tree*, he begins *to think of dying*. If this were the fact, is that to prevent the planting of trees? I have been planting of trees in every spot that I have ever *occupied*, all my life time'. For Cobbett, this activity was inseparable from his journalistic and educational endeavours, which all tended to the reform of a corrupt political system:

> All my plans in private life; all my pursuits; all my designs, wishes, and thoughts, have this one great object in view: *the overthrow of the ruffian Boroughmongers*. If I write grammars, if I write on agriculture; if I sow, plant, or deal in seeds; whatever I do has *first* in view the destruction of those infamous tyrants.[19]

While the connections between these activities were often obscure, Cobbett clearly viewed them as sharing a single purpose.

Kensington was also the starting point for Cobbett's 1820s tours of southern England, which would become his most enduring literary work. His accounts of these journeys first appeared in serial form in the *Political Register* before being published together in 1830 as *Rural Rides in the Counties of Surrey, Kent, Sussex, Hampshire, Wiltshire, Gloucestershire, Herefordshire, Worcestershire, Somersetshire, Oxfordshire, Berkshire, Essex, Suffolk, Norfolk, and Herefordshire: with Economical and Political Observations relative to matters applicable to, and illustrated by, the State of those Counties respectively*.[20] The first tour is titled, 'Rural Rides of a hundred and four miles, from Kensington to Uphusband; including a Rustic Harangue at Winchester[,] At a Dinner with the Farmers' and begins by announcing a self-consciously strenuous route and method:

> This morning I set off, in rather a drizzling rain, from Kensington, on horse-back, accompanied by my son James, with an intention of going to UPHUSBAND, near ANDOVER, which is situated in the North West corner of Hampshire. It is very true that I could have gone to Uphusband by travelling only about 66 miles, and in the space of about *eight hours*. But, my object was, not to see inns and turnpike-roads, but to see the *country;* to see the farmers at *home*, and to see the labourers *in the fields;* and to do this you must go either on foot or on horse-back.[21]

Cobbett's way of travelling prizes difficulty in pursuit of his mission ('to see the *country;* to see the farmers at *home*, and to see the labourers *in the fields*') and is presented as the only way to glean authentic knowledge of the countryside:

> Those that travel on turnpike roads know nothing of England.—From Hascomb to Thursley almost the whole way is across fields, or commons, or along narrow lanes. Here we see the people without any disguise or affectation. Against a *great road* things are made for *show*. Here we see them *without any show*. And here we gain real knowledge as to their situation.[22]

Cobbett's embrace of difficulty and obstacles reflects aspects of the human relationship with the natural world that David Fairer has described as constitutive of the georgic mode.²³

In *Rural Rides*, the pastoral exists only in fleeting and self-consciously staged moments in Cobbett's writing, as an alternative to his restless movement and political resolve. For example, in September 1826, Cobbett visited the Worcestershire estate of Stanford Court, at the invitation of Sir Thomas Winnington, an improving landowner and Member of Parliament for the county.²⁴ Declaring it to be 'one of the finest spots in all England ... and the park is every thing that is beautiful', Cobbett introduces a Mephisophelean dialogue:

> 'Well, then,' says the devil of laziness, 'and could you not be contented to live here all the rest of your life; and never again pester yourself with the cursed politics?' 'Why, I think I have laboured enough. Let others work now. And such a pretty place for coursing and for hare-hunting and woodcock shooting ... and never, never again to be stifled with the smoke that from the infernal WEN ascendeth for ever more and that every easterly wind brings to choke me at *Kensington!*' The *last word* of this soliloquy carried me back, slap, to my own study ... 'Go, George, and tell them to saddle the horses'; for, it seemed to me, that I had been meditating some crime.²⁵

Pastoral life, including rural retirement and country sports, is here a source of temptation, luring Cobbett away from his political commitments, until the abrupt end of his reverie. Such pastoral remnants are only transitory moments in *Rural Rides*; instead, the dominant mode is georgic, both in the tireless activity of Cobbett's writing and riding and in the agricultural labour he describes.²⁶

As Cobbett crossed and re-crossed the southern counties of England during the 1820s he built up a minute account of the English countryside and the state of rural labour, conditioned both by the aftermath of the long wars with France, including the economic dislocations and political agitation in the years after Waterloo, and by the context of accelerating industrialization. On one level, *Rural Rides* follows in the footsteps of Arthur Young's famous agricultural tours of the 1770s and 1780s and less well-known examples of the genre such as the radical orator John Thelwall's 'Pedestrian Excursion', serialized in the *Monthly Magazine* between August 1799 and November 1801, which included reports on the state of the crops, the rural economy and the condition of agricultural labourers. Cobbett does so, however, in a specifically post-war context. Writing about Wordsworth's poetry, Alan Liu has described georgic as 'the supreme meditational form by which to bury history in nature, epic in pastoral'.²⁷ Liu draws here on the historical context in which Virgil wrote the *Georgics*, in the aftermath of civil war, and the memorable image at the end of Book 1: 'Nothing surer than the time will come when, in those fields, a farmer ploughing will unearth rough and rusted javelins and hear his heavy hoe echo on the sides of empty helmets and stare in open-eyed amazement at the bones of heroes he's just happened on.'²⁸ As in Wordsworth's poetry of the 1790s, Cobbett often records his encounters with demobbed soldiers, fallen on hard times, travelling through the countryside and trying to make sense of their experiences:

> I met, at Worth, *a beggar*, who told me, in consequence of my asking *where he belonged*, that he was born in *South Carolina*. I found, at last, that he was born in the English army, during the American rebel-war; that he became a soldier himself; and that it had been his fate to serve under the Duke of York, in Holland; under General Whitlock, at Buenos Ayres; under Sir John Moore, at Corunna; and under 'the Greatest Captain' [Wellington], at Talavera! This poor fellow did not seem to be at all aware, that, in the last case, he partook in *a victory*! He had never before heard of its being a *victory*. He, poor fool, thought that it was a *defeat*. 'Why,' said he, 'we *ran away*, Sir.' Oh yes! said I, and so you did afterwards, perhaps, in Portugal, when Massena was at your heels; but it is only in *certain cases* that running away is a mark of being defeated; or, rather, it is only with certain commanders. A matter of much more interest to us, however, is that the wars for '*social order*,' not forgetting Gatton and Old Sarum, have filled the country with beggars, who have been, or pretend to have been, soldiers and sailors.²⁹

History is not buried in *Rural Rides*, but continually uncovered, as Cobbett seeks to challenge the dominant narrative of the war and show its continued effects in the English countryside.

When he reaches Dover, Cobbett surveys with rising incredulity and anger the coastal defences, built in readiness for invasion by Napoleon:

> Here is a hill containing probably a couple of square miles or more, hollowed like a honey-comb. Here are line upon line, trench upon trench, cavern upon cavern, bomb-proof upon bomb-proof ... more brick and stone have been buried in this hill than would go to build a neat new cottage for every labouring man in the counties of Kent and of Sussex!³⁰

Dismissing the utility of these defences, or the likelihood that Napoleon's armies would ever choose to land at Dover, Cobbett concludes that what Pitt's ministry wanted, 'was to prevent the landing, not of Frenchmen, but of French principles; that is to say, to prevent the example of the French from being alluring to the people of England'.³¹ If the cliffs of Dover have long been a symbol of English identity, serving, in Paul Readman's words, as 'a synecdoche of separateness from the Continent, of Britain's status as an island apart from the rest of Europe', Cobbett subverts this tradition, with an image instead of georgic communality:

> It is impossible to be upon this honey-combed hill; upon this enormous mass of anti-jacobin expenditure, without seeing the chalk-cliffs of Calais and the corn-fields of France. At this season, it is impossible to see those fields without knowing that the farmers are getting in their corn there as well as here; and it is impossible to think of that fact without reflecting at the same time, on the example which the farmers of France hold out to the farmers of England.[32]

Refusing any jingoistic celebration of Napoleon's defeat, Cobbett's view from Dover holds out the possibility of political reform in Britain, through the image of the French farmers getting in their corn – without, he pointedly observes, having to pay any tithes.

Elsewhere, Cobbett's journalism draws its terms and meanings from the agricultural practices he observes on the road, showing a characteristically georgic preoccupation with process and practical detail, while at the same time developing his own political lexicon:

> Mr. WINNAL has a large flock of sheep feeding on his cabbages, which they will have finished, perhaps, by January. This gentleman also has some '*radical Swedes,*' as they call them in Norfolk. A part of his crop is on ridges *five* feet apart with *two rows* on the ridge, a part on *four* feet ridges with *one* row on the ridge. I cannot see that anything is gained in weight by the double rows. I think, that there may be nearly twenty tons to the acre. Another piece Mr. WINNAL transplanted after vetches. They are very fine; and, altogether, he has a crop that any one but a '*loyal*' farmer might envy him.—This is really the *radical* system of husbandry. *Radical* means, *belonging to the root; going to the root*. And the main principle of this system (first taught by *Tull*) is, that the *root* of the plant is to be fed by *deep tillage*, while it is growing; and, to do this we must have our *wide distances*. Our system of husbandry is happily illustrative of our system of politics. Our lines of movement are fair and straightforward. We destroy all weeds, which, like tax-eaters, do nothing but devour the sustenance that ought to feed the valuable plants. Our plants are all *well fed;* and our nations of Swedes and of cabbages present a happy uniformity of enjoyments and of bulk, and not, as in the broad-cast system of Corruption, here and there one of enormous size, surrounded by thousands of poor little starveling things, scarcely distinguishable by the keenest eye, or, if seen, seen only to inspire a contempt of the husbandman. The Norfolk boys are, therefore, right in calling their Swedes *Radical Swedes*.[33]

This etymology for 'radical' takes the term away from urban political organization (its usual context in this period, in association with groups such as the London Corresponding Society) to deploy it instead in a georgic setting. The idea of '*belonging to the root; going to the root*' is at once a description of Cobbett's journalistic practice – digging below the surface, stripping away false layers of corruption – and an image of good husbandry. The crop produced serves also as an image for 'our system of politics', predicated on 'happy uniformity'.

On similar, egalitarian grounds, Cobbett repeatedly stresses a preference for variegated landscapes with woodlands and downs, which are less likely to be subject of new enclosures. After riding from Farnham to Alresford, he describes how, 'large sweeping downs, and deep dells here and there, with villages amongst lofty trees, are my great delight'; similarly, the countryside between Whitchurch and Burghclere is 'high, chalk bottom, open downs or large fields, with here and there a *farm-house in a dell*, sheltered by lofty trees, which, to my taste is the most pleasant situation in the world'.[34] By contrast, on the Isle of Thanet in Kent, he observes how

> the richer the soil, and the more destitute of woods; that is to say, the more purely a corn country, the more miserable the labourers. The cause is this, the great, the big bull frog grasps all. In this beautiful island every inch of land is appropriated by the rich. No hedges, no ditches, no commons, no grassy lanes: a country divided into great farms; a few trees surround the great farm-house. All the rest is bare of trees; and the wretched labourer has not a stick of wood, and has no place for a pig or cow to graze, or even to lie down upon. The rabbit countries are the countries for labouring men.[35]

For Cobbett, such monocultural systems of farming, which deprive the labourers of their customary rights, show the distance between the idealized England of his childhood and the present state of things across much of the country. By contrast, after crossing the High Weald, he is able to report, 'The labouring people look pretty well. They have pigs. They invariably do best in the *woodland* and *forest* and *wild* countries. Where the mighty grasper has *all under his eye*, they can get but little.'[36]

Not content to simply map the post-war countryside and record the deleterious changes to the lives of farmers and agricultural labourers, Cobbett produced an instruction manual for his readers to find their own redress. *Cottage Economy* (1821–2) advertised itself as an authoritative source of 'information relative to the brewing of BEER, making of BREAD, keeping of COWS, PIGS, BEES, EWES, GOATS, POULTRY AND RABBITS, and relative to other matters deemed useful in the conducting of the Affairs of a Labourer's Family'. This intensely practical work shows Cobbett in full georgic mode, taking the genre away from elite literary culture and down to the level of the cottage. His advice on these subjects always had a political aim in view, showing his readers how they could achieve a form of self-sufficiency by baking their own bread, brewing their own beer, reducing their wants, and avoiding taxed goods.[37] For Cobbett, independence was a political virtue: 'The great source of independence, the French express in a precept of three words, "*Vivre de peu*", which I have always very much admired. "*To live upon little*" is the great security against slavery.'[38] The spirit of *Cottage Economy* can be seen in many later attempts to return to the rural ideal, from Feargus O'Connor's Chartist Land Plan (1845–50), which aimed to resettle factory workers on smallholdings, to the back-to-the-land movements of the twentieth century.

On his rides, Cobbett draws attention to places where the effects of his writings can be directly observed. For example, in October 1825:

> I was going, to-day, by the side of a plat of ground, where there was a very fine flock of *turkeys*. I stopped to admire them, and observed to the owner how fine they were, when he answered, 'We owe them entirely *to you*, Sir; for, we never raised one till we read your COTTAGE ECONOMY.' I then told him, that we had, this year, raised two broods at Kensington, one black and one white, one of *nine* and one of *eight*.

He always remarks on places where his writings are read: at a paper-mill in the Forest of Dean, 'that set of workmen do, I am told, *take the Register*, and have taken it for years', 'at Cawston we stopped at a public house, the keeper of which had taken and read the Register for years'.[39] The radical Samuel Bamford famously located the rapid expansion of Cobbett's readership in 1816 with the launch of the cheap, unstamped edition of the *Political Register* in 'the manufacturing districts of South Lancashire, in those of Leicester, Derby, and Nottingham; also in many of the Scottish manufacturing towns'. Cobbett's urban and industrial readers are, however, strenuously denied by *Rural Rides*, and Cobbett insists instead on the reach of his writings in the agrarian communities of the south.[40] The complex dynamic at work, of historical belatedness, repression and longed-for recovery, is exemplified by the 'curious spectacle' Cobbett discovers on the road between Warminster and Westbury of unemployed weavers and spinners digging up a field. He seizes upon this single piece of evidence to argue that the direction of historical change has in fact been reversed: while political economists are urging '*the farmer labourers to become manufacturers*', the factories are '*throwing the people back again upon the land!*'[41]

If this was wishful thinking on Cobbett's part, Williams and other influential readers of Cobbett have framed this longed-for restoration in terms of a broader cultural nostalgia.⁴² In his biography of Cobbett, the twentieth-century guild socialist G. D. H. Cole sought to explain the apparent contradiction between Cobbett's rural subject matter and urban readership by arguing that industrial workers of the period may have 'been torn from the land, and flung into the factory' – echoing Cobbett's own violent metaphors – but 'kept, for a generation at least, the hearts and feelings of peasants, and responded more readily to a peasant's appeal than to programmes based on the acceptance of the new industrial conditions'.⁴³ This curious rationalization perhaps says more about Cole than it does about Cobbett or his audience: Clare Griffiths has suggested that Cole resorted to such an argument due to his own inability – writing a century after Cobbett – to imagine a radical, rural politics. Cole may have identified with Cobbett's ruralism through his own nostalgic temperament and attachment to the landscapes of southern England, but 'could not fully engage with the possibility of a countryside which might generate its own radicalism, as the urban, industrial world could'.⁴⁴

Cobbett's own later writings, however, show some accommodation with the reality of industrialization, through the lecture tours he made of the midlands, northern England, and Scotland. These journeys are included in G. D. H. and Margaret Coles's lavish centenary edition of *Rural Rides*, but stand in uneasy relationship to the earlier journeys: their focus is not primarily rural, but on towns and cities where Cobbett had been invited to lecture. He made the first of these tours at the end of 1829, accompanied by Anne and two of his sons. He initially shows his resistance to the whole idea, as in this revealing description of their approach through the snow to Birmingham, now travelling by stagecoach instead of on horseback:

> As we advanced on the way, the snow became deeper on the fields; and I really longed to be out in it, and thought much more, for the time, about the tracking of hares than about the making of speeches; and I could not help reflecting, and mentioning to my daughter, who was sitting with me, how strangely I had been, by degrees, pulled along, during my whole life, away from those pursuits and those scenes which were most congenial to my mind.⁴⁵

Cobbett is always ambivalent about travel and as he travels north his suspicions are intensified, this autobiographical moment linking the deepening of the snow and 'the tracking of hares' with his lifelong displacement from the 'scenes' he most values, which he is particularly conscious of while being 'pulled along' by the coach towards the towns and cities of the midlands and north. His later tour of Scotland is styled as a military advance on Edinburgh, the bastion of the hated political economy, while at other times he reverted to agricultural (and biblical) metaphors for his lecture tours: 'This is sowing the seeds of truth in a very sure manner: it is not scattering broad-cast; it is really *drilling the country*'.[46]

Cobbett was, however, delighted by the enthusiastic reception he received among those he had never considered his true constituency: in contrast to the picaresque roadside conversations of *Rural Rides*, he was surrounded by crowds of admirers and spoke to packed theatres and lecture halls. Indeed, his later, northern tours suggest that the focus in *Rural Rides* on meeting his readers as they worked the land in the south was an attempt to deny his increasing reliance on an audience in the towns and cities of industrial Britain. Cobbett may have known for years that many of his readers lived in the towns and cities of midland and northern England, but he had instinctively resisted this fact and mythologized a southern, agrarian readership. He now witnessed his own radical celebrity: 'great numbers assembled' just to see him change horses at Wakefield and Barnsley; at Ripley Castle 'I found myself at the most northerly point that I had ever been in my whole life' but he was still in some sense at home; and at Leeds, he reported, 'I have filled, and over-filled, the whole house, pit, boxes and galleries.'[47]

The experience of his northern tours also diminished his belief in the possibility of a universal model of 'cottage economy'. He visited a power-loom factory near Rochdale, emphasizing that, 'I never was induced to go into a factory, in England before', but admitted that 'owing to the goodness of the masters' the workers looked 'healthy and well-dressed'.[48] In Scotland, three years later, he was still emphasizing that 'I do not like to see manufactories of any sort', though once again qualifying his resistance: 'but that of Mr. MONTEITH, for the dyeing and printing of calicoes and shawls and handkerchiefs, and upon a scale of prodigious magnitude, I did go to see, and I saw it with wonder that I cannot describe'.[49] Wherever he went, he was reluctantly impressed: arriving in Sheffield at night, he saw 'the iron furnaces in all the horrible splendour of their everlasting blaze. Nothing can be conceived more grand or more terrific than the yellow waves of fire that incessantly issue from the top of these furnaces.' He often emphasizes the lack of good agricultural land, but concedes – an unlikely admission – that 'this is all very proper: these coal-diggers, and iron-melters, and knife-makers, compel us to send the food to them, which, indeed, we do very cheerfully, in exchange for the produce of their rocks, and the wondrous works of their hands'.[50] A new political vision had entered his writing, which extended beyond mere pragmatism: before the first election after the Reform Act, he wrote an open letter to the electors of Manchester, declaring 'our principal reliance must be upon the *great towns in the north*, beginning at Birmingham, and ending at Paisley and Glasgow', the first person plural now referring to a national class solidarity.[51] He was returned to parliament for Oldham, one of the newly created industrial constituencies, and announced his intention to write an autobiography under the title 'The Progress of a Ploughboy to a Seat in Parliament, as Exemplified in the Life of William Cobbett MP'.

On a later tour, he lectured at Newcastle and was particularly gratified to be asked to give another lecture, specifically on paper money, a subject he had been writing about for twenty years. This request produced an extraordinary retort to his southern audience:

> There, you chopsticks of the Isle of Wight and of Sussex and Kent! that's the way we do things i'the North! There, you Surrey chaps, that creep about amongst the sand-hills! that's the way that we go on in the country where the stuff comes from that warms your fingers in the winter. Faith! when I get back again, with all the additional '*antalluct*' that I am collecting here, I will not take things as I have done; I will rule you with a stiffer hand.[52]

The pronouns now place Cobbett alongside his northern audience, but the rhetorical extravagance suggests that no amount of acclaim in the cities of northern England and Scotland could make up for neglect from the readers he had addressed himself to for so long in the countryside of southern England. The popularity of Cobbett's journalism has been taken as evidence that, in Ian Dyck's phrase, 'the Regency farm worker was developing a political and class consciousness that rivalled that of the weaver, the miner and the cabinet-maker'.[53] Cobbett certainly saw his true audience in the agricultural communities that Patrick Wright has characterized as 'Deep England'.[54] He attempted to inhabit a rural ideal even as he recounted its erasure or increasing impossibility, with his own imprisonment, exile, and repeated dispossession standing for the experiences of many in a period of mass migration and emigration. Through his insistent focus on the value of agricultural labour, Cobbett presents a radicalized version of georgic, but this does not make him the insular or nostalgic writer that Williams and other commentators have often portrayed. Instead, his writings ultimately imagine a union between agricultural and industrial workers as the only possibility for genuine reform.

Notes

1 R. Williams, *The Country and the City* (1973; London: Vintage, 2016), p. 154. Kevin Gilmartin has recently explored Williams's long engagement with Cobbett, arguing that, for Williams, Cobbett was 'the leading figure among a group of Romantic-period visionaries who contested without fully comprehending the early impact of industrial capitalism'. In 1977, Williams asserted that 'Some of the questions then asked, more persistently by Cobbett than by anyone else, about the whole nature of the industrial project and the consequences for social relations, still have to be answered today'; '"In His Time and in Ours": Reading Cobbett (and Jane Austen) with Raymond Williams', in *Raymond Williams and Romanticism, Romantic Circles Praxis Series*, ed. J. Klancher and J. Sachs (2020), https://romantic-circles.org/praxis/williams/praxis.2020.williams.gilmartin.html. Accessed 3 September 2021.
2 Williams, *Country and the City*, pp. 161, 166.
3 See R. Williams, *Marxism and Literature* (Oxford University Press, 1977), ch. 8.
4 J. Austen, *Emma*, ed. James Kinsley and Adela Pinch (Oxford University Press, 2008), p. 283.
5 Austen, *Emma*, p. 24.
6 T. Carlyle, 'Sir Walter Scott', *The Works of Thomas Carlyle*, 30 vols. (1899), vol. XXIX, p. 39; K. Marx, letter to the *New York Daily Tribune*, 22 July 1853. For an earlier version of the argument here on Cobbett's rural radicalism and its connection to the 'revolution controversy' of the 1790s, see J. Grande, *William Cobbett, the Press and Rural England: Radicalism and the Fourth Estate, 1792–1835* (Basingstoke: Palgrave Macmillan, 2014).
7 W. Cobbett, *The Opinions of William Cobbett*, ed. J. Grande, J. Stevenson and R. Thomas (Farnham: Ashgate, 2013), p. 17; 'Proceedings in Parliament', *Cobbett's Weekly Political Register*, 10 January 1807, col. 36.
8 W. Cobbett, *A Year's Residence in the United States of America* (1819), p. vi.
9 This term first appears italicized in the *Political Register* on 28 March 1818 and then in capitals from 10 November 1821.
10 M. R. Mitford, *Recollections of a Literary Life, or Books, Places, and People*, 3 vols. (1852), vol. II, pp. 22–8.
11 Josephine McDonagh has written of how 'Mitford's name became synonymous with both a place – a village – and a style of writing that together epitomized English provincial life' but could also be exported abroad; *Literature in a Time of Migration: British Fiction and the Movement of People, 1815–1876* (Oxford University Press, 2021), p. 150. See also P. D. Edwards, *Idyllic Realism from Mary Russell Mitford to Hardy* (Basingstoke: Macmillan, 1988).
12 J. Barrell, 'Clare, Cobbett and the Changing Landscape', in *The New Pelican Guide to English Literature: From Blake to Byron*, ed. B. Ford (Harmondsworth: Penguin, 1982), p. 237; D. Simpson, *The Academic Postmodern and the Rule of Literature: A Report on Half-Knowledge* (University of Chicago Press, 1995), p. 141; L. Colley, 'I am the Watchman', review of L. Nattrass, ed., *William Cobbett: Selected Writings*, and Dyck, ed., *Rural Rides, London Review of Books*, 20 November 2003.

13 A. Cobbett, *Account of the Family* (London: William Cobbett Society, 1999), p. 36.
14 'A History of the Last Hundred Days of English Freedom', *Cobbett's Weekly Political Register*, 26 July 1817, col. 522.
15 Cobbett to W. Palmer, Kensington, 5 August 1825, papers of William Cobbett in the library of Nuffield College, Oxford, XX/12/1–5.
16 Cobbett to J. P. Cobbett, Kensington, 24 July 1821, Nuffield, XXX/147/1–4; Cobbett to J. P. Cobbett, Botley, 23 December 1819, Nuffield, XXX/68/1.
17 Cobbett to J. P. Cobbett, Kensington, 24 July 1821, Nuffield, XXX/147/1–4. See M. Townsend, *This Happy Land: William Cobbett on America, 1794–1835* (London: New European Publications, 2007), p. 325. Anne Cobbett wrote to her brother that the seed business 'will be our great object; for there is no knowing what may happen to all writing and printing' (London, 20 April 1820, Nuffield, XXX/80/1–2). Cobbett himself explained that 'I shall make them yield even more than my publications; for, one greatly assists the other' (Kensington, 13 September 1821, Nuffield XXX/153/1–2). Forced to increase the price of the *Political Register* at the end of 1819 by the Six Acts, Cobbett saw a dramatic fall in circulation compared to the 1816–19 circulation of the unstamped *Register* (the 'Twopenny Trash').
18 Cobbett to J. P. Cobbett, Brompton, 7 February 1821. Nuffield, XXX/140/1.
19 *Cobbett's Weekly Political Register*, 14 August 1819.
20 Clare Pettitt has argued that serial publications 'start to create the *feeling* of being part of a daily politics for more and more people' in this period; *Serial Forms: The Unfinished Project of Modernity, 1815–1848* (Oxford University Press, 2020), p. 8.
21 W. Cobbett, *Rural Rides*, ed. G. D. H. and M. Cole, 3 vols (London: Peter Davies, 1930), vol. I, p. 85.
22 Cobbett, *Rural Rides*, vol. I, p. 288.
23 D. Fairer, '"Where fuming trees refresh the thirsty air": The World of Eco-Georgic', *Studies in Eighteenth-Century Culture*, 40 (2011), 201–18.
24 See www.historyofparliamentonline.org/volume/1790–1820/member/winnington-sir-thomas-edward-1780–1839. Accessed 3 September 2021.
25 Cobbett, *Rural Rides*, vol. II, pp. 437–9.
26 Anthony Low's definition is a suggestive one for thinking about Cobbett's creation of a radical idea of Englishness: 'we may say that georgic is a mode that stresses the value of intense and persistent labor against hardships and difficulties; that it differs from pastoral because it emphasizes work instead of ease; that it differs from epic because it emphasizes planting and building instead of killing and destruction; and that it is preeminently the mode suited to the establishment of civilization and the founding of nations': *The Georgic Revolution* (Princeton University Press, 1985), p. 12.
27 A. Liu, *Wordsworth: The Sense of History* (Stanford University Press, 1989), p. 18.
28 Virgil, *Georgics* (Fallon), p. 23.
29 Cobbett, *Rural Rides*, vol. I, p. 155.
30 Cobbett, *Rural Rides*, vol. I, pp. 227–8.

31 Cobbett, *Rural Rides*, vol. I, p. 228.
32 P. Readman, *Storied Ground: Landscape and the Shaping of English National Identity* (Cambridge University Press, 2018), p. 34; Cobbett, *Rural Rides*, vol. I, p. 229.
33 Cobbett, *Rural Rides*, vol. I, p. 24.
34 Cobbett, *Rural Rides*, vol. I, pp. 297, 314.
35 Cobbett, *Rural Rides*, vol. I, p. 233.
36 Cobbett, *Rural Rides*, vol. I, p. 207.
37 See K. Castellano, *The Ecology of British Romantic Conservatism, 1790–1837* (New York: Palgrave Macmillan, 2013), ch. 5., 'Subsistence as Resistance: William Cobbett's Food Politics'.
38 W. Cobbett, *Advice to Young Men and (incidentally) to Young Women, in the Middle and Higher Ranks of Life* (1829), para. 17 [n. p.].
39 Cobbett, *Rural Rides*, vol. I, pp. 27, 47.
40 S. Bamford, *Passages in the Life of a Radical*, 2 vols (1844), vol. I, p. 7.
41 Cobbett, *Rural Rides*, vol. II, p. 405.
42 These paragraphs draw on Grande, William Cobbett, the Press and Rural England, pp. 164–5, 198–9.
43 G. D. H. Cole, *The Life of William Cobbett* (London: Collins, 1924), pp. 11–12.
44 Clare Griffiths, 'G. D. H. Cole and William Cobbett', *Rural History*, 10, 1 (1999), 91–104. See, similarly, Ian Dyck's verdict that, 'Cobbett was not without relevance to his industrial and urban audience. The fact that his writings appealed to industrial workers who aspired to return to the land meant that he articulated an agrarian ideal for industrial Radicals as well as a radical ideal for agrarians': *William Cobbett and Rural Popular Culture* (Cambridge University Press, 1992), 4.
45 Cobbett, *Rural Rides*, vol. II, p. 568.
46 Cobbett, *Rural Rides*, vol. II, p. 642.
47 Cobbett, *Rural Rides*, vol. II, pp. 607, 604.
48 Cobbett, *Rural Rides*, vol. II, p. 598.
49 Cobbett, *Rural Rides*, vol. II, p. 796.
50 Cobbett, *Rural Rides*, vol. II, pp. 607–8.
51 Cobbett, *Rural Rides*, vol. II, p. 691.
52 Cobbett, *Rural Rides*, vol. III, p. 724.
53 I. Dyck, *Cobbett and Rural Popular Culture* (Cambridge University Press), p. 75.
54 See P. Wright, *On Living in an Old Country: The National Past in Contemporary Britain* (London: Verso, 1985), pp. 81–7.

CHAPTER 10

Labour Isn't Working
The (F)ailing Georgics of Hardy's Wessex Novels
Andrew Radford

This chapter situates Thomas Hardy, and to a lesser extent his Wiltshire-born contemporary, Richard Jefferies, as case studies by which to assess broader environmental and social crises in the final decades of the nineteenth century.[1] My particular concern is with how the georgic sensibility, far from a patrician, anti-progressive or mannered enthusiasm 'of diminishing relevance' in late Victorian literature, has, in Hardy's view, a rare analytical power, persistence and cultural currency.[2] It allows him to probe moral and spiritual attitudes towards, and economic theories about, manual toil in an age of capitalist accumulation. Utilizing the commonplace of a poem as furrow – playing on the Latin *versus* as a turning from that of the plough to the turning of verse – the Wessex novels represent an alternative form of georgic labour. Hardy provides a fictional excavation of those partially concealed patterns of civic strife, exploitation and bare subsistence that comprise the farmer's lot, especially in the Depression years of the 1870s and 1880s – what *The Mayor of Casterbridge* calls a ceaseless and often traumatic 'battle of life'.[3] However, this locally focused attention to the challenges, inequalities and displacements of gruelling outdoor work – particularly the lived experiences of husbandmen with resisting, layered landscapes – was frequently downplayed in Victorian periodicals.[4] Jefferies was conscious that some of his fellow journalists elected to aestheticize the skills-based practical activities of farmers – such as planting, harvesting crops or managing livestock – thus supplying a reductive reading of the georgic as a paean to pristine nature. This is a tendency that Hardy's fiction – and essays such as 'The Dorsetshire Labourer' (1883) – firmly contests.

My aim here is not to reshape vexed – and vexing – critical debates regarding how we distinguish georgic from the classical pastoral. Brian Loughrey argues that the two modes of orientation to the land are 'so closely allied that they frequently impinge on one another'.[5] I am more preoccupied with how Hardy's carefully detailed portrayal of strenuous daily work with crops, soil and seed – and the beliefs that have grown up around it – refuses to offer utopian vistas, sentimental asides or glib solutions to tangled political dilemmas.[6] Instead, he explores the tensions, pressures and ambiguities inherent in fictional depictions of the countryside at a time when, according to Jefferies in 'Drought and Water' (1870), 'The Prospects of Farming' (1877) and 'Unequal Agriculture' (1877), foreign competition, a sharp decline in crop prices, shifting market trends and cutting-edge technologies 'founded upon theories rather than tradition' were causing unprecedented cultural ferment.[7]

The textual scholar Dennis Taylor, in his contribution to the 1993 essay collection *The Literature of Place*, posits that Michael Drayton's topographical poem *Poly-Olbion* (which Hardy read and diligently annotated), allowed Hardy to merge 'pastoral and georgic traditions' in his verse – ultimately shaping a fresh lyrical cadence.[8] This poetic cadence, especially in 'The Later Autumn' which deploys figurations from *Georgics* IV, illustrates not only prudent human oversight of, but even a rapt sense of umbilical attachment to an agrarian locale, reminiscent of the field worker who seems 'earth-born – autochthon' in Jefferies's *Red Deer* (1884).[9] However, Hardy's scrutiny of a question that dominates Jefferies's essays of the 1870s – how 'to farm in the best and most profitable manner' – strikes a markedly different and ominous note in the later fiction, especially *The Mayor of Casterbridge* and *The Woodlanders*.[10] These novels test the resonance of husbandry as a harmonious *being together* in a specific domain. Indeed, Angel Clare's declaration in *Tess of the d'Urbervilles* (1891) that 'we all are children of the soil' (human-and-animal) signals the residual romanticism of a fatuous scholar-gypsy, not the disabused view of practical doing and dwelling found in Hardy's ecologically sensitive poems such as 'The Pat of Butter', 'An August Midnight' or 'We Field Women'.

In *The Mayor of Casterbridge* and *The Woodlanders*, Hardy interprets georgic values, sources and motifs through his portrayal of the pugnacious 'corn king' Michael Henchard and the taciturn yeoman Giles Winterborne, respectively. These two texts make apt case studies because they ponder the contentious issue of how agrarian goods are produced. In both, Hardy documents an indigenous land-worker's increasingly fraught dispute with, and gradual supplanting by, a more ruthlessly hard-headed and savvy arriviste. On a cursory inspection, Henchard – a 'skilled countryman as distinct from' the 'general labourer'[11] – and the tree-planter Winterborne prompt comparison with Jefferies's notion of those adept 'in the operations of husbandry'. Such individuals, Jefferies avers in 'The Future of Farming', 'do not look upon' smallholding 'as a business in the same sense in which a merchant regards his trade. There is an amount of pleasure in contemplating such a picture as this; it is thoroughly English in its character'.[12] Jefferies proposes a 'good' husbandry here: environmental stewardship is a dignified, even patriotic pursuit that carries the cultural promise of augmented civic welfare. It is not solely concerned with measurable quantities (say, the corn yield in *The Mayor of Casterbridge* or wood as a source of fuel, medicine and lumber in *The Woodlanders*), but the affective and moral qualities of a farmer who develops a deep sense of kinship with the soil.

The problem is that Jefferies's conception of the stalwart 'English' farmer who makes the most of resources by sage management – Gabriel Oak in *Far from the Madding Crowd* (1874) – is reimagined in Hardy's later fiction as a tenuous fantasy. Although Casterbridge is described as 'a representative centre of husbandry',[13] these final Wessex novels reveal that 'good' husbandry is a bitterly contested concept. Hardy's Wessex becomes in effect a laboratory for experiments in more hard-nosed displays of agrarian capitalism that lauds profit-related productivity and bourgeois respectability over a profound and lasting connection to place that transcends ownership. The emphasis on land or property as a mere resource to be stripped and mined – number, weight and measure – is grimly captured in the opening pages of *The Mayor*. The 'reckless misadventurer' Henchard nullifies matrimonial and market protocol by scorning his own spouse and offspring as 'inferior animals', fit only for a swift 'sale by auction' at Weydon-Priors Fair.[14] Moreover, both Henchard and Winterborne flounder and die amid a natural milieu with whose agrarian attitudes, hallowed customs and seasonal rhythms they are supposed to have a close affinity. Henchard is a dyspeptic hay-trusser before his rise to the position of corn-merchant; Winterborne, whose arboreal gifts set him apart from other 'itinerant journey-workers'[15] is tasked with safeguarding Little Hintock's lore. Hardy situates these two husbandmen very deliberately then not as avatars of 'amazing' zest, but rather stagnant entities, out of touch with a 'fertile country'.[16] Neither is empowered through their farming principles and techniques – Winterborne seems incapable of reasserting what Gaston Bachelard terms 'the innermost energy of the manual labourer'.[17]

Dryden's seventeenth-century translation of the first lines of Virgil's *Georgics* – 'What makes a plenteous Harvest, when to turn | The fruitful Soil, and when to sowe the Corn' – carries a mordant resonance in *The Mayor*.[18] Indeed, Henchard's ability to foster ample, healthy crops, avow common interests and balance times of fruition and scarcity is limited at best, dysfunctional at worst. Although our initial glimpse of Henchard as 'First Citizen' is defined by festivities at the King's Arms and an imposing residence on Casterbridge's Corn Street, he ends up starving to death on Egdon Heath in a shack that augurs the woodcutter's fuel shelter under which Winterborne deteriorates. This downward trajectory reveals the irreversible erosion of any sense of husbandry as a 'happy' regenerative process. In the opening gambit of Virgil's *Georgics*, 'laetas' denotes 'delight', 'fecundity', 'luxuriance' and 'compost' – a term that distils the essence of 'a whole energy system', connecting human transactions to the seasonal calendar and the cosmos.[19] Yet Henchard and Winterborne are variously alienated from this venerable system, one that necessitates an intuitive grasp of the communal and symbolic implications and uses of crops and trees in diurnal vernacular contexts.

High-Pressure Agriculture

What these two novels of the 1880s demonstrate is that the georgic ethic – anchored in disciplined work habits, a holistic view of the human–animal relationship, and grave responsibility towards one's bucolic locale via resource conservation and sustainability – has been irredeemably infected by, among other things, insanitary housing, exposure, meagre fare and other cheerless conditions of labour in advanced capitalist modernity. Such conditions, scrutinized at length in Jefferies's trenchant rural sociology of the 1870s such as 'John Smith's Shanty' and 'Field-Faring Women', are viewed most poignantly in Susan Henchard's hardscrabble existence from *The Mayor*. Navigating a path between survival and destitution, Susan is so gaunt and careworn that she is nicknamed the 'ghost' by the children of Casterbridge.[20] If Hardy seeks to promote, like Jefferies in his spiritual autobiography *The Story of My Heart*, a recuperative sense of the numinous in taxing horticultural and agrarian endeavours, then the neurasthenic impact of these labour conditions – what Jefferies terms 'High-Pressure Agriculture' in an 1876 essay of the same name for *Fraser's Magazine* – effectively scuppers this undertaking. The eponymous protagonist of *Jude the Obscure* registers 'a true illumination; that here in the stone-yard was a centre of effort as worthy as that dignified by the name of scholarly study'. Yet this stress on the virtues of place-based artisanal engagement, informed by Jude's inquisitive intelligence, is poisoned by patterns of caste prejudice and sharp practice whose 'law' of 'mutual butchery' erodes obligations between neighbours.[21] In the 'antiquated borough' of Casterbridge, this 'law' has set Celt against Roman, Saxon against Norman, and now robber barons against landless labourers. Historic dissension is woven into the very fabric of archaeological survivals (the ruins of a Roman amphitheatre), festive diversions (a 'stage for boxing, wrestling, and drawing blood generally') and concludes with the 'trade-antagonism' between the factor Henchard and his Scottish protégé Donald Farfrae.²² This battle is conducted in the corn-market, the 'centre and *arena*' of the bustling county town (my italics).²³

So in *The Mayor* and *The Woodlanders*, the promise of multiplied perception through Virgil's *labor improbus* ('unremitting labour' amid the vagaries of natural phenomena) is replaced by an increasingly austere vision, a 'general drama of pain' marked by the compulsive calibration of the 'truly genteel' so often confused with individual worth.²⁴ It is this concern which separates the later Wessex novels from Hardy's evocation of agricultural techniques, rites and values in his published poetry. As Jefferies ruefully reflects in 'The Future of Farming' – which discusses, among other things, land usage and food production on smaller labour-intensive family farms – 'old methods of practice handed down are found incapable of meeting the strain put upon them'.²⁵

In *The Mayor*, Henchard personifies these 'old methods of practice' whose grievous insufficiencies are exposed when he enters into a protracted commercial spat with Farfrae. Although recent scholars have treated the quarrel between Henchard and the young Scottish usurper as a direct standoff between two antithetical types, it is better parsed as a collision of rival conceptions of georgic striving and responsible effort. In other words, the text challenges us to isolate the specific priorities and place-based duties synonymous with what Wordsworth's 1799 *Prelude* (line 453) calls 'honourable toil'. Henchard, seeking to secure his corn business against the stratagems of a wily pretender, repeatedly goads Farfrae to public displays of extrovert virility and agrarian flair, without apprehending that the two are not identical.

What the text implies here is that the older man's trapped rage, his 'volcanic fires' of affect and 'tigerish' approach to manual graft – which fuels his spiteful desire to embarrass Farfrae – should be channelled towards the cultivation of seed, which is a key aspect of a farmer's role in *The Mayor*. A 'farmer's income was ruled by the wheat-crop within his own horizon, and the wheat-crop by the weather. Thus, in person, he became a sort of flesh-barometer, with feelers always directed to the sky and wind around him.'²⁶ This portrayal of a farmer as 'flesh-barometer' echoes the neurasthenic Clym Yeobright's perceptual and sensuous apprehension of the Egdon slopes in *The Return of the Native* (1878). Clym finds a metaphysical balm and refuge through furze-cutting, a type of physical toil that makes 'the incipient marks of time and thought' less noticeable on his face.²⁷

Henchard cannot experience this arcane revelation of being. He is a 'corn king' displaced into, and ultimately nonplussed by, the more esoteric 'trade' of corn-dealing. Henchard is ill-equipped to handle this more convoluted agricultural 'arena', one increasingly splintered by the speculation of credit and the specialization of labour. He fails to keep pace with the radical transmutation of rustic *cycles* – built on exacting manual toil such as furze-cutting and hay-trussing – into *industries* shaped by labour-saving mechanical contrivances, such as Farfrae's seed drill. Henchard combines mayoral duties with being the foremost corn-factor. Yet by supplying inferior flour, he has failed to honour his civic obligations to the 'gentlepeople and such like leading volk'.[28] In a town described as the 'nerve-knot of the surrounding countryside', the crop yield is the populace's prime obsession. Topics of debate are 'sowing and reaping, fencing and planting' among shop-owners whose shelves boast a plethora of farming paraphernalia; and the rain seems to descend 'like meal' in a region where ancient burial mounds resemble 'the full breasts' of fertility deity 'Diana Multimammia'.[29] Yet the hubristic Henchard falls well short of Jefferies's lofty notion of the 'English' husbandman who looks beyond the mere 'business' of farming to embrace its sympathetic openness to other lifeforms, and its ability to bind manual workers together in an ambience of protective fellowship. Consequently, Henchard's hold over the corn-trade wanes: townspeople deplore the 'unprincipled' bread in this borough. The amateur antiquarian narrator employs this term, as well as 'wholesome crust', pointedly – capturing not just a vernacular vigour reminiscent of William Barnes's Dorset dialect poetry but, more importantly, also the *moral* texture of the manoeuvres by which Henchard becomes corn king and chief magistrate of Casterbridge.[30] Ironically, this would-be captain of industry has tainted the staff of life and is on the verge of fiscal ruin. Susan Henchard is advised that she 'may as well look for manna-food as good bread in Casterbridge just now'.[31]

Although Henchard once converted, with insolent swagger, his wife and child into cash at Weydon-Priors Fair, this former hay-trusser cannot make 'wholesome' the 'growed' grain (beginning to sprout in the ear before being gathered). Here the narrator impishly unravels the Judeo-Christian resonances of the lexis. He reminds us of the pungent, rum-laced concoction blended in a witch's cauldron at Weydon-Priors Fair, whose clammy furmity tent annuls farming etiquette to vaunt a more disquieting, heretical fecundity.

What Makes a Man of Character?

Culture, as Raymond Williams posits, 'in all its early uses was a noun of process: the tending *of* something, basically crops and animals'.[32] The volatile Henchard has become unmoored from the practical, knowledge-forming realities of this 'process'. Corn-dealing – conducting the delicate negotiations with the borough's many 'millers and bakers'[33] – is the 'arena' where the diplomatic Scot Farfrae shines because he compartmentalizes his feelings and promotes what Henchard construes as a strange and profoundly alienating bucolic order, one that, according to Jefferies, 'approaches nearer and nearer in methods of practice to those employed in manufacture'.[34] Under Farfrae's watch, the hay traffic thrives, and he improves the blighted seed – 'whatever he touched he prospered in'.[35] His 'curing' of the corrupted grain owes nothing to Midas-like sorcery but to positivist, pioneering experiments.

That there are fundamental differences between the agrarian practice of the two men is thrown into sharper relief by Henchard's intuitive and energetically eccentric *handiwork* – he measures 'his ricks by stretching with his arms' and judges 'his hay by a chaw'[36] – as opposed to Farfrae's rigorously cerebral sense of farming, quite literally, by the book. The pathos here is that Henchard's direct, assertive engagement with produce and soil via smell, taste and touch is closer to the Virgilian regard for a haptic and immersive approach to field management in *Georgics* II. To some extent these divergences mirror the transition from an oral to a predominantly literate culture in Wessex – what Jefferies portrays in *The Toilers of the Field* (1892) as a heady world 'of newspaper ... and current ideas'.[37] Henchard's coarse spontaneity of speech – his predilection for 'rough jest', 'telling good stories' and settling 'the price with a curse'[38] – is replaced by the permanency of print (soil surveys, cartographies, a codified set of observations on plant nutrition or seed preparation). Such reading matter becomes an external fund of data for Farfrae and other educated, class-conscious merchants and farmers in Casterbridge, furnishing clear guidelines on tilling the earth and fresh ways of visualizing it – ways which, the antiquarian narrator implies, strip the soil of symbolic grandeur and reframe it as a commodified background to potentially lucrative economic deals.

The subtitle of Hardy's novel – 'A Story of a Man of Character' – could apply equally to the ailing corn king, with his experience-based, locally derived awareness of Casterbridge, or his youthful successor whose controlled, verifiable experiments reflect the formative years of applied agricultural science. 'Character' in the closing phase of *The Mayor* suggests not only the moral fibre of a scrupulous farmer but also his level of practical and cultural literacy (a 'character' of written script). Henchard – analogous to the 'old-fashioned' husbandman with his tradition-laden knowledge of earth evoked by Jefferies's sketch 'John Smith's Shanty'[39] – is lamentably 'bad at letters'. For Henchard, 'penmanship' remains a 'tantalizing art', he cannot keep methodical accounts, being 'mentally and physically unfit for grubbing subtleties from *soiled paper*' (my italics).[40] The text reveals here, with a slyly sardonic pun, Henchard's visceral distaste for *book farming* as a thoroughly unnatural, mean, even dirty business. This episode is not so much concerned with beating swords into ploughshares and spears into pruning-hooks, as per the biblical maxim. Rather Farfrae's subtle 'letters' (theorizing about nutrition, organic composition, crop rotations and soil treatments) are converted into a formidable agrarian 'weapon' for 'mortal commercial combat'.[41] He claims victory in the 'war of prices'[42] and signs contracts of increasing intricacy while Henchard can only scoff at this bewildering interplay of legibility and legality. While the older man mocks Farfrae's effete fondness for the 'finnikin details' of agronomy, the Casterbridge 'plainer fellows' hail the Scot as the factor-philosopher of 'a new school who takes his contemporaries by storm'.[43] Henchard, by contrast, is treated as a shabby ethnographic relic who 'reckon[s] his sacks by chalk strokes in a row like garden-palings' and weighs 'his trusses by a lift'.[44] Even in death, Henchard's incapacity with written text matches his failure to join the ranks of farmers who are precise 'readers of Fate'. Henchard's will directs 'that no *flours* be planted on [his] grave'[45] (my italics). In this instance, the aberrant orthography signifies the tragic limitations of his husbandry, especially the age-old rustic industries of grain and flour.

The difficulty here is that Henchard, unlike the urbane yet watchful Scot, cannot 'catch his thoughts without pronouncing them'. Indeed, 'something fetichistic' underpins Henchard's local, experiential husbandry: the more frantic he becomes, the more farming seems like an exercise in magic to exploit fluctuations of the impersonal market.[46] Why else would he imperil his hard-won reputation as an abstemious corn-factor and churchwarden by secretly consulting a weather-prophet, Mr Fall, who occupies the seediest recess of the borough? Fall's nickname 'Wide-Oh', not only wittily alludes to the zero Henchard becomes to his exasperated fellow citizens and creditors, but also pinpoints his original transgression at Weydon-Priors Fair (he effectively *widows* himself for filthy lucre in a spasm of drunken fury).

Here the 'unlettered' Henchard has 'lost the plot' in every sense. His avid pursuit of individual honours and property ignores the virtues of civic interconnection as well as the customary rights and relations among his hard-pressed employees. By contrast, Farfrae's cultural credibility among the farmers and traders – especially his unflustered scrutiny of risk and management of grain-stores – reflects not merely Virgilian *parco* (thrift) and mutual obligation. His grasp of advanced forms of planting reveals cunning as well as a keen spirit of discovery: 'straightforward dealings don't bring profit – 'tis the sly and the underhand that get on in these times!' The profoundly placeless and itinerant Farfrae – having 'traversed strange latitudes'[47] his very Scottishness seems oddly manufactured – is aligned more with a functional reductionism than the august Virgilian verb of husbandry *cultor* as Hardy's narrator understands it (to occupy, to be a staunch friend, to revere the *genius loci* or spirit of place). Instead, Farfrae embodies technocratic managerialism anchored in a cautious use of 'ciphering and mensuration'.[48] Although he is introduced through his saccharine sub-Burnsian ditties which reduce Casterbridge topers to tears, can Farfrae really be, the narrator wonders, a community citizen for whom the 'dirt becomes god' and will thus give *Agricultura* the majesty of song in this region?[49] Or is the Scot's logistical strictness closer to Ted Hughes's formulation of the fastidious 'Puritan of the reformation, an idealist of rational control' who redefines the classical concept of *utilitas* as a lining of one's own pockets, instead of enriching the soil for the 'liege subjects of Labour'?[50]

Farfrae's enlightened toil is underpinned by formal chemical and mechanical erudition. He targets 'designs for placing the art of farming on a more scientific footing', which chimes with Richard Jefferies's admiring remarks on Scottish smallholders in 'The Prospects of Farming'.[51] In this 1877 article, Jefferies singles out these men for how they give their undivided 'attention' to their vocation, to the selection of seed and succession of crops that afford subsistence, especially the question of what harvests yield 'the best profits'.[52] This profit-related efficiency seems, at first glance, misaligned with the place-based concerns and cooperative relationship between human and non-human nature endorsed by a neo-georgic writer such as Wendell Berry. Yet then, *The Mayor* implies, are the pre-Christian rituals and brash styles of barter synonymous with Weydon-Priors any better than Farfrae's streamlined land practices, given the annual farming fair's illicit transactions and peepshows? Jefferies deplores such communal agrarian events as a 'chief cause of immorality' and personal 'ruin' in his 1872 *Times* article 'Wiltshire Labourers'.[53] What lends *The Mayor* a note of cryptic ambivalence here rather than any straightforwardly elegiac yearning for these archaic networks of bucolic (and bodily) commerce is the depiction of the Fair and indeed the black economy of Mixen Lane in Casterbridge as essentially squalid, even chaotic enclaves, over which the 'haggish' furmity woman presides, who crows of finalizing all sorts of shady deals 'with the richest stomachs in the land'.[54]

Reading the Leaves

The diffidence that characterizes the husbandry of Giles Winterborne in *The Woodlanders* could not furnish a more startling counterpoint to the public spectacles of intemperate folly and feral aggression synonymous with Henchard's handling of Casterbridge soil and seed. Yet Henchard's leaden 'glooms' and self-distancing drive are passed on to Winterborne, whose involvement in 'the apple and cider trade' is sketched in *The Mayor*:

> It happened that to-day there rose in the midst of them all two or three tall apple trees standing as if they grew on the spot; till it was perceived that they were held by men from the cider districts who came here to sell them, bringing the clay of their county on their boots.[55]

Winterborne, tasked with meeting Grace Melbury at Sherton Abbas in the planting season, displays in this market a ten-foot-high sample apple tree, which serves to some extent as his heraldic banner in *The Woodlanders*. This specimen tree, reminiscent of the tender cypress that the god Silvanus carries in Book I of Virgil's *Georgics*, also implies the 'woodwose' or 'Wild Man', a mythical creature synonymous with late medieval cultural production and believed to reside in – and preside over – remote forested areas. In what Jefferies calls 'the rude drama' of mumming in his 1878 essay 'Village Architecture', this grotesque entity is traditionally depicted – as in Joseph Strutt's *Sports and Pastimes of the People of England* (1801) – enveloped in leaves and vines, and clutching a large cudgel, or more frequently an uprooted tree.[56] Though Winterborne easily blends into the copses like a spirit of vegetation – he 'was the colour of his environment' – the cider-maker embodies neither Henchard's angry bravado nor the carnal vitality of his late medieval counterpart.[57] The cider-maker is everywhere shown to lack the corn king's bullish defiance, as he toils in vain – unable to exploit those 'better opportunities of rising in the social scale' that Jefferies affirms in the essay 'Wiltshire Labourers'.[58] Winterborne's efforts at arboreal cultivation, far from bolstering moral and physical wellbeing, culminate in dispossession and death, and cast a sobering sidelight on Andrew McRae's definition of the georgic as 'a mode that stresses the value of intensive and persistent labour against hardships and difficulties'.[59]

Winterborne's ineffectual labour is all the more notable because he has his own land experiences and philosophy that evoke Virgil's animistic depictions of saplings as sentient facets of the universe in Book 2 of *The Georgics*. Winterborne's work habits in this dense forest are, the text shows, markedly different from but more than equal to the leisurely regard of an environmental historian like Jefferies, or the pilgrim of fashion

Grace Melbury, and the first-generation romantic poets and painters she has studied at her expensive finishing school. Yet Winterborne's putative expertise – synonymous with the diligent nurture of plants – not only fails to counteract destructive organic processes in the forest but is also wilfully misconstrued and belittled by the timber-merchant Melbury and his 'cultivated' daughter Grace. As in *The Mayor of Casterbridge*, where the young hay-trusser Henchard is introduced as one 'pretending to read a ballad sheet', Winterborne's active engagement with soil is illustrated through vivid tropes of translating and writing the rural terrain ('hieroglyphs', 'alphabet').[60] On a cursory view the following passage prompts comparison with The Solitary's conception of the 'mute earth' as text in Wordsworth's most extensive experiment in the georgic, *The Excursion* ('If this mute earth | Were as a volume, shut, yet capable | Of yielding its contents to eye and ear' 5.250–54):

> The casual glimpses which the ordinary population bestowed upon that wondrous world of sap and leaves called the Hintock woods had been with these two, Giles and Marty, a clear gaze. They had been possessed of its finer mysteries as of commonplace knowledge; had been able to read its hieroglyphs as ordinary writing; to them the sights and sounds of night … were simple occurrences whose origin, continuance, and laws they foreknew … they had, with the run of the years, mentally collected those remoter signs and symbols which seen in few were of runic obscurity, but all together made an alphabet … The artifices of the seasons were seen by them from the conjuror's own point of view.[61]

Winterborne and his workmate Marty South's tending of this 'world of sap and leaves' is couched in terms of a combined decoding of a submerged animistic script. Winterborne, in marked contrast to the 'unlettered' Michael Henchard, whose struggles in relating to his land compel him to consult a 'conjuror' (Wide-Oh Fall), is himself invested with 'a gentle conjuror's touch' when examining 'the roots of each little tree, resulting in a sort of caress, under which the delicate fibres all laid themselves out in their proper directions for growth'.[62] The lexis here seems to resonate with standard assessments of Virgil's *Georgics*, II. 9–25, in that we are shown how the principles of *labour* are judiciously applied to the propagation of plants, trees and vines. Winterborne's compassionate yet instinctual 'caress' not only develops a variety of trees, but he apparently merges with them: 'the tree seemed to shiver, then to heave a sigh: a movement was audible, and Winterborne dropped almost noiselessly to the ground'.[63] However, when he strokes the flower that adorns Grace in the 'Autumn's very brother' scene – which appears to confirm our initial view of Winterborne as a wise 'reader' of organic nature's arcane inscriptions – his 'caress' reveals affective and vocational constraint. This is because *The Woodlanders* supplies a more disturbing account than *The Mayor* of an attenuated rustic domain in which seasonal activities such as 'barking' (the peeling of trees using ripping tools in chapter 19) not only defaces 'fine products of vegetable nature'[64] thus threatening biodiversity, but also fatally weakens that sustainable relationship with the cider districts that Winterborne tries to build.

The Demise of Autumn's Very Brother

The Woodlanders is then an unsettled and unsettling account of land-based life. This is partly due to the text's strange, mercurial moodiness of tone; it gestures at, while simultaneously querying, Winterborne's uncanny manipulation of the 'native soil', especially his 'marvellous power of making' the fruit-bearing and timber 'trees grow'.[65] Yet *The Woodlanders* is also concerned with the debasement of, even loss of faith in, a georgic lexicon, one that should acknowledge planting as a serious, substantial manifestation of human creativity. Instead, the text documents how the touristic Grace Melbury, and her 'Shelleyan' spouse Edred Fitzpiers – a figure of smirking insouciance – exploit a trite romantic register to depict the dynamic space of interaction between yeoman and Hintock earth, as well as sylvan phenomena more generally. If georgic labour is, on one level, the unending challenge to cultivate – to bring out the best via principled words and deeds – then *The Woodlanders* shows how the term 'cultivation' (thrice used in relation to Grace) has been drastically retooled to signify her recently acquired and ultimately pernicious gentility. She has been 'trained and tilled' at her voguish finishing academy into a profound 'foreignness of view'.[66] This educational 'polish' separates her irrevocably from the very practices, patterns and conventions of woodland work she seeks to laud. This is presented at its most complex in chapter 28 – the instance of Winterborne's ostensible transfiguration into 'Autumn's very brother'. In sharp contrast to Barber Percomb in the opening scenes, who does not 'belong to the country proper', Winterborne the stoical cidermaker suddenly takes on the guise of a magisterial woodland deity.[67] However, these sense-impressions are mediated through Grace's febrile gaze. In this Keatsian thought-adventure, Winterborne is not just reminiscent of an idealized 'happy husbandman' synonymous with *Georgics* II (458–60) but becomes a mystical recipient of the region's teeming ripeness. Illumined by sunbeams playing over the blades of his cider-production paraphernalia (a hint perhaps of Autumn's golden gleam which irradiates the world in James Thomson's *Seasons*), Winterborne's arboriculture implies – according to Jefferies's unsparing exposé of 'The Labourer's Daily Life' (1874) – that naively idyllic 'Arcadian beauty which is *supposed to prevail* in the country' (my italics).⁶⁸ Once again indicating the medieval folk myth of the 'Wild Man' covered in leafy vines, intertwined branches and garlands of flowers, the halting figure who earlier met Grace standing under his specimen tree is now smeared with the pips and rind of pressed apples:

> He looked and smelt like Autumn's very brother, his face being sunburnt to wheat-colour, his eyes blue as corn-flowers, his sleeves and leggings dyed with fruit stains, his hands clammy with the sweet juice of apples, his hat sprinkled with pips, and everywhere about him that atmosphere of cider which at its first return each season has such an indescribable fascination for those who have been born and bred among the orchards. Her heart rose from its late sadness like a released bough; her senses revelled in the sudden lapse back to Nature unadorned. The consciousness of having to be genteel because of her husband's profession, the veneer of artificiality which she had acquired at the fashionable schools, were thrown off, and she became the crude country girl of her latent, early instincts.
>
> Nature was bountiful, she thought. No sooner had she been cast aside by Edred Fitzpiers, than another being, impersonating chivalrous and undiluted manliness, had arisen out of the earth, ready to her hand.⁶⁹

This tableau both indulges and elaborates, while also debunking, Grace's florid terms of reference. The antiquarian narrator takes a macabre relish in the irony that if Winterborne's supposed talent for cider-production is pushed to its logical end, then this tutelary god of Grace's anodyne georgic *topos* is at risk of being pressed like his own 'crop of bitter-sweets'.⁷⁰

This is not an unschooled vision of a Virgilian, animistic cosmos, then. Rather it demonstrates to what degree Winterborne's local lore and sincere reactions to his land, work and neighbours have been repackaged as obfuscating suburban whimsy. Grace's rapt identification of Winterborne with the forest is described as an '*excursion of the imagination*' (my italics).⁷¹ The narrator invokes and indicts Wordsworth's long poem as part of a romantic literary bequest that hobbles those acts of sympathetic engagement which enrich historical awareness of a land-worker's plight. Grace's 'excursion' in the 'Autumn's very brother' episode bespeaks an anxiety of indolence: from a position of cosseted distance the young lady of leisure privileges the potent elemental appeal of Winterborne's husbandry over its irreducibly material grind, its hard-won insights by diurnal doing, and often paltry economic returns. Winterborne's labour-intensive life, as the text makes painfully clear, is 'not a Golden Age where apples drop freely from the boughs'.[72] Grace's reverie misrecognizes Winterborne's *labor* and operates to divest it of its unique properties – just as the trees themselves in this text are ultimately mutilated, denuded ('barked') and felled by Winterborne himself. Yet here as elsewhere, Winterborne is complicit in his own demise: he surveys himself through the prism of Grace Melbury's snobbish attitude to his vocation as pitiable, degraded and ancillary – agreeable only when garnished with imagery that dilutes or domesticates the earthy, arduous specifics of his rustic handicrafts.

Grace's 'Autumn's very brother' gloss is a dizzy rapture that not only fetishizes Winterborne but exposes her own condition as a rootless 'reader' of Nature – her 'imagination' can only *manufacture* a second-rate concept of an enduring, therapeutic relationship with Little Hintock's produce and people. Here Grace misconstrues Winterborne's place-based affect, his closeness to wild things, his deep respect for the immanent actuality of an organic locale and how arboreal objects anchor, encompass and coordinate collective and ceremonial activities such as Midsummer Eve (chapter 20). Though educated to a fine polish, Grace does not possess the grammar and syntax to furnish an honest, ecologically engaged appraisal of Winterborne's quiet sense of duty and history involved in devising tools to secure survival or moulding the terrain through the production of food. For her and her husband, the déclassé patrician Fitzpiers, the tools and terminology of Winterborne's arboriculture lack *poetry*. This is because Grace cannot grasp how the yeoman's active care for the plantations emerges through the gradual accretion of work experiences and sentiment. For her, by contrast, Little Hintock has become a stultifying backwater, the epitome of 'crude rusticity'.[73] So, she has to burnish Winterborne's indigenous attitudes, processes and principles – just as the sun illumines his cider-making apparatus and the reaper in Jefferies's short article 'The Beauty of the Fields' (1881) – with the gleam of holiness, using a hackneyed romanticism ironically funded by her socially climbing father. Melbury senior's muscle memory – the soreness in his 'left shoulder had come of carrying a pollard ... that in one leg was caused by the crash of an elm' – implies that this timber, spar and copse-ware merchant now seeks to inflict damage on an arboreal site that caused him such pain in his younger, less affluent days.[74] His lucrative line in 'barking' – which starves the roots of trees, rendering them 'half-dead' and 'hollow' – indicates the very instrumental and predatory attitude to the forest that might cause its eventual devastation, and foreshadows Wendell

Berry's notion of an agribusiness divorced from any moral obligation to sustainable communities set forth in *The Art of the Commonplace* (2002).

A Gentle Conjuror's Touch?

Grace Melbury's stylized framing of Winterborne's arboreal crafts acquires tragicomic force in the second half of *The Woodlanders* because he so conspicuously lacks the means to energize the sheltered recesses of Little Hintock. His uncertain position as tree-planter and cider-maker is partially explained by Richard Jefferies's description of a peculiar trait of the rural land-worker in 'The Labourer's Daily Life' for the November 1874 *Fraser's Magazine*. There is

> a singular and strongly marked characteristic of the agricultural class, taken generally. They work and live and have their being in grooves. So long as they can continue in that groove, and go steadily forward, without much thought or trouble beyond that of patience and perseverance, all goes well; but if any sudden jolt should throw them out of this rut they seem incapable of regaining it.[75]

'Patience' and 'perseverance' are the first articles of Winterborne's arboreal faith. The 'sudden jolt' that Jefferies portrays here has its analogue in the disastrous outcome of Winterborne's felling of the bedridden John South's totem-elm. The yeoman's operation on this tree not only undermines his status as a judicious warden of the forest, but also shows the narrator's resistance to Grace's smug feeling for a Wordsworthian 'Nature' as nurse, guide and guardian, shaped by her schoolroom reading of 'Tintern Abbey'. John South's trepidation indicates we are closer to the 'very malicious ... treacherous' elm depicted in Richard Jefferies's *Wood Magic: A Fable* (1881), which draws on this tree's legendary associations with mortality and the underworld (elm wood was traditionally used for making coffins).[76] South perceives the tree outside his cottage as an adversary, 'exactly his own age' emerging 'when he was born on purpose to rule him', to 'keep him as its slave'. These terms topple the political symbolism and benign, even sacramental overtones of trees in first- and second-generation romantic poetics, such as Thomas Paine's liberty tree, William Cowper's 'Yardley Oak' and John Clare's 'To a Fallen Elm'. South keeps time to the movements of his elm – 'As the tree waved South waved his head' – and believes it will fall and crush him. Winterborne, asked about the source of John South's petrified obsessiveness, concedes that 'others have been like it afore in Hintock'. Here the novel shows how Grace's fey woodland primitivism – anchored in a conception of Winterborne as zealous protector of biodiversity – is undercut by South's panicky fixation.[77] As the word 'my enemy' implies, South's hallucinations are fed by acute fear of the tree's decay lest it causes his own collapse. While Winterborne's arboriculture is grounded in care for each sapling on its own terms, Old South views the elm through the distorting lens of his egotistical and paranoid promptings.

What is at issue in these closing chapters – a melancholy sequence of 'timber-stories' – is Winterborne's capacity to bolster the community's respect for the material interconnectedness of human and arboreal lives through his 'gentle conjuror's touch', the centrepiece of his traditional husbandry.[78] Although this 'touch' with the trees and their by-products (apples, barks, spar-gads) implies he may be best situated to allay Old South's arboreal anguish, Winterborne is thwarted by the careerist physician Edred Fitzpiers, who rejects the old man's fraught reaction to the large elm as an insular atavism. Winterborne's hewing of South's tree is conducted upon Fitzpiers's clinical directive and deepens a chronicle of severance triggered by Barber Percomb's cutting of Marty South's luxuriant 'chestnut' tresses in the opening section. Yet Winterborne's arboriculture does not supply any reassuring sense that the quasi-mystical 'sympathy between himself and the fir, oak, or beech'[79] extends to the pruning or clearing outlined by Virgil (*Georgics*, II. 69–72, 80–2). Hardy exploits the more ominous associations of what is called 'shrouding' in *The Woodlanders* (lopping off the lowest branches of a tree). While pruning may be justified in arboriculture (see *Georgics*, II. 367–70), in *The Woodlanders* it necessitates the application of force against the natural conditions of the elm: '[e]ach [bough] quivered under *his attack*, bent, cracked, and fell into the hedge' (my italics).[80] If, as W. H. Auden's 1952 'Bucolics' poem implies, 'a culture is no better than its woods'[81] – implying how personal affect and collective memories become intermingled with and inseparable from the tangible soil – then Winterborne's 'shrouding' of Old South's elm will prove a hazardous act, given Hardy's attentive study of the desecration or unsanctioned use of ancient Greek and Roman woodland groves cited by J. G. Frazer's first edition of *The Golden Bough* (1890). After Winterborne's 'work' on the elm, John South suffers a fatal seizure. Although barked trees and extensive clearing are supposed to benefit civilized culture, according to Grace's father, *The Woodlanders* captures the echo of what has been ruptured and ruined in the process. This version of 'civilization' ultimately demoralizes and cripples, as the thoroughgoing 'cultivation' of Grace Melbury attests, given her transformation from ingenuous 'daughter of the woods' to an affectively sterile product of a suburban school.

Arboreal Anxieties

The closing chapters suggest that John South's arboreal dread, rather than Winterborne's supposed skill in working sustainably with the Hintock earth, is the more credible facet of woodland existence. The yeoman's immersion in the 'finer mysteries' of his homeland – highlighted by 'those young trees, so many of which he had planted' which '[send] out their roots in the direction that he had given them with his subtle hand'[82] – is repeatedly undermined by the myriad grisly descriptions of the operation of natural potencies within the Hintocks. Winterborne can do about as much to reverse such arboreal infections as Henchard can 'cure' the 'growed' grain in *The Mayor of Casterbridge*. Winterborne's failure to function as caretaker and custodian of this ecosystem is starkly apparent in the 'trees close together' at One-Chimney Hut, 'wrestling for existence', with 'wounds resulting from their mutual rubbings', and the 'dead boughs ... scattered about like ichthyosauri in a museum'.[83] The evocation of trees in terms of the 'Unfulfilled Intention', misshapen or marred by unwholesome rot, is a conceit whose severity cannot be ascribed to the narrator's fondness for chiaroscuro effects or to Grace Melbury's facile sense-impressions. Neither vitally beneficial nor beautiful, this conception of the forest – whose bizarre somatic imagery Hardy elaborates in the 'wilder' portions of Felice Charmond's estate – contrasts with *Under the Greenwood Tree* (1872), whose vision of the *genius loci* celebrates a precious cycle of recovery and resilience.

Like the trees to which he ineffectively ministers, then, Winterborne and his sylvan creed must be cleared away. His death (chapters 41 and 42) is not what gives this final section its tragic gravitas, however. *The Woodlanders* shows that in the entire run of the agrarian calendar, planting and harvesting, growth and decay, are equally crucial. The narrator's unnerving delineation of 'barren life' here is grounded in the sense that Giles Winterborne is not only the antitype of a robust, pagan 'Wild Man', but also a far cry from the Christian hermit 'Saint Giles', recalled in Book Four of Wordsworth's *Excursion* to watch over the forests of our native land (IV, lines 900–12).[84] Instead of a Wordsworthian priest of nature we view an emotionally inarticulate entity, whose 'sad powerlessness' is mirrored in his failure to accomplish fruitful 'manual labour'[85] in his era. He cedes control over the soil he tends and gains little from his arboreal practice except coarse fare and a basic wage. Ultimately, the yeoman can neither secure his modest property nor combat the blatant misuse of natural resources around him – symbolized by 'barking' – from which Grace's timber-merchant father profits. The problem is that the text has no alternative farmer-generated lore, community value or compelling georgic ethic to vouchsafe in Winterborne's wake – except Grace Melbury's shallow notions of an idealized arboriculture and the non-reciprocal, dominance-based relationship with Little Hintock espoused by her aristocratic neighbour Felice Charmond. When Grace is recovering from illness, she cleaves to her earlier, far-fetched 'cultivation' of Winterborne as a pip-smeared 'wood-god' from a forest of romance peopled with fauns and dryads. In this moment – a wan fantasy of the feeling of symbiosis that blurs boundaries between soul and soil – *The Woodlanders* illustrates the waning of a model of constructive husbandry whose actuality cannot be adequately traced since 'imagination' itself is liable to such grandiose and deceptive daydreams. Winterborne, like Henchard from *The Mayor*, typifies a once sturdy georgic regime which is doomed if it is compelled to adopt a new paradigm of agribusiness and its false consciousness of affective and forensic 'propriety'.[86]

Notes

1 There is evidence to suggest that Hardy met Richard Jefferies at a dinner in 1880, to which Matthew Arnold and Henry James were also invited. Hardy portrays Jefferies as 'a modest young man then getting into notice as a writer, through having a year or so earlier published his first successful book, entitled *The Gamekeeper at Home*'. See F. E. Hardy, *The Life of Thomas Hardy, 1840–1928* (London: Macmillan, 1965), pp. 134–5. As Roger Ebbatson explains, Hardy and Jefferies benefited from a number of mutual cultural contacts, such as the influential editor of *The Pall Mall Gazette*, Frederick Greenwood, and their first publisher, William Tinsley. See R. Ebbatson, *Landscape and Literature 1830–1914: Nature, Text, Aura* (Basingstoke: Palgrave, 2013), pp. 125–41; R. Ebbatson, *Landscapes of Eternal Return: Tennyson to Hardy* (Basingstoke: Palgrave, 2016).
2 G. Garrard, *Ecocriticism*, 2nd ed. (Abingdon: Routledge, 2004), p. 129.
3 T. Hardy, *The Mayor of Casterbridge*, ed. Dale Kramer (Oxford University Press, 1987), p. 161.
4 See T. Ziolkowski, *Virgil and the Moderns* (Princeton University Press, 1993), pp. 116–17.
5 B. Loughrey, ed. *The Pastoral Mode: A Casebook* (London: Macmillan, 1984), p. 11.
6 See I. Clark, *Thomas Hardy's Pastoral: An Unkindly May* (London: Palgrave, 2015), p. 10.
7 R. Jefferies, 'The Future of Farming', *Fraser's Magazine*, 8, 48 (1873), 687–97.
8 D. Taylor, 'Hardy and Drayton: A Contribution to Pastoral and Georgic Traditions', in *The Literature of Place*, ed. N. Page and P. Preston (London: Macmillan, 1993), pp. 40–63, at p. 40.
9 R. Jefferies, *Red Deer* (London: Longmans, Green and Co., 1894), p. 32.
10 R. Jefferies, 'The Labourer's Daily Life', in *Landscape with Figures: Selected Prose Writings*, ed. Richard Mabey (Harmondsworth: Penguin, 2012), p. 34.

11 Hardy, *Mayor*, p. 1.
12 Jefferies, 'Future of Farming', p. 688.
13 Hardy, *Mayor*, p. 257.
14 Hardy, *Mayor*, pp. 295, 8.
15 T. Hardy, *The Woodlanders*, ed. Dale Kramer (Oxford University Press, 1986), p. 58.
16 Hardy, *Mayor*, pp. 114, 64.
17 G. Bachelard, *Earth and Reveries of Will: An Essay on the Imagination of Matter*, tr. K. Haltman (Paris: Dallas Institute, 2002), p. 6.
18 Virgil, *Georgics* (Dryden), p. 155.
19 H. Kenner, *The Pound Era* (London: Pimlico, 1991), p. 171.
20 Hardy, *Mayor*, p. 27.
21 T. Hardy, *Jude the Obscure*, ed. P. Ingham (Oxford University Press, 1986), p. 60.
22 Hardy, *Mayor*, pp. 29, 104, 115.
23 Hardy, *Mayor*, pp. 72, 181.
24 Hardy, *Mayor*, pp. 335, 200.
25 Jefferies, 'The Future of Farming', p. 687.
26 Hardy, *Mayor*, pp. 235, 257.
27 T. Hardy, *The Return of the Native*, ed. S. Gatrell (Oxford University Press, 1986), pp. 205–7.
28 Hardy, *Mayor*, p. 33.
29 Hardy, *Mayor*, pp. 62, 330.
30 Hardy, *Mayor*, pp. 32, 43.
31 Hardy, *Mayor*, p. 44.
32 R. Williams, *Keywords: A Vocabulary of Culture and Society* (London: Fontana Press, 1976), p. 87.
33 Hardy, *Mayor*, p. 45.
34 R. Jefferies, 'High-Pressure Agriculture' (1876), p. 193.
35 Hardy, *Mayor*, p. 115.
36 Hardy, *Mayor*, pp. 112–13.
37 R. Jefferies, *The Toilers of the Field* (London: Longmans, 1892), pp. 242–3.
38 Hardy, *Mayor*, pp. 280, 40, 112–13.
39 R. Jefferies, 'John Smith's Shanty', *Fraser's Magazine*, 9 (1874), 147.
40 Hardy, *Mayor*, pp. 76, 80–4.
41 Hardy, *Mayor*, p. 178.
42 Hardy, *Mayor*, p. 179.
43 Hardy, *Mayor*, pp. 80, 54.
44 Hardy, *Mayor*, p. 113.
45 Hardy, *Mayor*, p. 353.
46 Hardy, *Mayor*, pp. 246, 17–19.
47 Hardy, *Mayor*, p. 9, 58.
48 Hardy, *Mayor*, p. 107.
49 A. Skea, *Ted Hughes: The Poetic Quest* (Armidale: UNE Press, 1994), p. 123.
50 T. Hughes, *Shakespeare and the Goddess of Complete Being* (London: Faber, 1992), p. 513; Hardy, *Mayor*, p. 27.

51 Hardy, *Mayor*, p. 278.
52 R. Jefferies, 'The Prospects of Farming' in *Agriculture and the Land: Richard Jefferies' Essays and Letters*, ed. R. Welshman (Edinburgh University Press, 2019), p. 105.
53 R. Jefferies, 'Wiltshire Labourers', in *Landscape with Figures*, ed. Mabey, p. 55.
54 Hardy, *Mayor*, pp. 8, 24.
55 Hardy, *Mayor*, pp. 250, 154.
56 R. Jefferies, 'Village Architecture', in *Landscape with Figures*, ed. Mabey, p. 64.
57 Hardy, *Woodlanders*, p. 142.
58 Jefferies, 'Wiltshire Labourers', p. 57.
59 A. McRae. *God Speed the Plough: The Representation of Agrarian England 1500–1660* (Cambridge University Press, 2002), p. 199.
60 Hardy, *Mayor*, p. 1.
61 Hardy, *Woodlanders*, pp. 297–8.
62 Hardy, *Woodlanders*, p. 59.
63 Hardy, *Woodlanders*, p. 87.
64 Hardy, *Woodlanders*, p. 155.
65 Hardy, *Woodlanders*, pp. 58, 56.
66 Hardy, *Woodlanders*, p. 189.
67 Hardy, *Woodlanders*, p. 1.
68 R. Jefferies, 'The Labourer's Daily Life', *Fraser's Magazine*, 10, 59 (November), 654–69.
69 Hardy, *Woodlanders*, pp. 185–6.
70 Hardy, *Woodlanders*, p. 47.
71 Hardy, *Woodlanders*, pp. 185–6.
72 W. Dowling, *Poetry and Ideology in Revolutionary Connecticut* (Athens, GA: University of Georgia Press, 1990), p. 36.
73 Hardy, *Woodlanders*, p. 108.
74 Hardy, *Woodlanders*, p. 33.
75 Jefferies, 'The Labourer's Daily Life', p. 654.
76 R. Jefferies, *Wood Magic: A Fable* (London: Longman, 1907), pp. 50–1.
77 Hardy, *Woodlanders*, pp. 92–3, 151, 135.
78 Hardy, *Woodlanders*, p. 129.
79 Hardy, *Woodlanders*, p. 58.
80 Hardy, *Woodlanders*, pp. 151–2.
81 W. H. Auden, 'Bucolics 2. Woods', *The Collected Poems of W. H. Auden*, ed. E. Mendelssohn (London: Faber, 1986), p. 560.
82 Hardy, *Woodlanders*, p. 293.
83 Hardy, *Woodlanders*, p. 280.
84 Hardy, *Woodlanders*, p. 168.
85 Hardy, *Woodlanders*, pp. 187, 56, 8.
86 Hardy, *Woodlanders*, pp. 249, 293, 172.

CHAPTER 11

Twentieth-Century Georgic
V. Sackville-West

Juan Christian Pellicer

V. Sackville-West's two formal georgics, *The Land* (1926) and *The Garden* (1946), are notable for their lyric beauty and exceptional for their popularity. They are the first successful poems of their kind since William Cowper's *The Task* (1785). Both georgics are in pentameter verse (mainly blank, but threaded with rhyme, and occasionally interspersed with lyrics in other metres) and arranged in four books to trace the seasonal cycle, which is itself the fundamental theme of both works. They each found a wide audience. Each was favourably reviewed, sold exceedingly well, and won a prestigious literary prize.[1] At the beginning of the twenty-first century, both poems were still in print. This chapter will focus on their poetic accomplishment, viewed as a form of engagement with the social and cultural pressures of their time. Sackville-West's representation of the agricultural life of her community, the Kentish Weald, is underwritten by her mastery of the formal traditions of Virgilian georgic as well as her understanding of local occupations. The form and the farm are best viewed stereoscopically.[2]

Figures of Virgilian Genres

The beginning of *The Land* announces cyclical repetition as one of its master tropes:

> I sing the cycle of my country's year,
> I sing the tillage, and the reaping sing,
> Classic monotony, that modes and wars
> Leave undisturbed, unbettered, for their best
> Was born immediate, of expediency. (p. 3)

The idea of 'classic monotony' remaining undisturbed by 'modes and wars' is a response to the Great War from the vantage-point of the early 1920s. *The Garden*, written during the Second World War, reverses the earlier position: 'of gardens in the midst of war | I boldly tell' (p. 13).[3] Yet the thing to notice at the beginning of *The Land* is the poet's careful fashioning of a tradition into which to inscribe herself. Her refrain through the georgic's long proem (which runs to the end of 'Winter Song', p. 11) is the epic trope 'I sing', inflected in a way that evokes the conventions of pastoral and georgic too: 'I sing once more | The mild continuous epic of the soil' (p. 3).[4] *Once more* is the note of pastoral, which plays on repetition: 'Yet once more, o ye laurels, and once more'. Yet the violent rhythms and gestures of shattering that launch Milton's *Lycidas* could not be farther away from the iambic regularity with which Sackville-West illustrates the unbroken continuity of agriculture and the seasonal cycle. The motif of the rural cycle itself distinguishes neither pastoral nor georgic, it is a common property of both. What instead identifies the mode of Sackville-West's proem as georgic is the poet's act of describing her own experience in her own voice. This georgic hallmark takes a lyric inflection; some readers have detected a Wordsworthian undersong.[5] 'I then, who as a wrestler wrought with earth | Bending some stubborn acres to my will, | Know that no miracle shall come to pass' (p. 8). However personal this voice, if not quite private, it is also said to issue from a reservoir of 'immemorial' knowledge, reflecting Sackville-West's patrician notion of hereditary kinship with the land ('I tell the things I know, the things I knew | Before I knew them, immemorially', p. 4). The voice itself need not be identified with any formal genre, and of course the purpose of picking out the various specialities of pastoral, georgic and epic is to observe these distinctive features working together, not separately, in the system of Virgilian genres. 'The mild continuous epic' neatly summarizes the repertoire of this generic triad.[6] 'Of the soil' establishes georgic as the master genre.

One Virgilian trope that Sackville-West does not employ is that of casting herself as the first to attempt her own particular endeavour. Whereas Virgil represents himself as the first to bring Hesiodic song to Roman towns ('Ascraeumque cano Romana per oppida carmen', *Georgics*, II. 176), Sackville-West suggests that poetic tradition is as continuously enduring as rural occupations themselves. Outlined against the sky, 'simple and classic', the figures of scythesman and shepherd 'rear their grave design | As once at Thebes, as once in Lombardy' (p. 3). Thebes is the capital of Hesiod's Boeotia; Virgil was from Mantua in Lombardy. When Sackville-West says of her immemorial scythesmen that they are as true to their classic design as the shape of their scythes, she is treating them as stylized figures, and so inviting us to read figuratively. When she says these scythesmen did not care 'what crop had ripened, whether oats in Greece | Or oats in Kent', she is writing metaphorically: real crops are not the issue. (Hesiod does not mention oats; Virgil's wild-oat flute is a reed made from a weed, see

Eclogues, I. 2 and *Georgics*, I. 154; and Sackville-West's manuscript reads, 'whether maize in Greece | Or oats in Kent'.⁷) Instead, Sackville-West uses the oat to combine the emblem of pastoral lyric, the *avena* or oaten reed, with the perennial quality of the crop cycle. Like the cut-outs of rural archetypes, the oat itself is a figure of pastoral, while 'oats in Greece | Or oats in Kent', specifying geographical location, is a figure of georgic. Read this way, Sackville-West's emblematic language accommodates Virgil's metapoetic dimension, as it also does at the close of *The Land*, in her imitation of Virgil's autobiographical 'seal' at the conclusion of the *Georgics* (IV. 559–66). Reflecting on Virgil's example, how 'from Mantua reft, | Shy as a peasant in the courts of Rome' he took the waxen tablets in his hand and 'out of anger cut calm tales of home', Sackville-West reconfigures Virgil, whose family home near Mantua was threatened by land redistributions, in her own self-image. Prevented by her sex from inheriting her own birthplace, the Sackville estate of Knole near Sevenoaks in Kent, and living in London (as well as visiting her husband the diplomat Harold Nicolson in Tehran in 1926, where she finished *The Land*), Sackville-West was bent on resurrecting her ancestral home in poetry (for she had not yet acquired Sissinghurst).⁸ The metapoetic reading of this autobiographical passage would have it represent the fact that Virgil used epic hexameter ('anger') to write on rural and Epicurean subjects.⁹ Indeed, all Sackville-West's evocations of Virgil seem deliberately stylized. In her haunting tercet

> My life was rich; I took a swarm of bees
> And found a crumpled snake-skin on the road,
> All in one day, and was increased by these. (*The Land*, p. 55)

it is tempting to discern an oblique Callimachean-style cameo of the Aristaeus epyllion in the fourth *Georgic*, which embeds the story of Eurydice (who, fleeing Aristaeus's embrace, was fatally bitten by a snake, then nearly rescued from Hades by her husband Orpheus) in Virgil's account of Aristaeus's discovery of a miraculous means to regenerate a beehive (*Georgics*, IV. 281–558).

Vernacular Georgic

Sackville-West maintained she had not yet read the *Georgics* when she conceived *The Land* in 1921, but she certainly read Virgil in the course of composition, between 1923 and 1926.¹⁰ Though she identifies Hesiod and Virgil as her main predecessors and groups the pair with Homer (p. 89), she takes Virgil as her principal model. Yet Sackville-West's affinity with the British georgic tradition, though less explicit, is arguably as important. Anyone familiar with Cowper's *Task* and with his predecessor James Thomson, as well as with Cowper's immediate successors, William Wordsworth and Charlotte Smith, will read Sackville-West with a sense of recognition. Didactic-descriptive pentameter verse about inhabiting the productive landscape, or topographical poetry that describes the speaker's passage through that landscape, represents a rich and varied tradition in British literature.[11] Sackville-West's prototype for both her georgics is Thomson's *Seasons*, the most thematically comprehensive, philosophically ambitious and scientifically curious of the British georgics, not least on account of her comparable focus on the seasonal round, each four-part poem progressing from winter to autumn.[12] Spoofed as 'The Oak Tree' in Woolf's *Orlando* (1928), the fictional counterpart of *The Land* is said by Woolf's critic Nicholas Greene to compare 'favourably' with Thomson: a barbed compliment, but unlike Greene's preceding remark ('it reminded him, he said as he turned over the pages, of Addison's *Cato*'), a comparison that holds true.[13] Sackville-West's Virgil is mediated through his British reception: naturalized, domesticated and given a lyrical dimension in the course of the seventeenth to nineteenth centuries in the accommodating and variegated traditions of the English country house poem and the blank verse georgic.[14]

Farm and Form

In both her georgic poems, from first to last, Sackville-West develops Virgil's fundamental idea that agriculture is an alternative form of warfare, waged not against human adversaries but against a recalcitrant natural world bent on speeding everything towards the worse ('in peius ruere', *Georgics*, I. 200). As Susanna Braund observes, Sackville-West's 'language of violence, struggle and toil vividly recalls that in *Georgics* I, especially the crucial lines (I. 145–6): "labor omnia vicit | improbus et duris urgens in rebus egestas"' – lines that are difficult to translate because the founding of toil's world dominion can be read as either a blessing or a curse.[15] *The Land* sings of the shrewd, practical 'means | That break the *unkindly* spirit of the clay' (pp. 3–4, my emphasis). A reviewer observed, 'Perhaps *The Land* leans a little to the gloomy side; but, then, the particular county of which the poet is singing is Kent, clayey Kent.'[16]

Sackville-West's practical knowledge of rural occupations is everywhere evident, but *The Land* 'is no more a didactic poem' than Virgil's *Georgics*.[17] For her epigraph, Sackville-West chose precisely the lines from Virgil's programmatic passage at the centre of *Georgics* III (284–93) that define the poet's work rather than the farmer's: 'nec sum animi dubius, *verbis* ea vincere magnum | quam sit et angustis hunc addere rebus honorem' ('And well I know how hard it is to win *with words* a triumph herein, and thus to crown with glory a lowly theme', *Georgics*, III. 289–90, my emphasis).[18] Sackville-West's point becomes even clearer when we consider that at proof stage she cancelled a second epigraph she had chosen: Hesiod's line 'There is no shame in working, but the shame is in not working' (*Works and Days*, line 311, David Grene's translation ; the Greek epigraph is untranslated, as is the Latin epigraph from Virgil that survived into print).[19] Contemporary reviewers took Sackville-West seriously on agricultural topics, as any critic should, and appreciated her acumen in these matters, but they acknowledged that poetry came first. Sidney Barrington Gates, the anonymous reviewer in *The Nation and Athenaeum* (6 November 1926) conceded that *The Land* 'could be read aloud in a country alehouse, and if it were not announced as poetry, its rough and racy wisdom would win a gruff assent' – only to insist, 'But it is a poem, and a very remarkable one'. Gates was himself a poet, as well as an aeronautical engineer. He praised not only 'the comely gravity and sweetness' of its music, but applauded that this music could sustain such an extensive work.[20]

Sackville-West describes the work of rural craftsmen as a correlative of poetic composition. The crafts of the thatcher, wheelwright, timber-master, plasterer, basket-maker, osier-weaver, bricklayer, shepherd and water-diviner – all these arts, described on pages 79–81, are described as analogues of the poet's craft, and vice versa:

> All craftsmen share a knowledge. They have held
> Reality down fluttering to a bench;
> Cut wood to their own purposes; compelled
> The growth of pattern with the patient shuttle;
> Drained acres to a trench.
> Control is theirs. They have ignored the subtle
> Release of spirit from the jail of shape.
> They have been concerned with prison, not escape;
> Pinioned the fact, and let the rest go free,
> And out of need made inadvertent art.
> All things designed to play a faithful part
> Build up their plain particular poetry.
> Tools have their own integrity; ...
> —So language, smithied at the common fire
> Grew to its use; as sneath and shank and haft
> Of well-grained wood, nice instruments of craft,
> Curve to the simple mould the hands require,
> Born of the needs of man.
> The poet like the artisan
> Works lonely with his tools...[21]

The idea that rural crafts may be understood as analogous to the art of poetry is implicit in parts of Virgil's *Georgics*, where the arts of grafting and beekeeping especially are susceptible to metapoetic interpretation, but in the *Eclogues* the idea is a defining feature, and was developed as a generic trope in the subsequent pastoral tradition.[22] 'These strains, Muses divine, it will be enough for your bard to have sung, as he sits and weaves a basket of slender willow', concludes the speaker of the tenth Eclogue ('Haec sat erit, divae, vestrum cecinisse poetam, | dum sedet et gracili fiscellam texit hibisco, | Pierides').[23] Since the fourth-century commentator Servius, Virgil's slender basket has been read allegorically. Its ideal 'gracilitas' or elegant simplicity may be taken to represent the Tenth Eclogue, or the *Eclogues* as a whole, or pastoral poetry, or even poetry full stop. We recognize the trope in Seamus Heaney's 'The Harvest Bow', where the 'frail device' plaited by the poet's father, and the reciprocal poem held in the reader's hands, may be read as emblems of each other. Representing rural occupations as parables of the poet's art distinguishes many other Heaney poems, for instance 'Thatcher' and 'Diviner', not to mention 'Digging' and 'Bogland'.[24]

Sackville-West develops a similar correspondence between the rural and the poetic arts, since she is a beneficiary of the progress narrative in ancient georgic, as well as its inflection in the eighteenth century as a narrative of social diversification. Virgil's so-called Jupiter theodicy in *Georgics*, I. 129–46, which reworks Hesiod's *Works and Days* as well as Lucretius, and concludes with the lines quoted earlier about the entry of 'labor' into the world and all our trials, projects from this foundational moment a narrative of the progress of civilization in which experience ('usus') is gradually beaten out ('extundit') into the various arts ('varias artes', I. 133).[25] In eighteenth-century georgic, a triumphal narrative of historical progress through the stages of economic diversification is given classic expression in Thomson's panegyric to Industry (*The Seasons*, 'Autumn', lines 43–150). John Dyer explores the ramifications of this grand narrative in *The Fleece* (1757), of all georgics the richest in social detail, by describing the remarkable variety of specialized trades and skills involved in the woollen industry.[26] The difference between Dyer's craftsmen and Sackville-West's is that Dyer's artisans and merchants (the artisans include carders, combers, spinsters, dyers, weavers, fullers, shearers and burlers) are figures of progress and modernity. Dyer is wedded to the idea of social 'improvement', and imagines that old and new technologies will continue to cooperate in the progress of industry and civilization.[27] By contrast, Sackville-West's thatcher, wheelwright, timber-master and the rest represent occupations on the brink of disappearing in the wake of modernizing technologies. They are figures of obsolescence, representing traditions that the poet wishes to honour, not memorializing them elegiacally but promoting their endurance in rural life by depicting their occupations. Sackville-West belongs to a culture that had absorbed Ruskin and Morris in myriad ways. Her aesthetics of rural craft and poetry has roots in the previous century.

'Playing the Farmer'

In *The Land*, however, her archaizing, traditionalist sensibility is vulnerable to the charge of what Raymond Williams called 'mystification': the obfuscation or distortion or disguise of real historical change by stylized forms of ahistorical representation, usually for politically conservative ends.[28] The accusation is serious, and few writers escape it entirely. We can begin with Virgil, whose first person speaker is, like Virgil himself, a landowner-poet who gives farming advice without ever acknowledging that the tasks he describes were routinely carried out by slaves.[29] This particular blind spot is not shared by Sackville-West, who never airbrushes labour or labourers out of her picture. On the contrary, she is uncommonly scrupulous about who does what and for whom, not merely about how they do it. Her farmer finds a use for the hours of winter darkness 'that keep his ploughman lusk' (a dialect word, 'idle', p. 19): the one is clearly working for the other. In *The Garden*, where in her dual role as gardener-poet she could easily have monopolized both parts, she does not displace the figure of the professional gardener in her employ. She speaks as a gardener, she addresses the reader as a fellow gardener, and describes the gardener as a stock figure ('the most dissatisfied of men', p. 16) to whom she attributes not only hard economic sense but a poetic imagination (pp. 26–9). In *The Land* she always represents figures such as the shepherd, farmer, bee-master and gardener as separate from herself, yet she participates emotionally, intellectually and, above all, poetically in the rural life they share in common: 'The country habit has me by the heart' (p. 5). We are rightly suspicious of such self-fashioning across class and occupation: in a different context, 'habit' could be taken in the sense of dressing up. Yet Sackville-West is no Marie Antoinette. No other self-confessed georgic poet in English approximates the rapture of Virgil's 'praises of the countryside' finale of *Georgics* II (475–542) with greater candour or verbal beauty.

What Sackville-West and Virgil have in common is the georgic game of 'playing the farmer', as Philip Thibodeau describes it in his book of that title (2011). Observing that Virgil and his contemporary readers were '*almost* farmers' – that is, mainly absentee landlords – Thibodeau not only investigates the poem's enabling 'economic fantasies', but also, more importantly in a literary context, inquires what these economic fantasies enabled the poet and his audience to conceive; for instance, the idea that the life of performing manual tasks could be dignified in philosophical art.[30] Virgil's georgic speaker invites the reader to imagine that they are both farmers, and that the act of mentally exploring the universe through the lens of agriculture is like actually engaging in the work of farming. 'Before our ploughshare cleaves an unknown plain', says Virgil ('prius ignotum ferro quam scindimus aequor'), we must first learn everything about the soil and climate (*Georgics*, I. 50–3). Virgil not only uses the first person plural, addressing the reader as a fellow farmer, but also speaks about agriculture in a way that invites the reader to imagine that the poet is also talking about something else. He uses a word for plain, 'aequor', that he also uses frequently of the sea.[31] As Mynors observes, the maritime parallel is 'not far below the surface'.[32] Plough and ship are both vessels of restlessly expansive cultivation. The imperialist implications are next illustrated, as the passage reviews the variety of produce yielded by the regions of the earth (*Georgics*, I. 56–9).[33] Yet since the ocean voyage is a common image of epic poetry, the maritime sense of 'aequor' also connects with the set of nautical metaphors Virgil uses to describe his own act of performing or composing the poem itself as a poetic sea voyage.[34] Sackville-West's geographic imaginary is rich too – Gates observes that she loves 'opening sudden windows on other lands' – and her scenes of travel and exploration invite the reader to join her in flights of the imagination.[35] Yet it is not until *The Garden* that she takes the plunge and follows Virgil in addressing the reader as a fellow cultivator. ('Come then', the Roman poet urges at I. 63, 'ergo age', start ploughing.)

Native and Foreign

'Hear first of the country that shall claim my theme', announces Sackville-West, 'the Weald of Kent', once the ancient forest of Andredsweald (the name the Jutes and Saxons derived from the Roman fort of Anderida), now 'a green, wet country on a bed of clay' (*The Land*, p. 11).[36] Sackville-West's mythic chorography may be compared with that of John Philips's *Cyder* (1708), which represents the poet's own part of Herefordshire between the Wye and the Monnow as Ariconium, the Roman name for the medieval Welsh kingdom of Ergyng or Archenfield, and traces its people to the pre-Roman Silures.[37] Yet unlike Philips's georgic, which celebrates the parliamentary Union of 1707, Sackville-West's Wealden poem quite lacks the pronounced British dimension that characterizes both Thomson and Dyer, and celebrates instead a distinctly English historical identity. ('England' and 'English' are used frequently and with emotion; 'Britain' and 'British', never.) Sackville-West's Kentish regionalism can be compared with the regionalisms of Victorian English novelists with regard to their implicit national dimension: 'By treating locations like Loamshire and Wessex with what Chapter 17 of *Adam Bede* calls a "faithful" and "Dutch" truthfulness they can then be made to seem English in a general as well as a local way.'[38] As Susan Bazargan observes, Woolf's title 'The Oak Tree' at a stroke reinserts *The Land* into the narrative of empire and nationhood from which Sackville-West's poem is at pains to separate itself – the narrative of Pope's *Windsor-Forest* (1713), in which the emblem of monarchy, the oak, is metamorphosed into shipmasts to bear Britain's commerce with her thunder and her cross.[39] For all Sackville-West's references to foreign travel, her notion of England itself is emphatically insular: the foreign is typically a figure of contrast, not of extension. The lines from *The Land* that Woolf quotes in *Orlando* are taken from a section in which erotically charged fritillaries – 'Sullen and foreign-looking, the snaky flower' – are compared with gypsies, and their seductive presence in an English field is recalled as a threat from which the speaker says she 'shrank' (pp. 48–50).[40] Woolf and Sackville-West both take gypsies as figures of lesbian seduction, and Sackville-West cherished the belief that her own Spanish grandmother Pepita was a gypsy, but this passage does suggest that such figures of foreignness are disconcerting in an English landscape.[41] In *The Garden*, however, Sackville-West relishes the foreignness of deceptively 'English' but actually 'cosmopolitan' tulips, 'Aliens, that Shakespeare never saw nor sang. | Alien Asiatics, that have blown | Between the boulders of a Persian hill' for centuries before reaching the Dutch and their great flower painters: 'Tulip, *dulband*, a turban; rare | Persian that wanders in our English tongue' (p. 78). Xenophobia has no part in this delighted contrast between the exotic and the native. What is missing, however, is the eighteenth-century delight in analysing the connecting nodes between the several scenes of production in increasingly complex and cosmopolitan processes of social organization. This particular absence in Sackville-West seems less georgic than Georgian.[42]

Languages

Sackville-West's language also cultivates the native by selection and exclusion. Her juxtaposition of *dulband* and *tulip* is typical of her promiscuous late style, not the artful chasteness of her style in the 1920s: '*The Land* seems to revel in its lexical parochialism.'[43] Instead of the Latinate Miltonic style that distinguishes eighteenth-century British georgics, she uses blank verse to cultivate a poetic idiom that uses 'local, dialect and archaic words and expressions' to reflect regional allegiances and the notion of a linguistic 'Englishness'. Sackville-West evidently took pains to prefer words of Germanic origin to words derived from Latin. For instance, at Woolf's suggestion she revised her draft of the poem's opening passage, changing 'profiles' (of the scythesmen and shepherds) to 'outlines'.[44] However, Sackville-West does not proscribe Latinisms: this is a poet who uses 'glaucous' with notable felicity (*The Land*, p. 14), as well as words such as 'asprous' (p. 5), 'sagacious' (pp. 9, 22) and the French-derived 'guerdon' (p. 10). Nor are her dialect words generally obtrusive. Readers familiar with Heaney and Muldoon will remain unfazed by 'thole', even as a noun:

> There's no beginning to the farmer's year,
> Only recurrent patterns on a scroll
> Unwinding; only use in step with need,
> Sharp on the minute when the minute's come;
> A watching, waiting thole,
> A reckoning by rule-of-thumb.[45]

'Thole' is not merely intelligible but wholly naturalized and in tune with the passage's conversational cadences, its nimble accents, alliterations and rhymes. (After more narrowly prescriptive georgics, how delightful to find, reading on: 'Therefore let no man say, "Peas shall be sown | This month or that"', p. 31, a verse paragraph in a characteristically pragmatic vein that resurfaces on p. 67.) Addison remains an excellent guide to the *Georgics*, but as for his warnings against the georgic poet's 'letting his Subject debase his Stile', or against admitting 'the low Phrases and Terms of Art, that are adapted to Husbandry' into 'a serious Poem' – such scruples were suited to their time, and incautious poets such as James Grainger ignored them at their peril (Grainger sang unguardedly of laxatives in *The Sugar-Cane*, 1764).[46] Yet decorum itself had changed by Hardy's day, not to mention Sackville-West's, and she heeded Addison in the spirit by ignoring the letter. After all, to describe a thatcher as 'proud of his stelch, and prouder of his eaves, | Proud of his skill to thatch an awkward pent' (p. 79) is arguably to elevate the language of a twentieth-century georgic rather than debase it. To observe of 'the old wheel-wright, punctual timber-master' that he 'could tell you whether wood were frow or doted | Before the trunk was opened' (pp. 79–80) is likewise an enrichment, unless one were to object that the poet is overdoing the 'Terms of Art'.[47] Yet that too seems overfastidious. Even a page as relatively thick with conspicuous words as page 20 comes off handsomely. The farmer we encountered earlier, laying plans while his ploughman is kept lusk, wonders, 'Shall the poor Roughets stand this year for hay?' The dialect word 'roughets' (waste fields) ventriloquizes; this is free indirect style. Less auspiciously, January is given an archaic name, 'the wolf-month'.[48] Yet the line rights itself by intensification, following through with a vivid and expressive dialect word, 'shrammed' (numb with cold): 'Now in the wolf-month, shrammed and gaunt'. A few lines on, the dung-cart's load is appropriately 'reasty' (rancid). 'The wedge-shaped hale of roots for winter feeding' ('hale', a feeder open at the sides) adroitly uses a dialect noun of Anglo-Norman origin, a word that has travelled from romance to the barnyard. And when the next page (21) brings a close-up of the farmer calculating with his pencil 'in the kitchen's hush' while 'in the dark shippon tranquil cattle crush | Sweet cake, sliced mangold; shift and blow, and champ', the dialect word 'shippon' (cowshed) is surely as poetic in its context as anything Addison could wish.[49] Above all, the verse in this poem is so continually varied that selective quotation from even a single page is likely to give an unreliable impression. Only five lines after the auditory vividness of 'cattle crush | Sweet cake, sliced mangold' we get an effect that is completely different, and equally memorable: 'Under the double spell of night and frost | Within the yeoman's kitchen scheme | The year revolves its immemorial prose'.

That last tercet corroborates Addison's observation that, precisely because a georgic's subject matter is prosaic, the poem itself must never be so. As we have seen, the Virgilian passage Sackville-West chose for her epigraph makes that very point ('And well I know how hard it is to win with words a triumph herein, and thus to crown with glory a lowly theme', III. 289–90). The *Georgics* is experimental specifically in a linguistic sense. That is why debate about georgic as a modern form has tended to be specifically concerned with matters of linguistic choice, especially in matters of translation.[50] (Unlike pastoral, georgic never became a flashpoint in the Augustan debate between the Ancients and the Moderns.) The protocol of georgic reception invites a reader to reflect critically on Sackville-West's word choices, as indeed she does herself, for her own self-awareness of lexical register is often evident. One example must suffice; it occurs after a gorgeous description of apple orchards on page 36:

> But though fair
> To him who leans upon the gate to stare
> And muse 'How delicate in spring they be,
> That mobled blossom and that wimpled tree',
> There is a purpose in the cloudy aisles
> That took no thought of beauty for its care.

Here we encounter 'mobled', an adjective usually heard in connexion with Hecuba, so that Polonius-like, we must decide whether 'mobled blossom' is 'good'. Since the archaism satirizes its speaker (an Osric-like aesthete, to judge by his words), our verdict, effectively pre-empted by the literary echo, may well come out as some version of 'faith, very good'. Yet the adjective does have a life independently of Shakespeare, and it remained in Sackville-West's vocabulary. *The Garden* describes the Guelder-rose as 'Mobled in roseate surprise | That in December hints at apple-blossom' (pp. 41–2). Polonius has ceased to be relevant, if indeed he ever was.

Although the speaker of 'mobled blossom' is twitted for supposing that orchards are laid out merely for aesthetic effect, beauty really is at the heart of Sackville-West's poetic concerns. Her manuscript notes for *The Garden* include a telling self-instruction: 'No vague imagination any use; must have precision and knowledge, and yet not allow them to impair sense of beauty. The connoisseur's lack of aesthetic taste. Possible to become too highbrow.'[51] Of the three Virgilian genres, only georgic is distinguished by its awareness of its own difficulty.

Campaigns of the Imagination

Sackville-West found her second georgic harder to write than her first, because, as she explained to her husband Harold Nicolson, she felt the topic of gardening lacked 'the inherent dignity of agriculture', and also because 'seed-boxes are not so romantic as tilth'.[52] *The Garden* begins by contrasting the metaphorical 'pretty treble' of gardening's plucked string with the full-voiced 'organ' music of *The Land*'s description of 'husbandry's important ritual' (*Garden*, p. 13). Sackville-West's initial sense of gardening's lesser stature is revealing of the nature of her task, for in persisting with her second georgic she abided by the Virgilian epigraph of her first. The challenge of georgic is linguistic first and last.

Whereas *The Land* begins with the notion of agriculture as man's war against the elements, 'undisturbed' by transitory 'modes and wars', the site of cultivation in *The Garden* is a war zone where bomb shelters are dug in the orchard (p. 95). Gardening is an act of resistance, 'a miniature endeavour | To hold the graces and the courtesies | Against a horrid wilderness', mirroring an endless cycle of 'advance, relapse, advance, relapse, advance':

> So does the gardener in little way
> Maintain the bastion of his opposition
> And by a symbol keep civility;
> So does the brave man strive

> To keep enjoyment in his breast alive
> When all is dark and even in the heart
> Of beauty feeds the pallid worm of death. (*Garden*, pp. 14–15)

Moreover, gardening is eroticized. Whereas *The Land* had celebrated the plough that 'Homer and Hesiod and Virgil knew' (p. 89), Sackville-West now describes the ploughshare and harrow as brutish instruments, preferring instead the 'smaller spade and hoe and lowly trowel | And ungloved fingers with their certain touch' (p. 13). A verse paragraph on this new topic on page 13 is held in the tender embrace of a parenthesis, describing the 'green-fingered lover' of the potting shed 'who scorned to take a woman to his bed'. Yet in wartime, when everyone finds themselves living 'as they had never lived before' (p. 14), the poet also operates on a heroic plane with a resourcefulness to match that of the soldier, or even (in a flight of exoticism) of the bullfighter. Sackville-West reminisces at length about the wartime summers, 'a strange, a fierce, unusual time' when civilians found themselves living 'exalted to a different clime' and performing 'not as spectators' but inside 'the stainèd ring' (p. 91).

The tones of voice in *The Garden* are even more various than in *The Land*, conveying a fuller sense of georgic plenitude. 'Winter', the poem's longest book, plumbs the depths of psychic terrors in wartime, yet also treats the season as a 'valuable and enforced retreat' that 'liberates the vision of the soul' from its darkness, existential as well as seasonal (p. 21). As Pomeroy observes, the whole poem is cast as 'a talisman against darkness'.[53] The imagination plays the crucial role. A set-piece that favourably compares 'imagined woods' to 'a vision | Seen by rare travellers on Tibetan hills' (pp. 27–8) is superficially reminiscent of the poetic circumnavigations of the globe in the fourth book of Dyer's *The Fleece*, but Sackville-West evokes the romance of scientific exploration not only to dignify and variegate her theme but also specifically to conjure an ideal of unseen beauty that can only be pictured in the imagination.[54] 'Think, and imagine', she urges her reader, 'this might be your truth; | Follow my steps, oh gardener, down these woods' (p. 29). (She admits that while she dreams, mixing lyrical 'impossibilities' with sober 'sense', the practical gardener sits apart 'in the lamplight'. Yet being herself a 'poor practised gardener', she knows as well as he 'the Yes and better still the No', p. 29.) Such set-pieces are knowingly escapist fantasies. 'Luxuriate in this my startling jungle', she proposes (p. 29). It is Sackville-West's lyrical rejoicement that still delights, as it must have rejoiced readers especially in the terrible winter of 1946–7 and the post-war years of austerity: 'Sun, shake out your locks, | That heavy fleece, that rowelled aureole' (p. 72).

The humour of georgic poetry is often underestimated, and Sackville-West is an antidote to po-faced reading. Her section on garden pests (pp. 73–5) invites comparison with Virgil as well as with John Philips. She enjoins the gardener's vigilance, 'for mischief buds at every joint and node', not only 'fungus and mildew, blight and spot and rust' (p. 73) but also pests such as the caterpillar, the aphis, the ant, the mole and the rabbit (p. 74). As in Virgil, the mock-heroic mode animates without quite undermining the topic's basic seriousness. 'The caterpillar that with hump and heave | Measures the little inches of his way' sounds like a figure from a children's storybook, but then the perspective zooms out to survey 'the insect enemies' horribly 'pullulating more than Tartar hordes, | Despoiling as they travel, procreation | Calamitous in ravage, multitude | Unnumbered' (p. 74). Next, a portrait out of Disney's *Bambi*:

> Moles from the meadow will invade your plot;
> Pink palm, strong snout, and velvet energy
> Tunnel a system worthy of a sapper;
> Heave monticules while you lie snug-a-bed,
> And heave again, fresh chocolate, moist mould (p. 74)

Again, the effect is not to minimize the threat of pests: the comedy of scale by which the mock-heroic operates also acts as a magnifying glass. Compare Virgil's mouse ('mus'), which is comically dwarfed by the polysyllabic adjective that describes him ('exiguus', I. 181), but whose unseen industry undoes the farmer's toil as handily as Virgil's blind moles (I. 183). Virgil's barnyard pests, which include the toad, the weevil and the ant, erupt from the earth as prodigies, 'monstra' (I. 185). This is unsettling language. The various plagues ('pestes') will mock you, Virgil warns (I. 181), and the verb matches the noun in strength: 'inludere' is also used to describe the baiting of a captured enemy at *Aeneid* II. 64. Yet Virgil's concluding portrait of the ant 'fearful of a destitute old age' ('inopi metuens formica senectae', I. 186) surely demands the tribute of a laugh. Virgil's sympathy with the hapless farmer, his addressee at I. 155–9, is likewise tinged with humour: 'heu' ('alas', I. 158) is surely a bit mocking, and the prospect of the starving farmer shaking oaks for mast replays a Golden Age topos with sardonic irony. Compare Sackville-West, who after describing the damage done by 'innocent' rabbits merely doing 'their duty' to stay alive, apostrophizes with sympathetic amusement, 'Poor gardener! Poor stubborn simpleton, | Others must eat, though you be bent on beauty' (p. 74). The georgic topos of agriculture as warfare is revisited in wartime with a grim smile: 'Gardener, | Where is your armistice? You hope for none. | It will not be, until yourself breed maggots' (p. 74).

It would be instructive to compare with Philips's cultivation of the mock-heroic in *Cyder*, though as Virgil says to Maecenas, I cannot embrace the whole theme here (*Georgics*, II. 42).[55] Suffice it to say that Philips is elaborate and baroque. He ingeniously suggests that 'Shoals' of snails 'that creep | O'er the ripe Fruitage, paring slimy Tracts | In the sleek Rinds, and unprest *Cyder* drink' can themselves be distilled in 'the warm Limbec' (alembic) to make medicinal snail water (I. 411–20). In her version of the war against garden pests, Sackville-West places her trust in native 'allies in this freakish scheme | Of nature's contradictions', such as the glow-worm with its 'little torch that bores its light | Into the shelly cavern of the snail' (p. 75).

Sackville-West is virtually the sole practitioner of formal georgic in her century, yet her poems are a great deal more various than any single treatment is likely to demonstrate. Variety itself is a primary formal feature of georgic, some would say its chief organizing principle.[56] For Sackville-West the other great structuring principle is the seasonal round, which not only marks the passing of time but also describes the tragic curve of the individual life, which cleaves to the shape of the scythe. Both poems begin with 'Winter', describing the gestation of life from darkness; in each poem this is the longest section. In *The Land*, the year of agricultural occupations describes a cycle that supports the poet's own sense of occupation, hence the work finishes with scenes of harvest and vintage leading into the Virgilian coda, in which the poet represents herself at mid-career. In *The Garden*, 'Autumn' is the poem's shortest part, sectioned by the sun-clock's mottos, all on the theme of *memento mori* ('IT IS ALREADY LATER THAN YOU THINK', p. 133). The poem's closing couplet depicts the aging poet and her friends drawing to the end of life as 'Travellers of the year, who faintly say | How could such beauty walk the common way?' (p. 135). It seems fitting to catch an echo of Shakespeare's Sonnet 65, 'How with this rage shall beauty hold a plea, | Whose action is no stronger than a flower?' Like Shakespeare's poem, Sackville-West's celebrates the labour of 'black ink'.

Notes

1 *The Land* won the Hawthornden Prize in 1927, and *The Garden* won the Heinemann Prize in 1946. By 1971, *The Land* had gone into twenty-two editions and sold around 100,000 copies. V. Glendinning, *Vita: The Life of Vita Sackville-West* (1983; London: I. B. Tauris, 2018), p. 166, and I. Blyth, 'A Sort of English Georgics: V. Sackville-West's *The Land*', *Forum for Modern Language Studies*, 45 (2009), 19–31, at 21.

2 'By using the interesting concept of "economic fantasy", Thibodeau rightly avoids separating (as many have done) form and farm, culture and agriculture in his new discussion of Vergil's agrarian poem.' A. Barchiesi, dustjacket text for P. Thibodeau, *Playing the Farmer: Representations of Rural Life in Vergil's Georgics* (Berkeley: University of California Press, 2011).

3 V. Sackville-West, *The Garden* (1946; London: Frances Lincoln, 2004). All references are to this edition.

4 'I sing' occurs seven times in the first seven verse paragraphs, pp. 3–8.

5 In the typescript/manuscript of *The Land*, 1926, Huntington Library HM 41088, the whole proem is first written using mainly third-person male pronouns in the past tense, with subsequent revisions rendering the first person present tense form of the published text. Originally the passage read, 'But he, the poet who had wrought with earth | Knew that no miracle should come to pass' (fol. 6). On the 'Wordsworthian' flavour: L. P. Wilkinson, who thought *The Land* 'perhaps the best of English georgics', described it as 'descriptive and contemplative rather than didactic, Wordsworthian rather than Miltonian in verse-style, self-consciously restrained in the manner of the 1920s, and dedicated to giving a true picture of rural life in the Weald of Kent'. *The Georgics of Virgil: A Critical Survey* (1969; Bristol Classical Press, 1997), p. 311. Shortly after publishing *The Land*, Sackville-West read *The Prelude* and declared, 'I HATE Wordsworth, the old prig, bore, preachifying old solemnity' (Glendinning, *Vita*, p. 168).

6 I read 'mild' and 'continuous' as emblematic, respectively, of pastoral and georgic. Other interpretations are possible: S. Braund instead takes 'mild' to denote the 'middle style' of georgic. S. Braund, 'Women and Earth: Female Responses to the *Georgics* in the Twentieth and Twenty-First Centuries', in *Reflections and New Perspectives on Virgil's Georgics*, ed. B. Xinyue and N. Freer (London: Bloomsbury, 2019), pp. 185–200, at p. 196. On the system of genres in Augustan poetry, see S. J. Harrison, *Generic Enrichment in Vergil and Horace* (Oxford University Press), 2007.

7 Typescript/manuscript of *The Land*, 1926, Huntington Library HM 41088.

8 S. Bazargan, 'The Uses of the Land: Vita Sackville-West's Pastoral Writings and Virginia Woolf's *Orlando*', *Woolf Studies Annual*, 5 (1999), 25–55, at 31.

9 *The Land* (1926; rev. ed. London: Heinemann, 1941, reset 1955, reprinted 1976), p. 107. References to this edition will henceforth appear parenthetically in the text.

10 Braund observes that Sackville-West's 1919 novel *Heritage* bears an untranslated epigraph from *Georgics*, IV. 559–61, 565–6, so the *Georgics* can hardly have been quite unknown to her ('Women and Earth', p. 194 and note p. 241).

11 See D. L. Durling, *Georgic Tradition in English Poetry* (New York: Columbia University Press, 1935) and Anthony Low, *The Georgic Revolution* (Princeton University Press, 1985).

12 Blyth, 'A Sort of English Georgics', p. 22. The kinship with Thomson was pointed out by J. C. Squire in his two reviews, 'Books of the Day: English Georgics', *Observer*, 10 October 1926, p. 6, and 'Poetry', *London Mercury*, January 1927, pp. 318–21, at pp. 318–19.

13 V. Woolf, *Orlando*, ed. Michael H. Whitworth (Oxford University Press, 2015), p. 163.
14 See A. Fowler, 'Country House Poems: The Politics of a Genre', *The Seventeenth Century*, 1 (1986), 1–14, and J. Chalker, *The English Georgic: A Study in the Development of a Form* (London: Routledge, 1969).
15 Braund, 'Women and Earth', p. 195. The Loeb translation reads, 'Toil triumphed over every obstacle, unrelenting Toil, and Want that pinches when life is hard'. See C. Perkell, 'The Golden Age and its Contradictions in the Poetry of Vergil', *Vergilius*, 48 (2002), 3–39, at 22. For a thorough discussion, see M. Gale, *Virgil on the Nature of Things: The Georgics, Lucretius and the Didactic Tradition* (Cambridge University Press, 2000), ch. 5, 'Labor Improbus'.
16 C. H. Warren, 'Gems and Coloured Glass', *Spectator Literary Supplement*, 30 October 1926, p. 758. A writer and broadcaster on agricultural topics, the reviewer was brought up in Kent; see G. Warren, 'C. Henry Warren: A Contented Countryman?', *Landscape*, 12 (2011), 1–23.
17 '[*The Georgics*] is no more a didactic poem than Ovid's *Ars Amatoria*': Wilkinson, *Georgics of Virgil*, p. 3.
18 On the title page bearing the title 'Husbandry' (cancelling an even earlier title, 'Work') in the typescript/manuscript of *The Land*, 1926, Huntington Library HM 41088, Sackville-West copies out the Latin epigraph together with Fairclough's Loeb translation (unrevised, naturally), which I quote.
19 Grene's translation in S. Nelson, *God and the Land: The Metaphysics of Farming in Hesiod and Vergil* (Oxford University Press, 1998), p. 17. See E. W. Pomeroy, 'Within Living Memory: Vita Sackville-West's Poems of Land and Garden', *Twentieth-Century Literature*, 28 (1982), 269–89, at 274.
20 S. B. Gates, in *The Nation and Athenaeum*, 6 November 1926, p. 188. The reviewer is identified by Virginia Woolf in a letter to Sackville-West, tentatively dated 12 October 1926; *The Letters of Virginia Woolf*, ed. N. Nicolson and J. Trautmann, 6 vols. (London: Hogarth Press, 1975–80), vol. III, p. 298 (no. 1679). See H. H. B. M. Thomas and D. Küchemann, 'Sidney Barrington Gates. 1893–1973', *Biographical Memoirs of the Fellows of the Royal Society*, 20 (1974), 181–212.
21 Sackville-West, *Land*, pp. 81–2; 'out of need made inadvertent art' (p. 81) recalls Virgil's 'Jupiter theodicy' at *Georgics*, I. 143–6. 'Release of spirit from the jail of shape' echoes Shakespeare's sonnet 129: see Pomeroy, 'Within Living Memory', p. 273.
22 J. Henkel, 'Vergil Talks Technique: Metapoetic Arboriculture in *Georgics* 2', *Vergilius*, 60 (2014), 33–66.
23 Virgil, *Georgics* (Fairclough), p. 95 (*Eclogue* X. 70–2).
24 Seamus Heaney, *Field Work* (London: Faber, 1979, reset 2001), pp. 55–6. For extended readings of Heaney's engagement with Virgilian traditions, see R. Falconer, *Seamus Heaney, Virgil and the Good of Poetry* (Edinburgh University Press, 2021) and J. C. Pellicer, *Preposterous Virgil: Reading through Stoppard, Auden, Wordsworth, Heaney* (London: Bloomsbury, 2022).
25 Gale, *Virgil on the Nature of Things*, pp. 28–35, and ch. 5.

26 J. Dyer, *The Fleece. A Poem in Four Books*, ed. J. Goodridge and J. C. Pellicer (Cheltenham: Cyder Press, 2007).
27 J. Barrell, *English Literature in History 1730–1780: An Equal, Wide Survey* (London: Hutchinson, 1983), pp. 90–109. The most comprehensive and exemplary treatment is J. Goodridge, *Rural Life Eighteenth-Century English Poetry* (Cambridge University Press, 1995), pp. 91–187.
28 R. Williams, *The Country and the City* (1973; London: Hogarth Press, 1985), p. 31. Developing this line of criticism, S. Raitt cites Williams, pp. 248 and 254, in *Vita and Virginia: The Work and Friendship of V. Sackville-West and Virginia Woolf* (Oxford: Clarendon Press, 1993), pp. 11–13. On Sackville-West's avowedly 'instinctive' Toryism, see p. 42.
29 For a refinement of this statement, see Thibodeau, *Playing the Farmer*, p. 45, and for an introduction to the topic, pp. 19–23. See also T. Geue, 'Soft Hands, Hard Power: Sponging Off the Empire of Leisure (Virgil, *Georgics* 4)', *Journal of Roman Studies*, 108 (2018), 115–40.
30 Thibodeau, *Playing the Farmer*: 'almost farmers', p. 19; 'economic fantasies', p. 40.
31 M. P. García Ruiz, '*AEQVOR*: The Sea of Prophecies in Virgil's *Aeneid*', *Classical Quarterly*, 64 (2014), 694–706, esp. 694–5.
32 Virgil, *Georgics*, ed. R. A. B. Mynors (Oxford: Clarendon Press, 1990, reprinted 2000), commentary on *Georgics*, I. 50–3.
33 C. Kerrigan, *Virgil's Map: Geography, Empire, and the Georgics* (London: Bloomsbury, 2020), pp. 21–30.
34 S. Harrison, 'The Primal Voyage and the Ocean of Epos: Two Aspects of Metapoetic Imagery in Catullus, Virgil and Horace', *Dictynna*, 4 (2007), paragraphs 15–20 (PDF, pp. 4–6); https://journals.openedition.org/dictynna/146 (accessed 18 March 2021).
35 Gates, *The Nation and Athenaeum*, p. 188.
36 K. P. Witney, *The Jutish Forest. A Study of the Weald of Kent from 450 to 1380* (London: Athlone, 1976), p. 7.
37 J. Philips, *Cyder: A Poem: In Two Books* (1708) (book 1, lines 73–80, 591; book 2, lines 668–9). John Dyer also celebrates 'Siluria', *The Fleece* (I. lines 57–9); see Goodridge, *Rural Life*, pp. 181–2.
38 D. Gervais, *Literary Englands: Versions of 'Englishness' in Modern Writing* (Cambridge University Press, 1993), p. 11, a page also cited in Bazargan, 'The Uses of the Land', p. 34. Blyth too observes that a 'metonymical shift, whereby "Kent" is understood to mean "England" (and vice versa), can be seen to be taking place in *The Land*' ('A Sort of English Georgics', p. 26).
39 Bazargan, 'The Uses of the Land', pp. 34–5. It is worth observing that, on the evidence of her published correspondence, Woolf seems never to have succeeded in reading through *The Land*, unless her repeated excuses merely served to avoid giving an assessment; 27 May 1931 (from Monk's House) finds her still making excuses to VSW for not reading it ('haven't got a copy here').

Woolf, *Letters*, vol. 4, p. 338 (no. 2378). Her final qualification in a letter to VSW of 27 January 1928 says it all: 'I've been reading the Land—so good, I think, some lines.' Woolf, *Letters*, vol. 3, p. 449 (no. 1849).
40 Woolf, *Orlando*, p. 154.
41 K. Blair, 'Gypsies and Lesbian Desire: Vita Sackville-West, Violet Trefusis, and Virginia Woolf', *Twentieth-Century Literature*, 50 (2004), 141–66, at 158–9.
42 See Williams, *Country and the City*, pp. 248–63.
43 Blyth, 'A Sort of English Georgics', p. 24.
44 Pomeroy, 'Within Living Memory', p. 274; Blyth, 'A Sort of English Georgics', p. 24. Woolf, *Letters* vol. III, p. 244 (no. 1622, 2 March 1926).
45 Sackville-West, *Land*, pp. 30–1; *OED* s.v. 'thole', n.2, 'obsolete, rare'; the sole instance is medieval. In the preface to his translation of *Beowulf* (London: Faber, 1999, pp. xxv–xxvi), Heaney describes his delight on encountering the verb 'thole' in a poem by John Crowe Ransom – a word he knew from local speech in Derry and was thrilled to rediscover in the Old English epic. The refrain of Paul Muldoon's elegy for Heaney is 'I cannot thole the thought of Seamus Heaney dead'; 'Cuthbert and the Otters', in *One Thousand Things Worth Knowing* (London: Faber, 2015).
46 J. Addison, 'Essay on the *Georgics*', Virgil, *Georgics* (Dryden), p. 149. Shaun Irlam is right, the example from Grainger is 'unpardonable'; '"Wish You Were Here": Exporting England in James Grainger's *The Sugar-Cane*', *ELH*, 68 (2001), 377–96, at 381. James Grainger, *The Sugar-Cane*, in John Gilmore, *The Poetics of Empire: A Study of James Grainer's The Sugar Cane (1764)* (London: Athlone Press, 2000), p. 152 (book IV, lines 516–7).
47 Sackville-West may have known George Sturt's *The Wheelwright's Shop* (1923), though as Paddy Bullard observes, Sturt points out that, on the contrary, one cannot know whether ash timber is 'frow' or 'doaty' before opening up the wood. P. Bullard, 'Restoring the Wheelwright's Shop', *The Journal of Modern Craft*, 13 (2020), 161–78, at 166–7.
48 Mercifully, the Anglo-Saxon 'Weod-monath' for August does not enter the poem except as a marginal rubric (pp. 74–5), and at p. 78 'the seremonth' is not ridiculous.
49 Addison, 'Essay on the *Georgics*', p. 149.
50 The debate about Dryden's translation is a case in point: see H. A. Mason, 'Milbourne "Redux"?', *Cambridge Quarterly*, 20 (1991), 223–57.
51 Quoted in Pomeroy, 'Within Living Memory', p. 283. Warm thanks to Alison Martin for kindly supplying the reference, Huntington Library, MS HM 43232.
52 Letter to Harold Nicolson dated Sissinghurst, 8 December 1942. H. Nicolson, *Diaries and Letters*, ed. N. Nicolson, 3 vols. (London: Collins, 1966–8), vol. II, p. 265.
53 Pomeroy, 'Within Living Memory', p. 282.

54 Sackville-West's heroes are the celebrated botanist/plant collectors and explorers George Forrest, Reginald Farrer, Robert Fortune and Frank Kingdon-Ward.
55 See J. C. Pellicer, 'Reception, Wit, and the Unity of Virgil's *Georgics*', *Symbolae Osloenses*, 82 (2007), 90–115.
56 On variety, see Wilkinson, *Georgics of Virgil*, ch. 4, *passim* but esp. pp. 71–5 and 142–3. See too W. Fitzgerald, *Variety: The Life of a Roman Concept* (University of Chicago Press, 2016); on English 'variety', Latin *varietas* and Greek *poikilia*, ch. 1, esp. 12–21, and on the idea of variety in *Georgics*, I. pp. 43–6.

CHAPTER 12

Rags and Tatters
Hughes, Oswald and Their Contemporaries

Jack Thacker

In the 1970s, an editor asked Ted Hughes if he could contribute a 'pastoral poem' for an upcoming edition of a magazine.[1] In response to the request, the poet went back to a journal he had kept on and off over a number of years which concerned his time spent farming in Devon earlier that decade. His plan, as he recalls in a recording for the BBC, was 'to see if [he] could dig up anything that might lend itself to re-shaping into a poem'.[2] While it makes sense that Hughes turned to his farming material when asked for such a contribution, it is revealing that the poem in question, the manuscript of 'February 17th', resisted Hughes's attempts to refine it; when he came to rework the piece, he soon discovered that by doing so he destroyed 'the fresh simple presence of the experience' of the original entry.[3] Later, when he published his farming journal as a sequence of poems – 'February 17th' foremost among them – he let them lie, as he puts it, 'in their rags and tatters'.[4] The poems – his 'bits & pieces from this other Eden' as he once described them – may be throwaway, the results of a literary experiment Hughes came to think of partly in negative terms, but their influence on the next generation of poets has been profound, especially where outdoor work, such as farming or gardening, constitutes a part of their writing processes.[5] This chapter examines what might be called a georgic strain in modern and contemporary poetry, the survival of which, either covertly or by accident, appears to be at least in part due to Hughes's efforts to make something, however unrefined, out of his farming experiences.

Rags and Tatters

When Hughes refers to his poems 'in their rags and tatters', in one sense he means how they remained rough around the edges and unedited from the first drafts, with him only making a few changes to the line breaks.[6] In another, the phrase captures the content and tone of the pieces themselves and is suggestive of the ways in which they represent the farming world. In 'February 17th' and throughout *Moortown Diary* (Hughes named the sequence after the farm he had purchased), he repeatedly draws on the imagery of tatters to describe the situation of farming.[7] In the poem 'Feeding Out-Wintering Cattle at Twilight', the farmer/speaker (which it is implied is Hughes himself) is feeding cattle in blustery winter weather as 'The hay blows luminous tatters from their chewings, a fiery loss, frittering downwind'.[8] 'A Monument', meanwhile, employs the image of a barbed wire fence to act as a memorial to the memory of Hughes's father-in-law, Jack Orchard, a farmer, depicting his 'raincoat in tatters, face fixed at full effort' as he constructed it (*CP*, p. 534). Hughes added a preface to the poems in the 1989 in which he decries the sorry state of modern agriculture, describing how due to modern pressures the 'deeply satisfying, self-reliant if occasionally gruelling way life had mutated' and how as a result he had settled on organic principles and 'keeping everything going on bailer twine' (*CP*, p. 1204). In a letter sent to his brother Gerald in 1974, however, he expresses how it was a 'miracle' he had not already gone bankrupt.[9] The 'fiery loss, frittering downwind' is economic as well as poetic.

It is not only the farm that threatened Hughes with diminishing returns. The origin of the *Moortown Diary* poems raises the question of what value they held – and still hold – in a literary context. Hughes may have felt they were too unwieldly and down-to-earth to be refashioned into pastoral pieces, but they remain luminous with significance, not least because they can be considered modern examples not of the pastoral but of the georgic, albeit a georgic in rags and tatters. Hughes states that his motivation for writing his farming material more generally was to 'write a whole book of deliberately "upbeat" poems'.[10] On reflection he found that 'some of them bear the signs of that effort', but he admits that on the whole it is 'extremely difficult to write about the natural world without finding your subject matter turning ugly'.[11] 'February 17th' is, according to Hughes, an example of the above difficulty. The poem describes how a 'lamb could not get born' (*CP*, p. 518) and Hughes's efforts to salvage something from the situation. Introducing the poem at a reading, he explains how 'when a small ewe tries to push out a large lamb, and that lamb fails to get his feet up with his nose ... the head of the lamb hangs outside the mother, while its shoulders are jammed against her pelvis inside'.[12] When conventional methods fail in such circumstances, he explains, the final resort is as documented in the poem. It describes how in this instance Hughes travelled

> Two miles for the injection and a razor.
> Sliced the lamb's throat-strings, levered with a knife
> Between the vertebrae and brought the head off
> To stare at its mother, its pipes sitting in the mud
> With all earth for a body. (*CP*, p. 519)

The poem concludes by detailing how Hughes proceeds to pull the headless corpse from the ewe, first by pushing it back inside and then by pulling it out again. The mood and the mode of the poem can be characterized as a push and pull between oppositions: 'upbeat' and 'ugly', the symbolic and the mundane, the fundamentals of life and death. The tension is also between the poem's literary and pragmatic elements. 'February 17th' can be read as an elegy for the dead lamb, but it also provides a practical guide for what to do as a farmer when the lambing process goes awry in this way, with Hughes managing to balance the necessary details – 'the injection and a razor' – with the symbolic image of the decapitated head with 'all earth for a body'. The poem's final image – 'And the body lay born, beside the hacked-off head' (*CP*, p. 519) – is a contradiction in itself but also aims to reconcile the preceding oppositions, to harvest something positive from a 'depressing' situation.

Commentators have called 'February 17th' authentic, 'artful', 'elegiac', 'ecological', and, significantly, georgic.[13] This particular poem is not unique in that regard. Citing an earlier observation by Thomas West, Iain Twiddy argues that when it comes to reading *Moortown Diary*

> the pastoral vision is limited. Hughes's collection, where the representation of agricultural existence is neither unconditionally natural (completely separate from human concerns), nor exclusively yoked to human relevance or artificially congenial, thus shares some common ground with the *Georgics*, along with their didacticism.[14]

Possibly the most important statement on the georgic quality of Hughes's work comes from his friend and fellow poet Seamus Heaney. In a posthumously published essay entitled 'Suffering and Decision', Heaney makes the claim that *Moortown* 'could be read as a local variation of the theme of Virgil's *Georgics*, insofar as it is [Hughes's] act of thanksgiving for the fulfilments he experienced in his middle and late years when he was integrated into the life and land of Devon'.[15] Although this claim is not Hughes's, no one would have understood better than Heaney – who had already developed an intimate friendship with Hughes by the time he had bought Moortown Farm – what the venture would have meant in terms of Hughes's life and writing. Like Twiddy, Heaney also understood the limitations of the pastoral, having previously ringfenced the term 'rural' for what he called 'the unselfconscious face of raggle-taggle farmland'.[16] If

Heaney himself appears to be at risk of pastoralizing Hughes's work with his talk of 'thanksgiving' and 'fulfilment', then this is because he knew – as any reader of Virgil knows – that in the *Georgics* acts of thanksgiving and suffering go hand in hand and that an animal's or a farmer's fortunes can change in an instant. Nonetheless, there is a cautious tone to both of these comparisons, as if to speak of Hughes's poems in the context of Virgil's *Georgics* – just as Hughes found when he tried to rework them into pastorals – risks undermining their 'fresh simple presence'.

Hughes may not have made the georgic connection himself, and it is unlikely that he directly imitated Virgil in his farming works. However, this does not preclude an interpretation of them in such a context, especially in those instances when other received modes, especially the pastoral, are not able to accommodate the gristlier details and downbeat moments which are all too familiar to the farmer and which Hughes makes no effort to hide as a poet. Twiddy's and Heaney's notions of 'common ground' and 'local variation' are fruitful, as they do not yoke Hughes's poems exclusively to Virgil. Yet there are limitations to these visions of the georgic. The important question is not the degree to which Hughes's work conforms to the conventions of the *Georgics* but the ways in which his poems influence our perception of the mode and other 'georgic' poems written in the years since.

The technological, environmental, and economic upheavals of the last fifty years have transformed farming almost beyond recognition. Over the same period, the georgic has survived at the margins of the literary mainstream, albeit in a diminished form and largely unrecognized – even by the poets in question themselves. If we are to appreciate the complexities which arise when farming and poetry combine, especially in a modern and contemporary context, then the term is worth reviving, redefining, and reimagining.

Theorists have employed a number of analogies to explain the presence of the georgic in English poetry beyond the vogue for the mode in the eighteenth century. Kurt Heinzelman offers the notion of georgic 'entailments' to describe Virgilian traces – no matter how buried or dispersed – in the Romantic era.[17] Kevis Goodman, who finds herself in agreement with Heinzelman concerning the post-eighteenth-century status of the georgic, comments on the mode's 'rhizomatic underpresence' across a variety of related genres up to the Romantic era and beyond.[18] Goodman also highlights the image at the end of Book I of Virgil's *Georgics*, in which a future farmer unearths the remnants of past battles, as a 'representative anecdote' for georgic influence.[19] By the latter half of the twentieth century, however, even such diverse and adaptable metaphors as these risk overstating its usefulness as a working category in English poetry. One precedent for the georgic in Hughes takes the form of a '*Georgics* of resistance', as identified by R. F. Thomas in the labouring-class poets John Clare and Patrick Kavanagh (and subsequently in Heaney) and which he characterizes as 'a georgic realism and a sense and use of agriculture as a grand metaphor for the problems of existence'.[20] 'February 17th' fits this description well, but even Thomas's counter strand of 'georgic realism' is in danger of aggrandizing the portrayal of farming that we find in Hughes.

In his preface to *Moortown Diary*, Hughes recounts how when he discovered the agricultural community in North Devon, the traditional way of life there seemed 'potent enough to overwhelm any stray infiltrations of modernity' (*CP*, p. 1203). He also captures 'how rapidly that changed within the next decade ... as the older generation died off and gave way to sons who were plunged into the financial nightmares, the technological revolutions and international market madness that have devastated farms, farmers and farming ever since' (*CP*, pp. 1203–4). The poems themselves do not directly address this devastation, but there are clear signs throughout the collection that the landscape Hughes worked on and wrote from is in decline. In the poem 'The Formal Auctioneer', Hughes provides a portrait of farmers at a livestock market, describing them in terms of a 'weathered, rooty, bushy pile of faces, | A snaggle of faces | Like pulled out and heaped-up old moots' (*CP*, p. 534). The pun on 'moot' here – a southern dialect word for a tree stump but more generally a 'meeting' or 'an assembly of people' (*OED*) – emphasises their precarious status: deeply rooted in the landscape and in the community but in the process of being uprooted by forces out of their control. In another poem, 'The day he died' (another elegy for Orchard), Hughes remarks that 'the land | Will have to manage without him ... With roots cut | And a great blank in its memory' (*CP*, p. 533). Hughes's georgic, then, if not a georgic of resistance, is a georgic of the remains – and is also relevant to *Remains of Elmet* (1979) – a hollowed-out version of the Virgilian model which reflects the fragmented and precarious nature of small-scale farming in recent times. Yet it is still a living archive of farming details, documenting as well as elegizing subjects which rarely matter in poetry – and matter even more for being rarely noticed.

In Hughes, the georgic is forever on the verge of being delivered fully formed but often results instead, to borrow a phrase from *Cave Birds* (1975), in 'the remains of something ... muddled as an afterbirth' (*CP*, p. 439). In the poem 'Ravens', for instance, he guides a three-year-old boy through a field of ewes and new-born lambs. One ewe, having given birth to a healthy lamb just a few moments before, trails her afterbirth behind her, described by Hughes as 'the tattered banners of her triumph' (*CP*, p. 517). The three-year-old, however, is more interested in one that has been born dead and already scavenged by ravens – 'a tattered bundle of throwaway lamb' (*CP*, p. 518). By insisting on the disasters as well as the triumphs, and by using the very same language to describe both, Hughes's Moortown poems arrive slightly muddled, but this does not diminish their worth as poems. 'A poem can survive stylistic blemishes', writes Heaney, 'but it cannot survive a still-birth.'[21] The georgic may be misshapen in Hughes, to the point that it is barely recognizable, but this a reflection of the conditions – both immediate and on a larger scale – in which the pieces were conceived and written. The stylistic blemishes turn out to be expressive of the muddled and compromised activity of farming itself and are in fact essential to the authenticity and liveliness of these unconventional yet highly regarded poems.

Weights and Checks

In 1980, Hughes wrote of *Moortown* that 'its growing into other people will be a slow business'.[22] Yet his forecast has turned out to be prophetic in the sense that the farming poems of that volume have proved to be influential as far as their georgic qualities is concerned. In her 2005 Ted Hughes Memorial lecture, the poet Alice Oswald singles out *Moortown Diary* for special praise among Hughes's works, stating that it is especially relevant to her own poetic project because he worked on it 'when he was spending almost every day outside, either gardening or farming'.[23] For Oswald, the situation of the farm in *Moortown Diary* keeps the poet's language grounded in the 'actual': she refers to the work as 'site-specific', highlighting Hughes's efforts to exclude 'the poetic process' with the aim of 'staying close' to his material.[24] In one of the first published statements by Oswald about her own work, written upon the publication of her debut collection of poems, *The Thing in the Gap-Stone Stile* (1996), there are clear indications that she adopts a similar approach:

> I've been a gardener for nearly seven years, I'm not a nature poet, though I do write about the special nature of what happens to exist. People are so delighted by the idea of gardening, but in the end it weathers you away. The inaccessibility of what you're working with becomes terrible. I do write about that.[25]

Given Oswald's insistence on the weathering effects of outdoor work, it is unsurprising that she holds Hughes's farming poetry in such high regard. Oswald is a gardener and not a farmer, but she understands as well as Hughes that cultivation is often more ugly than idyllic and what is required on behalf of the poet is a language which reflects this without sentimentalizing it. Oswald may object to the term 'nature poet', but this does not discount a georgic sensibility in her work – one modelled closely on Hughes – even if such a label might prompt a similar objection.

Before she first encountered Hughes's work, Oswald's reading about the natural world seemed to be in contrast to her experiences as a gardener; she recalls that '[she] thought [she'd] rather hear a gardener's or a farmer's account of the landscape than any poet's'.[26] Yet her preoccupation with authenticity is also a long-standing literary concern, deriving first and foremost from her studies of the classics. Oswald is well known for her reworkings of Homer's epic poetry in *Memorial* (2009) and *Nobody* (2019). Explaining her lifelong preoccupation with Homer in an interview with Max Porter in 2014, she states: '[Homer] just transmits life. No mediation. He describes a leaf and you don't get a description of a leaf, you get a proper leaf. That's always been my principle. You've got to make something living, and thinking isn't living.'[27] If thinking is not living, then for Oswald writers are predisposed to overthink things. An oral poet, on the other hand, much like an outdoor worker, is less inclined to render the natural world in an abstract sense. When it comes to Virgil's *Georgics*, however, Oswald is less admiring. In an interview with Fiona Cox in 2013, she expresses her ambivalence towards his poetry: 'I can't help loving the *Eclogues* and the *Georgics* and the *Idylls*', she says to Cox, 'but they're not quite enough.'[28] Like Hughes, Oswald defines her work against the refinement of pastoral conventions, but she remains in two minds about the distinction: 'it annoys me that I just love them', she adds, 'because in theory I don't'.[29] Oswald may not engage with Virgil 'in theory', grouping the *Georgics* alongside his *Eclogues* and Theocritus's *Idylls* in a tradition she firmly rejects, but once Hughes's influence has been taken into account, her relationship with the georgic is shown to have its own profound complexities.

Oswald's touchstone for outdoor work is gardening, but another case in which her perspective on the environment aligns closely with Hughes's – and therefore with a more down-to-earth and documentary style of writing – is in her 2002 book-length poem *Dart*, which takes its inspiration from the landscape of the Devon river. The poem features a range of voices as it follows the course of the Dart from source to estuary, one of which is of a fisherman:

> a thousand feet between Holne and Dartmeet and he climbs it,
> up the trickiest line, maybe
> maybe down-flowing water has an upcurrent nobody knows
> it takes your breath away,
> generations of them inscribed into this river[30]

Inscribed into Oswald's rendition of the fisherman recounting the journey of salmon is Hughes, a lifelong fisherman who fished the Dart himself and, as Mark Wormald has documented, came to regard salmon as 'an essential key to the principle of ecological interconnectedness'.[31] Reading the upcurrent of this influence in the above lines from *Dart*, it is possible to detect Oswald adopting a similar modal fluency as Hughes does in his poetry: the individual salmon's journey is conceived in epic and elemental proportions, while the demise of 'generations' is elegiacally 'inscribed' as a form of remembrance. As well as being a fisherman, Hughes had a farmer's knowledge of what goes into rivers, specifically the pollutants and run-off from industrialized agriculture, and his own river poems were written as part of a wider engagement with and advocacy for Devon's waterways.[32] In a report written while still working on *Dart* for the Poetry Society (who helped to fund the project), Oswald writes, in the spirit of Hughes, that one of her aims for the poem was 'to reconnect the Local Imagination to its environment – in particular, in these years of water shortages and floods, to increase people's awareness of water as a natural resource'.[33] In this respect, though, *Dart* has more in common with *Moortown Diary* than it does with Hughes's environmental protest poetry, in that its ecological message remains an undercurrent and, unlike the voice of the fisherman, is never fully vocalized. Oswald, who has expressed a suspicion of the term 'ecopoetry', prioritizes instead workaday and personal accounts of the river, sourced from those who know it at a local level.[34]

The fisherman's account is an example of a number of passages in *Dart* which are difficult to place in a literary sense, being neither pastoral nor ecopoetry but instead taking their inspiration from a deep-rooted, working knowledge of a real place. Despite the fact that the georgic elements also remain implicit in *Dart*, Tom Bristow has gone so far as to categorize it as a 'georgic memorial'.[35] Bristow's focus is on Oswald's documentations of lost industry in the account of the 'dairy worker' (*Dart*, p. 29) and in the catalogue of names of 'dead tinners' (p. 10). Oswald's georgics, however, do not merely memorialize – though this remains an important function – for as much as her poetry is focused on the historical, its emphasis is just as much on the vitality of the present and what it means to be alive (and survive) in a specific place. In her interim report, she provides a preliminary catalogue of the many voices that feature in the poem:

> I've spoken to a huge amount of people. Only a selection of these have found their way into the poem; forester, boat-builder, ecologist, stone-waller, sewage area-manager, canoe-instructor, seal watcher, fisheries officer, salmon fisher, archaeologist ... All are 'working' voices. This reflects my preoccupation with Work as a power-line for language.[36]

Oswald's original idea for *Dart* was to collate a series of poems written by the members of the Devon river community and 'to orchestrate it like a kind of jazz'.[37] As she writes in her report, she soon discovered that 'it was people's living, unselfconscious voices, not their poems, that were most awake to the river'.[38] For Oswald, work is 'a power-line for language' in the sense that it keeps her own writing unsentimental and animated: 'when a sewage worker talks of liquid being "clarified", when a fisheries officer talks of the water "riffling" or a stone-waller says "scrudging"', she proclaims, 'those words have never had such flare'.[39] *Dart* is positively awash with such instances, especially in the form of present participles and gerunds drawn from a rich and diverse pool of vocational dialects. To take just a few examples: 'coop-felling' (forester) (p. 11), 'tufting felting hanks tops spindles slubbings' (worker at Buckfast Woollen Mills, p. 19) and 'processing, separating, blending' (dairy worker, p. 29). In her early lyric poems, it is gardening as experienced first-hand by Oswald that informs the 'working' language of her poetry. In *Dart*, she sources this perspective from others from a wide range of occupations, professions and livelihoods.

In her Hughes lecture, Oswald makes a point of drawing attention to Hughes's use of present participles in his poem 'The Horses', highlighting the 'pile-up of words ending in "-ing": blackening, brightening, splitting, stumbling ... as if the language had only just been knocked up'.[40] Her appreciation of Hughes's language can be associated with the emphasis placed in *Dart* on the way in which 'work' itself *works* on language. It is a georgic appreciation, for, as David Fairer points out, 'the language of georgic is a working language – the language of work, and language consciously *at work*'.[41] Oswald's title for *Dart* attests to the idea of the river as a happening rather than an object: the verb 'dart' can mean 'to spear' or 'transfix', 'to throw, cast, shoot', 'to send forth, or emit, suddenly and sharply; to shoot out; to cast (a glance) quickly and keenly' and 'to move like a dart; to spring or start with a sudden rapid motion' (*OED*). Introducing *Dart*, she writes about how she 'wanted to give the poetic voice the slip, to get through to technical, unwritten accounts of water'.[42] The poem can therefore be seen as Oswald's attempt to balance the lyrical and the 'technical': too much poetry and she risks abstraction; too little and she risks ventriloquizing what Peter Howarth summarizes as 'the detached economistic resource management that [the poem] ostensibly opposes'.[43]

Dart may be framed as an expression of the eponymous Devon river, but unofficially the poem tells the story of the river's 'edgelands': its alluvium, borders, and floodplains, its agriculture, processing plants, powerlines, pylons, and the many other traces of long-established human activity along its banks. Mid-way through the poem, as the form of the river widens, larger scale industrial complexes flank its banks and begin to pollute the body of the text. In the case of the 'water abstractor', Oswald increases the didactic pressure upon the character, the poem, and the reader:

> have you any idea what goes into water?
> I have verified the calibration records
> have you monitored for colour and turbidity?
>
> I'm continually sending light signals through it, my parameters
>   are back to back
> was it offish? did you increase the magnetite?
> 180 tonnes of it. I have bound the debris and skimmed the supernatant
> have you in so doing dealt with the black inert matter?
>
> in my own way. I have removed the finest particles
> did you shut down all the inlets
> I added extra chlorine
> have you countervailed against decay?
>
> have you created for us a feeling of relative invulnerability?
> I do my best. (*Dart*, pp. 25–6)

The disembodied questions and the abstractor's answers take the form of instructions committed to memory, presumably for the purposes of following correct procedure. Yet the final phrase of the 'water abstractor' (whose job title relates to Oswald's suspicion of literary abstraction) – 'I do my best' – is an acknowledgement of individual limitations. These sentiments are echoed by the dairy worker and the sewage worker a few pages on: 'We have to think of our customers ... We've got weights and checks and trading standards' (dairy worker, *Dart*, p. 29); 'The whole place is always on the point of going under ... Not much I can do' (sewage worker, *Dart*, p. 30). Oswald's characters are frequently shown to be drowning under the administrative pressure of keeping industrial processes in check against the odds. Implicit in the relentless flow of the poem is an environmental awareness of the consequences, one that contradicts the level of 'invulnerability' assumed by the 'us' of the water-consuming population. Yet Oswald's didacticism falls short of any direct, larger message, except that to work with or against nature – at any level – is both messy and difficult and this is true for poets when working at the level of language. 'I have bound the debris and skimmed the supernatant' does not necessarily sound like poetry, but the value of such technical speak, no matter how broken and fragmented, lies in the way it reminds readers (and writers) of poetry that they too are implicated in the compromised world of work.

Clippings and Tags

In recent times, where the georgic has been overlooked, or in cases when it is actively resisted by poets, it has nonetheless survived by proving to be not only an adaptable but also a doggedly persistent mode. Reviewing Frost's *Selected Poems* in 1936, W. H. Auden identified 'two kinds of nature poets':

> the man who lives in the country because he has to, because he works there; and the sensitive who lives in the country because he can afford to and because he dislikes the city … The former can be divided again into two classes, the landed gentleman who is responsible for his land but does not work it with his own hands, such as Virgil of the Georgics, and the small farmer who works it himself. Of this last Robert Frost is almost the only representative.[44]

Auden's characterization of the poet's position in Virgil's *Georgics* may be accurate, if a little dismissive, but when it comes to the poem's afterlife in contemporary poetry the georgic can illuminate the work of those writing in the same class as Frost. If anyone stands as a testament to this it is Hughes, who was a farmer/poet in the strictest sense. In Geoffrey Hill's *Odi Barbare* (2012), presented as the fifth of six '*Daybooks*' in his 2013 volume *Broken Hierarchies*, poetic labour is once again equated with that of the farmer:

> What is far hence led to the den of making
> Moves unlike wildfire; not so simple-happy
> Ploughman hammers ploughshare, his *durum dentem*
> Digging the *Georgics*.[45]

In an essay on Dryden in *The Enemy's Country* (1991), Hill draws attention to the notion that 'there is at times in the digging and delving of the craft [of poetry] a blind complacency between "*otium*" [ease] and "*labor*" [toil]'.[46] He then proceeds to delve into Dryden's translation of the *Georgics*, hitting upon 'the easily "shining Share" … where Virgil has the "durum … dentem", the "hard tooth" of the "blunted share"'.[47] In Hill's summation, language must be 'worked on enough' so that 'time-saving prefabrications' do not undermine the gravity of a poet's situation.[48] It is a trap that he is wary to avoid in his own poetry, with its densely worded syntax and frequent, obscure allusions (in the case of *Odi Barbare* many of them to Virgil).⁴⁹ In Oswald's poetry, writing must be worked upon and inflected by work in order to do justice to the struggle of making a living outdoors. In Hill's account, 'a poet's words and rhythms are not so much his utterance so much as his resistance', but in his case they constitute an ethical rebuke to what he terms a poet's 'unhappy circumstances': 'the current reckonings of value in the society of his [or her] day'.⁵⁰

In *Mercian Hymns* (1971), Hill memorializes the industrial servitude of his grandmother in the West Midlands, 'whose | childhood and prime womanhood were spent in the | nailer's darg'.⁵¹ *Odi Barbare* finds the poet casting his mind back once more to his childhood in Worcestershire, remembering a time when 'Breathing hard we wrestled asbestos brake-pads'.⁵² In Hill's later work, the question is raised of how and why in a 'post-*Georgics*' age, it is worthwhile, arguably essential, to be channelling the '*labor*' of Virgil.⁵³ Hill may insist that the enterprise is one of the utmost seriousness, yet he too appears to wrestle with the inevitable '*otium*' that comes from taking pleasure in the crafting of poetry. Hill's ploughman is presented as 'not so simple-happy', but in the stanza the poet is 'Digging the *Georgics*' in another sense, with his onomatopoeic sounding of Virgil's Latin – '*durum dentem*' – hammering the point home melodiously, not just morally.

In *Moortown Diary*, Hughes captured the agricultural circumstances of his day, and of his day-to-day working life, by means of a verse diary. His journal poems find an echo in Hill's '*Daybooks*' in which, as Stephen James observes, there is a 'tendency to retain an impression of the notepad (or "daybook") jotting in the finished – or perhaps the insistently unfinishable – poem'.⁵⁴ The notion of a georgic 'daybook' is realized in Sean Borodale's *Bee Journal* (2012), which, in a homage to the apicultural instructions in Book IV of Virgil's *Georgics*, provides a detailed chronicle of the poet's experiences of beekeeping in Somerset. Like Hughes and Oswald before him, Borodale utilizes a journalistic 'note-poem' form in order to reduce the proximity between the finished work and the beekeeper's lived experience.⁵⁵ The book's blurb on its inside cover states that the poems within 'were written at the hive wearing a veil and gloves'. Meanwhile, on its back cover, an endorsement from Oswald echoes Hughes's 'Preface' to *Moortown Diary*: 'This book is a kind of uncut home-movie of bees. I like its oddness and hurriedness, its way of catching the world exactly as it happens in the split-second before it sets into poetry. These are pre-poems, note-poems dictated by phenomena.'

In a 2013 essay on 'Rural Realities and Rustic Representations', Nick Groom raises the question: 'how many poets, writers, artists, and film-makers of today's countryside will mention single farm payment, subsidies, set-aside, movement orders, DEFRA, ear-tagging, castration rings, veterinary bills, milk yields, rights of way, stock fencing, feed supplements, Azulox, silage and haylage, and purple spray, rather than the pastoral clichés that have tyrannized the land for decades, centuries even?'[56] In *Bee Journal*, Borodale does precisely this, with each poem documenting the highs and lows of beekeeping: the emotional peaks and troughs as well as the percentages and equations that, as the poet shows, have now become a fundamental aspect of apicultural husbandry.[57] In '14th August: Bee Inspector', for example, Borodale anticipates Groom's call for a poetics of 'DEFRA':

> Today a DEFRA bee inspector clipped the wings of our queen.
> What happened to those clippings?
> Her flightless life is in that box of ours:
> hoarded earth bit of her, no flight.[58]

Borodale's 'clippings' can be compared with Hughes's 'rags and tatters' and Oswald's verbal river debris: all are georgic scraps and are a testament to these poets' insistence on the untidier and less aesthetically pleasing, yet no less significant, features of working landscapes.

In her 2013 collection, *Red Devon*, the poet and former journalist Hilary Menos evokes livestock farming in the county where Hughes once lived, worked, and wrote (and where Oswald did the same), raising the same breed of cattle as Hughes did when he farmed livestock there. In the poem 'UK364195', which comes towards the end of the collection, Menos asks herself and her partner in the enterprise: 'what we've achieved … or more properly perhaps, what we have done?':

> Tinkered here and there; let well alone
> (though more by luck than judgement or design);
> learned more of what we can't do than what we can;
> passed on just a little of what we've learned.[59]

The poem takes the form of a sonnet, its rhyme scheme being simple (couplets) but also subtle: 'alone' rhymes with 'design' and 'can' with 'learned'. Its title, however, more bluntly refers (as a footnote to the poem explains) to the 'DEFRA herd/flock mark' of the poet's farm, a number which by legal requirement is stamped on the ear tags of each animal.[60] Menos's 'herd mark' recalls the inclusion of 'weights and checks and trading standards' in *Dart*. The presence of such features in a poem, then – whether a sonnet, a Hughes-esque 'note — poem', or a river-epic – provides a literary tag identifying it as georgic. At the end of her collection, Menos provides further notes in the style of Hughes's *Moortown Diary* on subjects ranging from 'Pesticides' to 'Super-weeds' to 'Agricultural run-off' to 'Growth hormones', but she imbues her notes with more of a pronounced environmental agenda, reflecting the adaptability of the georgic in the face of new developments and crises.[61]

Writing on the increasing disappearance of words from the environmental lexicon in the British Isles, the nature writer Robert Macfarlane declares that 'Nature has not now, nor has ever been, a pure category. We inhabit a post-pastoral terrain, full of modification and compromise.'[62] Macfarlane's reference to the post-pastoral is a useful one, suggesting that in recent times, more than at any other point in history, the state of the environment is critical, and that if we are to recognize this then our language must reflect it. Yet, if there was ever a literature of 'modification and compromise', then surely it is the georgic. The georgic of the last fifty years must be looked for – on farms, on riverbanks, under the microscope – but the signs are clear to see if one cares to look. Poets have themselves modified the georgic to suit the challenges of recent times, sometimes without even noticing they have done so. As a result, the georgic is less of a pure category today that it has ever been – if it ever was. Yet as these poets demonstrate in their work (both on and off the page), if language is going to keep working for us in the face of unprecedented challenges, it must be brought firmly, and kept, down to earth.

Notes

1 T. Hughes, 'February 17th', *Poetry Archive*, www.poetryarchive.org/poem/february-17th (accessed 13 June 2016), a transcript taken from an introduction to this poem in a recording for the BBC. The editor was Emma Tennant (1937–2017), who edited the avant-garde publication *Bananas* (1975–9).
2 Hughes, 'February 17th', *Poetry Archive*.
3 Hughes, 'February 17th', *Poetry Archive*.
4 Hughes, 'February 17th', *Poetry Archive*.
5 Hughes, 'To Glyn Hughes: [November 1979]', *The Letters of Ted Hughes*, ed. C. Reid (London: Faber, 2009), p. 430.
6 This is confirmed by Neil Roberts in *Ted Hughes: A Literary Life* (Basingstoke: Palgrave Macmillan, 2007), p. 122.
7 The sequence was published three times: first as a special edition entitled *Moortown Elegies* in 1978 (Rainbow Press), then as the title-sequence of the larger collection *Moortown* in 1979 (Faber & Faber), and finally with added notes a preface as *Moortown Diary* in 1989 (Faber & Faber). A number of the poems were also included in Michael Morpurgo, *All Around the Year* (London: John Murray, 1979).

8 T. Hughes, 'Feeding Out-Wintering Cattle at Twilight', in *Collected Poems*, ed. P. Keegan (London: Faber, 2005), p. 506. All further references to poems and prefatory material by Hughes, unless otherwise stated, will be from this edition, with citations in the text.
9 T. Hughes, 'To Gerald and Joan Hughes and family: 25 November 1974', in Hughes, *Letters*, ed. Reid, pp. 358–9, at p. 358.
10 A. Skea, 'Ted Hughes: "The Critical Forum" Series, Norwich Tapes Ltd. 1978', transcript by A. Skea, *Ann.Skea.com*, http://ann.skea.com/CriticalForum.htm (accessed 13 June 2016).
11 Hughes, cited in Skea, 'Norwich Tapes'. Hughes did produce a more 'upbeat' collection of poems based on his farming experiences in *Season Songs* (Faber & Faber, 1976). In a letter to Keith Sagar in 1977, Hughes comments upon a manuscript of what was to become 'Moortown Elegies', writing that he intended to put them in a collection 'in spite of their carelessness': 'I would have put more in Season Songs but somehow they are largely downbeat – and I deliberately made Season Songs up-beat, to buck me up. Diaries tend to record downs & disasters anyway': T. Hughes, '[21 April 1977]', in *Poet and Critic: The Letters of Ted Hughes and Keith Sagar*, ed. K. Sagar (London: British Library, 2012), pp. 55–6.
12 Hughes, cited in Skea, 'Norwich Tapes.'
13 On the poem's authenticity see T. Gifford and N. Roberts, *Ted Hughes: A Critical Study* (London: Faber, 1981), p. 251, and C. Robinson, 'The Good Shepherd: *Moortown Elegies*', in *The Achievement of Ted Hughes*, ed. K. Sagar (Manchester University Press, 1983), pp. 257–84, at p. 267; on its artfulness see Roberts, *A Literary Life*, p. 124; for its totemism see L. Webb, 'Mythology, Mortality, and Memorialization: Animal and Human Endurance in Hughes' Poetry', in *Ted Hughes: From Cambridge to Collected*, ed. M. Wormald, N. Roberts and T. Gifford (Cambridge University Press, 2013), pp. 33–47, at p. 39; for its 'elegiac ecological consolation' see E. Hadley, *The Elegies of Ted Hughes* (Basingstoke: Palgrave Macmillan, 2010), p. 73; and for a georgic assessment see I. Twiddy, *Pastoral Elegy in Contemporary British and Irish Poetry* (London: Bloomsbury, 2012), p. 104.
14 Twiddy, *Pastoral Elegy*, p. 64. Thomas West writes that Hughes's poems are 'too naturalistic to be pastorals' but goes on to say that they are 'occasionally georgic in so far as they show the ways and instruct in the techniques of country life': see T. West, *Ted Hughes* (London: Taylor & Francis, 1985), p. 104.
15 S. Heaney, 'Suffering and Decision', in *Cambridge to Collected*, ed. Wormald, Roberts and Gifford, pp. 221–37, at p. 225. What Heaney does not state explicitly, but which is implied by the content and context of the comparison, is that in this late essay he is also describing his own historical and creative life, especially during his 'late years', in which he returns to the 'celebration of farm work' in collections such as *Electric Light* (2001) and *District and Circle* (2006). I am grateful to Neil Corcoran for this observation.
16 S. Heaney, 'In the Country of Convention', in *Preoccupations: Selected Prose 1968–78* (London: Faber, 1980), pp. 173–80, at p. 173; originally published in *Times Literary Supplement*, 11 July 1975.

17 K. Heinzelman, 'Roman Georgic in the Georgian Age: A Theory of Romantic Genre', *Texas Studies in Literature and Language*, 33 (1991), 182–214.
18 K. Goodman, *Georgic Modernity and British Romanticism: Poetry and the Mediation of History* (Cambridge University Press, 2004), pp. 2, 10–11, 35–7.
19 Goodman, *Georgic Modernity*, p. 1.
20 R. F. Thomas, 'The "Georgics" of Resistance: From Virgil to Heaney', *Vergilius*, 47 (2001), 117–47, at 147.
21 S. Heaney, 'Feeling into Words', in *Preoccupations*, pp. 41–60, at p. 49.
22 T. Hughes, 'To Keith Sagar: 23 April 1980', in Hughes, *Letters*, pp. 431–2, at p. 432.
23 A. Oswald, 'Wild Things', *The Guardian*, 3 December 2005, www.theguardian.com/books/2005/dec/03/poetry.tedhughes/ (accessed 28 November 2016).
24 Oswald, 'Wild Things'; see Hughes, *Collected Poems*, p. 1205.
25 A. Oswald, '*The Thing in the Gap-Stone Stile*', in *Don't Ask Me What I Mean: Poets in their Own Words*, ed. C. Brown and D. Paterson (Basingstoke and Oxford: Picador, 2003), pp. 207–8, at p. 207; originally published in the *Poetry Book Society Bulletin*, 168 (Spring 1996).
26 Oswald, 'Wild Things'.
27 M. Porter, 'Interview with Alice Oswald', *White Review*, August 2014, www.thewhitereview.org/interviews/interview-with-alice-oswald/ (accessed 28 November 2016).
28 F. Cox, 'Interview with Alice Oswald', *Practitioners' Voices in Classical Reception Studies* (2013), www.open.ac.uk/arts/research/pvcrs/2013/oswald (accessed 28 November 2016).
29 Oswald, cited in Cox, 'Interview with Alice Oswald'.
30 A. Oswald, *Dart* (London: Faber, 2002), pp. 8–9. All further page references to *Dart* will be from this edition, cited in the text.
31 M. Wormald, 'Hughes and Fishing', in *Ted Hughes in Context*, ed. T. Gifford (Cambridge University Press, 2018), pp. 292–301, at p. 299.
32 Hughes became predisposed to protest poetry later in his career as he became more involved with environmental campaigns after he was made Poet Laureate in 1984. For specific works see 'If', '1984 on "The Tarka Trail"', *Rain Charm for the Duchy* (1992), and 'The Black Rhino'; for more on Hughes's campaigns, see Y. Reddick, *Ted Hughes: Environmentalist and Ecopoet* (Basingstoke: Palgrave Macmillan, 2017), pp. 245–67, 289–312.
33 A. Oswald, 'Alice Oswald Creates a River Dart Community Poem for the Millennium', *The Poetry Society*, www.poetrysoc.com/content/archives/places/dart/ (accessed 28 February 2017).
34 When asked by Garry Mackenzie on whether she considered *Dart* to be an 'ecopoem', she replies: 'that [label] has a cramping feeling. Sometimes if there's too much of an idea behind the writing the poem can't quite come alive': see A. Oswald, cited in G. MacKenzie, 'Poetry, Ecocriticism and Labour: The Work of Writing and Reading', *Green Letters*, 20 (2016), 183–96, at 190.

35 T. Bristow, *The Anthropocene Lyric: An Affective Geography of Poetry, Person, Place* (Basingstoke: Palgrave, 2015), p. 87.
36 Oswald, 'River Dart Community Poem for the Millennium'.
37 Oswald, 'River Dart Community Poem for the Millennium'.
38 Oswald, 'River Dart Community Poem for the Millennium'.
39 Oswald, 'River Dart Community Poem for the Millennium'.
40 Oswald, 'Wild Things'.
41 D. Fairer, 'Georgic', in *The Oxford Handbook of British Poetry, 1660–1800*, ed. Jack Lynch (Oxford University Press, 2016), pp. 457–72, at p. 467.
42 A. Oswald, '*Dart*', in *Don't Ask Me What I Mean*, ed. Brown and Paterson, p. 208.
43 P. Howarth, '"Water's Soliloquy": Soundscape and Environment in Alice Oswald's *Dart*', in *Poetry and Geography: Place and Space in Post-War Poetry*, ed. Neal Alexander and David Cooper (Liverpool University Press, 2013), pp. 190–203, at p. 201.
44 W. H. Auden, '[Robert Frost]', a review of Robert Frost, *Selected Poems* (1936), in *The Complete Works of W. H Auden*, ed. Edward Mendelson, 6 vols. (Princeton University Press, 1996–2015), vol. I, 137–41, at p. 138.
45 G. Hill, '*Odi Barbare*: XXI.V', in *Broken Hierarchies: Poems 1952–2012*, ed. Kenneth Haynes (Oxford University Press, 2013), p. 858.
46 G. Hill, 'Unhappy Circumstances', in *Collected Critical Writings*, ed. K. Haynes (Oxford University Press, 2008), pp. 176–91, at p. 182.
47 Hill, 'Unhappy Circumstances', p. 189; Virgil, *Georgics* (Dryden), p. 217.
48 Hill, 'Unhappy Circumstances', p. 182.
49 One of the epigraph's to Hill's *Odi Barbare* is taken from Virgil's *Aeneid*, II. 509–11. Elsewhere in the sequence, he refers to Virgil's love of bees, a reference to *Georgics*, IV (p. 836).
50 Hill, 'Unhappy Circumstances', p. 179. See also R. Macfarlane, 'Gravity and Grace in Geoffrey Hill', *Essays in Criticism*, 58 (2008), 237–56.
51 G. Hill, '*Mercian Hymns*: XXV', *Broken Hierarchies*, p. 107.
52 Hill, '*Odi Barbare*: XXVI', p. 860.
53 Hill, '*Odi Barbare*: XVI', p. 850.
54 S. James, 'The Nature of Hill's Recent Poetry', in *The Salt Companion to Geoffrey Hill*, ed. A. Roberts (Cambridge: Salt, forthcoming), https://research-information.bristol.ac.uk/files/47928644/James_Nature_of_Hill_s_Recent_Poetry.pdf (accessed 13 July 2018).
55 S. Borodale, *Bee Journal* (London: Cape, 2012).
56 N. Groom, '"Let's Discuss over Country Supper Soon": Rural Realities and Rustic Representations', *The Clearing*, 22 August 2013, www.littletoller.co.uk/the-clearing/lets-discuss-over-country-supper-soon-rebekah-brooks-and-david-cameron-rural-realities-and-rustic-representations-nick-groom/ (accessed 13 July 2018).
57 See in particular the poems '25th July: Brood Frame Check' (p. 20), '7th August: Brood Frame Check' (p. 24), '17th October: Audio Recording' (p. 67), and '6th January: Epiphany' (p. 80).

58 Borodale, '14th August: Bee Inspector', in *Bee Journal*, p. 25. The acronym 'DEFRA' stands for 'Department for Environment, Food and Rural Affairs', the governmental department in charge of agriculture, fisheries, food standards, rural communities and environmental issues.
59 H. Menos, 'UK364195', *Red Devon* (Bridgend: Seren, 2013), p. 61.
60 Menos, 'UK364195', p. 61.
61 Menos, *Red Devon*, p. 64.
62 R. Macfarlane, *Landmarks* (London: Hamish Hamilton, 2015), p. 7.

PART III
Territories

CHAPTER 13

Low Lands
Fen Georgic

Paddy Bullard

If Virgil had sat down to imagine an entirely georgic landscape, he might have pictured something like the modern East Anglian Fens. A 1,500-square-mile diamond of flat, low-lying land, the Fens are given over almost exclusively to agriculture. The very texture of its soil embodies the area's peculiar harmony of material form with georgic function: 'the beauty of that earth', writes the farmer-novelist Adrian Bell, 'was a thing one could have watched all day: the share divided it exactly; it fell away like the finest garden mould'.[1] 'Every thing grows well here', noted William Cobbett in 1830, 'earth without a stone so big as a pin's head; grass as thick as it can grow on the ground; immense bowling-greens separated by ditches; and not the sign of dock or thistle or other weed to be seen'.[2] Cobbett wrote this in the South Holland region of Lincolnshire, where the fields are now ploughed to within an inch of their drain edges, and every bit of soil is dedicated to farming. If John R. Stilgoe is right to trace the word 'landscape' to the Old Frisian *landschop* – 'shovelled land' formed by dykes against the sea – then the Fens are landscape in an especially pure sense.[3] South Holland is only dry enough for farmers to plough because in the seventeenth century Dutch engineers and Dutch shovellers embanked its rivers so that their waters are carried out above the land, much of which is at or below sea level, to the Wash.

If no van Ruisdael or Hobbema emerged at the time to celebrate this man-made region in landscape painting, it was not for want of encouragement from the local poets. '[W]hosoever would a Landskip rightly hit', promised Michael Drayton in *Poly-Olbion*,

> Beholding but my Fennes, shall with more shapes be stor'd,
> Then *Germany*, or *France*, or *Thuscan* can afford.[4]

Walking out into 'swampy fenland' on the western edge of the level, John Clare delighted himself by imagining how 'painters would feel exquisite to cull | Rich bits of landscape I have seen to day'.[5] The Fens are a perfect test case for thinking about georgic at the level of landscape. No other British region defines itself so distinctly and consistently: the black peatland around Ely may be different geologically from the silt marshland of Holbeach, but they are united in a singular and unremitting flatness, and by the same huge, dark-zenithed sky, which seems to swell and tuck itself over the horizon. Where other areas of British fen or marsh sit as features within a varied prospect, the Fens, stretching sixty-five miles from Boston, Lincolnshire at the top to Cambridge at the bottom, are wide enough to become their own context. One encounters throughout the same bleak and strenuous efficiency of field, drain and bank. It is a true industrial landscape: mechanized corridors of water suspending shelves of sheer soil; a huge factory-out-of-doors.

None of this gives obvious encouragement to literary description. Yet it does not follow that 'the fens are not a literary part of england', as Clare and others have assumed.[6] If the Fen landscape has no major Romantic voice to assert the dominating power of its character, like Emily Brontë's on Haworth Moor or Hardy's on Egdon Heath, that is only because John Clare happened not make such assertions. An ancient landscape that seems to forbid organic metaphor, the Fens can seem like perpetually unreclaimed literary ground. Yet since Caryl Churchill's *Fen* (1982) and Graham Swift's *Waterland* (1983) contemporary authors have found a more involving territory there than in more conventionally literary landscapes in the Lakes, the Yorkshire Moors or the Wessex uplands. Natural historians have always been drawn to marginal East Anglian flats. Among the new nature writing, Tim Dee's *Four Fields* (2013) is both a gazetteer of their work in the Fens and a defining modern portrait of the region.[7] Dee singles out two mid-twentieth-century writers who lived at the same time on Adventurer's Fen – part of the very low-lying and late drained area between Cambridge and Ely that also includes the National Trust's Wicken Fen – as opposing representatives of naturalist and georgic tendencies in the area: the naturalist E. A. R. Ennion wrote *Adventurers Fen* in 1942, while in 1944 the horticulturalist Alan Bloom published *Farm in the Fen*, his account of a doomed attempt to bring a particularly ill-favoured corner of the area into cultivation.

It is no surprise that this thoroughly georgic landscape should have associations with two important older English georgic poets. The most widely distributed of all British georgics was Thomas Tusser's *Good Pointes of Husbandrie* (1557), which sold so reliably through the sixteenth and seventeenth centuries that the Stationer's Company retained the copy as part of its gilt-edged English Stock.[8] When Tusser first published it he was tenant of the Abbey Farm, West Dereham, on the Norfolk fen edge: 'A place for wood, that trimlie stood', he called it later, 'With flesh and fish, as heart would wish'.[9] Several of his 'pointes' deal with the abundance of the Fens, the cheapness of their hay and bullocks, but there is a sense too that improvement is inevitable. Left in their natural marshy state the fens 'annoieth the meadowes' that abut them, providing a perpetual requirement for outward reclamation.[10] Another champion of fen improvement was John Dyer, who completed the most substantial English georgic, *The Fleece* (1757), in the rectory at Coningsby, a village perched on a spur of high ground that thrusts out of the Lindsey fen edge in Lincolnshire. Dyer was drawn to the most daring project of civil engineering then going ahead in the region, the draining of Deeping Fen by John Grundy Jr, who was installing fifty windmills to pump it dry:

> Moors, bogs, and weeping fens, may learn to smile,
> And leave in dikes their soon-forgotten tears.
> Labour and Art will every aim achieve
> Of noble bosoms ... See Deeping Fens,
> And the long lawns of Bourn. 'Tis art and toil
> Gives Nature value, multiplies her stores,
> Varies, improves, creates.[11]

Dyer is interested in the Fens as a landscape that demands a perpetual succession of technical innovations ('precept after precept', as Dyer translates Virgil's 'tum variae venere artes') together with a sustained effort of labour from its farmers, figured here both as triumphant ('every aim') and unremitting.[12] Dyer's Fen collocation of technology and toil is itself classically georgic.

It is an association that reoccurs in writing from the Fens. Here is a landscape in which an enormous human effort has all but subdued nature, and where nature's re-encroachment – floods from its artificially embanked rivers, marsh and woody carr if fields are left untended – is always anticipated. The draining of the Fens required a transregional coordination of administrative control, a cycle of enormous bets from private and public capital, and the integrated re-engineering of a million-acre landscape. Here the essentially local and punctual business of farming a particular farm in a given season is played out against cross-district politics and investment, not to mention the broader issues of labour flow and environmental policy. In the Fens these different scales of politics must be understood in terms of different scales of history. 'My humble model for progress', says Tom Crick, the history-teacher narrator of Graham Swift's *Waterland*, is the 'reclamation of land' from water:

> Which is repeatedly, never-endingly retrieving what is lost. A dogged and vigilant business. A dull, yet valuable business. A hard, inglorious business. But you shouldn't go mistaking the reclamation of land for the building of empires.[13]

Hilaire Belloc is one example of an empire-era fen tourist forever on the verge of that mistake: with 'every lesion in the continuity of our civilization', he wrote in 1906, 'the Fens suffered, for they always needed the perpetual attention of man to keep them fully inhabited, afforested, and cultured'. So the agrarian energies of Fenmen, Belloc concludes, are a modal variation on the expansive energies of British empire: 'they continue to extend and possess'.[14] Tom Crick's school classes on the French Revolution strike a chord with his pursuit of fen history. The agricultural writer Arthur Young made the same comparison in 1799, wondering how Fenmen 'living and fattening' under stable government could wish for 'a speculative legislation of a more popular cast'. Had any drainage scheme comparable to that in the Fens been executed in revolutionary France, he asked rhetorically?[15] The history of the Fens places often remote and lonely agricultural lives in a setting shaped by mighty human efforts against huge natural forces, especially those of river and sea. In the Fens it is easy for georgic writing to lose its human scale. Here both farmer and writer must make a reckoning with everything that the landscape has excluded.

John Clare and the Fen Sky

The Fens are a landscape described by a set of interrelated paradoxes. They are managed, human and artificial, and yet were until relatively recently one of the wildest places in the British Isles. They are tightly administered and engineered, and yet their social history is defined by episodes of resistance and dissent. In the early modern period they were a haven for enlightened antiquarians (typified by Maurice Johnson and William Stukeley of the Spalding Gentlemen's Society) and rational dissenters, and yet they retain an old association with witchcraft and superstition.[16] They are the fattest and wealthiest of British agricultural landscapes, and yet their literature describes lives of poverty, drudgery and social exclusion. These paradoxes often resolve themselves into contrasts between the georgic rigours of modern farming and the pastoral – or rather pastoralist – heritage of the Fens, harking back to an age when its people were wildfowlers, reed-cutters and eel-catchers. These contrasts reoccur in contemporary writings set in the Fens, but they are present as well in the work of the region's most widely read poet: John Clare.

Clare described Helpston, the parish where he was born in 1793, as 'a gloomy village in Northamptonshire, on the brink of the Lincolnshire fens'. In 1832 he went a step closer towards the edge of the Great Level, moving three miles east from Helpston to a smallholding in the neighbouring village of Northborough. Clare's editors and critics have not always maintained a distinction between the river-defined fen-edge parishes of Helpston or Northborough and the open reaches of Deeping Fen or Borough Great Fen that begin a few miles beyond them. The poem that Eric Robinson and David Powell call '[Winter in the Fens]' in *The Major Works*, beginning 'So moping flat and low our valleys lie', in which 'every village to an island grows' during a week of wet weather, is observed from the perspective of Clare's cottage garden in Helpston, not from the Fens as such. An attachment to wild wetland environments inspires Clare in poems such as the 'Song' that begins 'Swamps of wild rush beds', or in '[Patty]', which begins 'Ye swampy falls of pasture ground'. Yet both of these poems describe river margins, and Clare is more likely to be imagining the Welland as it flowed through the Westings flood meadows, pasturelands intercommoned between Helpston and four neighbouring parishes, than the dramatically open fenlands to the east.[17]

The distinction is significant because, when Clare does strike out into the open fen, a sense of transition from one landscape into another often structures his writing. The tiny dramas of curiosity and surprise that characterize his Northborough poems play out especially vividly when Clare ventures into the visionary dreariness of the Fens beyond Peakirk. The poem that Clare's editors call '[The Fens]' begins with another river-margin scene, but develops into his most sustained exploration of the open level beyond the Welland meadows. The ambulatory verses begin abruptly with Clare's 'shudder chill' on meeting a snake, who plops into the river before the poet and 'hissing with a forked tongue' swims away. As his natural history notes show, Clare associated snakes particularly with the Fens, and the encounter sets up a motif of deception and changeability that reoccurs in his treatment of the marshland landscape, slightly at odds with the openness of the scene.[18] It is easy to miss Clare's matching of the snake's tongue with a distant cloud formation, itself a visual deceiver, seventeen lines later:

> Theres not a hill in all the view
> Save that a forked cloud or two
> Upon the verge of distance lies
> & into mountains cheats the eyes
> & as to trees the willows wear

> Lopped heads as high as bushes are
> Some taller things the distance shrouds
> That may be trees or stacks or clouds
> Or may be nothing still they wear
> A zemblance where theres nought to spare[19]

Figuration emerges out of the nothing of the fen scene, where 'theres nought to spare' the eye. Clare's flatlander distance-scanning has been read for its difference from the conventions of early modern loco-descriptive poetry, which insists on hill-top elevation as the condition for visionary far-sightedness.[20] Yet that dualism is not Clare's, and his gaze towards the fen horizon – 'edged but not ended', as Tim Dee puts it – is a visual experience different categorically from that of the high-ground prospect.[21] Visitors to the Fens often report an unfamiliar sense that their personal height is determining how far they can see around the curve of the earth.[22] In this poem Clare is similarly conscious that the nothingness of the prospect is somehow obliging him to stand ('Nor een a molehill cushion meets | To rest on when I want a seat'). A related fenland experience captured by Clare is disorientation over distances. In the Fens any slight elevation towards a tallish object, to a tree or a church, 'seems to exaggerate their height', as Adrian Bell observed, 'and gives them a cathedral-like prominence, all their proportions and detail enhanced against the blinding sky'.[23] Objects many miles away take on a deceptive proximity: 'the sky seems to cleanse every outline', as Graham Swift puts it, 'and makes light of distances'.[24] In the middle ground, Clare allows himself to be confused further by measuring pollarded willows against overgrown bushes, much as he occupied himself at High Beaches by letting a distant city prospect sink into the 'brakes' or ferns at his feet: 'Thus London, like a shrub among the hills, | Lies hid and lower than the bushes here'.[25] Clare's experience of the landscape is that it makes his body the measure of its distances, while at the same time causing him to doubt his perception of the spaces they contain.

Another sort of cheat that raises Clare's suspicions in '[The Fens]' is a georgic one, the exploitation of land by the farmer, 'Who lives and triumphs in the plough.' Yet the sustained anger at agricultural 'tyrants' that animates Clare's famous enclosure poems, such as 'Helpston Green' or 'The Mores', is replaced here by a supple variability of tone. 'Gain mars the landscape every day', and each inch of green wildness is threatened by intensive cultivation. Yet Clare also notices the cheer of human prosperity taking a meaningful place amid the seasonal cycle of growth and production, of consumption and destruction:

> The meadow grass turned up & copt,
> The trees to stumpy dotterels lopt
> The hearth with fuel to supply
> For rest to smoke & chatter by
> Giving the joy of home delights
> The warmest mirth on coldest nights
> & so for gain that joys repay
> Change cheats the landscapes every day
> Nor tree no[r] bough about it grows
> That from the hatchet can repose
> & the orison stooping smiles
> Oer treeless fens of many miles
> Spring comes & goes and comes again
> And all is nakedness and fen.[26]

With a stooping, cheating smile the horizon gathers up the fen's nakedness and bleakness along with its productiveness, and even its comforts. The mood of the landscape shifts in these lines as rapidly as clouds and sunshine follow one another across a blustery fenland sky. '[The Fens]' is true to the poetics of disordered variability that Clare set out in his long manifesto-poem 'The Shadows of Taste', where the poet's living word promises to become 'a landscape herd and felt and seen | Sunshine and shade one harmonizing green'. In *The Georgics* Virgil suggests that 'the changeful Temper of the Skies' inspires wild animals in the same way that a heavenly soul inspires each human heart: 'As Rains condense, and Sun-shine rarifies; | So turn the Species in their alter'd Minds'.[27] Clare's admiration for the fen landscape is capacious enough to take in the resented gain-driven farmer along with everything else. Yet in the rapid and sensitive turns of his mind he is as close in spirit to Virgil's animals as he is to the rational and laborious farmer of *The Georgics*.

'The Powte's Complaint' and Fen Flood

John Clare's fen edges are above all a landscape lost in sky; other dwellers in the Great Level have focused more often on water as the area's dominant element. All cultivation in the Fens is threatened by inundation. Modern conservationists are only the most recent to argue that its lands should be left to the inevitable triumph of tide and flood. The 1695 edition of William Camden's *Britannia* warned that drained land would soon return to its original state, 'So that some think it the safest way, to follow the Oracle's advice in the like case, *Not to venture too far where heaven has put a stop*'.[28] Camden was taken to task for his scepticism by a later antiquary and fen native, William Stukeley, who insisted in 1724 that 'in the main the land is admirably good, hard and dry, produces excellent corn and grass, feeds innumerable sheep and oxen of a very large size'. Yet Stukeley also understood that this 'garden of *Eden*' demanded constant upkeep. He repeated the warnings of his friend, the projector Charles Kinderley, about the dangerously sluggish outfall channels of all the fenland rivers: if neglected 'this vast and rich tract must be abandon'd to eels and wild ducks'.[29] Life in the Fens before the nineteenth century was semi-submerged, especially if one was travelling from one part of it to another. In 1663 Samuel Pepys went to inspect some family estates at Parson's Drove, near Wisbech, and only got there 'with much ado, through the fens, along dikes, where sometimes we were ready to have our horses sink to the belly'.[30] 'Ye ffenns are full of water and mudd', reported the traveller Celia Fiennes a few years later. Her horse narrowly avoided falling into a deep dyke to one side of the causeway between Cambridge and Ely, which she found submerged.[31] The antiquary William Cole lost much of the value of his estate at Over in 1768 when the Bedford River burst its banks. His friend Horace Walpole begged him to sell up: 'We live at least on *terra firma* in this part of the world, and can saunter out without stilts. Then we do not wade into pools and call it going upon the water, and get sore throats.'[32]

It is fitting that this watery landscape, with its snakes and serpentine rivers, its false perspectives and treacherous mires, should sink the unwary reader so often into pools of plashy irony. Writing in the twelfth century, William of Malmesbury noticed that the fen people were 'so much disposed to a merry jest that they verge on insolence', and that spirit of humorous recalcitrance characterizes the region's popular tales and songs, just as it rubs off on more literary treatments.[33] In the drinking song 'The Draining of the Fens', which appeared in the miscellany *Wit and Drollery* (1661), Fenlanders race to drink up local beer supplies before thirsty Dutch engineers commandeer them. The latter have, after all, drained everything else: 'Our smaller rivers are now dry land, | The Eels are turned to serpents there'.[34] The poem prefigures some of the grim and pathetic fenland ironies played on by Graham Swift in *Waterland*. Swift's narrator Tom Crick has a love rival named Freddie Parr, a teenaged tippler, whose submerged body is found one morning in the lock for which Tom's father is keeper. Tom watches his father pumping on the drowned boy's back: 'And what else was my father doing on that July morning than what his forebears had been doing for generations: expelling water? Yet whereas they reclaimed land, my father could not reclaim a life.'[35] In their different ways all of these examples, both old and more recent, pivot ironically between drowning and dryness, between liquid dearth and drunken surfeit. The soggy landscape inspires a dryly humorous attitude to its dangers and discomforts.

A curious example of this tendency, and one that brings us back into the georgic sphere, is an anonymous satirical ballad known as 'The Powte's Complaint', preserved by the antiquary William Dugdale in his *History of Imbanking* (1662). Dugdale frames the ballad as belonging to a campaign by 'divers perverse-spirited people' – they 'brought turbulent suits in law' and 'made libellous songs' – against fenland drainage projects that were underway in the first two decades of the seventeenth century. The British Library holds manuscript copies of the ballad that predate the *History of Imbanking*, one of them attributing the satire to 'one Peny of wisbich 1619', which is consistent with Dugdale's association of it with resistance to works by the Commissioners of Sewers in the Wisbech area.[36] This 'Peny' remains unidentified, but his song has risen recently to prominence in Fen literature:

> Come, Brethren of the water, and let us all assemble,
> To treat upon this matter, which makes us quake and tremble;
> For we shall rue it, if't be true, that Fens be undertaken,
> And where we feed in Fen and Reed, they'll feed both Beef and Bacon.
>
> They'll sow both beans and oats, where never man yet thought it,
> Where men did row in Boats, ere undertakers bought it:
> But, Ceres, thou behold us now, let wild oats be their venture,
> Oh let the frogs and miry bogs destroy where they do enter.[37]

One sees from these opening stanzas why 'The Powte's Complaint' has become so attractive. Its defiance of commercial expansionism is gleeful and destructive: the 'Essex calves' imported where fen, reed and lake once had been are promised the revenge of 'Captain Floud': 'He bears down banks, and breaks their cranks and whirlygigs [ie. pumps and windmills?] asunder.' There are opportunities for conservationist readings as well. 'Today the poem makes an ongoing appeal', writes Mark Cocker, 'precisely because it grants insight into the ecological loss of one of the very creatures most affected. It is a piece of environmental art *avant la lettre*.'[38] The Powte of the title is the burbot (*Lota Vulgaris*), a kind of freshwater cod once common in fen waterways and only recently extinct in England. The fish gives a voice both to native Fenlanders whose livelihoods as anglers, fowlers and cutters of reed and peat are threatened by agricultural improvement, and to the animal species whose habitats will be destroyed by drainage. The angry apostrophe to Ceres in stanza 2 brings the song into the sphere of the anti-georgic: this is a prayer for the destruction of agricultural abundance. 'The Powte's Complaint' can be positioned precisely in the history of fenland riot and rebellion, giving some reason to take Dugdale's presentation of it as a rabble-rousing protest song at face value.

Yet the song itself fits its rebel billing unconvincingly. The Powte and his brethren are comical complainers. They 'quake and tremble' like Snug's 'smallest monstrous mouse' in *A Midsummer Night's Dream*, and their stubborn preference for 'boots and skatches [ie. stilts for crossing wet places]' to all the georgic comforts of beef, bacon, beans and oats seems to invite ridicule. For all their gleeful petulance, the invocations of destructive aid from Captain Flood, 'two-penny Jack' [ie. a pike], Eolus, Neptune and the moon summon natural forces that Cornelius Vermuyden and his Dutch drainage engineers had shown already they could overcome. Good cases were being made in the early seventeenth century against draining the Fens, but 'The Powte' adds little to their cause.[39] And how reliable a contextualizer was Dugdale? The *History of Imbanking* is a propagandist work. It was compiled to document the legal basis for the renewed drainage schemes of the Bedford Level Corporation, created the year after its publication by the General Drainage Act of 1663.[40] It is not unlikely that Dugdale either misunderstood or repurposed an old song that had been written originally to satirize the protesters, rather than to rally them. There was a fashion during the second decade of the seventeenth century for unpredictably ludic satire, such as the experimental mock-encomiums, macaronics and burlesques printed in Thomas Coryat's *Crudities* (1611).[41] Unsmiling antiquaries working fifty years later might well have misinterpreted such works. In 1662 the 'Powte' was more useful to Dugdale as a warning against popular insurrection than as a dubious satire. One of the manuscript miscellanies in which 'The Powte' survived, BL Add MS 23723, is full of mock-ballad exchanges between the universities and the Inns of Court, company that suggests it was collected and preserved as a *mock*-complaint, a well-established comic form. It appears in another miscellany, BL Bleinhem MS 61683, associated with two south Midlands families, the Hampdens and the Botelers, whose parliamentarian and gentry allegiances align them with pro-drainers such as the Earls of Bedford or Oliver Cromwell.[42] 'The Powte' does not afford its modern campaigning readers the firm footing they have assumed. It is a characteristically slippery, semi-submerged and ambiguous fenland text.

Waterland and Fen Bodies

Analogies between the farmer's body and the body of the land, between bucolic and human cultivation, are important for the georgic imagination. Like those who work upon it, land must be fallowed and fed: 'sweet Vicissitudes of Rest and Toyl', as Dryden has it in a compacted couplet that turns between farmer and field, 'Make easy Labour, and renew the Soil'.[43] Both are subject to diseases, to constitutional weaknesses, to cycles of vigour and decline. In the Fens, this metonymic convention of seeing land-as-body often takes a surreal turn. In 'The Powte' we are unsurprised to hear the voices of Fenmen issuing from the mouth of a fish, a creature immersed entirely in the waterscape. There is after all something artificial and perverse about every aspect of the fen region, including its soil. To however fat and profitable a temper '*Marsh-Earths*' may be brought with labour and exposure, for John Evelyn they remained non-descript: 'whether I may reckon this among the natural Earths', he wrote, 'I do not contend'.[44] Even the most optimistic fen writings, such as the georgical poem attributed to the economist Samuel Fortrey and printed in Sir Jonas Moore's *The History or Narrative of the Great Level of the Fenns* (1660), think about the miraculous fertility of fen silt-lands in terms of an underlying pathology: 'I sing of heaps of Water turn'd to Land', Fortrey declares:

> Like an *Elixir* by the Chymists hand
> Of Dropsies cur'd, where not one Limb was sound,
> The Liver rotted, all the Vitals drown'd.
> No late discover'd Isle, nor Old Plantation
> New Christned, but a kind of New Creation.[45]

No work of fen literature has explored these analogies of human body with agricultural landscape, and their potential for pathology or perversion, more thoroughly than Graham Swift's novel *Waterland* (1983). Swift shows us, as we have seen, the corpse of a drowned child being pumped dry by the operator of a drainage sluice. A local magnate in the grip of a breakdown switches his studies from fen topography to brain anatomy: where once Thomas Atkinson pored over the 'innumerable complexities of drainage, flood-control and pumping systems, he will pore over the even more intricate typography of the medulla and the cerebellum, which have, so he discovers, their own networks of channels and ducts and their own dependence of the constant distribution of fluids'.[46] Fen air is heavy with 'that smell which is characteristic of places where fresh water and human ingenuity meet ... a smell which is half man and half fish', the mention of ingenuity supplying here a georgic touch.[47] The fen family followed by Swift in his novel are hefted to the drained land in a peculiarly physical way. They are a 'fixed people ... perhaps they became amphibians'. Their georgic labours have worked them into the landscape, and its silty waters into their blood. Swift's metaphors of hybridized body and landscape set a mode of fenland Gothic that has been the starting point for literary representations of the region ever since.

Waterland is narrated by Tom Crick, obsolescent history teacher, forced into early retirement when his wife Mary snatches someone else's baby at a supermarket. Tom and Mary are fen natives, although they live now in south London. Their story is about their failure to escape the aftershock of childhood trauma – murder, sexual experiments gone wrong – and about the prefiguration of that failure in earlier generations of Crick's troubled family. Like his ancestors, Crick is blocked up with sclerotic memories. The prevailing landscape analogy is that of fenland watercourses obstructed by their own silt. Tom's elder brother Dick, a childlike and occasionally violent giant, works on a dredger, occupying himself with muddy 'sludgery-sloggery' that would 'sap even the stoutest spirit': the silt 'gathers, congeals, no matter what's going on in the busy world above … We have to keep scooping, scooping up from the depths this remorseless stuff that time leaves behind' (p. 299). For Tom's father Henry, shell-shocked veteran of muddy Flanders fields and 1917, the featureless landscape looks like forgetfulness. Yet it will not let Henry's memories drain away. 'And maybe that's just the point', Tom Crick speculates, 'it's oblivion he'd like to forget, it's that sense of the dizzy void he can't get away from. He could do without this feeling of nothing' (p. 193). The silt of the Fens represents memory as ungraspable liquid suspension and as reoccurring blockage. Displaced as sediment, it makes up the ground of the territory, but is still experienced as negation. What are the Fens, asks Crick,

> but a landscape which, of all landscapes, most approximated to Nothing? Every Fenman secretly concedes this; every Fenman suffers now and then the illusion that the land he walks over is *not there*, is floating. (p. 11)

This is a nothingness that somehow obtrudes upon and weighs down the human body, just as the emptiness of fen prospects has offered John Clare 'nought to spare the eye'. Swift's sense of this paradox was anticipated by Caryl Churchill in her play *Fen* (written 1982), which is about women gang labourers struggling together in the same harshly unsheltered workscape. One of them, Val, finds it impossible to get a rhythm in her agricultural tasks: 'It's like thick nothing', she complains, 'I can't get on. Makes my arms and legs heavy.'[48] The gang find themselves surrounded in the fields by the ghosts of their predecessors, nineteenth-century agricultural workers who belong to another class of spirit-nothingness deposited like sediment in the empty agricultural landscape.

Often the heavy nothing of work in the Fens turns writers to a central georgic theme, the paradox of 'labor improbus': agricultural labour as at once climactically triumphant and drudgingly wretched. *Waterland* recognizes the Fens as a farming landscape that is forever being reclaimed, and notices its demands ('sludgery-sloggery') on the bodies of those that toil there. On fen silt and peat work is in fact easier than on poor or heavy lands, but there always seems to be more of it, and it has a palpable history. Labour accumulates in this landscape. 'Men, women, horses, tractors, carts swarm all over it', Adrian Bell reported, 'There are, perhaps, dozens of farms in view, yet the whole might be one great farm.'[49] A little earlier in 1923 William Dutt had observed the sleek prosperity of men and beasts from these 'lush-grassed lowland pastures, where man and beast now reap the benefit of the old-time fenmen's arduous labours in reclaiming sea-soaked swamps and oozy meres'.[50] Half a century later, in Caryl Churchill's *Fen*, Frank is puzzled by Angela's wish to move to the country:

FRANK: 'What's this [the Fens] then?'
ANGELA: 'I like more scenery. The Lake District's got scenery. ... Real country is romantic. Away from it all. Makes you feel better.'
FRANK: 'This is real country. People work in it. You want a holiday'.

Later Frank is responsible for the death of Val, who speaks from beyond the grave about the ghosts of labourers she has now joined, crowds of lost lives that press in on her: 'There's so many of them all at once.'[51] For each of these writers the Fens are a landscape marked and made by the labour of human hands, and their emptiness somehow exaggerates the traces of the bodies of departed workers, making a vacancy that is the ghost of their lives. 'What do you do when reality is an empty space?' asks Tom Crick in *Waterland*, 'you can make things happen – and conjur up, with all the risks, a little token of Here and Now ... Or, like the Cricks, who out of their watery toils could always dredge up a tail or two, you can tell stories.'[52] In fen georgic, narrative is a desperate fling against emptiness: that is how this landscape reads itself back into literature.

The most common of all fen tropes that links bodies with landscapes – and also the most extreme – is that of incest and inbreeding. The secret at the heart of *Waterland* is that Tom's brother Dick is the child their mother had with their grandfather, Ernest Atkinson. As ever, fen waterways provide the controlling metaphor: 'Because when fathers love daughters and daughters love fathers it's like tying up into knot the thread that runs into the future, it's like a stream wanting to flow backwards.'[53] These images of knots and recursive streams evoke that other emblematic item of fen fauna: the writhing eel, a creature both phallic and impossible to sex. When the doomed schoolboy Freddie Parr assaults Mary, Tom Crick's wife-to-be, by thrusting a live eel into her knickers, there is a different sort of short-circuiting between human sex and natural environment:

> Whereupon Mary ... spirals, hunches her shoulders, digs her elbows into her ribs, holds out two quivering forearms on either side of her, takes in breath but making no other sound nor any other movement to relieve her situation (not having encountered it before) freezes stock-still and wide-mouthed while something squirms, twists, writhes inside her knickers and finally (because eels are adept at extricating themselves even from the most unlikely predicaments) squeezes itself out by way of a thigh-band, flops to the grass and with unimpaired instinct makes towards the Lode.

Mary's convulsive gestures mimic the fish – writhing, arms pressed quiveringly to sides – and Swift's long, squirming, paratactic sentence mimics her in turn. Fen writers have found these sorts of images and sexual associations hard to resist since *Waterland* was published in 1982. For example, the poet George Macbeth, holed up in West Norfolk during the later 1980s, imagined ancient knightly owners of the fenland estate he had recently restored:

> Taut seamen of dark slime,
> Whose eels ran in and out, they raped by rote,
> And starving daughters, fissured, owed them shame.[54]

Leslie Gaister's luridly Gothic novel *Honour Thy Father* (1990) features a tyrannical farmer, Pharoah, living in fenland squalor with four daughters. One has borne him a minotaurean son, George, who they keep locked up below ground level in a cellar. Jez Butterworth's play *The Night Heron* (2002) is set in another hovel, located somewhere north-east of Cambridge, and does for the Fens what his hit *Jerusalem* (2009) would do later for rural Wiltshire. Its main protagonist, the Beckettian everyman Wattmore, has fallen from the Edenic position of gardener at Corpus Christi College, where he once tended the English Summer Royal roses with an expert touch. He was sacked, we discover, under suspicion of a Peter Grimes-style crime involving the young son of the head gardener. Now Wattmore follows a local Christian cult led by Dougal, a charismatic preacher with Down's syndrome, the latest in a long line of fen characters with learning disabilities, often associated by implication with consanguineous parentage. A final example of contemporary fenland Gothic is Daisy Johnson's short story collection *Fen* (2016). It features a girl whose eating disorder culminates with her metamorphosis into an eel, a coven of female vampires who cannot digest the muddy blood of the local men they prey on, and a family of brothers who hunt over-weight fen foxes on foot. In each of these cases, strangely sexualized bodies are figured as emanations of the soil. They prove and pervert Tom Crick's speculation that 'sexuality reveals itself more readily, more precociously, in a flat land, in a land of watery prostration'.[55]

The Wake and Fen Depths

The sense that Clare, Churchill and Swift have of the Fens being like nothingness is similar to another common description of the area, as a 'thin place'. Merivel, the hero of Rose Tremain's novel *Restoration* (1989), washes up at New Bedlam, a Quaker mental hospital located somewhere north of March, and finds that in the Cambridgeshire Fens

> the crust of the earth appears thin, allowing water to seep and ooze upwards so that it is possible to imagine there are fishes and not worms in the soil. And it is a landscape of thin things – feathery marsh grasses and bullrushes and bending willows.[56]

Tim Dee has a similar feeling about the region: on the Great Level 'the world is spread thinly. The sky does most of the work.'[57] Paul Kingsnorth's novel *The Wake* (2014) is a desolate and anti-heroic reimagining of Hereward the Wake's fenland holdout against the eleventh-century Norman conquest. Here the lowness of the land and the shallowness of its waters is described as 'undeop' (the book is written in an adapted version of Anglo-Saxon), which captures the thinness again.[58] This fen un-depth goes with an exaggerated consciousness of what might be buried beneath the thin surface. *The Wake*'s narrator, the farmer-turned-partisan Buccmaster, recalls his grandfather taking him out onto the fen mere and showing him 'under the water and not so deop ... the stocc of a great blaec treow torn to its root lic a tooth in the mouth of an eald wif' – there is in fact 'a great eald holt' (old forest) just below their boat.[59] This image of shallow yet archaic submersion brings an urgent spiritual and personal revelation to Buccmaster. The underwater forest is the resting place of the old gods, drowned by Erce (the goddess of the ground itself) when Englishmen deserted the old house for Christianity, and to whom Buccmaster remains an isolated devotee. This detail of Kingsnorth's theogony is reminiscent of the classic fen folktale 'The Dead Moon', in which the moon is snagged on submerged wood and then trapped beneath a stone by evil creatures (later she is released by alert villagers).[60] For Buccmaster, the fen signifies interconnection between the farmer's body, spiritual identity and territory: 'my folc was in the fens before the crist cum to angland this ground is in our bodigs deop'.[61] The historical depths into which Kingsnorth's novel looks are profound, and yet Buccmaster can reach through them: they are environmental and personal, historical yet palpable.

Buccmaster occupies a specific social position, particular to his fen location: he is a substantial landholder, separate from both the Saxon and the Norman aristocratic orders (between which the rebel Hereward moves so much more confidently). The productiveness and isolation of his farm once helped secure that position. Buccmaster is a freeman-farmer rather than a warrior-thegn, and this lets Kingsnorth bleed his story dry of knightly heroism. He is vain, prickly, brutal, always skulkingly absent when action is afoot. He is proud of his seat on the local Wapentac, but otherwise has no obvious connection to the community or loyalty to his king or nation. His georgic possessions are essential to this precarious yet deep-rooted independence:

> Three oxgangs [perhaps 60 acres] of good land i had and two geburs [semi-servile tenants] to worc for me on it and four oxen of my own for the plough this was mor than any other man in this ham. Baerlic [barley] i had and rye sceap and hors also i had swine pasture holt my own water aeppels on many good treows.[62]

Buccmaster's farm is on the Lincolnshire fen edge somewhere between Clare's Northborough and Bourne, which was Hereward's family home. The fen setting is important and it makes sense of Buccmaster's special freedom, for he farms on a fen island: 'there is many ealonds in the fens what gifs us foda and good lifs', he explains: 'and as these ealonds is in meres on all side with paths what only fenn folks cnawen it is hard for those from other parts to cum in'.[63] This island farm is circumscribed and semi-secret, a distinct unit within the larger landscape. It is a more substantial version of the human-scale smallholding occupied by the Old Corycian in Virgil's fourth *Georgic*.

The novel's crisis is an attack by Norman soldiers while Buccmaster is away fishing for eels. His great house is burned down with his wife Odelyn in it. For Buccmaster her murder is only the worst element in a larger atrocity: the destruction *of a farm*, and with it the cancelling of his connection to the land. '[M]y land is gan', he laments, 'all heges down all barns beorned my swine cwelled bledan in the holt my oxen slit open my sceop all blaec and cwelled their heafods [heads] off my aeppel treows cut all to the ground'.[64] His absence during the attack seems accidental, but it fits a pattern of withdrawal and failure to act: he opposes his sons joining King Harold's armies and declines to join them himself; later he instructs his own small 'werod' of followers to skulk in the Brunnesweald (Bourne Wood) rather than attack the Normans as guerrillas; he forbids them to seek Hereward at Ely. In the end we learn that Buccmaster came into possession of his farm by parricide, and that he burned his father's and sister's bodies in a barn. The Norman violence that dispossesses him mirrors the violence by which he once took control of the land. This revelation casts a gloomy irony over Buccmaster's protests about the depth of his rootedness. The georgic dream of his life as a 'socman of the blaec fenns' is found at last to be as thin as marshland topsoil, and as shallow as the waters that cover his grandfather's drowned forest. Once again, no other British landscape could afford Kingsnorth such clear intimations of a paradox at the heart of the georgic life: that the farmer's experience of deep connection with the land can be a true one (the fen is 'the triewest place in angland') even while environmental or historical perspectives show us how precarious it really is.[65]

The themes of historical and environmental shallowness are brought together again in the final scene of *The Wake*. Returning to the site of his fen island farm, Buccmaster disinters from 'a scealo graef' his cache of ancient war gear, most spectacularly 'the eald war helm of my grand father all macd ofer with boars with seolfor and gold'.[66] His werod has captured a Norman bishop, whom Buccmaster plans to kill in a 'blud earn', a horrific Norse torture ritual. His plan fails, but the episode confirms how old things and buried histories lie just beneath the surface of the Fens. Buccmaster's buried armour recalls the foreboding final section of Virgil's first *Georgic*, where astonished farmers find javelins and helmets from forgotten battles tangling the prongs of their rakes, a few lines before 'crooked Scythes are streightned into Swords' once again.[67] In this thin landscape, narrative cycles of modernity and loss, of georgic reclamation and environmental catastrophe, are always on the verge of collapse into one another.

The shallowness of the landscape brings buried history readily to the surface, and it draws the prospect of climate change and rising sea levels – which may well inundate large portions on the Fens before the twenty-first century is over – closer as well. When W. H. Auden predicts the destruction of a modern fen-like landscape in 'A Summer Night' (1933), the sudden flood is followed with strange immediacy by a further cycle of environmental recovery and modernistic progress:

> Soon, soon, through dykes of our content
> The crumpling flood will force a rent
>   and, taller than a tree,
> Hold sudden death before our eyes
> Whose river dreams long hid the size
>   And vigours of the sea.
>
> But when the waters make retreat
> And through the black mud first the wheat
>   In shy green stalks appears,
> When stranded monsters gasping lie,
> And sounds of riveting terrify
>   Their whorled unsubtle ears.[68]

The riveters are back at work, and georgic wheat is sprouting, before the gasping washed-up Powtes (if that is what the monsters are) can expire. Nearly a century on from Auden's crumpling flood, it is hard now to see a future for the Fens in which the cycle of reclamation and decline will continue. Even Tim Dee's apprehension in 2013 of the sea's jealousy over its old waterline now seems optimistic. He sensed 'a keeping back of a wetter truth across the wider fens: it was once sea here and then was kept from being always-sea by being sometimes-sea'.[69] Will-be-sea is the more likely prospect today. The archaeologist and landscape historian Francis Pryor, who has charted the historical depths of the Fens more thoroughly than any other writer, ends his recent historical survey *The Fens* with a meditation on the medium-term prospect of the area's re-immersion by tide and flood: 'Had I been writing this twenty years ago I would have said "if"', he decides, 'Today, I am in no doubt whatsoever: it's a firm "when."'[70] *The Wake* is the first of a trilogy of novels by Paul Kingsnorth: in the third, *Alexandria* (2021), which is set on another fen edge far in the future, he imagines what may be the last human community on earth driven inland, and towards its final extinction, by suddenly rising sea levels. The *terminus ad quem* for the development of fen georgic is now in sight, and its future exponents are likely to fix their attention increasingly on the coming catastrophe.

Notes

1. A. Bell, 'Fens and Levels', in *The English Countryside*, ed. H. J. Massingham (London: Batsford, 1939), pp. 186–210, at p. 187.
2. *Cobbett's Political Register*, vol. 69, 2 January 1830 to 26 June 1830 (1830), p. 488.
3. J. R. Stilgoe, *What Is Landscape?* (Cambridge, MA: MIT Press, 2015), pp. 5–8.
4. M. Drayton, *The Works of Michael Drayton*, ed. J. W. Hebel, 5 vols. (Oxford: Blackwell, 1931–41), vol. IV, p. 515 (*Poly-Olbion*, XXV. 147–8).
5. J. Clare, 'A Walk', in *The Midsummer Cushion*, ed. K. Thornton and A. Tibble (Ashington: Carcanet 1980), pp. 461–2, at p. 461. Perhaps the nearest thing to a Fen successor to the Dutch Golden Age landscape artists was Clare's correspondent Peter DeWint, in whose Lincolnshire landscapes 'the blending & harmony of earth air & sky are in such a happy unison of greens and greys that a flat bit of scenery on a few inches of paper appear so many miles'; Clare to DeWint, 19 Dec. 1829, *The Letters of John Clare*, ed. M. Storey (Oxford: Clarendon Press, 1985), p. 488; see L. B. Pearce, 'John Clare and Peter DeWint', *John Clare Society Journal*, 3 (1984), 40–9.
6. J. Clare, 'Autobiographical Fragments', in *By Himself*, ed. D. Powell and E. Robinson, (Manchester: Carcanet Press, 1996) p. 115; cf. C. Taylor, 'Fenlands', in *The English Rural Landscape*, ed. J. Thirsk (Oxford University Press, 2000), pp. 167–87, at p. 170, whose list of fen writers is confined to Dorothy L. Sayers and Arthur Ransome.

7 T. Dee, *Four Fields* (London: Cape, 2013), pp. 30, 114, 216–18.
8 C. Blagden, *The Stationers' Company: A History, 1403–1959* (London: Allen and Unwin, 1960), p. 187; A. McRae, *God Speed the Plough: The Representation of Rural England, 1500–1660* (Cambridge University Press, 1960), pp. 146–51.
9 T. Tusser, *Five Hundred Points of Good Husbandry*, ed. G. Grigson (Oxford University Press, 1984), 'The Author's Life', p. 207.
10 Tusser, *Husbandry*, p. 106.
11 J. Dyer, *The Fleece. A Poem in Four Books*, ed. J. Goodridge and J. C. Pellicer (Cheltenham: Cyder Press, 2007), p. 55.
12 Dyer, *Fleece*, p. 26; Virgil, *Georgics* I. 145.
13 G. Swift, *Waterland* (1983; London: Picador, 1984), p. 291.
14 H. Belloc, *The Hills and the Sea* (London: Methuen, 1906), p. 125.
15 A. Young, *General View of the Agriculture of the County of Lincoln* (1799), p. 246.
16 I have not had an opportunity to examine the MS poetry collections, including georgic material, associated with the Spalding Gentlemen's Society: of three surviving volumes, two are in the Beinecke Library, Yale University, Osborn fc39 ('Manuscripts ... including numerous poems written for the Gentlemen's Society in Spalding, Lincolnshire'), while a third ('Miscellaneous Verses') remains in the Society's archives at Spalding (thanks to Dustin Frazier Wood, the Society's archivist, for drawing my attention to this material).
17 J. Clare, *Major Works*, ed. Eric Robinson and David Powell (Oxford University Press, 2004), pp. 46–7, 66; cf. B. Keegan, *British Labouring-Class Nature Poetry, 1730–1837* (Houndmills: Palgrave Macmillan, 2008), pp. 160–2; S. J. White, 'John Clare's Sonnets and the Northborough Fens', *John Clare Society Journal*, 28 (2009), 55–107.
18 J. Clare, *The Natural History Prose Writings of John Clare*, ed. M. Grainger (Oxford: Clarendon Press, 1983), p. 57.
19 J. Clare, *Poems of the Middle Period, 1822–1837, Volume V: Northborough Poems*, ed. E. Robinson, D. Power and P. M. S. Dawson (Oxford: Clarendon Press, 2003), pp. 27–8.
20 J. Barrell, *The Idea of Landscape and the Sense of Place 1730–1840* (Cambridge University Press, 1972), pp. 134–46.
21 Dee, *Four Fields*, p. 21.
22 Francis Pryor writes that the effect is 'one of the things I like about the flatness of the Fens' in *The Fens: Discovering England's Ancient Depths* (London: Zeus's Head, 2019), p. 293.
23 Bell, 'Fens and Levels', p. 188.
24 Swift, *Waterland*, p. 70.
25 J. Clare, 'London *versus* Epping Forest', *English Journal*, 22 (1841), 241.
26 Clare, *Middle Period*, pp. 29–30.
27 Virgil, *Georgics* (Dryden), p. 174 (*Georgics*, 1, ll. 419–20).
28 Camden, W., *Camden's Britannia Newly Translated into English*, ed. E. Gibson (London, 1695), 409.
29 W. Stukeley, *Itinerarium curiosum. Or an Account of the Antiquitys and Remarkable Curiositys in Nature and Art Observ'd in Travels thro' Great Britain* (1724), p. 15.

30 17 September 1663, *The Diary of Samuel Pepys*, ed. R. Latham, 11 vols. (London: Bell, 1970–83), vol. IV, p. 310.
31 C. Fiennes, *Through England on a Side Saddle … being the Diary of Celia Fiennes*, ed. E. W. Griffiths (1888), p. 127.
32 Walpole to Cole, 26 June 1769, *Horace Walpole's Correspondence with the Rev. William Cope*, ed. W. S. Lewis, 2 vols. (New Haven: Yale University Press, 1937), vol. I, p. 177.
33 William of Malmesbury, *Gesta Regum Anglorum, Vol. 1*. ed. R. A. B. Mynors, R. M. Thomson and M. Winterbottom (Oxford University Press, 1998), p. 395.
34 Anon., 'The Draining of the Fens', in T. Borlik, ed., *Literature and Nature in the English Renaissance: An Ecocritical Anthology* (Cambridge University Press, 2019), p. 457.
35 Swift, *Waterland*, p. 27.
36 T. A. Borlik and C. Egan, 'Angling for the "Powte": The Authorship, Provenance, and Manuscripts of a Jacobean Environmental Protest Poem', *ELR*, 48 (2018), 256–89.
37 W. Dugdale, *The History of Imbanking and Draining of Divers Fens and Marshes*, ed. Charles Nalson Cole (1662; 2nd ed. London, 1772), pp. 391–2.
38 M. Cocker, *Our Place: Can We Save Britain's Wildlife Before It Is Too Late?* (London: Vintage, 2019), p. 183.
39 See, for example, *The Anti-Projector or the History of the Fen Project* (1646).
40 F. Willmoth, 'Dugdale's History of Imbanking and Drayning: A "Royalist" Antiquarian in the Sixteen-Fifties', *Historical Research*, 71 (1998), 281–302.
41 M. O'Callaghan, *The English Wits: Literature and Sociability in Early Modern England* (Cambridge University Press, 2007), pp. 102, 119–27.
42 For Cromwell's ultimate support of drainage, see Darby, *Draining of the Fens*, p. 64.
43 Virgil, *Georgics* (Dryden), p. 158 (*Georgics*, 1. l. 79).
44 J. Evelyn, *A Philosophical Discourse of Earth* (1676), pp. 20–1.
45 'A True and Natural Description of the Great Level of the Fenns', in Sir Jonas Moore, *The History or Narrative of the Great Level of the Fenns, called Bedford Level with a Large Map of the said Level* (1660; 1685), p. 72.
46 Swift, *Waterland*, p. 68.
47 Swift, *Waterland*, p. 3.
48 C. Churchill, *Fen*, in *Plays: Two* (London: Methuen, 1990), p. 171.
49 Bell, 'Fens and Levels', p. 188.
50 W. A. Dutt, *Highways and Byways of East Anglia* (London: Macmillan, 1923), p. 265.
51 Churchill, *Fen*, p. 187.
52 Swift, *Waterland*, p. 52.
53 Swift, *Waterland*, p. 197.
54 G. Macbeth, 'The Vision of Gustavus Helsham, Esquire', in *Anatomy of a Divorce* (London: Hutchinson, 1988), pp. 20–7, at p. 22.
55 Swift, *Waterland*, pp. 157–8.

56 R. Tremain, *Restoration* (London: Vintage, 2020), p. 209.
57 Dee, *Four Fields*, p. 21.
58 P. Kingsnorth, *The Wake* (London: Unbound, 2014), pp. 34, 35, 108.
59 Kingsnorth, *Wake*, p. 51.
60 'The Dead Moon', in M. C. Balfour, ed., 'Legends of the Lincolnshire Cars', *Folk-Lore*, 2 (1891), 145–70, at 157–64.
61 Kingsnorth, *Wake*, p. 18.
62 Kingsnorth, *Wake*, p. 11.
63 Kingsnorth, *Wake*, p. 123.
64 Kingsnorth, *Wake*, p. 103.
65 Kingsnorth, *Wake*, p. 287.
66 Kingsnorth, *Wake*, p. 333.
67 Virgil, *Georgics* (Dryden), p. 178 (*Georgics*, II. l. 508).
68 W. H. Auden, 'A Summer Night', in *Collected Poems*, ed. E. Mendelson (London: Faber, 1976), p. 104.
69 Dee, *Four Fields*, p. 20.
70 Pryor, *Fens*, p. 398.

CHAPTER 14

Between the Georgic and the Pastoral
The British Weald

Suzanne Joinson

When the naturalist and author W. H. Hudson was fourteen, in 1855, he contracted typhus and was confined inside his father's ranch in Quilmes, Argentina. In bed, he read books he had picked up in a dusty second-hand bookshop in Buenos Aires: Gilbert White's *The Natural History and Antiquities of Selborne* (1789), James Thomson's *The Seasons* (1726) and Robert Bloomfield's *The Farmer's Boy* (1800), among others. These texts offered Hudson – nature-loving but unsuited to the brutalities of Argentine life – an alternative way to engage with his landscape. Rather than hunting he could mimic White and 'form a friendship with the fields and coppices, as well as with the birds, mice and squirrels who inhabit them'.[1] In Thomson's *The Seasons* he found shepherds depicted as 'real countrymen', echoing Virgil's 'courageous countrymen' labouring at the 'woolly ewes and straggly nannies' as well as Arcadian shepherd tropes.[2] Both versions provided powerful contrasts to his father's doomed attempts at sheep-farming on the Pampas. Hudson particularly identified with 'peasant poet' Robert Bloomfield who, like Hudson, foreshadowed Seamus Heaney's famous digging with a 'squat pen' by turning to the soil of poetry rather than the 'honourable toil', as Bruce Graver puts it, of working the land in the Virgilian sense:

> The Virgilian georgic attempts to chart how human beings, by diligent tendance of the natural world, can make a life for themselves in an uncertain and hostile universe.[3]

Hudson got from Bloomfield a sense of order and harmony that could be obtained from the continuity of the agricultural seasonal round. Generationally and geographically displaced – his grandparents having emigrated from Britain to America and his parents to South America – Hudson left the pampas at an early age knowing the open land was already being drained and enclosed, soon to be lost forever. Through these books a British pastoral calendar and a European georgic sensibility gave him what he was most in need of: a sense of home. When Hudson emigrated to England in 1874, aged thirty-three, he immediately dispatched to Selborne, trailing Gilbert White. Later he would embed himself in a house once inhabited by Richard Jefferies to write parts of the first of his successful rural-focused titles, *Nature in Downland* (1900), later followed by *Hampshire Days* (1903), *Afoot in England* (1909) and *A Shepherd's Life* (1910). It was as if he wished to burrow into adopted homesteads to locate himself in a version of the English landscape that might be called, in Edward Thomas's phrase, 'The South Country'.[4]

In this chapter I argue that Hudson came to England and created a prototype of creative non-fiction that drew on the tradition of country-themed books and was also influenced by the genre-blurring writing of Richard Jefferies, whose work is also discussed in Chapter 10 of this volume. Hudson's writing shifted into a highly idiosyncratic mode that strained away from the pastoral tropes typical of the perspective of the aesthetic tourist towards attempts to naturalize himself as an 'Englishman' and write himself into a georgic dwelling that might also be called a state of belonging.

In *Ecocriticism*, Greg Garrard locates the georgic within models of dwelling in the literature of farming and depictions of homesteads, exploring the relationship between dwelling on earth in relation to duty to and care of a place.[5] Hudson was without a homestead and wished to root himself in what Garrard calls a 'long-term imbrication of humans in a landscape of memory, ancestry and death, of ritual, life and work'.[6] This endeavour created a bridge between pastoral and georgic that in many ways reflects the hinterland nature of the 'threshold of England' of which Hudson writes. The South: always in the shadow of the metropolis and close, yet far, from the continent.

The appeal of Hudson's idealized rural England paved the way for many 'guides' to follow, including E. V. Lucas's *The Highways and Byways of Sussex* (1904) and Arthur Beckett's effusive *The Spirit of the Downs* (1909). These, alongside fiction titles prefiguring the rural 'mystic materialism' in Mary Webb's *Gone to Earth* (1917) and D. H. Lawrence's *The Rainbow* (1915) ultimately led the genre, I believe, into a cul-de-sac.[7] Agricultural-themed texts provoked charges of a reactionary ruralism, sentimentalism, or, worse, the beginnings of the evolution towards a contemporary form of popular writing that Richard Mabey describes as 'a vapid and repetitive strain of guidebooks and pop-science volumes whose overriding message is that we already know all those 'innermost secrets'.[8]

Those who followed Hudson's formula were usually London-based journalists, editors and illustrators aping the digressive meanderings of

Hudson but lacking his experience of displacement. As I will show later, this left the genre ripe for send up by Stella Gibbons, whose *Cold Comfort Farm* (1932) famously dismantles agricultural and rural tropes with such satirical skill that she brings the literature of agriculture in novels and non-fiction almost fatally to its knees.[9] However there is, I argue, a reversal route from the 'nature writing' cul-de-sac. As Jack Thacker points out, not all writers condemned rural tropes or targeted them with satire. Writing of Day Lewis, translator of a 1940 version of Virgil's *Georgics*, he states that 'for some writers the georgic proved fruitful as a transitional mode at the end of what Auden saw as a "low, dishonest decade" on the eve of war'.[10] T. S. Eliot, championing Day Lewis's translation, also equated the idea of agricultural labour with cultural work. As Thacker highlights, 'the work itself was one to which the author devoted "time, toil and genius"', showing that 'the "genius" of the *Georgics* became relevant to a modern situation'.[11]

Hudson, immune to unsettling signs of war, was certainly toiling. He side-stepped nationalism by virtue of his displacement despite eternally attempting to 'become English'.[12] He grounded his identity through an idolization of shepherds, presumably harking back to the Argentine ranch. In *Back to the Land* (1982), Jan Marsh quotes Hudson's *A Shepherd's Life*: 'it may be said that … speaking generally, the agricultural labourer is the healthiest and sanest man in the land, if not also the happiest as some believe'. Marsh comments, 'thus was the pastoral myth realized in the person of an English shepherd'.[13] Yet, much later when James Rebanks writes a memoir of sheep farming in the Lakelands he looks to Hudson's *A Shepherd's Life* for inspiration. In his almost identically titled *The Shepherd's Life* (2015), Rebanks explores shepherding lineage in England and his own family. Sharing stories of 'my grandfather, my father – everyone I knew and respected', he finds parallels with Hudson's narratives, and refutes Marsh's claim that Hudson's shepherds glorify the pastoral.[14] Both Hudson and Rebanks are in georgic territory: working shepherds, embedded in a landscape, and connected to a homestead.

In this chapter I explore a bridge that is created, I believe, from idyll to dwelling and from Weald to Lakeland. It reaches from Hudson's belief that 'only the rural workers still belong to the earth' and his sorrow at being displaced from this group, to Rebanks's assertion – much like Hudson's mourning of the enclosures of the pampas – that increased enclosure of British landscape leads to a profound cultural disconnection with the land. Rebanks does not see Hudson's shepherds as 'backward-looking' as Marsh describes them, but rather as part of a forward-looking

The Sound of the Scythe against the Whetstone

Loose in structure and geographically roaming, Hudson wrote *Nature in Downland* on short journeys made from London to the Downs between May and August 1899. The book skits through seasons and territories – church yards, marine areas, villages and forests – in no sequential order. Vistas remind Hudson of 'old days on horseback on the open pampas – an illimitable waste of rust-red thistles and the sky above covered with its million floating flecks of white' and he contrasts South American thistles with 'smaller, more fragile English thistle-down'.[15] His biographer, Jason Wilson, writes that with a foreigner's eyes he is 'like an explorer in the shires'.[16] For over a decade Hudson had been visiting Hampshire, the New Forest and Sussex whilst writing of lost and endangered habitats in *The Naturalist in the Plata* (1892). *Nature in Downland* was published in 1900, the year Hudson became a naturalized English citizen in order to be eligible for a civil pension, and by 1906 it was reprinted three times.[17] Later, in his revised *Birds of La Plata* (1920), Hudson wrote negatively about his choice to become English: 'When I think of that land so rich in bird life ... I probably made choice of the wrong road of the two then open to me'.[18] The experience of being an alien in London was so difficult and complex that Hudson rarely referred to it, but in one letter he wrote, 'It is no easy matter to become a citizen of this small country.'[19] It was within this atmosphere of loss and grief that he turned to an England of oxen-pulled carts and corn reaped with sickles, terrain that Prime Minister Baldwin later characterized by 'the sound of the scythe against the whetstone'.[20] Most totemic of Hudson's rural tropes is the shepherd who reoccurs in Hudson's books, a figure that he longs to know, or even be, but is forever distanced from. Admiringly, he watches him in situ:

> That solitary cloaked figure on the vast round hill, standing motionless, crook in hand, and rough-haired dog at heel, sharply seen against the clear pale sky, is one of those rare human forms in this land, which do not ever seem out of place in the landscape.[21]

Hudson asks himself if he wants to 'pry into and minutely examine the secret colour and texture of the mind' of a shepherd. He thinks not:

> In the case of the downland shepherd, this comparatively superficial knowledge which contents me has made me greatly admire him. That he differs

from others on the surface we cannot but see; and it would indeed seem strange if this had not been the case, since the conditions of his life are and have been for generations unlike those of other peasants; still, his best and sterling qualities are undoubtedly of the race.[22]

He is in anthropological mode, observing as if from a hide. Shepherds symbolize for him a simple and unchanging relationship to the earth. However, there is ambivalence. Hudson was a bird hunter in his early years in Argentina and only later turned conservationist, co-founding the RSPB.[23] Similarly to Jefferies, he is interested in the economical position of shepherds and the system of a shepherd 'paid a portion of his wages in kind' including a number of lambs, a portion of wool, and game and shooting rights. Hudson's earlier hunter and trader instincts can be glimpsed as he writes of the trapping and selling of wheatears, small birds once eaten as a luxury in the hotels of the coastal towns, and what 'was formerly a source of considerable profit to the shepherds of the South Downs'.[24]

Hudson, now English and a conservationist, is melancholy about the role shepherds played in catching birds in places such as Beachy Head and Rottingdean where 'shepherds made so many coops, placed at small distances apart, that the downs in some places looked as if they had been ploughed'.[25] Yet there is envy. Canny shepherds have intimate knowledge of wheatear migration patterns and behaviours. They know the catching places and how to make a healthy profit from Brighton poulterers and this ground-level familiarity indicates understanding of a local site that Hudson cannot attain. Shepherds become figures upon which Hudson projects his in-between status. Hudson no longer wanted to be a 'squatter', but he remained half foreigner and half of the city, destined to be on or beyond the bridging fence.[26]

Shepherds are most impressive to Hudson when seen against the backdrop of 'the vast sweep of parched ground', the empty Downs. The shepherd is an emblem of the seismic industrial shift still to come. Hudson's pessimism regarding urbanization always echoes with the loss of his bird-filled pampas and yet, as Adam Thorpe points out in an introduction to *A Shepherd's Life*, Hudson was mistaken in thinking of downland as natural:

> We now know that prehistoric people were as destructive of forests as we are, and that the downland's original tree cover, shallow-rooting in the chalk, was destroyed over a surprisingly short period – perhaps a few centuries.[27]

By 1910, when *A Shepherd's Life* is published, Hudson has gathered enough civic and national security to insert himself into the narrative and talk to the shepherd. *A Shepherd's Life* is an idiosyncratic oral history of a Wiltshire shepherd, William Lawes, whom Hudson calls Caleb Bawcombe to protect his identity. Hudson set about earning the shepherd's trust, allowing him to overcome his shyness and reluctance to speak:

> It is now several years since I first met Caleb Bawcombe, a shepherd of the South Wiltshire Downs, but already old and infirm and past work. I met him at a distance from his native village, and it was only after I had known him a long time and had spent many afternoons and evenings in his company, listening to his anecdotes of his shepherding days that I went to see his own old home for myself.[28]

Hudson would have been aware of the shepherds in Richard Jefferies's essays where Jefferies, as I will show later, effaced himself in the narrative in order to watch and observe. Hudson goes further, 'coaxing out his tales and jotting them in his notebook in the manner of the field naturalist'. Caleb's story includes tales of sheep-stealing, poaching, squires and family life, told in a looping, digressive style:

> I discovered that it was of little use to question him ... it was a very slow process, but it is not unlike the one we practise always with regard to wild nature.[29]

In taking an account of Caleb Bawcombe's life, Hudson draws a link from his childhood encounter with the Bloomfield and Sussex poet James Hurdis – who also wrote of wheatear trapping – and he extracts and assimilates Caleb Bawcombe's memories within his own narrative:

> The earlier of these memories were always the best to me, because they took one back sixty years or more, to a time when there was more wildness in the earth than now, and a bolder wild animal life.[30]

Hudson can only access a homestead or farm on the Downs as a visitor asking for a drink of water and so unearths shepherd narratives as a rooting exercise.[31] As his biographer Wilson puts it, 'writing about English shepherds was a secret therapy'.[32] In *A Shepherd's Life* Hudson is in residence, no longer a foreigner, writing that 'owing to a certain kind of adaptiveness in me, a sense of being at home wherever grass grows, I am in a way a native'.[33]

At the end of *Nature in Downland*, Hudson walks a few miles from a village in West Sussex with a 'man who was a native of the place' who wanted to tell him something: 'What he wanted to show me was the scenery amid which he had lived ... scenes familiar to him since his childhood.'[34] The message was that nowhere was prettier than his home and nowhere else made him happy. Hudson tried to disagree:

> the home feeling is in some degree universal in men born and bred amid rural scenes, but … the scenes for which they had pined had not been distinguished by beauty of any peculiarly attractive quality above others.³⁵

The 'native' had been 'anxious to make me understand the character and strength of the feeling that always drew him back … it was not any human tie – it was place'. Yet Hudson realizes his version of this sentiment – that all homes are the same, there is no special quality to any local spot – is wrong. He thinks of the other man's rural, idyllic home, and wonders at his mistake.

Hudson's knowledge of English rural life and place remained on the surface and his tragedy was that he knew it, despite literary accolades. Ford Madox Ford cited Joseph Conrad saying that Hudson's writing was 'like the grass that the good God made to grow and when it was there you could not tell how it came', and Arnold Bennett asked 'how many men know England, the actual earth and flesh of England, as Mr Hudson knows it?'³⁶ It is belonging, however, in the sense of knowing exactly how to work and manage the land, that Hudson wants but cannot access. Instead, he sketches what Macfarlane calls 'dream-maps', involving 'an act of imaginative cartography, a chart of longing and loss projected onto actual terrain', and as we follow Hudson through these maps, he leans deeply towards a homestead knowing it is always out of reach.³⁷

'Pigeon-Holed Finally as One Who Describes the Country'

'My bedroom on the first floor, with a view of the sea, is the one Jefferies occupied, but he died downstairs in one of the sitting-rooms', Hudson wrote in a letter about his stay in the house in Goring, West Sussex, where Jefferies wrote segments of his last work, *Amaryllis at the Fair*, published in 1887, the year he died of tuberculosis.³⁸ They were contemporaries, though they never met, and Jefferies' memory reaches back to an England already gone by the time Hudson arrived in the country:

> Some of the older shepherds still wear the ancient blue smock-frock, crossed with white 'facings' like coarse lace; but the rising generation use the great-coat of modern make, at which their forefathers would have laughed as utterly useless in the rain-storms that blow across the open hills.³⁹

Jefferies is difficult to classify. Ronald Morrison notes that 'critics have struggled to situate his works into meaningful and consistent genre categories and ideological frames' despite, as E. V. Lucas wrote in the introduction to Jefferies's children's book *Bevis*, his 'being pigeon-holed finally as one who describes the country'.⁴⁰ Yet contrary to the popular image of Jefferies as a deep-rooted countryman, he was a displaced person almost from birth, as Mabey says in an introduction to *Wild Life in a Southern County* (1879):

> Aged four, he was despatched from his family's declining farm to live with an aunt in Sydenham. When he was nine, he returned home ... When he was sixteen he ran away from home ... the smallholding was badly hit by cattle plague in 1865, he left school for good, and started work in Swindon on a new Conservative paper.[41]

This dislocation along with an impecunious existence both resonated with Hudson and repelled him.[42]

Jefferies made a living by writing of gamekeeping, farm-life and natural history, producing articles for *Pall Mall Gazette*, reprinted in 1978 as *The Gamekeeper at Home*, followed by *Wild Life in a Southern County* (1879) and *Nature Near London* (1883). In parallel, in 1880, he published *Hodge and His Masters*, focusing on agricultural matters. He should have been an English rural 'insider' but, as Mabey points out, 'at this stage in his life, Jefferies had not yet worked out which side of that "frontier line" he was on – anchored with civilisation, or on the wing with unrestrained nature'.[43] In 'The Breeze on Beachy Head', Jefferies stands on the precipice of the cliffs as if attempting to root himself in unchangeable coordinates, linking past to present:

> you cannot tell what century it is from the face of the sea. A Roman trireme suddenly rounding the white edge-line of chalk borne on wind and out from the Isle of Wight towards the gray castle at Pevensey (already old in the olden days), would not seem strange.[44]

On the 'tumulus' slope he is 'reclining on the grass', looking at the hollows of the land and the light. His account of the Beachy Head cliffs differs from Hudson's in that the author is not hiding, but rather becomes immersed in the scene:

> The edge and the abyss recall us; the boundless plain, for it appears solid as the waves are levelled by distance, demands the gaze.[45]

Jefferies has a changeable lens shifting from the panoramic, from the inside-looking-out, from Hudson's exiled margins, to extremely close-up. In 'The Southdown Shepherd', he explains how a shepherd's crook is often made from the barrel of a gun, echoing and inverting Virgil's famous and often misinterpreted line: 'they melt down the farmer's sickle into a sword'.[46]

> About a foot of the barrel being sawn off at the muzzle end, there was a tube at once to fit the staff into, while the crook was formed by hammering the tough metal into a curve upon the anvil. So the gun – the very symbol of destruction – was beaten into the pastoral crook, the emblem and implement of peace.[47]

This analysis of tool and object demonstrates a distinct difference between the georgic and the pastoral, as helpfully articulated by Richard Thomas, who states 'that there is little room for nostalgia in the former, which plays itself out in the context of the need for toil and toil as a form of warfare against resistant nature'.[48] Hence the use of weaponry-talk for farming matters.

Jefferies's focus on the materiality of tools also affords him more familiarity than Hudson's behind-the-trees lurking, yet Jefferies is still self-effacing. Rather than emphasizing the silhouette of the shepherd against the backdrop of the Downs, Jefferies concentrates on the georgic concern for the methods of working off, and on, the land. His 'burrowing' into detail enables him to distance the authorial self, becoming reporter of a scene whilst simultaneously drawing closer to the homestead. Jefferies echoes Richard Thomas's point that the catalogue of farm tools in Virgil's first *Georgic* 'gives pride of place to the plough, notably designated as currus, "chariot"'.[49] Jefferies goes on to describe the plough as an item that

> could scarcely have been invented; it must have been put together bit by bit in the slow year – slower than the ox; it is the completed structure of long experience. It is made of many pieces, chiefly wood, fitted and shaped and worked, as it were, together, well seasoned first, built up, like a ship, by cunning of hand.[50]

He returns to this idea of things put together 'bit by bit', a slowing down, smoothening, likening it to the 'spirit of art':

> There is not, perhaps, another homemade implement of old English agriculture left in use; certainly, none at once so curious and interesting, and, when drawn by oxen, so thoroughly characteristic.[51]

His words are like the tacks and parts of the plough, as if by each descriptive sentence Jefferies embeds himself in the individual components of the tools and working methods of the Downland soil, much as he immersed himself in the grassy slope of Beachy Head.

Jefferies does not often speak to the people he writes of, the drovers, tinkers and carters who work the land. When describing a sheep fair he does not say which one. He compares it to a fair he visited twenty-five years before. His prose is infused with melancholy: it is raining, 'the descending vapours close in the view on every side':

> It is just the same this year as last, like the ploughs and hurdles, and the sheep themselves. There is nothing new to tempt the ploughboy's pennies – nothing fresh to stare at.[52]

The minutiae of the observation (sheep, soil, furrows) is at odds with the lack of specificity regarding place. This tendency is echoed by Hudson's digressive sketches and jumps, and later by Edward Thomas's *The South Country* (1909). Thomas writes:

> This is not the South Country which measures about two hundred miles from east to west and fifty from north to south. In some ways it is incomparably larger than any country that was ever mapped, since upon nothing less than the infinite can the spirit disport itself.[53]

Likewise, Jefferies (and Hudson) slip between information gathering and breezy sketches of unnamed places. But Jefferies, writing about the South and London environs, was ahead of his time when it comes to bridging the hinterland, whether cultural or geographical. In the essay 'To Brighton' he writes:

> This Ditchling Beacon is, I think, the nearest and the most accessible of the southern Alps from London; it is so near it may almost be said to be in the environs of the capital. But it is alone with the wind.[54]

Like his shepherds who aren't quite brought in from the edges of his peripheral vision, he moves restlessly through the Weald and the South. For him, 'the agricultural home place', as Ronald Morrison describes it, 'is bound up in a complicated tangle of connections not only with the natural environment but also with economic, legal, cultural, and natural forces that all have a tremendous impact on individuals, human communities, and the land itself'.[55] In 'Village Architecture' included in *Wild Life in a Southern County* (1879), Jefferies's shepherd has a 'distinct individuality'. The author admires his ability 'to recollect all the endless fields in several square miles of country'.[56] He equates the shepherd's knowledge with a student's work in books: 'so the shepherd recalls *his* books, the fields; for he, in the nature of things, has to linger over them and study every letter: sheep are slow'.

Whilst Jefferies sketches nostalgic visions of the past, he is acute and practical-minded too. In his book *Richard Jefferies: His life and Work* (1909), Edward Thomas contextualizes Jefferies's 'nature writing' against the Victorian trend of encountering countryside through a hobby such as ornithology or amateur naturalism.[57] Thomas recognizes that Jefferies was working outside this pattern, writing of either 'doing nothing' out of doors or analysing and reflecting on agricultural matters.[58] In addition, there is a quality to Jefferies's writing that is underpinned with a unique element, perhaps born of illness and poverty, that echoes Hudson's exiled tones. Like Hudson, Jefferies is often out of kilter and out of place, but what pins him down is the georgic idea of 'toil' and 'work'.

Richard Thomas, writing of T. S. Eliot's interpretation of Day Lewis's *Georgics*, states that the poem 'desired to affirm the dignity of agricultural labour, and the importance of good cultivation of the soil for the well-being of the state both materially and spiritually'.[59] Just as Hudson could not work on the ranch, and Jefferies was displaced from his family homestead and could never earn enough to buy one back, both writers looked to the soil to find spiritual and physical well-being, but ultimately could not attain it.

In an essay exploring Virgil's Corycian in relation to Wendell Berry, W. R. Johnson depicts Virgil's independent gardener as marginal, like his land.[60] The place, much like the Weald of southern England, is neither wholly natural nor fully civilized and the countryside remains overshadowed by the metropolis. Virgil's 'marginalization gives him a unique and powerful vantage point, one borne of humility and local knowledge', according to Johnson. Jefferies would die and be buried in Worthing, Sussex, in 1887. Hudson asked to be buried in the same cemetery. Both were looking for a conscious return to land but, instead of a vantage point, their marginalization led to displacement. Jefferies's endeavours left him destitute, ill and unable to go out and join the natural landscape to which he so desperately wanted to belong. This was what haunted Hudson: the uncanny sense of walking in Jefferies's footsteps.[61]

Lovers of Unwrecked England

In *Highways and Byways of Sussex* (1904), the London-based journalist E. V. Lucas sings the praises of 'the unique character of the Sussex Downs' with invocations of W. H. Hudson's 'caustic' chapter on the town of Chichester's 'roughs and its public houses'.[62] The guide, published by Macmillan, was one of a number of publishing initiatives focusing on the 'country' in the late Edwardian period. The publishers J. M. Dent dispatched Edward Thomas to write about the South (*The South Country*, 1909) and Hilaire Belloc to write about London (*Historic Thames*, 1907) as part of their 'The Heart of England' series, and many others followed. These titles were popular but took Hudson's and Jefferies's idiosyncratic models in a bucolic, romantic direction.

Arthur Beckett begins *Spirit of the Downs* (1909) with a whimsical invocation to the titular Spirit ('Tell me, O spirit … !').[63] He leaves town, becomes healthy as he ventures through countryside, puts out a wish to be turned into a bird and the wish is granted. A review of the book in the *Spectator* was not keen on these fanciful digressions:

> We like Mr. Beckett better when he really does what he tells us in his introduction he set out to do,—when he walks from village to village through the open Downland, talking to shepherds and carters and tramps. We come nearer 'the Spirit' of Downland villages when we read of country soup made of buff fungus, and puff-balls named 'Satan's snuff-boxes'.[64]

Beckett was founder of the *Eastbourne Gazette and Herald* and the Society of Sussex Downsmen (begun in 1923) and he worked with Stanley Inchbold, an illustrator and landscape painter who produced books on Lebanon, Syria and Palestine. Guides were meant to shape aesthetic taste and travellers wished to partake in the same experience as those before them, following an expected and 'beautiful' route to connect to a larger experience. They were a curation of acceptable versions of rural England and the South and Weald presented an agreeable version of how 'English Country' landscapes should look. The creators of these books looked to the digressive, meandering forms of Hudson and Jefferies for a model. Later generations of post-war nostalgia-driven texts, such as Barclay Wills's *Bypaths in Downland* (1927), were less about belonging and more about idle perusing.

The country became a sentimentalized zone, removed from modernization, harking backwards to pastoral and nostalgic visions of lost England. Beckett 'the tramping traveller' compares the downland peasant to a pig ('they are simple and conservative') and his mention of 'the Gate of the West' in South Harting might be to the old town of Jerusalem.[65] Beckett also encounters shepherds, writing 'a gentleman had come to see his "stones"' of a shepherd met on Beachy Head who shows him Neolithic flint arrowheads picked up around the cliffs.[66] Yet Beckett does not want to hear memories, nor to understand how he is paid: he wants to stop the progression of time and reverse it. This is a fundamentally regressive position rather than a desire to belong to the place.

In the interwar years, titles worked hard to coax city-dwellers to a pastoral escape and the genre became a pastoral-georgic blur. Texts emerged that can be termed 'English Georgic', Virgilian imitations such as Vita Sackville West's *The Land* (1926) that looked to rural settings for sanctuary, or H. V. Morton's *In Search of England* (1927) that linked the countryside with nationbuilding.[67] These tendencies meant there was a turning against agricultural-themed works in some cultural quarters and as Macfarlane relates in *The Guardian*, the final 'death-blow' dealt to nature writing in Britain came in 1932 when Stella Gibbons published *Cold Comfort Farm*.[68] This had the effect of condensing all 'country writers' together and nailing them in one coffin, Hudson and Jefferies included.

Gibbons was a journalist, like Jefferies, Beckett and Lucas, and reviewing contemporary novels led her to infuse her text with in-jokes regarding the country books that landed frequently on her desk. She parodied the weather-filled landscapes heaving with sexual overtones so brilliantly that a straight-faced return to books such as *Sussex Gorse* by Sheila Kaye Smith (1916) was impossible. From *Cold Comfort Farm*:

> She [the hero Flora Poste] went down into a valley, filled with bushes of hazel and gorse, and made her way towards a little house built of grey stones, its roof painted turquoise-green, which stood on the other side of the Down. It was a shepherd's hut; she could see the stone hut close to it in which ewes were kept at lambing-time and a shallow trough from which they drank. If Mr Mybug had been there, he would have said that the ewes were paying the female thing's tribute to the Life Force. He said a woman's success could only be estimated by the success of her sexual life, and Flora supposed he would say the same thing about a ewe.[69]

The sending up of rural tropes – of landscapes sexualized, of nature anthropomorphized – puts *Cold Comfort Farm* in a somewhat contradictory position. Gibbons produces an excellent novel that dismantles the genre within which it operates. Similar to the imaginary version of rural Sussex that Thomas, Hudson and Jefferies all conjure, Gibbons's farm, as Macfarlane writes, is 'not on any map: true places never are'. He says:

> It lies somewhere on the high, hard ground of the Sussex hills in southern England, where the fields are 'fanged with flints' and the hedgerows entwined with 'sukebind'. 'Mud and rancid straw' carpet its yard. In the cowshed stands its herd: Feckless, Graceless, Pointless and Aimless, all milked by the local yokel, Adam Lambsbreath.[70]

Macfarlane cites A. N. Wilson's assertion that nature writing 'appeals to all that is gentlest and best in us, the lovers of unwrecked England'. Wilson links agricultural and soil-focused texts with nationbuilding ideologies, such as the 'spiritual ecologism' of Jorian Jenks, who farmed in West Sussex, and others such as H. J. Massingham's organicist project.[71] The country-genre cul-de-sac was therefore not only blocked in by satire, but also by the coupling of supposed georgic concerns with a preservation of the status quo and a regressive focus on imaginary past idylls.

Returning to Thomas's exploration of Day Lewis's translation of Virgil, Thomas traces this romanticization of agricultural notions back to Day Lewis, writing:

> The fascination of the Georgics for many generations of Englishmen is not difficult to explain. A century of urban civilization has not yet materially

modified the instinct of a people once devoted to agriculture and stock-breeding, to the chase, to landscape gardening, to a practical love of Nature. No poem yet written has touched those subjects with more expert knowledge or more tenderness than the Georgics. In our love of domestic animals, in the millions of suburban and cottage gardens, we may see the depth and tenacity of our roots in earth today. But the Georgics has little or nothing to say of the chase, landscape-gardening, domestic animals or suburban cottages, subjects which, however, are very much part of the British reception and distortion of the Virgilian Georgic.[72]

When Macfarlane insists that the unsatisfactory term 'nature writing' should not be seen as conservative, but rather a 'diverse, passionate, pluriform, essential, reviving tradition', he echoes Thomas's rallying complaint against the 'colossal underreading of Virgil' that has produced

a tedious and inert genre most of it rightly now relegated to the Rare Book Library. By focusing on and perpetuating tags and unexamined notions (life in the country is a golden age), a new genre was produced, visibly based in the *Georgics* (with pastoral blurring).[73]

Texts by Hudson, and to some degree Jefferies, are now being pulled out of the 'Rare Book Library' and placed back into the light. This tribute is exemplified by James Rebanks's successful *The Shepherd's Life*, which pays homage to Hudson and refocuses the country, or nature narrative, towards Virgil's poetry of 'labor improbus', or 'unremitting labour' as Day Lewis translates it.[74]

'We Are Nearly Home Now. The Sheep Can Sense It'

One day, I pulled *A Shepherd's Life* by W. H. Hudson from the bookcase as if it was a piece of junk. It was going to be lousy and patronizing, I just knew it. I was going to hate it like the books they'd pushed at us in school. But I was wrong, I didn't hate it. I loved it.[75]

James Rebanks writes in *The Shepherd's Life* (2015) about his life as a sheep farmer in the Lakelands. In a later book, *English Pastoral* (2020), he explains further that when young he left his family's farm in the Lake District to visit Australia, where his encounter with industrial-scale farming made him rethink his family's business at home in the Lakelands. Rebanks looks at a neighbour's soil and how it is fertilized the 'old fashioned' way with manure from cattle yards. He realizes that his is the healthiest soil, healthier than those coated in fertilizer and intensively farmed, his prose echoing Virgil's 'importance of good cultivation of the soil'.[76]

In *The Shepherd's Life*, Rebanks articulates his personal navigation between tradition and modernization, not unlike Jefferies who hovered between these two polarities and remains criticized today by some for not settling on one side or the other. Explaining how Herdwick sheep are the breed best suited to the landscape he works on, Rebanks writes, 'The first time I saw Herdwicks on our farm was as a child. Somehow they had more character than more modern sheep', and 'at that time, Herdwicks seemed to us noble, though like a thing from the past'.[77] He recounts a memory of buying lambs with his father and seeing drovers, 'some still wearing clogs, and all with sticks'. Now, rethinking his family's use of 'improved' modern breeds, he explores the renaissance of Herdwicks, 'the toughest mountain sheep in Britain' and the advantage of their inhabiting tougher land for lower cost.

Jan Marsh in *Back to the Land* sees the conversations between Hudson and Caleb Bawcombe as 'backward-looking … many of Bawcombe's memories were in fact stories told to him by his father, dating from around 1800 – which presents the shepherd's life as hard but happy'.[78] In contrast, Rebanks, thinking of the soil of his neighbour, does not see looking to traditional agrarian solutions as conservative or regressive. He explores sustainable options for the future and allows space for romantic notions of shepherding to sit alongside realities:

> There is a poetic fantasy that shepherds, and farmers, live a kind of isolated existence alone with nature. Wordsworth encouraged that idea, offering the world an image from his childhood of the shepherd alone in the fells with his dogs, at one with nature. At times this is physically true to life – men like my grandfather were sometimes alone with their sheep and the natural world. But it is equally true that shepherds don't exist alone, culturally or economically.[79]

Reading Hudson provided a tangible, cultural link for Rebanks based in work:

> I felt as if I could have worked with Caleb and talked sheepdogs, lame sheep or the weather. There is enough of the old shepherd in that book that I could forget that Hudson's pen was between us.[80]

Rebanks is an 'insider', as opposed to Jefferies's and Hudson's itinerant status, because he can claim lineage and heritage:

> I smile at the thought that the entire history of our family has played out in the fields and village stretching away beneath that fell, between Lake District and Pennines, for at least six centuries, and probably longer.[81]

This rootedness and proud territorial claim works hard to assert an authenticity in terms of a georgic dwelling that fights back against romantic pastoralism. 'Our farming way of life has roots deeper than five thousand years into the soil of this landscape', he states. By virtue of his birthright he is positioned to confidently claim a generic sensibility across what Hudson called a shepherding 'race'. Rebanks writes that shepherds 'consider themselves the equals of anyone' or 'shepherds have an unwritten rule' or 'shepherds hate other people's dogs'.[82] Where Jefferies was reporting on or immersing himself into a scene with a shepherd, and where Hudson transitioned from observing to interviewing shepherds, Rebanks is a shepherd and speaks for, and of, the vocation.

Being 'hefted', Rebanks says, is sheep being 'taught their sense of belonging by their mothers as lambs'.[83] He defines it as being linked, accustomed and attached to an area of land and one imagines that being hefted is exactly the element that was missing from Hudson's life. Rebanks's memoir shows us how focus on a georgic rethink of approaches to writing about farming can take us out of the pastoral–nationalist loop. Rather than being viewed through conservative nationalist tropes or idealized visions of pastoral or simple country idylls, we can bridge a new entry into a contemporary georgic by way of the landscape of the Weald and Lakeland. As Blake Morrison states, Rebanks's polemic can be overwhelming, but his profound sense of being embedded – hefted – within a homestead puts him squarely and confidently in a georgic terrain that is progressive and forward-facing.[84]

Hudson, and many of those who followed him, wrote to find a dwelling. Rebanks draws him out of the Rare Books Library into the dream-place he was trying to reach a century earlier. Despite the romantic projection onto both the Weald and Lakeland, there is a contemporary keenness to overcome the bucolic pastoral and to shift 'country writing' – and all that generic term includes – towards the georgic, meaning the practical day-to-day toil involved in working in a specific location. There is a shifting sense that small holdings and domestic farms can be sites of resistance, renewal and ecological regeneration. Books such as Isabella Tree's *Wilding: The Return of Nature to a British Farm* (2018) and John Lewis-Stempel's *The Running Hare* (2016) give us forward-looking narratives drawing deeply on place and site. Even satirical writers such as Gibbons are to some degree wanting to belong, straining for the emphasis of the old Corycian's 'knowing one's place in the landscape and what a particular environment might or might not sustain', in Johnson's words.[85]

In short, the writers examined here want not to be weekend visitors to the Weald and Lakes but included in the stewardship of the land in order to be of it. Hudson never found a homestead, but he understood the importance of tending place. His inheritor Rebanks insists that 'by remaining in a place, working on it and paying my dues' he is 'entitled to a share of its commonwealth'.[86] This insertion of his narrative, a Virgilian 'creating order out of disorder', into a located dwelling, anchors Hudson's peripatetic projected longings and brings the georgic, brightly, into contemporary relief.

Notes

1. R. Tomalin, *W. H. Hudson. A Biography* (London: Faber, 1982), p. 63.
2. Virgil, *Georgics* (Fallon), p. 60.
3. B. E. Graver. '"Honorable Toil": The Georgic Ethic of Prelude I', *Studies in Philology*, 92 (1995), 346–60.
4. E. Thomas, *The South Country* (Wimborne Minster: Little Toller, 2009).
5. G. Garrard, *Ecocriticism*, 2nd ed. (Abingdon: Routledge, 2012), p. 118.
6. Garrard, *Ecocriticism*, p. 118.
7. D. Matless, *Landscape and Englishness* (London: Reaktion Books, 1998), p 138. Matless describes the 'sexually charged mystic materialism of novelists such as John Cowper Powys and Llewelyn Powys' as targets for satire.
8. R. Mabey, 'Nature's Voyeurs', *The Guardian*, March 2002, www.theguardian.com/books/2003/mar/15/featuresreviews.guardianreview1 (accessed 10 April 2021).
9. See R. Macfarlane on Gibbons, 'Call of the Wild', *The Guardian*, December 2003, www.theguardian.com/books/2003/dec/06/featuresreviews.guardianreview34 (accessed 10 April 2021).
10. J. Thacker, 'The Farming of Verse: The Georgic Mode in the Poetry of Ted Hughes, Seamus Heaney, and Alice Oswald', unpublished PhD thesis, University of Bristol (23 January 2019), p. 11.
11. Thacker, 'Farming of Verse', p. 25 quoting T. S. Eliot, 'Virgil and the Christian World', in *On Poetry and Poets* (London: Faber, 1957), p. 125.
12. For an interesting exploration of Hudson's 'beyond the pale' status, see Wilson's reference to Hudson's letter to Cunninghame Graham in 1894 stating, 'he knew that the English reader had far less interest in gauchos (or Argentines) than in any people of races with the British Empire', in J. Wilson, *Living in the Sound of the Wind* (London: Constable, 2015), p. 249.
13. J. Marsh, *Back to the Land* (London: Quartet, 1982), p. 66.
14. J. Rebanks, *The Shepherd's Life: A Tale of the Lake District* (London: Allen Lane, 2015), p. 114.
15. W. H. Hudson, *Nature in Downland*, 2nd ed. (London: J. M. Dent, 1923), p. 3.
16. Wilson, *Sound of the Wind*, p. 257.
17. Tomalin, *Hudson*, p. 177.
18. Wilson, *Sound of the Wind*, p. 250.
19. Wilson, *Sound of the Wind*, p. 253.
20. In a speech to the Royal Society of St George in 1924 entitled 'What England Means to Me', https://spinnet.humanities.uva.nl/images/2013–05/baldwin1924.pdf (accessed 16 August 2021).

21 Hudson, *Nature in Downland*, p. 97.
22 Hudson, *Nature in Downland*, p. 98.
23 Tomalin, *Hudson*, pp. 147–52.
24 Hudson, *Nature in Downland*, p. 118.
25 Hudson, *Nature in Downland*, p. 122.
26 Wilson, *Sound of the Wind*, p. 255.
27 A. Thorpe, 'Introduction', W. H. Hudson, *A Shepherd's Life* (Wimborne Minster: Little Toller, 2018).
28 W. H. Hudson, *A Shepherd's Life* (London: J. M. Dent, 1936), p. 34.
29 Hudson, *Shepherd's Life*, p. 181.
30 Hudson, *Shepherd's Life*, p. 38.
31 In *Nature in Downland* (1900), he writes: 'That ancient notion of the value of a cup of cold water … if you approach any person wearing your look of one about to ask for some benefit, and your request is for a drink of water, you are sure to make him happy' (p. 166).
32 Wilson, *Sound of the Wind*, p. 260.
33 Hudson, *Shepherd's Life*, p. 3.
34 Hudson, *Nature in Downland*, p. 276.
35 Hudson, *Nature in Downland*, p. 278.
36 Conrad on Hudson referenced in 'Book Haven', November 2018, https://bookhaven.stanford.edu/2018/11/a-night-for-w-h-hudson-and-his-love-for-animals-was-deep-and-his-opinions-fierce/ (accessed 12 May 2021). Joseph Conrad, *A Personal Remembrance*. (n.p.: Kaf Publishing, 2013), Kindle edition.
37 R. Macfarlane, 'Introduction', in Thomas, *South Country*, p. 10.
38 Wilson, *Sound of the Wind*, p. 236.
39 R. Jefferies, *Wild Life in a Southern Country* (Wimborne Minster: Little Toller, 2011), p. 79.
40 E. V. Lucas, 'Introduction', R. Jefferies, *Bevis* (London: Cape, 1932), p. 15.
41 R. Mabey, 'Introduction', Jefferies, *Wild Life in a Southern Country*, p. 11.
42 See Wilson's biography for discussion on Hudson's reaction against Jefferies's *Story of my Heart*, Wilson, *Sound of the Wind*, p. 236.
43 R. Mabey, 'Introduction', Jefferies, *Wild Life in a Southern Country*, p. 11.
44 R. Jefferies, *Nature Near London* (London: Collins, 2012), p. 192.
45 Jeffries, *Nature Near London*, p. 197.
46 'They melt down the farmer's sickle into a sword' is quoted by R. Thomas who cites: *Georgics*, I. 508, 'et curvae rigidum falces conflantur in ensem'. R. F. Thomas, 'The "Georgics" of Resistance: From Virgil to Heaney', *Vergilius*, 47 (2001), 117–47, at 118. Peter Fallon's translation reads as: 'Scythes and sickles have been hammered into weapons of war'. Virgil, *Georgics* (Fallon), p. 60.
47 Jeffries, *Nature Near London*, p. 181.
48 Thomas, '"Georgics" of Resistance', p. 140.
49 Thomas, '"Georgics" of Resistance', p. 119.
50 Jeffries, *Nature Near London*, p. 186.
51 Jeffries, *Nature Near London*, p. 189.
52 Jeffries, *Nature Near London*, p. 186.

53 Thomas, *South Country*, p. 26.
54 Jefferies, *Nature Near London*, p. 179.
55 R. Morrison, 'Agriculture and Ecology in Richard Jefferies's Hodge and His Masters', *Victorian Writers and the Environment* (Abingdon: Routledge, 2016), p. 208.
56 Jefferies, *Wild Life in a Southern Country*, p. 80.
57 E. Thomas, *Richard Jefferies, His Life and Work* (Boston: Little, Brown, 1909), p. 108, https://archive.org/details/richardjefferiesoothomrich/page/338/mode/2up?q=ornithological+rambles (accessed 2 May 2021).
58 Thomas, *Jefferies*, p. 107.
59 Thomas, '"Georgics" of Resistance', p. 124.
60 W. R. Johnson 'Virgil's Corycian, Wendell Berry, and the Ecological Imagination', *Classical Association of the Middle West and South* (2004), https://camws.org/sites/default/files/meeting2016/234.VirgilBerry.pdf (accessed 20 April 2021), p. 125.
61 Johnson 'Virgil's Corycian', p. 125.
62 E. V. Lucas, *Highways and Byways of Sussex* (London: Macmillan, 1904), p. 33.
63 A. Beckett, *Spirit of the Downs* (London: Methuen, 1909). p. 2.
64 *Spectator*, 11 September 1909, p. 19, http://archive.spectator.co.uk/article/11th-september-1909/19/the-sussex-downs-an-author-who-writes-on-sussex-da (accessed 28 April 2021).
65 Beckett, *Spirit of the Downs*, pp. 71, 36, 58.
66 Beckett, *Spirit of the Downs*, p. 334.
67 See J. Thacker's useful outline of 'English Georgic', 'The Farming of Verse: The Georgic Mode in the Poetry of Ted Hughes, Seamus Heaney, and Alice Oswald', p. 16.
68 R. Macfarlane, 'Call of the Wild', *The Guardian,* December 2003, www.theguardian.com/books/2003/dec/06/featuresreviews.guardianreview34 (accessed 16 August 2021).
69 S. Gibbons, *Cold Comfort Farm* (London: Longmans, Green, 1932), p. 122.
70 R. Macfarlane, 'Something witty in the woodshed', *The Economist,* July 2015, www.economist.com/1843/2015/07/22/something-witty-in-the-woodshed (accessed 20 April 2021).
71 For further discussion of Jenks's and Massingham's organicism, see Matless, *Landscape and Englishness*, p. 109.
72 Thomas, '"Georgics" of Resistance', p. 125.
73 Thomas, '"Georgics" of Resistance', p. 130.
74 Thacker, 'Farming of Verse', p. 12.
75 Rebanks, *Shepherd's Life*, p .114.
76 Thomas, '"Georgics" of Resistance', p. 122.
77 Rebanks, *Shepherd's Life*, p. 57.
78 Marsh, *Back to the Land*, p. 66.
79 Rebanks, *Shepherd's Life*, p. 21.
80 Rebanks, *Shepherd's Life*, p. 115.
81 Rebanks, *Shepherd's Life*, p. 3.

82 Rebanks, *Shepherd's Life*, p. 257.
83 Rebanks, *Shepherd's Life*, p. 9.
84 B. Morrison, 'English Pastoral Review', *The Guardian*, September 2020, www.theguardian.com/books/2020/sep/03/english-pastoral-by-james-rebanks-review-how-to-look-after-the-land (accessed 30 May 2021).
85 Johnson, 'Virgil's Corycian', p. 2.
86 Rebanks, *Shepherd's Life*, p. 282.

CHAPTER 15

American Georgic

Sarah Wagner-McCoy

In 1847, Senator Daniel Webster welcomed the railway to his home state of New Hampshire in a speech celebrating American skill and industry. He praises the natural abundance of the landscape – the rich beauty of the Connecticut River valley, the water-power of the Merrimack, and the gorgeous fields and forests of his own farm – but refutes any connection between the local environment and the classical ideal: 'New Hampshire', he says, '... has no Virgil and no Eclogues.'[1] Invoking Virgil as a foil, Webster dismisses objections to the destruction of farmland and rural peace as mere nostalgia for an outmoded literary tradition, and exaggerates the contrast between Old World and New, 'otium' and 'negotium', fanciful poetry and real-world profits. Webster aligns rural appreciation and conservation with antiquated conventions, as out of place in the rapidly industrializing nation as the simple herdsmen and idyllic landscapes of Virgil's *Eclogues*.

In his foundational study of American pastoral, Leo Marx analyses Webster's contrast between the railroad and the rural idyll it threatens to disrupt as a touchstone of nineteenth-century US cultural history. Webster's enthusiasm for industrial progress captures the mainstream attitudes that Marx paraphrases:

> Pastoral poetry and the beauty of the landscape belong in one category, along with the peace and repose of rural life, but they are not to interfere with *serious* enterprises, with the activity of railroad promoters, men in touch with reality, whose 'business is to make a good railroad.' When Webster says, 'To be Serious, Gentlemen', it is with the serene assurance that his audience shares his definition of what is serious.[2]

Yet for many of Webster's countrymen, the pastoral ideal was serious. The pastoral defined 'the meaning of America ever since the age of discovery ... with an unspoiled hemisphere in view it seemed that mankind actually might realize what had been thought a poetic fantasy', Marx argues.[3] Over the course of the nineteenth century, however, the land once imagined as an attainable Arcadia produced a Gilded Age rather

316

than a Golden one. Webster's grasp of his historical moment proved true. Profit lay not in the 'stern climate and a stern soil' of New England but in the productive machinery that would connect the American West to an increasingly global economy.[4] In 1830, the United States had only 73 miles of railroad track; by 1860, 30,636 miles had been laid.[5] The Civil War accelerated the industrial boom, transforming the nation from a largely rural backwater into a technological, military and economic superpower. In *The Americanisation of the World* (1902), William Thomas Stead connected the 'advent of the United States of America as the greatest of world-Powers' to the rise of agribusiness: 'Europe is fed from day to day by the produce of American wheatfields and the slaughter-yards of Chicago.'[6] Technology revolutionized what remained of rural life. In the farmhouses of the fertile American interior, Frederick Law Olmsted observed, the 'railway timetable hangs with the almanac'.[7]

Narratives of the nineteenth-century shift from agriculture to industry have long been read through the lens of pastoral nostalgia. Analysing the iconic status of 'nature's nation' as a point of distinction from the traditions of the 'Old World', early studies of US literature simultaneously attest to the persistence of the rural ideal and to the inevitability of its decline.[8] From the literature of the 'American Renaissance' to Frederick Jackson Turner's frontier thesis (1893), discourses of exceptionalism have constructed a transatlantic dichotomy through the pastoral contrast of nature and culture, authenticity and artifice.[9] 'We will walk on our own feet; we will work with our own hands; we will speak our own minds', Ralph Waldo Emerson declares in a call for the emergence of a national literature; too long 'fed on the sere remains of foreign harvests' and inspired by 'the courtly muses of Europe', US writers must write about true nature rather than transplanting an oak into a flowerpot, or whittling away their pines, or carving shepherd and shepherdess figurines like 'Savoyards'.[10] Like Webster's disavowal of Virgil, Emerson's dismisses derivative pastoral as a means of asserting US independence, though to different rhetorical ends. Whereas Emerson hopes to 'fill the postponed expectation of the world with something better than the exertions of mechanical skill', Webster doubles down on exertion and mechanical skill as points of national distinction and pride. Turning not to nature but to a land transformed by Yankee ingenuity, Webster contrasts the idyllic landscape of Classical, Romantic and Transcendental nature appreciators with the autochthonous virtues of industrial progress in New England.

However, Emerson's and Webster's audiences would have been primed for their contrast between neoclassical convention and immersion in real nature by the wide circulation of popular British imports in a literary marketplace shaped by what Meredith McGill calls a 'culture of reprinting'.[11] Indeed, as Annabel Patterson argues, 'critical discourse from the beginning of the nineteenth century has been governed by the fiction that pastoral was either decadent, uninteresting, or dead', an easy target for Romantics such as Thomas Hood, who begins his humorous sketch 'May-Day' (1829) with a quip as dismissive as Webster's: 'The Golden Age is not to be regilt; Pastoral is gone out, and Pan extinct'.[12] Representing the call for a more authentic connection to nature as a break with the already discredited imitative pastorals of a previous generation, Wordsworth's 1800 Preface to *Lyrical Ballads* 'effectively buried a tradition that was already discredited', but Patterson also debunks the governing fiction of pastoral's extinction by tracing the continuity of the mode from the Romantic revolution onwards, noting that Wordsworth '*also* chose to preserve the term *pastoral* ... adding it to the title of the *Lyrical Ballads* of 1802 and building it as a subtitle into a few significant poems'.[13] In his analysis of Emerson's transatlantic sources, Lawrence Buell notes the *Nature* echoes *Lyrical Ballads* with 'an American-democratic twist ... Just as Wordsworth inverted the cultural authority of borderland and metropolis, so for Emerson the rustic postcolonial state that Europeans thought culturally impoverished seems a positive advantage.'[14]

Nor is Webster's praise of New Hampshire entirely homegrown. Interpreted at face value as a dismissal of *Eclogues*, the speech in fact adapts the central project of Virgil's *Georgics*, which represents agricultural labour and human ingenuity after the golden age. Webster's encomium to the 'indomitable industry ... without which the most fertile field by nature would remain forever barren' repurposes the language of Virgil and his imitators to promote the virtues associated, in the cultural imagination of the nineteenth-century United States, with the georgic tradition: 'sagacity, skill, and industry, the zealous determination to improve and profit by labor'.[15] The value of New Hampshire's rocky terrain lies not in its pastoral beauty, Webster claims, but in the georgic virtues acquired through its arduous cultivation. He lauds the marks of civilization by applying Virgil's apicultural metaphor to New Hampshire's school children, who cluster at schoolhouse doors 'as thick as bees', and cites John Denham's foundational English georgic, *Cooper's Hill* (1642), in a comparison of the Merrimack to the Thames.[16] Webster's New Hampshire may not have Virgil's *Eclogues*, but she does exemplify the virtues associated with Virgil's *Georgics* in its nineteenth-century US reception.

This chapter examines representations of American land and labour in the late nineteenth century as a complex engagement with the georgic mode. Aligning physical cultivation of the land with moral development of the self, US writers used georgic representations of economic, technological and imperial expansion to promote widely divergent visions of the ideal citizen and worker, from the virtuous husbandman of Thomas Jefferson's *Notes on the State of Virginia* (1785) to the bean-hoeing intellectual of Henry David Thoreau's *Walden* (1854). Although the georgic mode represents themes central to US cultural history, it is not merely a celebration of industry and labour; like Virgil's *Georgics*, which holds out the promise of progress in a fallen world but shows the human and environmental costs of the hard work it seems to promote, complex US adaptations of the georgic mode illuminate the destructive forces of agricultural labour, and the moral ambiguities of imperial expansion and racialized labour.

I begin by building on thematic accounts of American georgic writing in recent criticism to analyse the nineteenth-century reception of pastoral land and georgic labour. Encomiastic adaptations of both modes in a nation divided by a history of chattel slavery and expansionist conquest overlook the subtexts of enslavement, eviction and agricultural disaster in Virgil's first two poems. Although the representation of sectional difference before and after the Civil War generally maps divergent ideologies of Southern pastoral and Northern georgic onto competing myths of an Arcadian Old South and meritocratic Yankee industry, false narratives of agricultural improvement and civilizational hierarchy also used georgic discourses, justifying the theft of prime cotton land and expanding the slavocracy west of the Mississippi. Depictions of Choctaw, Chickasaw, Seminole, Creek, Quapaw, Caddoe and Cherokee land as either a vacant wilderness or the site of a prelapsarian golden age denies the long-standing and diverse traditions of cultivation by Tribal Nations. Yet Cherokee leaders also strategically invoke georgic ideologies to defend tribal sovereignty and protest US legislation of ethnic cleansing and forced removal. Frederick Law Olmsted's *Cotton Kingdom* (1861) contrasts Yankee georgic ideals with short-sighted Southern cultivation of land incentivized by the expansion of the Cotton Kingdom during the Trail of Tears. Destroying tracts of land and then moving west, the extractive capitalism of settlement undermines the ethics of georgic improvement and degrades the labour, skill and local knowledge of the enslaved. Invoking Virginia's tradition of didactic georgic writing, from John Smith to Thomas Jefferson, Olmsted's account of Virginia's self-destructive agricultural practices counters the false narratives of Southern pastoral and georgic adaptations alike, from nostalgic myths of the lost cause, which faulted the Civil War for ruining an Arcadian idyll that never was, to the claims of cultivation used to justify ethnic cleansing and maximize short-term profits, destroying rather than improving stolen land and civic society. I conclude the section with a rare example of georgic poetry, Charles Carter Lee's 'Virginia Georgics' (1858), which represents the state's environmental and economic decline in rhyming couplets. Focusing on the problem of tobacco monoculture by urging white landowners to improve their land rather than abandoning exhausted plantations and moving west, Lee barely acknowledges slavery or the looming war. Georgic functions, in this poem, to exonerate the enslavers. Representing Virginia's dire economic and environmental condition as a general and timeless struggle of farming in the fallen age, the adages of agricultural didacticism obscure historical causes and effects of systematic exploitation in plantation work camps and westward expansion.

Charles Chesnutt, by contrast, holds those who value short-term profits over human life responsible for the environmental ruin of Southern agriculture and the moral failures of its enslavers. In an early short story, 'A Tight Boot', Chesnutt explicitly alludes to Virgil's *Georgics* to counter the claims of Jeffersonian agrarianism, representing white supremacy as the cause of agricultural and economic ruin. Yet Chesnutt's regionalist fiction of North Carolina holds onto the hope of a golden age to come in which Black citizens who own the land they know and work might restore the earth and redeem the nation.

From American Pastoral to American Georgic

Beginning with European contact, American nature writers have drawn on Virgil and his imitators as both inspiration and foil, sometimes merging pastoral and georgic to celebrate the 'New World' as a union of an imagined ideal and a concrete rusticity, sometimes using the distinction to differentiate between nostalgic songs of lovesick herdsmen in idyllic Arcadia and didactic literature connecting farming to the project of moral cultivation. However, most Americanist scholarship uses pastoral to encompass both modes, interpreting pastoral broadly as a celebration of rural settings or nostalgia for rustic life. The designation tends to reflect thematic concerns rather than traditions of genre and convention. Lawrence Buell, for instance, defines pastoral broadly as 'all literature that celebrates an ethos of rurality or nature or wilderness over against an ethos of metropolitanism', a capacious understanding that has expanded the scope of environmental humanities.[17] Scholars of the pastoral mode such as Paul Alpers have pushed back on the 'ungoverned inclusiveness' of the term's usage, citing developments in US ecocriticism and British critical traditions dating back to William Empson's landmark reading of pastoral as 'putting the complex into the simple' in order to represent 'a beautiful relation between rich and poor'.[18] Yet the necessity of a loose definition of the mode in US literary studies stems in part from the historical loosening of generic constraints during the period of American literary emergence, as neoclassical distinctions between pastoral and georgic became blurred to the point of obfuscation.

Recent scholarship, however, shows a tendency to reassert the division between the two Virgilian traditions by reclaiming as georgic some of the environmental writing deemed pastoral by earlier critics. Timothy Sweet's *American Georgics: Economy and Environment in Early American Literature* offers the most comprehensive study to date. Rather than interpreting economic and technological development as a counterforce at odds with the pastoral ideal, Sweet uses the framework of georgic to connect the material and moral aspirations of North American settlement, reading representations of North American land as a 'site of labor' rather than a 'site of leisure', from the sixteenth-century promotions of colonization to the environmental writing of William Cooper and George Perkins Marsh.[19] The economic and environmental projects of settlement and agrarian nationalism are not, as pastoral designations suggestion, a retreat to nature but instead a georgic ideal of civilization grounded in the cultivation of the land. Other critics have revisited canonical works of US nature writing. Henry David Thoreau's *Walden* (1854), for example, is as much a didactic text on small-scale farming as it is an exercise in pastoral retreat, as Michael G. Ziser argues in 'Walden and the Georgic Mode', which reinterprets the fusion of intellectual and agricultural work as an explicitly georgic engagement with concrete environmental experience.[20] Critical interest in farm labour has also opened new avenues for generative analysis of African American georgic. Ian Finseth's book-length study of the role of nature in the development of racial ideologies argues for the prominence of georgic within African American cultural productions because it is 'more realistic, forward looking, and constructive than pastoral'.[21] Margaret Ronda applies a pessimistic reading of Virgil to the representation of racialized labour in Paul Laurence Dunbar's *Lyrics of Lowly Life* (1896), 'foregrounding its georgic strain [to] argue that Dunbar's poetry deemphasizes romantic portrayals of poetic enslavement or resistance in favor of an examination of labour's tragic, nonredemptive nature'.[22] In its emphasis on labour and economics, technology and empire, the georgic mode offers a generative framework for politically engaged studies of the cultural history of US agriculture and its representation.

Yet even as the critical turn to georgic seems to be contending for a more robustly materialist environmental criticism that would immunize the writing under view from the old charge against pastoral as escapist mystification or false consciousness, it is worth remembering that the *Georgics* is no less literary than the *Eclogues*. The 'ideological multivalence' of pastoral, as Buell terms it, applies equally to georgic: both modes have the potential to mystify hardship and injustice and both can describe the complexities of an environment and its rural inhabitants.[23] As I have argued previously, pastoral and georgic adaptations proliferated in the wake of the Civil War as a means of representing sectional and ideological divisions over contested land and racialized labour.[24] The construction of Southern regional identity through pastoral traditions has been well documented, as has the enduring influence of white supremacist fiction on US cultural history.[25] While plantation pastorals perpetuated nostalgia for a blissful idyll of leisure and natural abundance, the mode I identify as the Northern Georgics of Reconstruction represent the improvement of Southern land through a Yankee agenda of industrial progress and education, literalizing the moral didacticism of the mode in the project of Black uplift. John W. De Forest's *Miss Ravenel's Conversion from Secession to Loyalty* (1867) allegorizes reconciliation through the trope of cross-sectional romance, but represents teaching in a Black school as the turning point for the feisty southern belle, who initially resists her father's enthusiasm for implementing a georgic agenda of improved agricultural methods and labour practices on his federally sponsored Louisiana plantation.[26] In *Up From Slavery* (1901), Booker T. Washington represents the Tuskeegee Institute as an implementation of Thoreauvian georgic precepts, appealing to New England donors by connecting the cultivation of the land and the cultivation of his students through manual labour. Condemning the 'craze for Greek and Latin learning' as impractical and shallow, Washington recommends practical training in the fields associated with the georgic tradition.[27] Yet classical georgic literature also served as a touchstone for Black activists on the other side of the education debate, who advocated for equal access to the liberal arts curriculum. Later dubbed 'the Talented Tenth' by W. E. B. Du Bois, the Black elite viewed uplift as a project of self-cultivation through humanistic education, in which agricultural labour serves as a metaphor for literary pursuits, and the dignity of labour applies to the hard work of reading a Latin poem.[28]

A staple of US education, Virgil's texts were not only adapted on sectional lines but also interpreted, I argue, through the motifs of idyllic slavery and Yankee labour. Charles Anthon, a Columbia University classics professor whose textbooks were widely recognized throughout the nineteenth century as the 'standard authority in schools and colleges', maps the stereotype of the loyal retainer used by apologists for slavery on to the figure of Tityrus, imagining him not as a figure for Virgil but as the poet's slave.[29] 'His master, Virgil, goes to Rome, in order to obtain from Augustus the restoration of his lands; and Tityrus subsequently repairs to the same place for the purpose of procuring manumission from the former', Anthon explains, and the manumitted slave is 'filled with as much joy at the restoration of his master's fields as if they really belonged to himself'.[30] Anthon interprets the *Georgics* as a celebration of labour and industry, explaining the succession of the ages described in the first *Georgic* not as degeneration from the golden age but as progress towards empire and agricultural innovation: 'Before the time of Jove there was no cultivation of the fields. With the empire of Jove came in the various arts of civilized life.'[31] Although Virgil's aetiology of labour does suggest that the 'various arts' offer some compensation for the conditions of toil and want that characterize the Age of Jupiter, Anthon's gloss obscures the fundamental pessimism of the original lines: 'tum variae venere artes. labor omnia vicit | improbus, et duris urgens in rebus egestas' ('art followed hard or art. Toil triumphed over every obstacle, unrelenting Toil, and Want that pinches when life is hard').[32] These lines prove central to the celebration of all-conquering labour that characterizes the US reception of *Georgics* in the nineteenth century. Like the ingenuity and work ethic necessitated by New Hampshire's stern climate and stern soil in Webster's speech, hard work and technical skill are virtues born of struggle for Anthon; even 'improbus', an unambiguously negative word meaning 'bad, wicked, or vile', gets a positive spin in his translation – 'persevering industry'.[33] Anthon's notes sound less like Virgil than Emerson: 'I hear therefore with joy whatever is beginning to be said of the dignity and necessity of labour to every citizen', he says approvingly in his address. 'There is virtue yet in the hoe and the spade.'[34] Virgil's representations of loss and labour did not merely serve mainstream narratives' Southern nostalgia or Northern industry. I argue that Chesnutt finds in Virgil nuanced parallels between the histories of Augustan and US land and labour; he alludes to the poetry not only as a mark of cultural capital or a reflection the politics of educational access in the wake of Reconstruction, but also as an intertextual engagement with the enslaved herdsmen of *Eclogues* and the agricultural labour of *Georgics*. Debunking pastoral nostalgia for white leisure and georgic hope for white gain, Chesnutt adapts the cultural memories and mythic lore of rural communities in Virgil's first two poems to represent the experience of the Black labourers whose knowledge and skills shaped and were shaped by the land.

Although the divergence between the pastoral and georgic was used, especially during Reconstruction, to differentiate between the sectional characteristics of the North and the South, both modes converge in national narratives used to legitimize imperial expansion. Aligning Virgilian herdsmen and cultivators with white settlers obscures the resonance not only of slavery but also of displacement and claims to the land. Indeed, both modes facilitated the negation of Indigenous claims to land under the Lockean principles of US Law, erasing Indigenous labour through pastoral representations of a pre-contact golden age of natural abundance, and misrepresenting the land of Tribal Nations as vacant wilderness through georgic promotions of agricultural improvement and imperial progress. Yet Virgil's poems also resonate with counternarratives of nineteenth-century resistance to expansionist policies; Meliboeus's eviction in *Eclogue I* applies far more to the Trail of Tears than to the experiences of the white Southern enslavers who, occupying stolen lands, represented their nostalgia for antebellum leisure through pastoral analogies. Writing on the experience of exile, Vine Deloria Jr argues that no other group 'appears more deserving or representative of this status than North American Indians', given the history of forced removal from ancestral lands. The destruction of ceremonial life, he argues, leaves the exile 'thrust into a barren place where he has to abandon his former knowledge of the world'.[35] The epistemological, spiritual and material crisis of displacement in the wake of war is, in fact, the occasion for Virgil's *Eclogues*. Forced to relinquish the land to an 'impius … miles' (irreverent, unrighteous soldier) with no knowledge of the place or its gods, Meliboeus, heartsick, stays one last night with Tityrus, enumerating the pleasures of Arcadia and the suffering of being driven out. He has already lost the hope of his flock – twin goat kids dropped on bare flint during the migration – and he fears the contagious diseases and harmful vegetation he will not know to avoid in an unfamiliar land.[36] Worse than the loss of land is the loss of culture and community that results from war and displacement. In *Eclogues* IX, Lycidas and Moeris seek solace in old songs as they sit beneath trees marred by the fighting, but they falter, unable to remember the lyrics of the masterful singer Menalcas.[37] However, Virgil's project is not merely elegiac; the herdsmen sing new songs, and Meliboeus uses his lament to protest the conditions of exile and plan for his survival through adaptation, grafting his pear trees to grow in a new land. Although Arnold Krupat cautions against applying European genre categories to non-European literatures or seeking 'to find anything like a Pan-Indian uniformity of expressive response to death and loss', his analysis of diverse expressions of mourning, consolation and the continuation of the community in the face of loss suggests a wide range of potential avenues for comparative readings.[38] Long associated with the shallow Arcadian nostalgia of white supremacy and conquest, the pastoral mode resonates powerfully within counternarratives of collectivity, orality and resistance.

Georgic also cuts both ways: used as a premise for federal violence and political injustice to this day, the association of cultivation with moral virtue actually undermines the civilizational hierarchies of white supremacy asserted through agricultural representation. The practices of extractive capitalism destroyed land settled by US citizens. Rather than incentivizing the improvement of existing land through diversified agriculture, expansion rewarded a practice of exhausting the land, using up natural resources and then moving west to repeat the process. As James D. Rice observes, the narrative of European settlement in North America applies 'to much of the Americas across several centuries', a familiar story of 'the interplay of epidemics, the Columbian Exchange more broadly, and European colonialism in the conquest of Indigenous America; the transformative environmental effects of fire suppression, monoculture, and the imposition of a European-style "world of fields and fences,"' in William Cronon's evocative phrase.[39] Studies of the diverse agricultural practices of Tribal Nations, by contrast, show 'a mostly sustainable seasonal round of gathering, hunting, fishing, and cultivating domesticated plants and a complex set of commonly understood use rights to those resources'.[40] Despite ample documentation of the long history of Indigenous farming, however, the logic of nineteenth-century 'removal' (a sanitized term for the US's sustained programme of ethnic cleansing and land theft) is grounded in the imaginative traditions of georgic literature rather than the facts of American environmental history. As the Cherokee lawyer and playwright Mary Kathryn Nagle argues, the 'laws that eradicated tribal sovereignty, commodified Indigenous lands, and dehumanized Indigenous peoples' are premised on the contrast between white cultivation and the '"uncivilized" refusal to commercially exploit and abuse the land we live on'.[41] Citing the Supreme Court's 1823 decision in Johnson v. M'Intosh, Nagle argues that false narratives about farming as the basis of civilizational hierarchies shape the law to this day:

> In 1823, at a time when non-Indian corporate and colonial interests were demanding access to and ownership of tribal lands, the Johnson Court reasoned that '[c]onquest gives a title [to the Conqueror] which the Courts of the conqueror cannot deny', a claim now known as the Doctrine of Discovery. According to the Court in Johnson, Tribal Nations could not be left 'in possession of their country' because they were 'fierce savages whose occupation was war, and whose subsistence was drawn chiefly from the forest.' As a result, '[t]o leave them in possession of their country, was to leave the country a wilderness' ... *Johnson* has never been overturned, nor reversed.[42]

Ruling against the heirs of Thomas Johnson, a British citizen who had purchased land directly from the Piankeshaw, the Marshall Court granted the federal government exclusive rights to the conveyance of native land, eradicating the rights promised by treaties and written into the Constitution by appealing to a false narrative of white progress: 'As the white population advanced, that of the Indians necessarily receded. The country in the immediate neighbourhood of agriculturists became unfit for them. The game fled into thicker and more unbroken forests, and the Indians followed.'[43] Aligning agriculture with virtue, the essentializing claims of the Johnson court leverage the myths of Roman ethnography and literature to legitimize as inevitable a history of genocide and expansion.[44] The assumption that hunting is the economic basis of all Indigenous societies erases not only the distinctions among Tribal Nations but also the historical changes caused by the colonial fur trade, using an activity promoted and expanded by the incentives of European markets as evidence of unassimilability and unfitness for modern life. Moreover, Johnson v. M'Intosh inadvertently records the very history of Indigenous land use and improvement it seeks to erase. A minor passage in the text of the decision, for example, includes original place names to describe property conferred by one of the contested deeds. The history of Crab Tree Plains, Garlic Creek, Foggy Spring and Salt Lick Creek attest to the complex systems of forestry, wetland horticulture, water management and meat preservation long practised in the land mendaciously represented as unimproved wilderness.[45]

Whereas the Marshall Court's decision exposes the influence of georgic fiction over US legal history to this day, Cherokee responses to these civilizational hierarchies use georgic ideology to refute white supremacist claims. As Sweet argues, Cherokee speakers and writers used georgic rhetoric to protest the intensification of the US programme of ethnic cleansing during the 'Removal era'.[46] The 'Note' introducing the Cherokee Memorials to Congress deploys a georgic representation of Cherokee society to condemn proposed violations of tribal sovereignty as a destruction of 'the comforts and advantages of civilization' and the 'preservation and advancement in moral and civil improvement' on 'ancient territory' where they aim 'to pursue agriculture, and to educate their sons and daughters in the sciences and knowledge of things which pertain to their future happiness'.[47] Representing the Cherokee as a nation of farmers devoted to moral, civil and educational improvement won widespread support by appealing to white georgic ideologies, Sweet argues:

Whereas in the eighteenth century the Cherokees had explained themselves to whites using the image of the hunter, to argue against the land cessions that would disable the hunting activities that had become so economically useful to whites, in the nineteenth century, spokesmen such as Elias Boudinot, John Ridge, and David Brown presented the Cherokees as good farmers, again in hopes of holding onto the nation's land. This picture of Cherokee agrarianism affronted the white Georgians, who found it easier to argue for the removal of transient hunter-savages than of sedentary farmers.[48]

Nineteenth-century Cherokee agrarianism appealed to white concepts of domesticity, as dispersed family farming replaced the collective labour of Cherokee towns depopulated by wars and epidemics.[49] Viewed as a necessity in dealings with duplicitous traders, English-language education proved a valuable tool of protest, winning white support, and leaving a rich record of resistance in the newspaper the *Cherokee Phoenix* (1828–34), and the speeches, petitions and court cases brought in response to the crisis, but to little avail. The Removal Act passed by a narrow vote in 1830, authorizing President Andrew Jackson to claim prime cotton-land for the slavocracy under the guise of treaty negotiations with the Cherokee, Chickasaw, Choctaw, Seminole and Creek, as well as Quapaws and Caddoes. Forced to present-day Oklahoma by federal troops, the Cherokee lost over a quarter of their population on the Trail of Tears. Nor was 'Indian Territory' safe from imperialist incursion. In 1893, the year the government opened the Cherokee strip to settlement by land run, the editor of the *Oklahoma Farmer* proposed what would become the official state seal with a motto adapted from Virgil's *Georgics*: 'Labor Omnia Vincit' (labour conquers all).[50] With a simple tense change, the motto turns a description of hardship and necessity in the fallen age into a slogan for the power of hard work, representing the spoils of conquest as the just deserts of American meritocracy.

The End of the Rope: Virginia Georgics

In an 1828 letter to one of the sponsors of the Brainerd Mission, Nancy Reece, a Cherokee student, describes a conversation about forced displacement with younger children: 'if the white people want more land let them go back to the country they came from'; another says 'they have got more land than they use, what do they want to get ours for?'[51] There are many answers to this question, as Claudio Saunt argues, but the fundamental goal of the state-sponsored expulsion of 80,000 indigenous people was to expand US cotton production into the expropriated land and consolidate the power of Southern enslavers; the lands stolen by the federal government in the 'decade of deportation furnished nearly 160 million pounds of ginned cotton in 1850, equal to 16 per cent of the entire crop in the United States'.[52] In *The Cotton Kingdom: A Traveller's Observations on Cotton and Slavery in the American Slave States* (1861), Frederick Law Olmsted represents the Cotton Kingdom as an inversion of georgic cultivation, progress and industry, countering the narrative used to justify the Trail of Tears. His introduction, a chapter on 'The Present Crisis', argues that cotton has destroyed the agricultural productivity and self-sufficiency of the region, concentrated wealth in the hands of elite enslavers, undermined social ties and civic improvements, and expanded slavery, corroding the dignity of labour and the morality of white citizens.[53] Published shortly after the outbreak of the Civil War, *Cotton Kingdom* undermines the claims of plantation pastoral and Jacksonian georgic by depicting Southern agricultural and economic degeneration. The only evidence of wealth in a region destroyed by short-sighted cultivation and corrupted by greed, Olmsted shows, is the rising cost of the people enslavers claim as property.

Olmsted started researching the topic in 1852 as a special correspondent for the *New York Daily Times*. Publishing under the pseudonym 'Yeoman', his dispatches from the slave states became the basis of the three volumes he combined in *Cotton Kingdom*. He devotes nearly a quarter of the first volume, *A Journey in the Seaboard Slave States* (1856), to Virginia, contrasting its catastrophic situation not only with Yankee georgic ideals but also with the agrarian aspirations of Virginia's own georgic tradition, from John Smith's *Generall Historie* (1624) to Robert Beverley's *History and Present State of Virginia* (1705) to Jefferson's *The Notes on the State of Virginia* (1785). Immunizing himself against allegations of sectional bias, Olmsted cites warnings against the excesses of tobacco monoculture dating back to the first generation of Virginia colonists. Smith deplores the social disruption caused by the cultivation of the commodity, which encourages dispersed settlement and greed for short-term gain. Beverley documents the economic instability caused by price fluctuations for a staple crop, and advocates diversified production inspired by the 'georgic revolution' in England, criticizing, as Sweet argues, 'the settler culture's economy while proposing that proper management would sustain a well-ordered commonwealth'.[54] The decimation of the soil by the cash crop was well documented by the time Jefferson inveighed against its 'infinite wretchedness', and advocated replacing tobacco with wheat cultivation. Quoting directly from the state's homegrown tradition of instructive agricultural writing underscores the folly and greed of the enslavers Olmsted faults for extending tobacco monoculture west: 'As their exhausted fields failed to meet the prodigal drafts of their luxury, they only made further clearings in the forest, and "threw out," to use their own phrase, so much of the land as they had ruined. Year after year the process continued.'[55] Olmsted's description of extractive capitalism counters earlier georgic narratives of settlement and expansion. Instead of restoring existing farms or investing in civic life, white enslavers exhaust the land and the labourers they claim to own before pushing west to repeat the process of destruction.

Worse than the greed that ruins Southern land is the degradation of labour that ruins Southern society. Olmsted traces the indolence of the 'planting aristocracy' back to Smith's complaint that most of the gentlemen who immigrated on the first ships to Jamestown had never 'done a real day's work in their lives, before they left England'.[56] This vice is amplified, Olmsted argues, by the advent of slavery, 'the same year that the first cheerful labour by the voluntary immigrants to New England, by the May-Flower, was applied to the sterile soil of Massachusetts Bay'.[57] Grounding the value of cultivation not in the fertility of the soil but in the compensatory virtues of labour and ingenuity born of necessity, Olmsted echoes Webster's praise of the northeast's poor tillage as a source of moral improvement. Conversely, Virginia's natural abundance amplifies the greed and short-sightedness of its cultivation. Olmsted quotes in full Beverley's concluding paragraph, which appeals to georgic ideals to urge Virginians to reform:

> They depend upon the Liberality of Nature, without endeavoring to improve its Gifts by Art or Industry. They sponge upon the Blessings of a warm Sun and a fruitful Soil, and almost grutch [sic] the Pains of gathering in the Bounties of the Earth. I should be ashamed to publish this slothful Indolence of my Countrymen, but, that I hope it will some time or other rouse them out of their Lethargy, and excite them to make the most of all these happy Advantages which Nature has given them; and if it does this, I am sure they will have the Goodness to forgive me.[58]

Unpressured by want or necessity, Beverley's countrymen have no reason to labour for improvement, or to practise compensatory Art and Industry. Olmsted applies Beverley's anxiety about the indolence borne of excess to the problem of westward expansion; rather than learning the hard lesson of Jovian cultivation through the loss of a golden age, the enslavers responsible for the loss have access to an abundance of land that encourages further waste and degradation. The laws, Olmsted writes, have 'given free range, over millions of fertile acres, to essentially the same institutions of society which produced, and which still, spite of every advantageous surrounding, are still maintaining, in Virginia, that paralysis of enterprise and imbecility of industry, thus pathetically deplored a hundred and fifty years ago'.[59] Unlike Beverley, who speaks out despite the shame he feels for his countrymen, the Southerners Olmsted meets stay silent 'for the shame of publishing to the North the irreformable improvidence of the people'.[60] Even Beverley's tone of didactic candour proves unsustainable in the face of escalating sectional conflict, leaving Virginia devoid of georgic guidance as well as georgic virtues.

Olmsted's account of Virginia engages most extensively with the hypocrisy and fraudulence of Jeffersonian agrarianism. Instead of the nation of virtuous farmers envisioned in Jefferson's *The Notes on the State of Virginia*, the enslavers Olmsted encounters conceal the 'increasing poverty of the country under the ostentatious hospitality and pompous airs of the aristocracy'.[61] The profligate and lazy enslavers do not look 'to their own soil and industry' for subsistence, but depend on the people they claim to own for dwindling profits they waste on imported luxuries, sinking deeper into debt with every generation:[62]

> The sale of negroes, from time to time, to traders, who are now beginning to ship them off in considerable number, to the cotton plantations of the Southern Slave States, satisfies the most pressing demands for a few years, but only makes the ultimate catastrophe more accumulative and overwhelming. The end of the rope is finally reached, and the worn out and used up old plantations are going a begging for purchasers ... The iniquity of aristocracy is visited upon the children and upon the children's children.[63]

Olmsted introduces the passage with a quotation from Query XVIII of *The Notes on the State of Virginia* in which Jefferson ineffectually expresses his qualms about slavery's effect on the enslavers, 'nursed, educated, and daily exercised in tyranny'.[64] Jefferson fears that the moral corruption and indolence will be imitated by subsequent generations, perpetuating tyranny, the vice deplored by revolution. Invoking the language of aristocracy at odds with democratic citizenship, Olmsted shows that the situation is worse than Jefferson admits. Tyrants in their cruelty and aristocrats in their tastes, Virginia's enslavers fail their farms and abuse their labourers, widening the wealth gap and rendering even the land itself a beggar.

Moreover, Olmsted shows that Jefferson's agrarian ideal was always a sham. Even before tobacco monoculture exhausted the soil, Virginia's economy depended on capital and slavery rather than the cultivation and labour of the georgic ideal to generate wealth: 'The income from the land and labour became constantly smaller; not because of the substitution of grain for tobacco, but because of the gradual but constant deterioration of the soil, which that substitution marked.'⁶⁵ He explains his terminology with a scathing indictment of the fraudulence of Jeffersonian agrarianism:

> I use the awkward term, 'income from property in land and labor', instead of the simple one, 'profits of agriculture', because there never had yet been any legitimate profit of agriculture, in Virginia. From the beginning the planting aristocracy had merely been living on its capital; the whole labor of the country had been, and still, at the Revolution, continued to be engaged in nothing else but transmuting the soil of the country into tobacco—which was sent to England to purchase luxuries for its masters—and into bread for the bare support of its inhabitants, without making any return.⁶⁶

Virginia's plantation work camps not only fail to produce Jeffersonian virtues, but also fail to produce agricultural profits, undermining the democratic goals of revolution to support the greed of tyrannical enslavers.

I conclude this section on Virginia's tradition of agricultural representation by turning from the georgic ideologies expressed in prose writings to Charles Carter Lee's 'Virginia Georgics', a belated example of georgic poetry by the brother of the Confederate General Robert E. Lee. Although most scholarship on US georgic has focused on themes of agricultural and economic progress, celebrations of civic virtue and hard work, and practical guidance for cultivation, the formal conventions of georgic also shaped eighteenth-century US poetic traditions. Connecticut Wits such as Timothy Dwight and David Humphreys continued the tradition of revolutionary georgic inaugurated by Philip Freneau's 'The Rising Glory of America' (1772) to instil in citizens of the Young Republic the moral, religious and civic virtue of the idealized cultivator: 'The figure of the farmer in Virgil's *Georgics*, the exemplar of Roman virtue who must constantly stave off (if not quite "redress") the degenerative forces of both physical and human nature, is invoked throughout the poem as a paradigm for the American's struggle against corruption and social decay as he labours for the expansion of a United States Empire.'⁶⁷ Instructive georgic representations of individual crops in South Carolina, Charles Woodmason's fragmentary 'Indico' (1758) and George Ogilvie's account of rice production in *Carolina, or the Planter* (written in 1776 but published in 1790 in England, where he moved after the confiscation of his lands during the Revolutionary War, in 1790) adapt James Grainger's West Indian georgic, *The Sugar-Cane* (1764).⁶⁸ Written on the eve of succession, 'Virginia Georgics' seems both too late for the conventions of georgic imitation, long out of vogue by the mid-nineteenth century, and too early for the political work of georgic ideology, rebuilding unity and cultivation from the ruins of Civil War. 'In hindsight', Juan Christian Pellicer notes, 'the historical moment of 'Virginia Georgics' seems remarkably inauspicious for writing georgic'.[69] Yet the belatedness of its formal conventions is just one of several means through which the poem resists the chronological realities it claims to address.

Ostensibly, the poem engages georgic primarily as a didactic project. The four books detailing the proper care of soil, crops, livestock and garden offer practical guidance, extensively cited and footnoted, to reverse the environmental destruction of tobacco monoculture through progressive farming. Lee concurs in his account of the state's self-destruction with Olmsted on most points. Both fault extractive greed for ruining once-fertile land, worry that expansion disincentivizes environmental improvement, and offer practical advice to restore the golden age Lee idealizes in representations of pre-contact Virginia. However, Lee sees labour as the problem rather than the solution, inverting Virgil's aetiology by representing excessive 'toil' as the cause rather than the effect of a lost golden age:

> This new-world desolation was the toil
> Of labouring thousands withering out their soil—
> Of its most precious life-blood made to bleed
> To furnish distant nations with a weed,
> Which they would take in snuff—and laugh and joke
> And puff Virginia's life away in smoke …
> Then what we have to do is, if we can,
> To make the soil such as 'twas given to man.[70]

The compensation of art and learning also worsen the situation: 'Then Agricultural Societies grew, | And spoke and published what they thought they knew.' Indeed, the virtues of the *Georgics* function, in the extractive capitalism of Virginia, as forces of destruction rather than sources of improvement:

> The more his skill, the worse his labours end
> For as with greater art the plough is sped,
> The more the yield, and more the land is dead.

'Virginia Georgics' represents not the futility of labour but the threat posed by its capacity to exhausting resources too efficiently.

Throughout the poem, Lee credits his addressees for the work and agricultural skills they steal from the people they enslave: 'Let's recollect though from our sweat we eat, | The very labour makes the bread more sweet.' In this, he echoes Virgil, who decorously omits slavery from the *Georgics*, and refers to labourers euphemistically as 'socii' (companions), departing from other didactic agricultural writing.[71] The rare glimpses of slavery in the poem are nevertheless telling. After lamenting the loss of white families forced to abandon ruined farms and move west, he represents the people sold to prop up the declining fortunes of short-sighted enslavers as sorrowing for their beloved home state rather than for their loved ones:

> The very negroes have their laugh subdued—
> How gay it rung along James river's flood,
> And Rappahannock's, and the river of swans!
> You'd think 'the Quarters' bred flocks of black ones,
> So merrily their voices ring and chime!
> But exiled to that far and feverish clime,
> If one a joyous song should sing therein, he
> Would sing 'O, Carry me back to Old Virginny.'

The use of the passive voice, the curious syntax, and the layers of perception and misperception obscure not only the experience of communities held in slavery, but also the responsibility of the enslavers who 'subdued' and 'bred' families they claimed as property. Applying, in his use of 'very', a racial hierarchy of emotional sensitivity, the speaker imagines the suffering of 'exile' from the favourable clime of Virginia through the memories and beliefs of a white enslaver, who speculates about the experience of 'one' who might sing nostalgically about 'Old Virginny'. The unnamed 'one', an individual reduced to a numerical reference, echoes the dehumanizing description of Black children as 'flocks of black ones', using animal imagery that recurs in the poem's advice on rations:

> Another positive rule, alike of sense,
> And what is better still, benevolence …
> Is to keep fat, and to the utmost fed,
> Whatever on your farm is worked or bred.
> There is no maxim in economy's store
> Than this more precious—Nothing pays that's poor.
> When one condemns whate'er any one meets here,
> He does it in these words—'It's a poor creature!' …
> Poor creatures make poor farmers, these poor stock,
> And all poor lands, a miserable flock.

The language of 'benevolence' implies that this rule applies to humans claimed as property, exposing the chilling logic of enslavers who claim people as property to be 'worked or bred'. The application of the same rule to 'stock' and 'flock' as to Black people on a plantation work camp attests to dehumanizing practices of slavery, as does the application of the same depersonalizing terminology, such as 'whatever' and 'creature'. Yet the invocation of georgic didacticism represents the systemic conflation of human and animal life through the language of wisdom literature. Read as a maxim, the passage uses impersonal voice and general terminology which function not to mask but to transcend the particulars of chattel slavery.

Indeed, Lee uses the form of the adage throughout the poem to obscure the cause and effect of the sectional, agricultural and economic crises he details, as well as the humanitarian crisis he fails to acknowledge. Representing worsening calamities as timeless and universal struggles, 'Virginia Georgics' uses belatedness as a kind of wishful thinking; it is too late to reverse the ruin of tobacco monoculture, stop westward expansion, or compete with products brought by rail from industrial stockyards and granaries, just as it is too late to write a georgic poem. Yet, by offering solutions for problems that can no longer be solved, Lee indulges in a fantasy of escape from the historical reckoning he knows will come.

The Threshing Floor

The reckoning promised by reconstruction, however, is still to come, as Charles Chesnutt shows in his regional fiction of Patesville, a setting based on Fayetteville, North Carolina, where the author spent his formative years. Surrounded by long leaf pine forests and connected to Atlantic shipping routes by the Cape Fear River, Fayetteville became the inland hub of North Carolina's naval stores trade in the mid-nineteenth century, but the profits were short-lived. The decimation of the region's 'turpentine orchards' by extensive boxing left remaining trees vulnerable to insects and fire and destroyed the region's economy, pushing the industry south and costing North Carolina its dominance over the business. While wealthy investors cashed out, selling off used-up land and relocating to new tracts of forest in South Carolina, Georgia and Alabama, families such as Chesnutt's were left behind, struggling to rebuild what large producers had destroyed. The economic woes of the region, compounded by a generous policy of store credit, cost Chesnutt's father his grocery store business and left the family entirely dependent on a small farm with poor soil that 'required the most arduous toil to raise any kind of crop upon it'.[72]

Recent Chesnutt scholarship has illuminated the politics of both his classicism and his environmental representation, including his insightful critique of extractive capitalism in North Carolina's turpentine industry, strands that merge in his nuanced adaptations of Virgilian georgic.[73] Indeed, Chesnutt's commitment to post-war education, recorded in the journals he kept as a young man and well documented by scholars and biographers, was shaped by his experiences of agricultural labour in the region, and the historical injustice that forced Black farmers onto land exhausted by the greed of enslavers and industrial capitalists before and after the war. Chesnutt had to leave school at fourteen when his father's grocery store failed, working as an assistant teacher in town and, in the summers, leading classes for the children of rural sharecroppers in the region. His journals describe both agricultural and intellectual labour; he mentions Virgil more than any other classical author, reading his poetry at night after a day of teaching and farm chores, and copying out full passages of the *Aeneid* to memorize because he fears that he does not 'fully appreciate their beauties'.[74] 'I do not think that I will ever forget my Latin', he writes at the age of twenty: 'The labor I spend in trying to understand it thoroughly, and the patience which I am compelled to exercise in clearing up the doubtful or difficult points, furnishes[,] it seems to me, as severe a course of mental discipline as a college course would afford.'[75] Virgil functions not only as a substitute for elite education but also as a rich intertext for Chesnutt's fictions of contested labour and land. Representing the Black experience excluded from the celebratory tradition of American georgic, Chesnutt reveals the resonance of Virgilian difficulty and doubt in North Carolina.

Chesnutt's second story syndicated by S. S. McClure, 'A Tight Boot' (1886), centres on the misadventures of Bob, a bootblack at the Jefferson House, a rustic North Carolina hotel patronized not by virtuous farmers, as the name connotes, but by indolent enslavers with luxurious tastes. Rather than shining the shoes of an overnight guest as he should, Bob wears them to 'a colored dance at a cabin a mile from the hotel', violating the rules of the Jefferson House and the laws of the state forbidding an 'assemblage of slaves'.[76] Unable to remove the boots from his swollen feet the next morning, Bob incurs the wrath of the hotel owner in a scene infused with minstrel humour and slapstick violence. Yet the seemingly simple comic vignette begins with a description of the hotel's backyard that merges allusions to both *Notes on the State of Virginia* and the *Georgics* to represent the economic and moral truths of slavery behind the false agrarian ideals of a literal Jeffersonian facade.

In Query XIX, Jefferson explains why industrial self-sufficiency, the central principle of European political economy, should be sacrificed to preserve the morality of the virtuous republic he envisions. The costs of importing 'articles either of necessity, comfort, or luxury, which we cannot raise', will 'be made up in happiness and permanence of government' by preserving an ideal nation of farmers from the degeneracy of business, swayed by the 'casualties and caprice of customers. Dependence begets subservience and venality, suffocates the germ of virtue, and prepares fit tools for the designs of ambition.'[77] Although the up-country farmers who stop at the Jefferson House exchange crops for manufactures in accordance with this ideal, bringing cotton and tobacco to town and returning with 'money, and supplies of sugar, coffee, calico, and other luxuries which were not produced on their plantations', they exemplify the corruption Jefferson associates with manufacture. Chesnutt portrays all the hotel's white patrons as the dependent enslavers they are, capricious customers who laze in hammocks on the piazza, waited on hand and foot by Black men and women forced into the 'subservient' roles Jefferson ostensibly deplores.[78] Nor are the farmers 'a very large business' for the hotel. Instead, the busy 'season' is 'Court week', when judges, lawyers and county dignitaries 'came in from their plantations to attend Court'. Instead of representing justice, however, the County Court enforces laws used to claim people as property, explaining the presence of another type of hotel guest: 'the occasional "speculator", or dealer in human flesh, would come along through the country, picking up choice wares for the remote Southern market'. Revealing what lies behind the pastoral facade of 'broad piazzas' and the 'pleasant shade' of big elms 'fronting on the Court House square', Chesnutt ends his account not with a symbol of idyllic leisure or civic virtue but with a barren plot of land that ostensibly separates the enslavers and the enslaved: 'Back of the house, and separated from it by the clean-swept yard, stood the big red kitchen. The yard was perfectly innocent of grass or herbage of any kind ... and by constant trampling was as hard and white as an ancient threshing floor.'[79] On the simplest level, the simile compares the compacted soil of the barren yard, packed down as a by-product of the toing and froing of workers who minister to the hotel guests, to the deliberately flattened surface of the space used to thresh grain after a harvest. Like Virgil's epic similes, however, the comparison proves more complex than it might seem, especially in its repetition of two odd words alluding to *Notes on the State of Virginia*: 'herbage' and 'trampling.'

Advocating wheat as an alternative to tobacco, Jefferson deviates from the instructional tone detailing threshing practices and weevil prevention to praise through personification the benefits of a crop capable of 'cloathing the earth with herbage, and preserving its fertility'.[80] The yard in 'A Tight Boot' inverts Jefferson's metaphor on both fronts: the yard is naked and barren rather than fertile and clothed. Although innocent nudity connotes a prelapsarian state, the yard has no Edenic abundance; indeed, unlike the threshing floors Jefferson hoped Virginia would fill with grain, the yard is not barren by design but as a by-product of heavy traffic between the hotel and the kitchen, where Black men and women sleep. Alluding to the history of rape behind both Jefferson and the Jefferson House, the 'trampling' through which the yard is denuded of herbage literalizes the oppression described in Query XVIII:

> The whole commerce between master and slave is a perpetual exercise of the most boisterous passions, the most unremitting despotism on the one part, and degrading submissions on the other … with what execration should the statesman be loaded, who permitting one half of the citizens thus to trample on the other, transforms those into despots, and these into enemies, destroys the morals of the one part, and the amor patriae of the other … I tremble for my country when I reflect that God is just: that his justice cannot sleep for ever.[81]

Like Olmsted, Chesnutt invokes Jefferson's fear of despotism among enslavers to represent a situation far worse than he fears. Justice has departed from the earth, as Virgil describes at the end of the second *Georgic*, leaving her last footprints with the country farmers, not as vestiges of a golden age but as testimony to the history of rape, violence and exploitation that prepares the ground for a reckoning still to come. The Court House square and the leisurely idyll of the elm-shaded piazzas conceal the true symbol of Virginia's moral, environmental and economic ruin: a barren yard devoted to a fiction of racial segregation, harvesting nothing.

Describing the floor as 'ancient' not only connotes the biblical justice of threshing, but also the Virgilian threshing floor in the first *Georgic*. The maxim instructing the farmer to level the ground is brief, followed by a long digression on what can go wrong, from weeds and cracks in the floor to the 'variae … pestes' (various pests) that will consume the crop and render the farmer's labour futile.[82] As Richard Thomas argues, the passage 'inverts the focus' of conventions of agricultural didacticism adapted from Cato and Varro, devoting seven lines to the mouse, mole, toad, weevil and ant, but little attention to the threshing floor's construction and none to the primary problem of moisture. Virgil uses the creatures to 'represent rather the forces which attack man's work in the age of Jupiter, for the words "tum variae inludunt pestes" (181) clearly recall the statement 35 lines earlier, describing the advent after Saturn's departure of the phenomena associated with labor'.[83] The ancient threshing floor, hard and white, alludes both to Virgil's advice on the grain harvest and to the lines most frequently misinterpreted by Chesnutt's contemporaries: 'tum variae venere artes. labor omnia vicit | improbus, et duris urgens in rebus egestas' ('art followed hard or art. Toil triumphed over every obstacle, unrelenting Toil, and Want that pinches when life is hard').[84] The threshing floor underscores the inadequacies of even the most skilful labour in a fallen age, and reminds the attentive reader of the struggle omitted from laudatory nineteenth-century US georgics.

Chesnutt's subsequent writing fills in these gaps, advocating for the Black citizens who know and work the land in wide-ranging representations of agricultural history and economic injustice. Yet even in his unflinching depictions of a failed reconstruction, Chesnutt envisions an alternative to white supremacist systems through the image of a golden age of racial equality. Chesnutt concludes his second collection of short stories, *The Wife of His Youth, and Other Stories of the Color Line* (1899), with a seeming non-sequitur. In 'The Web of Circumstance', a hardworking blacksmith is falsely accused of stealing a costly whip and serves five years of court-ordered slavery, 'unrequited toil, and unspeakable hardship in convict camp'. Once an exemplar of uplift, the blacksmith returns to find that his wife is dead, his son has been lynched, and a white man now holds their property. He is murdered by the man responsible for the family's suffering, falling dead at the feet of an angelic white toddler who had offered aid. Vacillating between deterministic exposé of convict labour and domestic sentimentalism, the story ends with hope for a golden age still to come, a counterfactual alternative to the grim truths of the short stories in the collection:

> Some time, we are told, when the cycle of years has rolled around, there is to be another golden age, when all men will dwell together in love and harmony, and when peace and righteousness shall prevail for a thousand years. God speed the day, and let not the shining thread of hope become so enmeshed in the web of circumstance that we lose sight of it; but give us here and there, and now and then, some little foretaste of this golden age, that we may the more patiently and hopefully await its coming!

The golden age he longs for is not a pastoral idyll or a fiction of abundance but an ideal of citizenship, equality and justice promised by a failed Reconstruction. Contrasting the realities of the present with hope for a future, Chesnutt exhorts his readers to both speed and patience, demanding improvement here and now to await the fulfilment of an unfinished revolution as out of reach as the restoration of the golden age.

Notes

1 D. Webster, 'Opening of the Northern Railroad to Lebanon, N. H.', in *The Writings and Speeches of Daniel Webster*, 18 vols. (Boston: Little, Brown, 1903), vol. IV, p. 116.

2 L. Marx, *The Machine in the Garden: Technology and the Pastoral Ideal in America* (New York: Oxford University Press, 1970), p. 213.
3 Marx, *Machine in the Garden*, p. 3.
4 Webster, 'Opening of the Northern Railroad to Lebanon, N. H'., p. 116.
5 Marx, *Machine in the Garden*, p. 215.
6 W. T. Stead, *The Americanisation of the World; or, The Trend of the Twentieth Century* (London: Mowbray House, 1902), p. 5.
7 F. L. Olmsted, *Public Parks: Being Two Papers Read Before the American Social Science Association in 1870 and 1880, Entitled, Respectively, Public Parks and the Enlargement of Towns and A Consideration of the Justifying Value of a Public Park* (Brookline, MA, 1902), p. 7.
8 See P. Miller, *Nature's Nation* (Cambridge, MA: Harvard University Press, 1967); see also D. H. Lawrence, *Studies in Classic American Literature* (Cambridge, MA: Harvard University Press, 2003); Henry Nash Smith, *Virgin Land: The American West as Symbol and Myth* (Cambridge, MA: Harvard University Press, 1978).
9 F. O. Matthiessen, *American Renaissance: Art and Expression in the Age of Emerson and Whitman* (London: Oxford University Press, 1941); F. J. Turner, *The Frontier in American History* (New York: H. Holt and Company, 1920).
10 R. W. Emerson, 'The American Scholar', in *Nature and Selected Essays*, ed. L. Ziff (New York: Penguin Classics, 2003), pp. 83–106.
11 M. L. McGill, *American Literature and the Culture of Reprinting, 1834–1853* (Philadelphia: University of Pennsylvania Press, 2003). Prior to the passage of the International Copyright Law in 1891, cheap editions of foreign texts easily outcompeted domestic writing, but McGill argues that, rather than hampering the emergence of a national literature, rampant piracy democratized readership and created a mass market for widely circulated fiction and poetry.
12 A. M. Patterson, *Pastoral and Ideology* (Berkeley: University of California Press, 1987), p. 266. She cites 'May-Day' (1829), by the minor poet and humourist Thomas Hood.
13 Patterson, *Pastoral and Ideology*, pp. 269–71.
14 L. Buell, *Emerson* (Cambridge, MA: Harvard University Press, 2003), pp. 110–11.
15 Webster, 'Opening of the Northern Railroad to Lebanon, N. H.', p. 116.
16 Webster, 'Opening of the Northern Railroad to Lebanon, N. H.', p. 115. He quotes four famous lines of the poem:
    Though with those streams it no resemblance hold,
    Whose foam is amber and whose gravel gold,
    Its greater, but less guilty, wealth to explore,
    Search not its bottom, but survey its shore.
17 L. Buell, *The Environmental Imagination: Thoreau, Nature Writing, and the Formation of American Culture* (Cambridge, MA: Harvard University Press, 1995), p. 439 n. 4.
18 P. J. Alpers, *What is Pastoral?* (University of Chicago Press, 1996), p. ix.; W. Empson, *Some Versions of Pastoral* (New York: New Directions Press, 1974), p. 11.

19 T. Sweet, *American Georgics: Economy and Environment in Early American Literature* (Philadelphia: University of Pennsylvania Press, 2001), p. 2.
20 M. G. Ziser, 'Walden and the Georgic Mode', in *More Day to Dawn: Thoreau's Walden for the Twenty-first Century*, ed. S. H. Petrulionis and L. D. Walls (Amherst: University of Massachusetts Press, 2007), pp. 171–88.
21 I. F. Finseth, *Shades of Green: Visions of Nature in the Literature of American Slavery* (Athens: University of Georgia Press, 2009), p. 245.
22 M. Ronda, '"Work and Wait Unwearying": Dunbar's Georgics', *PMLA*, 127 (2012), 863–78, at 864.
23 Buell, *Environmental Imagination*, 36.
24 S. Wagner-McCoy, 'Virgilian Chesnutt: Eclogues of Slavery and Georgics of Reconstruction in the Conjure Tales', *ELH*, 80 (2013), 199–220.
25 Critics have variously read pastoral as the defining characteristic of Southern writing. Jan Bakker uses the pastoral as a way of complicating cavalier romance traditions in antebellum fiction (*Pastoral in Antebellum Southern Romance* (Baton Rouge: Louisiana State University Press, 1989)). Lucinda Hardwick MacKethan locates the heyday of Southern pastoral during Reconstruction when, threatened by the materialism and change of the 'New South,' 'post-Civil War portrayals of the antebellum Arcadia' flourished (*The Dream of Arcady: Place and Time in Southern Literature* (Baton Rouge: Louisiana State University Press, 1980), p. 11). John M. Grammer advances the idea of 'pastoral republicanism' as the 'collective myth of identity' (*Pastoral and Politics in the Old South* (Baton Rouge: Louisiana State University Press, 1996), p. 6).
26 J. W. De Forest, *Miss Ravenel's Conversion from Secession to Loyalty* (1867; New York: Penguin, 2000), p. 227. As Nina Silber argues, 'in treating reunion mainly as an amorous endeavor, this cultural recipe further contributed to the increasingly depoliticized assessment of the Civil War and its aftermath by hiding all political and sectional viewpoints behind the rubric of romance and sentiment' (*The Romance of Reunion: Northerners and the South, 1865–1900* (Chapel Hill: University of North Carolina Press, 1993), p. 110).
27 B. T. Washington, *Up from Slavery: Authoritative Text, Contexts, and Composition History, Criticism*, ed. W. L. Andrews (New York: Norton, 1996), p. 40.
28 W. E. B. Du Bois, *The Souls of Black Folk* (New York: Penguin, 1996), p. 435.
29 'Obituary, Charles Anthon, LL. D.', *New York Times*, 30 July 1867.
30 C. Anthon, 'English Notes, Critical and Explanatory', in *The Eclogues and Georgics of Virgil* (New York: Harper & Brothers, 1850), p. 104.
31 Anthon, *Eclogues and Georgics of Virgil*, p. 238.
32 Virgil, *Georgics* (Fairclough), pp. 108–9 (*Georgics*, I. 145–6).
33 Anthon, *Eclogues and Georgics of Virgil*, p. 238.
34 Emerson, 'American Scholar', pp. 83–106.
35 V. Deloria, Jr, 'Out of Chaos', in *For This Land: Writings on Religion in America* (New York: Routledge, 1998), p. 243.
36 Virgil, *Georgics* (Fairclough), pp. 30–1 (*Eclogues*, I. 70); Virgil uses shepherds to represent the noble landowners whose lands were expropriated (40–39 BCE) by Octavian and Antony as rewards for loyal veterans of the battle of

Philippi. Read as political allegory, the young man (*iuvenum*) who intervenes on Tityrus's behalf is Octavian, who reputedly protected Virgil from the Mantuan confiscations that threatened his family's land.

37 Virgil, *Georgics* (Fairclough), pp. 88–9 (*Eclogues*, IX. 51–5).
38 A. Krupat, '*That the People Might Live*': *Loss and Renewal in Native American Elegy* (Ithaca: Cornell University Press, 2012), p. 3.
39 J. D. Rice, 'Early American Environmental Histories', *The William and Mary Quarterly*, 75 (2018), 401–32, at 402. W. Cronon, *Changes in the Land: Indians, Ecology, and New England* (New York: Hill & Wang, 1983), p. 127.
40 Rice, 'Early American Environmental Histories', p. 401.
41 M. K. Nagle, 'On the Far End of the Trail of Tears', Center for Humans and Nature, 7 October 2020, www.humansandnature.org/on-the-far-end-of-the-trail-of-tears. Accessed 20 January 2021.
42 Nagle, 'On the Far End of the Trail of Tears'.
43 Johnson v. M'Intosh, 21 U. S. (8 Wheat.) 543 (1823), pp. 590–1.
44 See, for example, Z. Tan, 'Subversive Geography in Tacitus' "Germania"', *The Journal of Roman Studies*, 104 (2014), 181–204; C. B. Krebs, '"Imaginary Geography" in Caesar's "Bellum Gallicum"', *The American Journal of Philology*, 127 (2006), 111–36.
45 Johnson v. M'Intosh, pp. 552–3.
46 Sweet, *American Georgics*, pp. 122–52.
47 'Cherokee Memorials', in *Norton Anthology of American Literature*, ed. R. S. Levine, vol. B, 9th ed. (New York: W. W. Norton, 2017), p. 320.
48 Sweet, *American Georgics*, p. 123.
49 K. S. Smith, '"I Look on You … As My Children": Persistence and Change in Cherokee Motherhood, 1750–1835', *The North Carolina Historical Review*, 87 (2010), 403–30, at 412–15.
50 D. Pollio, 'Vergil and American Symbolism', *The Classical Outlook*, 87 (2010), 137–40, at 138.
51 Cited in Smith, '"I Look on You … As My Children,"' p. 424.
52 C. Saunt, *Unworthy Republic: The Dispossession of Native Americans and the Road to Indian Territory* (New York: Norton, 2020), p. 309.
53 F. L. Olmsted, *The Cotton Kingdom; a Traveller's Observations on Cotton and Slavery in the American Slave States. Based upon Three Former Volumes of Journeys and Investigations by the Same Author*, ed. Arthur M. Schlesinger (1861; New York: Knopf, 1953).
54 Sweet, *American Georgics*, pp. 75–6.
55 F. L. Olmsted, *A Journey in the Seaboard Slave States; With Remarks on Their Economy* (New York; London: Dix and Edwards; Sampson Low, Son & Co., 1856), p. 241.
56 Olmsted, *Seaboard Slave States*, pp. 272, 216.
57 Olmsted, *Seaboard Slave States*, p. 219.
58 Olmsted, *Seaboard Slave States*, 249. The quotation differs slightly from the passage in Beverley's text: 'Thus they depend altogether upon the Liberality of Nature, without endeavouring to improve its Gifts, by Art or Industry. They

spunge upon the Blessings of a warm Sun, and a fruitful Soil, and almost grutch the Pains of gathering in the Bounties of the Earth. I should be asham'd to publish this slothful Indolence of my Countrymen, but that I hope it will rouse them out of their Lethargy, and excite them to make the most of all those happy Advantages which Nature has given them; and if it does this, I am sure they will have the Goodness to forgive me'. See R. Beverley, *The History and Present State of Virginia, in Four Parts* (London, 1705), p. 83.

59 Olmsted, *Seaboard Slave States*, p. 249.
60 Olmsted, *Seaboard Slave States*, p. 251.
61 Olmsted, *Seaboard Slave States*, pp. 272–3.
62 T. Jefferson, *Writings*, ed. M. Peterson (New York: Literary Classics of the United States, 1984), p. 290.
63 Olmsted, *Seaboard Slave States*, pp. 273–4.
64 Olmsted, *Seaboard Slave States*, pp. 273–4.
65 Olmsted, *Seaboard Slave States*, p. 272.
66 Olmsted, *Seaboard Slave States*, p. 272.
67 L. Kutchen, 'Timothy Dwight's Anglo-American Georgic: "Greenfield Hill" and the Rise of United States Imperialism', *Studies in the Literary Imagination*, 33 (2000), 109–28, 109.
68 D. S. Shields, 'George Ogilvie's Narrative Poem "Carolina; Or, the Planter"', *The Southern Literary Journal*, 18 (1986) 5–20.
69 J. C. Pellicer, '"I Hear Such Strange Things of the Union's Fate": Charles Carter Lee's "Virginia Georgics"', *Early American Literature*, 42 (2007), 131–55, at 147.
70 C. C. Lee, *Virginia Georgics, Written for the Hole and Corner Club of Powhatan* (Richmond, VA: James Woodhouse and Company, 1858), https://leefamilyarchive.org/papers/books/georgics/01.html.
71 Virgil, *Georgics* (Fairclough), pp. 174–5 (*Georgics*, II. 528); Marcus Porcius Cato in *De Agri Cultura* and Marcus Terentius Varro in *Res Rusticae* include instruction on breeding and keeping slaves.
72 H. Chesnutt, *Charles Waddell Chesnutt: Pioneer of the Color Line* (Chapel Hill, NC: University of North Carolina Press, 1952), p. 8.
73 On Chesnutt and the environment, see M. Kuhn, 'Chesnutt, Turpentine, and the Political Ecology of White Supremacy', *PMLA*, 136 (2021), 39–54; K. Clasen, 'The Geography of Mandy Oxendine and the Emergence of Chesnutt's Environmental Ethos', *The South Carolina Review*, 46 (2014), 55–66; J. Myers, 'Other Nature: Resistance to Ecological Hegemony in Charles W. Chesnutt's "The Conjure Woman"', *African American Review*, 37 (2003), 5–20; on classicism, see J. L. Barnard, 'Ancient History, American Time: Chesnutt's Outsider Classicism and the Present Past', *PMLA*, 129 (2014), 71–86; C. Koy, 'African American Vernacular Latin and Ovidian Figures in Charles Chesnutt's Conjure Stories', *Litteraria Pragensia: Studies in Literature and Culture*, 21 (2011), 50–70.
74 C. W. Chesnutt, *The Journals of Charles W. Chesnutt*, ed. R. Brodhead (Durham, NC: Duke University Press, 1993) p. 90.

75 Chesnutt, *Journals*, p. 92.
76 C. W. Chesnutt, *The Short Fiction of Charles W. Chesnutt*, ed. S. L. Render (Washington D. C.: Howard University Press, 1981) p. 59.
77 Jefferson, *Writings*, pp. 290–1.
78 Jefferson, *Writings*, p. 290.
79 Chesnutt, *Short Fiction*, p. 58.
80 Jefferson, *Writings*, p. 293.
81 Jefferson, *Writings*, pp. 289–90.
82 Virgil, *Georgics* (Fairclough), pp. 110–11 (*Georgics*, I. 181).
83 R. Thomas, 'Prose into Poetry: Tradition and Meaning in Virgil's Georgics', *Harvard Studies in Classical Philology*, 91 (1987), 240–1.
84 Virgil, *Georgics* (Fairclough), pp. 108–9 (*Georgics*, I. 145–6).

CHAPTER 16

Environment and Empire
Georgic through Time

Charlie Kerrigan

In this chapter I would like to take a long view of the georgic tradition in order to suggest that there are meaningful consistencies which extend from its major ancient exemplar, Virgil's *Georgics*, through the eighteenth-century heyday of georgic poetry in English, and into the early twentieth century. Georgic poetry, I will argue, functions as a kind of archive, keeping alive obsolescent forms of agricultural and artisanal knowledge in the face of a rapidly advancing modernity, reminding the reader in the city of life in the country. Furthermore, georgic poetry can be understood in terms of political visibility. The georgic poet is never naïve, and is always looking beyond his or her immediate environment to the world beyond: for every 'here' there is an 'elsewhere', something the georgic poet uses to construct parallel images of self and other through the themes of patriotism, tourism and geography. This politics also extends to the poet's homeland, and it is useful to look around the landscape of georgic poetry and to ask who is seen by the georgic poet, who is not, and to what end. Georgic, that is, constructs an image of the countryside, and by extension the world, in political terms, in ways which make it a persistently modern form.

My argument will centre on three poems which are among the most well-known models in the georgic canon; it should be said that what follows is a necessarily selective treatment, meant to complement the diversity of the georgic mode attested to in preceding chapters. First is Virgil's *Georgics*, the poem written at Naples by an Italian poet at the beginning of the Roman empire (29 BCE). Hesiod is the first georgic poet in the canon, but it was Virgil who became the exemplar for later poets, with his four-book poem about the cultivation of land, the raising of livestock and the care of bees.[1] Second is James Thomson's *The Seasons*, published in increasingly expansive versions between 1726 and 1744, and indebted to Virgil's poem. Thomson – also the author of the words to *Rule Britannia* – yokes the georgic form to a nascent British empire in ways which, as will be seen, are similar to Virgil's own poetic project in the *Georgics*. His poem was one of the most popular in an eighteenth-century vogue for georgic poetry in English.² Third and last there is Vita Sackville-West's *The Land*, published in 1926 and another bestseller, which won the Hawthornden Prize in the year of its publication. Sackville-West's poem brings georgic into the postwar landscape of rural Kent, and is the most recent long-form georgic poem to match sustained Virgilian resonances with enduring popularity.³

I will suggest here that all three poems display similarities in their politics and, in particular, that there is much in Virgil's poem which directly anticipates the politics of the latter two. There is a view of Virgil's *Georgics* in older scholarship which sees it as a straightforward hymn to the countryside under a new political regime (that of Octavian, the future emperor Augustus), one which celebrates the smallholders of Italy.⁴ The identity of Virgil's farmers is never made clear in the poem, so readers have to decide for themselves who precisely is being celebrated in the famous lines which close its second book.⁵ In more recent scholarship, however, it has been argued that the poem's primary addressees are not small farmers at all, but rather the wealthy magnates of Roman Italy, greatly enriched at the time of the poem's publication by a system of slave-run agricultural estates and the Roman annexation of Ptolemaic Egypt (in 30 BCE).⁶ More broadly, the *Georgics* is deeply political at an imperial level, touring the Roman empire (and indeed the Roman known world) and constructing images of foreign peoples and their produce, celebrating the defeat of Octavian's enemies in orientalist terms and, it can be argued, the Roman imperial project. The *Georgics*, as I have argued elsewhere, is not simply a poem of peace.⁷

Viewed in this light, Virgil's poem appears much closer to the georgic poetry which appeared in English throughout the eighteenth century. In those poems, too, there is an interest in travel and geography, in making visible the world and its peoples in support of empire, most egregiously in a poem such as James Grainger's *The Sugar-Cane*, but also in Thomson's *The Seasons*.⁸ On the home front, Thomson's poem celebrates industry as the motor driving national prosperity, but this was a historical process which disenfranchised and immiserated large sections of the population even as it made its landed minority exceedingly wealthy: one could note in comparison the fact that the Italy which Virgil celebrates was a slave economy, enabled and supplied by Rome's increasing dominance of its Mediterranean world, as well as the above-mentioned argument that it also speaks to and for a landed minority.⁹ So while the 'georgic revolution' of individualism, hard work and empire, posited by Anthony Low and elaborated by Karen O'Brien, may have been novel in seventeenth- and eighteenth-century British terms, it had a definite antecedent in Virgil's

Georgics, in which a Roman poet took an earlier literary tradition and politicized it in a radical and patriotic direction.[10]

As we shall see, the politics of Sackville-West's *The Land* recalls its two predecessors, particularly in its themes of patriotism, travel and empire. Sackville-West signed her poem 'Ispahan [Isfahan], 1926', alluding to her travels in Iran in 1926 and 1927 which inform the poem and its imperial politics. *The Land*'s status as a post-war poem is ambivalent in much the same way as Virgil's *Georgics*: it is partly an elegy for what has been lost and a celebration of what survives, but it can also be read in the light of a post-war political settlement which, in the British context no less than the Roman, cloaked much looting and violence with the names of peace and reconstruction. The British empire reached its greatest territorial extent in the aftermath of the First World War, thanks to the assignations of the Versailles conference and the wartime work of British diplomats to ensure the maintenance and expansion of British (alongside French) power in the Middle East; Octavian's regime, meanwhile, was the result of decades of civil war in Roman Italy, and established an autocratic imperial system under the pretence of restoring the Roman Republic.[11] These three representative georgic poems, as I am calling them, thus have more in common politically than is sometimes recognized, and all three can be read usefully and productively in political terms.

Georgic Poetry as Archive

Georgic poetry begins with a love of the world which is its most salient feature; each of the three poems examined here combines, though in different degrees, attention to the details of the natural world with study of human life on the land. More than this, they record marginalized and at times obsolescent forms of knowledge and praxis, again with different emphases, forming what I suggest is a kind of georgic archive. Whether or not Virgil's poem addressed the landowners of Italian estates (there is no way of knowing for certain, and it seems reductive to assume just one kind of reader), it seems clear that the poem's primary audience on its publication was a metropolitan one: alongside its descriptions of nature, the *Georgics* is filled with dense and complex allusions to Greek and Alexandrian literary culture, as well as to elite Roman politics. That audience would not necessarily have been involved in day-to-day agricultural work, and so the poem's celebration of the countryside takes on a belated or oppositional aspect: reminding the reader in the city of the life and work of the countryside, and indeed of the world beyond the metropolis.[12]

In its keen appreciation of vines and fruit trees, the divinity of rivers and, most famously, the lives and care of bees, the *Georgics* represents what Seamus Heaney called 'a sustained, slightly mysterious performance', which, 'taken in parts or as a whole ... says "Glory be to the world"'.[13] To take just a few representative examples of Virgil's characteristic mix of playful curiosity, learned allusion and naturalist lore, there are citron trees from Persia (*Georgics*, II. 126–35), similar in appearance to a laurel tree and used by the Persians, we are told, to treat for asthma and bad breath; the lines are drawn from the Greek poet and philosopher Theophrastus but repurposed to Virgil's own ends.[14] There is an extended passage in book four in which the beekeeper Aristaeus ventures underground to visit his mother Cyrene, a nymph, whose cavernous home is also the source of the world's major rivers, which thunder through the rocks before they travel up into the world.[15] In the first *Georgic*, meanwhile, there is a description of offerings being given by country people to Ceres (goddess of agriculture) and Bacchus (god of wine) as they dance and sing in anticipation of a successful harvest and vintage; a kind of Roman harvest festival.[16]

This poetic appreciation does not need to imply that the *Georgics* was ever intended to be used for practical farming purposes, a question that has long interested readers and scholars of the poem.[17] Nevertheless, its appreciation of nature extends also to the mundane practicalities of life on the land and human subsistence. There are women who weave by winter candlelight, as well as descriptions of irrigation systems, cheese-making and how informed crop rotation increases nitrogen levels (and thus fertility) in the soil.[18] The potential loss of the harvest is a serious matter, as is the collapse and death of a beloved ox whilst in mid-harness.[19] Reading the *Georgics* in an urban, academic, twenty-first-century setting, I was grateful for these windows into real-life and millennia-old practices and perspectives for their implicit recognition of the interconnectedness of human, plant and animal life, a recognition which might be described as oppositional to conventional economic priorities which treat those three spheres as separate and unequal. This applies most strictly in a modern, twenty-first-century sense, but it is not unrealistic to apply it in a more limited sense to the metropolitan readers of ancient Rome, where there equally existed different levels of (dis)connectedness to the land.

In the *Georgics* there are also nihilistic scenes such as the cattle plague which closes the third book, rendering useless the poet's careful instructions for the raising and care of livestock which have occupied that book's first half. There are also several images of deforestation, both executed and threatened: in *Georgics* II and IV there appear ploughmen by turns angry ('iratus') and cruel ('durus') who fell trees and destroy nests in the name of agricultural productivity.[20] Large-scale forest fires are also described, either caused by the heedlessness of shepherds or, more menacingly, threatened by Aristaeus in a moment of impotent and angry confusion: this moment in particular, along with the destruction of the nightingale's nest in *Georgics*, IV. ll. 511–15, seem to say something about the links between environmental, economic and patriarchal violence.[21] The economic motives which destroy the natural world and disenfranchize its human communities are there already in the *Georgics*, that is, published in the booming slave economy of Roman Italy and read primarily by an urban and urbane audience. Deforestation in particular was a key process of imperial power in both the Roman and the British empires. The Roman state of Virgil's day was exploiting the forested hillsides of La Sila in modern Calabria – they appear in Virgil's poem – while the timber needs of the eighteenth-century British empire were supplied in large part by the woods of Ireland, an island which now ranks among the most deforested places in Europe.[22] Georgic in this instance is both elegy and rebuke.

Thomson's *The Seasons* spends far less time than the *Georgics* describing agricultural work practices, and, as in other eighteenth-century georgic poems, the hard edge and nihilism which colour Virgil's poem were jettisoned in favour of its more positive and patriotic moods.[23] While there are scenes here too of citron groves, rivers and harvest, the poem as a whole celebrates a nascent system of agricultural and industrial capitalism: 'All is the gift of Industry'.[24] Where Virgil is ambivalent, Thomson trumpets loudly, though it should be said that we have far more historical context in Thomson's case than in Virgil's. As has been noted by scholars, eighteenth-century georgic poetry aestheticized landscapes at home and abroad in ways which hid the ugliness and violence of Britain's political establishment and its policies. Britain became a green and pleasant land, so too did the islands of the Caribbean, as poetry and prose did the work of normalizing the violence of enclosure and slave-run plantations.[25] Nevertheless, there are moments in *The Seasons* when the elegiac mode comes to the fore. Matching Virgil, in 'Spring' Thomson gives the reader a description of the nightingale's distress at the loss of her nest and chicks (though, tellingly, in 'Autumn', deforestation has lost its negative connotation); there is also the extended harvest scene in 'Summer' and the 'pastoral Queen' who owes something to Perdita in Shakespeare's *The Winter's Tale*.[26] At such moments the reader finds the kind of communal social activity which the policies of the British landed elite were encroaching upon decade by decade; policies which Thomson appears to celebrate elsewhere in his poem.[27]

Georgic, then, is archival not only its in recognition of everyday agricultural practices (gleaning, for instance) and sustainable ways of life, but also in leaving us a record – in Virgil no less than in Thomson – of how those practices and ways of life are marginalized and destroyed. This rings true also in Sackville-West's *The Land*, which devotes more time than either of its two predecessors to describing not just the practices but also the people of the countryside. There are seasonal labourers who journey from London into Kent to pick hops, the thatcher stubbornly proud of his dying craft, as well as – in a moment of social commentary lacking in both Virgil and Thomson – an extended and sympathetic description of a homeless man and his death from exposure.[28] Sackville-West here puts back into georgic the nihilism which is there in Virgil but was largely forgotten in the English tradition. There is in Sackville-West's poem an opposition to modernity – here the post-war modernity of the 1920s – and a elegiac celebration of country practices that are being lost. Her tree-felling scene ('Autumn', pp. 93–4), echoing that in her two predecessors, is sustainable and productive in a way that neither Virgil's nor Thomson's is: every ten years, we are told, the woodman comes and from his felling produces poles, stakes and spiles (a word for a narrow strip of wood) for training hops and making fences. His craft takes place amidst an overall awareness of the ephemerality of both man and wood: 'But man to dust and trees to timber fall' ('Autumn', p. 94).

Georgic Visibility

It is my contention here that the politics of georgic as a literary form can usefully be understood in terms of visibility: who is seen by the georgic poet, who is not, and to what end. We can begin to see how the politics of visibility operates across the three poems under consideration by taking into account those normally excluded from agricultural discourse: women and slaves. Eleanor Scott has written of how women are largely written out of ancient Roman agricultural discourse, in particular the works of Cato the Elder, Varro and Columella, despite the fact that women did work the land in Roman Italy, whether free or unfree, as they have throughout history and still do across the globe.[29] This holds true also for Virgil's *Georgics*, the agricultural cast of which features women only when they are working indoors and managing the household, the productive outdoor life of the farm being an exclusively male sphere.[30] Women as they appear in Thomson's poem are dedicatees and muses, 'ruddy Maid[s]' or racialized 'full-form'd Maids of Afric', but are only rarely shown at work on the farm (see the housewife at the shearing, 'Summer', line 398).³¹ In Sackville-West's cast of characters also there is a preponderance of men, with women again more often objects of desire than productive labourers ('Spring', pp. 45–6, 'Summer', pp. 76–7, 'Autumn', p. 96). The undervaluation and obfuscation of women's work is thus a theme which runs through the georgic tradition, and reminds us that a georgic poem is always an image of the countryside, never the thing itself.

In terms of slaves and their (in)visibility on the farm, it is one of the most controversial points of Virgil's poem that slaves and slave-labour do not appear in its lines, at least explicitly: there are several characters named only by their role (e.g. the ploughman, the pruner) whom the original audience may have assumed were unfree.³² The charge against Virgil here is a charge that, again, could be levelled at the georgic genre as a whole: to what extent does the form prettify and gloss over unjust realities and systems of power? Italy in the *Georgics* is a place of 'eternal spring' and boundless fertility (II. 149–50), exactly the kind of language that the classically educated Edward Long used of Jamaica in his three volume *History* of the island, published in 1774.³³ *The Seasons* alludes several times to the slavery that underpinned the British empire and the Atlantic world in Thomson's day, but any sense of pathos in, for example, the passage detailing the sharks' attack on a stricken slave-ship ('Summer', p. 106, lines 1013–25), is outweighed by his championing of British power in the world and the way he constructs otherness in terms of climate and geography, to be discussed presently. In Sackville-West's *The Land*, the subject is the Kentish Weald and thus a society in which formal slavery was no longer practised. Nevertheless, there are moments in which the language of race and slavery do appear: Asia is a 'dark' place and in the woodman scene discussed earlier the felled tree is likened to 'a naked savage bound in chain'.³⁴

In general terms, then, georgic poetry appears historically as a genre which has privileged a perspective that is free and male; a particular and limited image of the countryside. I would like to move now to explore georgic's relationship to geography, patriotism and tourism; how it uses those three themes to construct images of home and abroad, and of self and other, doing in the process the work of empire. Virgil's *Georgics* brings the world to the reader, naming a range of places from across the known Roman world, from Britain to the Upper Nile and from Spain to the River Ganges. A centripetal dynamic acts to bring people, places and products within the bounds of Roman knowledge and Roman consumers: Chinese silk and Ethiopian cotton, Parthian warriors (from modern Iran) and tattooed Britons, the forests of northern Turkey and the deserts of Algeria and Libya.³⁵

Virgil himself does not adopt the persona of a tourist, rather he imagines himself lying at ease in Naples, composing his poem, while his patron Octavian 'thunders' by the banks of the Euphrates, bringing Roman rule to Syria and the Levant.[36] This juxtaposition reveals the political dynamic which underpins the *Georgics*'s world curiosity: the poem often turns its attention to real and imagined subjects of Roman imperial power, portraying them as either subjects of or threats to that power. There are rebellious Spaniards who threaten Roman colonial farms in the Iberian peninsula, frankincense from the 'soft' Sabaeans of modern Yemen – where the Roman state sent an army in the years following the poem's publication – as well as Indians, described alternately as 'unwarlike', 'thirsty' and 'coloured', a sustained construction of difference in climatic terms which anticipates both Thomson and Sackville-West as well as the early modern creation of the ideology of race.[37]

Within this diverse world, the Italian peninsula is given pride of place. No land on earth can compete with Italy in terms of its temperate climate, fertility and beauty, conditions which gave birth to the hardy and brave Italian peoples who now form the backbone of the Roman state and its world power. So the argument runs in what is the poem's most famous and influential passage, the 'praises of Italy' ('laudes Italiae') at *Georgics*, II, ll. 136–76. This is the part of the poem that British readers in the eighteenth, nineteenth and twentieth centuries prized above others, and this is the part of the poem that was excerpted, expanded and applied to Britain itself in the tradition of georgic poetry. Britain too, the argument went, enjoyed specific climatic conditions which had created a brave and industrious people fit for imperial rule, in contrast to the indolence bred by the oppressive heat of the tropics. Translators from John Dryden onwards consistently introduced the first person plural – not in Virgil's Latin – into their translations of book 2, collapsing the distinction between Italy and Britain. Italy became 'our land' and the poem's orientalist politics were adapted to the British empire: as late as 1940, Cecil Day Lewis's translation has Italy as 'this land of ours' (Virgil has simply 'these places') and the 'conquered cities of Asia' ('urbes Asiae domitas') in the original text become 'the cities of Asia we've mastered'.[38]

Added to this are particular details of Virgil's description of the Italian peninsula which facilitate comparison with the island of Britain, a comparison translators had no trouble in making: hilltop towns (*Georgics*, II, 156–7) became castles, the lakes of Italy (ll. 159–60) recalled the Lake District, while the Tyrrhenian and Adriatic (l. 158) became the Irish and North Seas.[39] The lines which speak of Octavian's naval prowess (ll. 161–4), meanwhile, would perhaps have chimed with late nineteenth- and early twentieth-century British readers' patriotic conceptions of the Royal Navy. In the case of one translator, Charles W. Brodribb (1878–1945), an Oxford Classics graduate who made a career as a journalist with *The Times*, the comparison was more than academic. In 1946 a volume of Brodribb's own poetry was published, and included are two short poems inspired by Virgil and the *Georgics*. 'Among the Lakes' playfully sets England against Italy in a patriotic terms (the lakes of England have 'nought to fear | From Como, Garda, or the Major Lake'), while 'Praises of Wiltshire', written in 1943, adapts the 'laudes Italiae' to an English context: 'But let not the forests of Scotland, harbour of horned deer, | Nor Cornwall's coastline nor green Shakespearean Arden | Muster against Wiltshire's praises'.[40]

For translators of the poem and their readers, then, Italy and Britain, their climates and their political prowess, were closely linked. This analogy was greatly enhanced by the phenomenon of British tourists travelling to Italy on the Grand Tour and experiencing the peninsula and its archaeological remains through the Classics which they had, in many cases, studied so intensively at school. Seminal in this regard is Joseph Addison – journalist, playwright and author of the essay on the *Georgics* first published in Dryden's 1697 translation – who travelled in Italy in the opening years of the eighteenth century and consistently reflected on his experiences through the lens of his classical education; Italy for Addison was 'Virgil's Italy'.[41] So too did nineteenth-century figures such as Mary Shelley, Thomas Babington Macaulay and William Gladstone travel in Italy with the *Georgics* in their minds.[42] Yet British writers, journalists and civil servants also travelled in the British empire at large and equated the naïvely happy farmers of Virgil's poem with the people they encountered, at times condescending to their perceived primitivism, at times suggesting that these people were reliant on, or in need of, the beneficent and civilizing presence of the British empire.[43] Analogies with Virgil's poem, that is, were not limited to Britain and its people, but were also extended to its colonial subjects and used to justify or advocate for their subjection.

I dwell on these contexts in order to highlight that over the course of the eighteenth, nineteenth and early twentieth centuries, the *Georgics* was a poem which informed how British readers thought about themselves, their empire and the world at large. The logic behind this process is one that is central to the tradition of georgic poetry, and is worth clarifying. It begins with patriotism inspired by the beauty of one's native land, which is seen to create a healthy population and to give rise to political supremacy. This political supremacy in turn gives the georgic poet access to the world, either as an actual tourist or as a surveyor from the imperial centre. From this access and the geographical information it bears, arguments are then made to justify, either implicitly or explicitly, the superiority of one's home country and the inferiority of others: a kind of circular justification for imperial rule. What I am arguing here is that this politics extends across three major poems in the georgic tradition, across, that is, Roman and British contexts, in different but substantially consistent ways. The georgic poet is a surveyor of the world and its peoples, bringing knowledge back from the edges of empire to its centre, and creating in the process a political justification for that empire. The temporal and cultural gap between Virgil's Rome and Britain is lessened, if not closed, by the fact that Britain's male elite were raised on the classics in general, and on Virgil in particular, giving that poet a cultural currency far beyond what he otherwise would have had.[44]

I have noted above how Virgil's *Georgics* fits into this scheme, and now I would like to consider how Thomson's *The Seasons* and Sackville-West's *The Land* can be seen to fit too. Beginning at 'Summer' (p. 125, line 1442) Thomson begins a praise of Britain, which owes much to Virgil's praise of Italy, a section of the poem that nearly doubled in length from its first to final version.[45] The patriotic connection between beauty, fertility and national prosperity is made immediately, in lines which describe Liberty walking abroad in 'Happy Britannia' (p. 125, lines 1438–45); by line 1595 Britain is an 'Isle of Bliss … At once the wonder, terror, and delight, | of distant nations' (p. 132, lines 1597–8). As ancient Italy produced great men like Camillus and the Scipios, so too does Britain have its 'Sons of Glory' who do service to the state and expand its empire.[46] By contrast, the wider world is home to 'barbarous nations, whose inhuman love | Is wild desire, fierce as the suns they feel', as well as 'Eastern tyrants' who 'from the light of heaven | Seclude their bosom-slaves'.[47] Thomson is echoing Virgil very closely here, linking temperateness of climate to civilization and juxtaposing enlightenment at home with barbarism abroad. *The Seasons* surveys the world even more extensively than the *Georgics* does, referencing rivers, peoples and places from Siberia to South America. Its politics of difference is most egregiously on display in lines which describe the Orinoco river and the people who live on its banks: we are shown a 'world of slaves', where no aspect of Western civilization (so perceived) has been able to reach, tyrannized by the 'Parent-Sun' himself.[48]

In both Virgil and Thomson, then, the apparent mundaneness of georgic subject-matter belies an intense and sophisticated interest in geography and empire. Both poems can be seen to do the work of empire in constructing ideas of difference in climatic terms, a process analogous to but distinct from the construction of racial ideologies that has marked human history from the early modern period to the present day. Imperial subjects are made visible, but only so that they can be labelled and at times dehumanized, their exploitation justified. Ostensibly, the contexts of Vita Sackville-West's poem are quite distinct, but this same process is evident in *The Land*, albeit in a more muted form. The *Land* was first published in 1926 and celebrates the English (specifically, the Kentish) countryside in an elegiac mode in the aftermath of the First World War. As mentioned previously, Sackville-West returns an element of nihilism to the georgic poem which had been forgotten in British poetry, and spends more time than Virgil or Thomson describing the people of the countryside.

In terms of patriotism, however, there is broad consistency between the three poets. England for Sackville-West, like Virgil's Italy and Thomson's Britannia, is a place of temperate fertility, and Kent is a place were classical ideals live on, where 'old Bacchic piety endures' among 'Homeric wagons' and 'Virgilian litanies'.[49] Italy is not alluded to specifically, but a contrast is developed between the lingering evening of England and the quick sunset of lower latitudes, a 'southern violence that burns away, | Ardent to live, and eager to be done.'[50] More pertinently, this England is implicitly compared with other parts of the world under the control of the British empire. Sackville-West was herself a tourist in the years up to and including the poem's publication, visiting India with Dorothy Wellesley, meeting the architect Edwin Lutyens in Delhi, before travelling on to Iran (then Persia) for the first of what would be two trips to see her husband, Harold, then His Majesty's Counsellor in the British Legation in Tehran.[51] Sackville-West's accounts of her travels show that she processed her experience of Iran in defensive and reactionary terms. For her Iran was an alien and primitive place, a 'savage, desolating country' which had been 'left as it was before man's advent'; it was 'certainly somewhere else' and existed 'far back in time'.[52] Though not formally part of the British empire, the discovery of oil in Iran in 1908 and the founding of the Anglo-Persian Oil Company (later BP) the following year meant that Britain would play an active role in Iranian politics for decades to come.[53]

This dichotomy of home and abroad can be read in certain passages of *The Land*, where scenes from India and Egypt (under full British political control until 1947 and 1922, respectively) are described in stereotypical and orientalist detail. A description of the Mughal palace at Fatehpur Sikri in Uttar Pradesh evokes a Mughal emperor who 'lolling on his throne, | Between his languid fingers crumbling spice, | Ordered his women to the chequered squares, | And moved them at the hazard of the dice' ('Spring', p. 40). Fritillaries, meanwhile, are like 'Egyptian girls', 'With foreign colour, sulky-dark, and quaint, | Dangerous too' ('Spring', p. 49). The contrast between England and these places of perceived exoticism, sensuality and danger is most apparent in the passage which opens 'Now you be thankful, who in England dwell' at the beginning of 'Summer': the object of poet's (and the reader's) gratitude is the rain which comes regularly in England to water and fertilize plants, crops and fields, a blessing upon which the Arab and the Persian cannot rely. The former 'watches in despair | The scrannel promise of his harvest parch', while the latter 'for all his pains | Sees roses languish with returning noon, | And in the heat of June | The leaves already flutter from the planes' ('Summer', pp. 61–2). As in Virgil's *Georgics* and Thomson's *The Seasons*, patriotism in Sackville-West's *The Land* does not exist in a vacuum; it implies and requires an elsewhere which is reassuringly inferior in climatic and political terms to one's native land. The world at large is an object of curiosity, but that curiosity is used to construct difference and to normalize unequal imperial relationships, whether Roman or British.

Georgic Modernity

Any commentary upon the georgic tradition is necessarily limited and selective, as is the case here. I have tried to suggest that there are meaningful consistencies which link the primary ancient model for georgic poetry with two of its successors in the English poetic canon, in full awareness that the georgic tradition extends far beyond these three poems. Georgic has been, in the examples under consideration here, implicated in imperial politics, imagining the world and its peoples from imperial centres in ways which appear to normalize and promote the subjection of imperial subjects. Themes of geography, travel and patriotism blend together in a poetic vision which is never naïve and which extends far beyond the immediate environment of farm or countryside, using other peoples and places to say something about 'home'. When the business of farm and countryside does appear, georgic has often privileged a (white, free) male perspective, minimizing or ignoring the women (not to mention children) who historically have been no less important to the work of many agricultural communities, as well as the slaves who, in both Roman Italy and the eighteenth-century Caribbean, did back-breaking work in inhuman conditions.

More positively, perhaps, the georgic tradition as a whole can be read as a kind of archive, implicitly celebrating forms of knowledge and practice often at odds with the economic status quo: Virgil's weavers, Thomson's gleaners and Sackville-West's thatcher; the value of healthy forests, clean rivers and sustainable use of the earth's natural resources. Georgic at its best marries intense appreciation of the natural world with an equally intense awareness of that world's fragility and precariousness. The economic contexts of Virgil's poem are hard to ascertain in full detail, but its seems clear that he wrote it at a moment when the Roman state was moving up the gears in economic and imperial terms, exploiting natural and human resources on an unprecedented scale. Thomson's poem, meanwhile, coincides with the beginning of the Industrial Revolution, and it is worth recalling what E. P. Thompson termed the 'truly catastrophic nature' of that revolution for the people of Britain, in that it accelerated the expropriation of common land, hastened the decline of centuries-old sustainable practices on the land, and embedded a factory-based capitalist system which greatly impoverished many of the population.[54] An awareness of what has been lost in this process is at the centre of Sackville-West's poem, published in 1926 yet drawing on a much older tradition and deliberately anachronistic in its use of language and Kentish dialect (on which see Chapter 11 in this volume).

In both its imperial and its archival aspects, it strikes me that georgic poetry as considered here is an inherently modern form. Many of the economic and environmental challenges facing the twenty-first-century world affect the countries of the Global South in vastly disproportionate ways, countries which have often borne the brunt of European and US imperialism in the past and labour under newer forms of imperialism in the present. These countries and their populations are the ones most affected by what Rob Nixon has termed 'slow violence', the way contemporary geopolitics exploits and works to hide the effects of Western economic policies and their environmental impacts on the world's poorer nations; to Nixon's thesis one could usefully add the caveat of Arundhati Roy, that there is 'no such thing as the "voiceless". There are only the deliberately silenced, or the preferably unheard.'[55] Roy and Naomi Klein have documented the contempt with which neoliberal policies and actors have treated communities and their lands in South America and India, while Jamaica Kincaid has written of the discrepancies of wealth and privilege that define modern tourism in the postcolonial Caribbean.[56] The same things that define the imperial aspect of the georgic tradition as considered in this chapter – here and elsewhere, those seen and unseen, unequal access to the world and its resources – also define modern environmental politics on a global scale.

Finally, at the more intimate level of text and reader, georgic puts centre stage the diversity of the world and historical ways of life on the land, keeping alive the memory of sustainable practices and offering alternatives to contemporary economic and agricultural arrangements often deemed by their champions to be inevitable or irresistible. It warns against taking for granted the beneficence of nature and its cooperation in human endeavours, and thus puts the human subject in reduced and humbling perspective; it is keenly aware of the interconnectedness of human, plant and animal life, and the destructive effects of powerful economic interests on all three. At a time when the effects of climate change are becoming increasingly visible in both frequency and scale, this would appear to be another way in which georgic's long-noted combination of beauty and utility – the way it 'raises in our Minds a pleasing variety of Scenes and Landskips, whilst it teaches us' – might be of use to its readers.[57]

Notes

1 Virgil, *Georgics* (Fairclough), pp. 98–260.
2 J. Thomson, *The Seasons*, ed. J. Sambrook (Oxford: Clarendon Press, 1981); quotations from the poem are by page number, season, and line number in this edition. For *Rule Britannia* and the popularity of *The Seasons*, see J. Sambrook, 'Thomson, James (1700–1748)', *ODNB*.
3 V. Sackville-West, *The Land*, new ed. (London: Frances Lincoln, 2004); quotations from the poem are by season and page number in this edition.
4 J. Chalker, *The English Georgic: A Study in the Development of a Form* (London: Routledge, 1969), pp. 7–8; A. Low, *The Georgic Revolution* (Princeton University Press, 1985), p. 69.
5 Virgil, *Georgics* (Fairclough), pp. 168–75 (*Georgics* II, ll. 458–540).
6 P. Thibodeau, *Playing the Farmer: Representations of Rural Life in Vergil's Georgics* (Berkeley, CA: University of California Press, 2011), pp. 106–15; T. Geue, 'Soft Hands, Hard Power: Sponging Off the Empire of Leisure (Virgil, *Georgics* 4)', *Journal of Roman Studies*, 108 (2018), 115–40.
7 C. Kerrigan, *Virgil's Map: Geography, Empire, and the Georgics* (London: Bloomsbury, 2020), pp. 7–20, 109–10. Here and throughout this chapter I use the term orientalist in the sense put forward by E. Said, *Orientalism*, new ed. (London: Penguin Classics, 2019).
8 J. Grainger, *The Sugar-Cane* (1764), at *Digital Grainger: An Online Edition of The Sugar-Cane*, https://digital-grainger.github.io/grainger/ (accessed 14 July 2021).
9 Thomson, *Seasons*, p. 149 ('Autumn', line 141); E. P. Thompson, *The Making of the English Working Class*, new ed. (London: Penguin, 2013); E. Meiksins Wood, *The Pristine Culture of Capitalism: A Historical Essay on Old Regimes and Modern States*, new ed. (London: Verso, 2015); K. Bradley, *Slavery and Society at Rome* (Cambridge University Press, 1994). Bradley (at pp. 29–30) estimates the slave population of Italy at the end of the first century BCE as having been between two and three million.

10 Low, *Georgic Revolution*; K. O'Brien, 'Imperial Georgic, 1660–1789', in *The Country and the City Revisited: England and the Politics of Culture, 1550–1850*, ed. G. Maclean, D. Landry and J. P. Ward (Cambridge University Press, 1999), pp. 160–79.

11 R. Syme, *The Roman Revolution* (Oxford: Clarendon Press, 1939); J. H. Morrow, 'The Imperial Framework', in *The Cambridge History of the First World War*, ed. J. Winter, 3 vols. (Cambridge University Press, 2014), vol. I, pp. 405–32.

12 On the poem's literary influences, see Thibodeau, *Playing the Farmer*, pp. 8–14, and Kerrigan, *Virgil's Map*, pp. 7–11. My conception of the poem's first audience is thus somewhat broader than that found in Thibodeau, *Playing the Farmer*, p. 4 ('The poet was himself a major landowner, writing for an audience of fellow landowners who relied on agriculturally based incomes to sustain lives of business and leisure'), though there too the poem's relationship to the day-to-day world of agriculture is explored.

13 S. Heaney, 'Glory be to the World', review article, *The Irish Times*, Dublin, 23 October 2004, p. D10, https://about.proquest.com/en/products-services/pq-hist-news/ (accessed 14 July 2021).

14 R. Thomas, ed., *Virgil: Georgics*, 2 vols. (Cambridge University Press, 1988), vol. I, pp. 178–9.

15 Virgil, *Georgics* (Fairclough), pp. 240–47 (*Georgics* IV, ll. 315–85).

16 Virgil, *Georgics* (Fairclough), p. 122 (*Georgics* I, ll. 338–50).

17 M. S. Spurr, 'Agriculture and the *Georgics*', *Greece & Rome*, 33 (1986), 167–87, at 167; Thibodeau, *Playing the Farmer*, pp. 17–19.

18 Virgil, *Georgics* (Fairclough), pp. 118–19, 126–27, 106–7, 204–5, 102–3 (*Georgics* I, ll. 293–94, 390–2, 111–17; *Georgics* III, ll. 400–3; *Georgics* I, ll. 71–6).

19 Virgil, *Georgics* (Fairclough), pp. 120–1, 212–13 (*Georgics* I, ll. 316–27; *Georgics* III, ll. 515–19).

20 Virgil, *Georgics* (Fairclough), pp. 118–19, 126–27, 106–7, 204–5, 102–3 (*Georgics* I, lines 293–4, 390–2, 111–17; *Georgics* III, ll. 400–3; *Georgics* I, ll. 71–6).

21 Virgil, *Georgics* (Fairclough), pp. 150–51, 242–23 (*Georgics* II, ll. 202–14, *Georgics* IV, ll. 329–32).

22 A fragment from the work of the historian Dionysius of Halicarnassus – active in Rome in the same years as Virgil – describes a thriving Roman logging industry in La Sila; both the place and the industry appear in the *Georgics* (II. 438 and III. 219–23); the fragment is translated in A. J. Toynbee, *Hannibal's Legacy: The Hannibalic War's Effects on Roman Life*, 2 vols. (Oxford University Press, 1965), vol. II, pp. 545–6. On deforestation in an Irish historical context, see F. Ludlow and A. Crampsie, 'Environmental History of Ireland, 1550–1730', in *The Cambridge History of Ireland*, ed. J. Ohlmeyer, 4 vols. (Cambridge University Press, 2018), vol. II, pp. 614–16.

23 R. Thomas, 'The *Georgics* of Resistance: From Virgil to Heaney', *Vergilius*, 47 (2001), 117–47, at 129–30.

24 Thomson, *Seasons*, p. 92 ('Summer', line 663: citron groves), p. 148 ('Autumn', line 121: the river Thames), p. 78 ('Summer', lines 352–70: the harvest scene), p. 149 ('Autumn', line 141: 'All is the gift of Industry').

25 O'Brien, 'Imperial Georgic', pp. 174–5; E. Bohls, 'The Gentleman Planter and the Metropole', in *Country and the City Revisited*, ed. MacLean et al., pp. 180–96.
26 Thomson, *Seasons*, p. 36 ('Spring', lines 714–28: the nightingale), p. 147 ('Autumn', line 81: deforestation), p. 78 ('Summer', lines 352–70: harvest), p. 79 ('Summer', line 401: the pastoral Queen). The debt to Shakespeare's *The Winter's Tale* is noted by Sambrook in Thomson, *Seasons*, p. 345.
27 O'Brien, 'Imperial Georgic', p. 169.
28 Sackville-West, *The Land*, p. 102 (hops-pickers), p. 79 (the thatcher), pp. 17–18 (the homeless man).
29 E. Scott, 'Roman Agriculture, Gender and Work, *or* Harvesting Women's Work from Roman Landscapes', unpublished paper, https://eleanorscottarchaeology.com/unpublished-papers (accessed 14 July 2021).
30 Virgil, *Georgics*, I. 293–4, I. 390–92, II. 524.
31 Thomson, *Seasons*, p. 2 ('Spring', line 5: Frances Thynne, Countess of Hertford), pp. 25 and 46 ('Spring', lines 483 and 936: 'Amanda' and 'Lucinda'), p. 78 ('Summer', line 355: the 'ruddy Maid'), p. 98 ('Summer', line 823: 'Maids of Afric'), and p. 79 ('Summer', line 398: the housewife).
32 Spurr, 'Agriculture and the *Georgics*', p. 175 n. 46. The *Georgics*' workforce includes a harvester ('messor', *Georgics*, I. 316), a shepherd ('pastor', *Georgics*, III. 402), a pruner ('putator', *Georgics*, II. 28), a digger ('fossor', *Georgics*, II. 264), a vineyard worker ('vinitor', Geoirgcs, II. 417) and a mule-driver ('agitator', *Georgics*, I. 273). Thibodeau, *Playing the Farmer*, p. 45 notes also the 'fuga' ('runaway') at *Georgics*, I. 286.
33 E. Long, *The History of Jamaica*, 3 vols. (London, 1774), vol. I, p. 373: 'Before the discovery of America, the romantic idea of a poet alone could expatiate on some utopian island, blessed with perennial verdure and unfading spring. In Jamaica we find the idea realized'. Bohls, 'Gentleman Planter', p. 190, comments: 'Turning slaves into happy reapers and canes into treasure, Long struggles to assimilate the grueling proto-industrial routine of the colonial plantation to the Utopian idyll that had long been prominent in discourse about the Americas.' Long was classically educated, and his *History* includes Latin quotations from Cicero and Horace, though not Virgil.
34 Sackville-West, *The Land*, 'Winter', p. 16 ('Dark Asia') and 'Autumn', p. 94: 'But man to dust and trees to timber fall, | And comes the hearse or comes the timber-wain, | With nut-brown team, patient to stand or haul, | And like a naked savage bound in chain, | With limbs once proud that now through ordure drag, | A captive moves his way in thrall'. Compare V. Sackville-West, *Twelve Days in Persia: Across the Mountains with the Bakhtiari Tribe*, new ed. (London: Tauris Parke Paperbacks, 2009), pp. 105–6: 'Persia does not lie on the road to any active or important centre, – nothing but the darkness of Central Asia stretches beyond it'.
35 Kerrigan, *Virgil's Map*, pp. 7–20.
36 Virgil, *Georgics*, IV. 559–66.

37 Virgil, *Georgics*, III. 408 (Spaniards), I. 57 ('molles ... Sabaei': 'soft Sabaeans'; for the Roman expedition see Kerrigan, *Virgil's Map*, p. 24 n. 26); II. 172, IV. 425 and IV. 293 (for Indians as 'unwarlike', 'thirsty' and 'coloured', with Kerrigan, *Virgil's Map*, p. 37).

38 Virgil, *Georgics* (Dryden), p. 188; J. R. D. Blackmore, *The Georgics of Vergil* (London: Low, 1871), p. 41; H. C. Gardner, *The Georgics of Virgil: Translated in English Verse by Lord Burghclere* (London: J. Murray, 1904), p. 65; C. W. Brodribb, *Virgil: The Georgics. in English Hexameters* (London: Ernest Benn, 1928); C. Day Lewis, *The Georgics of Virgil* (London: Jonathan Cape, 1940), pp. 39 and 56. Brodribb (*Georgics*, p. 27) outdoes Day Lewis in his racist conflation of Roman and British imperial power in India, translating 'imbellem ... Indum' (*Georgics*, II. 172, 'unwarlike Indian') as 'cow'd Hindoo'.

39 See Gardner, *Georgics*, p. 65, translating *Georgics*, II. 157–9: 'What rivers gliding past | Those time-worn battlements! | Or shall I tell | Of the great seas that wash our either shore? | Or sing the spacious glory of our lakes?' and Brodribb, *Georgics*, p. 27, translating *Georgics*, II. 158–9: 'And what of our two seas that lave our country on each side, | And those lordly lagoons'.

40 C. W. Brodribb, *Poems* (London: Macmillan, 1946), pp. 32 and 34–5.

41 J. Addison, 'A Letter from Italy, to the Right Honourable Charles, Lord Halifax. In the Year MDCCI', in *Remarks on Several Parts of Italy, etc. In the Years 1701, 1702, 1703*, 2nd ed. (1718), p. iv.

42 B. T. Bennett, *The Letters of Mary Wollstonecraft Shelley*, 2 vols. (Baltimore, MD: Johns Hopkins University Press, 1980), vol. I, p. 85; W. Thomas, ed., *The Journals of Thomas Babington Macaulay*, 5 vols. (London: Pickering and Chatto, 2008), vol. I, p. 47; M. R. D. Foot and H. C. G. Matthew, eds., *The Gladstone Diaries*, 14 vols. (Oxford University Press, 1968–94), vol. II, p. 445. The three receptions are discussed together at Kerrigan, *Virgil's Map*, pp. 68–9.

43 Kerrigan, *Virgil's Map*, pp. 67–95.

44 C. Stray, *Classics Transformed: Schools, Universities and Society in England, 1830–1960* (Oxford University Press, 1998); P. Vasunia, 'Virgil and the British Empire, 1760–1880', *Proceedings of the British Academy* (Oxford University Press, 2009), vol. 155, pp. 83–116; P. Vasunia, 'Greek, Latin, and the Indian Civil Service', in *British Classics Outside England*, ed. J. P. Hallett and C. Stray (Waco, TX: Alban, 2009), pp. 61–96.

45 Sambrook in Thomson, *Seasons*, pp. 358–9; O'Brien, 'Imperial Georgic', p. 169.

46 Virgil, *Georgics*, II. 169–79 and Thomson, *Seasons*, pp. 126–32 ('Summer', lines 1479–579).

47 Thomson, *Seasons*, p. 54 ('Spring', lines 1130–4).

48 Thomson, *Seasons*, p. 101 ('Summer', lines 875–85).

49 Sackville-West, 'Autumn', in *The Land*, p. 87.

50 Sackville-West, 'Autumn', in *The Land*, p. 106.

51 T. Otte, 'Nicolson, Sir Harold George (1886–1968)', *ODNB*.

52 V. Sackville-West, *Passenger to Teheran*, new ed. (London: Tauris Parke Paperbacks, 2009), pp. 67, 69, and 89–90; Sackville-West, *Twelve Days*, p. 66.

53 N. Keddie and M. Amanat, 'Iran Under the Later Qājārs, 1848–1922', in *The Cambridge History of Iran*, ed. P. Avery, G. R. G. Hambly, and C. Melville, 7 vols. (Cambridge University Press, 1991), vol. VII, pp. 174–212, at pp. 205–7.
54 Thompson, *Making of the English Working Class*, p. 217.
55 R. Nixon, *Slow Violence and the Environmentalism of the Poor* (Cambridge, MA: Harvard University Press, 2011), pp. 1–22; A. Roy, 'Peace & The New Corporate Liberation Theology', Sydney Peace Prize Lecture (University of Sydney: Centre for Peace and Conflict Studies, 2004), https://sydneypeacefoundation.org.au/wp-content/uploads/2012/02/2004-SPP_-Arundhati-Roy.pdf, p. 1 (accessed 14 July 2021).
56 N. Klein, *The Shock Doctrine: The Rise of Disaster Capitalism* (New York: Picador, 2008); A. Roy, 'The Road to Harsud', in *My Seditious Heart: Collected Non-Fiction* (London: Hamish Hamilton, 2019), pp. 309–28; J. Kincaid, *A Small Place* (London: Virago, 1988).
57 J. Addison, 'An Essay on the *Georgics*', in Virgil, *Georgics* (Dryden), p. 146.

Bibliography

Works issued before 1900 were published in London unless otherwise stated.

Select Primary Works

Addison, Joseph, 'An Essay on the *Georgics*', in *The Works of John Dryden. Vol. 5: Poems: The Works of Virgil in English, 1697*, eds. W. Frost and V. A. Dearing (Berkeley: University of California Press, 1987), pp. 145–53.
Addison, Joseph, 'A Letter from Italy, to the Right Honourable Charles, Lord Halifax. In the Year MDCCI', in *Remarks on Several Parts of Italy, etc. In the Years 1701, 1702, 1703*, 2nd ed. (1718), pp. i–x.
Anderson, Stephanie, *One Size Fits None: A Farm Girl's Search for the Promise of Regenerative Agriculture* (Lincoln, NE: University of Nebraska Press, 2019).
Archer, Fred, *When Village Bells Were Silent* (London: Hodder & Stoughton, 1975).
Armitage, Simon, *Still: A Poetic Response to Photographs of the Somme Battlefield* (London: Enitharmon Press, 2016).
Armstrong, John, *John Armstrong's The Art of Preserving Health*, ed. Adam Budd (Farnham: Ashgate, 2011).
Auden, W. H., *Collected Poems*, ed. Edward Mendelson (London: Faber & Faber, 1976).
Auden, W. H., *The Collected Poems of W. H. Auden*, ed. E. Mendelssohn (London: Faber, 1986).
Austen, Jane, *Emma*, ed. James Kinsley and Adela Pinch (Oxford University Press, 2008).
Bacon, Francis, *The Oxford Francis Bacon IV: The Advancement of Learning*, ed. M. Kiernan (Oxford: Clarendon Press, 2000).
Barrett, Hugh, *Early to Rise: A Suffolk Morning* (London: Faber and Faber, 1967).
Batchelor, Thomas, *Village Scenes: The Progress of Agriculture, and Other Poems* (1804).
Bates, H. E., *The Fallow Land* (London: Cape, 1932).
Beeson, Jane, *Scarhill* (London: Mandarin, 1995).
Bell, Adrian, *By-Road* (London: Bodley Head, 1937).
Bell, Adrian, *The Cherry Tree* (London: Cobden-Sanderson, 1932).

Bell, Adrian, *Corduroy* (London: Cobden-Sanderson, 1930).
Bell, Adrian, *Men and the Fields* (Wimborne Minster: Little Toller Books, 2009).
Bell, Adrian, *Silver Ley* (London: Cobden-Sanderson, 1931).
Beresford, Tristram, *We Plough the Fields: British Farming Today* (Harmondsworth: Penguin, 1975).
Berry, Wendell, *The Art of the Commonplace: The Agrarian Essays of Wendell Berry*, ed. N. Wirzba (Berkeley: Counterpoint, 2002).
Bloomfield, Robert, *The Farmer's Boy: A Rural Poem*, 3rd ed. (Vernor and Hood, 1800).
Blythe, Ronald, *Akenfield: Portrait of an English Village* (Harmondsworth: Penguin, 1969).
Borlik, Todd A., ed., *Literature and Nature in the English Renaissance: An Ecocritical Anthology* (Cambridge University Press, 2019).
Borodale, Sean, *Bee Journal* (London: Cape, 2012).
Brodribb, C. W., *Poems* (London: Macmillan, 1946).
Brodribb, C. W., *Virgil: The Georgics in English Hexameters* (London: Ernest Benn, 1928).
Bullough, Tom, *Addlands* (London: Granta, 2016).
Burnett, Emma-Jane, *The Grassling: A Geological Memoir* (London: Penguin, 2020).
Burnham Historians, *A Land Girl's Diary: Burnham 1948* (Taplow: Burnham Historians, 1999).
Butler, Charles, *The Feminine Monarchie or a Treatise Concerning Bees, and the Due Ordering of Them* (Oxford, 1609).
Camden, William, *Camden's Britannia Newly Translated into English*, ed. E. Gibson (1695).
Cato and Varro: On Agriculture, tr. W. D. Hooper and H. B. Ash (Cambridge, Harvard University Press, 1934).
Chatwin, Bruce, *On the Black Hill* (London: Cape, 1982).
Chesnutt, Charles W., *The Journals of Charles W. Chesnutt*, ed. R. Brodhead (Durham, NC: Duke University Press, 1993).
Chesnutt, Charles W., *The Short Fiction of Charles W. Chesnutt*, ed. S. L. Render (Washington, DC: Howard University Press, 1981).
Churchill, Carol, Fen, in *Plays: Two* (London: Methuen, 1990), pp. 144–92.
Clare, John, *By Himself*, eds. D. Powell and E. Robinson (Manchester: Carcanet Press, 1996).
Clare, John, *Major Works*, eds. Eric Robinson and David Powell (Oxford University Press, 2004).
Clare, John, *The Midsummer Cushion*, eds. K. Thornton and A. Tibble (Ashington: Carcanet, 1980).
Clare, John, *Natural History Prose Writings of John Clare*, ed. M. Grainger (Oxford: Clarendon Press, 1983).
Clare, John, *Poems of the Middle Period, 1822–1837. Volume V: Northborough Poems*, eds. E. Robinson, D. Power and P. M. S. Dawson (Oxford: Clarendon Press, 2003).
Clare, John, *The Shepherd's Calendar*, ed. Eric Robinson (Oxford University Press, 1993).

Clare, John, *The Village Minstrel and Other Poems*, 2 vols. (1821).
Cobbett, William, *The Opinions of William Cobbett*, ed. J. Grande, J. Stevenson and R. Thomas (Farnham: Ashgate, 2013).
Cobbett, William, *Rural Rides*, eds. G. D. H. Cole and M. Cole, 3 vols. (London: Peter Davies, 1930).
Cocker, Mark, *Our Place: Can We Save Britain's Wildlife before It Is Too Late?* (London: Vintage, 2019).
Collier, Mary, *The Woman's Labour: An Epistle to Mr Stephen Duck* (1739).
Collis, John Stewart, *Down to Earth* (London: Cape, 1947).
Collis, John Stewart, *While Following the Plough* (London: Cape, 1946).
Collis, John Stewart, *The Worm Forgives the Plough* (London: Charles Knight, 1973; reprinted by Penguin, 1975).
Columella, *On Agriculture, Volume I: Books 1–4*, tr. Harrison Boyd Ash (Cambridge, MA: Harvard University Press, 1941).
Columella, *On Agriculture, Volume II: Books 5–9*, tr. E. S. Forster and E. H. Heffner (Cambridge, MA: Harvard University Press, 1954).
Columella, *On Agriculture, Volume III: Books 10–12*, tr. E. S. Forster and E. H. Heffner (Cambridge, MA: Harvard University Press, 1955).
Cowper, William, *The Task*, in *The Poems of William Cowper*, eds. J. D. Baird and C. Ryskamp, 2 vols. (Oxford University Press, 1995), vol. II.
Crabbe, *The Complete Poetical Works*, eds. N. Dalrymple-Champneys and A. Pollard, 3 vols. (Oxford: Clarendon Press, 1988).
Darling, F. Fraser, *Island Farm* (London: Bell, 1943).
Dee, Tim, *Four Fields* (London: Cape, 2013).
Deloria, Vine, Jr., *For This Land: Writings on Religion in America* (New York: Routledge, 1998).
Dexter, Keith, and Derek Barber, *Farming for Profits* (Harmondsworth: Penguin, 1961; 2nd ed., London: Iliffe, 1967).
Dodsley, Robert, *Public Virtue: A Poem. In Three Books. I. Agriculture. II. Commerce III. Arts* (1753).
Drayton, Michael, *The Works of Michael Drayton*, ed. J. W. Hebel, 5 vols. (Oxford: Blackwell, 1931–41).
Dryden, John, *The Dryden-Tonson Miscellanies, 1684–1709*, eds. S. Gillespie and D. Hopkins, 6 vols. (London: Routledge, 2008).
Dryden, John, *The Works of John Dryden, Vol. 5: Poems; The Works of Virgil in English; 1697*, eds. W. Frost and V. A. Dearing (Berkeley: University of California Press, 1987).
Du Bois, W. E. Burghardt, *The Souls of Black Folk* (New York: Penguin, 1996).
Dugdale, William, *The History of Imbanking and Draining of Divers Fens and Marshes*, ed. C. N. Cole (1662; 2nd edn London, 1772).
Dyer, John, *The Fleece: A Poem in Four Books*, eds. J. Goodridge and J. C. Pellicer (Cheltenham: Cyder Press, 2007).
Elliott, Ebenezer, *The Splendid Village: Corn Law Rhymes; and Other Poems* (1833).
Evans, G. Ewart, *Ask the Fellows Who Cut the Hay* (London: Faber, 1956).
Evans, G. Ewart, *The Horse in the Furrow* (London: Faber, 1960).

Evelyn, John, *A Philosophical Discourse of Earth* (1676).
Fergusson, Robert, *The Works of Robert Fergusson* (Edinburgh, 1805).
Fiennes, Celia, *Through England on a Side Saddle ... being the Diary of Celia Fiennes*, ed. E. W. Griffiths (1888).
Firbank, Thomas, *I Bought a Mountain* (London: Harrap: 1940).
Ford, F. Madox, *It was the Nightingale* (London: Heinemann, 1934).
Ford, F. Madox, *No Enemy: A Tale of Reconstruction*, ed. P. Skinner (1929; Manchester: Carcanet, 2002).
Gay, John, *Poetry and Prose*, ed. Vinton K. D., 2 vols. (Oxford University Press, 1974–5).
Gibbons, Stella, *Cold Comfort Farm* (London: Longmans, Green, 1932).
Goldsmith, Oliver, *The Collected Works of Oliver Goldsmith*, ed. A. Friedman, 5 vols. (Oxford: Clarendon Press, 1966).
Grahame, James, *British Georgics* (Edinburgh, 1809).
Grainger, James, The Sugar-Cane (1764), in J. Gilmore, ed., *The Poetics of Empire: A Study of James Grainer's The Sugar-Cane (1764)* (London: Athlone Press, 2000).
Gyte, Maria, *The Diaries of Maria Gyte of Sheldon, Derbyshire, 1913–1920*, ed. G. Phizackerley (Cromford: Scarthin Books, 1999).
Hall, Daniel, Sir, *The Book of the Rothamsted Experiments* (London: John Murray, 1905).
Hallam Diaries, Berkshire Record Office, D/EX 1415.
Hallam, Isaac, *The Cocker: A Poem. In Imitation of Virgil's Third Georgic. Humbly inscrib'd to the Honourable Society of Sportsmen at Grantham* (Stamford, 1742).
Hardy, Thomas, 'The Dorsetshire Labourer', *Longman's Magazine, Vol. II* (May–October 1883), pp. 252–69.
Hardy, *Jude the Obscure*, ed. P. Ingham (Oxford University Press, 1986).
Hardy, Thomas, *The Mayor of Casterbridge*, ed. D. Kramer (Oxford University Press, 1987).
Hardy, Thomas, *The Return of the Native*, ed. S. Gatrell (Oxford University Press, 1986).
Hardy, Thomas, *The Woodlanders*, ed. D. Kramer (Oxford University Press, 1986).
Harrison, Melissa, *All Among the Barley* (London: Bloomsbury, 2018).
Hartlib, Samuel, *The Compleat Husband-Man: or, A Discourse of the Whole Art of Husbandry* (1659).
Hartlib, Samuel, *The Reformed Common-Wealth of Bees* (1655).
Houghton, John, *Husbandry and Trade Improv'd*, 4 vols. (1728).
Heaney, Seamus, *Field Work* (London: Faber, 1979).
Heaney, Seamus, *Preoccupations: Selected Prose 1968–78* (London: Faber, 1980).
Henderson, George, *Farmer's Progress* (London: Faber, 1950).
Henderson, George, *The Farming Ladder* (1944; London: Faber, 1956).
Hardy, Mary, *The Diary of Mary Hardy 1773–1809. Diary I, 1773–1781. Public House and Waterway*, ed. Margaret Bird (Kingston upon Thames: Burnham Press, 2013).

Heresbach, Conrad, *Foure Bookes of Husbandry*, tr. Barnabe Googe (1577).
Herrick, Robert, *The Complete Poetry of Robert Herrick*, eds. Tom Cain and Ruth Connolly, 2 vols. (Oxford University Press, 2013).
Hesiod, *The Georgicks of Hesiod ... Containing Doctrine of Husbandrie, Moralitie, and Pietie*, tr. George Chapman (1618).
Hesiod, *The Homeric Hymns, and Homerica*, tr. H. G. Evelyn-White (1914; Cambridge MA: Harvard University Press, 1982).
Hesiod, *Works and Days*, ed. M. L. West (Oxford: Clarendon Press, 1978).
Hill, Geoffrey, *Broken Hierarchies: Poems 1952–2012*, ed. K. Haynes (Oxford University Press, 2013).
Hodkin, William, *A Victorian Farmer's Diary. William Hodkin's Diary 1864–66. Life in and around Beeley on the Chatsworth Estate*, ed. T. A. Burden (n.p.: Derbyshire County Council Cultural & Community Services Department, 2003).
Holloway, William, *The Peasant's Fate: A Rural Poem* (Boston: Hosea Sprague, 1802).
Homewood, Robert A., *Three Farms* (London: Latimer House, 1947).
Hudson, William H., *Nature in Downland*, 2nd ed. (London: J. M. Dent, 1923).
Hudson, William H., *A Shepherd's Life* (Wimborne Minster: Little Toller, 2018).
Hughes, Ted, *Collected Poems*, ed. P. Keegan (London: Faber, 2005).
Jackson, Wes, 'Matfield Green', in *Rooted in the Land: Essays on Community and Place*, eds. W. Vitek and W. Jackson (New Haven: Yale University Press, 1996), pp. 5–103.
Jackson, Wes, 'Wilderness as Saint', *Aperture*, 120 (1990), 50–55.
Jago, Richard, *Edge-Hill, or, the Rural Prospect Delineated and Moralized* (1767).
Jefferies, Richard, *Agriculture and the Land: Richard Jefferies' Essays and Letters*, ed. R. Welshman (Edinburgh University Press, 2019).
Jefferies, Richard, *Bevis*, (London: Cape, 1932).
Jefferies, Richard, *Landscape with Figures: Selected Prose Writings*, ed. R. Mabey (Harmondsworth: Penguin, 2012).
Jefferies, Richard, 'The Future of Farming', *Fraser's Magazine*, 8, 48 (1873), 687–97.
Jefferies, Richard, 'The Labourer's Daily Life', *Fraser's Magazine*, 10, 59 (November), 654–69.
Jefferies, Richard, *Landscape with Figures: Selected Prose Writings*, ed. Richard Mabey (Harmondsworth: Penguin, 2012).
Jefferies, Richard, 'John Smith's Shanty', *Fraser's Magazine*, 9 (1874), 135–49.
Jefferies, Richard, *Nature Near London* (London: Collins, 2012).
Jefferies, Richard, *Red Deer* (London: Longmans, Green and Co., 1894).
Jefferies, Richard, *The Toilers of the Field* (Longmans, 1892).
Jefferies, Richard, *Wild Life in a Southern Country*, (Wimborne Minster: Little Toller, 2011).
Jefferies, Richard, *Wood Magic: A Fable* (London: Longman, 1907).
Jonson, Ben, *The Cambridge Edition of the Works of Ben Jonson*, eds. D. Bevington et al., 7 vols. (Cambridge University Press, 2012).
Kaye-Smith, Sheila, *Joanna Godden* (London: Cassell, 1921).

Kingsnorth, Paul, 'Learning What to Make of It', in *Confessions of a Recovering Environmentalist* (London: Faber, 2017), pp. 90–106.
Kingsnorth, Paul, *The Wake* (London: Unbound, 2014).
Lewis-Stempel, John, *Meadowland* (London: Black Swan, 2015).
Lewis-Sempel, John, *The Running Hare: The Secret Life of Farmland* (London: Doubleday, 2016).
Lively, Penelope, *Next to Nature, Art* (London: Heinemann, 1982).
McConnell, Primrose, *The Diary of a Working Farmer: Being the True History of a Year's Farming in Essex* (London: Cable, 1906).
McEntegart, Anne, *The Milk Lady at New Park Farm. The Wartime Diary of Anne McEntegart, June 1943–February 1945* (Sheffield: RMC Books, 2011).
Macfarlane, Robert, *Landmarks* (London: Hamish Hamilton, 2015).
Markham, Gervase, *The English Husbandman* (1613).
Marsh, Jan, *Back to the Land* (London: Quartet, 1982).
Marvell, Andrew, *The Poems of Andrew Marvell*, ed. N. Smith (London: Pearson Longman, 2003).
Monbiot, George, *Feral: Rewilding the Land, the Sea, and Human Life* (2013; London: Penguin, 2014).
Moore, John, *The Brensham Trilogy* (Oxford University Press, 1985), comprising *Portrait of Elmbury* (1945), *Brensham Village* (1946) and *The Blue Field* (1948).
Nicander, *The Poems and Poetical Fragments*, tr. A. S. F. Gow and A.F. Scholfield (1953; London: Bristol Classical Press, 1997).
Olmsted, F. Law, *The Cotton Kingdom; a Traveller's Observations on Cotton and Slavery in the American Slave States. Based upon Three Former Volumes of Journeys and Investigations by the Same Author*, ed. Arthur M. S. (New York: Knopf, 1953).
Olmsted, F. Law, *A Journey in the Seaboard Slave States; With Remarks on Their Economy* (New York; London: Dix and Edwards; Sampson Low, Son & Co., 1856).
Oswald, Alice, *Dart* (London: Faber, 2002).
Oswald, Alice, 'Wild Things', *The* Guardian, 3 December 2005.
Palladius, *Palladii Rutilii Tauri Aemiliani viri inlustris opus agriculturae*, ed. Robert H. R. (Leipzig: Teubener, 1975).
Pears, Tim, *The Horseman* (London: Bloomsbury, 2017).
Pears, Tim, *The Redeemed* (London: Bloomsbury, 2019).
Pears, Tim, *The Wanderers* (London: Bloomsbury, 2018).
Philips, John, *Cyder: A Poem: In Two Books* (1708).
Philips, John, *Cyder. A Poem. In Two Books*, eds. J. Goodridge and J. C. Pellicer (Cheltenham: Cyder Press, 2001).
Pope, Alexander, *Windsor Forest*, in *The Twickenham Edition of the Poems of Alexander Pope*, eds. J. Butt et al., 11 vols. (London: Methuen, 1939–69), vol. I.
Rebanks, James, *English Pastoral: An Inheritance* (London: Allen Lane, 2020).
Rebanks, James, *The Shepherd's Life: A Tale of the Lake District* (London: Allen Lane, 2015).

Rider Haggard, Henry, *Rural England: Being an Account of Agricultural and Social Researches Carried Out in the Years 1901 and 1902*, 2 vols. (1906; Cambridge University Press, 2011).
Ruck, Ruth Janette, *Place of Stones* (London: Faber, 1961).
Sackville-West, V., *The Garden* (1946; London: Frances Lincoln, 2004).
Sackville-West, V., *The Land* (London: Heinemann, 1926).
Sackville-West, V., *Passenger to Teheran*, new ed. (London: Tauris Parke Paperbacks, 2009).
Smart, Christopher, 'The Hop-Garden. A Georgic. In Two Books', in *The Poetical Works of Christopher Smart, Vol. 4: Miscellaneous Poems English and Latin*, ed. K. Williamson (Oxford University Press, 1987), pp. 41–65.
Smart, Christopher, 'The Hop-Garden: A Georgic', in *Poems on Several Occasions* (1752).
Smith, Charlotte, *Beachy Head: with Other Poems* (1807).
Smith, Katherine, *The Morville Hours: The Story of a Garden* (London: Bloomsbury, 2009).
Snyder, Gary, 'Reinhabitation', in *A Place in Space: Ethics, Aesthetics, and Watersheds* (Washington, DC: Counterpoint, 1995), pp. 183–92.
Spenser, Edmund, *The Faerie Queene*, ed. A. C. Hamilton, 2nd ed. (Harlow: Longman, 2007).
Spenser, Edmund, *The Shepheardes Calender: Conteyning Tvvelue Æglogues Proportionable to the Twelue Monethes*, in *The Poetical Works of Edmund Spenser*, ed. E. De Selincourt, 3 vols. (Oxford University Press, 1910), vol. I.
Speranza, Feliciano *Scriptorum Romanorum de re rustica reliquiae* (Messina: Università degli studi, 1974–).
Stovin, J., ed., *Journals of a Methodist Farmer 1871–1875* (London: Croom Helm, 1982).
Street, A. George, *Farmer's Glory* (London: Penguin, 1951).
Street, A. G., *Farmer's Glory* (1932; Oxford University Press, 1983).
Street, A. George, *Farming England* (London: Batsford, 1937).
Street, A. George, *The Gentleman of the Party* (London: Faber, 1936).
Street, A. George, *Strawberry Roan* (London: Faber, 1932).
Street, A. George, *Sweetacres* (London: Michael Joseph, 1956).
Stukeley, William, *Itinerarium curiosum. Or an Account of the Antiquitys and Remarkable Curiositys in Nature and Art Observ'd in Travels thro' Great Britain* (1724).
Sturt, George, *Change in the Village* (1912; Cambridge University Press, 2010).
Surtees, R. Smith, *Hillingdon Hall: Or, The Cockney Squire*, 3 vols. (1845).
Swan, W. Carter, *The Diary of a Farm Apprentice. William Carter Swan 1909–1910*, ed. Edmund E. S. (Gloucester: Alan Sutton, 1984).
Swift, Graham, *Waterland* (1983; London: Picador, 1984).
Swift, Jonathan, *The Cambridge Edition of the Works of Jonathan Swift. 16: Gulliver's Travels*, ed. D. Womersley (Cambridge University Press, 2012).
Taylor, John, *Taylors Pastorall, being both Historicall and Satyricall. or, The noble Antiquitie of Shepheards, with the Profitable Use of Sheepe* (1624).
Thomas, Edward, *Richard Jefferies, His Life and Work* (Boston: Little, Brown, 1909).

Thomas, Edward, *The South Country* (Wimborne Minster: Little Toller, 2009).
Thomas, R. Stuart, *An Acre of Land* (Newtown: Montgomeryshire Printing Co., 1952).
Thomson, James, *The Seasons*, ed. J. Sambrook (Oxford: Clarendon Press, 1981).
Tremain, Rose, *Restoration* (London: Vintage, 2020).
Tull, Jethro, *The New Horse-Houghing Husbandry: or, an Essay on the Principles of Tillage and Vegetation* (1731).
Turner, Ivan, *Riding on a Plough* (Upton upon Severn: Square One Publications, 1994).
Tusser, Thomas, *Five Hundred Points of Good Husbandry*, ed. G. Grigson (Oxford University Press, 1984).
Virgil, *Eclogues, Georgics, Aeneid I–VI*, tr. H. R. Fairclough, rev. G. P. Gould (1935; Cambridge, MA: Harvard University Press, 1999).
Virgil, *Georgics*, tr. Peter Fallon (Oxford University Press, 2009).
Virgil, *The Georgics of Virgil. Attempted in English Verse* (1750).
Virgil, *The Georgics of Virgil*, tr. T. Neville (Cambridge, 1767).
Virgil, *The Georgics of Virgil*, tr. David Ferry (New York: Farrar, Straus and Giroux, 2005).
Virgil, *The Georgics: A Poem of the Land*, tr. Kimberly Johnson (London: Penguin, 2010).
Virgil, *The Works of Virgil*, ed. J. Warton, 4 vols. (1753).
Virgil, *Virgil's Husbandry, or an Essay on the Georgics: Being the Second Book Translated into English Verse. ... With notes Critical, and Rustick*, tr. William Benson (1724).
Warren, C. Henry, *England is a Village* (London: Eyre and Spottiswoode, 1940).
Washington, Booker T., *Up from Slavery: Authoritative Text, Contexts, and Composition History, Criticism*, ed. W. L. Andrews (New York: Norton, 1996).
Williamson, Henry, *The Story of a Norfolk Farm* (London: Faber, 1941).
Xenophon, *Oeconomicus: A Social and Historical Commentary, with a New English Translation*, tr. S. B. Pomeroy (Oxford: Clarendon Press, 1994).
Young, Arthur, *The Farmer's Kalendar; or, a Monthly Directory for all sorts of Country Business: containing, Plain Instructions for Performing the Work of Carious Kinds of Farms, in Every Season of the Year* (1771).
Young, Arthur, *General View of the Agriculture of the County of Lincoln* (1799).
Young, Arthur, *A Six Months Tour through the North of England*, 4 vols. (1770).
Young, Arthur, *A Six Weeks Tour, through the Southern Counties of England and Wales* (1768).

Select Secondary Works

Allsobrook, David I., 'The Georgic Model of Middle-Class Education', in *Schools for the Shires: the Reform of Middle-class Education in mid-Victorian England* (Manchester: Manchester University Press, 1986).

Alpers, Paul J., *What is Pastoral?* (University of Chicago Press, 1996).
Anagnostakis, Ilias. *Geoponika: Farm Work,* tr. A. Dalby (Totnes: Prospect, 2011).
Anderson, David R., 'Sterling Brown and the Georgic Tradition in African-American Literature', *Green Letters*, 20 (2016), 86–96.
Andrews, Corey E., '"Work" Poems: Assessing the Georgic Mode of Eighteenth-Century Working-Class Poetry', in *Experiments in Genre in Eighteenth-Century Poetry*, ed. S. Jung (Lebanon, NH, 2011), pp. 105–33.
Astor, W. Astor, Viscount, and Murray of Newhaven, Keith Anderson Hope, Baron, *The Planning of Agriculture* (Oxford University Press, 1933).
Astor, W. Astor, Viscount, and Rowntree, B. Seebohm, in *The Agricultural Dilemma: A Report of an Enquiry* (London: P.S. King, 1935).
Astor, W. Astor, Viscount, and Rowntree, B. Seebohm, in *British Agriculture: the Principles of Future Policy* (Harmondsworth: Penguin, 1939).
Attié, K. Bootle, '"The Mettle of Your Pasture": Georgic Sensibility and English Identity in Henry V', *Studies in Philology*, 117 (2020), 769–800.
Baker, Samuel, 'The Maritime Georgic and the Lake Poet Empire of Culture', *ELH*, 75 (2008), 531–63.
Barrell, John, *English Literature in History 1730–1780: An Equal, Wide Survey* (London: Hutchinson, 1983).
Barrell, John, *The Idea of Landscape and the Sense of Place 1730–1840* (Cambridge University Press, 1972).
Bazargan, Susan, 'The Uses of the Land: Vita Sackville-West's Pastoral Writings and Virginia Woolf's *Orlando*', *Woolf Studies Annual*, 5 (1999), 25–55.
Beck, Rudolph, 'From Industrial Georgic to Industrial Sublime: English Poetry and the Early Stages of the Industrial Revolution', *The British Journal for Eighteenth-Century Studies*, 27 (2004), 17–36.
Bellanca, M. Ellen, *Daybooks of Discovery: Nature Diaries in Britain, 1770–1870* (Charlottesville: University of Virginia Press, 2007).
Bermingham, Ann, *Landscape and Ideology: The English Rustic Tradition 1740–1860* (London: Thames and Hudson, 1987).
Blunden, Edmund, *Nature in English Literature* (1929; rpt. Port Washington: Kennikat Press, 1970).
Blyth, Ian, 'A Sort of English Georgics: Vita Sackville-West's *The Land*', *Forum for Modern Language Studies*, 45 (2009), 19–31.
Borlik, Todd A., 'Bioregional Visions in *Poly-Olbion*', in *'Poly-Olbion': New Perspectives*, eds. A. McRae and P. Schwyzer (Cambridge University Press, 2020), pp. 89–111.
Borlik, Todd A., *Ecocriticism and Early Modern English Literature: Green Pastures* (London: Routledge, 2011).
Borlik, Todd A., and Clare Egan, 'Angling for the "Powte": The Authorship, Provenance, and Manuscripts of a Jacobean Environmental Protest Poem', *ELR*, 48 (2018), 256–89.
Brathwaite, Edward [Kamau], 'Creative Literature of the British West Indies during the Period of Slavery', *Savacou*, 1 (1970), 46–73, reprinted in *Roots* (Ann Arbor, MI.: University of Michigan Press, 1993).

Braund, Susanna, 'Women and Earth: Female Responses to the Georgics in the Twentieth and Twenty-First Centuries', in *Reflections and New Perspectives on Virgil's Georgics*, eds. B. Xinyue and N. Freer (London: Bloomsbury, 2019), pp. 185–200.

Bristow, Tom, *The Anthropocene Lyric: An Affective Geography of Poetry, Person, Place* (Basingstoke: Palgrave, 2015).

Bucknell, Clare, 'The Mid-Eighteenth-Century Georgic and Agricultural Improvement', *Journal for Eighteenth-Century Studies*, 36 (2013), 335–52.

Buell, Lawrence, *Emerson* (Cambridge, MA: Harvard University Press, 2003).

Buell, Lawrence, The Environmental Imagination: Thoreau, Nature Writing, and the Formation of *American Culture* (Cambridge, MA: Harvard University Press, 1995).

Bullard, Paddy, 'Restoring the Wheelwright's Shop', *Journal of Modern Craft*, 13 (2020), 161–78.

Bulman, James C., 'Shakespeare's Georgic Histories', *Shakespeare Survey*, (1985), 37–49.

Burke, Tim, 'The Romantic Georgic and the Work of Writing', in C. Mahoney, ed., *A Companion to Romantic Poetry* (Chichester: Wiley-Blackwell, 2011), pp. 140–58.

Caldwell, Tanya. '"A City Graced with Many a Dome": Hannah Cowley's Domestic Comedies, the Georgic Impulse, and the Female Arts', *Eighteenth-Century Life* 42 (2018), 28–57.

Caldwell, Tanya, *Time to Begin Anew: Dryden's Georgics and Aeneis* (Lewisburg: Bucknell University Press, 2000).

Castellano, Katey, *The Ecology of British Romantic Conservatism, 1790–1837* (New York: Palgrave Macmillan, 2013).

Cavaliero, Glen, *The Rural Tradition in the English Novel 1900–1939* (London: Macmillan, 1977).

Cavanagh, Dermot, 'Georgic Sovereignty in Henry V', in *Shakespeare Survey*, ed. P. Holland, vol. 63: *Shakespeare's English Histories and their Afterlives*, (Cambridge University Press, 2010), pp. 114–26.

Chalker, John, *The English Georgic: A Study in the Development of a Form* (London: Routledge and Kegan Paul, 1969).

Chambers, Douglas, *The Planters of the English Landscape Garden: Botany, Trees, and the Georgics* (London: Yale University Press for The Paul Mellon Centre for Studies in British Art, 1993).

Chambers, Douglas, '"Wild Pastorall Encounter": John Evelyn, John Beale and the Renegotiation of Pastoral in the Mid-Seventeenth Century', in *Culture and Cultivation in Early Modern England*, eds. M. Leslie and T. Raylor (Leicester: Leicester University Press, 1992), pp. 173–94.

Chesnutt, Helen M., *Charles Waddell Chesnutt: Pioneer of the Color Line* (Chapel Hill, NC: University of North Carolina Press, 1952).

Cohen, Ralph, 'Innovation and Variation: Literary Change and Georgic Poetry', *Neohelicon*, 3 (1975), 149–82.

Coolidge, John S., 'Great Things and Small: The Virgilian Progression', *Comparative Literature*, 17 (1965), 1–23.
Cooper, H., 'Pastoral and Georgic', in *The Oxford History of Classical Reception in English Literature Volume 2, 1558–1660*, eds. P. Cheney and P. Hardie (Oxford: Oxford University Press, 2015), 201–24.
Cooper, John R., *The Art of 'The Compleat Angler'* (Durham, NC: Duke University Press, 1968).
Corse, Taylor, 'Husbandry in *Humphry Clinker*, Tobias Smollett's Georgic Novel', *Studies in English Literature, 1500–1900*, 57 (2017), 583–60.
Craik, Katharine, '"These Almost Thingles Things": Thomas Moffat's *The Silkewormes*, and English Renaissance Georgic', *Cahiers Elisabéthains* 60 (2001), 53–66.
Crawford, Rachel, 'English Georgic and British Nationhood', *ELH*, 65 (1998), 123–58.
Crawford, Rachel, 'Forms of Sublimity: the Garden, the Georgic, and the Nation', in *A Concise Companion to the Restoration and Eighteenth Century*, ed. Cynthia Wall (Oxford: Blackwell, 2005).
Crawford, Rachel, *Poetry, Enclosure, and the Vernacular Landscape, 1700–1830* (Cambridge University Press, 2002).
Cronon, William, *Changes in the Land: Indians, Colonists, and the Ecology of New England* (New York: Hill and Wang, 1983).
Cronon, William, 'The Trouble with Wilderness; or, Getting Back to the Wrong Nature', in *Uncommon Ground: Rethinking the Human Place in Nature*, ed. W. Cronon (New York: Norton, 1996), pp. 69–91.
Dasgupta, Sukanta, 'Drayton's "Silent Spring": *Poly-Olbion* and the Politics of Landscape', *Cambridge Quarterly*, 39 (2010), 152–71.
De Bruyn, Frans, 'From Georgic Poetry to Statistics and Graphs: Eighteenth-Century Representations and the "State" of British Society', *Yale Journal of Criticism*, 17 (2004), 107–39.
De Bruyn, Frans, 'Reading Virgil's Georgics as a Scientific Text: The Eighteenth-Century Debate between Jethro Tull and Stephen Switzer', *ELH*, 71 (2004), 661–89.
Diaper, Jeremy, 'Farming and Agriculture in Literary Modernism', *Modernist Cultures*, 16 (2021), 86–113.
Diaper, Jeremy, 'Ill Fares the Land: The Literary Influences and Agricultural Poetics of the Organic Husbandry Movement in the 1930s–50s', *Literature and History*, 27 (2018), 167–88.
Diaper, Jeremy, *T.S. Eliot and Organicism* (Clemson University Press, 2018).
Dolan, Frances E., *Digging the Past: How and Why to Imagine Seventeenth-Century Agriculture* (University of Pennsylvania Press, 2020).
Doody, M. Anne, 'Insects, Vermin, and Horses: *Gulliver's Travels* and Virgil's *Georgics*', in *Augustan Studies: Essays in Honour of Irvin Ehrenpreis*, eds. D. L. Patey and T. Keegan (Newark: University of Delaware Press, 1985), pp. 147–74.
Drew, Erin, '"Iron War" as "Daily Care": Sustainability and the Dialectic of Care in Dryden's *Georgics*', *1650–1850: Ideas, Aesthetics, and Inquiries* 22 (2015), 217–38.

Durling, Dwight L., *Georgic Tradition in English Poetry* (New York: Columbia University Press, 1935).
Dyck, Ian, *William Cobbett and Rural Popular Culture* (Cambridge: Cambridge University Press, 1992).
Earnshaw, Katharine, 'Shelley's Georgic Landscape', in *Reflections and New Perspectives on Virgil's Georgics*, Bobby Xinyue and Nicholas Freer, ed (London: Bloomsbury Academic, 2019), pp. 169–84.
Eastin, Krisi A., 'Virgil and the Visual Imagination: Illustrative Programmes from Antiquity to John Ogilby', unpublished PhD thesis, Brown University (2009).
Ebbatson, Roger, *Landscape and Literature 1830–1914: Nature, Text, Aura* (Basingstoke: Palgrave Macmillan, 2013).
Ebbatson, Roger, *Landscapes of Eternal Return: Tennyson to Hardy* (Basingstoke: Palgrave Macmillan, 2016).
Ellis, Markman, '"The Cane-Land Isles": Commerce and Empire in Late Eighteenth-Century Georgic and Pastoral Poetry', in *Islands in History and Representation*, eds. Rod Edmond and Vanessa Smith (London: Routledge, 2003), pp. 43–62.
Ellis, Markman, 'Incessant Labour: Georgic Poetry and the Problem of Slavery', in *Discourses of Slavery and Abolition: Britain and its colonies, 1760–1838*, eds. Brycchan. Carey, Markman Ellis, and Sara Salih (Basingstoke: Palgrave Macmillan, 2004), pp. 45–62.
Empson, William, *Some Versions of Pastoral* (London: Chatto & Windus, 1935).
Fairer, David, 'A Caribbean Georgic: James Grainger's The Sugar-Cane', *Kunapipi: Journal of Post-Colonial Writing*, 25 (2003), 21–8.
Fairer, David, 'Georgic', in *The Oxford Handbook of British Poetry, 1660–1800*, ed. Jack Lynch (Oxford University Press, 2016), pp. 457–472.
Fairer, David, '"Where Fuming Trees Refresh the Thirsty Air": The World of Eco-Georgic', *Studies in Eighteenth-Century Culture* 40 (2011), 201–18.
Fairer, David, '"The Year Runs Round": The Poetry of Work in Eighteenth-Century England', in *Ritual, Routine, and Regime: Repetition in Early Modern British and European Cultures*, ed. Lorna Clymer (University of Toronto Press, 2006), pp. 153–71.
Falconer, Rachel, *Seamus Heaney, Virgil and the Good of Poetry* (Edinburgh University Press, 2021).
Feingold, Richard, *Nature and Society: Later Eighteenth-Century Uses of the Pastoral and Georgic* (New Brunswick: Rutgers University Press, 1978).
Finseth, Ian F., *Shades of Green: Visions of Nature in the Literature of American Slavery* (Athens: University of Georgia Press, 2009).
Fish, Stanley E., *Self-Consuming Artefacts: The Experience of Seventeenth-Century Literature* (Berkeley: University of California Press, 1972).
Freeman, Mark, 'The Agricultural Labourer and the "Hodge" Stereotype', *Agricultural History Review*, 49 (2001), 172–86.
Fowler, Alastair, 'The Beginnings of English Georgic', in *Renaissance Genres*, ed. Barbara K. Lewalski (Cambridge, MA: Harvard University Press, 1986).

Foy, Anna M., 'The Convention of Circumlocution and the Proper Use of Human Dung in Samuel Martin's *Essay upon Plantership*', *ECS*, 49 (2016), 475–506.

Foy, Anna M., 'Grainger and the "Sordid Master": Plantocratic Alliance in *The Sugar-Cane* and Its Manuscript', *RES*, 68 (2017), 708–33.

Fussell, George E., *The Classical Tradition in West European Farming* (Newton Abbot: David and Charles, 1972).

Fussell, George E., *The Old English Farming Books*, 5 vols. (London: Pindar, [1947?]–1991).

Genovese, Michael, 'An Organic Commerce: Sociable Selfhood in Eighteenth-Century Georgic', *Eighteenth-Century Studies*, 46 (2013), 197–221.

Gervais, David, *Literary Englands: Versions of 'Englishness' in Modern Writing* (Cambridge University Press, 1993).

Gifford, Terry, and Neil Roberts, *Ted Hughes: A Critical Study* (London: Faber, 1981).

Gill, Stephen, 'Wordsworth's Breeches Pocket: Attitudes to the Didactic Poet', *Essays in Criticism*, 19 (1969), 385–401.

Gillespie, Stuart, 'An Unknown English Translation of Virgil's Third Georgic (c.1800)', *Translation and Literature*, 24 (2015), 319–40.

Goodman, Kevis, *Georgic Modernity and British Romanticism* (Cambridge University Press, 2004).

Goodman, Kevis, '"Wasted Labor"? Milton's Eve, the Poet's Work, and the Challenge of Sympathy', *ELH*, 64 (1997), 415–46.

Goodridge, John, *Rural Life in Eighteenth-Century English Poetry* (Cambridge University Press, 1995).

Grande, James, *William Cobbett, the Press and Rural England: Radicalism and the Fourth Estate, 1792–1835* (Basingstoke: Palgrave Macmillan, 2014).

Graver, Bruce E., '"Honorable Toil": The Georgic Ethic of Prelude I', *Studies in Philology* 92 (1995), 346–60.

Graver, Bruce E., 'Wordsworth's Georgic Beginnings', *Texas Studies in Literature and Language* 33 (1991), 137–59.

Graver, Bruce E., 'Wordsworth's Georgic Pastoral: Otium and Labor in "Michael"', *European Romantic Review*, 1 (1991), 119–34.

Griffin, Dustin, 'Redefining Georgic: Cowper's *Task*,' *ELH*, 57 (1990), 865–79.

Griffiths, Clare, 'G. D. H. Cole and William Cobbett', *Rural History*, 10.1 (1999), 91–104.

Griffiths, Clare, 'Heroes of the Reconstruction? Images of British Farmers in War and Peace', in *War, Agriculture, and Food: Rural Europe from the 1930s to the 1950s*, eds. P. Brassley, Y. Segers and L. Van Molle (London: Routledge, 2012), pp. 209–28.

Groom, Nick, '"Let's discuss over country supper soon": Rural Realities and Rustic Representations', *The Clearing*, 22 August 2013, www.littletoller.co.uk/the-clearing/lets-discuss-over-country-supper-soon-rebekah-brooks-and-david-cameron-rural-realities-and-rustic-representations-nick-groom/

Hadley, Karen, '"Tulips on Dunghills": Regendering the Georgic in Barrett Browning's *Aurora Leigh*', *Victorian Poetry*, 52 (2014), 465–82.

Hammill, Faye, 'Cold Comfort Farm, D. H. Lawrence, and English Literary Culture Between the Wars', *Modern Fiction Studies*, 47 (2001), 831–54.

Head, Dominic, *Modernity and the English Rural Novel* (Cambridge University Press, 2017).

Heinzelman, Kurt, 'The Last Georgic: *Wealth of Nations* and the Scene of Writing', in *Adam Smith's Wealth of Nations: New Interdisciplinary Essays*, eds. Stephen Copley and Kathryn Sutherland (Manchester University Press, 1995), pp. 171–94.

Heinzelman, Kurt, 'Roman Georgic in the Georgian Age: A Theory of Romantic Genre', *Texas Studies in Literature and Language*, 33 (1991), 182–214.

Helgerson, Richard, 'The Land Speaks: Cartography, Chorography, and Subversion in Renaissance England', *Representations*, 16 (1986), 50–85.

Hiltner, Ken, *What Else Is Pastoral?: Renaissance Literature and the Environment* (Ithaca: Cornell University Press, 2011).

Hourihane, Colum, ed., *Time in the Medieval World: Occupations of the Months and Signs of the Zodiac in the Index of Christian Art* (Princeton University Press, 2007).

Howkins, Alun, *The Death of Rural England: A Social History of the Countryside since 1900* (London: Routledge, 2003).

Irlam, Shaun, '"Wish You Were Here": Exporting England in James Grainger's *The Sugar-Cane*', *ELH*, 68 (2001), 377–96.

Irvine, Robert, 'Labor and Commerce in Locke and Early Eighteenth-Century English Georgic', *ELH*, 76 (2009), 963–88.

Johnson, W. R., 'Virgil's Corycian, Wendell Berry, and the Ecological Imagination,' *Classical Association of the Middle West and South* (2004), https://camws.org/sites/default/files/meeting2016/234.VirgilBerry.pdf

Kaul, Suvir, 'On Intersections between Empire, Colony, Nation, and Province in Eighteenth-Century British Poetry', *Eighteenth-Century Novel*, 6–7 (2009), 138–44.

Keegan, Bridget, *British Labouring-Class Nature Poetry, 1730–1837* (Basingstoke: Palgrave Macmillan, 2008).

Keegan, Bridget, 'Georgic Transformations and Stephen Duck's "The Thresher's Labour"', *SEL: Studies in English Literature, 1500–1900*, 41 (2001), 545–62.

Keith, W. John, *The Rural Tradition: William Cobbett, Gilbert White and Other Non-Fiction Prose Writers of the English Countryside* (Hassocks: Harvester, 1975).

Kerrigan, Charlie, *Virgil's Map: Geography, Empire, and the Georgics* (London: Bloomsbury, 2020).

Krupat, Arnold, *'That the People Might Live': Loss and Renewal in Native American Elegy* (Ithaca: Cornell University Press, 2012).

Kuhn, Mary, 'Chesnutt, Turpentine, and the Political Ecology of White Supremacy,' *PMLA*, 136 (2021), 39–54.

Kutchen, Larry, 'Timothy Dwight's Anglo-American Georgic: 'Greenfield Hill' and the Rise of United States Imperialism,' *Studies in the Literary Imagination*, 33 (2000), 109–28.

Landry, Donna, 'Georgic Ecology' in *Robert Bloomfield: Lyric, Class, and the Romantic Canon*, eds. S. White, J. Goodridge, and B. Keegan (Lewisburg: Bucknell University Press), pp. 253–68.

Lee, C. Carter, *Virginia Georgics, Written for the Hole and Corner Club of Powhatan* (Richmond, VA: James Woodhouse and Company, 1858).

Lobis, Seth, 'Milton's Tended Garden and the Georgic Fall', *Milton Studies*, 55 (2014), 89–111.

London, April, *Women and Property in the Eighteenth-Century English Novel* (Cambridge University Press, 1999), Part 1, 'Samuel Richardson and Georgic'.

Long, Edward, *The History of Jamaica*, 3 vols. (London, 1774).

Low, Anthony, *The Georgic Revolution* (Princeton University Press, 1985).

McCarthy, J. Mathes, *Green Modernism: Nature and the English Novel, 1900 to 1930* (Houndmills: Palgrave Macmillan, 2015).

McDonald, Shirley, 'Settler Life Writing, Georgic Traditions and Models of Environmental Sustainability', *American Review of Canadian Studies*, 45 (2015), 283–98.

McRae, Andrew, 'Fashioning a Cultural Icon: The Ploughman in Renaissance Texts', *Parergon*, 14 (1996), 187–204.

McRae, 'Of Albion's "Sundry Varying Soyles": The Land and its Human Occupants in *Poly-Olbion*', in *'Poly-Olbion': New Perspectives*, eds. A. McRae and P. Schwyzer (Cambridge University Press, 2020), pp. 82–7.

McRae, Andrew, *God Speed the Plough: The Representation of Agrarian England, 1500–1660* (Cambridge University Press, 1996).

McRae, Andrew, 'Tree-Felling in Early Modern England: Michael Drayton's Environmentalism', *RES*, 63 (2012), 410–30.

MacKenzie, Garry, 'Poetry, Ecocriticism and Labour: The Work of Writing and Reading', *Green Letters*, 20 (2016), 183–96.

Major, William, 'The Agrarian Vision and Ecocriticism', *ISLE: Interdisciplinary Studies in Literature and Environment*, 14 (2007), 51–70.

Mannon, Ethan, 'Georgic Environmentalism in *North of Boston*: An Ethic for Economic Landscapes', *ISLE: Interdisciplinary Studies in Literature and Environment*, 23 (2016), 344–69.

Marland, Pippa, 'Rewilding, Wilding, and the New Georgic in Contemporary Nature Writing', *Green Letters*, 24 (2020), 421–36.

Marland, Pippa, McCracken, Davy and Somervell, Tess, '"Down on the Farm" – Introduction to the Special Issue on Agriculture and Environment', *Green Letters*, 24 (2020), 335–43.

Martz, Louis L., '*Paradise Regained*: Georgic Form, Georgic Style', *Milton Studies* 32 (2002), 7–25.

Martz, Louis L., '*Paradise Regained*: The Meditative Combat', *ELH*, 27 (1960), 223–47.

Marx, Leo, *The Machine in the Garden: Technology and the Pastoral Ideal in America* (New York: Oxford University Press, 1970).

Matless, David, *Landscape and Englishness* (London: Reaktion Books, 1998).

Moore-Colyer, Richard, 'Back to Basics: Rolf Gardiner, H. J. Massingham and "A Kinship in Husbandry"', *Rural History*, 12 (2001), 85–108.

Moore-Colyer, Richard and Conford, Philip, 'A "Secret Society"? The Internal and External Relations of the Kinship in Husbandry, 1941–52', *Rural History*, 15 (2004), 189–206.

Mounsey, Chris, 'Christopher Smart's *The Hop-garden* and John Philips's *Cyder*: A Battle of the Georgics? Mid-Eighteenth-Century Poetic Discussions of Authority, Science and Experience', *British Journal for Eighteenth-Century Studies*, 22 (1999), 67–84.

Murdoch, John, 'The Landscape of Labor: Transformations of the Georgic', in *Romantic Revolutions: Criticism and Theory*, eds. Kenneth R. Johnston et al., (Bloomington: Indiana University Press, 1990), pp. 176–93.

Nemoianu, Virgil, *Micro-Harmony: The Growth and Uses of the Idyllic Model in Literature* (Bern: Peter Lang, 1977).

Newby, Howard, *The Deferential Worker: A Study of Farm Workers in East Anglia* (London: Allen Lane, 1977).

Nixon, Rob, *Slow Violence and the Environmentalism of the Poor* (Cambridge, Mass.; Harvard University Press, 2011).

Nolan, Sean, '"The Task that Leads the Wilder'd Mind": Robert Bloomfield, Humble Industry, and Studious Leisure', *European Romantic Review*, 31 (2020), 573–85.

O'Briain, Katarina, 'Dryden's Georgic Fictionality', *Eighteenth-Century Fiction* 30 (2018), 317–38.

O'Brien, Karen, 'Imperial Georgic, 1660–1789', in *The Country and the City Revisited: England and the Politics of Culture, 1550–1850*, eds. Gerald MacLean, Donna Landry, and Joseph P. Ward (Cambridge University Press, 1999), pp. 160–79.

O'Hehir, Brendan, 'The Meaning of Swift's "Description of a City Shower"', *ELH*, 27 (1960), 194–207.

O'Hogan, Cillian, 'Irish Versions of Virgil's *Eclogues* and *Georgics*', in *Virgil and His Translators*, eds. Susanna Braund and Zara Martirosova. Torlone (Oxford University Press, 2018), pp. 399–411.

Oldenburg, Scott, 'Thomas Tusser and the Poetics of the Plow', *ELR*, 49 (2019), 273–303.

Patterson, Annabel, *Pastoral and Ideology* (Berkeley: University of California Press, 1987).

Patterson, Annabel, 'Pastoral versus Georgic: The Politics of Virgilian Quotation', in *Renaissance Genres*, ed. Barbara K. L. (Cambridge, MA: Harvard University Press, 1986), pp. 241–67.

Patterson, Annabel, 'Wordsworth's Georgic: Genre and Structure in *The Excursion*', *The Wordsworth Circle*, 9 (1978), 145–55.

Pellicer, Juan Christian, 'Celebrating Queen Anne and the Union of 1707 in Great Britain's First Georgic', *Journal for Eighteenth-Century Studies*, 37.2 (2014), 217–27.

Pellicer, J. Christian, 'The Georgic at Mid-Eighteenth Century and the Case of Dodsley's "Agriculture"', *RES*, 54, 213 (2003), 67–93.

Pellicer, J. Christian, 'Georgic as Genre: The Scholarly Reception of Vergil in Mid- Eighteenth-Century Britain', in *Reading Poetry, Writing Genre: English Poetry and Literary Criticism in Dialogue with Classical Scholarship*, eds. S. Bär and E. Hauser (London: Bloomsbury, 2019), pp. 79–93.

Pellicer, J. Christan, '"I Hear Such Strange Things of the Union's Fate": Charles Carter Lee's "Virginia Georgics"', *Early American Literature*, 42 (2007), 131–55.

Pellicer, J. Christian, 'Pastoral and Georgic', in *The Oxford History of Classical Reception in English Literature, Volume 3: 1660–1790*, eds. D. Hopkins and C. Martindale (Oxford University Press, 2012), pp. 287–322.

Pellicer, J. Christian, *Preposterous Virgil: Reading through Stoppard, Auden, Wordsworth, Heaney* (London: Bloomsbury, forthcoming 2022).

Pellicer, J. Christian, 'Virgil's Eclogues and Georgics in Charlotte Smith's Beachy Head', in *Romans and Romantics*, eds. T. Saunders, C. Martindale, R. Pite, and M. Skoie (Oxford: Oxford University Press, 2012), pp. 161–82.

Pellicer, J. Christian, 'Virgil's *Georgics* II in *Paradise Lost*', *Translation and Literature*, 14 (2005), 129–47.

Peterfreund, Stuart, 'Keats and the Fate of the Genres: The Troublesome Middle Term', *Genre*, 16 (1983), 249–77.

Pethers, Matthew, '"This Small Herculean Labor": Literary Professionalism, Georgic Work, and *Walden*', *Amerikastudien*, 54 (2007), 165–94.

Plasa, Carl, *Slaves to Sweetness: British and Caribbean Literatures of Sugar* (Liverpool University Press, 2009).

Pollio, David M., 'Vergil and American Symbolism', *The Classical Outlook*, 87 (2010), 137–40.

Pomeroy, Elizabeth W., 'Within Living Memory: Vita Sackville-West's Poems of Land and Garden', *Twentieth-Century Literature*, 28 (1982), 269–9.

Power, Henry, 'Virgil, Horace, and Gay's Art of Walking the Streets', *Cambridge Quarterly*, 38, (2009), 338–67.

Prince, Hugh, 'Art and Agrarian Change, 1710–1815', in *The Iconography of Landscape: Essays on the Symbolic Representation, Design and Use of Past Environments*, eds. Denis Cosgrove and Stephen Daniels (Cambridge University Press, 1988), pp. 98–118.

Randhawa, B. Puneet, 'The Inhospitable Muse: Locating Creole Identity in James Grainger's The Sugar-Cane', *ECTI*, 49 (2008), 67–85.

Readman, Paul, *Storied Ground: Landscape and the Shaping of English National Identity* (Cambridge University Press, 2018).

Reddick, Yvonne, *Ted Hughes: Environmentalist and Ecopoet* (Basingstoke: Palgrave Macmillan, 2017).

Rice, James D., 'Early American Environmental Histories,' *William and Mary Quarterly*, 75 (2018), 401–32.

Robinson, Craig, 'The Good Shepherd: *Moortown Elegies*', in *The Achievement of Ted Hughes*, ed. Keith Sagar (Manchester University Press, 1983), pp. 257–84.

Rogers, Pat, 'John Philips, Pope, and Political Georgic', *Modern Language Quarterly*, 66.4 (2005), 411–42.
Ronda, Margaret, '"Work and Wait Unwearying": Dunbar's Georgics,' *PMLA*, 127 (2012), 863–78.
Røstvig, Maren-Sofie, *'The Happy Man': Studies in the Metamorphoses of a Classical Ideal. Vol. I: 1600–1700*, 2nd ed. (Oslo University Press, 1962).
Sandberg, Julianne, 'The Georgic Mode and "Poor Labours" of George Herbert', *Renaissance Studies*, 30, 2 (2016), 218–35.
Sandiford, Keith, *The Cultural Politics of Sugar: Caribbean Slavery and Narratives of Colonialism* (Cambridge University Press, 2000).
Saunt, Claudio, *Unworthy Republic: The Dispossession of Native Americans and the Road to Indian Territory* (New York: Norton, 2020).
Sayre, Laura, 'Locating the Georgic: From the *Ferme Ornée* to the Model Farm', *Studies in the History of Gardens and Designed Landscapes*, 22 (2002), 167–92.
Sayre, Laura, 'The Politics of Organic Farming: Populists, Evangelicals, and the Agriculture of the Middle', *Gastronomica*, 11 (2011), 38–47.
Schenck, C. Marguerite, *Mourning and Panegyric: The Poetics of Pastoral Ceremony* (University Park: Pennsylvania University Press, 1988).
Schoenberger, Melissa, *Cultivating Peace: The Virgilian Georgic in English, 1650–1750* (Lewisburg: Bucknell University Press, 2019).
Schoenberger, Melissa, 'The Sword, the Scythe, and the "Arts of Peace" in Dryden's Georgics', *Translation and Literature*, 23, 1 (2014), 23–41.
Schulz, Max F., *Paradise Preserved: Recreations of Eden in Eighteenth and Nineteenth-Century England* (Cambridge University Press, 1985).
Scodel, Joshua, *Excess and the Mean in Early Modern English Literature* (Princeton: Princeton University Press, 2002), Part 2, 'Means and Extremes in Early Modern Georgic'.
Scott, Charlotte, *Shakespeare's Nature: From Cultivation to Culture* (Oxford University Press, 2014).
Sessions, William A., 'Spenser's Georgics', *English Literary Renaissance*, 10 (1980), 202–38.
Sharpe, Matthew, 'Georgics of the Mind and the Architecture of Fortune: Francis Bacon's Therapeutic Ethics', *Philosophical Papers*, 43 (2014), 89–121.
Shields, David, *Oracles of Empire: Poetry, Politics, and Commerce in British America, 1690–1750* (University of Chicago Press, 1990).
Shaw, M., 'Cold Comfort Times: Women Rural Writers in the Interwar Period', in *The English Countryside Between the Wars: Regeneration or Decline?*, eds. P. Brasslet, J. Burchardt and L. Thomson (Woodbridge: Boydell Press, 2006), pp. 73–86.
Silva, Cristobal, 'Georgic Fantasies: James Grainger and the Poetry of Colonial Dislocation', *ELH*, 83 (2016), 127–56.
Smith, C. Weiss, *Empiricist Devotions: Science, Religion, and Poetry in Early Eighteenth-Century England* (University of Virginia Press, 2016).
Smith, Virginia F., 'Frost on the Apple', *ISLE: Interdisciplinary Studies in Literature and Environment*, 23 (2016), 677–93.

Snell, K. D. M., *Annals of the Labouring Poor: Social Change and Agrarian England, 1660–1900* (Cambridge University Press, 1985).

Spate, O. H. K., 'The Muse of Mercantilism: Jago, Grainger, and Dyer', in *Studies in the Eighteenth Century: Papers Presented at the David Nichol Smith Memorial Seminar, Canberra 1966*, ed. R. F. Brissenden (University of Toronto Press, 1968), pp. 119–31.

Spurr, M. S., 'Agriculture and the *Georgics*', *Greece & Rome*, 33 (1986), 167–87.

Sweet, Timothy, *American Georgics: Economy and Environment in American Literature, 1580–1864* (Philadelphia: University of Pennsylvania Press, 2001).

Thacker, Jack, 'The Farming of Verse: The Georgic Mode in the Poetry of Ted Hughes, Seamus Heaney and Alice Oswald', unpublished PhD thesis, University of Bristol, (23 January 2019).

Thibodeau, Philip, *Playing the Farmer: Representations of Rural Life in Vergil's Georgics* (Berkeley: University of California Press, 2011).

Thirsk, Joan, gen. ed., *The Agrarian History of England and Wales*, 8 vols in 11 (Cambridge University Press, 1967–2000).

Thirsk, Joan, 'Plough and Pen: Agricultural Writers in the Seventeenth Century', in *Social Relations and Ideas: Essays in Honour of R.H. Hilton*, eds. T. H. Aston et al., (Cambridge University Press, 1983), pp. 295–317.

Thomas, Richard F., 'Didaxis and Aesthetics in the Georgics Tradition', in *Calliope's Classroom: Studies in Didactic Poetry from Antiquity to the Renaissance*, eds. A. Harder, A. A. MacDonald, and G. J. Reinink (Leuven: Peeters, 2007), 71–102.

Thomas, Richard F., 'The Georgics of Resistance: From Virgil to Heaney', *Vergilius*, 47 (2001), 117–47.

Thorne, Christian, 'William Cowper, the Georgic, and the Unwritten Literature of the 1780s', *Boundary 2*, 44, 3 (2017), 73–98.

Trevisan, Sara, "'The murmuring woods euen shuddred as with feare': Deforestation in Michael Drayton's *Poly-Olbion*', *The Seventeenth Century*, 26 (2011), 240–63.

Tulloch, Elspeth, 'Husbandry, Agriculture and Ecocide: Reading Bessie Head's *When Rain Clouds Gather* as a Postcolonial Georgic', *European Journal of English Studies*, 16 (2012), 137–50.

Turner, James, *The Politics of Landscape: Rural Scenery and Society in English Poetry 1630–1660* (Oxford University Press, 1979).

Twiddy, Iain, *Pastoral Elegy in Contemporary British and Irish Poetry* (London: Bloomsbury, 2012).

Tylus, Jane, 'Spenser, Virgil, and the Politics of Poetic Labor', *ELH*, 55 (1988), 53–77.

Van Sant, Ann, 'Crusoe's Hands', *Eighteenth-Century Life*, 32 (2008), 120–37.

Vasunia, Phiroze, 'Virgil and the British Empire, 1760–1880', *Proceedings of the British Academy*, 155 (Oxford University Press, 2009), pp. 83–116.

Vespa, Jack, 'Georgic Inquisitiveness, Pastoral Meditation, Romantic Reflexivity: "Nutting" and the Figure of Wordsworth as Poet', *Genre*, 38 (2005), 1–44.

Wagner, Jeffrey, 'American Georgics and Globalization: Literary and Economic Co-Evolution in Three Enclosure Movements', *ISLE: Interdisciplinary Studies in Literature and Environment*, 20 (2013), 71–84.

Wagner-McCoy, Sarah, 'Virgilian Chesnutt: Eclogues of Slavery and Georgics of Reconstruction in the Conjure Tales', *ELH*, 80 (2013), 199–220.
Wall, Wendy, 'Renaissance National Husbandry: Gervase Markham and the Publication of England', *Sixteenth Century Journal*, 27 (1996), 767–85.
Wallace, Andrew, 'Virgil and Bacon in the Schoolroom', *ELH*, 73 (2006), 161–85.
Wallace, Anne D., 'Farming on Foot: Tracking Georgic in Clare and Wordsworth', *Texas Studies in Literature and Language*, 34 (1992), 509–40.
Wilkinson, L. Patrick, *The Georgics of Virgil: A Critical Survey* (Cambridge University Press, 1969).
Wilkinson, L. P., *The Georgics of Virgil: A Critical Survey* (Bristol Classical Press, 1997).
Williams, Raymond, *The Country and the City* (1973; London: Vintage, 2016).
Wilson-Okamura, D. Scott, *Virgil in the Renaissance* (Cambridge University Press, 2010).
Zimmerman, D. Mark, 'The Last Georgic, or James Grahame's Revision of Eighteenth-Century Rural Labour', *Scottish Studies*, 45 (2010), 244–52.
Ziolkowski, Theodore, *Virgil and the Moderns* (Princeton University Press, 1993).
Zwierlein, Anne-Julia. 'Milton Epic and Bucolic: Empire and Readings of *Paradise Lost*, 1667–1837', in *The Oxford Handbook of Milton*, eds. McDowell, N. and N. Smith (Oxford University Press, 2011), pp. 669–86.

Index

Addison, Joseph
   'Essay on the Georgics', 3, 10–12, 66, 100, 123, 124, 126, 150–2, 159, 161, 166, 171, 238, 244, 245, 352
   Spectator, 12
Aemilianus, 48
Africa, 40
   Carthage, 39, 40
   Egypt, 40, 345, 354
Alcidamas, 46, 47
Alpers, Paul, 320
America, 201, 202
America, states of
   Carolina, 200, 205, 320, 334–6
   Connecticut, 316, 331
   Kentucky, 26
   Mississippi, 319
   New England, 317, 322, 329
   New Hampshire, 323
   Virginia, 136, 319, 320
Americans, First Nation, 319, 325–7
Anderson, James, 161, 168
Anthon, Charles, 322–3
Aristaeus, 51, 157, 237
Armitage, Simon, 3
Armstrong, John, 157, 164
Ascham, Roger, 6
Aubrey, John, 71
Auden, W. H., 230, 265, 291, 292, 298
Austen, Jane, 16, 197, 200
Austen, Ralph, 10

Bacon, Francis, Lord Verulam, 7, 8, 13, 121, 122, 124, 126, 127, 167
   Baconianism, 9
Baldwin, Stanley, 20–1, 299
Bamford, Samuel, 208
Barrett, Hugh, 103, 105
Bassus, 43
Batchelor, Thomas, 187
Bates, H. E., 104

Bathurst, Bella, 23
Beachy Head, 17, 180, 191–4, 300, 303, 304, 307
Beckett, Arthur, 306
Beeson, Jane, 111
Bell, Adrian, 20, 99, 104–5, 275, 280, 287
Belloc, Hilaire, 278, 306
Bennett, Arnold, 302
Benson, Richard, 111
Beresford, Tristram, 103
Berry, Wendell, 26–7, 223, 229, 306
Beverley, Robert, 328–30
Bible, The, 40, 61
Blackwell, Alexander, 157
Blith, Walter, 7–10, 141
Bloom, Alan, 276
Bloomfield, Robert, 19, 184–91, 296, 301
Blythe, Ronald, 22, 105, 111, 116
Borodale, Sean, 266–7
Boyle, Robert, 10
Bruegel, Jan, 61
Buell, Lawrence, 318, 320, 322
Bullough, Tom, 24, 111
Burnett, Elizabeth-Jane, 23
Butler, Charles, 7, 9
Butterworth, Jez, 288

Caesar Augustus, also known as Octavian, 49–51, 125, 345, 346, 351
Caesar, Julius, 49, 163
Camden, William, 281
Canada, 105, 199
Carew, Thomas, 3
Caribbean, 14, 25, 166, 348, 355, 356
Carlyle, Thomas, 199
Carson, Rachel, 111
Carter Swan, William, 79, 82
Cato the elder, 47–50, 54, 157, 160, 238, 337, 349
Cecil, Robert, 127
Chapman, George, 121–2, 131, 136

Charles I, 141, 142
Chatwin, Bruce, 111
Cherrington, John, 109, 110
Chesnutt, Charles, 25, 26, 320, 323, 334–8
Churchill, Caryl, 276, 286–7, 289
Clare, John, 14, 16, 17, 19, 58, 67–9, 83, 84, 177, 178, 182, 189, 209, 229, 259, 275, 276, 279–81, 286, 289, 290
Cobbett, William, 16, 197–211, 275
Cocker, Mark, 283
Cole, G. D. H., 209
Cole, William, 282
Collier, Mary, 13, 65
Collis, John Stewart, 107–8
Columella, 48–9, 51, 147, 157, 349
Common Agricultural Policy, 5
Conrad, Joseph, 302
Corn Laws, 17
Coryat, Thomas, 284
Countryfile, 23
Court, Arthur, 110, 111
Cowley, Abraham, 146–9
Cowper, William, 57, 69–71, 74, 159–61, 172, 179, 184, 229, 235, 238
Crabbe, George, 17, 184, 185
Crawford, Rachel, 179, 189
Cromwell, Oliver, 10, 141–3, 284
Cronon, William, 26, 325
cummings, e. e., 3

Daniel, Samuel, 8
Day Lewis, Cecil, 298, 306, 308, 309, 351, 359
De Forest, John W., 322
Dee, Tim, 276, 280, 289, 292
DEFRA, 267
Democritus of Abdera, 41
Demosthenes, 44, 47
Denham, John, 158, 318
Dickinson, Emily, 3
didactic, 1, 3, 5, 6, 10, 15, 22, 25, 51, 123, 124, 148, 152, 156, 160, 161, 163, 178–80, 183, 184, 186–90, 238, 264, 319–21, 330, 332, 333
Dimock, Cressy, 9
Dionysius of Utica, 43
Dodsley, Robert, 14–15, 157, 165, 170–2
Donaldson, Jack and Frances, 103
Douglas, Gavin
    Eneados, 6
Drayton, Michael, 121, 122, 129, 135
    Poly-Olbion, 8–9, 121, 131, 133–6, 216, 275
Dryden, John, 10–11, 27, 50, 123, 126, 150–2, 163, 173, 217, 265, 271, 284, 351, 352
Du Bois, W. E. B., 322
Duck, Stephen, 13, 65, 162, 182, 185, 186
Dugdale, William, 283–4

Dunbar, Paul Laurence, 321
Dyer, John
    The Fleece, 14, 157, 165, 185, 240, 277

ecocriticism, 126
ecopoetry, 262
Edgeworth, Maria, 198
Eliot, T.S., 3, 22, 50, 298, 306
Elizabeth I, 23, 125, 127
Elliott, Ebenezer, 184
Elyot, Thomas, Sir
    The Governour, 6
Emerson, Ralph Waldo, 317–18, 323
empire, 14, 24, 49, 52, 125, 156, 243, 278, 321, 323, 344–6, 348, 350–5
Empson, William, 321
England, counties of
    Berkshire, 200
    Buckinghamshire, 87, 110
    Cambridgeshire, 276, 289
    Cheshire, 106
    Cornwall, 352
    Derbyshire, 79
    Devon, 23, 106, 255, 257, 259, 261–5, 267
    Dorset, 108, 220
    Essex, 283
    Hampshire, 65, 80, 197–9, 203, 297, 299
    Herefordshire, 69, 80, 242
    Kent, 69, 85, 203, 205, 207, 211, 235–8, 242, 243, 253, 345, 349, 350, 354, 356
    Lancashire, 106, 135, 208
    Lincolnshire, 79, 134, 275–7, 279, 290
    Middlesex, 135
    Norfolk, 3, 16, 18, 79, 108, 206, 277, 288
    Northamptonshire, 17, 135, 279
    Oxfordshire, 109
    Shropshire, 21, 68
    Somerset, 106, 110, 266
    Suffolk, 17, 22, 104, 105, 111
    Surrey, 18, 197, 199, 211
    Sussex, 21, 72, 73, 79, 87, 104, 107, 205, 211, 297, 299, 301, 302, 306–8
    Wiltshire, 105, 110, 135, 215, 223, 224, 288, 300, 301, 352
    Worcestershire, 204, 266
    Yorkshire, 3, 24, 276
England, regions of
    Cotswolds, 108, 135
    Dartmoor, 261, 263, 264
    Fens, 134, 277
    Lake District, 4, 106, 112, 287, 298, 309–12, 351
    Thames valley, 125, 167, 306, 318
    Wessex, 215, 217, 219, 221, 243, 276
Ennion, E. A R., 276

environment, 2, 5, 17, 95, 106, 111, 126, 133–6, 178, 224, 261, 262, 268, 287, 305, 311, 316, 322, 344, 355
epic, 4, 7, 10, 42, 45, 49–51, 121, 131, 135, 148, 149, 151, 179, 204, 236, 237, 242, 261, 262, 267, 336
Epicureanism, 8, 237
ethnicity, 80, 320, 322, 323, 333–8
Euripides, 44
Evelyn, John, 9, 30, 140, 144, 285

Fairer, David, 156, 165, 178, 183, 191, 204, 263
Fallon, Peter, 22
farming
 apiculture, 9, 40, 42, 50, 51, 58, 61, 69, 74, 94, 237, 240, 241, 266, 267, 318, 344, 347
 apple and cider production, 10, 69, 202, 224, 226, 228, 229, 245
 cereal production, 21, 23, 44, 50, 63, 67, 85, 90, 91, 108, 110, 160, 186, 219, 236, 283, 292, 328, 336
 crop rotation, 9, 50, 222, 347
 dairy and milk production, 20, 64, 65, 99, 100, 105–8, 110, 132, 265, 308, 347
 enclosure, 13, 16, 18, 127, 129–31, 177, 179, 182, 184, 280, 298, 348
 grafting, 50, 63, 69, 170, 240, 324
 livestock, 4, 17, 48, 49, 50, 63, 72, 82, 85, 90, 91, 101, 104–8, 110–12, 127, 134, 141, 156, 162, 166, 184, 188, 206, 215, 245, 256, 259, 260, 267, 282, 296, 298, 301, 304, 305, 309–11, 332, 344, 347
 ploughing, 3, 4, 20, 21, 58, 61, 64, 67, 86, 88, 91, 104, 108, 123, 127, 128, 130, 131, 155, 160, 168, 199, 215, 247, 275, 280, 290, 304, 332
 scything, 65
 silviculture, 52, 59, 60, 62, 63, 67, 69, 74, 82, 83, 85, 89, 93, 94, 133, 144–6, 163, 178, 200–3, 207, 216, 218, 224–32, 239, 240, 245, 279, 324, 334, 347–50
 soil fertility and manuring, 11, 44, 70, 101, 109, 130, 155, 159–60, 170, 222, 309, 332, 334, 347
 sowing, 41, 59, 65, 70, 72, 105, 168, 210, 215, 220
 specialist crops, 128, 130
 sustainability, 5, 26, 133, 191, 218, 226, 229, 299, 310, 325, 349, 355, 356
 threshing, 59, 65, 67, 99, 101, 105, 336, 337, 338
 tractors, 82–8, 91, 95, 99, 104–9
 viticulture, 39, 52, 57, 59, 62, 63, 65, 66, 69, 70, 73, 75, 141, 146, 224, 225, 227, 347
Fergusson, Robert, 181, 182
Ferry, David, 140, 142, 150, 172
Fiennes, Celia, 282

Firbanks, Thomas, 106
Fortrey, Samuel, 285
Fowler, Alastair, 10, 122, 123, 133, 135, 136
Fraser Darling, Frank, 107
Frazer, J. G., 230
Fream, William, 101
Freneau, Philip, 331
Frost, Robert, 265
Fuller, Thomas, 8

Gaister, Leslie, 288
Gardiner, Rolf, 108
Gates, Sidney Barrington, 239, 242, 253
Gay, John
 Trivia, 1, 12
georgic themes
 craft, 221
 digression, 45, 158, 166, 171, 337
 rural craft, 26, 171, 179, 215, 239–41, 244, 265, 323, 332, 349
 turning, 57–9, 62, 65–7, 68, 122, 131, 145, 151, 183, 192, 197, 215, 307, 322, 331
georgic time
 annual cycles, 4, 58, 59, 66, 67, 105, 163
 daily cycles, 80, 81, 103, 201, 218, 228
 seasonal cycles, 3, 4, 13, 45, 61, 62, 64–7, 173, 180, 185, 189–91, 217, 218, 226, 235, 236, 238, 245, 247, 249, 280, 281, 296, 325, 348, 349
Gibbons, Stella
 Cold Comfort Farm, 21, 104, 298, 307, 308
Goldsmith, Oliver, 17, 180, 182–4, 186, 190, 192
Goodman, Kevis, 192, 258
Googe, Barnabe, 6, 124
Grahame, James, 184, 185, 188–90
Grainger, James
 The Sugar-Cane, 14, 25, 157, 160, 166, 170, 244, 331, 345
Gray, Thomas, 182, 192
Greece, xii, 17, 39, 54, 55, 236, 358
 Athens, 41
 Peloponnese, The, 41
Groom, Nick, 266
Grundy, John, Jr., 277
Gyte, Maria, 79, 86

Hakluyt, Richard, 126
Hallam, William, 81
Hamilton, James, 156, 161
Hardy, Mary, 79, 86
Hardy, Thomas, 2, 18, 21, 99, 216–19, 221, 223, 230, 244, 276
 Jude the Obscure, 218
 Mayor of Casterbridge, 216–17, 225, 231

Tess of the d'Urbervilles, 216
The Woodlanders, 216, 217, 219, 224, 226, 229–32
Harman, Tony, 110, 111
Harrison, Melissa, 23, 111
Harrison, Ruth, 112
Hart, Christopher, 111
Harte, Walter, 15, 156
Hartlib, Samuel, 5–10, 12
Heaney, Seamus, 22, 240, 257, 296, 347
Heinzelman, Kurt, 15, 165, 194, 258
Henderson, George, 108
Heresbach, Conrad, 6, 124
Hereward the Wake, 289–90
Hesiod, 43–7, 50–3, 61, 66–7, 70, 72, 74, 121–2, 124, 131, 136, 150, 157, 165, 236, 237, 239, 240, 247, 344
Hill, Geoffrey, 265, 266
Hockney, David, 3, 4
Hodkin, William, 79
Holloway, William, 184
Holme, Constance, 104
Homer, 43–7, 237, 247, 261
Homewood, Robert, 107
Hood, Thomas, 318
Horace, 132, 147, 177, 183
Houghton, John, 11
Hudson, W. H., 296–312
Hughes, Ted, 22, 223, 255, 260
Hunter, Alexander, 157
Hurdis, James, 301

India, iv, 354, 356
Iran
Tehran, 354
Italy, 48, 49, 50, 53, 55, 158, 345, 346, 348–53, 355
Calabria, 348
Naples, 344, 351
Rome, xii, 39, 40, 43, 47–9, 126, 145, 151, 237, 323, 347, 353

Jackson, Wes, 26
Jago, Richard
Edge-Hill, 14, 158
James I, 122, 130, 132, 133, 136
Jefferies, Richard, 18, 215–21, 223, 224, 227–9, 297, 300–10
Jefferson, Thomas, 25, 319, 328, 330, 335–7
Johnson, Daisy, 288
Johnson, Maurice, 278
Johnson, Samuel, 4, 202
Jonson, Ben, 121–2, 129–34, 135

Kames, Henry Home, Lord, 172
Kavanagh, Patrick, 22, 259

Kaye-Smith, Sheila, 21, 104, 308
Keats, John, 179
Kincaid, Jamaica, 356
Kinderley, Charles, 282
Kingsnorth, Paul, 26, 289–92
Kinship in Husbandry, 108
Klein, Naomi, 356

labour, 1, 4–6, 8, 10, 14, 15, 20, 22, 24, 26, 57, 59, 63, 66, 69, 79–81, 84, 85, 91, 95, 99, 108, 109, 121, 122, 125–6, 128, 129, 131, 132, 135, 142, 148–50, 156, 158, 162–6, 171, 172, 178, 179, 181–6, 189, 191, 192, 197, 198, 201, 204, 211, 215, 218–20, 224, 226, 228, 231, 241, 249, 265, 277, 285–7, 298, 306, 309, 318, 319, 321–3, 327, 328, 329, 330, 332, 335, 337, 338, 350, 356
Laity, John, 109
land reform, 9
landscape, 2, 3, 5, 6, 8, 17, 22, 27, 61, 67, 79, 84, 89–96, 99, 112, 122, 127, 132, 134, 135, 142, 152, 158, 167, 185, 191, 192, 198, 238, 243, 259, 261, 275–82, 285, 286, 289–92, 296–8, 306–8, 311, 316, 344
Lawrence, D.H., 21, 297
Lee, Charles Carter, 25, 320, 331
levellers, 130
Lewis-Stempel, John, 95, 311
Lisle, Edward, 15
Lively, Penelope, 111
Low, Anthony, 123, 140, 345
Lucretius, 240

Mabey, Richard, 297, 303
Macbeth, George, 288
Macfarlane, Robert, 268, 307, 308
Madox Ford, Ford, 22, 57, 71, 72, 302
Mago, 40, 41, 43, 48, 157
Marc Antony, 49
Marcus Aurelius, 43
Markham, Gervase, 8–9, 124, 125, 129, 130
Marsh, Jan, 298, 310
Marshall, William, 169–71
Marvell, Andrew, 10, 142–4, 150
Marx, Leo, 316
Massingham, H. J., 108, 308
Maxey, Edward, 7
McClure, S. S., 335
McConnell, Primrose, 101, 103
McEntegart, Anne, 79, 84–6, 88–91
Menos, Hilary, 267
Meres, Franes, 124
Mills, John, 167
Mills, Magnus, 111

386   Index

Milton, John, 1, 10, 123
    Paradise Lost, 10, 70, 148, 150
    Paradise Regained, 1, 10, 149
Mitford, Mary Russell, 199–201
modernity, 2–4, 9, 23, 24, 61, 66, 70, 96, 105, 157, 171, 172, 181, 218, 240, 245, 256, 259, 291, 326, 344, 347, 349–51, 353, 356
Monbiot, George, 24, 25
Moore, Jonas, Sir, 106, 205, 285
More, Thomas, St.
    Utopia, 6, 127
Morrison, Ronald, 302, 305
Morton, H. V., 307
Muldoon, Paul, 244
Musonius Rufus, 42

Nagle, Mary Kathryn, 325
National Trust, 23, 276
Newton, Isaac, Sir, 13
Nicander, 42, 48, 50
Norden, John, 7, 130
North, Sam, 111
nostalgia, 5, 19, 172, 179, 181, 182, 190, 209, 304, 307, 316, 317, 320, 322

Ogilvie, George, 331
Olmsted, Frederick Law, 25, 317, 319, 327–32, 337
Orpheus, 3, 44, 51, 237
Oscott Psalter, 59
Oswald, Alice, 22, 260

Palladius, 48, 52
Pandora, 45
pastoral, 4, 6, 8, 49, 50, 91, 95, 111, 123, 125, 127, 128, 132, 136, 143, 149, 151, 177, 186, 188, 190, 192, 193, 199, 201, 204–5, 215, 216, 236, 237, 240, 245, 255–8, 261, 262, 267, 268, 278, 296, 297, 303, 304, 307, 309, 311, 315–20, 320–3, 328, 336, 338, 348
Patterson, Annabel, 8, 318
Payne Knight, Richard, 185
Pears, Tim, 111
Penshurst, Kent, 131, 132
Pepys, Samuel, 282
Philips, John
    Cyder, 12, 14, 69, 71, 157, 160, 163–4, 170, 171, 185, 242, 248, 249
Plato, 41, 44, 46, 47
Plattes, Gabriel, 9, 12
Platts, Hugh, Sir, 7
Pliny the Elder, 42
Politian, 52
Pope, Alexander, 12, 14, 158, 167, 243
Pound, Ezra, 22, 72

Powys, T. F., 21, 104
Proteus, 51
Pryor, Francis, 292
Purchas, Samuel, 126

Queen Mary's Psalter, 60

Raisin, Ross, 24
realism, 4, 180, 181, 185, 259
Rebanks, James
    English Pastoral, 4, 5, 27
    Shepherd's Life, 4, 297, 298, 300, 309, 310
Reece, Nancy, 327
retirement, rural, 69, 156, 172, 204, 266
Rider Haggard, Henry, 18, 19, 102
Rothamsted research station, 102
Rowe, Nicholas, 181
Roy, Arundhati, 356
Royal Society, 9, 11, 161
    Georgical Committee, 9, 11, 71, 140
Ruck, Janette, 109

Sackville-West, Vita, 19, 20, 66, 68–9, 73, 74, 104, 244, 235–49, 307, 345, 346, 349–51, 353–6
Schama, Simon, 57
Scot, Reynolde, 6
Scott, Thomas, 164
Scott, Walter, 198, 200
Shakespeare, William, 123, 125, 126, 243, 246, 249, 348
Smart, Christopher, 157
    'The Hop Garden', 14
Smith, Adam, 165
Smith, Ali, 3
Smith, Charlotte, 17, 180, 238
    Beachy Head, 191–4
Smith, John, 328
Smith, Sidney, 89
Snyder, Gary, 26
Spalding Gentlemen's Society, 278
Spenser, Edmund, 6, 58, 123, 125, 136
Sprat, Thomas, 140, 161
Stead, William Thomas, 317
Stephens, Henry, 101
stewardship, 5, 26, 217, 311
Stewart, Chris, 72
Stoicism, 8, 42
Stovin, Cornelius, 79, 80, 85, 86, 89, 90
Strange, Doreen, 80
Street, A.G., 19, 20, 99, 100, 102, 105, 109
Stukeley, William, 278, 282
Sturt, George, 18–20
Surtees, R.S., 17

Swift, Graham, 276, 277, 280, 282, 285, 286, 288, 289
Swift, Jonathan, 12, 13
Swift, Katherine, 57, 68
Swing Riots, 16
Switzer, Stephen, 13, 155

Taylor, Dennis, 216
Taylor, John, 125
Tennyson, Alfred, Lord, 17
Thelwall, John, 204
Theocritus, 50, 181, 261
Thirsk, Joan, 7
Thomas, Edward, 297, 304–6
Thomas, R. S., 99
Thomas, Richard F., 22
Thompson, E. P., 356, 361
Thompson, Flora, 22
Thomson, James, 71
  Seasons, 1, 13, 19, 67, 158, 172, 185, 192, 227, 238, 240, 296, 344, 345, 348, 350, 353, 355
Thoreau, Henry David, 25, 319, 321
Tonson, Jacob, 11, 151
traditional knowledge, 5
Tree, Isabella, 311
Tremain, Rose, 289
Tull, Jethro, 13, 155, 156, 161, 162, 170, 206
Turner, Frederick Jackson, 317
Turner, Ivan, 80, 83, 86
Tusser, Thomas, 6, 62–5, 67, 73, 76, 124–5, 129–31, 276

utopia, 9, 216

Varro of Reate, 48–50, 61, 62, 147, 337, 349
Vermuyden, Cornelius, 284
Virgil, 61
  Eclogues, 58, 123, 181, 237, 240, 261, 316, 318, 322–4
  Georgics, 1–4, 7, 12–14, 17, 19, 26, 49, 50, 52, 57, 58, 66, 74, 79, 122–4, 126, 132, 136, 140, 141, 144, 151, 155, 157, 160, 162, 163, 166, 178, 184, 187, 189, 191, 217, 218, 224, 225, 237, 238, 240, 257, 258, 261, 265, 266, 290, 291, 298, 304, 307, 309, 318–20, 327, 331, 337, 344–50, 353, 355

Walpole, Horace, 282
Walton, Izaac, 10
Warren, C. Henry, 107
Washington, Booker T., 322
Waugh, Evelyn, 21
weather, 43, 57, 64, 68, 70, 81, 178, 180, 185, 219, 222, 256, 279, 308
Webb, Mary, 20, 21, 104, 297
Webster, Daniel, 316–18
Weston, Richard, Sir, 9, 10
White, Gilbert, 197, 296, 297
Wilkinson, L. P., 52, 166
William of Malmesbury, 282
Williams, Raymond, 19, 21, 22, 57, 128, 132, 179, 197, 201, 220, 241
Williamson, Henry, 108
Wilson, Edmund, 22
women's labour
  agricultural, 80, 85, 87, 149, 216, 218, 286, 287, 349, 350, 355
  domestic, 46, 59, 64, 65, 347
Woodhouse, James, 179
Woodmason, Charles, 331
Wordsworth, William, 17, 179, 204, 205, 219, 225, 227, 229, 231, 236, 238, 310, 318
Worlidge, John, 10
Wright, Patrick, 211

Xenophon, 41, 42, 44, 47–50, 124

Young, Arthur, 16, 162, 168, 172, 204, 278

For EU product safety concerns, contact us at Calle de José Abascal, 56–1°,
28003 Madrid, Spain or eugpsr@cambridge.org.

www.ingramcontent.com/pod-product-compliance
Lightning Source LLC
LaVergne TN
LVHW011755060526
838200LV00053B/3606